Climate Change and Vulnerability

Climate Change
and Vulnerability

Edited by
Neil Leary, Cecilia Conde, Jyoti Kulkarni,
Anthony Nyong and Juan Pulhin

London • Sterling, VA

First published by Earthscan in the UK and USA in 2008

Climate Change and Adaptation: ISBN 978-1-84407-470-9
Climate Change and Vulnerability: ISBN 978-1-84407-469-3
Two-volume set: ISBN 978-1-84407-480-8

Typeset by FiSH Books, Enfield
Printed and bound in the UK by Antony Rowe, Chippenham
Cover design by Susanne Harris

For a full list of publications please contact:

Earthscan
8–12 Camden High Street
London, NW1 0JH, UK
Tel: +44 (0)20 7387 8558
Fax: +44 (0)20 7387 8998
Email: earthinfo@earthscan.co.uk
Web: **www.earthscan.co.uk**

22883 Quicksilver Drive, Sterling, VA 20166-2012, USA

Earthscan publishes in association with the International Institute for
Environment and Development

A catalogue record for this book is available from the British Library

Library of Congress Cataloging-in-Publication Data

Climate change and vulnerability / edited by Neil Leary ... [et al.].
    p. cm.
  ISBN-13: 978-1-84407-469-3 (hardback)
  ISBN-10: 1-84407-469-2 (hardback)
  1. Climatic changes. 2. Climatic changes—Developing countries. I. Leary, Neil.
  QC981.8.C5C5625 2007
  304.2'5—dc22

                                                                      2007034503

The paper used for this book is FSC-certified and
totally chlorine-free. FSC (the Forest Stewardship
Council) is an international network to promote
responsible management of the world's forests.

FSC
Mixed Sources
Product group from well-managed
forests and other controlled sources
Cert no. SGS-COC-2953
www.fsc.org
© 1996 Forest Stewardship Council

Contents

List of Figures and Tables

Figures

Tables

Acknowledgements

The two volumes *Climate Change and Vulnerability* and *Climate Change and Adaptation* are products of Assessments of Impacts and Adaptations to Climate Change (AIACC), a project that benefited from the support and participation of numerous persons and organizations. AIACC was funded by generous grants from the Global Environment Facility, the Canadian International Development Agency, the US Agency for International Development, the US Environmental Protection Agency and the Rockefeller Foundation. The initial concept for the project came from authors of the Third Assessment Report of the Intergovernmental Panel on Climate Change (IPCC) and was championed by Robert Watson, Osvaldo Canziani and James McCarthy, the IPCC chair and IPCC Working Group II co-chairs, respectively, during the Third Assessment Report. The productive relationship between AIACC and IPCC was continued and nurtured by Rajendra Pachauri, the current Chair of the IPCC, and Martin Parry, who joined Dr Canziani as co-chair of IPCC Working Group II for the Fourth Assessment Report.

The project could not have succeeded without the very capable and dedicated work of the more than 250 investigators who undertook the AIACC case studies, many of whom are authors of chapters of the two books. The project also benefited from the valuable and enthusiastic assistance of the many committee members, advisers, resource persons and reviewers. These include Neil Adger, Ko Barrett, Bonizella Biagini, Ian Burton, Max Campos, Paul Desanker, Alex De Sherbinin, Tom Downing, Kris Ebi, Roland Fuchs, Habiba Gitay, Hideo Harasawa, Mohamed Hassan, Bruce Hewitson, Mike Hulme, Saleemul Huq, Jill Jaeger, Roger Jones, Richard Klein, Mahendra Kumar, Murari Lal, Liza Leclerc, Bo Lim, Xianfu Lu, Jose Marengo, Linda Mearns, Monirul Mirza, Isabelle Niang-Diop, Carlos Nobre, Jean Palutikof, Annand Patwardhan, Martha Perdomo, Roger Pulwarty, Avis Robinson, Cynthia Rosenzweig, Robert Scholes, Ravi Sharma, Hassan Virji, Penny Whetton, Tom Wilbanks and Gary Yohe. Patricia Presiren of the Academy of Sciences of the Developing World (TWAS) and Sara Beresford, Laisha Said-Moshiro, Jyoti Kulkarni and Kathy Landauer of START gave excellent support for the administration and execution of the project.

Finally, thanks are owed to Alison Kuznets and Hamish Ironside of Earthscan and to Leona Kanaskie for assistance with copy-editing and production of the books.

Foreword

Climate change is increasingly recognized as a critical challenge to ecological health, human well-being and future development, as underscored by the award of the Nobel Peace Prize for 2007 to the Intergovernmental Panel on Climate Change (IPCC). The award recognizes the substantial advances in our shared understanding of climate change, its causes, its consequences and its remedies, which have been achieved by more than 20 years of work by the thousands of contributors to the IPCC science assessments, and which draw from the research and analyses of an even larger number of scientists and experts. This work has culminated in the unprecedented impact of the Panel's most recent report, the Fourth Assessment Report.

The Fourth Assessment Report advances our understanding on various aspects of climate change based on new scientific evidence and research. A major contribution in this regard has come from the work promoted under the project Assessments of Impacts and Adaptation to Climate Change (AIACC). The AIACC project was sponsored by the IPCC to fill a major gap in the available knowledge about climate change risks and response options in developing countries that existed at the completion of the Third Assessment Report in 2001. Twenty-four national and regional assessments were executed under the AIACC project in Africa, Asia, Latin America and small island states in the Caribbean, Indian and Pacific Oceans. The two volumes *Climate Change and Vulnerability* and *Climate Change and Adaptation* present many of the findings from the AIACC assessments.

The findings not only give us a fuller scientific understanding of the specific nature of impacts and viable adaptation strategies in different locations and countries, but have contributed to a much better appreciation of some of the equity dimensions of the problems as well. In simplified terms, the biggest challenge in confronting the negative impacts of climate change lies in the developing world, where people and systems are most vulnerable. Not only are these negative impacts likely to be most serious in the subtropics and tropics, where most developing societies reside, but the capacity to adapt to them is also limited in these regions.

An important element in understanding vulnerabilities to climate change is in linking current and projected exposures to climate stresses with other existing stresses and conditions that are responsible for hardship and low levels of economic welfare. Climate change often adds to these existing stresses, increasing the vulnerability of such communities and ecosystems. Unfortunately, limited research is carried out in developing countries on likely impacts and appropriate responses related to climate change. This is where the knowledge provided by the assessments of the AIACC has been particularly valuable.

There is considerable interest in interpretation of Article 2 of the United

Nations Framework Convention on Climate Change (UNFCCC), the focus of which defines the ultimate objective of the Convention, namely that of preventing a dangerous level of anthropogenic interference with the climate system. Research on impacts of climate change focusing on specific parts of the world that are highly vulnerable enhances our understanding of what may constitute a dangerous level of anthropogenic interference with the world's climate system. In the absence of such knowledge, any value judgement defining a dangerous level would apply to, and be determined by, knowledge only from particular regions of the world, primarily the developed nations. Understanding the critical nature of impacts in some of the most vulnerable parts of the world, which are largely in developing countries, will assist our determination of what might constitute a dangerous level of interference with the earth's climate system. Such knowledge would help appropriately to include and consider those locations which are perhaps much closer to danger than was known earlier.

The record and outputs of the AIACC are impressive. The project, funded by the Global Environment Facility and coordinated by the Global Change System for Analysis, Research and Training (START), the Academy of Sciences for the Developing World (TWAS) and the United Nations Environment Programme (UNEP), engaged investigators from more than 150 institutions and 60 countries to execute the assessments. The quality of the assessments is demonstrated by the more than 100 peer-reviewed publications produced, which benefited substantially the IPCC's Fourth Assessment Report. In view of this success, it is imperative that we build on the experience and achievements of AIACC and develop the next phase of such work to help advance new knowledge for a possible Fifth Assessment Report of the IPCC.

While the material contained in the two volumes from AIACC and the substantial amount of knowledge developed through the case studies presented in the following pages are valuable, the need for further work is enormous. There remain many countries in the developing world where very little is known about the nature and extent of the impacts of climate change, and these gaps would not permit the development of plans and programmes to address climate change risks or to put in place response measures that would help communities and ecosystems to adapt to the impacts of climate change. These clearly would get much more serious with time unless suitable mitigation measures are taken in hand with a sense of urgency. Yet, even with the most ambitious mitigation actions, the inertia of the system will ensure that the impacts of climate change will continue for centuries, if not beyond a millennium. Knowledge of impacts and the manner in which they would grow over time is therefore critical to the development of capacity and measures for adaptation to climate change. The work of the AIACC provides an extremely important platform to take such steps, but there is yet very far to go to meet the challenges ahead. It is hoped that the material contained in this volume is just the start of a process that must expand and continue in the future.

R. K. Pachauri
Director General, The Energy and Resources Institute (TERI)
and Chairman, Intergovernmental Panel on Climate Change (IPCC)

Part I:

Introduction

For Whom the Bell Tolls:
Vulnerabilities in a Changing Climate

Neil Leary, James Adejuwon, Wilma Bailey, Vicente Barros, Punsalmaa Batima, Rubén M. Caffera, Suppakorn Chinvanno, Cecilia Conde, Alain De Comarmond, Alex De Sherbinin, Tom Downing, Hallie Eakin, Anthony Nyong, Maggie Opondo, Balgis Osman-Elasha, Rolph Payet, Florencia Pulhin, Juan Pulhin, Janaka Ratnisiri, El-Amin Sanjak, Graham von Maltitz, Mónica Wehbe, Yongyuan Yin and Gina Ziervogel

No man is an island, entire of itself; every man is a piece of the continent, a part of the main. If a clod be washed away by the sea, Europe is the less, as well as if a promontory were, as well as if a manor of thy friend's or of thine own were: any man's death diminishes me, because I am involved in mankind, and therefore never send to know for whom the bell tolls; it tolls for thee.

JOHN DONNE, 1623

Introduction

People have evolved ways of earning livelihoods and supplying their needs for food, water, shelter and other goods and services that are adapted to the climates of the areas in which they live. But the climate is ever variable and changeable, and deviations that are too far from the norm can be disruptive, even hazardous.

Now the climate is changing due to human actions. Despite efforts to abate the human causes, human-driven climate change will continue for decades and longer (IPCC, 2001a). Who is vulnerable to the changes and their impacts? For whom does the bell toll? We ask, against the oft-quoted advice of the poet John Donne, because understanding who is vulnerable, and why, can help us to prevent our neighbour's home from washing into the sea, a family from suffering hunger, a child from being exposed to disease and the natural world around us from being impoverished. All of us are vulnerable to climate change, though to varying degrees, directly and through our connections to each other.

The propensity of people or systems to be harmed by hazards or stresses, referred to as vulnerability, is determined by their exposures to hazard, their sensitivity to the exposures, and their capacities to resist, cope with, exploit, recover from and adapt to the effects. Global climate change is bringing changes in exposures to climate hazards. The impacts will depend in part on the nature, rate and severity of the changes in climate. They will also depend to an important degree on social, economic, governance and other forces that determine who and what are exposed to climate hazards, their sensitivities and their capacities. For some, the impacts may be beneficial. But predominantly harmful impacts are expected, particularly in the developing world (IPCC, 2001b).

To explore vulnerabilities to climate change and response options in developing country regions, 24 regional and national assessments were implemented under the international project 'Assessments of Impacts and Adaptations to Climate Change' (AIACC). The case studies, executed over the period 2002–2005, are varied in their objectives, geographic and social contexts, the systems and sectors that are investigated, and the methods that are applied. They are located in Africa, Asia, Latin America, and islands of the Caribbean, Indian and Pacific Oceans. The studies include investigations of crop agriculture, pastoral systems, water resources, terrestrial and estuarine ecosystems, biodiversity, urban flood risks, coastal settlements, food security, livelihoods and human health.

One factor that is common to most of the studies is that they include investigation of the vulnerability of people, places or systems to climatic stresses. Vulnerability studies take a different approach from investigations of climate change impacts. The latter generally emphasize quantitative modelling to simulate the impacts of selected climate change scenarios on Earth systems and people. By contrast, vulnerability studies focus on the processes that shape the consequences of climate variations and changes to identify the conditions that amplify or dampen vulnerability to adverse outcomes. The climate drivers are treated as important in vulnerability studies, but drivers related to demographic, social, economic and governance processes are given equal attention. Understanding how these processes contribute to vulnerability and adaptive capacity in the context of current climate variations and extremes can yield insights regarding vulnerability to future climate change that can help to guide adaptive strategies (Leary, 2002).

This volume presents a collection of papers from the AIACC case studies that address questions about the nature, causes and distribution of vulnerability to climate change. In this first chapter we introduce the case studies and present a synthesis of lessons from our comparison of the studies. A companion to this volume, *Climate Change and Adaptation* (Leary et al, 2008), explores options for adapting to climate change, capacities for implementing these and obstacles to be overcome.

Our synthesis of lessons about vulnerability is a product of a week-long workshop held in March 2005. During the workshop we applied a three-step risk assessment protocol previously used by Downing (2002). In the first step we identified domains of vulnerability that correspond to resources or systems that are important to human well-being, are very likely to be affected by climate change, and are a focus of one or more of the case studies. Four major domains were selected, around which we organized our discussions in the workshop and which have been used to structure both this chapter and the book as a whole: 1) natural resources, 2) coastal areas and small islands, 3) rural economy and food systems, and 4) human health.

In the second step, outcomes of concern within each domain were identified and ranked as low-, medium- or high-level concerns. In selecting and ranking outcomes, we attempted to take the perspective of stakeholders concerned about national-scale risks. Outcomes are included that our studies and our interpretation of related literature suggest are plausible, and that would be of national significance should they occur. Our rankings of low-, medium- and high-level concerns are based on the following criteria: potential to exceed coping capacities of affected systems, the geographic extent of damages, the severity of damages relative to national resources, and the persistence versus reversibility of the impacts. The rankings do not take into account the likelihood that an outcome would be realized. They represent the degree of concern that would result if the hypothesized outcomes do materialize. While we have not formally assessed the likelihood of the different outcomes, each is a potential result under plausible scenarios and circumstances.

In step three we identified the climatic and non-climatic factors that create conditions of vulnerability to the outcomes of concern within each domain. Where climatic and non-climatic drivers combine to strongly amplify vulnerability, the potential for high-level concern outcomes being realized is greatest. Conversely, where some of the drivers interact to dampen vulnerability, outcomes of lower-level concern are likely to result.

The lessons produced from this protocol are presented below in this chapter. The case studies from which they are derived are elaborated on in the chapters that follow.

Natural Resources

Natural resources, under pressure from human uses, have undergone rapid and extensive changes over the past 50 years that have resulted in many of them being degraded (MEA, 2005). Population and economic growth are likely to intensify uses of and pressures on natural resource systems. Global climate change, which has already impacted natural resource systems across the Earth, is adding to the pressures and is expected to substantially disrupt many of these systems and the goods and services that they provide (IPCC, 2001b; IPCC, 2007; MEA, 2005). Our case studies investigated vulnerabilities to climate hazards for a variety of natural resources, which are grouped into the contexts of water, land, and ecosystems and biodiversity.

Water

Population and economic growth are increasing water demands, and many parts of the world are expected to face increased water stress as a result (Arnell, 2004). Water resources are highly sensitive to variations in climate and, consequently, climate change will pose serious challenges to water users and managers (IPCC, 2001b). Climate change may exacerbate the stress in some places but ameliorate it in others, depending on the changes at regional and local levels.

Vulnerabilities from water resource impacts of climate change are addressed by several of the case studies. Outcomes of concern for water resources from these studies and the climatic and non-climatic drivers of the outcomes are identified in Table 1.1. Scenarios of future climate change indicate that many of the study regions, including parts of Africa and Asia, face risks of greater aridity, more variable water supply and periods of water scarcity from drought. In contrast, scenarios suggest that the climate may become wetter and water supply greater in southeastern South America and southeastern Asia.

Changes in water balances will impact land, ecosystems, biodiversity, rural economies, food security and human health; vulnerabilities to these impacts are discussed in later sections of this chapter. The outcomes are strongly dependent on factors such as the level and rate of growth of water demands relative to reliable supplies; water and land-use policies, planning and management; water infrastructure; and the distribution and security of water rights. Where water becomes less plentiful and climates drier, the changes have the potential to retard progress towards the Millennium Development Goals.

The impacts that can result from persistent and geographically widespread declines in water balances have been demonstrated all too frequently. Osman-Elasha and Sanjak (Chapter 12) and Nyong et al (Chapter 11) examine the impacts of decades of below average rainfall and recurrent drought in two parts of the Sudano-Sahel zone with case studies in Sudan and Nigeria respectively. The reduced availability of water in these arid and semi-arid areas has resulted in decreased food production, loss of livestock, land degradation, migrations from neighbouring countries and internal displacements of people. The effects of water scarcity have contributed to food insecurity and the destitution of large numbers of people; they are also implicated as a source of conflict that underlies the violence in Darfur.

Non-climate factors that have contributed to the severity of impacts of past climatic events in Sudan and Nigeria create conditions of high vulnerability to continued drying of the climate and future drought. Both studies find that large and growing populations in dry climates that are highly dependent on farming and grazing for livelihoods, lack of off-farm livelihood opportunities, reliance of many households on marginal, degraded lands, high poverty levels, insecure water rights, inability to economically and socially absorb displaced people, and dysfunctional governance institutions create conditions of high vulnerability to changes in water balances. While projected water balance changes for the Sahel and Sudano-Sahel zones are mixed (Hoerling et al, 2006), they include worrisome scenarios of a drier, more drought-prone climate for these regions.

Table 1.1 *Water resource vulnerabilities*

Level of Concern	Outcomes of Concern	Climate Drivers	Other Drivers	AIACC Studies
High	• Collapse of water system leading to severe and long-term water shortage	• Persistent and severe decline in water balance due to reduced rainfall and/or higher temperatures • Sea level rise causing salt-water intrusion into shallow aquifer of small island • Disappearance of glaciers	• Lack of alternative water sources • High and growing water demand relative to reliable supply • Failure of water and land-use policy, planning and management • High dependence on single vulnerable water source	
	• Water scarcity that retards progress on Millennium Development Goals and threatens food security	• Persistent, regional decrease in rainfall, increase in aridity • More variable rainfall and runoff • More frequent severe drought events	• High dependence on subsistence or small-scale rain-fed crop farming and herding • Land degradation • High poverty rate • Insufficient investment in rural development • Inequitable access to water • Lack of social safety nets • Governance failures • High and growing water demand relative to reliable supply	• Sudan (Osman-Elasha and Sanjak, Chapter 12) • Northern Nigeria (Nyong et al, Chapter 11) • Mongolia (Batima et al, Chapter 4) • Mexico (Eakin et al, Chapter 13)
Medium	• Losses from reallocations of water among competing users • Non-violent but costly conflict among competing water users	• Persistent and moderate decrease in rainfall, increase in aridity • More variable rainfall and runoff • More frequent severe drought events • Changes in timing of runoff and water availability	• High and growing water demand relative to supply • Extensive land use changes • Pollution from industrial, agricultural and domestic sources • Undefined or insecure water rights • Poor performance of institutions for water planning, allocation and management	• Western China (Yin et al, Chapter 5) • Philippines (Pulhin et al, Chapter 15) • South Africa (Callaway et al, 2006)
	• More frequent flood events that increase loss of life, damage to infrastructure, loss of crops and disruption of economic activities	• Increase in heavy precipitation events	• Growth in populations and infrastructure in flood-prone locations • Poorly managed land-use change, including clearing of vegetation and filling of wetlands that can provide flood protection • Ineffective disaster prevention, preparedness, warning and response systems	• Argentina (Eakin et al, Chapter 13) • Argentina (Barros et al, Chapter 6) • Thailand and Lao PDR (Chinvanno et al, Chapter 16) • Philippines (Pulhin et al, Chapter 15)
Low	• Losses to water users from localized, temporary and manageable fluctuations in water availability	• Seasonal droughts	• More severe effects kept in check by: • Effective management, planning and policies for water demand and supply	• Philippines (Pulhin et al, Chapter 15) • Western China (Yin et al, Chapter 5) • Thailand and Lao PDR (Chinvanno et al, Chapter 16) • South Africa (Callaway et al, 2006)

The Heihe river basin of northwestern China has experienced more modest drying over the past decade (Yin et al, Chapter 5). But with increasing development in the basin, water demands have been rising and intensifying competition for the increasingly scarce water. As a result, water users in the basin have become more vulnerable to water shortage, reduced land productivity and non-violent conflict over water allocations. These effects illustrate outcomes of medium- and low-level concern. A drier climate, as some scenarios project for the region, would exacerbate these conditions and could result in outcomes of higher-level concern if future development in the basin raises water demand beyond what can be supplied reliably and sustainably.

For the case study regions in the eastern part of the southern cone of South America (Conde et al, Chapter 14; Eakin et al, Chapter 13; Camilloni and Barros, 2003), the Philippines (Pulhin et al, Chapter 15), and the Lower Mekong river basin (Chinvanno et al, Chapter 16), climate change projections suggest a wetter climate and increases in water availability. In the southern cone of South America, increased precipitation over the past two decades has contributed to the expansion of commercially profitable rain-fed crop farming, particularly of soybeans, into cattle ranching areas that were previously too dry for cropping. While this has generated significant economic benefits, the increased rainfall has also brought losses from increases in heavy rainfall and flood events. In the future, a wetter climate in these regions would also bring benefits from increased water availability, but may cause damages from flooding and water-logging of soils (Eakin et al, Chapter 13). Furthermore, farmers may face greater risks from greater rainfall variability in South America that could include both heavier rainfall events and more frequent droughts (IPCC, 2001a).

In the Pantabangan–Carranglan watershed of the Philippines, increases in annual rainfall and water runoff would benefit rain-fed crop farmers, irrigators, hydropower generators and other water users. But changes in rainfall variability, including those related to changes in ENSO variability, could intensify competition for water among upland rain-fed crop farmers, lowland irrigated crop farmers, the National Power Corporation and the National Irrigation Administration (Pulhin et al, Chapter 15). Changes in flood risks are also of concern in the watershed. In the Lower Mekong, while increases in annual rainfall may bring increases in average rice yields, shifts in the timing of rainy seasons and the potential for more frequent flooding are found to pose risks for rice farmers (Chinvanno et al, Chapter 16). Those most vulnerable to changes in variability in the Lower Mekong and in Pantabangan–Carranglan are small-scale farmers with little or no land holdings, lack of secure water rights, limited access to capital and other resources, and limited access to decision-making processes.

Land

The quality and productivity of land is strongly influenced by climate and can be degraded by the combined effects of climate variations and human activities. Land degradation has become one of the most serious environmental problems, reducing the resilience of land to climate variability, degrading soil fertility, undermining food production and contributing to famine (UNCCD, 2005a). Seventy per cent of the world's drylands, including arid, semi-arid and dry sub-humid areas, are degraded, directly affecting more than 250 million people and placing 1 billion people at risk (UNCCD, 2005b).

Human-caused climate change is likely to affect land degradation processes by altering rainfall averages, variability and extremes, and by increasing evaporation and transpiration of water from soils, vegetation and surface waters. The effects on land will depend in part on how the climate and water balances change. But they will also depend strongly on non-climate factors that shape human pressures on land. The human consequences will, in turn, be shaped by the ability of people to cope and respond to the effects and to reduce the human pressures that drive land degradation.

Two of our case studies, one in Sudan (Osman-Elasha and Sanjak, Chapter 12) and the other in Mongolia (Batima et al, Chapter 4), have land degradation as a central focus. Other studies also examine land degradation as both a potential outcome as well as an amplifier of climate change vulnerability in the Philippines (Pulhin et al, Chapter 15), Tlaxcala, Mexico (Ziervogel et al, Chapter 9) and Tamaulipas, Mexico, and the Argentine Pampas (Eakin et al, Chapter 13).

Table 1.2 lists some of the outcomes of concern from the studies that are related to land degradation. The ranking of outcomes is based on the spatial extent, severity of impacts, and the reversibility or irreversibility of land degradation. The climate drivers of land degradation outcomes are increases in aridity and increases in the frequency, severity and duration of droughts. Non-climate drivers include population growth and economic incentives that create pressures to intensify land uses, expand farming and grazing activities into marginal lands, and clear vegetation. Contributing to this are land tenure systems, land policies and market failures that limit incentives for good land and water management. Widespread poverty, breakdown of local support systems and ineffective governance institutions heighten the vulnerability of populations to income and livelihood losses, food insecurity and displacement from their homes as a result of land degradation.

In northern and central states of Sudan, the dry climate, sandy soils and heavy human pressures on the land create conditions of high vulnerability to desertification. Below average rainfall over the past 20 years and growing land-use pressures have degraded grazing and crop lands in North Darfur and reduced food and fodder production and the availability of water (Osman-Elasha and Sanjak, 2005). The scarcity of these lifelines has triggered southward migrations of people and their livestock within North Darfur. In addition, people fleeing civil war in neighbouring Chad also migrated into western Sudan.

The resulting rapid increases in human population and the number of livestock have intensified pressures on the already fragile environment, including over-grazing and excessive cutting of gum arabic (Acacia senegal) trees to clear land for cultivation and provide fodder and firewood. The reduction in vegetation cover has increased vulnerability to loss of soil and soil fertility by

Table 1.2 *Land vulnerabilities*

Level of Concern	Outcomes of Concern	Climate Drivers	Other Drivers	AIACC Studies
High	• Widespread desertification of lands with irreversible changes to soil structure or nutrient status	• Arid, semi-arid or sub-humid climate • Persistent decrease in rainfall, increased aridity • Increase in climate variability, including more frequent extreme droughts	• Severe overuse of land, including overly intense cropping with poor soil management, poor irrigation practices, extension of cropping into marginal lands, overgrazing of rangelands, removal of vegetation and deforestation • Land tenure systems, land-use policies, market failures and globalization forces that create pressures for overuse and limit incentives for good land management • Population pressure • Breakdown of support systems • Poverty • Poor, erodable soils	• Sudan (Osman-Elasha and Sanjak, Chapter 12) • Northern Nigeria (Nyong et al, Chapter 11)
	• Widespread but reversible desertification of lands	• Arid, semi-arid or sub-humid climate • Increase in climate variability, including more frequent extreme droughts	• Intensive use of land that degrades land productivity during dry periods but does not irreversibly alter soils • Population pressures • Poverty • Inability of land management systems to adapt to climate variations	• Sudan (Osman-Elasha and Sanjak, Chapter 12) • Northern Nigeria (Nyong et al, Chapter 11) • Mexico (Eakin et al, Chapter 13)
Medium	• Land degradation of limited geographic extent that is irreversible	• Increased aridity of limited geographic extent • Increase in climate variability, including more frequent extreme droughts	• Locally severe overuse of land • Population pressures • Poverty	• Mongolia (Batima et al, Chapter 4) • Mexico (Eakin et al, Chapter 13) • Philippines (Pulhin et al, Chapter 15)
Low	• Localized but reversible land degradation	• Moderate, temporary drying of localized extent	More severe effects kept in check by: • Tenure systems and land policies that promote good land management • Households that have sufficient resources with which to cope with reduced food and fodder production • Social systems that function to absorb shocks	• Mexico (Eakin et al, Chapter 13) • Philippines (Pulhin et al, Chapter 15)

exposing soils to wind erosion and encroachment of desert sands. Similar processes are degrading lands in Sudan's North Kordofan state (Ziervogel et al, Chapter 9). The human consequences of drought and land degradation in Sudan are explored later in this chapter. If, as some climate projections suggest, the future climate of the region becomes drier and the frequency and severity of droughts increase, desertification processes would be exacerbated.

Mongolia, a nation for which livestock herding is the dominant livelihood activity, is also experiencing serious land degradation (Batima et al, 2005). Over the past 40 years, although rainfall has stayed relatively constant, increases in mean temperatures ranging from near 1°C in the low mountains and on the plains of the Gobi Desert to more than 2°C in the high mountains have resulted in drying of the climate and soils. With the dryer climate, pasture production has declined by 20 to 30 per cent over the same period. Overstocking and overgrazing of pastures in the drier conditions, driven in part by institutional changes that have turned Mongolia's pastures into an open access commons, has led to degradation of lands in parts of Mongolia. Climate projections indicate that temperatures will continue to rise and suggest that the region may continue to become drier. Such scenarios would likely worsen problems of land degradation in Mongolia.

Ecosystems and biodiversity

Habitat change, overexploitation, invasive alien species, pollution and climate change are identified by the Millennium Ecosystem Assessment as presently the most important drivers of ecosystem change and biodiversity loss. By the end of the 21st century, it is possible that climate change may become the dominant driver (MEA, 2005). Case studies in South Africa (von Maltitz and Scholes, Chapter 2) and the Philippines (Lasco et al, Chapter 3) investigate the potential changes in the spatial extent of ecosystem types and biodiversity loss for scenarios of climate change. The findings of these studies are summarized here. Other studies examine the impacts of climate change on the productivity of ecosystems and the consequences for human livelihoods; these are examined in sections of this chapter on water, land, coastal systems and the rural economy.

Outcomes of high, medium and low levels of concern from the South African and Philippine studies are presented in Table 1.3. At the high end of the scale, the two studies find that loss of some entire ecosystems, along with extinction of many of their species, is probable for changes in climate that are projected for a doubling of atmospheric concentration of carbon dioxide.

In the South African example, projected increases in aridity in the western half of the country would cause current biomes to contract and shift towards the eastern half of the country. A large proportion of South Africa would be left with a habitat type that is not currently found in the country. The impacts vary by location and biome type, and for individual species.

The savanna systems of South Africa and their species are found to have relatively low vulnerability to climatically driven extinctions. By comparison, species of the fynbos biome are potentially more vulnerable to climate change

Table 1.3 *Ecosystems and biodiversity vulnerabilities*

Level of Concern	Outcomes of Concern	Climate Drivers	Other Drivers	AIACC Studies
High	• Collapse or loss of entire ecosystem and extinction of many of the system's species	• Rapid rate of change in mean temperature • Changes in water balance across an ecosystem's geographic distribution that are beyond tolerance limits of dominant species • Changes in seasonal climate extremes, variability and means	• Narrow climate tolerances of dominant species of an ecosystem • Extensive habitat loss and fragmentation due to land-use change • Severe pressure from overgrazing, over-harvesting, over-fishing, etc • Severe competition from invasive species • Severe pressure from pollution • Changing fire regimes • Physical barriers to species migration (e.g. islands, mountain tops, isolated valleys) • Changes in grass–tree interactions due to increased CO_2 in atmosphere	• South Africa (von Maltitz and Scholes, Chapter 2) • Philippines (Lasco et al, Chapter 3)
Medium	• Species loss and retrogressive succession	• Greater water stress from higher temperatures and lower precipitation	• Moderate pressure on ecosystems due to habitat loss and fragmentation, overexploitation, competition from invasive species and pollution • Changing fire regimes • Changes in grass–tree interactions due to increased CO_2 in atmosphere	• South Africa (von Maltitz and Scholes, Chapter 2)
	• Species loss and change in habitat compositional structure	• Slow changes in climate that allow most species to migrate	• Sufficient connections of suitable habitat persist across the landscape to enable species to migrate	• South Africa (von Maltitz and Scholes, Chapter 2)
Low	• Genetic loss • Loss of genetic variability, loss of sub-species and varieties	• Slow changes in climate • Small absolute changes in temperature and precipitation that do not fundamentally alter water balances	More severe effects kept in check by: • Managing pressures on ecosystems to a low level • Connections of suitable habitat enable species to migrate	• South Africa (von Maltitz and Scholes, Chapter 2

than are those of the savannas. The fynbos is the major vegetation type of the Cape Floral Kingdom, which is the smallest of the world's six floral kingdoms. It is located entirely in South Africa, has the highest concentration of species of any of the floral kingdoms and has a species endemism rate of 70 per cent. While the fynbos biome is projected to have relatively little loss in spatial extent, climatic habitats would move for many individual species and some climatic habitats would disappear completely. Model simulations suggest that many species of the fynbos will be able to migrate with their moving habitats, but some would not and would be lost.

The situation for the succulent karoo biome is more dire. The succulent karoo is an arid ecosystem of southwestern South Africa and southern Namibia that is also rich in biodiversity and high in species endemism. Model simulations for climate change scenarios corresponding to a doubling of carbon dioxide project that almost the entire extent of the succulent karoo would be lost to a new climatically-defined habitat type. Extinction of many of the species endemic to the biome would probably result.

In the Philippines, increasing temperature and rainfall are projected by Lasco et al (Chapter 3) to result in the dry forest zone being completely replaced by wet forests and rainforests. They estimate that a 50 per cent increase in precipitation would cause dry forests, which occupy approximately 1 million hectares, to disappear completely from the Philippines and moist forests, which occupy 3.5 million hectares, to decline in area by two thirds. Most of these forest areas would become wet forests, which would more than double their area from their present size. If precipitation were to increase by 150 per cent, which is within the range of climate model projections for the end of the century, all dry and moist forests would disappear, wet forests would decline by half and rain forests, a forest type not currently present in the Philippines, would grow to 5 million hectares. The warmer, wetter climate that is projected for the Philippines would increase the primary productivity of the forests and produce associated benefits. But the disappearance of dry and possibly moist forest types would result in loss of species.

Coastal Areas and Small Islands

Coasts and small islands are highly exposed to a variety of climate hazards that may be affected by global climate change. The climatic hazards converge with local and regional human pressures in coastal zones to create conditions of high vulnerability, particularly in areas with high concentrations of people and infrastructure along low-lying coasts. Barros et al (Chapter 6) investigate flood risks from storm surges along the Argentine coast of the Río de la Plata. Nagy et al (Chapter 7), also working in the Río de la Plata basin, examine changing dynamics of the estuarine ecosystem and their implications for fisheries on the Uruguayan side. Payet (Chapter 8) explores problems of coastal erosion and also risks to tourism in the Seychelles, while Mataki et al (2005 and 2006) assess the vulnerability of coastal towns of Fiji to flooding. Outcomes of concern from these studies are summarized in Table 1.4.

Table 1.4 *Coastal area and small island vulnerabilities*

Level of Concern	Outcomes of Concern	Climate Drivers	Other Drivers	AIACC Studies
High	• More frequent and greater loss of life, infrastructure damage, displacement of population and disruption of economic activities	• Increase in frequency and intensity of extratropical and tropical storms • Sea level rise	• Large and growing population and infrastructure in exposed coastal areas • Lack of land-use policies to avoid/reduce exposures • Lack of maintenance of flood control infrastructure • Loss of wetlands and reefs • Ineffective disaster prevention, preparedness, warning and response systems	• Central America (Project LA06, www.aiaccproject.org) • Argentina (Barros et al, Chapter 6)
	• Loss of tourism-related income, export earnings and jobs	• Changes in number of wet days and frequency of storms	• Damages to infrastructure, beaches, water supply and ecosystems that provide tourism-related services • High dependence on tourism for income and employment	• Seychelles (Payet, Chapter 8)
	• Severe coastal erosion	• Increase in frequency and intensity of extratropical and tropical storms • Sea level rise	• Intensive land uses in the coastal zone • Loss of coastal wetlands and bleaching of coral reefs	• Seychelles (Sheppard et al, 2005; Payet, Chapter 8) • Fiji (Mataki et al, 2005 and 2006)
Medium	• Damage to coastal ecosystems and their services and resulting impacts on fishing livelihoods	• Sea level rise • Changes in winds, water temperatures, and freshwater inflow to estuaries and coastal waters	• Pollution discharges into waters • Nutrients carried into coastal waters by runoff • Use of fertilizers that runoff into coastal waters • Removal of vegetation that increases erosion • Hardening of shoreline to protect against storm surges • Over-harvesting of fish and shellfish	• Uruguay (Nagy et al, Chapter 7)

Table 1.4 (continued)

Level of Concern	Outcomes of Concern	Climate Drivers	Other Drivers	AIACC Studies
	• Diminishing and less reliable water supply	• Sea level rise • Changes in water balance and ENSO and monsoon variability	• Increasing water demand from growing population and economic activity • Increasing extraction of groundwater	• Fiji (Mataki et al, 2005 and 2006)
Low	• Modest acceleration of coastal erosion and modest infrastructure damage	• Increase in frequency and intensity of extra-tropical and tropical storms • Sea level rise	More severe effects kept in check by: • Low concentrations of population and infrastructure in areas exposed to erosion • Intact coastal wetlands and inland vegetation • Good coastal policies and management practices	• Argentina (Barros et al, Chapter 6)

Barros and colleagues find that sea level rise would permanently inundate only small and relatively unimportant areas along the southern coast of the Río de la Plata during this century. However, the area and population that would be affected by recurrent flooding from storm surges would increase considerably. They estimate that sea level rise and changes in wind fields would increase the population affected by storm surges with a five-year return period from 80,000 persons at present to nearly 350,000 in 2070. For storm surges with a 100-year return period, the population affected would rise from 550,000 at present to nearly 900,000 by 2070. Economic costs resulting from real estate damage and increased operational costs of coastal public facilities are estimated to range between 5 and 15 billion US dollars for the period 2050–2100, depending on the rate of sea level rise. These estimates are based on the current population and development in the basin. Continuation of trends that have been concentrating both people and infrastructure on the coast would increase the number of people exposed and the potential economic damage.

Coastal erosion is common to all coasts, but the level of concern that it engenders ranges from low to high depending on local circumstances. The study by Barros and colleagues finds that coastal erosion is presently of little concern in the Río de la Plata basin, though concern could rise if newly accreted lands in the Parana delta are allowed to be settled and developed. In contrast, Payet finds that concern about coastal erosion is high in the Seychelles and Mataki, and colleagues make the same conclusion for Fiji and the Cook Islands. In each of these cases, infrastructure and resources are more exposed to the impacts of erosion than is the case in the Río de la Plata. Another recent study of the Seychelles (Sheppard et al, 2005) found that coastal erosion is significantly heightened as a result of coral bleaching events that reduce the ability of reefs to dissipate wave energy. The authors conclude that areas that have experienced mass bleaching are at a higher risk from coastal erosion under accelerated sea level rise.

In the Seychelles, as in many island states, tourism is a major contributor to incomes. The attributes that make the Seychelles and other islands attractive tourist destinations can be highly sensitive to climate stresses. The high economic dependence on tourism and the sensitivity of tourist resources to climate create a situation of high socioeconomic vulnerability to climate change (Payet, Chapter 8). Climate change can impact tourism by accelerating beach erosion, inundating and degrading coral reefs, damaging hotels and other tourism-related infrastructure, and discouraging tourists from visiting because changes in climate reduce an area's appeal. In a scenario that assumes a substantial increase in the number of wet days per month, Payet estimates that tourist visits would be reduced by 40 per cent. They also estimate that the decrease in tourist visits would reduce tourism expenditures by 40 million US dollars and cause over 5000 jobs to be lost, representing 15 per cent of the national labour force. The effects would be felt in all areas of the economy.

The trophic state of the estuary of the Río de la Plata has degraded since the mid-1940s. The eutrophication of the estuary is due primarily to nutrients introduced by increased fertilizer use and changes in human land uses, but climatic factors such as changes in river flows and wind patterns have also contributed (Nagy et al, Chapter 7). A consequence of the eutrophication is an increase in the frequency of harmful algae blooms in the last decade, resulting in considerable economic harm to commercial fisheries and tourism as well as negative impacts on public health in Uruguay. Climate change would impact the estuary through changes in freshwater input from tributaries and changes in winds that would modify the circulation, salinity front location, stratification and mixing patterns. These changes would, in turn, alter oxygen content, nutrients and primary production in the estuary.

Many of the estuary's services would be altered. But the specific changes are difficult to predict as they depend on the balance of multiple and complex interactions. One of the concerns is the sustainability of fisheries in the Río de la Plata. A case study of an artisanal fishery located on the northern coast of the estuary finds the fishermen and the fishing settlement to be vulnerable to climate driven shifts in the salinity front location and other changes in the estuary that would alter fish catch or the effort and cost required to catch fish.

Rural Economies and Food Security

Several of the case studies investigate the vulnerability of rural livelihoods to climate variability and change, and the implications for rural economies and food security. Rural livelihoods and economies are based on and dominated by agricultural, pastoral and forest production systems that are highly sensitive to climate variations. Climate change can and will have both positive and negative impacts on the productivity of these systems, which will, in turn, impact incomes, costs of production, supplies of food and other commodities, stores of food, livestock and financial savings, and food security. Table 1.5 highlights some of the potential negative outcomes identified as concerns by the studies. The focus is on negative outcomes because our interest is in understanding who is vulnerable in rural economies, how they are vulnerable and why.

The productivity of farm fields, pastures and forests will be impacted by exposures to changes in the averages, ranges and variability of temperatures and precipitation, water balances and frequencies, severities of droughts, floods and other climate extremes, and the ameliorating effects of higher carbon dioxide concentrations on plant processes. One of the common findings of the studies is that systems with similar exposures to climate stimuli can vary considerably in their vulnerability to damage from such exposures.

The particular factors that determine vulnerability are context-specific and vary from place to place. But some commonalities can be identified. Rural households' sensitivity to climate shocks and capacity to respond vary according to their access to water, land and other resources and the condition and quality of these resources. Large and growing populations, a high proportion of households engaged in subsistence or small-scale farming and herding, land degradation, high poverty rates and governance failures create conditions of vulnerability for rural economies and households. Declining local authority, lack of social safety nets, violent conflict, gender inequality and competition from market liberalization are also factors that add to vulnerability in the different case study areas. These issues are developed in the sections below.

Table 1.5 *Rural economy vulnerabilities*

Level of Concern	Outcomes of Concern	Climate Drivers	Other Drivers	AIACC Studies
High	• Violent conflict • Famine	• Persistent below average rainfall, increased aridity • Severe, multi-year, geographically widespread drought events	• Tensions among rival groups • Migrations of herders into lands of sedentary farmers • Collapse of local authorities • Governance failures • Scarcity of food, water and other resources	• Sudan (Osman-Elasha and Sanjak, Chapter 12) • Northern Nigeria (Nyong et al, Chapter 11)
	• Multi-year collapse of rural production systems • Widespread and persistent loss of livelihoods and impoverishment • Chronic hunger and malnutrition for large percentage of population • Long-term or permanent out-migration on large scale	• Persistent below average rainfall, increased aridity • Severe, multi-year, geographically widespread drought events	• Large and growing population in dryland areas • High percentage of households engaged in subsistence or small-scale farming and herding on lands with poor soils and no irrigation • Overuse or clearing of lands leading to land degradation • Lack of or insecure water rights • High poverty rate • Lack of off-farm livelihood opportunities • Lack of social safety nets • Governance failures	• Sudan (Osman-Elasha and Sanjak, Chapter 12) • Northern Nigeria (Nyong et al, Chapter 11) • Mongolia (Batima et al, Chapter 4)
Medium	• Loss of export earnings • Loss of national income • Loss of jobs	• More frequent climate extremes over large portion of growing area of key export crops • Changes in average climate or shifts in rainy season that stress export crops	• High dependence on small number of agricultural commodities for export earnings, national income and employment • Declining or volatile export crop prices • Insufficient investment in research, development and diffusion of agricultural technology	• Sri Lanka (Ratnasiri et al, Chapter 17)

Table 1.5 (*continued*)

Level of Concern	Outcomes of Concern	Climate Drivers	Other Drivers	AIACC Studies
	• Increased rural poverty rates • Declining and more variable net farm incomes for many rural households • Failures of small farms • Accelerated rural-to-urban migration	• Region-wide increase in frequency of climate extremes that cause losses of crops, livestock and income • Changes in average climate or significant shifts in rainy season that stress traditionally grown crops and available substitutes	• Declining output prices (e.g. due to trade liberalization) • Rising input prices (e.g. due to removal of subsidies) • Lack of income diversification of rural households • Lack of access to credit by small farmers • Stagnant rural development • Poor rural infrastructure (e.g. roads, water storage) • Lack of social safety nets	• Argentina and Mexico (Eakin et al, Chapter 13) • South Africa, Nigeria, Sudan and Mexico (Ziervogel et al, Chapter 9) • Thailand and Lao PDR (Chinvanno et al, Chapter 16) • Philippines (Pulhin et al, Chapter 15)
Low	• Declining and more variable net farm incomes for some rural households • Decreased and more variable quality of crop and livestock output • Temporary migrations as strategy to obtain off-farm incomes	• Increase in frequency of climate extremes that cause losses of crops, livestock and income • Changes in average climate or shifts in rainy season that are less optimal for traditionally grown crops	More severe effects kept in check by: • Robust and diversified rural development • Equitable access to resources (e.g. improved seed varieties) • Adequate household savings • Maintenance of social safety nets • Political stability • Well maintained rural infrastructure and services • Access to credit and insurance	• Argentina and Mexico (Eakin et al, Chapter 13) • Thailand and Lao PDR (Chinvanno et al, Chapter 16) • Philippines (Pulhin et al, Chapter 15) • Sri Lanka (Ratnasiri et al, Chapter 17)

Household access to resources

Access or entitlements to land, water, labour and other inputs to rural production processes are important determinants of the vulnerability of rural households. They shape the sensitivity of households' livelihoods and food security to variations in climate and land productivity. They also underpin the capacity of households to withstand and respond to the impacts.

Ziervogel et al (Chapter 9) compare the determinants of food insecurity from four case studies: Mangondi village in Limpopo Province, South Africa; Gireigikh rural council in North Kordofan, Sudan; Chingowa village in Borno State, Nigeria; and Tlaxcala State, Mexico. Each of the study sites has a dry, drought-prone climate and exposure to declining average precipitation and frequent drought are sources of risk to household food security. Comparison of the cases demonstrates that household characteristics related to resource access play a dominant role in determining household vulnerability. These include household income, income diversification, area of land cultivated, soil quality, household labour per hectare cultivated and the health status of household members. Factors external to the household also control access to resources needed to cope with and recover from climate shocks. These include the existence of formal and informal social networks, availability and quality of health services, and prices of farm inputs and outputs. In each of the case studies, labour available to the farm household is adversely affected by rural–urban migration and infectious disease such as HIV/AIDS and malaria.

Adejuwon (Chapter 10) compares the vulnerability of peasant households to climate shocks in different states of Nigeria using household census data. He finds that the percentage of households employed in agriculture, poverty rate, dependency ratio, access to potable water, health status and educational attainment are important determinants of vulnerability. Also important is the aridity of the climate and quality of soils. The comparison identifies households in the northern states of Nigeria as the most vulnerable in the country. Nyong et al (Chapter 11) conduct detailed surveys of households in these northern states to identify household characteristics that determine vulnerability. Key characteristics include ownership of land and livestock, area and quality of land cultivated, sufficiency of annual harvest relative to household food needs, dependency ratio, cash income, livelihood diversification, gender of household head, and connections to family and social networks. Women in this patrilineal society can be particularly vulnerable.

In the Pantabangan–Carranglan watershed of the northern Philippines, households are exposed to variability in rainfall and water supply as well as to flood events (Pulhin et al, Chapter 15). The vulnerability of households to these exposures is found to be correlated with variables that determine access to and control of resources: ownership of land, farm size, farm income, gender, and status as a native or migrant to the basin. Large landowners are less vulnerable to variable incomes and other impacts of climate events than are smallholder farmers due to their greater resources for coping and recovery, their ability to live in locations that are less exposed to flooding and erosion, and their ability to capture more of the benefits from development projects due to their ties to the institutions that implement these projects. Projections of future climate change suggest the potential for greater precipitation in the Philippines, which would ease water scarcity in most years. However, flooding may become a more frequent stress and would likely impact poor, smallholder farmers of the basin the hardest.

Chinvanno et al (Chapter 16) similarly find that land ownership and other indicators of economic vitality are important determinants of the vulnerability of rice farmers in the Lower Mekong basin. Farmers of rain-fed rice in Thailand and Lao People's Democratic Republic (PDR) are exposed to varia-tions in rice harvests and other impacts from seasonal flooding, shifts in the dates of onset and cessation of the rainy season and variations in rainfall amounts. Farm households with small land holdings produce low volumes of rice and incomes from rice, which are often only enough to sustain the house-hold on a year-to-year basis. As a result, smallholder farm households have very limited buffering capacity to deal with losses or to cope with anomalies during the crop season. Small land holdings also limit the ability of the farmer to implement other activities to diversify their income sources.

Comparing farm households from the Thai study sites with those at the Lao PDR sites, Chinvanno and colleagues find that a larger proportion of the Thai farmers are at high risk from climate shocks despite their higher monetary incomes. They attribute this to higher food costs relative to farm income, lack of income diversification, little savings in the form of financial assets, livestock or food stores, and high debt relative to income among farmers at the Thai sites. Farmers at the Lao PDR study sites also have the advantage of being able to supplement their food supplies with harvests of various products from rela-tively healthy natural ecosystems adjacent to their farms, an option that is not available at the Thai sites.

Land degradation

Land degradation is both an outcome of climate stress and a source of addi-tional stress that can amplify the vulnerability to climate impacts of people making a living from the land. It is found to be an important factor in several of the case study areas, including Mongolia (Batima et al, Chapter 4), Sudan (Osman-Elasha and Sanjak, Chapter 12), northern Nigeria (Nyong et al, Chapter 11), the Philippines (Pulhin et al, Chapter 15), and Argentina and Mexico (Eakin et al, Chapter 13).

In the grazing lands of Mongolia, land degradation has been severe due to the harsh and variable climate, drying of the climate over a 40-year period, and heavy grazing pressures. As noted earlier, these conditions have depressed pas-ture productivity and livestock production. Batima et al (Chapter 4) find that these stresses, combined with the effects of profound economic and institu-tional changes that accompanied Mongolia's transition from a socialist to a market system, have increased vulnerability among herders to climate extremes, as was demonstrated by events in 1999–2003. Several years of sum-mer droughts and severe winter conditions (called *zud*) combined to drastically reduce pasture production, animal weights at the start of winters and stores of fodder for winter months. Approximately 12 million head of livestock died as a result, roughly a quarter of Mongolia's herds. Thousands of families lost animals, an important source of savings, which increased poverty and reduced further the capacity of livestock-dependent households to cope with shocks. Many lost their livelihoods with their animals and migrated to urban centres where unemployment is high and few opportunities awaited them. Climate scenarios suggest the potential for further drying of the climate and Mongolia's herders continuing to be in a state of high vulnerability to the effects of land degradation, drought and *zud*.

In the Philippines' Pantabangan–Carranglan watershed, reforestation and community development projects were implemented to reverse land degradation problems and provide other benefits. However, the projects developed a dependency on external assistance for livelihoods. Many of the jobs associated with the development projects ended when the projects were terminated. Affected households have resorted to charcoal making and *kaingin* (slash and burn) farming, which are damaging the fragile environment of the watershed, including the reforested areas, and increasing vulnerability to flooding (Pulhin et al, Chapter 15).

Food insecurity is increasing in Tlaxcala, Mexico, for a variety of causes, including a shortage of farm labour due to out-migration of young males, declining maize prices and severe soil erosion problems (Ziervogel et al, Chapter 9). The shortage of farm labour constrains the use of soil conservation practices, which are labour-intensive, and leads to the expansion of mono-cropping of maize, a system that increases soil erosion.

Eakin et al (Chapter 13) find that mono-cropping has contributed to land degradation and heightened vulnerability in their study areas in Mexico and Argentina. In Tamaulipas, Mexico, mono-cropping of sorghum, which is resilient to water stress, was promoted by the national government as a strategy for managing drought risks. However, farming of sorghum under persistent drought conditions in the 1990s may have resulted in degradation of soils that is adding to farmers' risks from drought. Now the government is using incentive payments to farmers to encourage them to switch to other alternatives. In the Argentine Pampas, the dramatic expansion of soybean mono-cropping is also observed to be associated with land degradation. This contributes to flood problems and raises concern about the long-term sustainability of soybean farming in the region.

Conflict

Persistent low rainfall, recurrent drought, land degradation, high population growth, governance failures and other factors have deepened poverty and resulted in food and resource scarcity in the Sahel. The scarcities have contributed to tensions between competing groups and tribes. Cereal production in the region has grown at a meagre 1 per cent per annum over the past decade, while the population has grown at an estimated 2.7 per cent. Against this backdrop of generally tightening food scarcity, climatic and other events have created conditions of crisis. Responses can and have inflamed tensions that contribute to violent conflict, compounding the vulnerability of populations to climatic and other stresses.

Events in Sudan's North Darfur State illustrate a case of extremely high vulnerability of the population to loss of livelihoods, livestock, lands and personal security leading to destitution, hunger, famine and violent death (Osman-Elasha and Sanjak, Chapter 12). The drivers of this human misery are multiple and complex. Among them are 20 years of below average rainfall that has severely reduced the availability of water, food and fodder in this dry region of infertile soils. The drying climate and human pressures on the land, exacerbated by migrations of people and their livestock into the area, are degrading the land. Traditional land management systems and practices have been disrupted, bringing nomadic and sedentary tribes into more frequent contact and conflict over land and other scarce resources. These resource conflicts are an important factor behind the widespread violence that has taken tens of thousands of lives in Darfur and forced many more to flee their homes. The lack of physical security and access to resources have devastated livelihoods, eroded capacities to cope with climate and other stresses, and threaten people of the region with famine.

Farmers and herders of northern Nigeria face similar pressures. In their case study of northern Nigeria, Nyong et al (Chapter 11) find that food scarcity and rising food prices have led to intensification of farming and grazing and expansion of these activities into more marginal lands. The greater land-use pressures, combined with the persistent decline in average rainfall, have added to land degradation problems. The productivity of grazing lands has declined in the north. In response, herders have migrated south into sedentary farmers' lands. The resulting conflicts have led to the loss of lives, the destruction of crops, livestock and farmlands, and food insecurity for those affected.

Commodity export-oriented economies

The sensitivity of cash crop yields to climate variability and change is of considerable importance to countries that depend heavily on the contribution of cash crops to national income and foreign exchange earnings. In Sri Lanka, coconut and tea production are the largest sources of export earnings, major contributors to national income and significant employers of labour. Ratnasiri et al (Chapter 17) investigate the effects of past climate variations on the plantation tea sector of Sri Lanka and develop crop models to simulate yield responses to future climate change. Tea yields are affected by variations in both precipitation and temperature. The 1992 drought in Sri Lanka caused a 25 per cent decline in tea production and a corresponding 22 per cent decline in foreign exchange earnings from tea. Projections of future climate change indicate warmer temperatures and both increases and decreases in precipitation. In the lowlands, where temperatures are near the optimum for tea yields, warming would decrease yields. In the cooler uplands, tea yields would increase with warming. Hence the lowland plantations, owned largely by smallholders with low adaptation capacity, are more vulnerable than the upland plantations, which are owned by large companies. An important factor for vulnerability in these cash crop sectors will be the effect of climate change on climate variability, particularly the frequency of drought, which, as shown by past events, is a significant source of risk for these sectors.

Market forces and social safety nets

The case studies by Eakin et al (Chapter 13) of crop and livestock farms in Cordoba, Argentina, and Tamaulipas, Mexico, demonstrate the influences of international market integration and government social programmes on the vulnerability of farmers. Both countries have pursued policies of trade liberalization, privatization and deregulation. The policies have opened access to international markets and foreign investments, allowing, for example, the profitable expansion of soybean farming in Argentina. But competition from overseas producers and removal of price supports and input subsidies have created a 'price squeeze' for farmers, particularly for maize farmers in Mexico.

In this highly competitive environment, farm households have less margin for absorbing shocks, including crop and livestock losses from climate extremes, and so are more vulnerable. The pressures are leading to greater concentration of farms into larger-scale commercial operations as smaller family farms face a number of disadvantages, including higher cost of credit, lack of access to technical skills, high dependence on crop income, greater problems with pests and lack of economies of scale. The problems for small farmers are compounded by cutbacks in state-supported social security mechanisms, resulting in declining rural incomes and increasing inequality between small and large landholders. In Tamaulipas, communal and private tenure small farmers are responding to declining and uncertain farm incomes by diversifying into off-farm sources of income, a trend that is reducing their vulnerability to direct climate impacts.

Mongolia's transition from a socialist to market system in the early 1990s brought dissolution of the collectives through which the livestock sector was managed and subsidized services delivered to herders and their families. As described in Batima et al (Chapter 4), herders received livestock for private ownership but found themselves lacking access to health, education, veterinary, water and marketing services, facing higher prices for transport, fodder and fencing materials, and lacking institutions to regulate access to pastures (which remain state owned), enforce seasonal migration of herds or reserve pastures for emergency use. The dissolution of the social safety nets heightened the vulnerability of pastoralists to climate and other hazards. Traditional customary institutions of the pre-socialist era are beginning to re-emerge and to fill some of these needs.

Human Health

The paths by which climate can affect human health are diverse and involve both direct and indirect mechanisms. The most direct mechanisms operate through human exposures to climatic extremes that can result in injury, illness and death. Climate and climate change also affect human health by influencing human exposure to infectious disease through effects on the biology, habitats and behaviours of disease pathogens, hosts and vectors. Even less directly, climate and climate change can affect human health through impacts on the resources that individuals and communities need to maintain good health. Health outcomes of concern highlighted in the synthesis workshop are summarized in Table 1.6.

Many vector-borne infectious diseases are climate-sensitive and epidemics of these diseases can occur when their natural ecology is disturbed by environmental changes, including changes in climate (McMichael et al, 2001). For example, observations of numbers of malaria and dengue cases vary with inter-annual variations in climate (Wandiga et al, Chapter 18; Heslop-Thomas et al, Chapter 19; Kilian et al, 1999; Lindblade et al, 1999). In the Lake Victoria region of East Africa, significant anomalies in temperature and rainfall were recorded during the El Niño period of 1997–1998 and these were followed by severe malaria outbreaks. A similar association of dengue fever occurrences with ENSO variability has been observed in Jamaica. Other infectious diseases that have been observed to be sensitive to climate variability and change include other insect-borne diseases such as encephalitis, yellow fever and Leishmaniasis and water-borne diseases such as cholera, typhoid and diarrhoea (Aron and Patz, 2001; McMichael et al, 2001).

Projected changes in rainfall and temperature have the potential to expose more people to vector-borne diseases by expanding the geographic range of vectors and pathogens into new areas, increasing the area of suitable habitats and numbers of disease vectors in already endemic areas, and extending transmission seasons. For example, average temperature and precipitation in the East African highlands are projected to rise above the minimum temperature and precipitation thresholds for malaria transmission and extend malaria into areas from which it has been largely absent in the past (Githeko et al, 2000). Other studies suggest that if El Niño events continue to increase in frequency, the elevated temperatures and precipitation would increase malaria transmission (Kilian at al, 1999; Lindblade et al, 1999). In rural communities of the highlands studied by Wandiga et al (Chapter 18), risks for developing malaria and complications from the disease are amplified by low utilization of hospitals and clinics because of distance, cost and low incomes.

The health outcome identified as the highest-level concern is sustained or often repeated in geographically widespread epidemics with high mortality rates. At medium and low levels of concern are more frequent epidemics or outbreaks of infectious disease that may be associated with mortality but which are geographically and temporally limited. Another concern is that changes in climate may allow more virulent strains of disease or more efficient vectors to emerge or be introduced to new areas.

Whether changes in climate result in greater infectious disease incidence or epidemics, the geographic extent and severity of epidemics or outbreaks that might result depend on complex interactions that include not just the effect of climate stresses on the ecology of infectious disease, but also on demographic, social, economic and other factors that determine exposures, transmission,

Table 1.6 *Human health vulnerabilities*

Level of Concern	Outcomes of Concern	Climate Drivers	Other Drivers	AIACC Studies
High	• More frequent geographically widespread and sustained epidemics of infectious and waterborne disease with high human mortality	• Geographically widespread changes in climate that increase the geographic area and number of disease vectors • More frequent heavy rainfall and drought events that disrupt water supply and sanitation and expose people to waterborne pathogens	• Severely degraded or collapsed healthcare system • Poor and declining immunity, nutritional and health status of large portion of population • High poverty rates that limit access to healthcare • Poor or non-existent programmes for disease surveillance, vector control and disease prevention • Large portion of population lack reliable access to potable water and sanitation • Land-use changes that increase habitat for disease vectors and reservoirs for zoonotic diseases	• East Africa (Wandiga et al, Chapter 18) • Caribbean (Heslop-Thomas et al, Chapter 19)
Medium	• Emergence of new or more virulent strains of infectious disease and more efficient disease vectors • More frequent but geographically and temporally limited epidemics with high or moderate mortality • Increase in number of infectious disease cases and mortality in endemic areas and seasons	• Changes in climate that alter disease and vector ecology and transmission pathways • Changes in climate that moderately increase exposures by expanding endemic areas and seasons	• Land-use changes that increase habitat for disease vectors and reservoirs for zoonotic diseases • Crowding • Drug resistance • International migration, travel and trade • Water storage and sanitation practices • Poor programmes for disease surveillance, vector control and disease prevention • Declining quality and increasing cost of healthcare	• East Africa (Wandiga et al, Chapter 18) • Caribbean (Heslop-Thomas et al, Chapter 19)
Low	• More frequent but geographically and temporally limited epidemics with no mortality • Increase in number of isolated infectious disease cases that are not life-threatening	• Changes in climate that alter disease and vector ecology and transmission pathways • Changes in climate that moderately increase exposures by expanding endemic areas and seasons	More severe effects kept in check by: • Access to healthcare • Effective disease surveillance, vector control and disease prevention • Good nutritional and health status of population • Access to potable water and sanitation	• East Africa (Wandiga et al, Chapter 18) • Caribbean (Heslop-Thomas et al, Chapter 19)

results of infection, treatment and prognosis. Vulnerability to severe health outcomes are greatest where the healthcare system is severely degraded, large numbers of people lack access to healthcare, the immunity, nutritional and health status of the population is low, and effective programmes for disease surveillance, vector control and disease prevention are lacking (see Table 1.6). Where the converse of these conditions holds, the likelihood that the most severe health outcomes would be realized is much diminished.

Many of the climate change impacts described in previous sections can also have health impacts by reducing individuals' resilience to disease, the resources available to maintain and protect their health and obtain access to healthcare, and the ability of their communities to deliver quality healthcare services. Examples of these indirect effects include households placed at greater risk of illness as a result of loss of livelihood, assets and support networks from severe and persistent drought, health risks associated with displacement and crowding of populations that migrate in response to climate impacts, healthcare systems being overburdened by increases in case loads as a result of direct health effects of climate change, and impacts of climate extremes on healthcare infrastructure and personnel. The severity of the indirect health outcomes that are realized will depend on the geographic extent, persistence and return period of the triggering climatic event, the severity of impact on resource productivity, livelihoods and healthcare infrastructure, and the resilience of the affected area as indicated by the diversity of economic opportunities, poverty rate, health status and capacity of the healthcare system relative to the population.

Conclusion

In all of the case studies, climate hazards are a significant danger now, not just in the distant future. Potential outcomes from exposure to climate hazards and climate change identified as high-level concerns include water scarcity that retards progress towards development goals, land degradation, losses of entire ecosystems and their species, more frequent and greater loss of life in coastal zones, food insecurity and famine, loss of livelihoods, and increases in infectious disease epidemics. All of these are plausible outcomes of exposure to climate hazards. Whether they are likely outcomes will vary and will depend on the degree and nature of vulnerability of the exposed systems.

Vulnerability to impacts from climate variation and change is shown by our case studies to have multiple causes. The causes include not only exposure to the climatic stressors, but also to stressors that derive from interactions among environmental, demographic, social, economic, institutional, political, cultural and technological processes. The state and dynamics of these processes differ from place to place and generate conditions of sensitivity, adaptive capacity and vulnerability that differ in character and degree. Consequently, populations that are exposed to similar climatic phenomenon are not necessarily impacted the same.

Differences in vulnerability are also apparent for different sub-populations or groups inhabiting a region, and even from household to household within a group. Factors such as sources and diversity of a household's livelihood, experience and skills, level of wealth, ownership and access to land, water and other resources, support from social networks, and access to technical assistance and knowledge give rise to differences in vulnerability between households.

Our synthesis focuses on four domains of vulnerability: natural resources; coasts and small islands; rural economies and food security; and human health. A common finding across the domains of vulnerability is that impacts ranked as high-level concerns generally are not likely to result from climate stress alone. They are most likely to be realized when multiple stresses act synergistically to create conditions of high vulnerability. A climate shock or stress has the potential to do the most damage in a context in which natural systems are being severely stressed and degraded by overuse and in which social, economic or governance systems are in or near a state of failure and thus not capable of effective responses.

Unfortunately, such conditions exist in many parts of the world, particularly the developing world. Places where this is true are consequently vulnerable to some of the high-level concern outcomes from exposure to climate stresses, both now, from current climate variations and extremes, and increasingly in the future as the climate changes. An exception is the potential loss of some ecosystems or their biodiversity, which might, in some instances, be triggered by climate change alone. For example, the rate of climate change is a key factor that threatens the succulent karoo biome of South Africa, and a rapid rate of change could, by itself, be sufficient to cause its demise. But for many other ecosystems it will be the interaction of a changing climate with pressures from human uses, and management of land and other resources that will probably determine their fate.

More optimistically, our studies suggest that the potential severity and risk of many of the outcomes are less where social, economic and governance systems function in ways that enable effective responses to prevent, cope with, recover from and adapt to adverse impacts. For example, a healthcare system that is effective in delivering services to a population, combined with public health programmes that promote preventive behaviours, disease monitoring and disease vector control, can substantially limit the risk that climate change would cause widespread and persistent epidemics. Disaster prevention, preparedness, early warning and response systems can similarly help to limit the extent of harm from changes in the frequency or severity of extreme climate events. Poverty reduction can provide households with access to all manner of resources that can help them to cope with and overcome climate-related impacts.

These and other examples indicate that improving the performance of human systems can reduce vulnerability. Doing so can yield near-term payoffs, as we improve our management of existing climate risks, as well as the longer-term benefits associated with building resilience to a changing climate. But optimism should be tempered by the reality of how challenging it has been to achieve even minimal progress where key human systems have been dysfunctional.

References

Arnell, N. W. (2004) 'Climate change and global water resources: SERES emissions and socioeconomic scenarios', *Global Environmental Change*, vol 14, pp31–52

Aron, J. L. and J. A. Patz (2001) *Ecosystem Change and Public Health: A Global Perspective*, John Hopkins University Press, Baltimore, MD

Callaway, J., D. Louw, J. Nkomo, M. Hellmuth and D. Sparks (2006) 'The Berg river dynamic spatial equilibrium model: A new tool for assessing the benefits and costs of alternatives for coping with water demand growth, climate variability and climate change in the Western Cape', AIACC Working Paper No 31, International START Secretariat, Washington, DC, www.aiaccproject.org

Camilloni, I. A. and V. R. Barros (2003) 'Extreme discharge events in the Parana river and their climate forcing', *Journal of Hydrology*, vol 278, pp94–106

Donne, J. (1623) *Devotions Upon Emergent Occasions*, Meditation No 17, available at www.incompetech.com/authors/donne/bell.html

Downing, T. E. (2002) 'Linking sustainable livelihoods and global climate change in vulnerable food systems', *Die Erde*, vol 133, pp363–378

Githeko, A. K., S. W. Lindsay, U. E. Confaloniero and J. A. Patz (2000) 'Climate change and vector-borne disease: A regional analysis', *Bulletin of the World Health Organization*, vol 78, no 9, pp1136–1147

Hoerling, M., J. Hurrell, J. Eischeid and A. Phillips (2006) 'Detection and attribution of 20th century northern and southern African monsoon change', *Journal of Climate*, vol 19, pp3989–4008

IPCC (2001a) *Climate Change 2001: The Scientific Basis*, J. T. Houghton, Y. Ding, D. J. Griggs, M. Noguer, P. J. van der Linden, X. Dai, K. Maskell and C. A. Johnson (eds), contribution of Working Group I to the Third Assessment Report of the Intergovernmental Panel on Climate Change, Cambridge University Press, Cambridge, UK, and New York

IPCC (2001b) *Climate Change 2001: Impacts, Adaptation and Vulnerability*, J. J. McCarthy, O. F. Canziani, N. A. Leary, D. J. Dokken and K. S. White (eds), contribution of Working Group II to the Third Assessment Report of the Intergovernmental Panel on Climate Change, Cambridge University Press, Cambridge, UK, and New York

IPCC (2007) 'Summary for policymakers', in M. Parry, O. Canziani, J. Palutikof and P. van der Linden (eds) *Climate Change 2007: Impacts, Adaptation and Vulnerability*, contribution of Working Group II to the Fourth Assessment Report of the Intergovernmental Panel on Climate Change, Cambridge University Press, Cambridge, UK, and New York

Kilian, A., P. Langi, A. Talisuna and G. Kabagambe (1999) 'Rainfall pattern, El Niño and malaria in Uganda', *Transactions of the Royal Society of Tropical Medicine and Hygiene*, vol 93, pp22–23

Leary, N. (2002) 'AIACC, contributing to a second generation of climate change assessments', *START Network News*, no 7, May

Leary, N., J. Adejuwon, V. Barros, I. Burton, J. Kulkarni and J. Pulhin (eds) (2008) *Climate Change and Adaptation*, Earthscan, London

Lindblade, K., E. Walker, A. Onapa, J. Katunge and M. Wilson (1999) 'Highland malaria in Uganda: Prospective analysis of an epidemic associated with El Niño', *Transactions of the Royal Society of Tropical Medicine and Hygiene*, vol 93, pp480–487

Mataki, M., K. Koshy and V. Nair (2006) 'Implementing climate change adaptation in the Pacific islands: Adapting to present variability and extreme weather events in Navua, Fiji', AIACC Working Paper No 34, International START Secretariat, Washington, DC, www.aiaccproject.org

Mataki, M., K. Koshy, R. Lata and L. Ralogaivau (2005) 'Vulnerability of a coastal township to flooding associated with extreme rainfall events in Fiji', unpublished working paper, University of the South Pacific, Suva, Fiji

McMichael, A., A. Githeko, R. Akhtar, R. Carcavallo, D. Gubler, A. Haines, R. S. Kovats, P. Martens, J. Patz and A. Sasaki (2001) 'Human health', in J. J. McCarthy, O. F. Canziani, N. A. Leary, D. J. Dokken and K. S. White (eds) *Climate Change 2001: Impacts, Adaptation and Vulnerability*, Cambridge University Press, Cambridge, UK, and New York

MEA (2005) *Ecosystems and Human Well-being: Synthesis*, Millennium Ecosystem Assessment, Island Press, Washington, DC

Sheppard, C., D. Dixon, M. Gourlay, A. Sheppard and R. Payet (2005) 'Coral mortality increases wave energy reaching shores protected by reef flats: Examples from the Seychelles', *Estuarine, Coastal and Shelf Science*, vol 64, pp223–234

UNCCD (2005a) 'Fact Sheet 3: The consequences of desertification', www.unccd.int/publicinfo/factsheets

UNCCD (2005b) 'Fact Sheet 1: An introduction to the United Nations Convention to Combat Desertification', www.unccd.int/publicinfo/factsheets

Part II:

Natural Resource Systems

2

Vulnerability of Southern African Biodiversity to Climate Change

Graham P. von Maltitz and Robert J. Scholes

Introduction

Southern Africa, and in particular South Africa, is home to a vast variety of endemic flora and fauna which, besides its intrinsic value, is vital for sustaining human livelihoods as well as many formal and informal economic sectors. Seven broad terrestrial ecological zones (biomes) occur in this region: the savanna, grassland, nama karoo, succulent karoo, forest, desert and fynbos biomes (Rutherford and Westfall, 1994). Some authorities also recognize an eighth biome, the thicket biome (Low and Rebelo, 1996). Of these, the fynbos biome in the Cape region and succulent karoo biome in the succulent karoo region possess particularly high levels of plant biodiversity and are two of the eight centres of plant endemism identified within southern Africa (Cowling and Hilton-Taylor 1994; Cowling and Hilton-Taylor, 1997).

The biomes of southern Africa are characterized by unique climatic parameters, though edaphic (soil related) factors are also important in defining the habitats of individual species (Rutherford and Westfall, 1994). Early assessments using simple biome-level climatic envelope models have confirmed that global climatic change is likely to severely impact future biome distribution patterns (Scholes, 1990; Rutherford et al, 1999), with existing biomes likely shifted eastwards and compacted into the eastern half of the country (Figure 2.1). Based on projections of the HadCM2 (including and excluding sulphates) and CSM scenarios, by 2050, 38–55 per cent of the current area of South Africa would have a climatic envelope that did not match any current biome. Consequently, future climate conditions will possibly produce species assemblages with no counterpart in present communities (Hannah et al, 2002) and wide-scale species loss is also probable (see, for example, Thomas et al, 2004).

The succulent karoo biome is of particular concern since it would likely be almost entirely replaced by an area with hotter and dryer conditions (Rutherford et al, 1999). In addition, the main area of its future distribution is predicted to be disjunct from its area of current distribution, being separated

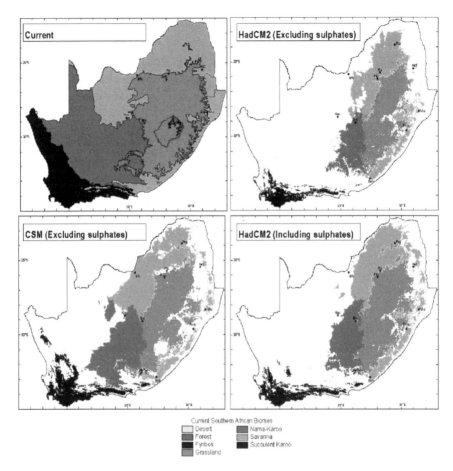

Figure 2.1 *Current and future predicted distributions of the major South African biomes (fynbos, succulent karoo, nama karoo, savanna and grassland), generated using simple bioclimatic modelling techniques based on five ecologically important bioclimatic parameters*

Source: Rutherford et al (1999).

by a range of mountains. The extents of other biomes – savanna, grasslands and nama karoo – are also reduced, with both the savanna and nama karoo invading into some grassland areas. The fynbos is the only biome to show limited changes in total extent, but there is evidence that many individual species may be impacted. The forest biome is very small and dispersed, and the most likely scenario is that only its distribution in the north-eastern part of the country would be impacted. Very little desert is presently found in South Africa, though its extent may increase in future due to desertification caused by climate change.

In order to better understand the potential impacts of climate change on biodiversity in southern Africa, we selected three of these biomes – fynbos, succulent karoo and savanna – as pilot study sites primarily on the basis of the following important characteristics:

- Though the spatial extent of the fynbos is less likely to be reduced as much as other biomes, it is very important in terms of its biodiversity and there is significant concern about individual species response to climate change within this biome.
- The succulent karoo, which has a unique biodiversity, is likely to experience some of the most severe impacts from climate change based on the results of previous modelling studies.
- The savanna is a widespread biome in Africa and is very important from a livelihood perspective. It possesses a unique co-dominance of tree and grass lifeforms, which makes it perfect for studying systems-level responses of functional groups of plants to climate change.

Furthermore, data on the three biomes are also readily available from previous and ongoing work in these areas, which facilitates the analysis of their vulnerability to climate change.

Description of the Biomes Studied

Fynbos

Fynbos, literally meaning fine-leaved bush, is a local term for the heath-like vegetation found in areas of South Africa that have a Mediterranean-type climate with winter rainfall (Cowling et al, 1997). Evergreen, fire-prone vegetation on a low-nutrient substrate is a key feature of the fynbos. It is largely confined to the rugged and steep quartzitic Folded Mountains in the Cape Floristic region[1] located in the south-western tip of South Africa and occupies an area of about 71,000km². This biome has exceptionally high species richness, with an estimated 7300 species, of which 80 per cent are endemic (Cowling and Hilton-Taylor, 1994 and 1997). Altitude, rainfall, aspect and soil are important determinants of vegetation structure, while stochastic factors such as fire frequency and intensity play an important role in determining species composition (Cowling et al, 1997). There is a strong dependency on insects as pollinators and some species depend on ants as seed dispersers (myrmecochory). Others depend on the wind or are passively dispersed. Most species have specific strategies to ensure regeneration from seeds after fires, although a few species can also resprout following fire. Species that do not resprout after fire but are limited by seeds for recruitment face a high risk of extinction if their pollinator or disperser mutualisms collapse (Bond, 1984).

    With respect to species composition, approximately 40 per cent of the fynbos plant species are comprised of the highly speciated ericoid family. It is, however, the Proteaceae family that makes up the bulk of the shrub biomass and holds ecological and economic importance. The standing biomass of the Proteaceae is a major driver of the fire regime and though a few protioids can resprout after fire, the majority are obligatory reseeders. This is an important factor when considering climate change impacts on the fynbos (Bond and Breytenbach, 1985).

Succulent karoo

The succulent karoo biome is an area of about 100,000km^2 that stretches along the west coast of southern Namibia and South Africa and as a narrow band across the northern edge of the fynbos. It is found predominantly on coastal plains and intermountain valleys, mostly at an altitude of less than 1000m. The biome receives only 20–290mm of annual rain, more than 40 per cent of which falls in winter. It is the high summer aridity and the finer grained and more nutrient-rich soils that differentiate this area from the fynbos. The biome has more than 5000 plant species, of which about 50 per cent are endemic (Milton et al, 1997).

The unique feature of the karoo vegetation is the high concentration of leaf-succulents of the two dominant families, Mesembryanthemaceae and Crassulaceae. Most species are insect pollinated and seed dispersal occurs mostly by wind or water, with long-lived perennials and short-lived annuals having different seeding strategies. The annuals use a number of mechanisms to delay germination to periods of suitable rainfall and different species respond to different timing of rain. Generally, annuals have a high proportion of seedlings reaching reproductive maturity, whereas long-lived species tend to have a very low annual recruitment rate (Milton, 1995; Rosch, 1977; van Rooyen et al, 1979). Disturbance of the landscape also promotes the establishment of annuals. The re-establishment of long-lived plants onto disturbed areas is, in contrast, very slow and may take up to 80 years (Beukes et al, 1994; Dean and Milton, 1995). Fire is not a feature in the succulent karoo but the vegetation is susceptible to drought, which can kill off many of the perennials. Once again, annuals tend to recover rapidly from drought while perennials recover very slowly (Milton 1995).

Savanna

The co-dominance of trees and grass is what distinguishes the savanna from other biomes. Savannas cover 54 per cent of the land area of southern Africa and 60 per cent of sub-Saharan Africa. They are found in predominantly frost-free regions with a moist hot season (Scholes and Walker, 1993; Scholes, 1997). The species richness of the Savanna is second only to the fynbos in southern Africa, with about 5780 species in an area of about 600,000km^2. Although plant diversity at the small plot scale ('alpha diversity') is high, the species turnover ('beta diversity') and landscape ('gamma') diversity are generally low (Scholes, 1997). In other words, adjacent patches tend to have very similar species. This is in sharp contrast to the fynbos, which has high beta and gamma diversity.

The savanna grasses largely depend on animals or wind for seed dispersal, whereas trees have ballistic dispersal, wind dispersal and animal dispersal. The herbaceous layer is a mix of annual and perennial forbs[2] and grass species, with annuals being more dominant in arid areas. Trees can be exceptionally long lived (a few centuries in some species) and many species are able to resprout if damaged by animals or fire. Fire is a common occurrence, and its frequency and intensity are largely governed by rainfall and herbivory. Fire and herbivory play an important role in determining the proportional representation of trees and grasses in the savanna (Scholes, 1997).

The savannas are home to most of Africa's large mammals and support an important tourism industry. They also house a large livestock ranching industry. Historically, the savannas have supported most of the indigenous human populations of Africa and the area still plays an important role in supporting subsistence economies through the supply of grazing, fuelwood and other natural resources (Scholes, 1997).

Research Framework and Methodology

Three different approaches were developed to assess the vulnerability of biodiversity to climate change in the succulent karoo, fynbos and savanna. We also attempted to determine the potential impacts of this vulnerability on biodiversity-dependent human communities in these biomes.

For the fynbos biome a 'time-slice' modelling approach was used to investigate the migratory corridors required for individual species to track climate change (for details see Midgley et al, 2006; Williams et al, 2004). The Proteaceae were used as representative species because of the ready availability of detailed distribution data and their economic importance and because their distributions have been shown to be closely correlated with the distributions of other fynbos species. Species distribution data were obtained from the *Protea* Atlas Project database (http://protea.worldonline.co.za/default.htm). Climate data were interpolated for the one-minute grid (Schulze et al, 1997) and future projections were based on the HadCM2 general circulation model, using IS92a emissions scenarios (Schulze and Perks, 1999). Soil categorization, species nomenclature and species dispersal modes were some of the other data obtained.

In the karoo case study, a simpler approach was taken to examine the link between a single animal species and its habitat and food resources. Two species, the highly endangered riverine rabbit (*Bunolagus monticularis*) from the nama karoo and the padloper tortoise (*Homopus singnatus*) from the succulent karoo (for details see Hughes et al, 2005a and b) were used for this purpose.

The savanna study, on the other hand, investigates key functional properties – tree cover, fire frequency, grass and browse production, and carrying capacity – for major guilds of herbivores and carnivores, rather than individual species interaction. A model based on the Lotka–Volterra approach (Lotka, 1925; Volterra, 1926) was developed for this purpose (Scholes, 2005) and attempts were made to predict the functional responses of grasses and trees to changes in temperature, rainfall and CO_2 levels.

Vulnerability of Different Biomes and Species to the Impacts of Climate Change

The primary factors affecting the vulnerability of individual species are the magnitude of climate impacts and the adaptive capacity of species. Different global circulation models (GCMs) and emission scenarios result in a range of projections for future climate in southern Africa. Common to all is an increase in temperature, but the magnitude of this change varies from under 1°C to up to 3.5°C for 2080 (Scholes and Biggs, 2004).

There is less agreement between GCMs regarding the impacts of climate change on rainfall. Most models project reduced rainfall in the western half of southern Africa, though there may be increased rainfall in the eastern subcontinent (Scholes and Biggs, 2004). From the perspective of plants, an increase in temperature combined with reduced rainfall greatly decreases the available moisture for growth. In other words the ratio of rainfall to potential evaporation tends to decrease, resulting in more desert-like conditions. The fertilization effect of increased CO_2 may, to some extent, offset the impacts of this increased aridity.

The fynbos as a biome appears less affected by climate change than many of the other southern African biomes (Rutherford et al, 1999). In a study of climate impacts using the Proteaceae as an indicator group, Midgley et al (2002a) reported that 17 of the 28 *Protea* species examined would experience potential range contraction, while 5 species would likely experience range elimination. Changes in climatic factors were predicted to have a greater impact than land transformation as the Proteas tend to move to areas of higher altitude in the mountains that are not likely to be impacted by land transformation. This study was repeated for 330 *Protea* species (Midgley et al, 2002b), with similar results. A loss of 51 per cent to 65 per cent of the area extent of the fynbos biome was predicted, depending on the climate scenario used. One third of the *Protea* species were found to have complete range dislocation (in other words there is no overlap between their future range and their current range). Only 5 per cent would retain more than two thirds of their current range, while 10 per cent of the species would have no predicted range in the future scenario.

To further examine *Proteaceae* responses to climate change we developed a dynamic movement model to determine whether the Proteas could disperse from their current distribution to predicted 2050 habitats (Williams et al, 2004). The model assumed a shorter migration range for *Protea* species with ant-dispersed seeds rather than those whose seeds are wind dispersed. A time-sliced approach was used to see whether suitable 'stepping stone' habitats existed to allow the *Protea* to move from their current distribution to their future distribution. The study found that, of the 282 species investigated, 262 maintained overlapping habitats and did not need to disperse (though their range may be reduced), 18 species were obligatory dispersers (those that would have to move to new habitats) and could reach their new habitats, while 2 species were unable to disperse because of land transformation. Thirty-four species were removed from the analysis, as they had no future habitat and would therefore likely become extinct unless ex situ conservation was initiated.

These detailed studies on the Proteas are unique and other genera of the fynbos have not been subjected to similar scrutiny. Although Proteas may serve as an example to represent general trends, they only account for a small proportion of the actual diversity, and the rest still need more detailed analysis. Additionally, the many assumptions and uncertainties associated with climatic envelope modelling in general and the dynamic movement models in particular have not been taken into account in the current results.

The succulent karoo biome is expected to suffer the greatest impact from climate change, losing almost all of its current range according to studies by Rutherford et al (1999). The small area of future range is projected to be disjunct from the current range, separated by mountain escarpments (Rutherford et al, 1999). In the Namibian portion of the succulent karoo, many species are also highly localized endemics that probably lack the ability for long-distance migration, even though their projected future habitats may bear similarities to their present habitats. So far a decline has already been observed in the population of *Aloe dicotima*, one of the most conspicuous species of the succulent karoo (Foden, 2002).

Among animals in the succulent karoo, the padloper tortoise will likely adapt to the impacts of climate change because it has a broad range of plant food sources growing over a widespread area. In contrast, the riverine rabbit from the nama karoo is predicted to become extinct because its specialized habitat and food requirements are unlikely to be met under future climate conditions (Hughes et al, 2005a and b).

The core of the savanna case study was an investigation of the dynamics of trees and grasses, given climate change. Trees and grasses have different responses to both changes in soil moisture and temperature, and increased atmospheric CO_2 concentrations, which tend to have a growth promoting effect. The CO_2 effect is more pronounced in trees than in tropical grasses, but in both cases begins to saturate at around 500ppm under natural conditions (Scholes et al, 1999). According to preliminary model runs for the northeastern lowveld savanna, the negative impacts of the decrease in soil moisture and increase in temperature would more than compensate for the small advantage trees have from elevated CO_2 levels. A slight increase in woodiness is, however, predicted. It is also predicted that habitat suitability for browsers and grazers is likely to remain relatively constant in the 50-year timeframe, provided appropriate management of fire and elephant population, the key controls of future habitat structure. Overall, the carrying capacity for large herbivores is projected to decrease by about 10 per cent.

Other Factors Likely to Influence Ecosystem and Species Vulnerability

Flatness of topography

Altitudinal gradients and aspect both affect local climate conditions. In hilly topography with steep environmental gradients, plants and animals would only have to move short distances to find new habitats (Cowling et al, 1999). For example, *Protea* species are expected to move up altitudinal environmental gradients in response to climate change (Williams et al, 2004). A potentially negative consequence of such higher altitude 'escapes' is that species may be trapped on these 'islands' and their dispersal into new areas might be prevented. By contrast, on a flat topography like that of the succulent karoo, the horizontal rate of climatic envelope shift would be more rapid, making it extremely difficult for plants to disperse fast enough to track a changing climate. While this may not be a problem for widespread species adapted to long-distance seed dispersal and rapid establishment, it is likely to be devastating for species with localized distributions, short-range seed dispersal or slow rates of establishment (in other words many of the long-lived perennial species).

Availability of refugia

Small climatically suitable refugia could potentially support remnant populations of a species in an otherwise changed climate; for example, a cooler and moister south slope of a mountain (in comparison to a hot north slope) or a deep river gorge that provides moisture and temperature regulation and protection from fire. The fynbos biome and the savanna biome are more likely to have a number of refugia options than the karoo biome.

Edaphic barriers

Most plant species are adapted to specific soil (edaphic) conditions and are unlikely to be able to move over barriers of unsuitable soils. Similarly, the large mammals and birds of the savanna biome tend to be either 'fertile soil' specialists or 'infertile soil' specialists. Factors such as texture, water holding capacity, nutrient status and acidity are likely to be the most important in terms of soil suitability. An example is *Colophospernum mopane*, a common species of the low-lying and hot savanna areas which is predicted to expand extensively with global warming on the basis of its climate envelopes (Rutherford et al, 1999) but which may, in practice, show little or no response as the species appears to be limited to the heavy soils of river valleys (Scholes, 1997). Similarly, mountains are likely to form barriers, especially if the substrate on the mountains greatly differs from that of the surrounding plains, as is the case of the Cape Folded Mountains, which separate the existing succulent karoo from areas of future suitable habitat.

Land transformation and habitat fragmentation

The combined impacts of habitat loss due to land transformation (into cropland) and climate change will make some species exceptionally vulnerable. Land transformation is typically most severe in the relatively flat areas suitable for crop production (Haplin, 1997). The west coast renosterveld[3] of the fynbos, for instance, has already lost an estimated 97 per cent of its habitat (Low and

Rebelo, 1996) and just 100m of cropland may be sufficient to prevent dispersal of some *Protea* species (Williams et al, 2004).

Life history characteristics

A number of life history characteristics of species are likely to influence their vulnerability to climate change, more so in the case of plants than animals. Some of the key characteristics are discussed below:

- *Niche specialists versus generalists*: Species with broad climate tolerances are less likely to be impacted than specialist species with narrow habitat niches. For example, a large number of Proteas as well as the padloper tortoise are likely to maintain habitats into the future while a few Proteas and the riverine rabbit would likely lose their habitat niche (see Williams et al, 2004; Midgley et al, 2002a and b; Hughes et al, 2005a and b).
- *Species movement*: In plants, the mechanism of seed dispersal will determine the distance that species can migrate per generation. This can be hundreds of metres or even kilometres where wind, animals, birds or water are the dispersal agents. Many seeds lack long-distance dispersal mechanisms and tend to concentrate very close to the parent plant. For instance, many of the Proteas have ant-dispersed (myrmecohory) seeds (Bond and Slingsbey, 1983), which limits the distance they can move to about a few metres per generation (Bond, 1984). In the case of animals and insects, some birds and large mammals may travel hundreds of kilometres, while others may be limited because of mobility or reluctance to cross changed habitats. Samango monkeys, for example, though highly mobile, will not cross extensive open ground to move from one forest patch to another.
- *Species interactions – competition and facilitation*: Species do not move as total habitats (Hannah et al, 2002); rather, individual species move at different rates. In a new area, a species is likely to experience new competition from those species already present. The impacts of this are exceptionally difficult to understand or model.
- *Dependency on pollinators and dispersers*: Where species have a mutual dependency on a pollinator or seed disperser, both organisms would have to adapt simultaneously to climate change for their long-term sustainability. Obligatory pollinators and seed dispersers are common in the fynbos and succulent karoo, but relatively rare in the savanna (see, for example, Milton et al, 1997; Cowling et al, 1997). The risk is far less where there are generic pollinators such as the honeybee.
- *Species establishment*: The establishment niche (Grubb, 1977) will be a key limiting process for many plant species because, once established, many species can cope with slightly modified climatic niches (for example, the numerous garden trees that grow way outside of their natural climatic niche). Additionally, plants that require many years to mature and fruit may be more vulnerable to climate impacts than annual species.
- *Species longevity*: It is probable that many established plant species might be able to persist in a changed climate, especially long-lived species that

might persist for centuries and possibly regenerate if climate mitigation is successful and optimal conditions return. Short-lived species are likely to be more severely impacted and could become extinct within a few generations.

- *Seed ecology*: Some plant species require a cool period to stimulate germination and climatic warming could negatively affect their ability to germinate. In the succulent karoo, plant species appear to be dependant on seasonal rainfall for germination.

Impacts of alien invasive species

Alien invasive species pose a strong threat to some biomes, especially the fynbos. Any indigenous species attempting to establish itself in a new habitat may have to compete with alien vegetation simultaneously moving into the new niche. It has been suggested that invasive alien species may invade more rapidly under conditions of climatic change, as they are frequently opportunistic species adapted to a wide range of habitats (Macdonald, 1994).

Impacts of fire

Both the fynbos and savanna are fire-dependent ecosystems (Cowling et al, 1997; Rutherford and Westfall, 1994; Scholes, 1997), and any changes in fire frequency or intensity would change the dynamics of these systems. On the other hand, the succulent karoo is not adapted to fire and its spread into habitats where fire occurs would therefore be limited.

Impacts of misaligned conservation strategies

Strategic conservation planning typically attempts to ensure that all current habitat types are conserved in at least one location. It does not take into consideration possible impacts of climatic change that will result in new species assemblages and changes in the spatial location of at least some species. The current conservation network may thus prove inadequate for protecting biodiversity in the future. It may be poorly aligned to facilitate the movement of biodiversity and may not provide sufficient protection of important areas that could serve as biodiversity refugia. Therefore, a better solution would be to protect gradients and transitional areas in addition to core areas (Peters and Darling, 1985; Haplin, 1997; Hannah et al, 2002; Williams et al, 2004). This would require a strategic expansion of the conservation network, including enhancing conservation outside of protected areas (also referred to as managing the matrix). This has been studied in detail only in the case of the fynbos biome (Williams et al, 2004), where it was determined that for effective conservation, a doubling of the current conservation network is needed. The conservation of 'persistence areas', or areas that remain suitable over time despite climate change, is also recommended.

Of the three biomes considered, species in the succulent karoo are likely to be more vulnerable to climate change than those of the savanna or fynbos, primarily because of the potential extent of climate impacts on this habitat, but also because of other factors that compound climate change impacts such as the relatively flat topography, edaphic conditions, specialist pollinators and the slow rate of re-establishment of long-lived perennial species.

Impacts on the fynbos will, to some extent, be mitigated by the mountainous terrain, though species loss is still probable. The high level of land transformation in the lowland fynbos habitats makes species in these habitats especially vulnerable. In contrast, the savannas, as a system, are considered less vulnerable to climate change, with most functional aspects likely to be maintained. Direct impacts on individual species are less certain and still unexamined. According to our study on the vulnerability of biodiversity in the savanna, the widespread and generalist nature of most savanna species is likely to result in less severe impacts when compared to the fynbos and karoo biomes.

Human Dependencies on Biodiversity

In addition to the intrinsic value of biodiversity, there are also direct and indirect benefits that contribute to human livelihoods. So far the value of biodiversity to human well-being has been poorly researched and therefore we have made an initial attempt to predict the likely impacts of climate-induced biodiversity change on livelihoods in our three case study biomes.

Succulent karoo

This near-desert area has low plant production potential and a very low human population density. It has historically been used prominently for livestock grazing, though even with borehole water it is still an inhospitable environment. Livestock stocking rates have decreased over the last couple of decades and this is attributed to species changes in response to herbivory (Dean and McDonald, 1994; Milton et al, 1997). It can be assumed that with increasing aridity, as predicted by most climate models, this area will become less suited to livestock production. Changes in the global economics of livestock production are likely to exacerbate this impact.

The succulent karoo is also an increasingly popular ecotourism spot during its annual periods of wild flower blooms. These blooms are all from annual species, mostly of the Asteraceae, Liliaceae and Mesembryanthemaceae families, and are dependent on seasonal rainfall. A decline in rainfall or shift in seasonality of rainfall may therefore have a direct impact on the tourism industry.

Fynbos

In contrast to the succulent karoo, the fynbos is an area of high human population in the plains, while the mountains have a relatively low population density. Land transformation for agriculture and settlement has had strong impacts on biodiversity, but natural biodiversity per se is not the basis of the main economic activity in the biome. There are, however, individual species of the fynbos that are extensively used for the cut flower and dry flower industry, for flavouring brandy (buchu) and for herbal tea (rooibos tea). The vegetation is also used for fuelwood, though much of this is from alien invasive species. Any changes in the availability and location of such commercial species would directly impact these industries. In addition, the fynbos is also a major tourist attraction, though the relationship between tourism and species biodiversity is unclear and is unlikely to be linear.

Savanna

The savanna biome is very important in terms of livelihood benefits, especially for the rural poor (see, for example, Campbell, 1996; Shackleton et al, 2004) and is used predominantly for livestock grazing and wildlife management, including nature-based tourism. Within South Africa, most of the communally managed areas occur in the savannas and these house extensive rural communities that depend on the natural biodiversity of the savanna for a large proportion of their livelihoods. This trend is even more prominent in other southern African countries where there is a smaller cash economy and a poorer state social support network. By far the most important resources from the savannas to these subsistence communities are fuelwood and grazing, although many other resources, including construction timber, edible plants, medicinal plants and craft material, are also collected. In the future it is likely that the range of services derived from savannas would still be maintained (possibly at a somewhat lower level), though there may be a change in specific species. However, the change in climate may cause these areas to become less suitable for crop production and hence reliance on natural products may increase.

The wildlife-based tourism industry in the savannas is expected to survive the impacts of climate change, as is the livestock industry, although climate change may accelerate a switch from livestock to wildlife management. This is due to the greater resilience of wildlife to a hot environment and also the possibility of increased pathogen infestations in livestock due to climate change.

Conclusion

The vulnerability of individual species to climate change depends on the interaction between the magnitude of the impact and the adaptive capacity of the species. Of the three South African biomes considered, the fynbos and succulent karoo are predicted to be the most vulnerable to projected climate changes in the 21st century, while the savanna is predicted to be more resilient. The plant species-rich succulent karoo is at risk partly because of the magnitude and nature of the projected climate change (in the most extreme scenarios, its current climate niche is not represented in the future) but also because of the relatively flat topography, which does not provide altitudinal or aspect-based refugia. This means that species need to disperse very rapidly to keep track with a changing environment. Their capacity to do so is constrained by their strong soil specificity in this geologically complex location. Additionally, the slow establishment rates of many long-lived species places them at greater risk than annual species with more rapid establishment and greater seed dispersal. Not only is there a large probability of extensive species loss in the succulent karoo, but the biome's ability to support livelihoods is also expected to decline.

Within the fynbos, the extent of species loss may exceed that predicted from habitat loss alone but it is expected to be less severe than in the succulent karoo. The complex reproduction ecology of many of the species adds to their vulnerability and this is not taken into consideration in simple climatic envelope-based modelling. Species loss is an important concern given that this biome is an international biodiversity hotspot. The mountainous terrain will, to some extent, assist in adaptation to climate change. Economic sectors dependent on the biodiversity in this biome, such as the wild flower industry, may suffer severe impacts from climate change.

A key consideration in both the fynbos and succulent karoo biomes is the close and obligatory association between species; for instance, between plant species and their pollination and seed dispersal agents. The entire suite of organisms would have to move jointly in response to a changing environment for the long-term integrity and viability of the community and its constituents. The current knowledge base and models are unfortunately inadequate to analyse future climate impacts on these relationships.

The savanna biome is predicted to have relatively limited functional or species change. Though the biome overall is species-rich, the mean range size of the organisms is large (in other words the same species are found over extensive areas and across a wide climate niche). The diverse mammals and birds for which this biome is world-renowned are relatively mobile and not highly dependent on particular plant species, but on broad functional categories of plants, which are projected to persist. There is some evidence that enhanced CO_2 may promote C3 trees over C4 grasses[4], but our models suggest that this effect may be overwhelmed by differences in temperature and water response functions between trees and grasses. Coupled with changing fire regimes and elephant densities, these impacts could result in a structurally changed savanna, which would, in turn, have consequences on habitat structure and species proportions in the community, though not necessarily their persistence. The ability of the savanna biodiversity to support rural subsistence livelihoods or the wildlife and tourism industry is not expected to change very substantially, although climate change may accelerate the current shift from cattle to wildlife ranching.

From a human vulnerability perspective, it is the savannas that have the highest density of human settlements and it is in these areas where there is a high dependency on the use of savanna resources, particularly fuelwood, but also numerous other livelihood-enhancing products. These areas are also exceptionally important for nature-based tourism and wildlife-based production. In contrast, the fynbos and succulent karoo have a lower level of subsistence livelihood dependency, though a number of enterprises have developed around the commercial harvesting of particular plant species such as *Proteaceae* for the flower market and herbal teas and brandies.

Notes

1   The Cape Floristic region is a biodiversity hotspot with Mediterranean-type climate and is one of the only two hotspots that encompass an entire floral kingdom (for details see www.biodiversityhotspots.org/xp/Hotspots/cape_floristic/).
2   Forbs are non-grass, broad-leaved plants with little or no woody material and are usually found on fields, prairies or meadows. This group includes most herbs, vegetables, and wild and garden flowering plants.
3   Renosterveld vegetation is a type of fynbos that dominates on the flatlands of the western Cape. It is dominated by the daisy family (Asteraceae) and has low levels of typical fynbos genera such as Proteas, Ericas and Restios, It has been extensively cleared to make way for agricultural crops and housing development (Low and Rebelo, 1996).
4   C3 plants produce a three-carbon compound during photosynthesis and include most trees and common crops like rice, wheat, barley, soybeans, potatoes and vegetables. The C4 plants produce a four carbon compound during photosynthesis and include grasses and crops like maize, sugar cane, sorghum and millet. Under increased atmospheric concentrations of CO_2, C3 plants have been shown to be more responsive than C4 plants (see IPCC, 2001).

References

Beukes, P. C., R. M. Cowling and F. Ellis (1994) 'Vegetation and soil changes across a succulent karoo grazing gradient', *Arid Zone Ecology Forum Abstracts*, Foundation for Research Development, Pretoria, South Africa, p23

Bond, W. (1984) 'Fire survival of Cape Proteaceae: Influence of season and seed predation', *Vegitatio*, vol 56, pp65–74

Bond, W. and G. J. Breytenbach (1985) 'Ants, rodents and seed predation in Proteaceae', *South African Journal of Zoology*, vol 20, pp150–155

Bond, W. and P. Slingsbey (1983) 'Seed dispersal by ants in shrublands of the Cape Province and its evolutionally implications', *South African Journal of Science*, vol 79, pp213–233

Campbell, B. (ed) (1996) *The Miombo in Transition: Woodlands and Welfare in Africa*, CIFOR, Indonesia

Conservation International (no date) 'Cape Floristic region, Biodiversity hotspots', www.biodiversityhotspots.org/xp/Hotspots/cape_floristic/

Cowling, R. M. and C. Hilton-Taylor (1994) 'Patterns of plant biodiversity and endemism in southern Africa: An overview', in B. Huntley (ed) *Botanical Diversity in Southern Africa,* National Botanical Institute, Pretoria, South Africa

Cowling, R. M. and C. Hilton-Taylor (1997) *Phytogeography, Flora and Endemism*, in R. M. Cowling, D. M. Richardson and S. M. Pierce (ed) *Vegetation of Southern Africa*, Cambridge University Press, Cambridge, UK

Cowling, R. M., R. L. Pressey, A. T. Lombard, P. G. Desmet and A. G. Ellis (1999) 'From representation to persistence: Requirement for a sustainable reserve system in the species-rich Mediterranean-climate deserts of southern Africa', *Diversity and Distributions*, vol 5, pp1–21

Cowling, R. M., D. M. Richardson and P. J. Mustart (1997) 'Fynbos' in R. M. Cowling, D. M. Richardson, and S. M. Pierce (eds) *Vegetation of Southern Africa*, Cambridge University Press, Cambridge, UK

Dean, W. R. J. and I. A. W. McDonald (1994) 'Historic changes in stocking rates of domestic livestock as a measure of semi-arid and arid rangeland degradation in the Cape Province South Africa', *Journal of Arid Environments*, vol 26, pp281–298

Dean, R. and S. J. Milton (1995) 'Plant and invertebrate assemblages on old fields in the arid southern karoo, South Africa', *African Journal of Ecology*, vol 33, pp1–13

Foden, W. (2002) 'A demographic study of Aloe dichotoma in the Succulent Karoo: Are the effects of climate change already apparent?', Unpublished MSc thesis, Percy Fitzpatrick Institute of African Ornithology, University of Cape Town, Cape Town, South Africa

Grubb, P. J. (1977) 'The maintenance of species richness in plant communities: The importance of the regeneration niche', *Biological Reviews*, vol 52, pp107–145

Hannah, L., G. F. Midgley and D. Millar (2002) 'Climate change-integrated conservation strategies', *Global Ecology and Biogeography*, vol 11, pp485–495

Haplin, P. N. (1997) 'Global climate change and natural-area protection: Management responses and research directions', *Ecological Applications*, vol 7, pp828–843

Hughes, G. O., W. Thuiller, G. F. Midgley and K. Collins (2005a) 'A fait accompli? Environmental change hastens the demise of the critically endangered riverine rabbit (*Bunolagus monticularis*)', Unpublished report, South African Botanical Research Institute, Cape Town, South Africa

Hughes, G. O., V. J. T. Loehr, W. Thuiller, G. F. Midgley and T. E. J. Leuteritz (2005b) 'Global change and an arid zone chelonian: The case of *Homopus signatus*', Unpublished report, South African Botanical Research Institute, Cape Town, South Africa

Lotka, A. J. (1925) *Elements of Physical Biology*, Williams and Wilkins, Baltimore, MD, US

Low, B. and A.G. Rebelo (eds) (1996) *Vegetation of South Africa, Lesotho, and Swaziland*, Department of Environmental Affairs and Tourism, Pretoria, South Africa

Macdonald, I. A. W. (1994) 'Global change and alien invasion: Implications for biodiversity and protected area management', in O. T. Solbrig, P. G. van Emden and W. J. van Oordt (eds) *Biodiversity and global change*, CAB International, Wallingford, UK

IPCC (2001) 'Glossary of terms' in J. McCarthy, O. Canziani, N. Leary, D. Dokken and K. White (eds) *Climate Change 2001: Impacts, Adaptation and Vulnerability*, Contribution of Working Group II to the Third Assessment Report of the Intergovernmental Panel on Climate Change, Cambridge University Press, Cambridge, UK and New York, US

Midgley, G. F., L. Hannah, D. Millar, W. Thuiller and A. Boot (2002a) 'Developing regional species-level assessments of climate change impacts on biodiversity in the Cape Floristic region', *Biological Conservation*, vol 112, pp87–97

Midgley, G., F. L. Hannah, D. Millar, M. C. Rutherford and L. W. Powrie (2002b) 'Assessing the vulnerability of species richness to anthropogenic climate change in a biodiversity hotspot', *Global Ecology and Biogeography*, vol 11, pp443–451

Milton, S. J. (1995) 'Spatial and temporal patterns in the emergence and survival of seedlings in the arid karoo shrubland', *Journal of Applied Ecology*, vol 32, pp145–156

Milton, S. J., R. I. Yeaton, W. R. J. Dean and J. H. J. Vlok (1997) 'Succulent karoo', in R. M. Cowling, D. M. Richardson and S. M. Pierce (eds) *Vegetation of Southern Africa*, Cambridge University Press, Cambridge, UK

Peters, R. L. and J. D. Darling (1985) 'The greenhouse effect and nature reserves', *Bioscience*, vol 35, pp707–717

Rosch, M. W. (1977) 'Enkele plantekologiese aspekte van die Haster Malan-natuurreservaat', MSc thesis, University of Pretoria, Pretoria, South Africa

Rutherford, M. C. and R. H. Westfall (1994) 'Biomes of Southern Africa: An objective characterisation', *Memoirs of the Botanical Survey of South Africa*, vol 63, pp1–94

Rutherford, M.C., G. F. Midgeley, W. J. Bond, L. W. Powrie, R. Roberts and L. Allsopp (1999) *Plant biodiversity: Vulnerability and Adaptation Assessment*, South African Country Study on Climate Change, National Botanical Institute, Cape Town

Scholes, R. J. (1990) 'Change in nature and the nature of change: Interactions between terrestrial ecosystems and the atmosphere', *South African Journal of Science*, vol 86, pp350–354

Scholes, R. J. (1997) 'Savanna' in R. M. Cowling, D. M. Richardson and S. M. Pierce (eds) *Vegetation of Southern Africa*, Cambridge University Press, Cambridge, UK

Scholes, R. J. and R. Biggs (2004) 'The regional scale component of the Southern African Millennium Ecosystem Assessment', Millennium Ecosystem Assessment, CSIR, Pretoria, South Africa

Scholes, R. J. and B. H. Walker (1993) *An African Savanna: Synthesis of the Nylsvley Study*, Cambridge University Press, Cambridge, UK

Scholes, R. J., E. D. Schulze, L. F. Pitelka and D. O. Hall (1999) 'The biogeochemistry of terrestrial ecosystems', in B. H. Walker, W. L. Steffen, J. Canadell and J. S. I. Ingram (eds) *The Terrestrial Biosphere and Global Change*, Cambridge University Press, Cambridge, UK, pp88–105

Schulze, R. E., M. Maharaj, S. D. Lynch, B. J. Howe and B. Melvil-Thompson (1997) *South African Atlas of Agrohydrology and Climatology*, Water Research Commission, Pretoria, South Africa

Schulze, R. E. and L. A. Perks (1999) *Assessment of the Impact of Climate*, School of Bioresources Engineering and Environmental Hydrology, University of Natal, Pietermaritzburg, South Africa

Shackleton, C. M. and S. E. Shackleton (2004) 'Use of woodlands resources for direct household provision' in M. J. Lawes, H. A. C. Ealey, C. M. Shackleton and B. G. S. Geach (eds) *Indigenous Forests and Woodlands in South Africa: Policies, People and Practice,* University of Kwazulu-Natal Press, Scottsville, South Africa

Thomas, C. D., A. Cameron, R. E. Green, M. Bakkenes, L. J. Beaumont, Y. C. Collingham, B. F. N. Erasmus, M. F. de Siqueira, A. Grainger, L. Hannah, L. Hughes, B. Huntley, A. S. van Jaarsveld, G. F. Midgley, L. Miles, M. A. Ortega-Huerta, A. T. Peterson, O. L. Phillips and S. E. Williams (2004) 'Extinction risk from climate change', *Nature*, vol 427, pp145–148

Van Rooyen, M. W., G. K. Theron and N. Grobbelaar (1979) 'Phenology of the vegetation in Hester Malan Nature Reserve in Namaqualand Broken Veld: The Therophyte population', *Journal of South African Botany*, vol 45, pp433–452

Volterra, V. (1926) 'Variations and fluctuations of the number of individuals in animal species living together', reprinted (in 1931) in R. N. Chapman (ed) *Animal Ecology*, McGraw-Hill, New York, US

Williams, P., L. Hannah, S. Andelman, G. Midgley, M. Araujo, G. Hughes, L. Manne, E. Marinez-Meyer and R. Pearson (2004) 'Planning for climate change: Identifying minimum-dispersal corridors from the Cape Proteaceae', *Conservation Biology*, vol 19, no 4, pp1063-1074

Yee, T. W. and N. D. Mitchell (1991) 'Generalized additive models in plant ecology', *Journal of Vegetation Science*, vol 2, pp587–602

3

Forest Responses to
Changing Rainfall in the Philippines

*Rodel Lasco, Florencia Pulhin, Rex Victor O. Cruz,
Juan Pulhin, Sheila Roy and Patricia Sanchez*

Introduction

Among the world's forests, tropical forests have critical importance in terms of their natural resources, the enormous variety of biodiversity they house and their vast potential to conserve existing carbon pools and serve as carbon sinks (Brown et al, 1996). Forests are highly dependent on climate since they are limited by water availability and temperature. The IPCC Fourth Assessment report concludes that the resilience of natural ecosystems could be exceeded due to projected climate change in the next century coupled with multiple stresses (Fischlin et al, 2007). In addition, a global warming of more than 2–3°C above pre-industrial levels could lead to substantial changes in the structure and functioning of terrestrial ecosystems.

Philippine forests have extremely high floral and faunal diversity, being one of the biodiversity 'hot spots' of the world (McNeely et al, 1990). They harbour about 13,000 species of plants, comprising 5 per cent of the world's total plant species (DENR/UNEP, 1997). The main strategy in biodiversity conservation is through the implementation of the National Integrated Protected Area System (NIPAS) Law of 1992, which has provided a stronger legal basis for the establishment and management of protected areas. To date, 18 terrestrial and marine reserves have been proclaimed as initial components of NIPAS. However, many of these areas are protected merely on paper because of a lack of resources.

The major land-cover types in the Philippines in terms of area coverage are classified into six categories (Lasco et al, 2001): upland farms, secondary forests, protected forests, brush lands, grasslands and tree plantations. About 70 per cent (21Mha) of the Philippines' total land area was covered with lush forests at the end of the 19th century (Garrity et al, 1993) but only about 5.789Mha (20 per cent) of forest remains (Earth Trends, 2003), with less than 1Mha of old-growth forests (FMB, 1998; Lasco et al, 2001). The current status of primary land-cover types in the Philippines is described as follows (Lasco et al, 2001):

- *Old growth and other protected forests*: Since 1992, the Government of the Philippines has banned logging on all old-growth forests, mossy forests and forests above 100m asl (above sea level) and with slope greater than 50 per cent as part of NIPAS. In 1995, the area of forest under protection was estimated at 2.7Mha, consisting of mossy forests (1.1Mha), old-growth Dipterocarp forests (0.8Mha), pine forests (in high elevation areas, mainly *Pinus kesiya*), mangroves and sub-marginal forests.
- *Post extraction secondary forests*: Logging is permitted only in the post extraction secondary Dipterocarp forests since these forests are the main source of wood in the country. There were about 2.8Mha of post extraction secondary forests in the country as of 1997 (FMB, 1998).
- *Upland Farms*: It is estimated that there are 5.7Mha of upland farms in the Philippines, consisting of forest tree-based farms, swidden fallow secondary forests, coconut plantations (typically intercropped) and fruit orchards. However, large portions of the swidden fallow areas are probably devoted to annual crops and are therefore not true swidden fallow systems. There is therefore uncertainty regarding the exact distribution of upland farms and the related swidden fallow secondary forest since these systems are highly dynamic. In response to the problem of shifting cultivation in the uplands, the government is promoting agroforestry as the main alternative production system (Agroforestry Communications, 1986; Lasco and Malinao, 1993; Nera, 1997).
- *Tree Plantations*: The rehabilitation of vast denuded areas through reforestation activities and private commercial tree plantations is a primary objective of the Philippines Government. Typically, fast growing species such as *Gmelina arborea*, *Acacia* spp. and *Eucalyptus* spp. are used. In government reforestation activities, trees planted are intended primarily for establishing a permanent forest cover and are not to be harvested. On the other hand, the commercial plantations established by private developers on farms are usually harvested after about 10–15 years. The rate of establishment of tree plantations was estimated at 65,233ha in 1995 (FMB, 1998; Lasco et al, 2001). There is no accurate estimate of the total area actually planted. Official records show that from 1976 to 1995, 1.3Mha were planted, but of this area only 0.6Mha can be assumed to exist (Lasco and Pulhin, 1998).
- *Grassland*: There are no natural grasslands in the Philippines except in very small patches located in high-altitude areas and human-induced and maintained grassland ecosystems (about 2Mha) that are usually the result of severe land degradation (Earthtrends, 2003). These areas are expected to regenerate back to tropical forests if protected, but regular burning (for example, the slash-and-burn method commonly practised in the Philippines) prevents plant succession.
- *Brushlands*: As of 1997, there were 2.4Mha of brushland areas in the Philippines, consisting essentially of remnants of tropical forests progressively degraded by excessive cutting. Forest cover in these areas is less than

20 per cent and the vegetation consists of relic trees, shrubs and grasses. Like grasslands, brushland areas are expected to regenerate back to mature forests if adequately protected.

Not all global vegetation models agree on whether tropical forests will increase or decrease in extent as a result of climate change. But any major shift in rainfall pattern will affect distribution of vegetation types. Shifts in rainfall patterns could increase conversion of forests to agricultural land by increasing migration from areas affected by drought, erosion and so on. Productivity will increase or decrease depending on rainfall. Temperature change could affect the climate of a certain area drastically, leading to a loss of a few species of plants and animals that may significantly drain the biodiversity resources of these forests. A 2–3°C increase in temperatures will have marginal effects in the tropics but extended exposure to temperatures of 35–40°C combined with water shortage may damage plant tissue (Hudson and Brown, 2006).

To date, there has been no study that quantifies the effects of climate change on Philippine forests. It was earlier hypothesized that under various GCM scenarios, tropical forest areas in the Philippines will likely expand as temperature and precipitation increase in many parts of the country (Cruz, 1997). At the same time a change in temperature could potentially result in significant biodiversity losses. It is also possible that species may adapt to stresses in the environment over the period of time during which climate change occurs, resulting in no significant changes in biodiversity.

In response to this lack of scientific information on the potential implications of climate change for Philippine forests, a quantitative assessment of the impact of climate change scenarios on Philippine forest types was undertaken with the following objectives:

- to determine the potential vegetative cover of the Philippines without human intervention using the Holdridge life zones; and
- to simulate changes in present vegetative cover as a result of climate change using GIS tools and the Holdridge life zones.

Methodology

Simulating potential forest types using the Holdridge life zones

The Holdridge life zones are an ecological classification system based on the three climatic factors: precipitation, heat (biotemperature) and humidity (potential evapotranspiration ratio) (Holdridge, 1967). Holdridge (1967) defined a life zone as a group of associations related through the effects of these three major climatic factors. Figure 3.1 shows the classification of the most common life zones on the Earth based on these parameters. All Philippine forests can be classified under the tropical belt because the biotemperature here is always greater than 24°C. Thus, the main determinant of life zone classification in the Philippines would be precipitation (expressed as mean annual rainfall).

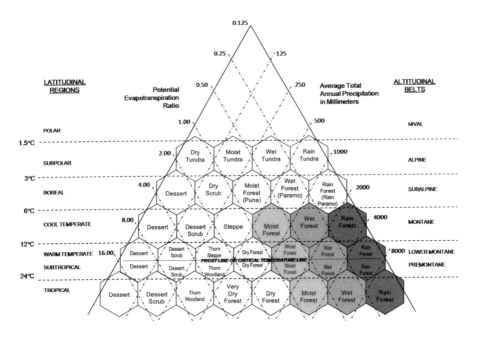

Figure 3.1 *The Holdridge system of vegetative cover classification*

Source: Holdridge (1967).

The mean annual biotemperature is the measure of heat that is utilized in the life zone chart. The biotemperature mean is the average of the temperatures in Celsius at which vegetative growth takes place relative to the annual period. The range of temperatures within which vegetative growth occurs is estimated to lie between 0°C as a minimum and 30°C as a maximum. The positive temperatures within this range must be averaged out over the whole year in order to make it possible to effectively compare a given site with any other on Earth. The biotemperature is thus calculated as:

$$\text{Mean annual biotemperature (MAB)} = \Sigma \ (0 < T < 30)/365 \text{ days}$$
(or divide by 12 rather than 365 to use months rather than days as units).

The third climatic factor that determines the boundaries of life zones is humidity, best described by the potential evapotranspiration (PET) ratio. PET is the theoretical quantity of water given up to the atmosphere within a zonal climate and on a zonal soil by the natural vegetation of the area throughout the growing season. Both evaporation and transpiration are directly correlated with temperature, and other factors being equal, the mean annual PET in millimetres at any site may be determined by multiplying the mean annual biotemperature by the factor 58.93.

The PET ratio is determined by dividing the value of the mean annual PET in millimetres by the value of the mean annual precipitation in millimetres. The PET ratio is thus a measure of the humidity that can be utilized for comparing distinct sites. It can be expressed as:

PET ratio = mean annual PET/mean annual precipitation,

where mean annual PET = MAB × 58.93.

The Holdridge life zones can also be graphically represented by means of the Holdridge life zone chart, created on the basis of annual temperature and precipitation values, to demonstrate relationships between different vegetation types. The classification of forest types in the Holdridge model for a given set of temperature and precipitation conditions can be considered as rough estimates of the potential forest types that would thrive under those conditions in the future.

Climate change impacts on Philippine forest cover

Based on the three parameters, Holdridge life zones for the Philippines were identified using the ArcView 3.2 GIS program. Changes in temperature (1°C, 1.5°C and 2°C increases from current values) and precipitation (25 per cent, 50 per cent and 100 per cent increases from current values) based on the projections of climate scenarios were next used to determine the future distribution of forest types in the Philippines (Table 3.1). These precipitation and temperature scenarios are within the limits of GCM projections for the country (Government of the Philippines, 1999).

Table 3.1 *Synthetic climate change scenarios used in the study*

Increase in Rainfall (% relative to present)	Increase in Temperature (°C)		
	1	1.5	2.0
25	Scenario 1a	Scenario 1b	Scenario 1c
50	Scenario 2a	Scenario 2b	Scenario 2c
100	Scenario 3a	Scenario 3b	Scenario 3c

The various maps generated by ArcGIS 8.1 for the classification of Holdridge life zones for the Philippines include a rainfall map, a Thiessen map generated using temperature data and a land-use map. The rainfall map was based on the data collected by the Philippine Atmospheric, Geophysical and Astronomical Services Administration (PAGASA). Average annual rainfall in the Philippines ranged from 1000mm to 4000mm in 1961–1990. Temperature data were also obtained from the PAGASA and a Thiessen map was created from the 55 weather stations throughout the Philippines. The average diurnal temperature in the Philippines ranged from 19.3°C to 28.2°C in 1949–2002.

The land-use map is based on the 1993 map prepared by the Presidential Task Force on Water Resources Development and Management. Presently there are only about 6 million hectares of forests left (excluding brushland and man-made forest plantations), a mere 20 per cent of the country's total land area. Of these, 1.6 million hectares are non-production and less than 1 million hectares are old growth forest. This land-use map served to delineate the boundaries of Philippine forests and was used as an overlay on the calculated Holdridge life zone in the Thiessen map.

Results and Discussion

Potential vs actual life zones

In the absence of any anthropogenic influence, simulation of potential forest types for current temperature and precipitation showed that the Philippines would be dominated by the dry tropical, moist tropical and wet tropical forest life zones (Figure 3.2). Such a condition probably existed when the Spanish colonizers first set foot in the Philippines in 1521. At that time it is estimated that 90 per cent of the country was covered with lush tropical rainforest. By 1900, there was still 70 per cent or 21Mha of forest cover (Garrity et al, 1993). However, by 1996 there was only 6.1Mha (20 per cent) of forest cover remaining (FMB, 1998). The average deforestation rate from 1969 to 1973 was 170,000 hectares per year (Forest Development Center, 1987) while over the past 20 years it has been about 190,000 to 200,000 hectares per year (Revilla, 1997). However, the average rate of deforestation in the more recent past years has declined somewhat (largely due to reduced logging and stronger reforestation and forest protection efforts) and is in the vicinity of 100,000 hectares per year (Lasco and Pulhin, 1998; Pulhin et al, 2006). In the Philippines, the direct and indirect causes of deforestation include shifting cultivation, permanent agriculture, ranching, logging, fuel wood gathering and charcoal making (Kummer, 1992).

Using ArcView, we overlaid the actual forest cover of the Philippines in 1993 over the potential life zones predicted by the Holdridge system. As might be expected, all the forest types showed a decline, with the highest decline in dry forests and the least decline in wet forests (Table 3.2).

Effects of the synthetic climate change scenarios on vegetative cover

When the temperature and precipitation projections generated by climate change scenarios were considered, the change in forest cover was found to vary depending on the magnitude of change in climate parameters. For a 25 per cent increase in precipitation for the entire range of temperature increases (1°C, 1.5°C and 2°C), the following changes in forest cover were observed (Figures 3.3 and 3.4):

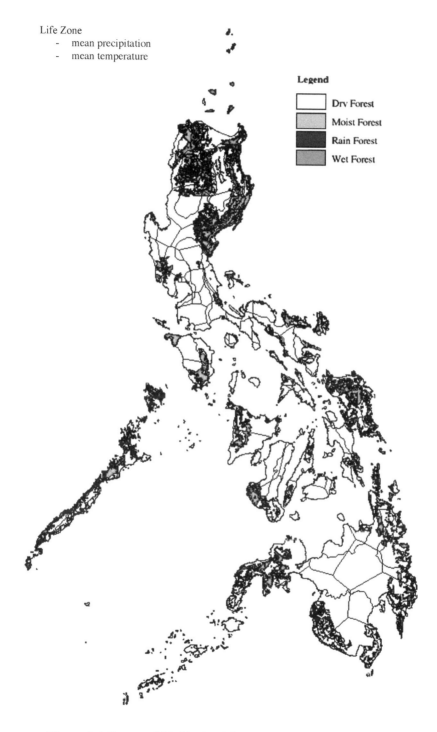

Life Zone
- mean precipitation
- mean temperature

Legend

☐ Dry Forest
☐ Moist Forest
■ Rain Forest
▨ Wet Forest

Figure 3.2 *Potential Holdridge life zones in the Philippine forests
without human influence*

Table 3.2 *Comparison of potential and actual (1993)*
life zones in the Philippines

Life Zone Type	Area Distribution (ha)		Percentage Distribution	
	Potential	1993 Life Zone	Potential	1993 Life Zone
Dry Forest	8,763,696.10	1,082,197.20	29.65	3.66
Moist Forest	15,149,315.26	3,534,636.30	51.25	11.96
Wet Forest	5,646,414.43	2,266,455.20	19.10	7.67
TOTAL	**29,559,425.79**	**6,883,288.71**	**100.00**	**23.29**

- a total loss of all dry forests even at the lowest temperature change of 1°C this was expected considering the increase in available water;
- a 30.5 per cent increase in moist forest across all temperatures; and
- a negligible (0.1 per cent) increase in wet forest.

It is noteworthy that the temperature increase had negligible drying effects on the life zones in the Philippines. Normally, even slight increases in temperature (even by 0.5°C) can give rise to the El Niño phenomenon in some areas of the country. This is probably because all parts of the country already fall within the tropical belt under the Holdridge system (>24°C) and the precipitation estimates for the different scenarios are quite large, negating any effect on the increase in temperature.

A 50 per cent increase in precipitation results in the following changes in the Holdridge life zones (Figures 3.3 and 3.5):

- total loss of all dry forests even at the lowest temperature change – this is again expected considering the increase in available water;
- a 47 per cent decline in moist forests across all temperatures;
- an increase in rainforests from non-existent under current conditions to 365,000ha under a 1°C increase in temperature – as temperature increases, there is a slight decline in rainforest area; and
- a 106 per cent increase in wet forest cover as a result of greater precipitation.

It is assumed in this study that the total forested area remains fixed in the analysis. In other words, we assumed that non-forested areas could never revert back to forests because of human influence (for example, agriculture and settlements).

Finally, a 100 per cent increase in precipitation will result in the following changes in the life zone pattern in the Philippines (Figures 3.3 and 3.6):

Forest area by type for different climates

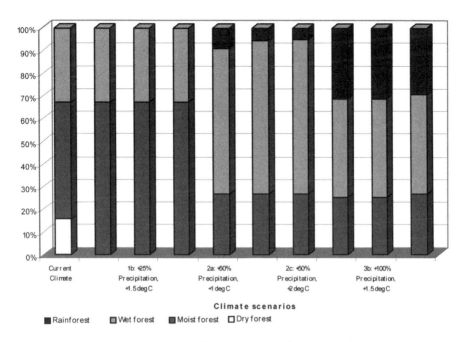

Figure 3.3 *Projected change in area of existing life zones in the Philippines under various climate change scenarios (25%, 50% and 100% increase in precipitation)*

- total loss of all dry forests (>1Mha);
- a 50 per cent decline in moist forests area;
- a significant rise in the area of rainforests from zero under current conditions to more than 2Mha; and
- a 32 per cent increase in wet forests, about one-third of the increase under Scenario 2.

As in the previous scenarios, the impact of temperature change is observed to be minimal due to the very high precipitation increases that mask any temperature effects. The impacts of the various climate change scenarios on Philippine forest ecosystems are presented in Figure 3.3. Overall, the simulation study showed that increases (of 25 per cent, 50 per cent and 100 per cent) in precipitation and temperature would result in a redistribution of forest types as classified by the Holdridge scenarios. The dry forests are the most vulnerable. They could be totally wiped out even under a 25 per cent increase in precipitation. Moist forests are also vulnerable, especially under a higher precipitation increase. On the positive side, there will be a significant increase in rainforest types as precipitation levels increase.

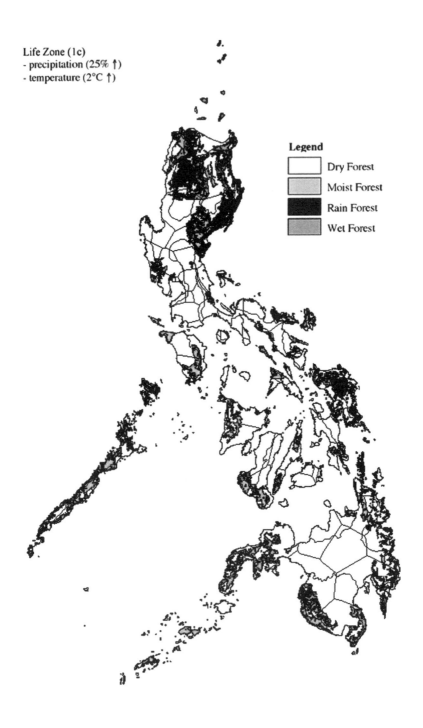

Figure 3.4 *Holdridge life zones in the Philippine forests under Scenario 1 (25% increase in rainfall) and with a 2°C temperature increase*

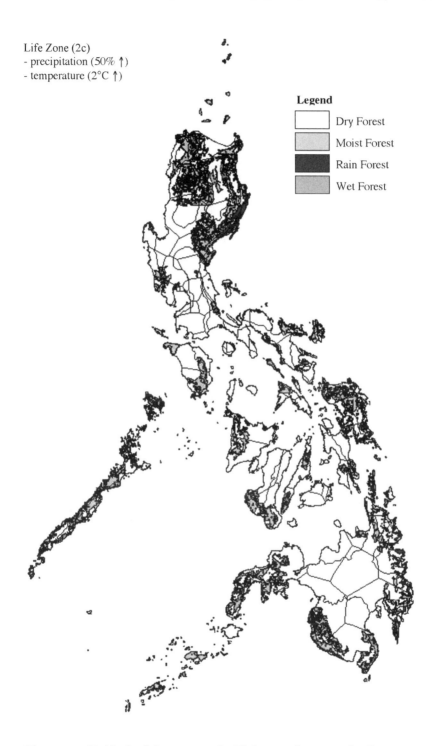

Life Zone (2c)
- precipitation (50% ↑)
- temperature (2°C ↑)

Legend

☐ Dry Forest

☐ Moist Forest

■ Rain Forest

☐ Wet Forest

Figure 3.5 *Holdridge life zones in the Philippine forests under Scenario 2 (50% increase in rainfall) and with a 2°C temperature increase*

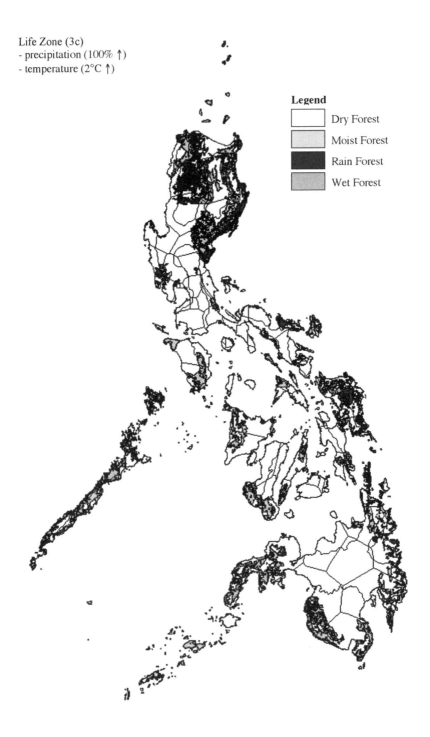

Life Zone (3c)
- precipitation (100% ↑)
- temperature (2°C ↑)

Legend

Dry Forest

Moist Forest

Rain Forest

Wet Forest

Figure 3.6 *Holdridge life zones in the Philippine forests under Scenario 3 (100% increase in rainfall) and with a 2°C temperature increase*

The results of the study are generally consistent with the findings of the IPCC's Third Assessment Reports (McCarthy et al, 2001). At the eco-physiological level, while the net effect of climate change on the net primary productivity (NPP) of the Philippine forest system is not yet clear, there is generally a positive correlation between NPP and temperature. However, if rainfall is not sufficient, water stress could be a problem.

Global vegetation models (for example, BIOME, MAPSS and IMAGE) do not agree on whether tropical forests will increase or decrease (McCarthy et al, 2001), but any major shift in rainfall pattern will affect distribution of vegetation types. Under enhanced CO_2 conditions, tropical evergreen broadleaf forests could readily establish after deforestation. On the other hand, shifts in rainfall patterns could increase conversion of forests to agricultural land by increasing migration from areas affected by drought, erosion and so on. Productivity will increase or decrease depending on the amount of rainfall.

Adaptation Strategies and Options for Philippine Forests

National policy framework and potential adaptation strategies

To date, there has been little consideration of an overall climate change adaptation strategy and options for the Philippine forest ecosystems. The 1999 Philippines Initial National Communication contains adaptation options for watershed management that partly apply to forest ecosystems. These are mainly contained in the laws and policies governing the use and conservation of forest resources in the Philippines, which include the following:

- Presidential Decree 705 of 1975 (Revised Forestry Code of the Philippines) – embodies the general mandate of the Constitution in managing and conserving forest resources.
- DENR Administrative Order No 24, Series of 1991– promulgates the shift of logging from old-growth forests to secondary (residual) forests, effective as of 1992. Prior to this, logging was confined to old-growth forests.
- Republic Act No 7586 – 'National Integrated Protected Areas Systems Act of 1992' – stipulates that the management, protection, sustainable development and rehabilitation of protected areas shall be undertaken primarily to ensure the conservation of biological diversity. However, not all of the remaining natural forests are covered by NIPAS. All remaining old-growth forests are protected but logging is still allowed in secondary forests.
- Republic Act No 8371 – 'Indigenous People's Rights Act of 1997' – recognizes the vested rights of indigenous peoples over their ancestral lands within forestlands, including secondary forest. The implementing guidelines of this law are still being finalized.
- Executive Order 363 of 1995 – adopts community-based forest management (CBFM) as a national strategy to ensure the sustainable development of the country's forests and promote social justice.

- Executive Order 318 of 2004 – 'Promoting Sustainable Forest Management in the Philippines' – is an attempt to revise Presidential Decree 705 and aims to attain sustainable forest management in the country's production forests.

All of the above provide the overall framework for climate change adaptation in the Philippines forest sector. Watershed management, forest conservation and greater local community participation are strategies that could also contribute towards climate change adaptation. For example, protecting existing forests allows for natural adjustment to a new climate regime. Greater local community involvement could minimize the financial cost to state agencies of adaptation.

In terms of actual activities on the ground, the government has been actively pursuing several initiatives in spite of its limited resources. These include:

- conservation of remaining forests in NIPAS sites and watershed areas;
- reforestation and rehabilitation of barren upland areas through tree planting and agroforestry; and
- community-based forestry activities such as community organizing and development.

The private sector is less involved today compared to their involvement during the height of logging activities in the 1950s and 1960s. However, civil society is more involved as community-based programmes increase.

The incorporation of climate change concerns in planning for forest resources is unfortunately not yet a priority for the government. The more urgent concern is the protection of remaining forests from human exploitation, which is viewed as the more imminent threat. However, the incorporation of climate change concerns early on in the planning process might help to avert some of the negative impacts and improve the coping capacity of forest ecosystems. As we have shown earlier in the results of our analysis based on the Holdridge life zone system, certain forest types in the Philippines, especially the dry forest types, are highly vulnerable and could, in future, be entirely replaced by other types of forests. The laws and regulations mentioned above may therefore need to be reassessed and updated to focus more on how forest management can be improved to mitigate climate change impacts, with special focus on areas classified as dry forests, such as areas in Northern Luzon, Negros, Cebu, Palawan, Basilan and General Santos.

In this light, a national adaptation strategy should probably focus on identifying forested areas that are more at risk and the unique species they harbour. Specific adaptation options could include conservation and management of vulnerable species and assisting local communities that are highly dependent on forests at risk, among others.

Adaptation Strategies Identified by Stakeholders

Local stakeholders in the Philippines that depend to various extents on forest resources generally have little awareness about climate change issues. However, they have abundant experience in coping with climate variability and extremes such as tropical storms and high rainfall and drought brought about by the ENSO phenomenon. Their current adaptation strategies to such extreme events might serve as a guide to their possible responses to the impacts of future climate change, under the implicit assumption that adaptation options to the impacts of climate variability could be applicable to the impacts of climate change.

Stakeholder responses to current climate events were gauged on the basis of stakeholder interactions during a workshop held in the Pantabangan–Carranglan watershed of the Philippines in 2004 aimed at identifying the impacts of climate variability and extremes and determining local coping strategies. Thirty participants from different organizations within the Pantabangan–Carranglan watershed – the National Power Corporation, the National Irrigation Authority, local government units, non-government organizations and people's organizations – attended the workshop.

A wide variety of adaptation options were identified by stakeholders. These centred on the use of appropriate species/crops, scheduling, technical innovations (for example, water conservation), capacity building and law enforcement (see Table 3.3). The high degree of knowledge on adaptation options exhibited by participants indicates a relatively strong level of awareness on adjusting to climate variability and extremes. This existing knowledge base could have the potential to serve as a building block for the determination of future climate change adaptation strategies.

In general, the adaptation options identified are consistent with those recommended in the Philippines Initial National Communication (1999) and the IPCC Third Assessment Report (McCarthy et al, 2001). Since these adaptation options were identified in response to climatic variability at a particular site, their applicability to other areas would have to be determined.

Conclusions

Under potential climate change scenarios, forest types in the Philippines could change dramatically, especially with increasing precipitation levels. The most vulnerable are the dry forests and to a lesser degree the moist forests, which could be completely eliminated with the rise in precipitation. They would most likely be replaced by the rainforest type.

At the national and local levels, climate change issues are not yet considered in the planning and implementation of forestry activities. However, there is a set of laws and regulations at the national level that could provide a framework for the implementation of adaptation options. At the local level, stakeholders have been adapting to climate variability and extremes for a long time and their strategies could also serve to inform future adaptive responses to climate change.

Table 3.3 *Adaptation options to climate variability and extremes for forest lands in the Pantabangan–Carranglan watershed, Philippines*

Land Use	Adaptation Options
Tree plantation	Adjusted silvicultural treatment schedules and proper silvicultural practices Plant species that can adjust to variable climate situations Proper timing of tree planting projects or activities Construction of fire lines Controlled burning Supplemental watering
Natural forest	Safety net measures for farmers by local and national government Cancellation of logging permits (total logging ban)
Grasslands	Reforestation – adaptation of contour farming in combination with organic farming Promote community-based forest management Increased funds for forest protection and regeneration from national government Increase linkages among local government, national government and non-governmental organizations Introduction of drainage measures Controlled burning Introduction of drought resistant species Intensive information dissemination campaign among stakeholders

It is recommended that future studies examine the impacts of climate change and the accompanying changes in forest types on biodiversity at the species level, with a special emphasis on rare, threatened and endangered species. It is also recommended that a thorough review of existing policies on managing forest ecosystems in the country be conducted in order to be able to assess their effectiveness in terms of addressing the projected future impacts of climate change and safeguarding the country's forest resources from irreparable damage.

References

Agroforestry Communications (1986) *The Philippine Recommendations for Agroforestry*, PCARRD, Los Baños, Laguna

Brown, S., J. Sathaye, M. Cannel and P. Kauppi (1996) 'Management of forests for mitigation of greenhouse gas emissions', in R. T. Watson, M. C. Zinyowera and R. H. Moss (eds) *Climate Change 1995: Impacts, Adaptations and Mitigation of Climate Change: Scientific-Technical Analyses*, Contribution of Working Group II to the Second Assessment Report of the Intergovernmental Panel on Climate Change, Cambridge University Press, Cambridge and New York, pp775–797

Cruz, R.V.O. (1997) 'Adaptation and mitigation measures for climate change: Impacts on the forestry sector' in *Proceedings of the Consultation Meeting for the International Conference on Tropical Forests and Climate Change*, Environmental Forestry Programme (ENFOR), CFNR, UPLB, College, Laguna, Philippines

DENR/UNEP (Department of Environment and Natural Resources/United Nations Environment Program) (1997) *Philippine Biodiversity: An Assessment and Action Plan*, Bookmark Inc, Makati City, Philippines

Earthtrends (2003) 'Earth trends country profiles: Forests, grasslands, and drylands: Philippines', World Resources Institute, http://earthtrends.wri.org

Fischlin, A., G. F. Midgley, J. T. Price, R. Leemans, B. Gopal, C. Turley, M. D. A. Rounsevell, O. P. Dube, J. Tarazona and A. A. Velichko (2007) 'Ecosystems, their properties, goods, and services', in M. L. Parry, O. F. Canziani, J. P. Palutikof, P. J. van der Linden and C. E. Hanson (eds) *Climate Change 2007: Impacts, Adaptation and Vulnerability*, Contribution of Working Group II to the Fourth Assessment Report of the Intergovernmental Panel on Climate Change, Cambridge University Press, Cambridge, UK, pp211–272

FMB (1998) *Forestry statistics (1997)*, Forest Management Bureau, Quezon City, Philippines

Forest Development Center (1987) *Towards a Successful National Reforestation Program*, Policy paper no 24, UPLB College of Forestry and Natural Resources, Laguna, Philippines

Garrity, D. P., D. M. Kummer and E. S. Guiang (1993) *The Upland Ecosystem in the Philippines: Alternatives for Sustainable Farming and Forestry*, National Academy Press, Washington, DC

Government of Philippines (1999) *Philippines Initial National Communication to the UN Framework Convention on Climate Change*, Government of Philippines, Manila

Holdridge, L. R. (1967) *Life Zone Ecology (Revised Edition)*, Tropical Science Center, San Jose, Costa Rica

Hudson, J. C. and D. Brown (2006) 'Rethinking Grassland Regionalism', University of Minnesota website, www.geog.umn.edu/Faculty/brown/grasslands/RGR1.htm

Kummer, D. M. (1992) *Deforestation in Post-war Philippines*, Ateneo de Manila University Press, Philippines

Lasco, R. D. and E. P. Malinao (1993) 'Height growth and herbage production of seven MPTS uses as hedgerows in alley cropping system: An on-farm experiment', *Sylavatrop: The Technical Journal for Philippine Ecosystems and Natural Resources*, vol 3, no 1, pp97–107

Lasco, R. D. and F. P. Pulhin (1998) *Philippine Forestry and CO$_2$ Sequestration: Opportunities for Mitigating Climate Change*, Environmental Forestry Programme (ENFOR), CFNR, UPLB, College, Laguna, Philippines

Lasco, R. D., R. G. Visco and J. M. Pulhin (2001) 'Secondary forests in the Philippines: Formation and transformation in the 20th century', *Journal of Tropical Forest Science*, vol 13, pp652–670

Nera, B. S. (1997) 'Agroforestry of DENR's social forestry program', in *Developments in Agroforestry Research*, Book Series Number 160/1997, Philippine Council for Agriculture, Forestry and Natural Resources Research and Development, Los Baños, Laguna, Philippines, pp35–44

McCarthy, J., O. Canziani, N. Leary, D. Dokken and K. White (eds) (2001) *Climate Change 2001: Impacts, Adaptation and Vulnerability*, Contribution of Working Group II to the Third Assessment Report of the Intergovernmental Panel on Climate Change, Cambridge University Press, Cambridge, UK and New York, US

McNeely, J. A., K. R. Miller, W. V. Reed, R. A. Mittermeier and T. B. Werner (1990) *Conserving the World's Biological Diversity*, IUCN, Gland, Switzerland and Washington, DC

Pulhin, J. M., U. Chokkalingam, R. J. J. Peras, R. T. Acosta, A. P. Carandang, M. Q. Natividad, R. D. Lasco and R. A. Razal (2006) 'Historical overview', Chapter 2 in U. Chokkalingam, A. P. Carandang, J. M. Pulhin, R. D. Lasco, R. J. J. Peras and T. Toma (eds) *One Century of Forest Rehabilitation in the Philippines: Approaches,*

Outcomes and Lessons, Center for International Forestry Research (CIFOR), Bogor Barat, Indonesia

Revilla, A. V. (1997) 'Working paper for the forestry policy agenda for the incoming administration', UPLB College of Forestry and Natural Resources, Laguna, Philippines

4

Vulnerability of Mongolia's Pastoralists to Climate Extremes and Changes

Punsalmaa Batima, Luvsan Natsagdorj and Nyamsurengyn Batnasan

Introduction

Over a million of Mongolia's roughly 2.7 million inhabitants live in rural areas, most herding livestock for their livelihood. More than three quarters of the country's land area is used for grazing livestock, making pasture by far the largest category of land use. Herding on the open pastures of Mongolia is very risky, however. The climate is one of harsh extremes such as summer drought, severe winter conditions called *zud*, spring and autumn frost, dust storms, blizzards, heavy snowfall and cold rain. These and other climate hazards negatively impact herders' livelihoods by reducing access to forage, fodder and water, weakening livestock and limiting their weight gain, and even killing large numbers of animals.

Mongolian pastoralists adopted nomadic practices long ago as an adaptation that provides resilience to the highly variable climate and productivity of Mongolia's grasslands. But, as our study shows, Mongolia's pastoralists have become more vulnerable to climatic hazards.

This condition of high and increasing vulnerability is cause for serious concern given the potential consequences of future climate change. Mongolia is heavily reliant on the pastoral system and impacts on it will be felt throughout Mongolian society and the Mongolian economy. The livestock sector, which includes not only herders but also processors and distributors of livestock products, employs almost 50 per cent of the population, produces roughly 35 per cent of agricultural gross production and accounts for 30 per cent of the country's exports (National Statistical Office, 2001). Recent experiences have demonstrated that severe and widespread drought and *zud* that impact livestock herds can trigger large internal migrations of people, cause widespread unemployment, deepen poverty, sharply reduce export earnings and impact incomes throughout the economy.

The growing vulnerability to climate hazards is driven by institutional and government policy changes and by recent climate changes. The transition to a market economy in the early 1990s brought important changes to the institutions of Mongolia's pastoral system and to government policies that have contributed to growing vulnerability. Changes have also been observed in the climate of the region which have had negative impacts on Mongolia's grasslands, livestock and herders.

In our study of the vulnerability of Mongolia's pastoralists to climate change we constructed indices of recent trends in drought and severe winters from observational data, examined the impacts of a drying climate and severe weather events on grassland productivity, livestock and livelihoods, and developed maps of current vulnerability to climate extremes. The effects of changing institutions and policies on vulnerability to climate hazards were also explored. The potential impacts of future climate change were investigated using model simulations of changes in grassland productivity, grazing behaviour of animals and animal weight gain for different scenarios of future climate. Our research also included assessment of options for adapting to changing climate stresses. We present here in this chapter our findings on the changing vulnerability of Mongolia's pastoralists; findings about adaptation options are reported in Batima et al (2008).[1]

Changing Climate: Observed Trends

Mongolia's climate is semi-arid to arid and is characterized by a long-lasting cold winter, a dry and hot summer, low precipitation, large temperature fluctuations between day and night and between summer and winter, and a relatively high number of sunny days (an average of 260 days per year). There are four sharply distinct seasons and the months in each season are quite different. January, the coldest month, averages -30 to -34°C in the high mountain areas of Altai, Khangai, Khuvsgul and Khentii, -20 to -25°C in the steppe, and -15 to -20°C in the Gobi Desert. July, the warmest month, averages 12–15°C in the mountain areas and 20–25°C in the southern part of the Eastern steppe and the Gobi Desert. Annual mean precipitation is 300–400mm in the mountain regions, 150–250mm in the steppe, 100–150mm in the steppe desert, and 50–100mm in the Gobi Desert. About 85 per cent of total precipitation falls from April to September, of which 50–60 per cent falls in July and August.

The clear skies in winter due to high anticyclone dominance over Mongolia results in low snowfall. Snow contributes less than 20 per cent of the annual precipitation. The first snowfall typically occurs from the middle of October to the beginning of November. It is usually short-lived and disappears because of late-autumn warming and wind, but sometimes a late-autumn first snowfall persists through the winter as snow cover in mountainous regions.

Climate change studies conducted in Mongolia show a gradually increasing trend in air temperature and a slightly decreasing trend in precipitation. During the past 60 years, the annual mean air temperature has increased by 1.80°C. Clear warming started in the 1970s and intensified from the end of 1980s. Thirty of the years during the period 1940–2003 had positive air temperature anomalies, with 23 of these occurring after 1970. Similarly, all eight years that exceeded a 1°C anomaly were observed after 1990, including three consecutive years in 1997, 1998 and 1999. The year 1998 was the warmest year ever measured instrumentally in Mongolia.

The warming has been most pronounced in winter, with a mean temperature increase of 3.61°C. The spring and autumn temperature has also increased from 1.4 to 1.5°C. Geographically, more intensive spring and autumn warming of >2°C was observed at high altitudes in mountainous regions while warming of <1°C was observed at lower altitudes, as well as in the steppe and the Gobi Desert.

With the warming there has been a corresponding increase in the number and duration of hot days. For example, heat wave duration has increased by 8 to 18 days, depending on location. The greatest increase, of 15–18 days, was recorded in the mountainous regions, while in the Gobi Desert, heat-wave duration increased by only 6–8 days. In 1998, heat-wave duration reached 70 days in the high mountains and 30 days in the Gobi Desert, which was the most anomalous event that has occurred in the past 40 years.

Changes in annual precipitation averaged over the entire country are small and not statistically significant, but some trends have been observed at regional scales. In the central region, annual precipitation decreased by 30–90mm, but it increased by 2–60mm in the far western area and by 30–70mm in the extreme southeastern part of the country. The magnitude of these changes ranges from 5 to 25 per cent of normal precipitation. Seasonally, autumn and winter precipitation increased by 4–9 per cent while spring and summer precipitation has decreased by 7–10 per cent (Batima, 2006).

With the higher temperatures and mixed trends for precipitation, evaporative demand has increased and the climate of Mongolia has become slightly drier. To examine trends in drought conditions, an index of summer drought was constructed using data from 64 meteorological stations distributed evenly across the country (Batima, 2006). The index is calculated as a function of anomalies of mean monthly temperature and precipitation for summer months from long-term averages:

$$S_{\text{summer}} = \sum_{i=1}^{n} \sum_{j=1}^{4} \left(\frac{T - \bar{T}}{\sigma_T} \right)_{ij} - \sum_{i=1}^{n} \sum_{j=1}^{4} \left(\frac{P - \bar{P}}{\sigma_P} \right)_{ij}$$

where T and P are the j monthly mean temperature and precipitation at i meteorological station, $\bar{T}$ and $\bar{P}$ are the long-term average temperature and precipitation at the same meteorological station, σ_T and σ_P are standard deviations of temperature and precipitation.

Analysis of the drought index shows a clear increasing trend over the period 1940 through 2002 that is significant at the 95 per cent confidence level (see Figure 4.1). The increase in drought conditions is most pronounced over the last decade of the available time series, with four consecutive years of summer drought from 1999 through 2002 that affected 50–70 per cent of the territory. Such long-lasting and widespread drought had not been observed in Mongolia in the previous 60 years. During these 4 years, about 3000 water sources, including 680 rivers and 760 lakes, dried up (Ministry of Nature and Environ-ment, 2001 and 2003).

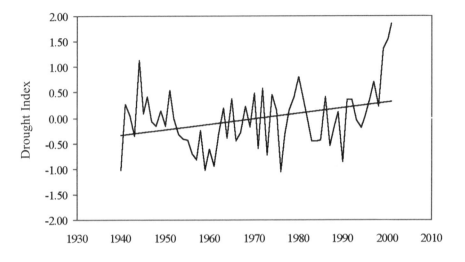

Figure 4.1 *Summer drought index, 1940–2002*

Harsh winter conditions called *zud* pose the greatest climate hazard for herders in Mongolia. The *Mongolian Language Vocabulary Dictionary* defines *zud* as 'a very severe situation of food insufficiency for both people and animals caused by natural factors in winter' (Tsevel, 1966). *Zud* has been described as 'live-stock famine' and can result in mass death of animals from hunger, freezing and exhaustion. It comes in a variety of forms that include heavy snowfall or ice cover that prevents animals from grazing, lack of snow cover and water, and extreme cold.

   An index of the severity of winter is constructed as a function of monthly mean temperature and precipitation anomalies for winter months:

$$S_{\text{summer}} = \sum_{i=1}^{n} \sum_{j=1}^{4} \left(\frac{T - \overline{T}}{\sigma_T} \right)_{ij} - \sum_{i=1}^{n} \sum_{j=1}^{4} \left(\frac{P - \overline{P}}{\sigma_P} \right)_{ij}$$

where T and P are winter j monthly mean temperature and precipitation at i meteorological station, $\overline{T}$ and $\overline{P}$ are long-term average temperature and pre-cipitation at the same meteorological station, σ_T and σ_P are standard deviation of temperature and precipitation. The winter severity index is calculated using data from the same 64 stations as for the summer drought index. Analysis of the winter index shows slightly decreasing occurrence of severe winter condi-tions. The normalized values of the winter indices for the country are shown in Figure 4.2.

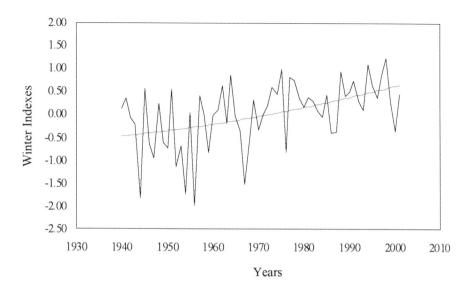

Figure 4.2 *Winter severity index, 1940–2002*

As can be seen from Figure 4.2, climatic conditions for winters in Mongolia grew milder as measured by the index. This is consistent with the observed winter warming of 3.61°C since 1940, which is twice the rate of warming of any other season (Natsagdorj et al, 2005). One might argue that herders should benefit from warmer winters, but unfortunately, this is not what has been observed. While the nationally averaged index for winter severity shows a trend toward milder conditions, the frequency of *zud* covering more than 25 per cent of the country's territory doubled in 1980–1990 and tripled in 1990–2000 compared to the 1960s. This important spatial pattern is hidden by the nationally averaged data.

In many cases, the warmer winter temperatures were accompanied by a number of unusual or unseasonal weather phenomena. For example, usually there are no wind storms during winter in Mongolia. But in recent years, wind storms have become more common in December and January. Wind storms during the coldest period of the year cause drifting of snow over a large area, causing animals to run long distances to avoid wind-drifted snow. Many animals die of exhaustion as a result. Air temperatures that rise rapidly to anomalous levels for short (3–7 day) periods and then fall to levels that are normal for the winter months cause rapid melting of snow cover and refreezing into an ice sheet that may cover a large area and prevent grazing. Animals also show temperature stress from short-period temperature fluctuation. Thus, despite the trend toward milder winter temperatures, herders' exposure to *zud* conditions has been increasing.

Climate, Environment and Livelihood

In normal years, pasture growth begins in late April; standing biomass reaches its peak in August and decreases to 70–80 per cent of the peak by late autumn, 50–60 per cent in winter and 30–40 per cent in spring. Between August and spring, the quality of the vegetation, measured by the carbon:nitrogen ratio, decreases by a factor of 2–3 and protein content falls by a factor of 3–4.

The productivity of Mongolia's grasslands, measured as standing peak biomass, varies from 100 to 1000kg per hectare (ha), decreasing from the north to the south of the country. Grassland productivity declined by 20 to 30 per cent over the latter half of the 20th century as temperatures and a tendency towards drought conditions increased. Standing plant biomass, monitored since 1964 in a national network of 25m × 25m fenced stations, declined at rates of 2 to 7kg/ha/yr in the different biomes of Mongolia (Table 4.1). Standing biomass has also decreased for the critical months of April and May, when animals weakened by the long winter need to rebuild their strength. In the steppe and forest steppe, April peak standing biomass has decreased by 10–20 per cent and the May peak has decreased by 30 per cent (Tserendash et al, 2005).

Because observations of pasture biomass were carried out in fenced fields, the reduction is considered to be the result of climate change. The decline in pasture productivity observed in the monitoring stations is consistent with wider trends as shown by analysis of normalized difference vegetation index (NDVI) changes for the last 10 days of each July for the period 1982–2002, which shows a clear decline of NDVI in 69 per cent of the country's territory over the past 20 years.

Table 4.1 *Standing peak biomass by ecosystem type, 1960–2000*

Ecosystem	No of stations	Length of time series (years)	Average peak biomass (kg/ha)	Change in peak biomass (kg/ha/yr)
Forest-steppe	18	16–31	590	-6
Steppe	13	19–34	300	-5
Desert-steppe	18	17–29	220	-3
Desert	2	18–21	170	-7
Altai Mountains	5	17–24	170	-2

Animal breeds native to Mongolia have small body sizes and low productivity relative to exotic breeds. But they are well adapted to the severe climatic conditions of Mongolia's winter and spring, as well as to various diseases. Even so, an average of 2.4 per cent of the total livestock population dies each year. When the climate is extreme, the results can be disastrous. Climate hazards such as summer drought, *zud*, spring and autumn frost, strong dust storms, blizzards, heavy snowfall and cold rain can cause mass death of animals and weaken the livelihood of herding families.

Mongolian livestock obtains over 90 per cent of its annual feed intake by grazing year-round on open pastures. The animals start to gain weight in early summer, when high quality grass is available, and attain their maximum weight by the end of autumn. By winter, animals can take in only 40–60 per cent of their daily feed requirements by grazing because of the decreased quantity and quality of forage. They lose weight during this time and reach their minimum weight in the spring. In the case of ewes, the weight loss from autumn to spring is approximately 34 per cent. March and April are usually the most difficult months for livestock and are when livestock losses are greatest because animals are weakened and hay and fodder are in short supply. It is still cold, dry and extremely windy, with frequent dust storms and occasional snowfall, and new grass has not yet grown. Spring is also the time when animals bear young, and pregnant animals that are weakened are at particular risk. Spring plant growth is critical for animals to rebuild strength lost during winter and to produce milk for newborns.

The observed decreases in the productivity of Mongolia's grasslands have negatively impacted livestock, as indicated by decreases in animal weights. Observations of animal weights made at three sites in three different biomes over the period 1980–2001 indicate that average weights of ewes, goats and cattle have fallen. Ewe weight has declined by 4kg on an annual basis, or roughly 8 per cent, since 1980. An even greater decline, of 8kg, has been observed for springtime. Animal weight is an indicator of biocapacity for surviving harsh winter and spring conditions. The observed weight declines are evidence of decreased biocapacity and increased vulnerability to climate variations and extremes.

Another factor contributing to declining animal weights may be the impact of high summer temperatures on animal grazing behaviour. When midday summer temperatures exceed certain thresholds, animals cease grazing, reducing the amount of time spent grazing per day and thus food intake. Over the period 1980–2001, the time spent grazing decreased by an average 0.8 hours per day for the months of June and July (Bayarbaatar et al, 2005).

Drought impacts

The growing season in Mongolia is very short, lasting from May to September, and pasture productivity can vary widely depending on summer rainfall and temperatures. Dry summers and droughts have been observed to decrease rangeland productivity by 12–48 per cent in the high mountains and by 28–60 per cent in the desert steppe (Tserendash et al, 2005. But drought is not commonly perceived as a natural hazard in Mongolia because it is not the proximate cause of significant livestock mortality during or immediately following a summer of below normal rainfall.

Nevertheless, drought does result in decreased pasture vegetation, decreased palatable plant species, reduced water availability, an absence of grass on pasture and increased prevalence of pests. Furthermore, drought prevents herders from preparing hay and other supplementary feed for animals and dairy products for themselves. These effects of drought reduce the availability of forage and fodder for livestock. Most importantly, in drought years animals are unable to build up the necessary strength or biocapacity during the summer and autumn that is necessary to cope with the harsh, cold winter and spring, making them more vulnerable to mortality in those months. Some of the first- and second-order impacts of drought are described in Table 4.2.

Table 4.2 *First- and second-order impacts of drought*

Affected activity	First-order impacts	Second-order impacts
Animal husbandry	Insufficient vegetation on pasture Drying of water sources Increased number of hot days and heat-wave duration	Animals cannot take the necessary energy and nutrients Animals cannot graze on pasture because of hot weather and decrease daily intake Decreased animal weight Decreased biocapacity of animals to survive winter and spring
Grazing and supplemental feed production	Reduced hay making area Grazing areas normally preserved for winter/spring used during the summer	Limited forage produced and reserved for winter Reduced food reserves for livestock Reduced winter pasture
Livelihood	Reduced livestock productivity; Reduced production of milk, dried curd, clotted cream, butter	Reduced food reserves Reduced cash income Food insecurity and malnutrition
Conservation of pasture	Increase in pests (e.g. Brandt's vole and grasshoppers) Increase frequency of fire in forest and steppe Soil erosion and loss of nutrients	No grass on affected area No hay on affected area Degradation of pasture land

Animal weight is an important indicator of animal biocapacity and changes in weight integrate the effects of multiple environmental changes on biocapacity. There is a direct correlation between our drought index and sheep and goat weights, which demonstrates the negative impact of drought on animals' biocapacity (Figure 4.3).

Zud impacts

Winter *zud* represents a high risk both to livestock and to humans who depend on livestock for income, food, transportation, fuel, and materials for clothing and shelter. The impacts of *zud* are illustrated in Figure 4.4, which shows a positive correlation between our index of winter severity and livestock mortality.

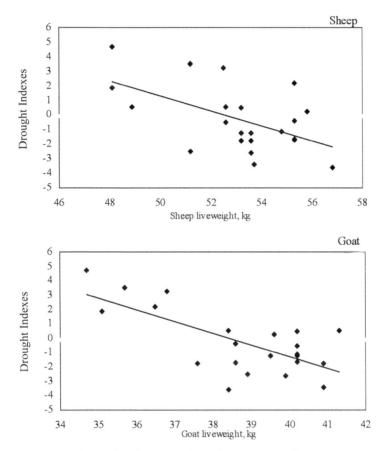

Figure 4.3 *Relationship between drought indexes and summer/autumn live-weights of sheep and goats*

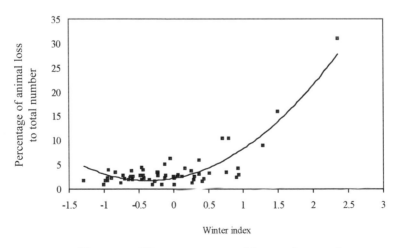

Figure 4.4 *Winter severity and livestock mortality*

There are several forms of *zud*, depending on their characteristics, contributing factors, and causes: *tsagaan* (white), *khar* (black), *tumer* (iron), *khuiten* (cold), *khavsarsan* and *tuuvaryin zud*. These are described in Table 4.3. *Zud* can last from one to several months. Mongolian herders are practised at coping with *zud* when it occurs in a small area and is of short duration. But *zud* that covers a large area and is long in duration strains the coping capacity of herders and their livestock and can cause high animal mortality. Very severe *zud* occurred in the years 1944–1945, 1967–1968, 1978–1979 and 1999–2002, during which abnormally high numbers of animals were killed. Nearly one third of livestock in Mongolia, 8.8 million animals, died during the *zud* of 1944 and 12 percent, or 2.6 million animals, died in the 1967–1968 *zud*.

Table 4.3 Zud *forms and their description*

Zud Form	Description	Climatic Criteria
Tsagaan (white) *zud*	Results from high snowfall that prevents livestock from reaching the grass. Herders used to leave the *zud* area if the area was small. Can cause a very serious disaster if it covers a large area. *Tsagaan* is the most common and disastrous form of *zud*.	Long lasting: large amount of snowfall in the beginning of winter. Short lasting: large amount of snowfall at the end of winter.
Khar (black) *zud*	Occurs when lack of snow in grazing areas leaves livestock without any unfrozen water supplies where wells are not accessible. Both human and animals suffer from lack of water to drink. This form usually happens in the Gobi Desert region.	Very little or no snowfall in winter. No winter forage on pasture because of drought in summer. No winter forage on pasture due to overgrowth in number of voles (*Microtus brandtii*) and grasshoppers or increased incidence of forest and steppe fire.
Tumer (iron) *dzud*	Occurs when snow cover melts and refreezes to create an impenetrable ice-cover that prevents livestock from grazing.	Short rapid warming in wintertime (3–7°C higher than monthly mean temperature) followed by return to sub-freezing temperatures.
Khuiten (cold) *zud*	Occurs when air temperature drops to very low levels for several consecutive days. Extreme cold temperatures and strong freezing wind prevent animals from grazing; the animals expend most of their energy in maintaining their body heat.	Air temperature falls by 5–10°C lower than the monthly mean.
Khavsarsan (combined) *zud*	A combination of at least two of the above phenomena occurring at the same time.	
Tuuvaryin zud	Geographically widespread white, black, iron or cold *zud* combined with overcrowding of livestock and migration of livestock over certain territory that results in overgrazing and depletion of pasture land resources.	Geographically widespread *zud*.

Mongolian herders experienced the worst *zud* of the last 30 years in 1999–2000 and then faced severe *zud* in 2000–2001 and 2001–2002 as well. This period also coincided with severe and extensive summer droughts. More than 50 per cent of the territory was affected and over 12 million livestock animals died, representing 25 per cent of the total (National Statistical Office, 2001). More than 12 thousand herders' families lost their entire herds, while thousands more were pushed to subsistence levels below the poverty line by their loss of animals. Such long-lasting winter *zud* for three consecutive years combined with summer droughts had not happened in Mongolia for 60 years. The government's disaster relief funding for a disaster of this magnitude was inadequate to meet the urgent demands of the affected population and Mongolia requested international relief assistance in February 2000.

The mass death of livestock significantly affected the herders' daily lives. Many people lost their means of transportation, which prevented them from moving away from the affected areas. Those who could move from their normal grazing areas placed an additional burden on areas not directly affected by the *zud*. Overgrazing in these areas increased the geographical extent of the impacts of the *zud*. Herders also faced an insufficient supply of heating materials (manure), food and cash income, which negatively affected their health. The elderly and newborn are the most vulnerable during a *zud* and mortality rates rose for these groups.

Massive death of livestock not only affects the herders' livelihood but also causes severe socioeconomic damage to the whole country. Many herders migrated from rural to urban areas, reversing the trend of net urban to rural migration of the 1990s and raising the urban population of Mongolia from just under 50 per cent in 1999 to over 57 per cent. Unemployment and poverty rose in the urban areas. Gross agricultural output in 2003 was 40 per cent below the 1999 level and its contribution to national gross domestic product decreased from 38 to 20 per cent (National Statistical Office, 2003).

Regions vulnerable to *zud* and drought

Zud represents the greatest single climatic hazard for Mongolia's herders. But, as demonstrated by the 1999–2002 events, the joint occurrence of summer drought and winter *zud* can have even greater impacts. Data from the Institute of Meteorology and Hydrology are used to calculate the frequency of white *zud*, black *zud* and drought conditions for the Mongolian landscape and classify the degree of vulnerability of each area as shown in Table 4.4.

The classifications of frequencies of different extremes have been mapped and the results of an overlay of black and white *zud* are shown in Figure 4.5. As can be seen from this map, almost 60 per cent of the country's territory is classified as having high, very high or severe vulnerability to *zud*. When drought is included (Figure 4.6), 90 per cent of the county is revealed to be vulnerable to natural disasters. Especially vulnerable are the western edge of the Khangai Mountains and the Altai Mountains, including the Great Lakes basin and the Gobi Desert. The Altai and Khangai mountain regions, including the Great Lakes basin, fall within the Altai-Sayan ecoregion, which is designated

Table 4.4 *Frequency of extremes and levels of vulnerability*

Vulnerability Level	Drought Frequency	White *Zud* Frequency	Black *Zud* Frequency
Slight	No drought	No *zud*	No *zud*
Moderate	1–20%	1–10%	1–10%
High	21–40%	11–20%	11–20%
Very high	41–60%	21–40%	21–40%
Severe	61–70%	41–70%	41–60%

as a Global 200 Ecoregion by the World Wildlife Fund for its outstanding biological diversity. Thus an increased incidence of drought and *zud* under climate change would affect not only the livestock sector but also some of the unique ecosystems and biodiversity of Mongolia (Batima et al, 2004). During the disastrous period of 1999–2002, the regions that lost more than half of their animals (from 800,000 to 1,400,000 animals) correspond to the areas classified as severely vulnerable to drought and *zud*.

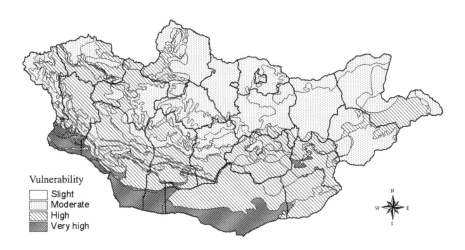

Vulnerability
- Slight
- Moderate
- High
- Very high

Figure 4.5 *Areas vulnerable to black and white* zud

Changing Institutions, Policies and Resources

Thousands of years of traditional pastoral practices were fundamentally changed with collectivization of the livestock sector in the early 1960s. Prior to this, allocation of pasture land, sharing of labour and resources, and the settle-

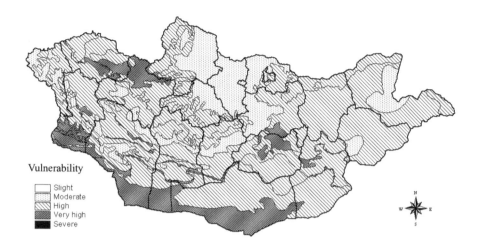

Figure 4.6 *Areas vulnerable to drought, black* zud *and white* zud

ment of disputes were organized through a hierarchy of customary institutions such as the *khot ail* (a group of 2 to 12 households that camp together), *neg nutgiinkhan* or 'people of one place' (a neighbourhood-level group of 20–50 households) and *bag* (group of 50 to 100 households) (Chuluun et al, 2003). Through these institutions a nomadic system of seasonal migration of households and livestock herds operated such that access to forage was provided year round, grazing pressures were regulated and drought and *zud* risks managed.

In 1960 the livestock sector was collectivized and pasture land, animals and tools of production became the property of collectives called *negdels*. The *negdels* took over the regulatory functions of the traditional customary institutions for allocating pasture and resources and enforcing seasonal movement of herds. Within the *negdel*, each herding family specialized in the production of a single animal species and sometimes age class of animals (Chuluun et al, 2003). The *negdel* was the management and economic unit responsible for supplying inputs, consumer goods, fodder, transport, health services, education and veterinary services to its members. The government, through the *negdel*, provided inputs for fencing, veterinary services, cross-breeding to improve livestock breeds and irrigated forage production, all at greatly subsidized prices. A State Emergency Fodder Fund was established to provide supplementary feed during hazardous weather events.

During the collectivized period of 1960–1990, income inequality was low, poverty was virtually unknown, access to primary healthcare was nearly universal and adult literacy reached 97 per cent (Mearns and Dulamdary, 2000). The collectively supplied and subsidized services and resources reduced the exposure and sensitivity of herders' livelihoods to climate hazards and provided the means for coping with climate-driven variability in their production system and recovering from shocks to their production. However, herders became dependent on centralized and heavily subsidized services and inputs.

In the beginning of the 1990s, the country was transformed from a socialist system to a market economy. With the transition came dissolution of the *negdels*, an end to state subsidies to the livestock sector, and privatization of livestock, shelter, wells and other tools of production, while pasture land remained the property of the state. The transition was accompanied by a loss of external subsidies from the Soviet Union, collapse of the state budget, retrenchment of state employment, drastically reduced provision of health and education services, and deep cuts in investment in basic infrastructure. The end of the 1990s also saw deterioration in terms of trade and loss of export earnings as prices fell for Mongolia's three main exports (copper, gold and cashmere) and oil prices rose. As a result, Mongolia experienced a widening of income inequality, unemployment, a doubling of maternal mortality, declining literacy and a rapid rise in poverty that has put more than one third of the population below the poverty line (Mearns and Dulamdary, 2000).

Privatization of livestock created a large number of herders with small animal herds who constitute the bulk of the poor. During the socialist period, there was some private ownership of animals, which provided a supplement to herders' incomes and diet, but almost no herders owned more than 100 animals. With the end of the socialist system, privately owned animals provide most of a herder's income and diet, and poverty in the rural areas is tightly linked to the number of animals owned by a household. In the market economy era, households with fewer than 50 animals are considered by the government to be poor and those with 51–100 animals are considered to be vulnerable to poverty. Households in these two categories, about 60 per cent of herders, are highly vulnerable to climate hazards because severe events such as *zud* can eliminate their herds or reduce herd sizes below levels needed for a subsistence income. Households with 101–200 animals, approximately 25 per cent of herders, are usually able to generate sufficient income to support a comfortable life, yet they are still vulnerable to events that cause a large loss of animals and reduce their incomes to subsistence levels or below. Thus nearly 85 per cent of herder households are vulnerable to climate extremes such as the series of severe droughts and *zud* from 1999 through 2002 that devastated livestock herds.

Many of the poorer herder households were newcomers who migrated in the early 1990s from urban to rural areas in response to reduced state employment, economic contraction and the opportunity to receive private livestock (Mearns and Dulamdary, 2000). The migration was large enough to reverse the earlier rural-to-urban migration trend and more than double the number of herders and their households during the 1990s (Chuluun et al, 2003). The newcomers typically have small herds with low diversity of herd structure, are young, have high dependency ratios, have little herding experience and lack knowledge of local customary arrangements. This latter characteristic impeded them from assimilating and gaining access to social networks, informal credit sources, wells, pastures and winter shelters, creating a condition of high vulnerability to climate and other shocks (Mearns and Dulamdary, 2000). Many of these herders were forced to migrate back to urban areas when they lost their herds during the 1999–2002 period of drought and *zud*.

The dissolution of the *negdels* left a vacuum in which the use of pasture is largely unregulated and customary rights weakened. Pasture effectively became an open access commons in which herders lack incentives to conserve pasture or make investments in land, water and other infrastructure. Without the *negdels* or appropriate incentives, investment has been lacking and infrastructure such as winter shelters, wells, marketing systems, veterinary services and production of feed supplements has deteriorated. Herders responded to the open access nature of pastures by increasing the numbers of animals stocked and grazed. Many reduced the frequency and distance of movement of herds, trespassed into pastures traditionally reserved for use only during climate calamities, moved herds closer to urban centres with services that were increasingly unavailable in rural areas and even grazed herds on the same pasture year round. As a result, pastures in some areas have been overstocked and degraded and have reduced productivity (Chuluun et al, 2003).

The changes since 1990 outlined above have diminished the capacity of Mongolia's pastoralists to cope with climatic, economic and other shocks. The elimination of subsidies and services to the livestock sector, the loss of the safety nets of the socialist system, and the contraction of opportunities due to the economic downturn and deteriorated terms of trade eroded the livelihood resources available to pastoralists. A large class of poor households with small herds, insufficient human capital and lack of access to social and financial capital has been created in the rural areas. The dismantling of socialist collective institutions has resulted in a loss of critical infrastructure and transformed the landscape into an open access commons that is susceptible to misuse and degradation. As a result of these changing conditions and pressures, the vulnerability of pastoralists has been exacerbated.

On the positive side, some customary institutions such as the *khot ail* are re-emerging to fill the vacuum left by the dissolution of the socialist collective system. Herders are organizing themselves into traditional communities to share common seasonal camps and water resources, share labour, regulate access to pastures, and support traditional practices such as seasonal migration of herds and maintenance of reserve pastures. Herders are also diversifying their herds to include multiple species and age classes, which helps them to hedge against climate and market risk. These customary institutions offer a potential model for reducing vulnerability to climate and other risks, and enabling adaptation (Batima et al, 2008).

Climate Change: Future Projections and Impacts

The most recent assessment of the Intergovernmental Panel on Climate Change (IPCC) concludes that increases in annual mean temperature will be well above the global mean in the Tibetan Plateau and above the mean in East Asia (Christensen et al, 2007). The 25th to 75th percentiles of projections of annual mean temperature change between 1980–1999 and 2080–2099 from 21 models reviewed by the IPCC for the A1B emission scenario range between 3.2 and 4.5°C, with a median of 3.8°C for the Tibetan Plateau. In East Asia, the 25th–75th percentile range is 2.8–4.1°C and the median is 3.3°C. Greater warming is projected for winter than summer and for higher altitudes. Longer, more intense and more frequent heat-waves as well as fewer very cold days are very likely.

Precipitation increases are considered likely for winter and summer in East Asia and very likely for winter in the Tibetan Plateau. The 25th–75th percentile range of precipitation changes for the 21 models is +6 to +17 per cent in winter, +5 to +11 per cent in summer and +4 to +14 per cent annual average in East Asia over the 100 year period. In the Tibetan Plateau, the projected changes are +12 to +26 per cent in winter, 0 to +10 per cent in summer and +2 to +13 per cent annual average. More frequent intense precipitation events are very likely in the region.

In our analyses of the possible impacts of climate change on pasture productivity and livestock, we used climate projections from three general circulation models (GCMs), HadCM3, ECHAM4 and CSIRO-Mk2b, for two scenarios of future emissions (A2 and B2) to construct scenarios for Mongolia (Natsagdorj et al, 2005). Our scenarios of temperature and precipitation changes derived from these model experiments are presented in Table 4.5.

Table 4.5 *Projections of temperature and precipitation changes in Mongolia relative to 1961–1990 baseline for SRES A2 and B2 emission scenarios*

Model	A2 – medium-high emissions						B2 – medium-low emissions					
	2020		2050		2080		2020		2050		2080	
	T,°C	P,%	T,°C	P,%	T,°C	P,%	T,°C	P,%	T,°C	P,%	T,°C	P,%
Winter												
HadCM3	0.9	23.6	2.4	38.7	3.9	67.0	1.0	16.5	1.7	34.4	2.5	54.7
ECHAM4	3.6	59.0	5.7	80.9	8.7	119.4	3.7	11.5	6.0	82.0	6.6	90.3
CSIRO-Mk2b	1.7	12.6	2.9	27.2	5.2	49.0	1.7	14.2	2.7	24.9	3.7	36.8
Summer												
HadCM3	2.0	−2.5	3.5	7.1	6.4	6.4	2.2	3.1	3.3	8.7	4.7	4.5
ECHAM4	1.9	7.2	3.7	6.5	6.6	11.3	2.1	7.6	3.8	5.7	4.9	8.6
CSIRO-Mk2b	1.3	−2.1	2.9	0.5	5.5	−2.3	1.9	0.4	3.0	−1.4	4.1	−1.3

The scenarios constructed from all three GCM projections yield greater warming in both winter and summer and much wetter winters than is suggested by the IPCC's 2007 assessment. The ECHAM4-derived scenarios are the warmest and wettest while the CSIRO-Mk2b-derived scenarios are less warm and less wet. According to all the scenarios, summers in Mongolia will be hotter and drier. The projected evapotranspiration is higher than the projected increase in precipitation, which will dry the soil. Future winters are projected to have milder temperatures but greater snowfall.

The impacts of the climate change scenarios on rangelands are simulated using the CENTURY 4.0 model (Metherell et al, 1993). The model yields estimates of above ground biomass and carbon:nitrogen ratio in the vegetation. Results are presented in Tables 4.6, 4.7 and 4.8 for the time periods 2020, 2050 and 2080. Above-ground biomass in 2080 is negatively impacted in the steppe and forest steppe biomes for all scenarios, as is forage quality, represented by the carbon:nitrogen ratio. The reductions in biomass range from -5 to -22 per cent in the steppe and -14 to -37 per cent in the forest steppe. The most severe reductions are for the HadCM3- and ECHAM4-derived scenarios because of their drier summers. In contrast to the steppe and forest steppe, increases in biomass are projected for the high mountains and desert steppe. In most cases, decreases in forage quality are projected for the high mountains and desert steppe. Given the relative importance of the steppe and forest steppe biomass, the overall impact of climate change on Mongolia's pastures is expected to be negative.

Table 4.6 *Estimated changes in above-ground biomass and carbon:nitrogen ratio for scenarios derived from the HadCM3 climate model*

Ecosystem zones	A2			B2		
	2020	2050	2080	2020	2050	2080
Above-ground biomass						
Forest steppe	−3.8	−6.0	−37.2	−10.4	−11.9	−27.8
Steppe	−2.9	−5.0	−19.9	−0.6	−0.6	−7.1
High mountains	20.2	24.9	25.3	2.5	26.2	27.9
Desert steppe	16.9	40.6	46.8	18.9	43.7	52.1
Carbon:nitrogen ratio						
Forest steppe	−1.2	−1.4	−10.4	−2.8	−3.8	−7.1
Steppe	−1.7	−0.7	−7.2	−1.9	−1.7	−3.9
High mountains	−1.2	−1.4	−2.8	−2.1	−1.7	−2.2
Desert steppe	−1.0	−0.7	−2.0	−0.9	−0.4	−0.7

Reduced pasture productivity and forage quality would negatively impact livestock. Livestock would also be negatively impacted by the effects of warmer temperatures on the amount of time they can graze. Models of animal grazing behaviour project decreased grazing time in summer and increased time in winter over much of the land area. Estimates of combined effects of changes in pasture yield, forage quality and grazing time on summer–autumn ewe weight for the HadCM3 scenarios are presented in Table 4.9. Substantial reductions in animal weight are projected for the steppe and forest steppe zones, with modest reductions in the high mountains and nearly no change in the desert steppe.

Table 4.7 *Estimated changes in above-ground biomass and carbon:nitrogen ratio for scenarios derived from the ECHAM4 climate model*

Ecosystem zones	A2			B2		
	2020	2050	2080	2020	2050	2080
Above-ground biomass						
Forest steppe	8.5	−7.2	−22.3	7.9	−10.1	−14.0
Steppe	11.8	3.8	−11.0	14.0	−0.4	−5.5
High mountains	90.8	77.6	74.0	104.4	71.4	74.9
Desert steppe	50.6	57.0	52.1	60.8	51.1	31.7
Carbon:nitrogen ratio						
Forest steppe	0.6	−3.1	−9.1	1.5	−4.5	−5.0
Steppe	0.8	−1.4	−5.7	1.4	−2.6	−3.1
High mountains	4.0	2.4	−0.5	5.6	1.5	1.1
Desert steppe	0.5	−0.4	−2.2	1.1	−1.0	−1.5

Table 4.8 *Estimated changes in above-ground biomass and carbon:nitrogen ratio for scenarios derived from the CSIRO-Mk2b climate model*

Ecosystem zones	A2			B2		
	2020	2050	2080	2020	2050	2080
Above-ground biomass						
Forest steppe	−4.6	−6.8	−30.8	−7.6	−12.7	−16.9
Steppe	−4.2	−1.6	−21.9	−7.3	−11.4	−15.2
High mountains	11.3	34.0	34.8	11.0	8.5	62.7
Desert steppe	11.1	36.9	53.0	27.9	25.9	57.6
Carbon:nitrogen ratio						
Forest steppe	0.6	−3.1	−9.1	1.5	−4.5	−5.0
Steppe	0.8	−1.4	−5.7	1.4	−2.6	−3.1
High mountains	4.0	2.4	−0.5	5.6	1.5	1.1
Desert steppe	0.5	−0.4	−2.2	1.1	−1.0	−1.5

Conclusions

Mongolia's pastoralists historically have been strongly impacted by the extremes of the region's climate. They are highly vulnerable to climate hazards and their vulnerability has grown in recent decades. Warming and drying of the climate has reduced the quantity and quality of forage on Mongolia's pasture lands and this has negatively affected livestock and herders' livelihoods. Despite the warmer temperatures, spatially extensive winter *zud* events increased significantly in frequency in the 1980s and 1990s relative to the

1960s. More than 60 per cent of the country's land has been shown to be vulnerable to climate-driven extremes.

Table 4.9 *Projected changes in ewe weight (%) with combined effects of changes in pasture productivity, forage quality and grazing time for HadCM3 climate change scenarios*

Ecosystem zones	A2			B2		
	2020	2050	2080	2020	2050	2080
Forest steppe	−10.68	−34.40	−57.75	−26.97	−38.33	−53.99
Steppe	−12.85	−31.67	−39.50	−15.86	−24.10	−34.37
High mountain	−2.92	−3.05	−9.03	−2.76	−3.64	−3.77
Desert steppe	2.02	3.87	−0.18	2.18	0.96	−0.36

These climatic and environmental changes have happened against a backdrop of tremendous social and economic change as Mongolia transformed itself from a socialist to a market-oriented system. The social and economic changes created greater vulnerability to climate and other shocks within the pastoral communities. Economic opportunities and income contracted, subsidized inputs and services to the livestock sector were eliminated, socialist institutions for the organization and management of livestock production were dissolved, overgrazing degraded pastures in some areas, investment was insufficient to maintain critical infrastructure in the rural areas, and a new class of poor rural households was created. These changes reduced the ability of herders' households to cope with *zud*, drought, market variations and other stresses, and increased their vulnerability. New opportunities and new institutions are emerging, and these are helping to reduce vulnerability. Yet vulnerability remains high.

This is a worrying situation as Mongolia faces a climate that is changing because of human actions. Our analyses of the future impacts of climate change suggest that pasture yields and forage quality will continue to decline and that these will negatively impact livestock. Our analyses have not taken into account possible changes in *zud* in the future. As temperatures warm, winters will become milder, offering the potential for less frequent and severe *zud* events. However, *zud* is a complex phenomenon that is not simply a function of mean temperature. Higher projected winter precipitation could result in more frequent and greater snowfall. Changes in patterns of daily temperature variability, frequencies of wind storms and other climate parameters will affect *zud* occurrence. Recent decades have been a time of warming, yet as noted previously, the frequency of *zud* events that impact more than 25 per cent of Mongolia has increased substantially. How human-driven climate change will affect the frequency, intensity or spatial extent of *zud* is highly uncertain, but the outcome will have important consequences for all Mongolia. It will be critical for Mongolia to take up this challenge and explore options for adapting to a changing climate, a challenge that we examine elsewhere (see Batima et al, 2008).

Note

1   Details of this research are reported in Batima (2006).

References

Batima, P. (2006) 'Climate change vulnerability and adaptation in the livestock sector of Mongolia', Final Report, Project AS06, Assessments of Impacts and Adaptations to Climate Change, International START Secretariat, Washington, DC, US

Batima, P., N. Batnasan and B. Lehner (2004) *The Freshwater Systems of Western Mongolia's Great Lakes Basin: Opportunities and Challenges in the Face of Climate Change*, ADMON, Ulaanbaatar, Mongolia

Batima, P., B. Bat, S. Tserendash and B. Myagmarjav (2008) 'Adapting to drought, zud and climate change in Mongolia's grasslands', in N. Leary, J. Adejuwon, V. Barros, I. Burton, J. Kulkarni and R. Lasco (eds) *Climate Change and Adaptation*, Earthscan, London, UK

Bayarbaatar, L., G. Tuvaansuren and D. Tserendorj. 2005. 'Climate Change and Livestock'. In P. Batima and B. Bayasgalan, eds, *Vulnerability and Adaptation Assessment for Grassland Ecosystem and Livestock Sector in Mongolia: Impacts of Climate Change.* ADMON. Ulaanbaatar (in Mongolian)

Christensen, J. H., B. Hewitson, A. Busuioc, A. Chen, X. Gao, I. Held, R. Jones, R. Koli, W. Kwon, R. Laprise, V. Rueda, L. Mearns, C. Menendez, J. Raisanen, A. Rinke, A. Sarr and P. Whetton (2007) 'Regional Climate Projections', in S. Solomon, D. Qin, M. Manning, Z. Chen, M. C. Marquis, K. Averyt, M. Tignor and H. L. Miller (eds) *Climate Change 2007: The Physical Science Basis*, Contribution of Working Group I to the Fourth Assessment Report of the Intergovernmental Panel on Climate Change, Cambridge University Press, Cambridge, UK and New York, US

Chuluun, T., A. Enkh-Amgalan and D. Ojima (2003) 'Tragedy of the commons during transition to market economy and alternative future for the Mongolian rangelands', *African Journal of Range and Forage Science*, vol 20, no 2, p115

Mearns, R. and E. Dulamdary (2000) 'Sustaining livelihoods on Mongolia's pastoral commons', Presented at the 8th Biennial Conference of the International Association for the Study of Common Property, Bloomington, Indiana, May 31 – June 4, Digital Library of the Commons, http://dlc.dlib.indiana.edu/archive/00000574/

Metherell, A. K., L. A. Harding, C. V. Cole and W. J. Parton (1993) *CENTURY Soil Organic Matter Model Environment*, Technical Documentation Agroecosystem, version 4.0., Colorado State University, Fort Collins, CO, US

Ministry of Nature and Environment (2001) *Annual Report on Environmental Resources*, Ministry of Nature and Environment, Ulaanbaatar, Mongolia

Ministry of Nature and Environment (2003) *Report on Water Resources Inventory*, Ministry of Nature and Environment, Ulaanbaatar, Mongolia

National Statistical Office (2001) *Mongolian Statistical Yearbook 2001*, National Statistical Office, Ulaanbaatar, Mongolia

National Statistical Office (2003) *Mongolian Statistical Yearbook 2003*, National Statistical Office, Ulaanbaatar, Mongolia

Natsagdorj, L., P. Gomboluudev and P. Batima (2005) 'Climate change in Mongolia', in P. Batima and B.Myagmarjav (ed) *Vulnerability and Adaptation Assessment for Grassland Ecosystem and Livestock Sector in Mongolia: Current and Future Climate Change*, ADMON, Ulaanbaatar (in Mongolian)

Tserendash, S., B. Bolortsetseg, P. Batima, G. Sanjid, M. Erdenetuya, T. Ganbaatar and N. Manibazar (2005) 'Climate change and pasture', in P. Batima and B. Bayasgalan (eds) *Vulnerability and Adaptation Assessment for Grassland Ecosystem and Livestock Sector in Mongolia: Impacts of Climate Change*, ADMON, Ulaanbaatar (in Mongolian)

Tsevel (1966) *The Mongolian Language Vocabulary Dictionary*, Academy of Sciences, Ulaanbaatar, Mongolia

5

Resource System Vulnerability to Climate Stresses in the Heihe River Basin of Western China

Yongyuan Yin, Nicholas Clinton, Bin Luo and Liangchung Song

Introduction

China's Western Region Development Strategy, announced in 1999, aims to accelerate economic growth in the western provinces and close disparities between the eastern and western regions. The vast region of 6.85 million square kilometres encompasses 71 per cent of the land area of China and is home to 355 million people, or 28 per cent of the total population (Liu and Nielson, 2004). The region is rich in many natural resources, but is poor in fertile land and water, is subject to highly variable precipitation, and its soils suffer constant wind erosion. Western lands account for 80 per cent of China's total eroded lands (Glantz et al, 2001).

These features have been and will continue to be important limiting constraints on development of the region. Human-caused climate change is likely to affect the availability of water, agricultural productivity and soil fertility, and could make resource and environmental constraints more biting in the future. Successful development of the west that attains economic and other goals in a sustainable manner will need to be cognizant of the current constraints and how they may evolve with a changing climate. This requires information about vulnerability to current and changing climate hazards, including its nature and causes, its distribution among the population, and its spatial distribution across the landscape, that can be used by decision makers to reduce vulnerability and improve the adaptive capacity of resource systems to cope with climate change.

In this chapter we present an approach that we have developed for the assessment of water and land resource system vulnerability along with preliminary results from its application to the Heihe river basin of northwestern China. The basin is a region of predominantly arid and semi-arid climate with highly variable rainfall, scarcity of water and fragile ecological systems. The basin is poor in financial resources, infrastructure, education levels, and access to technology and markets, creating a situation of low adaptive capacity relative to the coastal region of China. People in the region are facing substantial and multiple stresses, including rapidly growing demands for food and water, poverty, land degradation, water pollution and conflicts over resources. Our analysis shows that resource-related stresses and conflicts result in a high degree of vulnerability in the basin to climatic risks and that these risks may be amplified by climate change. The growing resources vulnerability poses a big challenge for government agencies to manage natural resources more effectively while facilitating development in the basin.

Assessing Resource System Vulnerability

We define the vulnerability of a system to climate variation and change as its propensity to undergo impacts from climate perturbations that disrupt the nominal functionality of the system. Our focus is on the vulnerability of natural resource systems, specifically water and land, which provide the physical basis for human life and society. Our conception of natural resource systems encompasses not only the physical resources themselves, but also human interactions with and use of these resources. Natural resources provide three groups of functions: 1) raw materials and energy as inputs of economic production; 2) services that support recreation, amenity wilderness and non-use values and 3) air, water, food and waste assimilation required as life-support for human society. Vulnerability of natural resource systems is concerned with shocks or stresses that disrupt any of these functions.

Vulnerability to climate hazards has been described by different authors as having three dimensions: exposure, sensitivity and adaptive capacity (see, for example, Kasperson et al, 2002). Exposure relates to the frequency, intensity and nature of climate events or phenomena with which elements of the system of study come into contact. Sensitivity describes the degree to which a resource system is affected by exposure to climate stimuli. It is obvious that the sensitivity of a system to environmental stresses is influenced by the properties of the system, including its state or condition. A system that is in a degraded, weakened or fragile state from previous exposure to climate or other stresses is often highly sensitive to new exposures. Environmental risk is mainly determined by exposure and sensitivity.

Adaptive capacity is the ability of a system to respond to exposures and their effects so as to limit harm, or even to benefit. It is related to resilience, which is the ability of the exposure unit to resist or recover from the damage associated with the convergence of multiple stresses. Smit et al (1999) and Downing et al (1997) use 'coping range' to characterize a system's adaptive capacity. It is suggested that a system will not be seriously damaged as long as the environmental change or variation falls within a system's coping range, while changes beyond the boundaries of the coping range can result in severe or even disastrous consequences. Smit et al (2000) suggest that defining a coping range can help to measure the adaptive capacity of the system.

Resource vulnerability and environmental risk

Resource system vulnerability is closely linked to environmental risk, which can be expressed as:

$$R = P(e) \times D$$

where R is environmental risk, e is exposure to an environmental perturbation or hazard, P(e) is the probability or likelihood of exposure to the hazard, and D is the damage or consequence of exposure, which is a function of the intensity of the exposure, the sensitivity of the system and its adaptive capacity. In similar fashion we define vulnerability in probabilistic terms:

$$V = P(s) \times P(e) \times [1-P(a)]$$

where V is the vulnerability of the system, P(s) is the probability that the system is sensitive to the hazard, P(e) is the probability of exposure to the hazard and [1-P(a)] is the probability that the system lacks capacity to cope with or adapt to the hazard. In this construction, vulnerability is the joint probability that the system is sensitive, that it will be exposed and that it lacks the capacity to adapt, assuming independence among exposure, sensitivity and adaptive capacity. Values of V would lie in the interval [0, 1]. With zero probability of any one of the component factors, the system is not considered to be vulnerable. An alternative conception would be to interpret each of the components as an index number, normalized to lie between 0 and 1, whose value is the proportion of the maximal degree of exposure, sensitivity or capacity.

Statistical measurement methods

Climate risk also has been expressed as a statistical measure of the extent or duration of a resource system failure under climate stresses, should a failure occur. The extent of a system failure is the amount an observed statistical value exceeds or falls short of a critical threshold. For example, water system vulnerability can be measured as the volume of water by which supply falls short of meeting demand for a certain amount of water for a municipality, or to continually release water above a minimum flow rate from a reservoir. Water system vulnerability can also be measured as the average deficit occurring during failures to meet a target, as well as the severity of failures. For example, if we use river flow, F, as an indicator to measure vulnerability, the water system vulnerability can be calculated by:

$$EV_f = Max\ [0,\ LF_t - F_t,\ F_t - UF_t]$$

where EV_f is the water system's maximum-extent vulnerability based on the river flow indicator; LF_t and UF_t are the lower and upper critical thresholds of the coping range respectively; and F_t is the observed river flow (ASCE and UNESCO/IHP, 1997). If the observed data for the system performance indicator values lie within the upper and lower thresholds (within the coping range), we assume that the range of values is satisfactory, acceptable or not vulnerable. Statistics or observed data above the upper threshold or below the lower limit are considered as unsatisfactory or vulnerable. It should be noted that these coping ranges may change over time.

Using indicators to measure resource vulnerability

In resource vulnerability assessment, indicators are used as decision criteria or standards by which the degree or the group of resource vulnerability class can be identified. ASCE and UNESCO/IHP (1997) suggest a list of vulnerability indicators that can be used for water resource vulnerability assessment. Each indicator is composed of a number of attributes or variables which are measurable by using existing sources of information in most cases. For example, Lane et al (1999) define reservoir system vulnerability as the magnitude of a water supply failure relative to annual yield.

The South Pacific Applied Geoscience Commission (SOPAC) developed an environmental vulnerability indicator (EVI) that uses a hierarchical structure to aggregate 47 individual indicators (Kaly et al, 1999). The purpose of the EVI is to evaluate the significance of environmental vulnerability of a nation facing alternative stresses or hazards. The EVI includes three levels. The top level, the EVI, consists of three composite sub-indices: a risk exposure sub-index (REI), an intrinsic resilience sub-index (IRI) and an extrinsic resilience index (ERI). Each sub-index is constructed from a number of indicators used to measure different determinants of the environmental vulnerability of a nation.

The Famine Early Warning System (FEWS) of the US Agency for International Development (USAID) adopted various methods to conduct comprehensive assessments of vulnerability in poor southern African countries (USAID, 1997). FEWS uses an indicator method to identify geographic locations which are vulnerable to climate variables and stresses. The results are used to classify areas as slightly, moderately, highly or extremely vulnerable to famine. A vulnerability analysis mapping (VAM) project was also used by the same study in Mozambique for vulnerability assessment. The VAM applied classification methods to generate flood risk maps, drought risk maps, food systems maps, land-use maps, market access maps, and health and nutritional profile maps.

Vulnerability assessment approach developed for this study

The climate vulnerability assessment in this study, outlined in Figure 5.1, has four components: 1) climate scenarios, 2) sensitivity analysis, 3) vulnerability indicators and 4) system vulnerability to climate stimuli. Given the large amount of research and literature on climate change scenario development and climate sensitivity analysis, we focus in this chapter on the selection of vulnerability indicators, their integration into an assessment of vulnerability and mapping of vulnerability.

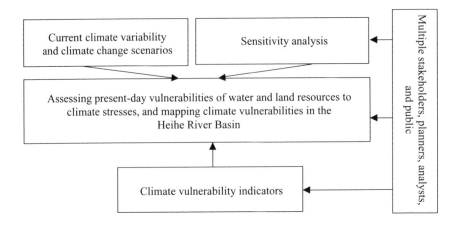

Figure 5.1 *Flow-chart of the general research approach*

Several key vulnerability indicators are selected to measure resource vulnerability under current climate conditions in the Heihe river basin. GIS (geographic information system) is used to identify the spatial distribution of water resource vulnerability by combining the indicators of domestic water deficit (Srdjevic et al, 2003) and irrigation deficit (Qi and Cheng, 1998) into a composite indicator. Maps, tables and figures provide visual displays of resource system vulnerability, which can help policymakers identify the most vulnerable subunits. It should be pointed out that there have been few practical applications of such an approach, particularly in climate vulnerability research.

Results of our assessment of vulnerability to current climate variation establishes a baseline set of measurements and observations that could be used to measure progress toward reducing vulnerability to future climate change. The various vulnerability indicators can be applied to project potential vulnerabilities of the resource systems in the future using climate change scenarios. In this way, the research on present vulnerabilities of resource systems can provide insights into potential impacts and vulnerabilities associated with future climate change. The methodology developed and applied by our study provides, we hope, a useful approach that could be replicated and extended in other studies.

Case Study of the Heihe River Basin

The Heihe river basin is located in a region bounded by latitudes 35.4 and 43.5°N and longitudes 96.45 and 102.8°E. A map of the study region is shown in Figure 5.2. The study area is the second largest inland river basin in the arid region of northwestern China. The basin includes parts of two provinces, Qinghai and Gansu, and the Inner Mongolia Autonomous Region. With an area of 128,000 square kilometres, the basin accommodates a population of 1.8 million living in 11 counties, three small cities and five prefectures. The region is composed of diverse ecosystems, including mountain, oasis, forest, grassland and desert. The Heihe river flows from a headwater in the Qilian Mountain area to an alluvial plain with oasis agriculture, and then enters deserts in Inner Mongolia, representing the upper, middle and lower reaches of the basin respectively. The total length of the Heihe river is 821 kilometres.

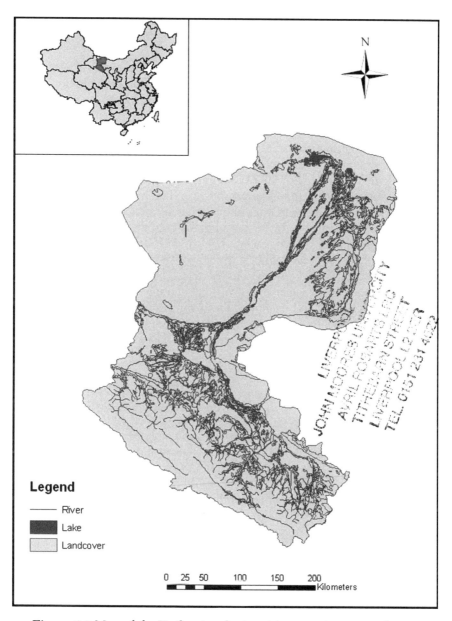

Figure 5.2 *Map of the Heihe river basin with approximate population distribution shown in shades of grey (black is highest population density)*

The Heihe river basin has a typical arid and semi-arid continental climate, characterized by low and irregular rainfall, high evaporation and recurrent drought. The basin can be divided into three typical climate zones following the altitudinal gradient. On the southern slope of the Qilian Mountain, the climate is wet and cold with a mean annual precipitation ranging from 300 to 500mm. In the middle reach, the climate becomes much drier and the mean annual precipitation is only 100–200mm. In the lower reach, the average annual precipitation is less than 60mm, making it one of the driest areas at the same latitude on Earth (Digital River Basin, undated).

Great temporal variations in temperature and precipitation also exist over the Heihe River Basin, with about 50–70 per cent of the precipitation recorded during the summer. Mean daily temperature ranges from −14°C to 3°C in January and from 11°C to 27°C in July (Gansu Meteorological Bureau, 2000).

The Heihe river basin is a poor region in China with a harsh environment and fragile ecological systems. The region is critically short of water and arable land, deficient in educated, technical and scientific personnel, and far from even domestic markets. The major economic sector in the region is agriculture, and irrigation is crucial for crop production. The leading crops are wheat, potatoes and corn. The oasis agriculture relies on irrigation from the Heihe river and its tributaries. While the basin has fostered the development of much oasis agriculture in the middle reach, rangeland farming in the upper reach and herdsmen in the lower reach, towns, small hydropower plants, a large number of rural communities, and government agencies, climate stresses have imposed considerable economic, social and environmental impacts.

With a resource-based economy, the study region is very sensitive to climate. People in the basin face substantial and multiple stresses, including rapidly growing demands for food and water, large populations at risk of poverty, degradation of land and water quality, and other issues that may be amplified by climate change.

Drought is one of the main climate hazards in the basin, with characteristics of high frequency and significant damage. For example, droughts occurred in the middle reach in about 50 per cent of the years since 1951. During drought years, while the precipitation volume of May and June is remarkably lower than the mean, the annual evaporation demand remains at 2000 to 2650mm (Chen and Qu, 1992). Under climate change conditions, periods of drought are likely to become more frequent and severe, and water shortages may increase water-use conflicts. Land degradation problems and limited water supplies restrict present agricultural production and threaten the food security of the region. Climate change may cause negative impacts on food and fibre production in the region (Shi, 1995). In addition, decreases in water availability and food production would lead to indirect impacts on human health. Kang et al (1999) suggested that spring outflow at the mountain outlet would increase while summer flow would decline by 2030 under climate change scenarios. Irrigation demand in the summer accounts for more than 70 per cent of the total agricultural water consumption in the region. This seasonal shift of water supply will affect agricultural production considerably.

There is already some evidence of an observed positive trend in temperatures over the past 50 years, with a more significant rise in the Qilian Mountain area. During this period, annual average temperature increased more than 1°C in Sunan County and 0.9°C in upper mountain areas. The Qilian Mountain glaciers are already undergoing a rapid retreat at a rate of about one metre annually. The region depends on spring melt from the glaciers for the main water supply (Cheng, 1997). A declining water supply has already affected land resources, with large areas of farmland undergoing desertification (Digital River Basin, undated).

Climate exposure

In identifying present-day climate risks, existing climate variation patterns need to be specified. The climate change trend in northwest China for the past 50 years was investigated by analysing temperature and rainfall data from 1951 to 2004 (Wang, 2005). Climate change scenario specification for this study represents the possible future climate conditions under various assumptions. Based on eight coupled global atmospheric and oceanic circulation models (AOGCMs), the climate change projection over west China for the 21st century was calculated by the NCC/IAP (National Climate Center/Institute of Atmospheric Physics) T63 simulation model (Xu et al, 2003). Ding et al (2005) applied a regional climate model (Ncc/RegCM2) nested with a coupled GCM (NCCT63L16/T63L30) and Hadley Center model (HadCM2) for climate change studies. Outputs of the Chinese regional-scale climate model were used to design scenarios (Li and Ding, 2004). Results for western China from the regional climate experiment for the IPCC SRES AS emission scenario project an increase of 0.4°C in mean annual temperature for the period 2020–2030, with greater warming in summer, and a slight decrease in precipitation (Yin, 2006).

Sensitivity analysis

The purpose of sensitivity analysis is to identify those climate variables possessing relative importance in determining resource system vulnerability. In addition, sensitivity analysis can indicate those key aspects of resource systems which are sensitive to certain climate variables. Since the relations between climate variables and various system aspects are based on historical statistics or experience, this kind of information can be derived from experts or stakeholder consultation. In this connection, stakeholder workshops and surveys were carried out to provide sensitivity information. The consultation with stakeholders on climate sensitivity is also part of the capacity-building process of the study. In the consultation process, stakeholders identified key climate stresses, vulnerability indicators and critical thresholds they use in resource management.

Climate sensitivity analysis through stakeholder consultation in this study followed an approach used in the Hunter Valley case study (Hennessy and Jones, 1999). A potential sensitivity matrix was generated during a stakeholder workshop to identify climate variables with the greatest forcing and activities with the broadest sensitivity to climate in the study region. The sensitivity results indicate that water shortage is the main concern of the study region. Rainfall variability and soil moisture levels have the greatest impact, while temperature has only a moderate effect. Obviously, rural resource-use activities are very sensitive to climate events.

Identification of critical vulnerability indicators

The research procedure follows with an identification of indicators to measure resource vulnerability in the study. To select critical indicators for vulnerability assessment, the first major source of information used for the study was government reports, documents and other published materials on resource issues. Based on existing key policy concerns in the region, indicators for measuring resource vulnerability under climate stimuli were identified. Some operationally useful key indicators in vulnerability and adaptive capacity assessment are listed in Table 5.1.

Table 5.1 *Potential determinants (climate and other variables with forcing) and resource indicators*

Climate and Other Related Factors	Resource Vulnerability Indicators
Rainfall variability	Food security
Maximum temperature	Farm income
Soil moisture	Water scarcity (withdrawal ratio)
Minimum temperature	Drought hazards
Wind	Palmer drought severity index (PDSI)
Cold snap	Water use conflicts
Heat stress days	Arable land loss
Accumulated degree days	Groundwater stress
Cropping area	Salinity
Population growth	Soil erosion
Economic growth	Grassland deterioration
Technology	
Consumption	
Urban expansion	
Resource management	
Government policies	

The preceding discussion indicates that climate risks and vulnerabilities are determined by many factors, including climate stimuli, system sensitivity to climate, adaptive capacity and other response options to deal with risks. The factors that influence the system exposure risk (Table 5.1, left column) can mainly be divided into climate stimuli (rainfall variability, temperature extremes and so on), properties of the resource use systems (resource management), and economic and social forces (economic and population growth). These factors affect the spatial distribution of climate impacts and adaptive capacity which could result in significant differences in climate risks and vulnerabilities geographically.

Since resource system vulnerability is related to failures of the resource system to provide economic, social and ecological functions to meet societal demands, indicators listed in the right column of Table 5.1 reflect some aspects of these functions. It is obvious that farm income is one of the most important indicators for measuring vulnerability. Improvements in economic return will also reduce system vulnerability (Yohe and Tol, 2002).

In China, providing enough food for the country's 1.3 billion people is always a big challenge, and there is increasing concern about China's food security or its ability to feed itself. The provision of adequate food on a continual basis is a major indicator of regional sustainability. The food security indicator reflects the ability to achieve higher levels of self-sufficiency, and it can be used to check whether the resource base can provide enough food supply.

Early in 2000, the Chinese central government launched a major new initiative to develop China's poor, underdeveloped western regions. China's Western Region Development Strategy has opened a new chapter of economic growth and expansion in China's western provinces. The motivations behind the Western Region Development Strategy are aimed at rapid changes in western China over the next few decades and easing the income disparities between coastal and interior China. Stimulated by this new development strategy, many industrial and housing developments have been sited in productive farmland, forestry and wilderness areas. How to slow down the conversion of farmland to urban and industrial uses is critical for regional sustainability in western China. Thus a further indicator, to protect and conserve arable land, reflects this concern.

It is now generally realized that environmental concerns should be incorporated in decision making in an effort to achieve sustainable development (World Commission on Environment and Development, 1987). There are a large number of parameters that can be used as indicators of ecological vulnerability. In Table 5.1, environmental concerns are reflected by the indicators for salinity, soil erosion and grassland deterioration.

There is an increasing concern about the implications of climate change for water management (Gleick, 1990) and water-use conflicts in the semi-arid region of western China (Kang et al, 1999). Dealing with potential water-use conflicts under changing climate is therefore considered as an important indicator. The competition over access to water resources in the Heihe river basin has led to disputes, confrontation and many cases of violent clashes. Changing water supply induced by climate warming may increase water-use conflicts in the region.

In order to improve the reliability of the information on indicators derived from existing sources, workshops and surveys with stakeholders and decision makers in the region were conducted to discuss major policy issues related to climate change and environmental risks. Various government officials and experts were invited to workshops in the Heihe river basin. Stakeholder representatives were consulted to identify key concerns related to resource use in the region and to prioritize these indicators. These representatives included officials from various ministries of Gansu Province, bureaus of municipal governments, research institutes, women's groups and universities. It was indicated during these workshops that water shortage was the key problem relating to sustainable development in the region. Almost all the problems of ecological unsustainability are caused by water shortage in the region.

Mapping vulnerability

Mapping the spatial distribution of system vulnerability is useful in helping policymakers identify the most vulnerable subunits. To show the geographical distribution of the vulnerability levels using indicators, several spatial scales have been considered, ranging from square kilometres, the county level and the sub-basin level to the whole basin, based on data availability and other logistical reasons. For test purpose, this study applied a GIS mapping technique to illustrate resource system vulnerabilities using existing and modelled data at different scales.

The probabilistic concept of vulnerability is directly applicable to the geographic assessment of vulnerability and facilitates interdisciplinary synthesis of geographic information. For example, outputs from climate models in the form of projected mean temperatures and precipitation provide an indication of future exposure to potentially deleterious environmental conditions. These outputs are commonly available as geographically referenced grids, which can be used to calculate probability of exposure based on the distributional assumptions of climate model accuracy. Similarly, social information, by county, jurisdiction or other geographic entity, can be collected and assembled into indicators of adaptive capacity (or lack thereof). The probability of adaptive capacity could be inferred from [0,1] scaled indices or percentage of a threshold level for the index (percentage of threshold revenue, for example). Adopting this approach, we have undertaken to map sensitivity as a geographic data set (layer) to be integrated as above with layers that represent exposure probability and lack of adaptive capacity probability.

As discussed earlier, the requisite ingredients for vulnerability to a particular event include exposure to the event, sensitivity to events of that magnitude and duration, and lack of adaptive capacity to handle events of that type. Any lack of these key ingredients means the system is not vulnerable. For example, if P (exposure to event) = 0, then vulnerability = 0, and the same applies for the other terms. A map of vulnerability is created by multiplying (using map algebra, a form of overlay analysis for rasters in which the maps are multiplied cell by cell) the input maps of probability of exposure, sensitivity and lack of adaptive capacity. Thus teams with different emphases can produce maps that are easily integrated under this conceptual framework. While probability maps may be readily created (of frequency of observable or projectable events, for example), indicators may also be used as a proxy. The following sections illustrate the use of geographic data to create maps of sensitivity to be integrated with the results of climate simulations and social studies of adaptive capacity.

Preliminary Results of Resource Vulnerability in the Heihe River Basin

For illustration purposes, measurements of some key vulnerability indicators were carried out in the case study. While all indicators listed in Table 5.1 were investigated by the research team, this study only calculated resource vulnerability indicators of water withdrawal ratio, water-use conflicts and Palmer Drought Severity Index (PDSI), as well as conducting vulnerability mapping. Based on data availability, PDSI was calculated at river reach level; water withdrawal ratio and water conflict (events of disputes, confrontation and violent clashes for accessing water resources) were measured at the basin scale. Results presented here are for water system vulnerability under current climate conditions. Vulnerability assessments for other indicators and under climate change scenarios are presented in the final report for the research project (Yin et al, 2006).

Water withdrawal ratio

One important water vulnerability indicator is the water withdrawal ratio, defined as the ratio of average annual water withdrawal to water availability. Critical thresholds for indicators were set to enable the comparison of indicator values for different areas and to identify their vulnerability levels. If indicator values do not exceed the threshold level, it is assumed that the system will have a relatively benign experience under climate stresses, but beyond the threshold level, the system will suffer significant stress under climate variation and/or change. For example, a critical threshold level for the drought indicator can be determined by the amount of rainfall required in a specific region. It also can be set using more complex methods such as the accumulated deficit in irrigation allocations over a number of seasons (Jones and Page, 2001).

For the annual water withdrawal ratio indicator, the World Meteorological Organization (WMO) suggests that values exceeding 20 and 40 per cent of annual water availability be considered as medium and high water stress respectively (WMO, 1997). In northern China, however, 60 per cent is considered by the government to be the threshold for high water stress (Xie, 2000; Gansu Meteorological Bureau, 2000).

Annual water availability, water withdrawal and water withdrawal ratios in the Heihe river basin for the years 1991 to 2000 are presented in Table 5.2. The current water withdrawal ratios are extremely high, ranging between 80 and 120 per cent, far exceeding the critical threshold levels set by both the WMO and the Chinese Government. These values suggest very high levels of water stress in the basin. Water stress in the region might intensify in the future because of growing water withdrawals (driven by population and economic growth) and/or decreasing water availability as a result of climate change.

Table 5.2 *Water withdrawal ratio in the Heihe river basin, 1991–2000*

Year	1991	1992	1993	1994	1995	1996	1997	1998	1999	2000
Water Availability ($10^8 m^3$)	35.90	34.33	35.46	35.57	34.04	34.64	34.63	34.33	34.70	34.84
Total water withdrawal ($10^8 m^3$)	29.02	27.38	35.40	28.81	29.55	35.76	28.01	41.35	35.45	32.33
Water withdrawal ratio (%)	124	125	100	124	115	96.9	124	83	97.9	108

The Palmer Drought Severity Index

The Palmer Drought Severity Index (PDSI) is used as an indicator of the frequency of drought hazards over time. The PDSI was introduced by Palmer (1965) for measurement of meteorological drought. It has been widely used in different regions of the world to study severity of drought hazards (Briffa et al, 1994; Kothavala, 1999; Ntale and Gan, 2003). Because the PDSI can simulate monthly soil moisture content, it is suitable for comparing the severity of drought events among regions with different climate zones and seasons (Makra et al, 2002).

The computation of the PDSI begins with a climatic water balance using historic records of monthly precipitation and temperature. Soil moisture storage is considered by dividing the soil profile into two layers. The indicator operates on a monthly time series of precipitation and temperature to produce a single numerical value. Negative PDSI values indicate drought conditions and positive values indicate wet conditions relative to normal conditions for an area. Index values in the range –0.5 to 0.5 represent near normal conditions, –0.5 to –1.0 an incipient dry spell, –1 to –2 a mild drought, –2 to –3 a moderate drought, –3 to –4 a severe drought and beyond –4 an extreme drought. We calculate the PDSI using time series data for monthly temperature and monthly precipitation from 15 meteorological stations in the basin obtained from the meteorological service of Gansu Province.

In order to identify spatial variations of drought conditions within the Heihe river basin, the basin is subdivided into four areas based on land use, population distribution and climatic conditions. The low reach is covered by desert and wetland; the lower part of the middle reach includes degraded land; the upper part of the middle reach has most of the agricultural land and includes the majority of the population in the basin; and the upper reach is mountains covered by snow and glacier. The calculated point PDSI values are interpolated into these four areas.

Growing season temperature has been increasing gradually in recent decades in the low reach of the Heihe river basin, while growing season precipitation has trended downwards. This implies an increasing tendency for drought conditions. Figure 5.3a shows the growing season PDSI values in the low part of the basin. The averaged PDSI value is –0.546, which confirms a tendency towards drought conditions during the past decades.

In the lower and upper parts of the middle reach of the Heihe river basin, both temperature and precipitation have trended upwards. The growing season PDSI in the lower part of the middle reach was negative in most years of the study period, as shown in Figure 5.3b, which indicates that that part of the basin has had a preponderance of drought conditions. In contrast, drought conditions have not dominated in the upper part of the middle reach, though calculated PDSI values are highly variable for the period 1961–2000, as shown in Figure 5.3c.

Both temperature and precipitation were increasing during the growing season in the upper reach during the study period. The calculated growing season PDSI values show that wet conditions have prevailed over the region, as shown in Figure 5.3d. This is partly due to high annual precipitation in that mountainous area.

Water-use conflict

Water use conflicts are disputes, confrontations and violent clashes about accessing water resources. The number of these events can be traced to show a system's failure in supplying a certain amount of water for multiple users. In the Heihe river region, various water-use policies and plans have been implemented or designed to limit or prohibit the utilization of water by sectors or regions. Controversies have occurred, of course, as a result of such policies. For the water diversion policy in the Heihe river basin, farmers in the upper and middle reaches of the river already argue that less water for irrigation has led to detrimental consequences in the agricultural sector, while others have indicated that the new policy has been able to revive a dried lake located in the downstream region. Obviously, water policies or regulations may make some sectors or regions worse off and others better off because of their redistributive nature. It is this redistributive nature of policies that often aggravates water-use conflicts.

Figure 5.4 illustrates the trend of water-use conflict in the study basin. It shows that the trend of water-use conflict has been increasing in the past decade. The trend of this social indicator suggests that water shortage in the growing season is becoming more and more serious because of decreased water supply and increasing population and per capita water use.

Mapping vulnerability in the Heihe river basin

The following indicators were computed from a wide variety of ancillary data sets. These data will be described for each indicator. The indicators focus on weather, agriculture and water resources. Although numerous assumptions are made in the analysis, it is important to keep in mind that the objective is to elucidate geographic patterns. Thus, relative differences between areas are the important trend under investigation.

The agricultural sector relies heavily on irrigation water, mainly from river flow and groundwater sources, due to the aridity of the region. For this reason, vulnerability of this sector is largely a function of water resources. To evaluate agricultural vulnerability, both crop water demand and water resource availability were assessed.

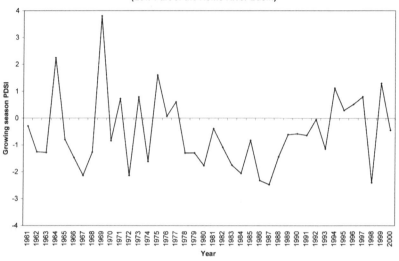

a

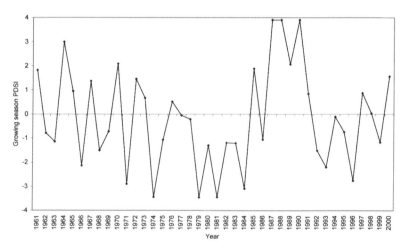

b

Figure 5.3 *Growing season PDSI for the Heihe river basin, 1961–2000:*
a) lower reach; b) lower part of middle reach

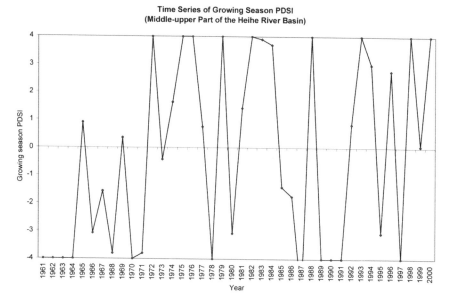

c

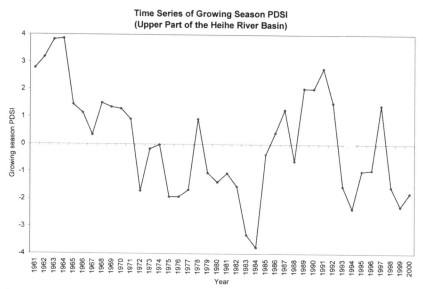

d

Figure 5.3 *Growing season PDSI for the Heihe river basin, 1961–2000:*
c) upper part of middle reach; d) upper reach

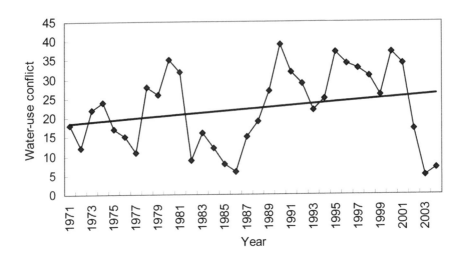

Figure 5.4 *Trend of water-use conflicts (number of violent events in competition for water) in the study basin*

Precipitation and temperature data were collected from meteorological stations distributed through the Heihe river basin. The data were averaged, on a monthly basis, over the period from 1995 to 2000 in order to represent current conditions. Using a method similar to that of Tan et al (2002), these data were interpolated to one-kilometre grid cells and partitioned into infiltration and runoff fractions (in millimetres) using the 'rational' method in which runoff is estimated from rainfall, catchment size and infiltration. Rational runoff coefficients were created from inputs of a digital elevation model (DEM), soil type and land cover using the method described as follows. Unique combinations of soil type and land cover were determined from spatial data sets over the project area. Each soil/land cover combination was assigned a United States Department of Agriculture Natural Resources Conservation Service (USDA/NRCS) 'curve number' for characterizing soil infiltration and runoff (USDA/NRCS, 1999). The curve numbers were converted to rational runoff coefficients using Tan et al's (2002) Equation 3 and the DEM on the project area. Runoff was computed based on the rational runoff equation $Q = cIA$, where Q is discharge, I is rainfall (assumed at constant intensity) and A is catchment area. The runoff was routed to a theoretical channel network (derived from the DEM) to assess monthly values of discharge, geo-located at one-kilometre resolution. The difference between estimated runoff and monthly rainfall was assumed to be infiltration.

The spatial distribution of the cropland map of the Heihe river basin was created from data of the International Geosphere-Biosphere Program (IGBP). Crop types were also based on the data in the land cover data set from the IGBP. Estimated crop evapotranspiration was computed using the FAO method described in FAO Drainage and Irrigation Paper 56 (Allen et al, 1999).

The FAO Crop Water Requirement (or CROPWAT) model can be used to estimate some critical values of crop growth and water requirements. The computation of indicators of crop stress or yield index can be achieved using the relationship Yield Index = ETc-stressed/ETc-max (Allen et al, 1999).

Weather conditions were based on a combination of the measured data and the CLIMWAT database, which is a set of weather records from observation stations distributed globally. The simulated evapotranspiration data were compared to the estimated rainfall on a monthly basis. It is assumed that all infiltrated rainfall is available for crop growth, while runoff is not. This analysis indicates areas of crop water deficit, meaning that the infiltrated rainfall is insufficient to meet crop demand. Thus, the deficits indicate the amount of irrigation water needed to maximize crop growth. Areas of high deficit will place more pressure on irrigation infrastructure and neighbouring areas of surplus. Figure 5.5 shows the distribution of these high-demand areas.

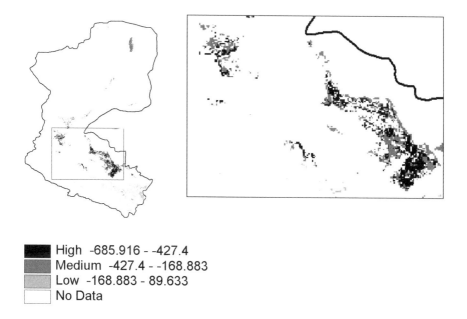

High -685.916 - -427.4
Medium -427.4 - -168.883
Low -168.883 - 89.633
No Data

Figure 5.5 *Areas with high irrigation water demand (negative units are in millimetres of deficit)*

The map indicates that there are geographic differences in demand for irrigation. This is due to the combination of crop type under cultivation (some crops require more water) and local variation in climate conditions, particularly rainfall, temperature and humidity. The areas where high crop water demand and low rainfall converge are areas with high irrigation demand. In the likely event of climate change, areas with high water deficits, as shown in Figure 5.5, will be more affected by fluctuations in the supply of irrigation water. Thus, this deficit can serve as an indicator of vulnerability.

However, irrigation will compete with humans for available water. The Landscan data set was utilized in the analysis of per capita water supply in the Heihe river region (Dobson et al, 2000). It was assumed that none of the infiltrated water was available for humans and that human consumption would rely entirely on runoff. Thus, the per capita water resources index was computed as the annual runoff (supply) divided by the population (demand). Where this index is very low, it indicates that either there are a lot of people or there is a low supply, or a combination of the two. Similar to the analysis of crop water requirements, the areas of low per capita water yield indicate areas of high demand from external sources. These areas may exert more pressure on neighbouring regions with a surplus of water resources. However, there may be cumulative impacts associated with high demand for water for both domestic and agricultural use. Figure 5.6 indicates the areas of high demand for domestic water supplies.

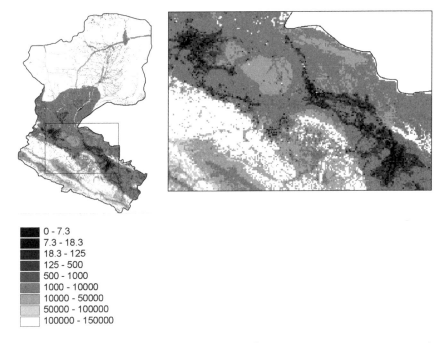

■	0 - 7.3
■	7.3 - 18.3
■	18.3 - 125
■	125 - 500
■	500 - 1000
■	1000 - 10000
■	10000 - 50000
■	50000 - 100000
□	100000 - 150000

Figure 5.6 *Per capita water resources (in cubic meters per capita per annum)*

Note: Areas of low value (dark colours) indicate a high demand for water resources not available through local supply.

Source: The break points are taken from values in Feitelson and Chenoweth (2002).

A simple comparison of available runoff and population – what Feitelson and Chenoweth (2002) call 'annual per capita internal renewable water resources' – indicates the geographic areas of high demand. Figure 5.6 shows areas where the local demand for water is not met by a 'readily available' local supply (from local runoff). The 'dependence ratio' indicator suggested by Lane et al (1999) describes this deficit as the fraction of the local demand that must be met through water transfers. Areas of supply deficit are likely to be of varying degrees of vulnerability based on the extent of local resources available for remedying this supply/demand imbalance (in other words, the adaptive capacity). For example, the income per capita and the existing level of water supply infrastructure development will determine how well these areas can import water from elsewhere or otherwise provide local people with a safe source of water. This map should be interpreted as the sensitivity of the system, rather than the vulnerability, which is a function of sensitivity, exposure and lack of adaptive capacity. It is notable that some areas are barely at the subsistence level in terms of access to water. Similar to the indicator for the agricultural sector, the areas of high demand for water will be more affected by any fluctuations in supply that result from changes in climate.

The above metrics are fairly indirect indicators of sensitivity of the system. Its potential exposure to climate change to future climate change can be illustrated by current trends in weather and climate. The following indicators of exposure – the number of months during which rainfall was 20 per cent lower than the long-term average for that month and the number of days during which the maximum temperature was more than 5°C higher than the mean monthly maximum – are based on the analysis of weather at seven observation stations between 1999 and 2003. These indicators are computed based on the methods proposed in Kaly and Pratt (2000).

It is notable that the periods of dry weather are in the upper indices of vulnerability, while the 'heat-wave' indicator is much higher than anything discussed in Kaly and Pratt (2000). While Kaly and Pratt (2000) describe the indicators for 'vulnerability', here we are using them for exposure. We also created a map to show the number of months over the five-year period during which rainfall was 20 per cent lower than the long-term average for that month. This is an indicator of drought stress and, as such, should be considered in conjunction with the per capita domestic water indicator and the crop water deficit indicators as shown in Figures 5.5 and 5.6. Similarly, another map was created to show the number of days over the five-year period during which the maximum temperature was more than 5°C higher than the mean monthly maximum. This is a 'heat-wave' map that should also be considered in conjunction with the other indicators, in terms of illustrating the areas of likely weather extremes. The exposure indices we have used are for historical and illustrative purposes. Ideally, gridded GCM output regarding future exposure to climate extremes would be used to predict areas of likely future vulnerability.

These indicators can be scaled and multiplied to obtain a geographic amalgam of vulnerability using the probabilistic framework. To do this, the weather indicators (dry periods and hot periods) were divided by their relative maxima and multiplied to obtain a composite indicator of weather extremes on a scale of [0,1], with 1 representing areas with more frequently observed extreme weather. This composite was used in the construction of two additional indicators, one representing the vulnerability of agriculture to weather extremes (the agricultural vulnerability indicator) and the other representing the vulnerability of domestic water availability to weather extremes (the domestic vulnerability indicator). The per capita water indicator and crop water deficit indicators were normalized to [0,1], with 1 (most vulnerable) corresponding to the lowest per capita water availability and the highest irrigation deficit respectively.

Each normalized indicator was then multiplied by the composite weather indicator in the manner described by the probabilistic equation of vulnerability (and assuming each area to have equivalent adaptive capacity) to obtain two indices of vulnerability for the respective water uses. Here we assume adaptive capacity is constant across the project area; it is therefore not included in the analysis. However, this additional characteristic could be readily incorporated into the analysis given suitable geographic data.

By using the scaled indicators as proxies for probability estimates, the vulnerability indices represent the likelihood of there being a confluence of extreme weather and 'marginal' conditions in the form of very low water availability or a high irrigation deficit on local cropland. This interpretation is justified by the fact that these marginal conditions will be aggravated by hot weather increasing evapotranspiration of crops and evaporation of water from channels or other impoundments, and by a lack of rainfall that restricts replenishment of supply. As agricultural and domestic water are competing uses, it is logical to combine these two vulnerability indictors into a composite indicator that reveals in what areas there are likely to be shortages and conflicts when there are adverse weather conditions. The composite indicator was created by adding the agricultural and domestic vulnerability indicators, summing over a rectangular 3-pixel neighbourhood and scaling to [0,1]. The rationale behind this manipulation is based on the assumption that in a three-kilometre neighbourhood, competing water uses will compound each other and result in a localized area of higher vulnerability (of both uses) to adverse weather conditions. This composite indicator is shown in Figure 5.7.

In keeping with our probabilistic conceptual framework, Figure 5.7 can be interpreted as the likelihood of water resource system vulnerability, a critical system in this arid region. The high vulnerability areas (values close to one) are determined by the confluence of water resource system sensitivity and exposure to environmental extremes. Since domestic and agricultural uses compound each other (are additive effects) in this analysis, having a low vulnerability in either of these sectors does not render the area not vulnerable, but vulnerability is reduced by the absence of competing uses. Of course, the vulnerability is relative to the scale of analysis, since the indicators were normalized based on regional extremes. By expanding the scope of the analysis, it is likely that new extremes would be introduced and the indices would automatically adjust themselves accordingly.

The obvious area of high vulnerability in the southeast portion of the region consists of a population centre, with high agricultural production, in an area that has historically experienced deleterious climate conditions (not enough rain and too hot). Areas of very low vulnerability may be due to either the absence of extreme weather conditions or the absence of an irrigation deficit and a high per capita water supply. This is consistent with what we would expect for this region, but with one caveat. As noted earlier, we did not incorporate a lack of adaptive capacity indicator in this analysis. Therefore, the vulnerability of rural areas with no means of coping with climatic extremes and high sensitivity may be underestimated. Similarly, the vulnerability of relatively urban areas with more extensive infrastructure, monetary resources and/or political clout may be over estimated.

It is notable that there is a large portion of Figure 5.5 (irrigation deficit) that shows the 'No Data' value but that this value has not made its way into Figure 5.7, the map for vulnerability. This is explained by the fact that the map sources we used do not show agriculture in the 'No Data' areas (at the one kilometre resolution scale). We therefore assume that there is no demand for irrigation water in those areas. The infiltrated water would probably be used by local vegetation or enter the groundwater, but is, nevertheless, assumed to be unavailable for humans.

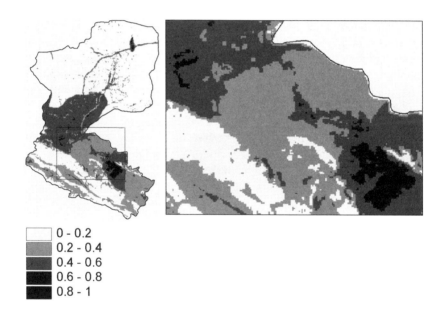

0 - 0.2
0.2 - 0.4
0.4 - 0.6
0.6 - 0.8
0.8 - 1

Figure 5.7 *Geographic distribution of vulnerability to adverse weather conditions in the Heihe river basin*

Reduced water availability resulting from low rainfall is compounded by the decreased quality of the diminished supply (Qi and Cheng, 1998). While the demands for water resources increase as populations and economies grow, the availability of water is being reduced by climate variation (See Figure 5.3). The competition over access to water resources in the Heihe river basin has led to increasing disputes, confrontation and many cases of violent clashes (See Figure 5.4). The growing water-use conflicts have posed a big challenge for local government agencies to implement effective water allocation policies.

The composite indicator represents the vulnerability of both agricultural and domestic water users to unfavourable weather conditions in the form of long hot and dry spells. It should not be interpreted as an absolute measure of vulnerability, rather as a way of identifying areas of high relative vulnerability within the region. The frequency distribution of different vulnerability levels is shown in Figure 5.8. The histogram illustrates a bimodal distribution with values concentrated in the lower range and a fairly small number in the upper range. This is appropriate given that the analysis was designed to identify areas of high vulnerability for the purpose of building the adaptive capacity in those areas.

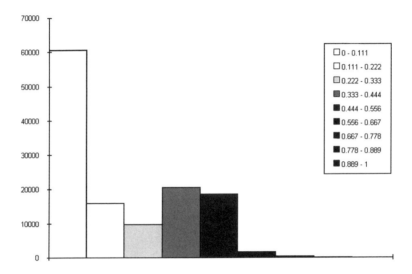

Figure 5.8 *Histogram of composite water-use vulnerability levels in the Heihe river basin*

Note: Vertical axis is frequency of grid cell values.

Conclusions

The chapter seeks to provide answers to some important questions in relation to climate vulnerability assessment. It provides information on the geographical distribution of current climate vulnerability levels in the Heihe river basin region. The results indicate the relative vulnerability levels of water and land resources in different areas exposed to current climate stimuli. The vulnerability indicator measurements for resource systems can be applied to project potential vulnerabilities of the resource systems to future climate change scenarios. In addition, the chapter contributes to methodological development in vulnerability assessment and mapping.

By using vulnerability indicators, the climate vulnerability of the study region under current climate conditions has been investigated. The methods for the compilation of indicators, geographic allocation and synthesis are valid for other regions as well. By taking a probabilistic approach, the framework automatically scales up due to the consistency of the [0,1] scale. If true probability measures are unavailable (though they frequently are available), the analysis is automatically normalized to regional extremes. Thus, the method should be viewed as portable, but intra-region comparisons will not, in general, be valid. The applications presented here are intended to benefit future studies that aim to assess resource system vulnerability. The consideration of scale will be important in the determination of what indicators are necessary and feasible for inclusion in any potential climate vulnerability assessment.

In vulnerability and adaptive capacity measurement, many of the indicators can be expressed in numerical terms, particularly for climate and physical variables. It is also recognized in the case study, however, that many indicators cannot be quantified and that many of the threshold levels can only be qualitatively described. As a result, some data used in the case study are fairly abstract and not particularly meaningful out of context. It is also notable that the indicator is only mapped over areas of agriculture, as the crop indicator was included in the composite, and is undefined over areas without agriculture. However, assuming food production to be an important element of society and a logical starting point for vulnerability reduction, this composite indicator is informative. Specifically, the areas of highest vulnerability, as evidenced by the indicators, have been narrowed down to several square kilometres. Assuming constraints to the adaptive capacity of the entire region, these places could be designated as high priority in terms of implementing effective adaptation strategies to prevent long-term damage from climate change.

For examining system vulnerability to climate change, a natural resource system representing particular future conditions needs to be proposed. For example, water resource system design, operation and management policy can be specified over time. The specification will include assumptions regarding system design, operation, and hydrologic and other inputs and demands that are all key aspects of a water system scenario representative of what could occur in the future. Incorporated into that scenario are key indicators of resource vulnerability. The uncertainties arising in estimating future demand or operational changes can be comparable to those associated with projecting climate change, and can be equally complicated for vulnerability assessments.

As a pilot study, the methods here can be critiqued. When applying vulnerability assessment methods in the study, vulnerability indicator selection and vulnerability measurement were not carried out in a comprehensive and systematic way. This is in large part a result of spatial data availability over the study area. However, these methods are effective in vulnerability assessment and mapping spatial distributions of resource system vulnerability. When future climate change and socioeconomic scenarios are available, these methods can also be applied to estimate indicator values in the future. This will produce future vulnerability data for each indicator.

References

Allen, R. G., L. S. Pereira, D. Raes and M. Smith (1999) *Crop Evapotranspiration: Guidelines for Computing Crop Water Requirements*, FAO Irrigation and Drainage Paper No. 56, Food and Agriculure Organization of the United Nations

ASCE and UNESCO/IHP (1997) *Sustainability Criteria for Water Resource Systems*, Task Committee on Sustainability Criteria, Water Resources Planning and Management Division, American Society of Civil Engineers and Working Group of UNESCO/IHP IV Project M-4.3

Briffa, K., P. Jones and M. Hulme (1994) 'Summer moisture availability across Europe, 1892–1991: An analysis based on the Palmer drought severity index', *International Journal of Climatology*, vol 14, pp475–506

Chen, L. H. and T. G. Qu (1992). 'Rational development and utilization on water and soil resources in the Heihe region' (in Chinese with English abstract), Science Press, Beijing, pp143–176

Cheng, G. (ed) (1997) *Assessing Climate Change Impacts on Snow Pack, Glaciers and Permafrost in China*, Gansu Culture Press, Lanzhou, China (in Chinese)

Digital River Basin (undated) 'Digital River Basin', Heihe River Basin website, http://heihe.westgis.ac.cn (accessed July 2007)

Ding, Y. H., Q. P. Li and W. J. Dong (2005) 'A numerical simulation study of the impacts of vegetation changes on regional climate in China' *Acta Meteorological Sinica*, vol 63, no 5, pp604–621 (in Chinese)

Dobson, J. E., E. A. Bright, P. R. Coleman, R. C. Durfee and B. A. Worley (2000) 'LandScan: A global population database for estimating populations at risk', *Photogrammatic Engineering and Remote Sensing*, vol 66, pp849–857

Downing, T. E., L. Ringius, M. Hulme and D. Waughray (1997) 'Adapting to climate change in Africa', *Mitigation and Adaptation Strategies for Global Change*, vol 2, pp19–44

Feitelson, E. and J. Chenoweth (2002) 'Water poverty towards a meaningful indicator', *Water Policy*, vol 4, pp263–281

Gansu Meteorological Bureau (2000) *Agricultural Ecosystem Database*, report, Gansu Meteorological Bureau, Lanzhou, China

Glantz, M. H., Q. Ye and Q. Ge (2001) 'China's western region development strategy and urgent need to address creeping environmental problems', *Arid Lands Newsletter*, vol 49 (http://ag.arizona.edu/OALS/ALN/ALNHome.html; accessed July 2007)

Gleick, P. H. (1990) 'Vulnerabilities of water system', in P. Wagonner (ed) *Climate Change and US Water Resources*, John Wiley and Sons, New York, pp223–240

Hennessy, K. J. and R. N. Jones (1999) *Climate Change Impacts in the Hunter Valley: Stakeholder Workshop Report*, CSIRO Atmospheric Research, Melbourne

Jones, R. N. and C. M. Page (2001) 'Assessing the risk of climate change on the water resources of the Macquarie river catchment', in F. Ghassemi, P. Whetton, R. Little and M. Littleboy (eds) *Integrating Models for Natural Resources Management Across Disciplines, Issues and Scales*, vol 2, Modelling and Simulation Society of Australia and New Zealand, Canberra, Australia, pp673–678

Kaly, U. L., L. Briguglio, H. McLeod, S. Schmall, C. Pratt and R. Pal (1999) *Environmental Vulnerability Index (EVI) to Summarise National Environmental Vulnerability Profiles*, Report to NZODA, SOPAC, Suva, Fiji

Kaly, U. and C. Pratt (2000) *Environmental Vulnerability Index: Development and Provisional Indices and Profiles for Fiji, Samoa, Tuvalu, and Vanuatu*, Phase II Report for NZODA, SOPAC Technical Report 306, SOPAC, Suva, Fiji

Kasperson, J. X., R. E. Kasperson, B. L. Turner, W. Hsieh and A. Schiller (2002) 'Vulnerability to global environmental change', in A. Diekmann, T. Dietz, C. Jaeger and E. Rosa (eds) *The Human Dimensions of Global Environmental Change*, MIT Press, Cambridge, MA, US

Kothavala, Z. (1999) 'The duration and severity of drought over eastern Australia simulated by a couple ocean-atmosphere GCM with a transient increase in CO_2', *Environmental Modelling and Software*, vol 14, pp243–252

Lane, M. E., P. H. Kirshen and R. M. Vogel (1999) 'Indicators of impacts of global climate change on US water resources', *Journal of Water Resources, Planning and Management*, vol 125, pp194–204

Li, Q. P. and Y. H. Ding (2004) 'Multi-year simulation of the East Asian monsoon and precipitation in China using a regional climate model and evaluation', *Acta Meteorologica Sinica*, vol 62, no 2, pp140–153 (in Chinese)

Liu, D. and W. Neilson (eds) (2004) *China's West Region Development: Domestic Strategies and Global Implications*, World Scientific Publishing, Singapore

Makra, L., Sz. Horváth, P. Pongrácz and J. Mike (2002) 'Long-term climate deviations: An alternative approach and application on the Palmer drought severity index in Hungary', *Physics and Chemistry of the Earth*, vol 27, pp1063–1071

Ntale, H. K. and T. Y. Han (2003) 'Drought indices and their application to east Africa', *International Journal of* Climatology, vol 23, pp1335–1357

Palmer, W. C. (1965) 'Meteorological drought', Research Paper, vol 45, Weather Bureau, US Department of Commerce

Qi, F. and G. Cheng (1998) 'Current situation, problems and rational utilization of water resources in arid North-Western China', *Journal of Arid Environments*, vol 40, pp373–382

Shi, Y. (1995) *Impacts of Climate Change on Water Resources in North-western and Northern China*, Shandong Science and Technology Press, Jinan, China

Smit, B., I. Burton, R. J. T. Klein and R. Street (1999) 'The science of adaptation: A framework for assessment', *Mitigation and Adaptation Strategies for Global Change*, vol 4, pp199–213

Smit, B., I. Burton, R. J. T. Klein and J. Wandel (2000) 'An anatomy of adaptation to climate change and variability', *Climatic Change*, vol 45, pp223–251

Srdjevic, B., Y. D. P. Medeiros and A. S. Faria (2003) 'An objective multi-criteria evaluation of water management scenarios', *Water Resources Management*, vol 18, pp35–54

Tan, C. H., A. M. Melesse and S. S. Yeh (2002) 'Remote sensing and GIS in runoff coefficient estimation in China, Taipei', *Proceedings of the 23rd Asian Conference on Remote Sensing*, Kathmandu, Nepal, November, www.gisdevelopment.net/aars/acrs/2002/pos3/217.pdf

USAID (1997) *FEWS Project: Vulnerability Assessment*, published for USAID, Bureau for Africa, Disaster Response Co-ordination, Arlington, VA

USDA/NRCS (1999) 'SCS Runoff Equation', Employee Training Module 205, www.wcc.nrcs.usda,gov/hydro/hydro-training-course.html

Wang, Z. Y. (2005) 'Climate change analysis for Western China: 1951–2004', PhD thesis, China Meteorological Administration, Beijing, China

WMO (1997) *Comprehensive Assessment of the Freshwater Resources of the World*, overview document, World Meteorological Organization, Geneva

World Commission on Environment and Development (1987) *Our Common Future*, Report of the World Commission on Environment and Development, Oxford University Press, Oxford, UK

Xie, J. (ed) (2000) *Northwestern China Arid Climate Change Research and Projection, Volume II: Drought and Flooding Indicators*, China Meteorological Press, Beijing (in Chinese)

Xu Y., Y. H. Ding, Z. C. Zhao and J. Zhang (2003) 'A scenario of seasonal climate change of the 21st century in Northwest China', *Climatic and Environmental Research*, vol 8, no 1, pp19–25 (in Chinese)

Yin, Y. Y. (2006) 'Vulnerability and adaptation to climate variability and change in Western China', Final Report, AIACC Project No AS25, International START Secretariat, Washington, DC, US, www.aiaccproject.org

Yohe, G. and R. S. J. Tol (2002) 'Indicators for social and economic coping capacity: Moving toward a working definition of adaptive capacity', *Global Environmental Change*, vol 12, pp25–40

Part III:

Coastal Areas

6

Storm Surges, Rising Seas and Flood Risks in Metropolitan Buenos Aires

Vicente Barros, Angel Menéndez, Claudia Natenzon,
Roberto Kokot, Jorge Codignotto, Mariano Re, Pablo Bronstein,
Inés Camilloni, Sebastián Ludueña, Diego Rios and
Silvia G. González

Introduction

The metropolitan region of Buenos Aires, which is the political, financial and cultural centre of Argentina, is located on the Argentine coast of the Plata river and is home to nearly a third of the country's population. The total number of people living along the Plata river coast, including the Buenos Aires region, is almost 14 million. A considerable portion of this coastal area is low-lying land, between 2.8 and 5m above mean sea level, and is often subject to recurrent storm surge floods, which are common to this region due to the unique features of the Plata river estuary. Such storm surge floods, locally known as *sudestadas*, are expected to become more frequent as the mean sea level rises due to global climate change. The very low-lying areas will, in fact, probably be permanently flooded by the end of this century. These areas are, however, largely uninhabited due to their frequent exposure to storm surges and, as a result, the social impact of future permanent flooding is expected to be small. Climate change vulnerability in this coastal zone would therefore be mostly conditioned by its future exposure to extreme storm surges, especially in the densely populated areas of metropolitan Buenos Aires, where this phenomenon is presently not as common.

This potential future vulnerability of the socioeconomically important Argentine coast therefore raises several important questions regarding the exact nature of the climate change impacts and their specific implications for population, infrastructure and the economy, namely:

*   How many people and how much infrastructure and real estate are presently affected by storm surge floods with different return periods?

• What are the present conditions of this population in terms of social vulnerability and exposure to storm surge floods?
• Under climate change scenarios, how will the return period of these floods change during the present century and, consequently, how much additional population will be affected at each return period? What will be the extent of damage to real estate and infrastructure?

Responses to these questions are critical for the assessment of the strengths and weaknesses of current socioeconomic and governance systems in this region and for the evaluation of their ability to manage the present and future impacts of extreme storm surges and flooding events due to climate change. We have therefore attempted to fill this important knowledge gap using various investigative techniques with the objective of developing an informative resource that can effectively advise the planning process in the region and help shape appropriate responses to the threat of climate change impacts on the physical, social and economic spheres.

The Physical System

The Plata river is a freshwater estuary with unique features. It begins with a width of 50km and widens to 90km at the Montevideo–Cape Piedras section (Figure 6.1), also known as the inner Plata river. The salinity front between fresh- and saltwater is a little downstream of a line connecting Montevideo and Cape Piedras. From here the salinity gradually increases towards the boundary line between Punta del Este and Cape Rasa, where it reaches the ocean's level of salinity. This 200km-wide boundary line is considered the outer border of the Plata estuary.

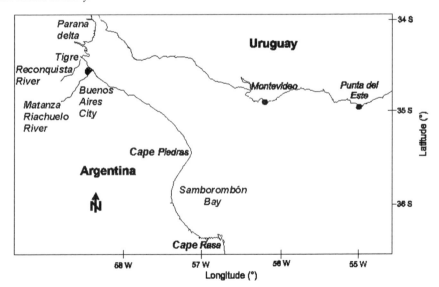

Figure 6.1 *The Plata river estuary*

The dimensions and shape of the Plata river estuary, together with its very small slope (of the order of 0.01m/km), create quasi-maritime dynamic conditions due to the effects of wind as well as astronomical tides from the sea, which tend to grow in size as they propagate towards the shallower and narrower, inner part of the estuary. Wind storms generated by southeasterly winds are associated with some of the highest wind speeds and when combined with astronomical tides result in events locally known as *sudestadas* that flood low-lying areas along the coast (Escobar et al, 2004). The floods are more severe on the Argentinean coast than on the Uruguan side because of the Coriolis effect[1] and also because the Argentine coast is lower and therefore subject to frequent flooding, especially at Samborombóm Bay. Other low-lying coastal areas are to the south of Greater Buenos Aires, in the floodplains of the Matanzas-Riachuelo and Reconquista rivers and at the tip of the Paraná delta.

In the city of Buenos Aires, the alert level due to flooding by *sudestadas* is not raised until water reaches a height of 2.30m above mean sea level because much of the area near the shore is located at an elevation of 1m or more above the mean high water line, which, in turn, is located at 0.99m above the mean sea-level at the Buenos Aires port. Floods caused by *sudestadas* typically last from a few hours to two or three days. Table 6.1 shows details of flood events, including their return periods and water heights, calculated from a 50-year tide record at the Buenos Aires port. These values are only representative for this particular location, since the coastal storm surge varies at different locations along the coast, intensifying as it progresses towards the interior of the estuary.

Table 6.1 *Water heights (above mean sea level) at the Buenos Aires port for return periods*

Return Period (years)	Height Above Mean Sea Levels (m)
2.5	2.50
5	2.80
11	3.10
27.5	3.40
79	3.70
366	4.00

Source: Adapted from D'Onofrio et al (1999).

Three primary factors that can influence water levels in the Plata river estuary include sea-level forcing, wind forcing and tributary forcing. A hydrodynamic model of the estuary was therefore used to assess the response of the river water level to changes in the mean sea level, the direction and intensity of surface winds, and tributary contributions (Barros et al, 2003). The physical influences of these variables on the Plata river estuary are outlined below:

- **Sea-level forcing**: Because of the small slope and the exceptionally high ratio between the width and length of the estuary, model simulations suggest that sea-level increases will propagate towards the inner part of the estuary without great alteration. A decrease is expected only in the inner portions of the Plata river, and at the Paraná delta front the increase is likely to be only 10 per cent of the initial height (Re and Menéndez, 2003).

- **Wind forcing**: Wind tension over the surface of the Plata river drags water into or out of the estuary, depending on wind direction, and plays a significant role in modifying water levels. Hydrodynamic model simulations forced by wind data from the National Center for Environmental Prediction/National Center for Atmospheric Research (NCEP/NCAR) (Kalnay et al, 1996) indicate that changes in wind direction and intensity during 1951–2000 due to a southward displacement of the South Atlantic high pressure belt (Escobar et al, 2003), explain about 5cm of the 13cm rise observed at the Buenos Aires port during the 20th century. Model simulations also indicate that the approximately 15cm difference between the summer and winter water levels is caused by the directional shift of wind between these seasons (Re and Menéndez, 2003).

- **Tributary forcing**: The mean discharge from the Plata river is about 25,000m³/s, which includes 20,000m³/s from the Paraná River and 5000m³/s from the Uruguay river, its two main tributaries. However, the impact of changes in tributary stream flows was not observed to be proportional. The most extraordinary flooding from both tributaries totalled 80,000m³/s in 1983 (Re and Menéndez, 2003), but the effect of this massive stream flow on the Plata river level was almost insignificant in the outer part of the estuary and was very small in its inner part, except for the Paraná delta front. At Buenos Aires, streamflows greater than 75,000m³/s cause only a 5cm rise in the water level (Barros et al, 2003).

Assessing Present and Future Vulnerability to Recurrent Floods

A multidisciplinary approach that accounted for both physical and socioeconomic factors was employed for assessing vulnerability along the Plata river coast in Argentina. Statistical data on physical and social aspects was integrated in a geographical information system (GIS), which was then used to estimate, for different return periods of flood, the population and the public infrastructure (schools, hospitals and so forth) affected and the damage to real estate.

A two-dimensional hydrodynamic model with high spatial (2.5km) and temporal (1 minute) resolution and based on the HIDROBID II software (Menéndez, 1990) was used to represent mean and storm surge levels. The model was forced with the astronomical tide at the southern border, the river discharges at the upstream border and the wind field over the whole domain. The model's capacity to reproduce water-level distribution at the Buenos Aires port for the 1990–1999 period was first verified (Figures 6.2 and 6.3), followed by the estimation of extreme tide values along the coast of the Plata river, thus overcoming the lack of basic data (Figure 6.4). Future sea-level data and future wind data from the Intergovernmental Panel on Climate Change's (IPCC's) HADCM3 A2 scenario were then used to determine future scenarios of mean water level in the Plata river estuary. For sea-level data other IPCC model outputs were also considered (Church et al, 2001).

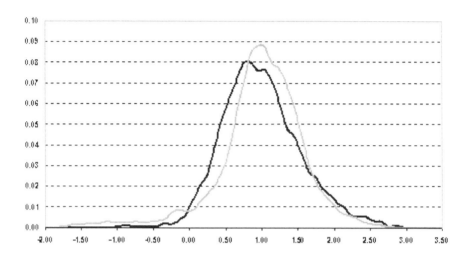

Figure 6.2 *Frequency of levels (m) above mean sea level at the Buenos Aires port, 1990–1999*

Note: Observed frequency is shown by heavy line; simulated frequency by the HIDROBID II model is shown by light line.

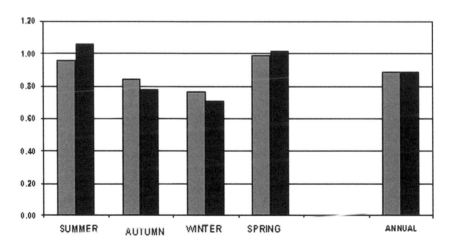

Figure 6.3 *Mean Plata river level (m) calculated by the HIDROBID II at the Buenos Aires port, 1990–1999*

Note: Modelled level is shown in black and observed level is shown in grey.

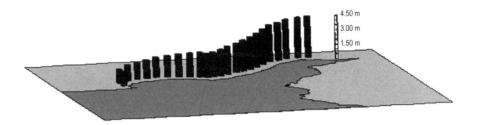

Figure 6.4 *Maximum heights calculated for the storm surge tide with return period of 100 years in the Buenos Aires port*

For calculating the return periods of floods over land, a surface-level model was constructed with adequate vertical and horizontal resolution. The topography was put together with data from different sources: topographic maps of the Military Geographical Institute, altitude measurements taken by the Buenos Aires city authorities at certain points, field measurements with a differential GPS, and altitude maps constructed with satellite radar.

The susceptibility of public buildings was evaluated by means of surveys in each of the 27 administrative districts of the Plata river basin that have territory under the 5m above sea level boundary. Present and future risk to public service infrastructure (including water supply, the sewage network, power facilities, highways and railroads) was assessed, as was the risk to real estate. Costs were estimated as a function of the Plata river level rise over its mean present level and its implications for infrastructure and real estate. Figure 6.5 shows the function of the cost of each flood event, including its depreciation effect on real estate as a function of the rise of the Plata river over its present level. Similar functions were calculated for each component of infrastructure. The sum of costs per event for each of these components was then used to determine the mean annual costs of flooding and, in combination with modelled flood recurrence and duration data, enabled the assessment of damages.

Social vulnerability was estimated at the district scale due to the lack of data at smaller sub-levels, recognizing that this option leads to only a first-order approximation of the geographical distribution of this vulnerability. Social data was obtained from the census and a modest one per cent annual population growth rate was assumed for future scenarios. A social vulnerability index (SVI) was calculated using indicators related to demography, living conditions of the population, and structural production and consumption processes. Values ranging from 1 (lower vulnerability) to 5 (higher vulnerability) were assigned to each indicator. Next an index of social risk (SRI) was developed by multiplying the SVI by an index of exposure to floods (EFI). The latter was calculated from the recurrence of floods at each 1km^2 cell and is approximately the inverse of the return period of flooding (RPF).

Damage (M USD)

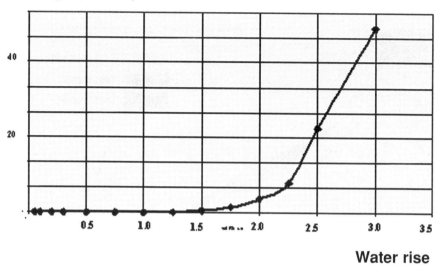

Water rise

Figure 6.5 *Damages in real estate per event in millions of US dollars as a function of the water-level rise over the mean present level*

Present and Future Vulnerability

Flood risk

Our findings suggest that the areas at permanent flood risk during the 21st century along the Greater Buenos Aires coast due to climate change-related sea-level rise are very small. The only major concern with regard to permanent flooding could be for the few and sparsely populated very low lying areas at the tip of the Paraná delta and for the new lands that could be added to it in the next few years.[2] Therefore, climate change impacts in this region are expected to be mostly due to the increasing inland reach of storm surges or *sudestadas* in the heavily populated areas.

Figure 6.6 shows the flood return periods for the present time. The areas more affected by *sudestadas* are the southeastern coast of Buenos Aires and the district of Tigre. In both areas, there is a mix of low income communities and upper middle class gated communities. The differences in the storm surge return periods for the 2070/2080 A2 scenario in comparison to present conditions are shown in Figure 6.7. No significant change is observed in the Plata river coast of Buenos Aires and in the districts located immediately to the north, but towards the south of the city and in the Tigre district a significant increase in exposure to recurrent floods can be seen. The A2 scenario predicts a considerable reduction in flood return periods in the valleys of the

Reconquista and Matanzas-Riachuelo rivers, where a socially vulnerable population predominates.

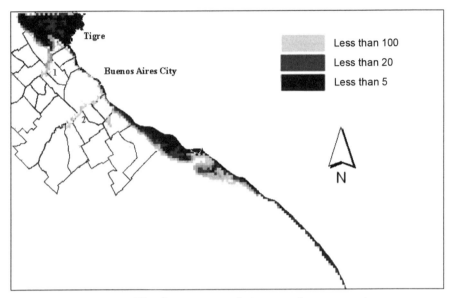

Figure 6.6 *Flood return periods in years for present time*

Note: The number 1 denotes an area below the Reconquista valley and the number 2 denotes the Matanzas-Riachuelo valley; lines show the boundaries of the districts of the metropolitan area of Buenos Aires.

The survey of public properties in the area that could be affected by floods at least once in 100 years in the 2070/2080 A2 scenarios indicates that there are 125 administrative public offices, 17 social security offices, 205 health centres, 928 educational buildings, 92 security buildings and 306 recreational areas, including parks and squares, at risk. In addition, there are also 1046 private industries potentially at risk.

Assuming little change in population density and distribution, under the scenario of maximum sea-level rise during the 2070 decade (2070_{max} scenario), the number of people living in areas at flood risk with a return period of 100 years is expected to be about 900,000, almost double the present at-risk population. The relative increment of affected population is even larger for a flood recurrence time of 1 to 5 years, which more than triples for the 2070_{max} scenario in comparison to the present period (Table 6.2). It must be noted that these figures were calculated without considering any growth in population. When a modest 1 per cent annual population growth over the next 70 years is assumed, maintaining the present geographical distribution, the number of people affected for each return period in the 2070s would be double the values in Table 6.2. This means that the population exposed to some risk of flood recurrence every 100 years would be about 1,700,000.

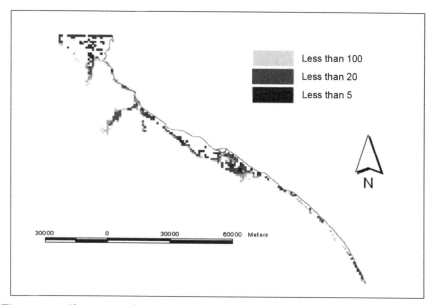

Figure 6.7 *Changes in the return period between 2070–2080 and present time in years*

Table 6.2 *Present population living in areas that are, or will be, flooded under different scenarios*

	Return Period (years)					
	1	5	10	20	50	100
1990–2000	33,000	83,000	139,000	190,000	350,000	549,000
2030–2040	102,000	297,000	390,000	500,000	643,000	771,000
2070–2080	113,000	344,000	463,000	563,000	671,000	866,000

Cost of damages

Current real estate damage was estimated at US$30 million/year; assuming no socioeconomic changes or no construction of defences, it would reach US$80 and US$300 million/year by 2030–2040 and 2070–2080 respectively under an anticipated 1.5 per cent annual growth rate in the infrastructure. These figures do not include losses to the upper middle class gated communities that are increasingly being built in the coastal areas and neither do they include working hours lost, which could be significant given the size of the population likely to be affected. The figures therefore should be considered as very conservative estimates.

Social vulnerability and risk

In tandem with increasing storm-surge risk, the communities that display the highest social vulnerability are those that currently experience a relatively low recurrence of floods and are therefore densely occupied. They are populated by varying social classes, ranging from the upper middle class to the socially vulnerable. The increased inland reach of floods due to the impact of an increased recurrence of *sudestadas* or storm surges is expected to result in significant economic impacts for these neighbourhoods, including important real estate losses. As previously mentioned, the two most socially vulnerable areas in this region that are highly susceptible to floods are not located directly on the coast of the Plata river, but in the flood valleys of two of its tributaries, the Reconquista and the Matanzas-Riachuelo.

The low-lying areas along the coast of the Plata river, which are more exposed to frequent floods and storm surges and are at risk of permanent flooding, are, on the other hand, relatively less vulnerable because they are quite sparsely occupied. Vulnerability in these areas is high only in the few places that are occupied by poor squatter settlements that lack many basic needs as well as any access to social security, and have a child mortality rate higher than the national average. Many households in these settlements are also headed by women. Crime insecurity, unemployment and violence are among the common social issues faced by these communities. The existing social vulnerability of this small group of people is further worsened by the impacts of floods, which are expected to become more severe as the mean sea level rises due to climate change.

In contrast to the poor squatter settlements in the flood risk zones of the Plata river and its tributaries, a more recent trend is the occupation of these suburban coastal areas by upper middle class gated communities. These include the southern coast of the Plata river, 20 to 50km to the southeast of Buenos Aires, and the county of Tigre, immediately to the south of the Paraná delta. Beginning in the 1980s, and especially since the 1990s, these zones have been increasingly occupied by upper middle class private gated communities built at an artificially elevated level, above the impact of storm surges. These developments have been largely driven by security concerns about living in the city; the attractions of nature, countryside and greenery (Ríos, 2002); and the enticing view offered by the shorelines. The increased accessibility to these areas, aided by new highways, further fuelled the growth of these private communities. In the early 1990s, private neighbourhoods occupied an area of about 34.4km²; by 2000, this area had grown nearly 10 times to about 305.7km². In the district of Tigre, 90 private residential developments were authorized in 1998, of which 50 have already been constructed. About 40 per cent of the district's population now lives in these gated communities. New projects are continually springing up all along the coast, both in the southeastern and in the northern extremes of the Buenos Aires metropolitan area and even in the Paraná delta front (Ríos, 2002).

The construction of these gated communities in low-lying lands, historically frequently flooded, requires a massive transformation of the terrain and of the surface drainage, with the associated destruction and replacement of the original ecosystems, in order to obtain an elevation which is assumed to be secure from flood waters. Most of these private neighbourhoods are constructed at an altitude of 4.4m above sea level, which is considered to be a level safe from the impacts of floods. However, this assumption may not hold true in the future, when the impacts of climate change may result in more intense storm surges and increase the inland reach of floods. Therefore, though these communities are secure in terms of crime and other social hazards, they now face a new risk from climate change. Outside these gated communities are some of the original squatter settlements, which now face an increased susceptibility to flooding due to the massive land transformation and changes to surface drainage resulting from the construction of these elevated communities, which has effectively destroyed the natural drainage systems in the region.

Figure 6.8 shows the current social risk index derived from social vulnerability and flood exposure. This figure is similar to the flood return period figure because of the coincidence of the areas of maximum exposure and social vulnerability. However, there is an important difference in the district of Tigre, in the north, where there is little social vulnerability despite it being a high flood risk zone. This is because these areas are less populated and the occupants are presently the well-to-do private gated communities that are situated at an elevated level, along with perhaps a few poor squatter communities. Therefore, the area of maximum social risk is to the south of this district and in the Reconquista river valley, which is home to the socially vulnerable communities.

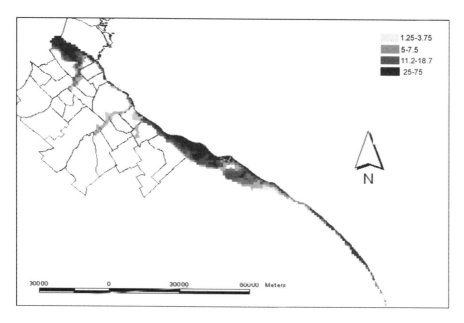

Figure 6.8 *Social risk index: Present conditions*

Note: The varying ranges of the social risk index are represented by the various shades of grey (e.g. the darkest shade stands for the range of 25 to 75).

In comparison, in the 2070–80 A2 scenario (Figure 6.9), there is a change in the social risk index due to an increase in flood risk and a worsening of the situation of the more socially vulnerable areas along the Reconquista and Matanza-Riachuelo valleys and to the south of Greater Buenos Aires in a zone relatively far from the coast where few gated communities are expected. There is also a slight worsening of the social risk index of the areas of gated communities in the Tigre district and to the southeast of Buenos Aires due to the increased reach of extreme storm surges, possibly above the secure height of these communities.

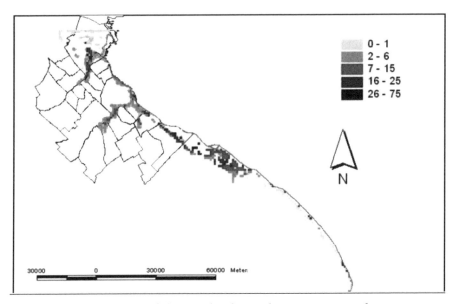

Figure 6.9 *Variation of the social risk map between 2070 and present*

Note: Values as in Figure 6.8.

An interesting observation made during the course of this investigation was that, in some cases, future social vulnerability to increased flooding may also be exacerbated by the status of current adaptive measures employed by some communities living in flood-prone areas. This could be due either to the changing dynamics of the communities or to the inadequacy of existing strategies to manage floods. Examples of such communities include the La Boca neighbourhood in the Buenos Aires district and the Avellaneda District, both of which are situated close to downtown Buenos Aires. These two communities have existed since the late 19th century and have historically lived with frequent flood impacts. Of these, the La Boca neighbourhood is an old harbour town built on a marshy area to the left of the mouth of the Riachuelo river. It has historically been one of the poorest areas of the city of Buenos Aires and the main climatic hazards it faces are floods due to *sudestadas* and intense rainfall. The Avellaneda District is an old urban industrial town situated on a flood plain to the south of La Boca on the other side of the Riachuelo river. It is also greatly impacted by floods as well as water and air pollution.

In these neighbourhoods, a critical element of adaptation to storm surge floods has traditionally been informal networks among neighbours that support local practices and strategies that aid in anticipating the arrival of floods (including an early warning system and self-help and evacuation strategies) and tend to diminish local vulnerability. However, of late there has been an increasing influx of newcomers into these areas, which is gradually eroding the collective memory of these cultural practices of adaptation and could increase the vulnerability of this population to the more severe floods in the future. Moreover, the construction of the coastal defence structure for the city of Buenos Aires, including the La Boca neighbourhood, during the last decade has successfully provided protection against recent floods, but this has also unfortunately created a sense of complacency among the local population regarding the threat. This could prove dangerous in the long run as the coastal defences, built with current flooding levels in mind, may be insufficient protection against the higher future flood levels resulting from climate change (Gentile, 2002). By this time the collective knowledge of flood coping strategies would also have been lost and institutional responses would likely have been significantly weakened.

Other Factors that Enhance Social Vulnerability to Climate Change

Other factors that tend to increase vulnerability to climate change impacts or hamper the processes of adaptation are those that are common to many developing countries and include issues such as lack of basic information; physical, social or institutional weaknesses; and a lack of public awareness about climate change and its consequences. The specific manner in which these factors play out in the Argentine context is briefly outlined below.

Lack of basic information

Determination of vulnerability to climate change impacts in developing countries can often be hampered by the lack of data necessary for such efforts. Long-term data on many variables critical to the determination of vulnerability is often found to be insufficient or absent. This is especially true for data on variables that change rapidly. In this study two critical variables for which useful and sufficient data were lacking were land altitude maps or records for some locations and tide data for the Plata river coast. As a result a new digitized model of land altitude had to be specially developed to generate proxy data on land altitude that would otherwise either have been impossible or taken a very long time to obtain. Similarly for tide data a hydrodynamic model had to be developed to fill the information gaps.

Institutional weakness

The vulnerability of coastal areas in Argentina is also impacted by the weak institutional structures, which have so far been unable to effectively put in place policies and programmes to reduce the risk of current and future flood impacts. Frequent changes in the national government tend to make the various institutions responsible for aspects of flood management very unstable in terms of their persistence, and even when they do persist, their policies change often. In the case of flood management, whatever little planning has been done or the few successful programmes and projects that have been implemented have unfortunately not always been continued with each change of government. One example of this is the Emergency Federal System created in the 1950s. Since then, it has been moved several times to and from different ministries and has had its plans and policies variously altered. In general, the current institutional management style, typical of the national culture, is not adequate for long-term planning.

There is also a lack of coordination and poor communication between the different institutions that hold responsibility for flood management. As a result their policies and measures are often fragmented and lack coherence in totality, thus generating a high degree of uncertainty. Communication between institutions and the general public is also poor and civil participation in the determination of flood defence strategies tends to be nominal, with decision making being largely top–down.

Lack of public awareness

Awareness among the general public about climate change and its potential risks is also found to be very low, largely due to the absence of any instituted programmes and measures to communicate this kind of information publicly. In fact, government officials, investors and engineers who make decisions that affect the coastal area also possess no knowledge of climate change impacts and of the dynamics of the system they are altering. As a result, the development of the entire coastline has been undertaken without accounting for the rising water level, which rose 17cm during the last century and is now rising even faster. There is also a high level of interest in the development of the new land environments that have been created over the past 300 years at the tip of the Paraná delta, which is now advancing over the Plata river at a pace of 70m per year. Plans are being made to use these new lands for real estate development, and disputes over the nature of their use, jurisdiction and property have already begun among various sectors of civil society. Despite this significant business interest there is little awareness that these are also one of the most vulnerable areas in the region to rising water levels. A continuation of this sort of poor coastal management would, in future, necessitate new investments in expensive remedial structures.

Conclusion

Future climate change risk to coastal areas along the Greater Buenos Aires coast is expected primarily from the greater inland reach of recurrent storm surge floods or *sudestadas*, rather than due to the impact of permanent flooding. This is because the area likely to be permanently flooded in the future due to an increase in the level of the Plata river is very small and is sparsely populated. Therefore, unless there is a change in the population distribution resulting in a much greater inhabitation of this low-lying area, the risk due to permanent flooding in this century is expected to be relatively minor.

The greatest impact from increased storm surge recurrence will be felt in those neighbourhoods that presently have a relatively low recurrence of floods and are therefore densely occupied. As a result, large social damages and substantial real estate losses can be expected. These neighbourhoods are currently occupied by a wide social spectrum, ranging from the upper middle class to a socially vulnerable population. In the absence of any adaptation measures, the lower limit of the total infrastructure losses, including real estate, for the Buenos Aires region is calculated to range between 5 and 15 billion US dollars for the period 2050–2100, depending on the speed of the sea-level rise and the increase in the infrastructure value.

The increasing popularity of gated communities in low-lying, flood-prone coastal areas is an additional factor that will add to the future real estate risks due to more frequent and intense storm surges if climate change impacts continue to be ignored in the planning of these neighbourhoods. The massive land transformation brought on by these construction activities is destroying the critical natural hydrological drainage capacity of the area and endangering not only the rich occupying the gated communities but also the poor squatters outside. Some non-governmental organizations have now begun calling for an urgent regulation of the Plata river coastal zones in the Greater Buenos Aires region. In order to be effective, such regulation must include consideration of future climate change scenarios and the associated Plata river levels.

At the moment, unfortunately, institutional preparation to deal with either current or future climate impacts is almost non-existent, and the ability to develop an effective flood management strategy is quite weak. Moreover, many of the historical collective adaptation strategies to floods among the local population are also gradually being eroded due to a sense of complacency arising out of the construction of flood control structures around Buenos Aires, which unfortunately may not afford adequate protection in the future. This cultural loss can also be attributed to the increasing influx of newcomers into these areas.

Given these risks, the dissemination of the findings of this research (Barros et al, 2005) in collaboration with a local non-governmental organization, Fundacion Ciudad, can help to fill the knowledge gap about the impacts of and vulnerability to climate change in the region and generate awareness about the associated issues, especially among decision makers. These findings can serve as effective tools to guide institutions in the determination of strategies and implementation of programmes that can help in adapting to the impacts. They can also assist individuals and private developers in making appropriate decisions regarding future property development. These findings therefore also underline the importance of scientific research in helping develop and maintain the collective awareness of both present and future climate hazards.

The preliminary results of this study have so far been presented at a forum for stakeholders and at numerous other institutional meetings. These activities are successfully contributing to a gradual awareness building among key individuals and have already resulted in frequent consultations. It is hoped that the continuation of these efforts will eventually build an increased understanding about the implications of climate change for this region at the public and institutional levels, and will lead to the development of effective adaptation strategies for the Plata river coast.

Notes

1 The Coriolis effect is an impact of the Earth's rotation which causes the deflection of winds to the right of their direction of travel in the northern hemisphere and to the left of their direction of travel in the southern hemisphere. This effect was first described by the French scientist Gaspard-Gustave Coriolis in 1935.
2 The Paraná delta is growing over the Plata estuary by the addition of sediments brought by the Paraná river. This is a natural process that is probably being enhanced by deforestation processes in part of the basin.

References

Barros, V., I. Camilloni and A. Menéndez (2003) 'Impact of global change in the coastal areas of the Río de la Plata', *AIACC Notes*, vol 2, International START Secretariat, Washington, US, pp9–11, www.aiaccproject.org
Barros, V., A. Menéndez, and G. Naggy (eds) (2005) *Climate Change in the Plata River*, Center for Atmospheric and Ocean Research, Buenos Aires, Argentina (in Spanish)
Church, J. A., J. M. Gregory, P. Huybrechts, M. Kuhn, K. Lambeck, M. T. Nhuan, D. Qin, and J. L. Woodworth (2001) 'Changes in sea level', in J. T. Houghton, Y. Ding, D. J. Griggs, M. Noguer, P. J. van der Linden and D. Xiaosu (eds) *Climate Change 2001: The Scientific Basis*, Contribution of Working Group I to the Third Assessment Report of the Intergovernmental Panel on Climate Change, Cambridge University Press, Cambridge, UK and New York, US
D'Onofrio, E., M. Fiore and S. Romero (1999) 'Return periods of extreme water levels estimated for some vulnerable areas of Buenos Aires', *Continental Shelf Research*, vol 4, pp341–366
Escobar, G., V. Barros and I. Camilloni (2003) 'Desplazamiento del anticiclón subtropical del Atlántico Sur' ['The shift of the South Atlantic subtropical high'], *X Congreso Latinoamericano e Ibérico de Meteorología*, Proceedings of Tenth Latin American and Iberic Congress of Meteorology, Latin American and Iberic Federation of Meteorological Societies, La Habana, Cuba
Escobar, G., W. Vargas and S. Bischoff (2004) 'Wind tides in the Río de la Plata estuary: Meteorological conditions', *International Journal of Climatology*, vol 24, pp1159–1169
Gentile, E. (2002) 'La incorporación de la gestión del riesgo por inundaciones en la

gestión urbana pública: El caso del barrio de La Boca' ['The inclusion of flood risk in the urban public management: The neighbourhood of La Boca case'], Instituto Gino Germani, Buenos Aires, Argentina

Kalnay, E., M. Kanamitsu, R. Kistler, W. Collins, D. Deaven, L. Gandin, M. Iredell, S. Sha, G. White, J. Woollen, Y. Zhu, M. Chelliah, W. Ebisuzaki, W. Higgins, J. Janowiak, K. C. Mo, C. Ropelewski, J. Wang, A. Leetmaa, R. Reynolds, R. Jenne and D. Joseph (1996) 'The NCEP/NCAR 40-year reanalysis project', *Bulletin of the American Meteorological Society*, vol 77, pp437–471

Menéndez, A. N. (1990) 'Sistema HIDROBID II para simular corrientes en cuencos' ['HIDROBID II System to simulate currents in basins'], *Revista Internacional de Métodos Numéricos para Cálculo y Diseño en Ingeniería* (International Magazine of Numeric Methods for Calculation and Engineering Design), vol 6, pp1–6

Re, M. and A. Menéndez (2003) 'Modelo numérico del Río de la Plata y su frente marítimo para la predicción de los efectos del cambio climático' ['Numeric model of the Plata River and its marine front for the prediction of the effects of the climate change'], *Mecánica Computacional*, vol 22 (M. Rosales, V. Cortínez and D. Bambill, eds), Bahía Blanca, Argentina

Ríos, D. (2002) 'Vulnerabilidad, urbanizaciones cerradas e inundaciones en el partido de Tigre durante el período 1990–2001' ['Vulnerability, closed urbanizations, and floods in the Tigre District during the period 1990–2001'], thesis, Facultad de Filosofía y Letras, University of Buenos Aires, Buenos Aires

7

Climate and Water Quality in the Estuarine and Coastal Fisheries of the Río de la Plata

Gustavo J. Nagy, Mario Bidegain, Rubén M. Caffera,
Frederico Blixen, Graciela Ferrari, Juan J. Lagomarsino,
Cesar H. López, Walter Norbis, Alvaro Ponce,
Maria C. Presentado, Valentina Pshennikov,
Karina Sans and Gustavo Sención

Introduction

The Third Assessment Report of the Intergovernmental Panel on Climate Change (McCarthy et al, 2001) identified two main environmental problems in South America: land-use changes and El Niño Southern Oscillation (ENSO) variability. A good example is the Río de la Plata basin and estuary, an area that has been substantially influenced by human activities in recent decades and is highly sensitive to both climate extremes and changing precipitation patterns.

The Río de la Plata basin, which measures 3,100,000km^2, includes the Uruguay river basin, which in turn covers an area of 297,000km^2 in Brazil, Argentina and Uruguay, and has a human population density of 25 persons/km^2. The population increased by almost 90 per cent between 1961 and 1994 (Baethgen et al, 2001), which led to increasing pressure on watersheds due to their extensive use for agriculture and water storage, fertilizer application, and the heavy discharge of wastewater from point sources (wastewater from domestic use is about 20 per cent) and of nutrients from non-point sources (Pizarro and Orlando, 1985; Tucci and Clarke, 1998; Nagy, 2000; Nagy et al, 2002a).

The main climatic changes reported in the Río de la Plata basin include an increase in inter-annual variability, especially of ENSO variability and precipitation ($\geq$20 per cent change in recent decades); the southward displacement of the quasi-permanent Atlantic subtropical high-pressure circulation; and associated changes in frequency of the prevailing winds, increased surface air and water temperatures ($\geq 0.8°C$), runoff, soil moisture and the Pantanal's extent (Díaz et al, 1998; Camilloni and Barros, 2000; Escobar et al, 2004; Bidegain and Camilloni, 2004; Liebmann et al, 2004).

The Río de la Plata river and estuary is a large (38,000km²) and wide funnel shaped (30–240 km width) coastal plain system. In this study, we focus on the estuarine frontal zone related to the salt intrusion limit (Figure 7.1). This productive ecosystem sustains the ecological and biogeochemical processes (nutrient assimilation, denitrification and production of organic matter) that determine the goods (fisheries) and services (fish reproduction, CO_2 fixation and denitrification) obtained from the estuary.

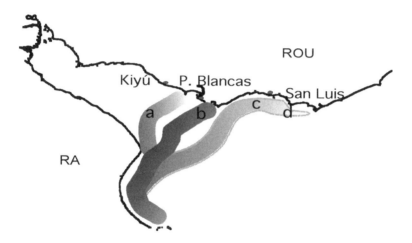

Figure 7.1 *Río de la Plata estuarine front location under different ENSO conditions: a) strong La Niña event (1999–2000), b) typical, c) moderate El Niño (winter 1987), d) strong El Niño 1997–1998/2002–2003*

Note: RA – República Argentina; ROU – República Oriental del Uruguay.
Source: Modified from Nagy et al (2002b).

Goal

In this chapter the current biophysical and human vulnerability and the adaptive capacity to deal with impacts of climate variability and change in the estuarine waters of the Uruguayan coast of the Río de la Plata are synthesized. The main questions addressed are as follows:

- How sensitive is the system to climate variability and change?
- Is eutrophication related to climate change and variability?
- Is the coastal fishery system sustainable under increased river flow variability?

ENSO-related inter-annual rainfall variability and associated river discharge fluctuations and changes in wind patterns are examined using observational records of recent decades. Our attempt is to understand the ecosystem response to climatic and anthropogenic influences and to estimate potential future impacts and vulnerability due to trophic state changes (increase in symptoms of eutrophication) and coastal fisheries activity. The associated livelihood potential from the present to the next several decades is also assessed. Specifically, we summarize the overall climatic background, develop future climate scenarios, and reference projections for a range of climate and non-climate factors and related vulnerability scenarios for future decades based on analysis of indicators of impacts and vulnerability. The basic data are the observational record from the past 30 years; some climatic and environmental trends (precipitation and drivers of eutrophication) are based on longer-term records from 1940.

Our analytic approach includes:

1   multi-level indicators of vulnerability to climate change and a driver-pressure-state-impact-response (DPSIR) index for water resources, ecosystem and coastal fisheries, and settlement adapted from Moss (1999) and the Stockholm Environment Institute (SEI) (2001);
2   calculations of vulnerability indicators, indices and vulnerability matrices, related regression models, and economic analysis of fishing activity, a combination of objective values (such as net income and education, wind speed, and ENSO-related sea-surface temperature (ENSO 3.4 index)) and the use of expert judgement in order to assess social, economic, environmental and legal indicators of sensitivity of fishermen and to assess the impacts of harmful algal blooms (HABs);
3   use of the IPCC's Special Report on Emissions Scenarios (SRES) A2/B2 climatic scenarios and Hadley CM3/ECHAM-4 global climate models (GCMs) (Bidegain and Camilloni, 2004).

Río de la Plata Basin Climate Baseline (1961–1990)

The mean annual temperature in the Río de la Plata basin ranges from around 15°C in the south to more than 25°C in the mid-western Chaco region (Figure 7.2, left panel). In the austral (southern hemisphere) winter, monthly mean temperatures have a clear north–south gradient. In July, for example, the mean temperature over the northwest part of the basin is more than 20°C, while that in the province of Buenos Aires is around 10°C less. In the austral summer the gradient is more zonal, reacting to the land–ocean distribution. In January, maximum mean temperatures reach over 27.5°C in western Argentina, while they are less than 22.5°C along the coastlines of southern Brazil, Uruguay and Buenos Aires (Hoffmann, 1975).

The eastern zone of the Río de la Plata basin is dominated by the influence of the South Atlantic high pressure (Figure 7.2, middle panel), whereas the northern portion shows a typical low pressure system (the Chaco low) that is

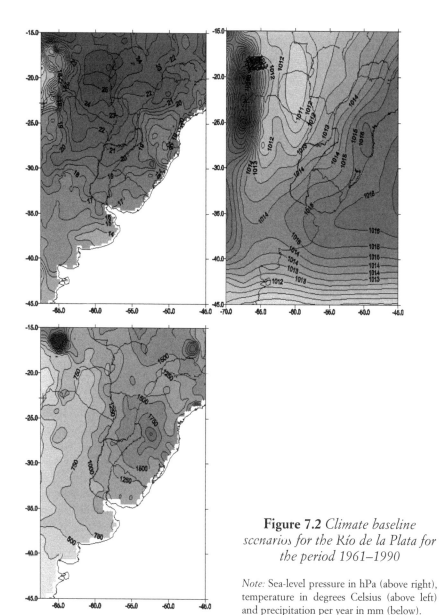

Figure 7.2 *Climate baseline scenarios for the Río de la Plata for the period 1961–1990*

Note: Sea-level pressure in hPa (above right), temperature in degrees Celsius (above left) and precipitation per year in mm (below).

more intense in the austral summer. Surface winds are northerly over most of the region, with a maximum in the northeastern sector; to the south, westerlies are present throughout the year but are strongest during the austral winter (Kalnay et al, 1996).

The annual average precipitation in the region is about 1100mm (Figure 7.2, right panel). Annual mean rainfall tends to decrease both from north to south and from east to west. Amounts range from 1800mm in the maritime uplands along the Brazilian–Paraguayan border to 400mm along the western boundary of the region. The amplitude of the annual cycle in rainfall decreases from north to south. The northern part of the region has a well-defined annual cycle with maximum precipitation during summer (December to February). The central region (northeast Argentina/southern Brazil) has a more uniform seasonal distribution, with maximum precipitation occurring during the southern spring and autumn.

The Río de la Plata River Estuary: Setting, Subsystems and Sectors

The funnel-shaped Río de la Plata is a coastal plain estuary with a river paleo-valley (called Canal Oriental) along the northern coast (López Laborde and Nagy, 1999) that behaves as a conduit channel for water and particles to the coastal ocean (Nagy et al, 2002b). Microtidal systems like the Río de la Plata estuary characteristically have low mixing capacity, primarily due to the prevailing wind; hence river inflow to the coastal zone is the 'master variable' that controls stability (defined as a function of the vertical difference in salinity as a function of depth, nutrient excess, flushing time of water and particles, stratification and gravitational circulation, salinity, and bottom-water hypoxia) (EPA, 2001; Nagy et al, 2002b; Nagy, 2003 and 2005).

Total freshwater inflow (Q_V) to the Río de la Plata, estimated as the sum of the discharges of the Paraná (Q_P) and Uruguay (Q_U) rivers, typically varies from 1500 to greater than 3000m³/s for strong La Niña and El Niño years respectively. A strong relationship has been reported between the ENSO SST 3.4 Index (defined as the temperature anomaly in ENSO Regions 3 and 4 in the Pacific Ocean) and freshwater inflow, especially the Uruguay river flow during 1998–2002. Both the location and structure of the estuarine front and salinity off Montevideo closely follow river flow on monthly to inter-annual timescales (Severov et al, 2004) and have important effects on most ecological and biogeochemical processes in the estuarine waters and resources (Nagy et al, 2002a and b; Nagy et al, 2003). However, total freshwater inflow extremes also depend on other climatic and human-driven factors which are not considered in the analysis presented here.

Freshwater inflow has increased by about 35 per cent over the past 50 years because of increased precipitation and runoff and land-use changes (García and Vargas, 1998; Tucci and Clarke, 1998; Kane, 2002; Nagy et al, 2002a; Menéndez and Re, 2005) and closely follows inter-annual fluctuations of ENSO events (Figure 7.3) as shown for the long-term series for the Uruguay river (Nagy et al, 2002a and b).

Small changes in precipitation are reflected as doubled streamflow, though this amplification of signal varies on inter-annual to inter-decadal time scales (Berbery and Barros, 2002), revealing a high vulnerability of the region to increased precipitation (Figure 7.3). These physical factors dictate the nutrient condition of the Río de la Plata estuary. Hence consideration of the related trophic state change is a valuable exercise.

Eutrophication is the process by which a body of water is enriched with organic material (Nixon, 1995). The change in trophic state associated with

River Uruguay flow

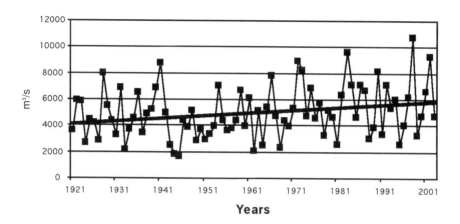

Figure 7.3 *River Uruguay discharge at Salto from 1921 to 2003*

Source: Bidegain et al (2005).

nutrient excess is driven by physical driving forces such as increase in human population density and related economic activities such as the use of synthetic fertilizers (Seitzinger et al, 2002). The balance between production and respiration of organic matter dictates the magnitude and direction of air–sea flux of biologically active elements (Gordon et al, 1996).

The occurrence of eutrophication includes effects or symptoms such as excess algal biomass, hypoxia and harmful algal blooms (HABs) that are indications that the system cannot cope with the available nutrient inputs (NRC, 2000; De Jonge et al, 2002). The main factors in the expression of symptoms of eutrophication are 1) flushing time (ft), 2) turbidity, 3) nutrient inputs (N_I) and 4) mixing state (stratification–destratification cycle) (De Jonge et al, 2002; Nagy et al, 2002b). The expression of these symptoms depends on both nutrient inputs (NCR, 2000; De Jonge et al, 2002) and the balance between river flow (Q_V) and wind stress (W), which determine mixing and transport processes (EPA, 2001; Nagy, 2003; Nagy et al, 2004).

According to Seitzinger et al (2002), by 2050, export of nitrogen over South America will have increased nearly two to three fold from current values. Generically, the temperate regions export less than half the nitrogen from anthropogenic sources compared to tropical regions, which is partially explained by lower precipitation. However, ENSO variability and other hydroclimatic drivers also play a major role in controlling the trophic state changes in the Río de la Plata basin (Nagy et al, 2003b, 2004 and 2005).

Since 1940, the trophic state changes in the Río de la Plata region have been due to increasing trends in pressure indicators and a shift of state indicators during the 1980s (Nagy et al, 2003b; López and Nagy, 2005; Calliari, Gomez and Gomez, 2005). For example, eutrophic concentrations of nitrate and chlorophyll were observed during extreme floods (1983 El Niño and 1999 La Niña respectively) (Nagy et al, 2002a and b). Human-driven land-use change and changing climatic drivers have indirectly altered trophic state. Continued trends of these parameters suggest that vulnerability and impacts may increase over the next few decades.

As an indicator of this symptom, HABs have occurred since at least 1980, becoming more frequent and causing great economic damage due to their impacts on molluscs and fish, on the tourism industry, and on public health in Uruguay (Méndez et al, 1996; Méndez et al, 1997; Ferrari and Nagy, 2003). Freshwater cyanobacterial blooms have also multiplied in recent years, becoming persistent during the summer (López and Nagy, 2005). The occurrence of HABs is closely connected to changes in freshwater inflow or Q_V (Méndez et al, 1996; Nagy et al, 2002b; López and Nagy, 2005).

Not far from the Plata river estuary is the mouth of the Santa Lucia river estuary, which lies within the same estuarine frontal zone, located a few miles to the west of Pajas Blancas (see Figure 7.1), close to a major fishing area. This system is eutrophic because of nutrient excess derived mostly from fertilizer application. The inter-annual variability of water height and river flow (Q_{SL}) here are related to ENSO effects that predominate during August to February. Since 1979, yearly means of Q_{SL} and persistence of floods have increased by about 25 per cent because of the increase in precipitation in the basin (Caffera et al, 2005). Such river discharge fluctuations can greatly influence local variability of salinity, sea level, turbidity, nutrient content and trophic state during the peak of primary productivity and fishing activity.

The evolution of the trophic state in the Santa Lucia river estuary was related to the river flows of both the Santa Lucia and the Uruguay rivers (Q_{SL} and Q_U) during the studied period (October 2002 to May 2004). We selected one state/impact variable of trophic state (chlorophyll-a) to show the response and coping capacity of the ecosystem to ENSO events. The increase in both Q_{SL} and Q_U decreased salinity from about 5 per cent to 1 per cent, blocking the expression of trophic state symptoms (chlorophyll-a <5µg/l), whereas during normal flows, salinity increased to about 10 per cent and chlorophyll-a increased to eutrophic levels (>20µg/l) (Nagy et al, 2004; Caffera et al, 2005). To summarize:

- within normal river flow and salinity ranges the system expresses symptoms of trophic state change;
- when river flow is high (for example, 2002–2003 El Niño years) the river does not develop symptoms of trophic state change because both water and nutrients are exported to the Plata river estuary; and
- hydrological fluctuations associated with ENSO events seem to exert some control on the coping capacity of the ecosystem.

These results are in close agreement with previous observations for the adjacent waters of the Plata river (Nagy et al, 2002a and b), which showed that during La Niña years and low river flow (1999–2000), the system would be prone to increased trophic state changes.

Indicators of Susceptibility, Impact and Vulnerability

Indicators of the susceptibility of the trophic state for both cross-system and long-term comparisons as well as for the assessment of the impact of nutrient excess in estuaries (NRC, 2000; De Jonge, Elliott and Orive, 2002; EPA, 2001) are an important component of this kind of analysis. Nagy et al, (2002b and 2004), Nagy (2003) and Ferrari and Nagy (2003) have developed such indicators for fresh and estuarine waters of the Uruguayan coastal zone. Their analysis suggests that some expected impacts and responses under current and future scenarios would be an increase in hypoxia, HAB events and changes in biodiversity. In the present analysis, the following variables are considered:

1   **susceptibility** (for example, flushing and residence times of water, buoyancy and mixing state);
2   **drivers** (population density, fertilizer use, point sources and Q_V);
3   **pressure** (nitrogen (N), phosphorus (P) and silicon (Si) load);
4   **state variables** (N, P); and
5   **response/impacts or symptoms** (such as changes in algal biomass (Chlorophyll-a), dissolved oxygen (O_2), occurrence of HABs, nutrient ratios (N/P and N/Si) and dominant species).

Some variables can be both state and impact (Figure 7.4).

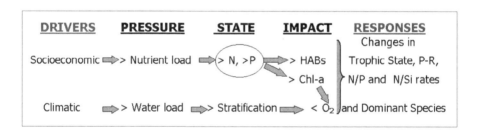

Figure 7.4 *DPSIR framework of trophic state and symptoms of eutrophication for the Río de la Plata estuary*

Note: N = nitrogen; P = phosphorus; HABs = harmful algal blooms; Chl-a = chlorophyll-a; Si = silicon.

Table 7.1 shows an example of an impact matrix of an important symptom of trophic state changes (HAB occurrence) developed by Ferrari and Nagy (2003) for the Uruguayan coastal zone of the Plata river for the decade 1991–2000. Four indicators were estimated and aggregated: 1) intensity of HABs (cells/l), 2) persistence (months), 3) extension along the coast (percentage of coverage) and 4) toxicity (toxin concentration from low to very high). Both freshwater (cyanobacteria HABs, for example, *Mycrocystis aeruginosa*) and estuarine/marine species as well as toxic and noxious species were considered.

Table 7.1 *Aggregated impact matrix of HABs in the Uruguayan coastal zone of the Río de la Plata for the period 1991–2000*

| Indicators | 0 | Prevailing | | | Extreme |
		1	2	3	4
Intensity (cells/l)	0	10^2	10^3	10^4	10^5
Persistence (months)	0	0.25	0.75	1–6	>6
Extension (% of coverage)	0	10	25	50–75	>75
Toxicity (concentration)	0	Low	moderate	high	very high

A second aggregated impact matrix was then built in order to take into account the occurrence of the four main HAB species weighted from absence (0) to very high (4) according to the criteria defined in Table 7.1; weights of the HAB species were summed and ranked from 0 to 100 (very low to very high). Weighting criteria were based on both the literature (EPA, 2001) and local occurrence range according to the expert judgement of the authors (Table 7.2). The ENSO SST 3.4 index, which is well correlated with the Uruguay river flow Q_U, is also reported on an annual basis (from March to February) (see Table 7.2).

Table 7.2 *Aggregated impact index of HABs for the Río de la Plata, 1991–2000*

Year	SST 3.4	1 Alexandrum tamarense	2 Gymnodium catenatum	3 Dinophysis acuminata	4 Mycrocistis aeruginosa	Σ	Index 0–100	Impact
1990–1991	0.3	3	0	0	0	3	21	low
1991–1992	1.0	2	3	2	2	9	64	high
1992–1993	0.4	2.75	2.75	0	0	5.5	39	low
1993–1994	0.4	1.25	2.25	1.5	2.75	7.75	55	medium
1994–1995	0.6	2	2.25	0	0	4.25	30	low
1995–1996	-0.4	3	2.25	1.5	0	7	50	medium
1996–1997	-0.3	1.25	1.5	0	3	6	43	medium
1997–1998	1.8	0	2	0	0	2	14	very low
1998–1999	-0.7	1.25	1.25	0	2	4.5	32	Low
1999–2000	-1.3	1.0	1	0	0	2	14	Very low
Average	**0.2**	**1.75**	**1.83**	**0.5**	**0.98**	**4.7**	**36**	**Low to medium**

Finally, these indicators were weighted taking into account their impacts on three sectors (human health (-H); economic activity (-Ec), specifically molluscs' consumption; and environmental health (-Ev)) according to the expert judgement of the authors. Coefficient weights were 0.75, 0.50 and 0.25 for H, Ec and Ev respectively, which were multiplied by the values reported in Table 7.2. Thus a weighted aggregated impact index of persistence/extension/toxicity (IPET) was built (Table 7.3). An impact coefficient was assigned for each of the four species. Relative impact of each indicator (IPET from 0 to 1) is shown for each species and sector. Extreme values are toxicity of *Gymnodinium* for human health and intensity of *Dinophysis* for the environment (Table 7.3).

Table 7.3 *Weighted aggregated impact index of HABs (index of persistence/extension/toxicity, IPET) for each species and sector on the northern coast of the Río de la Plata, 1991–2000*

Species	Weighted Index for each sector (0–1)		
	Health: 0.75	Economic activity: 0.50	Environment: 0.25
Gymnodinium 0.50	T: 0.37	T: 0.25	P: 0.13
Alexandrum 0.42	E: 0.32	P: 0.21	E: 0.11
Microcystis 0.33	P: 0.25	E: 0.17	T: 0.08
Dinophysis 0.22	I: 0.19	I: 0.13	I: 0.06

The overall impact of HAB occurrence was moderate, with only one high-impact year (1992) and two low-impact years (1998 and 2000), which coincide with strong ENSO events (1997–1998 and 1999–2000 respectively). The only species that reached high values in 1991 and 1993 (*Alexandrium tamarense*) was due to both the northward displacement of the Malvinas current, where *Alexandium* is present, and a low freshwater inflow or Q_V (Méndez et al, 1996), especially because of a low Q_U (Nagy et al, 2002b). Usually, both drivers are associated with El Niño and La Niña years respectively, which reduces the vulnerability of the Plata river to the presence of these blooms. To date HABs have occurred during spring time, but they could be potentially dangerous to human health if they were to occur during summer.

Such examples – the blooms of *Alexandrium*, the relatively high index of El Niño multi-year events (1991–1994), and the extreme events of 1998 and 2000 – suggest some hydroclimatic control on HAB occurrence. Recent years (2001 and 2003, not shown here) have shown a marked increase in cyano-HABs (López and Nagy, 2005) at intensities higher (>3) than those found during the past decade. El Niño and La Niña events could stimulate cyano-blooms, the former by advecting freshwater and the latter by decreasing it.

Coastal Fishery System Vulnerability in the Pajas Blancas Fishing Community

An artisanal fleet exploits fisheries 5–7 miles off the Uruguayan coast in the estuarine zone of the Río de la Plata close to the Santa Lucia river mouth. The main community is based at Pajas Blancas (see Figure 7.1) within the estuarine front (EF). The peak of the fishing period, October to December (Figure 7.5), is controlled by Q_V (especially by Q_U) and wind rotation (Norbis, 1995; Nagy et al, 2003a; Norbis et al, 2004).

The location of the estuarine front displaces as a function of:

1   total river flow Q_V (which, in turn, is strongly associated with both seasonal and ENSO-related inter-annual variability in precipitation); and

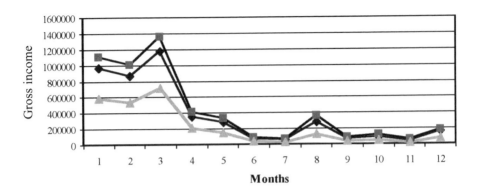

Figure 7.5 *Long-term gross income of fishermen (local currency-1999)*

Note: Average – black; strong ENSO years – light grey; maximum – dark grey. Months: 1 (October)–12 (September).
Source: Nagy et al (2003a).

2   offshore and onshore winds on a weather development timescale (1–10 days) (Norbis et al, 2004).

Climatic stimuli (river flow and wind) thus displace the estuarine front upward and downward (Framiñán and Brown, 1996; Severov et al, 2003 and 2004), out of the fishing area. Displacement of the estuarine front induces changes in the spatial distribution of fish and their recruitment. Frequency patterns of winds have also changed over the past few decades (Pshennikov et al, 2003), with an increase in onshore east–southeast winds (Escobar et al, 2004). During strong ENSO events, the estuarine front tends to be located far from the Pajas Blancas community of fishermen (see Figure 7.1).

In spite of the increase in the variability of the Plata and Uruguay river flows (Q_P and Q_U) and related extreme locations of the estuarine front, as well as the increase in onshore winds, fishermen have shown good adaptive capacity since 1988. Many of them have migrated seasonally or permanently away from the estuarine front along the coast following resources (Hernández and Rossi, 2003; Norbis et al, 2003) in order to reduce their long-term vulnerability to the fluctuations of Q_V and avoid bad years (Norbis et al, 2004).

Sensitivity and vulnerability of coastal fisheries

We estimated proxy variables, classified and valued respectively as low (1), moderate (2) and high (3), in order to assess social, economic, environmental and legal indicators of sensitivity of the fishermen's community (Table 7.4). The sum of all indicators (non-weighted index of vulnerability) suggests that the community is subject to moderate to high vulnerabilities yet seems to be resilient. Only those strong ENSO events whose effects are noticeable during the peak of the fishing period (El Niño 1992, 1997 and 2002 and La Niña 1989

Table 7.4 *Assessment of the vulnerability of the coastal fishing community*

Proxy variable	Vulnerability		
	High (3)	Moderate (2)	Low (1)
Social			
Family		X	
Education		X	
Housing		X	
Employment		X	
Health		X	
Social organization	X		
Sub-total: 2.2/3			
Economic			
Boats		X	
Engines		X	
Fishing gear			X
Communications		X	
Refrigeration	X		
Catch		X	
Prices		X	
Net income		X	
Subtotal: 2.0/3			
Environmental			
Climate – ENSO	X		
Winds	X		
Storm surges/Flooding		X	
Eutrophication		X	
Habitat loss			X
Subtotal: 2.2/3			
Legal/Institutional			
Laws		X	
Territorial planning		X	
Coast Guard controls	X		
Conflicts with industrial fleet	X		
Conflicts with neighbours		X	
Legal organization X			
Subtotal: 2.5/3			
Total: 2.2/3			

Note: Unweighted total index of vulnerability (IV) = 2.2 (scale 1–3).

Source: Modified from Nagy et al (2003a) and Norbis et al (2004).

and 1999) seem to impact fishing activity and net income. Therefore, less than one third of the peak fishing periods are considered to be very bad in economic terms (when the net income of fishermen is estimated to be reduced by ~60 per cent with regard to normal years as shown in Figure 7.5) (Nagy et al, 2003a; Norbis et al, 2004).

The question regarding the sustainability of coastal fisheries was thus empirically answered because the fishing activity remains sustainable regardless of their (estimated) high vulnerability. Our analysis suggest that their resiliency is (or was) due to:

- the combination of planned and reactive adaptation measures to hydroclimatic variability (for example, migration to escape from the high variability of the estuarine front);
- the good fishing performance of most fishermen – many fishermen have acquired a high level of appropriate skills and developed a high capacity to understand weather and environmental conditions, for instance, they usually conduct exploratory samplings of bottom waters with hand-made domestically produced hand-made equipment (Hernández and Rossi, 2003); and
- their (dominant) cautious behaviour (to avoid weather-related risks in spite of economic losses), which reduced their vulnerability. Fishermen do not risk fishing for at least one day after unfavourable wind conditions occur, even if fish are often then available (Norbis, 1995). Even if this behaviour should be considered a bad practice in terms of cost–benefit analysis, it has not significantly affected long-term income. However, real-time weather forecasting applied to fisheries would be a good adaptation practice, provided fishermen can trust the information, which is not always up-to-date.

Thus, the following question arises: Will fishermen have the adaptive capacity to continue to be successful under increasing climatic and economic pressures such as those that occurred in 2002?: which consisted of:

- severe economic crisis;
- increase in fuel prices;
- a moderate El Niño year that decreased surface salinity at Pajas Blancas to close to zero because of the seaward displacement of the estuarine front; and
- increase in the occurrence of unfavourable wind conditions for fishing activity (>8m/s) (Nagy et al, 2003a; Norbis et al, 2004).

According to Norbis (1995) and Norbis et al (2003) southern winds (SW to SE) of >8m/s are not favourable for fishing and, as mentioned above, most fishermen prefer not to risk fishing on the first day of favourable conditions after bad weather, usually losing one favourable day. In fact, fishing activity for the 1998–1999 period shows that the number of fishing boats and fish haul increased during the favourable days, suggesting that there is no resource limitation and that the community tends to follow the advice of the fishermen who are the leaders (i.e. the expert fishermen or fishermen who perform well) (Norbis et al, 2004 and 2005).

Generally, the average wind speed in the region is 5–6m/s, but it increases to >6m/s during spring and summer because of the prevailing SE winds (Nagy et al, 1997; Escobar et al, 2004). This means that fishermen are both highly exposed and resilient to developing their activity within a narrow wind range close to the limit of 8m/s. However, the overall conditions during 2002 forced fishermen to change their no-risk behaviour (Nagy et al, 2003a; Norbis et al, 2004 and 2005).

Scenarios of coastal fisheries activity

Norbis et al (2005) developed an empirical scenario of fishing activity and productivity based on both the long-term yearly fishing activity gross income (see Figure 7.5) and the fishing period 1998–1999. This economic scenario was built for:

- 30 boats;
- fishing period (2, 3 and 4 months);
- monthly fishing days (8, 14 and 17 days); and
- efficiency of fishing units (26, 38 and 46 boxes).

Thus, nine different empirical scenarios were developed using various combinations of the first three sets of assumptions in the list above (i.e. number of boats, fishing period and monthly fishing days). These scenarios represent maximum (1) and minimum (9) fishing activity within the range of observed conditions during 1998/1999, for each variable. Of these, six scenarios yield captures greater than the maximum observed in 1998/1999 and the most successful are those based on four- and three-month seasons of fishing activity. It must be noted that these scenarios do not include captures during the low fishing activity period (February to September, see Figure 7.5), when many fishermen migrate seaward of the estuarine front to San Luis (see Figure 7.1).

Both the observations and the economic scenario suggest that:

- the longer the peak of the fishing period the greater the capture, which depends mainly on hydroclimatic conditions (the ENSO-induced estuarine front location);
- the number of fishing days per month is crucial and this is highly dependent on the occurrence of southern winds (wind induced estuarine front location and mixing state);
- the sustainability of the fishing activity depends on several factors for which thresholds have been estimated: fishing activity must be ≥15 days/month and the fishing period must be >2 months;
- in the event of an increase in climatic constraints only the most able fishermen would be able to maintain present net income; and
- it will be necessary to continue this analysis for at least two more years with different climatic, environmental and socioeconomic conditions, as well as to incorporate anthropological research.

Future Climate Scenarios and Some Environmental Impacts

Future climate changes for the Río de la Plata were extracted from global circulation model (GCM) runs (Bidegain and Camilloni, 2004). Estimates of future changes in mean temperature and precipitation over the region, for the baseline period 1961–1990, are based on two recent GCMs: the HADCM3 model from the Hadley Centre (UK) and the ECHAM4 model from the Max

Planck Institute (Germany) run with the IPCC SRES emission scenarios A2 (medium high) and B2 (medium low). Based on the model results, changes in annual precipitation across the Río de la Plata are expected to vary between +0.1 and +0.2mm/day by the 2050s according to HADCM3 and between +0.0 and +0.6 mm/day by the 2050s according to ECHAM4 for the high emissions scenario (A2). In the case of the low emissions scenario (B2) it should vary between +0.0 and +0.3 mm/day by the 2050s according to HADCM3 and by +0.0 to +0.5mm/day by the 2050s according to ECHAM4.

Annual temperature across the region would rise between +1.5°C and +3.0°C by the 2050s according to HADCM3, or by +0.5°C to +2.0°C by the 2050s according to ECHAM4, for the high emissions scenario (A2). For the low emissions scenario (B2) it should rise by +1.3°C to +2.5°C by the 2050s according to HADCM3, or +0.4°C to +2.0°C by the 2050s according to ECHAM4. Annual sea-level pressure across the Plata river basin by the 2050s, according to ECHAM4, indicates a southern displacement of the Atlantic sub-tropical high pressure. Under this scenario, and projecting the trends observed over the past three decades (changes in South Atlantic high pressure and sea-level pressure) and the increase in east and southeast winds reported by Escobar et al (2004), we can assume an increase in the frequency of onshore winds.

Some Conjectures about Climate Scenarios, Environmental Vulnerability and Impacts

Current environmental scenarios (1971–2003) in the Plata river basin and estuary discussed in this chapter are dominated by the following main stresses:

- increase in temperature, precipitation, streamflow, sea level and onshore winds;
- increase in population, use of natural resources and export of nutrients;
- increase in economic activities, land-use changes, soil erosion and runoff/infiltration ratio; and
- increase in symptoms of eutrophication.

Current climate and future scenarios (time horizon 2020–2050) presented in the previous sections for the Plata river basin and estuary suggest a potential change (since the 1961–1990 baseline conditions) in precipitation within the range +5 per cent to +20 per cent and in temperature from +1°C to +2°C. During the last few decades these changes have been observed to be +20 to +25 per cent for precipitation and +0.5°C to +0.8°C for temperature, along with a +25 to +40 per cent change for total river flows (Q_V).

Trends for Q_V are very difficult to estimate because of both the uncertainty of regional human drivers (for example, land-use change) and the varied regional scenarios from different GCMs. Both the GCM scenarios used here i.e. the HADCM3 and ECHAM-4, have systematically underestimated the baseline precipitation over the region (i.e. estimated precipitation values lower than the observed baseline precipitation for 1961–1990), but not necessarily the increase in it. Indeed, during the past few decades the observed increase in precipitation (Liebmann, 2004) was associated with the observed increase in river flow. Moreover, small changes in precipitation are doubled in the stream-flow signal (Berbery and Barros, 2002). Tucci and Clarke (1998) have suggested that one third of observed increases in streamflows were attributable to land-use changes.

From an environmental point of view, under one future scenario (for 2020–2050) in which streamflow remains similar or slightly lower (0 per cent to -10 per cent) with regard to present values, we do not expect a significant increase in present environmental stresses on the estuarine system (which are already moderately high).

Our concern is about a future scenario where total river flow Q_V increases within the range 10–25 per cent, together with projected temperature increases, for which significant impacts are expected in the estuarine and coastal systems (increase in the vulnerability to trophic state changes and air–water and sediment–water gas and nutrient exchanges), besides changes in the shelf and contour current circulation (water temperature changes and ocean-driven HABs).

Thus, the following question arises: Is such a scenario (increase in temperature and river flow) plausible under projected changes in temperature (of +1–2°C) and precipitation (~5–20 per cent), taking into account the consequent increase in evapotranspiration?

Some assumptions are as follows: 1) about a third of Q_V changes may be due to land-use changes (Tucci and Clarke, 1998); 2) observed vs projected changes are of the same sign in all variables; and 3) the expected value for temperature change is 2 to 4 times greater than that formerly observed. A key question relates to the relative amounts of potential and actual evapotranspiration rates in the future. This uncertainty makes it very difficult to establish any coherent scenario about future streamflow, especially if current land-use changes continue increasing the runoff/infiltration ratio (which could reduce the impact of temperature rise on evapotranspiration).

Considering the fact that seasonal temperature, precipitation and stream-flow cycles are not superposed, any changes should modify seasonal circulation, stratification and mixing patterns, inducing further environmental shifts (such as changes in gas and nutrient exchanges), with a probable increase in both the degree and occurrence of hypoxic events (estimated to be about 20 per cent) in deep bottom waters and denitrification (emission of N_2 to the atmosphere) (Nagy et al, 2002a and b; Nagy et al, 2003b), as well as an increase in the vulnerability of fishermen and low-lying areas.

The long-term evolution of salinity off Montevideo (Nagy et al, 2002a; Bidegain et al, 2005) and the monthly evolution during the period 1998–2002 (Scverov et al, 2004), as well as the evolution of the estuarine fronts location within the Río de la Plata estuary and adjacent shelf since 1998 (Severov et al, 2003 and 2004) allow the development of a conceptual model (not detailed here) for annual as well as monthly time periods: when the Uruguay river flow or Q_U is 4000m³/s, typical yearly salinities are >10–12 per cent, when Q_U is

>5500m³/s they are ~7–9 per cent (present average: ~8 per cent) and when Q_U is >7000m³/s salinity is <5 per cent on timescales greater than weather development, whereas when Q_U is >10,000m³/s freshwater prevails in most of the Uruguayan coast and the estuarine front is displaced tens of miles to the mouth.

Under a hypothetical environmental scenario for 2020–2050, based on climate models outputs, past trends, reference projections and expert judgement, some predictions can be made. Both long-term and monthly analysis of recent years suggests that a hypothetical increase in the Q_U of ~20 per cent should reduce average salinity at Montevideo by 2–3 ppt or parts per thousand (reaching 5 or 6 ppt) and displace riverward the estuarine front. If these changes were coupled with a plausible increase in onshore winds, especially during spring months, when ENSO is active, and biological processes and goods are in their activity peak period, significant changes in both the structure and location of the several fronts of the Río de la Plata as well as of the biological and biogeochemical functions (including fish reproduction, fishing activity and biogeochemical dynamics) can be expected (Severov et al, 2004; Nagy et al, 2004; López and Nagy, 2005; Lappo et al, 2005).

If projected scenarios of human drivers (for example, +70–100 per cent population and ~150–200 per cent N input) (Nagy et al, 2003b) as well as land-use changes for the Uruguay river basin are to be accounted for, significant changes in symptoms of eutrophication and coastal fisheries livelihood can be expected.

We need to assume a plausible pessimistic point of view. Taking into account the evolution, variability and extremes of temperature, precipitations, river flow and trophic state variables change during the past 10 to 30 years, and projecting them through the next 10–30 years, significant environmental impacts and changes can be expected soon.

Conclusion

- The overall vulnerability of the region and the impacts on the fresh and estuarine waters, coastal zone, ecosystem goods, processes and services on the Uruguayan coast of the Río de la Plata are primarily associated with ENSO-related climate variability.
- In addition, human and climatic shifts are drivers of environmental pressure and state variables within the Río de la Plata basin and sub-basins at different spatial scales and timescales, which produce, stimulate or trigger impacts, ecosystem responses and shifts within the estuarine waters of the Río de la Plata and its coastal zone.
- Increase in precipitation plays a major role in controlling buoyancy, eutrophication and production and respiration (P-R) processes of organic matter, since sensitivity to trophic state changes depends on the balance between river flow and winds.
- Projected scenarios for 2050 will increase vulnerabilities of the exposed sectors, and some of them will likely be heavily impacted and/or will

become unsustainable. While we have limited our discussion to the impacts on coastal fisheries in this chapter, other sectors affected include low-lying wetlands and beaches, tourism and supply of drinking water. The impacts on these sectors could be the subject of future studies.

- Changes in climate and the resulting changes in river flow will modify the circulation, stratification and mixing patterns of water in the Río de la Plata estuary, inducing further environmental impacts and increasing the vulnerability of fishermen.

References

Baethgen, W., V. Barros, E. Berbery, R. Clarke, H. Cullen, C. Ereño, B. Grassi, D. P. Lettenmeier, R. Mechoso, and P. Silva Dias (2001) 'Climatology and hydrology of the Plata Basin', WRCP/VAMOS, www.clivar.org (also available from www.atmos.umd.edu/~berbery)

Berbery, E. and V. R. Barros (2002) 'The hydrologic cycle of the La Plata basin in South America', *Journal of Hydrometeorology*, vol 3, pp630–645

Bidegain, M. and I. Camillloni (2004) 'Performance of GCMs and Climate Baselines Scenarios for Southeastern South America', paper presented at Latin America and Caribbean Assessment of Impacts and Adaptation to Climate Change (AIACC) Workshop, Buenos Aires, Argentina

Bidegain, M., R. M. Caffera, V. Pshennikov, J. J. Lagomarsino, G. J. Nagy and E. A. Forbes (2005) 'Tendencias climáticas, hidrológicas y oceanográficas en el Río de la Plata y costa Uruguaya', in V. Barros, A. Menéndez and G. J. Nagy (eds) *El Cambio Climático en el Río de la Plata*, vol 14, Centro de Investigaciones del Mar y la Atmósfera (CIMA) – Universidad de Buenos Aires (UBA), Buenos Aires, pp137–143

Caffera, R. M., M. Bidegain, F. Blixen, J. J. Lagomarsino, G. J. Nagy, K. Sans, G. Dupuy, and R. Torres (2005) 'Vulnerabilidad presente de los recursos hídricos y estado trófico del Río Santa Lucía a la variabilidad climática', in V. Barros, A. Menéndez and G. J. Nagy (eds) *El Cambio Climático en el Río de la Plata*, vol 14, Centro de Investigaciones del Mar y la Atmósfera (CIMA) – Universidad de Buenos Aires (UBA), Buenos Aires, pp33–39

Calliari, D., M. Gómez and N. Gómez (2005) 'Phytoplankton biomass and composition in the Río de la Plata estuary: Large-scale distribution and relationship with environmental variables', *Continental Shelf Research*, vol 25, pp197–210

Camilloni, I., and V. Barros (2000) 'The Paraná river response to El Niño 1982–1983 and 1997–1998 events', *Journal of Hydrometeorology*, vol 1, pp412–430

De Jonge, V., M. Elliott and E. Orive (2002) 'Causes, historical development, effects and future challenges of a common environmental problem: Eutrophication', *Hydrobiologia*, vol 475/476, pp1–19

Díaz, A. F., C. D. Studzinski and C. R. Mechoso (1998) 'Relationship between precipitation anomalies in Uruguay and Southern Brazil and sea surface temperature in the Pacific and Atlantic Oceans', *Journal of Climatology*, vol 11, pp251–271

EPA (US Environmental Protection Agency) (2001) *Nutrient Criteria Technical Guidance Manual: Estuarine and Coastal Marine Waters*, Government Printing Office, Washington, DC

Escobar, G., W. Vargas and S. Bischoff (2004) 'Wind tides in the Río de la Plata estuary: Meteorological conditions', *International Journal of Climatology*, vol 24, pp1159–1169

Ferrari, G. and G. J. Nagy (2003) 'Assessment of vulnerability of trophic state in estuarine systems: Development of a highly aggregated impact index', paper presented at the First AIACC regional workshop for the Latin America and the Caribbean, San Jose, Costa Rica, Assessments of Impacts and Adaptations to Climate Change, International START Secretariat, Washington, DC, US, www.aiaccproject.org

Framiñán, M. B. and O. B. Brown (1996) 'Study of the Río de la Plata turbidity front: Part I: Spatial and temporal distribution', *Continental Shelf Research*, vol 16, pp1259–1282

Garcia, N. O. and W. M. Vargas (1998) 'The temporal climatic variability in the Río de la Plata basin displayed by the river discharges', *Climatic Change*, vol 38, pp359–379

Gordon, D. C. Jr, P. R. Boudreau, K. H. Mann, and T. Yanagi (1996) 'LOICZ Biogeochemical Modelling Guidelines', *LOICZ Reports and Studies*, vol 5, LOICZ, Texel, The Netherlands

Hernández, J. and P. Rossi (2003) 'Characterization of the artisanal fishermen settlements of the frontal zone of the Río de la Plata', in *Research for Environmental Management, Fisheries Resources and Fisheries in the Saline Front*, vol 16, EcoPlata, Montevideo, Uruguay, pp217–234

Hoffman, J. A. J. (1975) *Atlas Climático de América del Sur*, vol I, WMO-UNESCO-Cartographia, Geneva

Kalnay, E., M. Kanamitsu, R. Kistler, W. Collins, D. Deaven, L. Gandin, M. Iredell, S. Saha, G. White, J. Woolen, Y. Zhu, M. Chelliah, W. Ebisuzaki, W. Higgins, J. Janowiak, K. C. Mo, C. Ropelewski, J. Wang, A. Leetma, R. Reynolds, R. Jenne and D. Joseph (1996) 'The NCEP/NCAR 40-Year reanalysis project', *Bulletin of the American Meteorological Society*, vol 77, pp437–471

Kane, R. P. (2002) 'Precipitation anomalies in southern America associated with a finer classification of El Niño and La Niña events', *International Journal of Climatology*, vol 22, pp357–373

Lappo, S. S., E. Morozov, D. N. Severov, A. V. Sokov, A. A. Kluivitkin and G. Nagy (2005) 'Frontal Mixing of River and Sea Waters in Río de la Plata', *Transactions of the Russian Academy of Sciences* (Earth Science Section), vol 401, pp267–269, (in Russian)

Liebmann, B. C., L. Vera, L. Carvalho, I. Camilloni, M. Hoerling, D. Allured, V. Barros, J. Baez and M. Bidegain (2004) 'An observed trend in Central South American precipitation', *Journal of Climatology*, vol 17, pp4357–4367

López Laborde, J. and G. J. Nagy (1999) 'Hydrography and sediment transport', in G. M. Perillo, E. M. Pino and M. C. Piccolo (eds) *Characteristics of the Río de la Plata: Estuaries of South America: Their Geomorphology and Dynamics*, Springer-Verlag, Berlin, pp137–159

López, C. H. and G. J. Nagy (2005) 'Cambio global, evolución del estado trófico y floraciones de cianobacterias en el Río de la Plata', in V. Barros, A. Menéndez and G. J. Nagy (eds) *El Cambio Climático en el Río de la Plata*, vol 16, CIMA-UBA, Buenos Aires, Argentina, pp157–166

McCarthy, J. J., O. F. Canziani, N. A. Leary, D. J. Dokken and K. S. White (eds) (2001) *Climate Change 2001: Impacts, Adaptation, and Vulnerability*, Contribution of Working Group II to the Third Assessment Report of the Intergovernmental Panel on Climate Change, Cambridge University Press, Cambridge, UK

Méndez, S., D. N. Severov, G. Ferrari and C. Mesones (1996) 'Early spring *Alexandrium tamarense* toxic blooms in Uruguay waters', in Y. T. Oshima and Y. Fukuyo (eds) *Harmful and Toxic Blooms*, Intergovernmental Oceanographic Commission of UNESCO, Paris, pp113–117

Méndez, S., M. Gómez and G. Ferrari (1997) 'Planktonic studies of the Río de la Plata and its oceanic front', Chapter 4 in P. Wells and G. Daborn (eds) *The Río de la Plata: An Environmental Overview*, EcoPlata Project Background Report, Dalhousie University, Halifax, Nova Scotia

Menéndez, A. and M. Re (2005) 'Hidrología del Río de la Plata', in V. Barros, A. Menéndez and G. J. Nagy (eds) *El Cambio Climático en el Río de la Plata*, vol 7, CIMA-UBA, Buenos Aires, Argentina, pp69–83

Moss, R. (1999) *Vulnerability to Climate Variability and Change: Framework for Synthesis and Modeling: Project Description*, Battelle Pacific Northwest National Laboratory, Richland, WA, US

Nagy, G. J. (2000) 'Dissolved inorganic NP budget for the frontal zone of the Río de la Plata system: Estuarine Systems of South American Region: Carbon, nitrogen, and phosphorus fluxes', in V. Dupra, S. Smith, L. I. Marshall-Crossland and C. J. Crossland (eds) *LOICZ Reports and Studies 15*, LOICZ, Texel, The Netherlands, pp40–43

Nagy, G. J. (2003) 'Assessment of vulnerability and impacts to global change: Trophic state of estuarine systems', paper presented at the First AIACC regional workshop for the Latin America and the Caribbean, San Jose, Costa Rica, Assessments of Impacts and Adaptations to Climate Change, International START Secretariat, Washington, DC, US, www.aiaccproject.org

Nagy, G. J. (2005) 'Vulnerabilidad de las aguas del Río de la Plata: Cambio de estado trófico y factores físicos', in V. Barros, A. Menéndez and G. J. Nagy (eds) *El Cambio Climático en el Río de la Plata*, vol 15, CIMA-UBA, Buenos Aires, Argentina, pp145–155

Nagy, G. J., M. Gómez-Erache and A. C. Perdomo (2002a) 'Río de la Plata', in T. Munn (ed) *The Encyclopedia of Global Environmental Change*, vol 3 (Water Resources), John Wiley and Sons, New York, US

Nagy, G. J., M. Gómez-Erache, C. H. López and A. C. Perdomo (2002b) 'Distribution patterns of nutrients and symptoms of eutrophication in the Río de la Plata estuarine system', *Hydrobiologia*, vol 475/476, pp125–139

Nagy, G. J., G. Sención, W. Norbis, A. Ponce, G. Saona, R. Silva, M. Bidegain and V. Pshennikov (2003a) 'Overall vulnerability of the Uruguayan coastal fishery system to global change in the estuarine front of the Río de la Plata', Poster Session, The Open Meeting Human Dimensions of Global Environmental Change, Montreal, Canada, October

Nagy, G. J., C. H. López, F. Blixen, G. Ferrari, M. C. Presentado, A. Ponce, J. J. Lagomarsino, K. Sans, and M. Bidegain (2003b) *El Cambio Global en el Río de la Plata: Escenarios, Vulnerabilidad e Indicadores de Cambio de Estado Trófico en la Costa Norte*, V Jornadas Nacionales de Ciencias del Mar, Mar del Plata, Argentina

Nagy, G. J., J. J. Lagomarsino, K. Sans and E. Andrés (2004) 'Evaluación de las Cargas Contaminantes a la Costa Uruguaya del Río de la Plata y Atlántico. Evaluación del Estado Trófico (Nutrientes, Clorofila, Oxígeno disuelto e Indicadores Tróficos)', final report, FREPLATA Project, Montevideo, Uruguay

National Resource Council (2000) *Clean Coastal Waters: Understanding and Reducing the Effects of Nutrient Pollution*, Ocean Studies Board and Water Science and Technology Board, Commission on Geosciences, Environment, and Resources, National Research Council, National Academy of Sciences Press, Washington, DC,

Nixon, S. W. (1995) 'Coastal marine eutrophication: A definition, social causes, and future concerns' *Ophelia*, vol 41, pp199–219

Norbis, W. (1995) 'Influence of wind, behaviour and characteristics of the croaker (*Micropogonias furnieri*) artisanal fishery in the Río de la Plata', *Fisheries Research*, vol 22, pp43–58

Norbis, W., J. Verocai and V. Pshennikov-Severova (2003) 'Artisanal fleet activity in relation to meteorological conditions (synoptic scale) during the fishing period October 1998–March 1999', in *Research for Environmental Management, Fisheries Resources and Fisheries in the Saline Front*, vol 14, EcoPlata, Montevideo, Uruguay, pp191–197

Norbis, W., G. Saona, V. Pshennikov, G. J. Nagy, and G. Sención (2004) 'Vulnerability

of Uruguayan artisanal fisheries of the frontal zone of the Río de la Plata to River
Flow and wind variability', paper presented at the Second AIACC regional work-
shop for the Latin America and the Caribbean, Buenos Aires, Argentina,
Assessments of Impacts and Adaptations to Climate Change, International START
Secretariat, Washington, DC, US, www.aiaccproject.org/meetings/meetings.html

Norbis W., A. Ponce, D. N. Severov, G. Saona, J. Verocai, V. Pshennikov, R. Silva, G.
Sención and G. J. Nagy (2005) 'Vulnerabilidad y capacidad de adaptación de la
pesca artesanal del Río de la Plata a la variabilidad climática', in V. Barros, A.
Menéndez and G. J. Nagy (eds) *El Cambio Climático en el Río de la Plata*, vol 3,
CIMA, BsAs, Argentina, pp181–187

Pizarro, M. and A. Orlando (1985) 'Distribución de fósforo, nitrógeno y silicio disuelto en el Río de la Plata', Serv. Hidr. Naval. Secr. Marina, Publ. H-625, pp1–57

Pshennikov, V., M. Bidegain, F. Blixen, E. A. Forbes, J. J. Lagomarsino and G. J. Nagy
(2003) 'Climate extremes and changes in precipitation and wind patterns in the
vicinities of Montevideo, Uruguay', paper presented at the First AIACC regional
workshop for the Latin America and the Caribbean, San Jose, Costa Rica,
Assessments of Impacts and Adaptations to Climate Change, International START
Secretariat, Washington, DC, US, www.aiaccproject.org

Seitzinger, S., C. Kroeze, A. F. Bouwman, N. Caraco, F. Dentner and R. V. Styles (2002)
'Global patterns of dissolved inorganic and particulate nitrogen inputs to coastal
systems: Recent conditions and future projections', *Estuaries*, vol 25, pp640–655

Severov, D., G. J. Nagy, V. Pshennikov and E. Morozov (2003) 'SeaWifs fronts of the
Río de la Plata estuarine system', *Geophysical Research Letters*, vol, 5, p01914

Severov, D. N., G. J. Nagy, V. Pshennikov, M. De los Santos and E. Morozov (2004)
'Río de la Plata estuarine system: Relationship between river flow and frontal variability', paper presented at 35th COSPAR Scientific Assembly, Paris, France, July

Stockholm Environment Institute (2001) 'Framework for vulnerability', The George
Perkins Marsh Institute at Clark University and The Stockholm Environment
Institute, Research and Assessment Systems, Stockholm, Sweden

Tucci, C. E. M. and R. T. Clarke (1998) 'Environmental issues in the La Plata basin',
Water Research Development, vol 14, pp157–174

8

Climate Change and the Tourism-Dependent Economy of the Seychelles

Rolph Antoine Payet

Introduction

The Seychelles is a small island state of 115 islands spread over an exclusive economic zone covering an area of 1.37 million square kilometres in the Indian Ocean. They share characteristics with other small island states that, in the judgement of the Intergovernmental Panel on Climate Change (IPCC), make small islands especially vulnerable to the effects of climate change, sea-level rise and extreme events (Mimura et al, 2007). With a total land area of just 455.3 square kilometres, most of the population, infrastructure and economic activities of the Seychelles are concentrated on the coasts of three large islands. These islands are among the granitic group of 43 islands with mountainous peaks that rise steeply and constrain development to the very narrow 1 to 2km-wide coastal plains. The people and infrastructure that are concentrated in these coastal plains are highly vulnerable to storm surges and coastal erosion. The economy is heavily dependent on tourism and, to a lesser extent, on fisheries, both of which have their main infrastructure located in the exposed coastal plains and are dependent on natural resources such as coral reefs and freshwater supplies that are sensitive to climate variations, sea-level rise and other stressors.

Tourism plays a role of unmatched importance in the economy of the Seychelles and any shocks that negatively impact the tourism industry are felt throughout the islands. This situation is not unique to the Seychelles and is a feature of the economies of many other small island states. Yet the vulnerability of tourism-dependent island states to climate change has been largely unstudied. Because of the importance of this issue, we undertook an analysis of the potential impacts of climate change on the tourism industry of the Seychelles. Results of the analysis and their implications for vulnerability for the wider economy and society are presented in this chapter. Also addressed are adaptation strategies for managing climate risks to the tourism industry.

Past Climate Events and their Impacts

The impacts of the 1997–1998 El Niño and the 1998–2000 La Niña events demonstrate the sensitivity of the economy of the Seychelles to climate events (Payet, 2005). Combined losses in monetary terms caused by these events amounted to an estimated US$22 million, or 4 per cent of GDP. Figure 8.1 shows the distribution of losses by sector of the economy. Fisheries suffered the greatest loss, accounting for 45 per cent of the total, followed by agriculture, with 28 per cent of the losses. The tourism sector suffered an estimated US$2.6 million loss, or 12 per cent of the total.

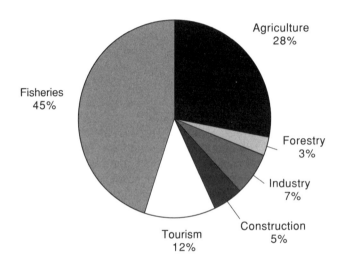

Figure 8.1 *Share of economic losses by sector from the 1997–1998 El Niño and 1998–2000 La Niña events in the Seychelles*

Source: Payet (2005).

Other impacts included damage to coastal infrastructure such as roads and airstrips, as well as to the natural environment, including coral reefs, beaches and forests. Increased recession of the coastline has been observed since that period, primarily because of the destabilizing nature of higher tide levels and resulting damage to dune vegetation. Critical infrastructure necessary to support the economy and human welfare, such as houses, hospitals, power stations, electric supply, communication networks, emergency response centres, water supplies and schools, all located in the low-lying areas, were also affected by the torrential floods of August 1998.

Intense rainfall events, nearly all of which are directly or indirectly associated with the Intertropical Convergence Zone and tropical cyclones in the region, are a significant climate hazard in the Seychelles. The Indian Ocean is the most prolific of all oceans in generating tropical cyclones. Tropical cyclones do not directly impact the granitic islands of the Seychelles as they lie too close to the equator. But the passage of cyclones to the south can result in the deepening of the intertropical convergence, culminating in feeder bands which can bring in heavy rainfall to the island of Mahe. Heavy rainfall events in Mahe of more than 200mm within 24 hours are shown in Table 8.1. Such heavy rainfall can lead to flooding and landslides resulting in loss of property and significant damage to agricultural crops on the granitic islands.

Table 8.1 *Intense rainfall events of above 200mm in a 24-hour period over the island of Mahe, Seychelles, 1972–1997*

Region	District	Amount (mm)	Date Occurred	Weather Event
West Mahe	Barbarons	210.0	4 November 1996	ITCZ
	Anse Boileau	266.5	15 August 1997	Storm (El Niño)
	Tracking Station	284.8	21 December 1986	Storm (El Niño)
	Tea Factory	291.5	4 November 1986	Storm (El Niño)
	Grand Anse	480.0	15 August 1997	Storm (El Niño)
East Mahe	La Misere	232.4	3 February 1984	Tropical cyclone
	Cascade	242.0	21 May 1990	TC 'Ikonjo'
	Seychelles Airport	245.1	2 February 1981	ITCZ
North Mahe	La Gogue	240.0	30 January 1991	Storm (El Niño)
	Belombre	247.5	30 January 1991	Storm (El Niño)
	North East Point	279.2	29 January 1991	Storm (El Niño)
	Le Niol	282.0	15 August 1997	Storm (El Niño)
South Mahe	Val D'Endore	202.6	15 August 1997	Storm (El Niño)
	La Plaine	215.6	15 August 1997	Storm (El Niño)
South Mahe (cont.)	Anse Forbans	216.5	15 August 1997	Storm (El Niño)
	Anse Royale	220.5	15 August 1997	Storm (El Niño)
Central Mahe	New Port	240.0	28 January 1978	Tropical cyclone
	St. Louis	277.4	4 November 1996	ITCZ
	Rochon	281.1	4 November 1996	ITCZ
	Hermitage	288.2	27 January 1987	El Niño/ITCZ

Note: ITCZ – Intertropical Convergence Zone; TC – tropical convergence.
Source: Seychelles Meteorological Services.

Analysis of the frequency of cyclones and tropical depressions for the period 1959–1980 shows that there are three peak periods of activity: the last 10 days of December, the 10–20th of January and almost the whole month of February. No correlation is found between the activity in any one year and occurrence of El Niño.

Tourism in the Seychelles

The tourism industry in the Seychelles is based on the natural beauty of its islands, the uncrowded beaches, clear coastal waters and year-round sunshine.

A study undertaken in 2004 found that more than 65 per cent of tourists choose to visit the Seychelles for the predominantly pristine nature of their coastal resources and the natural beauty in general (Cesar et al, 2004). Tourism has grown from a mere 3000 annual visitor arrivals in the early 1970s to over 132,000 in 2002. With an average length of stay of 10 days, the number of visitor nights spent by tourists in the Seychelles is roughly 1.3 million per year (Figure 8.2). This growth in tourism has been a principal driver of economic growth in the Seychelles. Tourism now accounts for about 29 per cent of foreign exchange earnings, 20 per cent of GDP and one third of employment.

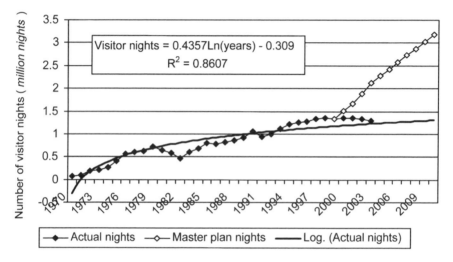

Figure 8.2 *Number of tourist nights per year in the Seychelles –
Actual number of tourist nights and predictions from the Vision 2 master
plan and a statistical model are shown*

Source: Cesar et al (2004).

However, tourist travel to the Seychelles is very sensitive to external market forces and regional political stability. For example, tourism numbers declined sharply from 1980 to 1983 as a result of economic recession in European markets (Gabbay and Gosh, 1997) and in 1991–1992 and 2003 during the two wars in the Persian Gulf region. The terrorist attacks of 11 September 2001 and the recent SARS outbreak (2004) also caused a drop in tourist arrivals. In the late 1990s, competition from other destinations also affected the performance of tourism in the Seychelles. The industry is also sensitive to changes in climate, as demonstrated by our study and described later in this chapter.

The industry faces a number of challenges, including the need to:

1   compete more effectively with other destinations by providing greater value for money and enhanced quality levels;

2   improve air access and airport infrastructure;
3   diversify attractions and activities;
4   address shortages of trained and qualified personnel; and
5   protect the environment (MTT, 2001).

The Seychelles have traditionally demonstrated a strong development policy aimed at ensuring that tourism is environmentally sustainable. But with growing development pressure, many of these policies are being reviewed.

The benefits of a policy to promote environmentally sustainable tourism have been significant in terms of allowing many areas of the country to remain undisturbed and retain most of the original landscape. With its pure white beaches that hug the granitic coastline, the Seychelles have been described by many tourist magazines as among the most beautiful paradise islands in the world, coining the tagline 'unique by a thousand miles'. Consequently, the policy of the government has been to exploit the comparative advantages of the Seychelles as an ecotourism destination by promoting a wide range of nature-based attractions and activities related to the Seychelles' unique natural environment. However, climate change can impact on the very resources that today are the basis for tourism.

Tourism and Climate

Climate can and does impact tourism through its effects on the resources and infrastructure that are critical to tourism services and on the climate-related amenities that tourists seek when visiting destinations such as the Seychelles. The effects of climate change on tourism in small islands are expected to be largely negative (Mimura et al, 2007). The projected changes will expose the Seychelles to rising sea level, warmer temperatures and, probably, increasing rainfall (Christensen et al, 2007). The intensity of precipitation events is projected to increase generally, and, in particular, in tropical areas that experience increases in mean precipitation, where extremes are projected to increase more than the mean. Projections also suggest that tropical cyclones are likely to become more severe, with greater wind speeds and higher mean and peak intensity of precipitation (Meehl et al, 2007).

Sea-level rise and greater intensities of rainfall and tropical cyclones would accelerate coastal erosion and beach erosion, threatening one of the primary tourist attractions of the Seychelles. Sea-level rise, rising sea surface temperatures, increased tropical cyclone intensity and changes in ocean chemistry from higher carbon dioxide concentrations are likely to negatively impact the health of coral reef systems, another major tourist attraction of the Seychelles and also important to the islands' fisheries and conservation of biodiversity. Increased coral mortality would also accelerate coastal erosion, as demonstrated by the effects of coral mortality over the past decade in the Seychelles (Sheppard et al, 2005). Damage to or disruption of infrastructure located in the highly exposed coastal plains, such as the airport, hotels, roads, communication and electrical networks, water works and health facilities, would strongly and negatively impact tourism. Tourism places heavy demands on the scarce water supplies of the Seychelles and the industry is highly vulnerable to climate events that disrupt the supply of water (Payet and Agricole, 2006).

Traditional economic tools have been used to estimate in monetary terms the direct and indirect impacts of climate on welfare, but most of this work is confined to temperate regions. Exceptions to this are estimates of losses from coral bleaching. Westmacott et al (2000) estimate that the tourism industry of the Maldives suffered a financial loss of more than US$3 million from severe coral bleaching in the Indian Ocean as a result of the 1997/1998 El Niño event. Aish and Cesar (2002), using the contingent valuation method, estimate an economic welfare loss of US$5 million from the mass coral bleaching of 1996. Cesar et al (2004) go on to estimate the welfare changes for scenarios of future coral reef bleaching. In their baseline scenario, there is no further bleaching and the coral reef environment is assumed to recover. Recovery of the reef is estimated to yield benefits of US$5 million to US$10 million over the next 25 years. An alternate scenario assumes that bleaching events continue and that there is no adaptation response. The result is catastrophic, with a potential loss of more than US$500 million over the next 25 years.

Viner and Agnew (1999) examined the potential impacts of climate change on tourism in the Maldives and concluded that the main impacts would come from sea-level rise, elevated sea-surface temperatures and seawater intrusion on coastal lands. These changes in the coastal environment are expected to have impacts on tourism demand and also tourism resources such as beaches, coral reefs and water. Changes in the natural capital of tourism, as Viner and Agnew project for the Maldives as a result of climate change and which are likely in other small island destinations, would cause changes in the tourism attractiveness of a destination and tourist revenues.

A number of studies have investigated the effects of climate on tourism demand. Research in the UK by Agnew (1995) and Benson (1996) shows that the main driver for sun-sea-sand tourism was primarily linked to climatic conditions in the UK, with people taking more tropical holidays to escape the cold European winters. This is confirmed by the UK Department of Environment and Transport study that found temperature to be the most important climate variable influencing annual domestic holiday tourism (Agnew, 1998). Similarly, work by Giles and Perry (1998) links increases in domestic tourism spending in the UK, and corresponding decreases in international travel, to warmer than usual summers at home. These examples indicate that both local and destination climate factors play a role in tourism demand in long-haul destinations such as the Seychelles.

In a study of the German tourist market for travel to both local and international destinations, Hamilton (2003) found temperature, humidity and rainfall at the destination site influence tourism demand for those destinations. A positive relationship is found between demand and average temperature during the period of travel until the optimum mean temperature is reached, estimated to be 24°C, after which demand decreases for temperatures in excess of the optimum. Hamilton also estimates that 11.5 wet days per month is optimal, with demand falling when the number of wet days exceeds that amount.

Studies for the tourist markets in the UK (Maddison, 2001) and The Netherlands (Lise and Tol, 2002) also find that temperature influences tourist travel and estimate optimal temperatures of 29°C and 21°C for British and Dutch travellers respectively. Neither of these studies found precipitation to have a significant effect.

A Survey of Tourists to the Seychelles

We conducted a survey of 400 tourists in the Seychelles to investigate their sensitivity to various climate variables such as precipitation, sea temperature, sunshine and cloud cover, state of the sea and wind conditions. The first part of the survey asked questions about the different activities that respondents might undertake during their stay in the Seychelles and how changes in climatic conditions might affect their overall satisfaction with the destination. The second part documented basic demographic variables of the interviewees. Written questionnaires were prepared in English, French, German and Italian; other tourists were all interviewed in English. The surveys were undertaken at the airport in the departure lounge (thus the tourists would also be able to comment on their level of satisfaction).

Among the factors cited by respondents as their primary reasons for visiting the Seychelles include sunshine, tranquility, culture, clear waters, nature and food. Approximately 20 per cent of the tourists surveyed came to the Seychelles to enjoy the sun, while 18 per cent did so to enjoy peace and tranquility (see Figure 8.3). Because sunshine is closely linked to the number of wet days and cloudiness, the responses suggest that an increase in rainy days will affect the satisfaction of tourists in the Seychelles. Roughly 35 per cent of the respondents did state that their enjoyment of their stay would have been affected by rainfall, whereas only 10 per cent said that cloudiness would affect their enjoyment. The Seychelles experience an average of 12.6 wet days per month, or 42 per cent of the year, and considerably higher than the optimum estimated by Hamilton (2003), suggesting that increases in numbers of wet days would have a negative affect on tourist visits to the Seychelles.

Tourists were asked about their attitude to rain days, including the number of rainy days they would tolerate during the period of their stay and the point at which rain days would cause them to change their travel plans. Almost 50 per cent of tourists reported concern about the number of rainy days during their stay, while the other half were not bothered. Very few tourists would change their plans following one day of rainfall, while 18 per cent of those surveyed indicated that they would change their travel plans after three consecutive days of rainfall.

Temperature is an important factor for tourists visiting the Seychelles, but not as critical as rainfall. Tourist activities are primarily focused on the beach during the day and in the hotels in the evenings. The survey results indicate that, on average, tourists spend approximately 4.2 hours a day on the beach and about another 3 hours hiking, diving or sightseeing. Average daily temperature in the Seychelles is 27°C, which exceeds the estimated optimal

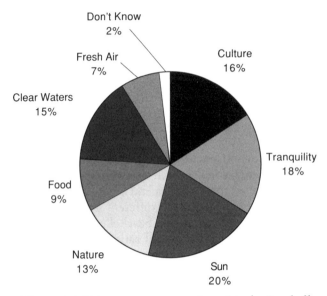

Figure 8.3 *Primary reasons tourists visit the Seychelles*

temperatures sought by travellers from Germany and The Netherlands. Increases in daytime temperatures during the hours when tourists are active would be likely to adversely affect comfort levels. Warmer evening temperatures would also probably reduce comfort levels at night because of the high humidity, but this could be ameliorated by cooling of indoor spaces.

When asked about preferences for cooling during the night-time, such as fans and air-conditioning, 41 per cent stated that they would prefer to use air-conditioning while only 28 per cent would prefer the ambient air temperature. One reason stated for the preference for the use of air-conditioning in the evening is the relatively high humidity levels, which may make it uncomfortable to sleep.

Data collected in this survey show that tourists increasingly verify meteorological information for their travel destinations, either with their travel agent before planning a holiday or using the internet. Of the 400 tourists surveyed, 37 per cent undertake their own research into the climatic conditions prevailing in their destination of choice, while 30 per cent depend on the advice of their travel agent. Information presented and available on climate conditions such as rainfall or warm sunny periods can therefore influence the length and quality of the tourist visits to the Seychelles.

A Statistical Model of Tourist Visits to the Seychelles

Results of the survey, as well as an examination of the literature on tourism demand, were used to specify a statistical model of climate effects on tourist visits to the Seychelles. Tourist arrivals are modelled as a logarithmic function of annual average air temperature, hours of sunshine, precipitation and relative humidity. Many other variables that are likely to influence demand for travel to the Seychelles are omitted due to lack of data. The model was estimated using data for the period 1972 to 2000.

The results of the multivariate analysis are presented in Table 8.2. The partial coefficient for temperature shows a positive relationship with tourist arrivals, while sunshine hours and relative humidity show negative correlations. However, none of the estimated coefficients are statistically different from zero.

Table 8.2 *Results from estimation of the model of tourist demand*

Predictors	Unstandardized Coefficients		T	Sig.	95% Confidence Interval for B	
	B	Std. Error			Lower Bound	Upper Bound
Constant	4.880	2.763	1.766	0.121	−1.653	11.414
Temperature	0.024	0.036	0.660	0.530	−0.061	0.108
Sunshine	−0.051	0.063	−0.806	0.447	−0.200	0.098
Precipitation	0.000	0.001	−0.204	0.844 −	0.002	0.001
Relative humidity	−0.015	0.031	−0.466	0.655	−0.088 0	.059
R Square	0.281					
Adjusted R Square	−0.13					
Standard error of the estimate	0.054					

The lack of a statistically significant effect of climate variables on tourist arrivals in the Seychelles contrasts with the results of Hamilton (2003), Maddison (2001), Lise and Tol (2002) and others, as well as with the findings of our own survey of tourists. A key difference between our analysis and that of the other cited works is that these other studies estimated demands for travel to multiple destinations using cross-sectional data. In multiple destination, cross-section models, differences in the average climate conditions of the different destinations result in different demands for travel to the different destinations. In that context, climate does influence tourists' choice of travel destinations. Our analysis sought to use time-series data of inter-annual climate variations to explain annual variations in travel to a single destination. The results suggest that inter-annual variations in climate do not strongly influence tourist travel to a destination.

Implications for the Seychelles Economy

Hypothetical scenarios of increases in the number of wet days and in average temperatures are constructed to illustrate the sensitivity of the Seychelles economy to possible impacts of climate change on tourism. In constructing the scenarios it is assumed that the optimal number of wet days is 11.5 days per month, as estimated by Hamilton (2003), and that the optimal temperature is 29°C, as estimated by Maddison (2001). The average number of wet days per month is assumed to increase from the present average of 12.5 to 14.3 days by 2020. The increase is based on extrapolation of recent trends in the number of wet days. Such a scenario is plausible given climate model projections of rainfall increases in the Indian Ocean. We assume, as a worst case scenario, and based on responses to our survey, that the increase in wet days would decrease tourist arrivals by 39 per cent.

Average temperature is assumed to increase from the present average of 27°C to 31°C in 2020, an increase that is extreme in comparison to recent estimates from the IPCC (Christensen et al, 2007). Estimates from Maddison imply that average temperatures at a destination site 2°C in excess of the optimum would cause 10 per cent of tourists to opt for local tourism, and that of those who do go, 24 per cent would prefer to remain inactive during the day due to discomfort. Additional effects would be an increase in the use of air-conditioning, estimated at 28 per cent, and an increase in water demand, estimated at 2 per cent.

The economic impacts are measured as estimated changes in tourism earnings and the social impacts are measured as effective job losses, which includes losses in tourism and its multiplier effect in the economy. The results are shown in Table 8.3. Economic costs would amount to approximately US$72 million in net present-value terms. This works out at approximately US$743 per capita. The impact would be felt in all areas of the economy. Hotel developers would face reduced occupancy rates, revenues and profits. Government receipts from tourism would be reduced by US$13 million in net present-value terms, which would, in turn, affect social programmes and infrastructure investments. Recreational revenue losses could undermine the management and protection of many protected areas, including marine parks, which would result in additional welfare losses. Increases in the consumption of water and electricity would cost over US$3 million.

The estimated economic and social impacts are based on hypothetical scenarios that make some rather extreme assumptions. However, they are useful for understanding the sensitivity of the Seychelles economy to climate impacts on tourism and also as a benchmark of the scale of potential losses. Omitted from these estimates are potential losses from impacts on coral reefs, beaches, water supplies and other natural resources, as well as impacts to infrastructure.

Adaptation Strategies

Tourism in the Seychelles and the wider economy of the islands are vulnerable to impacts of climate change on tourism demand and on the natural resources that support the tourism industry. While further research is needed to address many unanswered questions about how global climate change will affect the climate of the Seychelles, and how resources and tourism will be impacted,

Table 8.3 *Social and economic impacts from increases in average number of wet days and temperatures*

Scenario assumptions	Tourist response	Annual Economic Cost (US$ million)	Annual Effective Job Losses (US$ million)	Net Present Value* (US$ million)
Increase in number of wet days (>11.5 days/month)	39% of tourists may cancel their trip	−52.3	−21.0	−46.9
Increase in temperature during the active hours of the day (>29°C)	Local tourism favoured over long-haul, 10% tourists may opt for a local holiday	−13.4	−5.4	−12.1
	Increased periods of inactivity, est. 24% loss by recreational sector	−12.5	−2.7	−9.8
	Increased use of A/C – power demand increased by 28%		+0.4	−3.0
	Increase in water demand by 2% above normal demand rate	−0.4		−0.3

*Discounted over 15 years at 3 per cent net present value.

action is needed to prepare for a changing climate. Four adaptation strategies for tourism in small island states are proposed. Each is needed and would yield significant benefits whether or not climate change brings new or greater hazards to the Seychelles. But the threat of climate change gives greater impetus and urgency to their consideration and implementation, which would build necessary resilience for coping with climate change.

Long-term sustainable planning and management of tourism infrastructure

The importance and long-term benefits of planning for tourism development have been demonstrated in many countries, including small island states. Planning for sustainable tourism development involves the harnessing of the powerful earning power of tourism to promote sound environmental management, economic development and social progress, without compromising the integrity of existing support systems. In the Seychelles, several poorly planned tourism developments are now being used as lessons for the future. One example includes a hotel that was built too close to the beach – with increasing erosion, the costly undertaking of maintaining the coastal infrastructure is decreasing the overall profits of the company. As a result, the hotel is finding

it difficult to obtain further financing for hotel improvements and enhance-
ments for its staff.

Poor practices such as this reduce the ability of tourism infrastructure to
face the emerging hazards in the changing global climate. While tour operators
and other support services can easily exit tourism markets, hotels cannot do so,
because of their huge investments in immovable property. Hence the need for
proper policies that ensure those properties retain their maximum ecological
and tourism value over time. Several hotels in the Seychelles have dedicated
conservation programmes in which they allocate a certain amount of their profits towards habitat restoration and protection on or adjacent to their property.
A number of new hotels also provide examples of good practice, having been
built with good set-back distances from the beach with adoption of proper
beach management plans, better architectural design and landscaping to promote cooler garden spots and living environment for tourists, as well as energy
conservation through better building design.

Modification of coastlines for private hotel services such as marinas and
slipways, including removal of coral rock and discharge of pollution, all contribute to stress on vital coral reef ecosystems. In addition to the biodiversity
and fisheries supported by coral reefs, they also play an effective role in protecting coastlines against extreme events. Protection of the reefs will be
important for preventing coastal erosion in the long term. In the Seychelles, the
effective implementation of environmental impact assessment regulations has
been crucial in redressing some of the past mistakes (Payet, 2003). Stresses on
reef systems from sea-level rise and warmer sea surface temperatures can be
addressed through improved building and landscape design as well as maintenance of green areas and beach vegetation.

Diversify recreational tourism resources

Many of the resources in small island states are undervalued in terms of their
ecotourism services. The recent mass coral bleaching event which threatened to
collapse the diving industry in the Maldives highlighted the fact that many small
island states have too many of their eggs in one basket. Although diversification
can be another challenge in itself, many Caribbean island states have become
financial and banking centres, which provide additional sources of revenue.
Other island states like the Seychelles have diversified their economies into fisheries and offshore services with the aim of reducing dependency on tourism.
However, in many cases, and certainly in the Seychelles, tourism will remain the
mainstay of the economy in the next 25 to 50 years. Consequently, it is important that all tourism activities cause minimum impacts on the environment and
ecotourism activities are as non-intrusive as possible.

Involvement of the local communities in local tourism development and
diversification is a proven method to develop adequate resilience when external shocks in the tourism industry propagate to a small island state. Such
efforts will optimize revenue from recreational activities and also ensure that
all members of local communities benefit. In turn, they can better commit to
the protection of the coastal resources.

Opportunities for diversification in other types of marine ecotourism are available but, as with any ecotourism activities, proper guidelines and policies will need to be agreed on and proper training given. In 2001 the Seychelles Government adopted an ecotourism strategy to improve and diversify tourism experiences as part of a policy of encouraging ecotourism (MTT, 2001). Opportunities such as whale, dolphin, whale shark and turtle watching provide tremendous opportunities for small island states to recover from losses as a result of coral bleaching. Creating artificial reefs, which later can become areas for diving, is still an expensive option for many small island states but worth consideration. On the other hand, making substantial investments in the protection and management of important coral reef areas is critical for future re-growth of the coral reefs (Engelhardt, 2002). The Seychelles are also studying opportunities for developing low-scale eco-lodges on some of the inhabited outer islands in an effort to ensure proper management and conservation of those islands.

Offer unique experiences and refrain from tourism intensification

As discussed earlier, with a gradual warming in the European region, many potential long-haul tourists would be induced to stay in Europe and take local holidays. However, beaches in Europe would be likely to become so crowded that making a long-haul trip to a non-crowded, quiet and unique beach destination would become an increasingly attractive option. This was especially emphasized by tourists interviewed in our survey, who ranked tranquility and cultural experiences as major motivations for visiting the Seychelles. The uncrowded beaches and unspoiled environment of the Seychelles may command an increasing premium in the tourist market, provided that development is properly managed to preserve the attributes that give the Seychelles an advantage.

The survey also indicates that some tourists are insensitive to climatic variables such as rainfall and temperature, as long as the destination promises to offer a unique and thoroughly holistic rejuvenation for the city dweller. The current proliferation of spas and other holistic treatment centres are too focused on infrastructure; nothing beats a spa in a natural environment. While city-based spas are also successful, island destinations can offer such unique experience in a non-aggressive environment and, in many cases, enable the development of community services in terms of providing such goods as herbal extracts and other possibilities.

Capacity building and coordination

The cornerstone of any adaptation strategy is the ability to build resilience across the entire population strata. Capacity building for sustainable management needs to penetrate government agencies, the private sector, non-governmental organizations and civil society. Achievements in the first three adaptation strategies will not be sustainable if these are not driven by sustainability principles, efficiency gains across the various sectors of the economy, improved coordination of activities aimed at restoration of particular degraded habitats and human values.

Implementing the different strategies will require significant financial and technical resources. Implementing sustainable planning and management of the tourism sector is estimated to cost US$600,000 annually. Diversification of tourism resources and offering unique tourist experiences would cost US$300,000 and 500,000 per year respectively, while capacity building costs are estimated at roughly US$1 million per year. The total net present value of costs to implement these strategies over the next 15 years is US$21 million. It is expected that through such comparatively small investments, tourism losses as a result of the two climate variables considered in this study may be greatly minimized. Although it is not possible to avoid all potential losses due to limitation in adaptation, such strategies will yield a net benefit of more than the adaptation investment made.

Because tourism is a very dynamic industry, with fierce competition and high risks, achieving common ground and translating these plans into action is a challenge, and one by which varied political, business and community interests will be affected. The integrated coastal zone management framework provides a good platform for such approaches to be effectively implemented, and many successful coastal zone management plans are now in place in various parts of the world, including many small island states.

References

Agnew, M. (1995) 'Tourism', in J. Palutikof, S. Subak and M. Agnew (eds) *Economic Impacts of the Hot Summer and Unusually Warm Year of 1995*, Department of the Environment, Norwich, UK, pp139–147

Agnew, M. D. (1998) 'Domestic holiday tourism', in *Indicators of Climate Change in the UK: A Pilot Study for the Global Atmosphere Division*, Department of Environment and Transport, ITE, Penicuik, Scotland, pp49–51

Aish, A. and H. Cesar (2002) *Economic Analysis of Coral Bleaching in the Indian Ocean Phase II*, report no 0-02/08, prepared for the World Bank in support of the coral reef degradation in the Indian Ocean (CORDIO) Programme, Institute for Environmental Studies, Amsterdam, The Netherlands

Benson, K. (1996) 'Focus on weather economics', in *Window on the Economy*, Kleinwort Benson Research, London, UK, pp4–22

Cesar, H., P. Van Buekering, R. A. Payet and E. Grandcourt (2004) *Evaluation of the Socio-Economic Impacts of Marine Ecosystem Degradation in the Seychelles*, World Bank/GEF/Government of Seychelles, Seychelles

Christensen, J. H., B. Hewitson, A. Busuioc, A. Chen, X. Gao, I. Held, R. Jones, R. Koli, W. Kwon, R. Laprise, V. Rueda, L. Mearns, C. Menendez, J. Raisanen, A. Rinke, A. Sarr and P. Whetton (2007) 'Regional climate projections', in S. Solomon, D. Qin, M. Manning, Z. Chen, M. C. Marquis, K. Averyt, M. Tignor and H. L. Miller (eds) *Climate Change 2007: The Physical Science Basis*, Contribution of Working Group I to the Fourth Assessment Report of the Intergovernmental Panel on Climate Change, Cambridge University Press, Cambridge, UK and New York, US

Engelhardt, U., M. Russel and B. Wendling (2002) 'Coral communities around the

Seychelles Islands 1998–2002', in O. Linden, D. Souter, D. Wilhelmsson and D. Obura (eds) *Coral Reef Degradation in the Indian Ocean: Status Report 2002*, COR-DIO, Univeristy of Kalmar, Sweden, pp212–231

Gabbay, R. and R. Ghosh (1997) 'Tourism in the Seychelles', Discussion Paper 97.08, Centre for Migration and Development Studies, Department of Economics, University of Western Australia, Perth, Australia

Giles, A. and A. Perry (1998) 'The use of a temporal analogue to investigate the possible impact of projected global warming on the UK tourist industry', *Tourism Management*, vol 19, pp75–80

Hamilton, J. M. (2003) *Climate and the Destination Choice of German Tourists*, Working Paper FNU-15 (revised), Research Unit Sustainability and Global Change, Centre for Marine and Climate Research, University of Hamburg, Hamburg, Germany

Lise, W. and R. Tol (2002) 'Impact of climate on tourist demand', *Climatic Change*, vol 55, pp429–449

Maddison, D. (2001) 'In search of warmer climates? The impact of climate change on flows of British tourists', *Climatic Change*, vol 49, pp193–208

Meehl, G., T. Stocker, W. Collins, P. Friedlingstein, A. Gaye, J. Gregory, A. Kitoh, R. Knutti, J. Murphy, A. Noda, S. Raper, I. Watterson, A. Weaver and Z. Zhao (2007) 'Global climate projections', in S. Solomon, D. Qin, M. Manning, Z. Chen, M. C. Marquis, K. Averyt, M. Tignor and H. L. Miller (eds) *Climate Change 2007: The Physical Science Basis*, Contribution of Working Group I to the Fourth Assessment Report of the Intergovernmental Panel on Climate Change, Cambridge University Press, Cambridge, UK and New York, US

Mimura, N., L. Nurse, R. McLean, J. Agard, L. Briguglio, P. Lefale, R. Payet and G. Sem (2007) 'Small islands', in M. Parry, O. Canziani, J. Palutikof and P. van der Linden (eds) *Climate Change 2007: Impacts, Adaptation and Vulnerability*, Contribution of Working Group II to the Fourth Assessment Report of the Intergovernmental Panel on Climate Change, Cambridge University Press, Cambridge, UK and New York, US

MTT (Ministry of Tourism and Transport) (2001) *Vision 21: Tourism development in Seychelles 2001–2010*, Government of Seychelles, Seychelles

Payet, R. A. (2003) 'Effectiveness of the environment impact assessment process in managing tourism development in Seychelles', in B. Chaytor and K. R. Gray (eds) *International Environmental Law and Policy in Africa*, Environment and Policy Series vol 36, Kluwer Academic Publishers, Amsterdam, The Netherlands, pp327–349

Payet, R. A. and W. Agricole (2006) 'Climate change in the Seychelles: Implications for water and coral reefs', *AMBIO*, vol 35, no 4 pp182–189

Sheppard, C., D. Dixon, M. Gourlay, A. Sheppard and R. Payet (2005) 'Coral mortality increases wave energy reaching shores protected by reef flats: Examples from the Seychelles', *Estuarine, Coastal and Shelf Science*, vol 64, pp223–234

Viner, D. and M. Agnew (1999) *Climate Change and Its Impact on Tourism*, Report Prepared for WWF-UK, Climatic Research Unit, University of East Anglia, Norwich, UK

Westmacott, S., H. Cesar, and L. Pet-Soede (2000) 'Socio-economic assessment of the impacts of the 1998 coral reef bleaching in the Indian Ocean: A summary', in D. Souter, D. Obura, and O. Lindén (eds) *Coral Reef Degradation in the Indian Ocean, status report*, CORDIO, Stockholm, Sweden, pp143–159

Part IV:

Rural Economy
and Food Security

9

Household Food Security and Climate Change: Comparisons from Nigeria, Sudan, South Africa and Mexico

Gina Ziervogel, Anthony Nyong, Balgis Osman-Elasha, Cecilia Conde, Sergio Cortés and Tom Downing

Introduction

Food security, which became a catch phrase in the mid-1990s, can be defined as the success of local livelihoods in guaranteeing access to sufficient food at the household level (Devereaux and Maxwell, 2001). The failure of early solutions to the problem of food insecurity in the 1970s and 1980s was largely attributed to their technological bias, stressing production rather than equitable distribution, access, affordability and utilization. Since then, it has become clear that food security revolves around complex issues that encompass a wide range of interrelated environmental (and climatological), economic, social and political factors. Addressing food security, therefore, requires an integrated approach (as highlighted in Chapter 1 of this volume) that can enable many regions to find adequate and effective solutions to food access and availability issues.

Early models projecting world food demand and supplies into the 21st century generally showed that global food supplies would match or exceed global food demand at least within the next two to three decades (Devereux and Edwards, 2004). One shortcoming of these models, however, is that their scales are very coarse and conceal regional disparities that are a major concern for already food-insecure regions (Stephen and Downing, 2001). Another shortcoming is that the models paid little or no attention to climate variability and change. Climate variability and change are major threats to food security in many regions of the developing world, which are largely dependent on rain-fed and labour-intensive agricultural production (Parry et al, 1999 and 2004; Döös and Shaw, 1999; McCarthy et al, 2001; Gregory et al, 2005).

Although there is research on the impact of climate on food production, there is limited understanding of how climate variability currently impacts food systems and associated livelihoods (Downing, 2002; Ziervogel and Calder, 2003; Gregory et al, 2005). This needs to be better understood before assessing the impact of climate change on food security. Variability is a measure of the frequency distribution of the value of climate variables and their range over a given time period. Temperature and precipitation are the most critical climate variables to measure with regard to food systems. Not only does the range between high and low values matter, but also the frequency at which these extremes occur and the intensity of the events. The focus in this chapter is on the impact of below-normal rainfall and drought on food security. The Third Assessment Report of the Intergovernmental Panel on Climate Change (Watson et al, 2001) projects that areas that are currently dry might experience an average increased dryness with global warming. It is important to note that with a climate that is warmer on average, even if there is no change in the amplitude of El Niño, the risk of droughts and floods that occur with El Niño will increase. In southern Africa, there is evidence that the drought experienced during the second half of the 20th century has been influenced by greenhouse gases, and drying trends are projected to continue (Hoerling et al, 2006). Variability is also expected to increase with more rain falling in intense-rainfall events, larger year-to-year variations in precipitation in areas where increased mean precipitation is projected and increased variability of Asian summer monsoon precipitation (Watson et al, 2001). Although the issue of food security is directly linked to climate variability and change (Winters et al, 1999; Reilly, 1995), it must be noted that climate is not the single determinant of yield, nor is the physical environment the only decisive factor in shaping food security (Parry et al, 2004).

Despite understanding the multidimensional nature of food insecurity, it remains a key concern affecting the livelihoods of marginal groups. Therefore, understanding the impacts of climate variability, as well as the possible changes in this variability on food security, is critical to making improvements in food security. Food insecurity at the household level often results in resources being diverted. For example, resources that might have been used to support the development of livelihoods (for example, education, healthcare and employment) get reallocated to ensure that basic food needs are met. The acquisition of food for marginal groups often entails a delicate balance of producing food for the household under stressed conditions at the same time as drawing on social and economic resources to access available food. When conditions in the environment vary (for example, climate, soil and water characteristics and land-use changes), this can place an additional stress on food production (McConnell and Moran, 2000).

There are many levels at which a food system can be examined (Stephen and Downing, 2001). Food policy, trade and resource use are governed by decisions at national, regional and global levels. Global climate is part of a global system but influenced by the actions of individual large countries such as the US, China and India. The boundaries between these systems are not clear. And this is true for the impact of these global, regional and national systems on the local level of food systems. Yet it is at the local, individual and household levels that food is used, and it is people who must ensure their access to food; otherwise, they can become food insecure. Although individual access depends on factors at numerous scales, the first level of analysis that determines the nature of food insecurity is the local level of household livelihoods.

In this chapter, we examine household food security from a livelihood perspective for a number of regions around the world where food insecurity is a stress to rural livelihoods. We draw on case studies from semi-arid regions in Nigeria, Sudan, South Africa and Mexico,[1] and tease out the commonalities and differences from the case studies to learn some lessons about climate variability and food security on a livelihood scale. Although vulnerability to climate change, including vulnerability to food insecurity, is highly differentiated across continents, countries and livelihood systems, it is important to explore common strands across regions regarding food security and its determinants.

Although each of the regions selected for this study is a drought-prone region, they are not all equally vulnerable to drought. Some, through various policies and adaptation strategies, have reduced their food insecurity resulting from droughts. Sharing their experiences could help other vulnerable regions deal with their food insecurity. Furthermore, in a globalizing world economy, regional integration is commonly being adopted to solve environmental problems. Identifying regional drought-related food insecurities could also lead to devising regional solutions to tackle such problems.

The four case studies use different research approaches, yet all of the projects focus on food security, climate variability and climate change. Data for the studies were collected from households using ethnographic and interview research techniques. The household was adopted as the unit of analysis, as the household level tends to be where decisions about household production, investment and consumption are made in most agrarian societies, particularly under long-lasting drought conditions. Questions that this paper seeks to answer include:

- What factors determine a household's vulnerability to food insecurity?
- What are the differences and commonalities with respect to these factors across the study regions? and
- What are the implications of these in addressing climate policy as related to food insecurity at regional or country-wide scales?

Climate Variability and Change and Food Security

Food security depends on availability of food, access to food and utilization of food (FAO, 2000). Food availability refers to the existence of food stocks for consumption. Household food access is the ability to acquire sufficient quality and quantities of food to meet all household members' nutritional requirements. Access to food is determined by physical and financial resources, as well as by social and political factors. Utilization of food depends on how food is used, on whether food has sufficient nutrients and on whether a balanced diet can be maintained. It is these three facets of the food system that all need to be met in order for food security to be realized. Each of these facets can be impacted by climate variability (Gregory et al, 2005); these impacts are discussed below.

Impact of climate variability and change on food availability

The consensus of scientific opinion is that countries in the temperate, high-latitude and mid-latitude regions are generally likely to enjoy increased agricultural production, whereas countries in tropical and subtropical regions are likely to suffer agricultural losses as a result of climate change in coming decades (Arnell et al, 2002; Devereux and Edwards, 2004). It should be noted that the favourable assessment for temperate and high-latitude regions is based primarily on analyses of changes in mean temperature and rainfall; relatively little analysis done to date takes account of changes in variability and extremes. Impact of climate variability on crop production should be a priority given that analyses of agricultural vulnerability indicate that the key attributes of climate change are those related to climatic variability, including the frequency of non-normal conditions (Bryant et al, 2000; Smit et al, 2000).

Climate variability directly affects agricultural production, as agriculture is inherently sensitive to climate conditions and is one of the most vulnerable sectors to the risks and impacts of global climate change (Parry et al, 1999). Climate change could impact on growing season and plant productivity (Gregory et al, 2005). Many factors impact the type of policies implemented at a national level (such as domestic politics, redistribution of land/wealth, exchange rates and trade issues). Climate variability should be factored into these policies, as these policies can impact the availability of staple foods, for example, by providing incentives to grow crops appropriate for the climate conditions.

In the case study sites, the two major forms of agricultural production are arable farming and pastoralism. Because of the limited amount and uneven distribution of rainfall over both time and geographic scope at the study sites, rainfall represents the most limiting factor for agricultural and livestock production. Its consequences are well known to local populations: the drying out of water sources, scarcity of grazing land, shortage of dairy products, loss of wild plants for gathering, migration of grazers, bad harvests and livestock losses, among others. For instance, it has been estimated by the World Bank that around 10 per cent of the population of Sub-Saharan Africa is primarily dependent on their animals, while another 58 per cent depend to varying degrees on their livestock. Increasing population pressures, interacting with declining rainfall and reduced pasture, have already begun to impact the livestock sector negatively. Rangeland condition is directly affected by the climate (as highlighted in the section on desertification in Chapter 1 of this volume) and, in turn, directly affects the quality and quantity of small and large livestock and associated livelihood activities.

Impact of climate variability and change on food access

Individuals have sufficient access to food when they have 'adequate incomes or other resources to purchase or barter to obtain levels of appropriate foods needed to maintain consumption of an adequate diet/nutrition level' (USAID, 1992). Food access depends on the ability of households to obtain food from purchases, gathering, current production or stocks, or through food transfers from relatives, other members of the community, the government or donors. Intra-household distribution of these resources is an important determinant of food security for all household members. Food access is also influenced by the aggregate availability of food in the market, market prices, productive inputs and credit (USAID, 1992). Poor market infrastructure and an unfavourable policy environment may lead to high and variable prices for food and inputs, further undermining agricultural productivity, food supplies and derived incomes.

Access depends on both physical factors and social and economic factors. After food is produced, it needs to be moved from the point of production to the point of consumption. This often depends on transport systems. In many developing countries, inefficient and ineffective transport systems retard delivery and increase the price of food. Climate change is expected to place a strain on transport systems (McCarthy et al, 2001). For example, increased heat stress may reduce the life of roads, and windstorms can impact transit at air and sea terminals as well as damaging infrastructure which may create delays (Perry and Symons, 1994). During droughts, people are known to move into marginal lands. Most of these marginal lands may not have good road access, and transporting food from such marginal farms poses a huge challenge.

Impact of climate variability on food utilization

Adequate food utilization is realized when 'food is properly used, proper food processing and storage techniques are employed, adequate knowledge of nutrition and child care techniques exists and is applied, and adequate health and sanitation services exist' (USAID, 1992). Food utility involves how food is used. This can include how often meals are eaten and of what they consist. Constraints on food utilization include loss of nutrients during food processing, inadequate sanitation, improper care and storage, and cultural practices that negatively impact consumption of nutritious foods for certain family members.

In many areas where food is produced and consumed locally, food utility changes with seasonal variation and food availability changes throughout the year. The hungry season is the time before the planted crops are ready to be eaten. Similarly, at harvest time, there might be festivals and a lot of food consumed. If there has been a drought and food availability is low, the range of food available often decreases, and so the meal frequency can decrease and the balance of nutrients can be inadequate. This can lead to malnutrition in children. It is also important to note that climate can have an impact on food utility indirectly. For example, if there are hot dry days, crops and vegetables may be dried so that they can be used later in the year. At the same time as seasonal crop production, many households face fluctuations in cash and in-kind income, both within a single year and from year to year. Agricultural households may face seasonal fluctuations in income related to crop cycles. Year-to-year fluctuations in income can result from varying agroclimatic conditions and climate variability.

Household food security and livelihoods

Livelihoods can be considered as the combined activities and available social and physical assets that contribute to the household's existence (Carney, 1998). Each individual has his or her own means of securing a livelihood, and the individuals together make up the household's packages of livelihood assets and strategies. These strategies are pursued within a larger context that often determines whether these strategies will succeed or fail.

The livelihoods approach is useful for understanding food insecurity as it emphasizes the importance of looking at an individual's capacity for managing risks, as well as the external threats to livelihood security, such as drought (Chambers, 1989; Scoones, 1998; Carney, 1998; Moser, 1998). It enables the agency of individuals to be captured in their decision-making process (Ziervogel, 2004). For example, if one household has a member who works in the city and remits money and the household has a productive field, access to food sources may be spread through own production and food purchasing. If there is a drought and crops fail, the household may still have access to food if money continues to be remitted. If a household absorbs more children through the death of family members, then utilization of the existing food sources may be stressed and the number of meals reduced. This may result in a family being forced to remove children from school so that they can work to try and increase access to food that will result in improved utilization. A government grant may ameliorate this impact. It is clear that food insecurity depends on the agency of individuals and the components of household livelihoods that are interlinked with the three facets of food security, as explained above.

Livelihoods of households can be compared if similar characteristics and activities in household livelihoods are grouped together to cluster livelihood typologies. Examples of typologies might include small-scale farming livelihoods or informal trade-based livelihoods. These help focus on an intermediate system level that draws from the local but has a unit of analysis which is greater. Recognizing livelihood typologies is a useful construct for comparing livelihood systems between regions (Dixon et al, 2001). A number of livelihood typologies can coexist and can vary in their geographical extent. In some instances, a livelihood typology may draw on certain environmental resources, such as coastal resources for fishing; in other instances, they may cross national boundaries, such as livestock-based livelihoods. The predominant livelihood typology for each case study is expanded in detail in the following case studies section.

Case Studies

Case studies examining food security in Nigeria, Sudan, South Africa and Mexico are compared to identify commonalities and differences in how local food systems are impacted by global environmental change.[1]

Case Study 1: Mangondi village, Limpopo Province, South Africa

Mangondi village is situated within the Vhembe district, Limpopo Province, in the northeast region of South Africa. Many of the previously disadvantaged farmers in the area have begun increasing the size of their production to try and enter into the fruit and vegetables market. Although there has been an increase in productivity among some previously disadvantaged farmers, there are still many constraints that are faced, and many of the poorer households remain food-insecure and do not have access to production or employment opportunities.

A key constraint on farming in this area is high climate variability, as numerous droughts and floods have occurred in recent decades (for example, the 2000 floods or the 2002/2003 drought). Managing this climate variability as well as possible is of paramount importance when many other stressors (such as land access, political instability, market fluctuations, globalization and HIV/AIDS) enter into the equation (Ziervogel and Calder, 2003). Marketing is also a key concern. Although former subsistence farmers have started growing products for sale, particularly when they have access to irrigation, it is challenging to find markets that will buy products consistently, due to variable demand, prices and quality of produce. It is also hard for the producers to ensure quality and quantity of supply, as credit is limited and input and environmental conditions vary (Ziervogel et al, 2006).

A communal farming project was initiated in Mangondi village in 1993 that aimed to support women in the production of vegetables to combat malnutrition among children (Archer, 2003). In the first year, subsistence crops were planted; in later years, vegetables were planted with the intention of selling them. Through the years, the success of the project has fluctuated. In some years, the farmers have had a functional irrigation scheme and money for inputs and have made profits. In other years, the irrigation pump has failed, people have not planted, and harvest and marketing has been poor.

Research in this village has been undertaken since 1999 to examine the role of seasonal forecasts and agricultural support among smallholder farmers. Surveys, participatory approaches and computer-based knowledge elicitation tools have been used to determine the types of adaptive strategies followed under certain conditions and why, with a focus on the role of climate, market and livelihood needs (Bharwani et al, 2005). This is supported by the knowledge of household livelihood profiles, local responses to climate, availability of forecast information over time and access to information sources such as market demand and technical knowledge (Ziervogel et al, 2006).

Food security

This research has focused on participants involved in the communal garden scheme. The available data, therefore, do not represent the entire village. However, extensive work has been done in the area that enables a picture of food security to be painted. The members involved in the scheme have identified an increase in food security since the project started. Participants have stated that they now have vegetables to eat, which they did not have before there was an irrigation project, and that, as a result, health has improved and vegetables can be sold and the money used to send children to school. When there are surplus vegetables, they dry them so they can be used in months when vegetables are not readily available. The availability of vegetables has also impacted on the quality of livelihoods, as participants now spend less time travelling to nearby markets to obtain them.

The disadvantage has been that the irrigation project relies on a pump that is often broken, primarily because it is too small for the garden area (Archer 2003). This has meant that time and resources have been invested in the garden area, and when the pump is broken these resources are wasted. It is also uncertain when the pump will be fixed, which makes it hard to plan and hard to market crops. The limitations of the pump can therefore make people more vulnerable when they are expecting and investing in a harvest that does not materialize.

The food security of members not involved in the project depends on individual situations. The land is relatively fertile and there are numerous fruit trees. Many households have some livestock (such as cattle or chickens). The field crops can provide food when rains are good, but it is not uncommon for whole crops to fail when the rain is insufficient and irregular. Farmers who produce surplus are able to sell some of their vegetables, but marketing is a key constraint, and there are not large consistent markets. There are many households in the area in which members are sick, and households struggling to survive as they do not have access to labour for production or access to alternative employment. In South Africa, there is a grant system that supports many households and enables them to buy food. Grants are available in the form of pensions, child grants (for each child up to eight years old if household income is below a certain amount) and disability grants. Disability grants are available for the physically disabled, which includes people who are unable to work because of AIDS. The increased occurrence of HIV/AIDS has an impact on food security, as increased amounts of food and appropriate nutrition are needed, while labour decreases and resources are spent on health rather than agricultural production.

Case Study 2: Gireigikh Rural Council of Bara Province, North Kordofan State, Sudan

The Gireigikh area lies in North Kordofan State in drought-prone western Sudan, typified by the semi-arid and desert scrub of the African Sahel region. The area is characterized by harsh climatic conditions and erratic seasonal rainfall. The predominant socioeconomic grouping consists of a mix of agro-pastoralists and transhumants, who are extremely vulnerable to drought. The key ongoing pressures are the degraded rangelands and strong sand dust storms in the region. The current vulnerabilities result from changes in climate variability, particularly aggravated by the long-term and intense droughts. Hoelzmann et al (1998) found that much of what is desert in Africa today used to be covered in steppe vegetation, and that many small lakes and streams existed above a latitude of 23°N, where they currently do not exist. This desertification is combined with problems of soil erosion and failing livestock and crop production. These factors directly affect the food security situation, which leads to loss of rural livelihoods and displacement of the rural people.

Food security

The Community-Based Rangeland Rehabilitation Project was implemented in Bara Province of North Kordofan State, a semi-arid land that receives a long-term average rainfall of 275mm annually (Dougherty et al, 2001). This amount used to be sufficient to maintain people's livelihood and establish their staple food crops, which are mainly millet and sorghum, in addition to raising animals. However, the area was affected by drought episodes three times between 1976 and 1992, with the most severe drought occurring in 1984. The drought of 1980–1984 highlighted the basic problems that have been ignored for too long: family and tribal structures and their autonomous traditional practices of resource management and land tenure had broken down (Dougherty et al, 2001). Two tribes inhabit the study area: the *Gawama'a* and the *Kawahla*. The *Kawahla* are a nomadic tribe that settled in Gireigikh after they lost their herds due to a drought that hit their previous areas of settlement in Eastern Kordofan during the period 1967–1973. The *Gawama'a* were originally farmers and herders of cattle, sheep, camels and goats. After continuous drought cycles hit the area, the *Gawama'a* lost all their cattle and most of their sheep, camels and goats and were forced to shift from keeping livestock to farming crops.

In the semi-arid Gireigikh area the majority of the interviewed farmers indicated that production declined and vast tracts of land became completely barren with no trees and all the below-canopy herbaceous species removed. The amount that was produced was not enough to sustain their food requirement for the whole year, and they often ended up with severe food shortages. To make up for the meagre income made from this kind of agricultural practice, young men had to travel, leaving the women behind, to seek jobs in nearby towns or in the capital city of Khartoum.

With the droughts, water quantity became a limiting factor for the people to practise any alternative livelihood activities, for example, growing vegetables or fruits or raising poultry. Women were known to walk long distances to fetch meagre quantities of water from a hand-dug well, which was both time and health consuming. To address these problems, a project titled 'Community-Based Rangeland Rehabilitation for Carbon Sequestration and Biodiversity Conservation in North Kordofan State' was initiated by the United Nations Development Programme (UNDP) Global Environment Facility (GEF) during the period 1994–2000. The project objectives were 1) to sequester carbon through the implementation of a sustainable, local-level natural resources management system that prevents degradation of, rehabilitates or improves rangelands, and 2) to reduce the risks of production failure in the drought-prone area by providing alternatives for sustainable production, increasing the number of livelihood alternatives so that out-migration would decrease and population would stabilize.

The reported outcomes from the Bara case study (Osman-Elasha, 2006) include:

- the establishment of local institutions, such as the village community development committees, to coordinate community natural resource management and community development activities;
- the development of land-use master plans to guide future resource use and implementation of sustainable rotational grazing systems and establishment of community mobilization teams to conduct outreach and training;
- the reforestation and stabilization of 5km of sand dunes to halt desert encroachment and soil erosion;
- the restocking of livestock by replacing goat herds with more resilient and less resource-damaging sheep;
- the creation of a water management subcommittee to better manage wells;
- the establishment of 17 women's gardens to produce vegetables for household consumption, with surplus sold at local markets;
- the establishment of five pastoral women's groups to support supplemental income-generating activities (including sheep fattening, handcrafts, milk marketing); and
- the planting of 195km shelterbelts around 130 farms to act as windbreaks, to improve soil moisture and to increase fertility (Dougherty et al, 2001).

Figure 9.1 shows the profound change from the poor financial conditions that used to prevail before the project to the much improved situation after the intervention (up to 80 per cent level of financial sustainability was observed as compared to the less than 10 per cent level of financial sustainability before). Information on indicators such as effectiveness of credit repayment revealed that the money from the revolving fund was primarily used for buying animals for fattening and marketing them in large state markets, hence fetching higher prices. Moreover, it offers necessary funds for the Natural Resources Committee to support other activities such as seed distribution for women's irrigated gardens and the purchase of improved stoves. This has led to the conclusion that the improvement of financial capital could contribute to the improvement of other livelihood capitals, such as natural, human and physical. Moreover, the presence of reliable local-level institutional structures (for example, the Sudanese Environment Conservation Society (SECS) Bara Branch, along with the Community Credit Committees and Coordination Committee) has provided a guarantee to the local community that has enabled their access to credits.

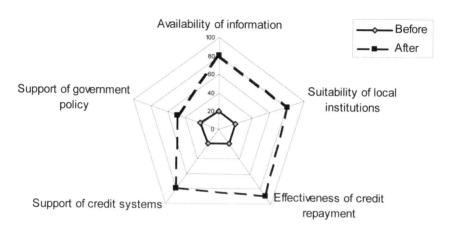

Figure 9.1 *Assessment of sustainability of financial capital before and after intervention of the Rangeland Rehabilitation Project, based on availability of information, effectiveness of credit repayment, suitability of local institutions, and support of credit systems and government policy to income-generating activities*

Case Study 3: Chingowa village, Magumeri Local Government Area, Borno State, Nigeria

Chingowa village is located in the Magumeri Local Government Area of Borno State in the Sahel zone of northeastern Nigeria. It has a mean annual rainfall of 600mm, which falls in the four months of the rainy season, which lasts between June and September. Agriculture, which is rain-fed, is primarily supported during the short rainy season, except around the oasis, which supports perennial vegetable farming. The vegetation consists mainly of shrub grassland, which is favourable for extensive grazing.

Drought has been a recurrent feature in the Sahel, with records of drought dating back to the 1680s. The magnitude and intensity of these droughts have been on the increase over the last 100 years, however, and consequently so has the resulting destruction (Hulme et al, 2001). The lack of water, in association with high temperatures (up to 45°C at certain periods of the year), is the most limiting factor for agricultural productivity in the village. The main crops cultivated in the village include maize, millet, sorghum and beans. Farmers are predominantly smallholders using traditional farming systems, which mix food crops and cash crops on the same farming unit. Because crop farming is largely rain-fed in the village, the increase in the magnitude and intensity of droughts will result in a shift from the production of certain traditional crops, with all the possible negative consequences that this may bring to the local people. The rearing of livestock is a very important aspect of life in the village, as it represents livelihood, income and employment. Recurrent droughts have forced some pastoralists to dispose of their cattle and lose their livelihood systems, which ultimately increases their vulnerability. The southward movement of the isohyets has also resulted in the southward migration of pastoralists into lands formerly occupied by sedentary farmers. This has been a major source of conflict in the village, leading to widespread destruction of farmlands and cattle, with adverse implications for food security.

The methodology used for this case study included data collection through the administration of questionnaires, focused group discussions, stakeholder analyses and field sampling. The case study looks at vulnerability to food insecurity in Chingowa village in Borno State of Nigeria, where questionnaires were administered to 30 farm households in the village. The research shows that one of the main concerns among the respondents is the fear of famine, which highlights the problem of food insecurity.

Food security

In assessing food insecurity in the village, various factors that predispose households to being vulnerable were examined. These factors include agricultural productivity and production, labour availability and land tenure, food storage and processing, transportation and distribution, population factors, income and conflicts.

The size of the landholding that a household cultivates directly affects their production and hence food security. Population growth has led to a high level of fragmentation of land in the village. Hence, acquiring a relatively large tract or tracts of land for farming is a difficult task. A majority of the farmers in the village (61.2 per cent) are smallholders who cultivate less than 5 hectares of land. Only about 19 per cent of the respondents used irrigation, with just less than a third of them irrigating more than half of their total farm lands.

The existing tenurial arrangements in the village also affect agricultural production in the village and pose a constraint on sustainable food security. There are sociocultural factors that prevent women from having title to land in many parts of the country, including Chingowa village. In Chingowa, ownership of farmland is predominantly acquired through paternal inheritance, which, to a large extent, excludes the women. However, some respondents cultivate lands that are communally owned, purchased outright, rented or borrowed.

Other factors that affect agricultural productivity in the village include the unavailability of inputs, particularly fertilizer and improved seeds, and poor transportation infrastructure, which has adversely affected market access. Chingowa village is situated about 1.5km from a good road and 6km from a daily market.

With low agricultural productivity in the village, the population has had to continue to rely on other sources of income in order to meet household demand for food and other needs. In addition to arable farming, pastoralism is a major economic activity in the village. The most common domesticated animals in the village are cattle, poultry, goats and sheep.

Labour is a critical input in the traditional, subsistence farming system practised in the village. The farmers plant very small areas at a time, using crude implements and labour-intensive practices. As a result, the demand for labour is generally very high at the time of planting, weeding and harvesting.

Two main factors that affect the availability of labour in the household are rural–urban migration and the quality of the household, conceptualized as the ratio of healthy working members of the household over the sick members, as captured in the dependency ratio. With the spread of killer diseases such as malaria, HIV/AIDS and cerebrospinal meningitis, the quality of available household labour is seriously compromised.

The problem of inadequate storage facilities has compounded the problem of food security in the village. It is estimated that about 15–20 per cent of cereals and up to 40 per cent of perishable crops produced are lost before they can be consumed. This situation is made worse by the dearth of any agro-processing industry close to the village. It also has a discouraging effect on the farmers as the struggle to sell most of their crops immediately after harvest results in very unprofitable competition and lower prices.

The village has witnessed several communal crises, largely between the pastoralists and the sedentary farmers. These conflicts have largely arisen through the struggle for resources, which has been exacerbated by the frequent droughts and the downward shifts of the isohyets, and are a major constraint to food security in the village. The crises usually occur during the planting, weeding or harvesting periods, and with the flight of farmers from the area, irrespective of the stage of farming, food security is threatened as most, if not all, the crops are lost. The pastoralists also suffer significant losses of livestock.

Case Study 4: Rain-fed maize production in Tlaxcala, Mexico

Rain-fed maize production is the most important agricultural activity for the majority of subsistence farmers in Mexico. The maize is traditionally cultivated on a surface called *milpa*, which includes other cultivars (such as beans and chillies) and plants used for medical and food preparation purposes. This activity is strongly affected by climate variability, particularly drought events, which have forced farmers to apply different coping strategies (Florescano, 1995). In Mexican history, hunger and famine have been common and are related to severe drought events, in which great losses in maize production have affected both rural and urban populations. The impacts of these events have been exacerbated during the most important civil wars in the country (the War of Independence and the Mexican Revolution).

Nowadays, farmers who rely on rain-fed crops apply different strategies to cope with drought, including switching to more pest-resistant maize varieties, changing cultivars, seeking temporary jobs in urban areas, renting their fields, or even emigrating to the capital city of the state, cities in other states or the US.

In 2004, 10.23 million Mexican migrants lived in the US, a population that has grown at an annual rate of 4.2 per cent since 1994 (CONAPO, 2004). In the same year, 16,613 million US dollars were sent by migrants to Mexico (Banco de Mexico, 2004). This flux of income has represented a basic support to preserve or enhance the levels of nutrition, health and education of the rural population, particularly for rural villages with less than 2500 inhabitants (Lozano, 2005).

This situation was mainly forced by the aggressive changes in governmental policies related to the economic liberalization of agriculture, particularly since the North American Free Trade Agreement (NAFTA) came into effect in 1994 (Nadal, 2000).

In the last decade, basic grain imports have increased by almost 40 per cent and maize imports have doubled, even though in NAFTA it was established that the total liberation of maize (and beans) imports will occur by 2008 (Bartra 2003). In general, the structural reforms in the agricultural sector have implied the removal of subsidies for seeds, agrochemicals, energy and water, the reduction of credits, and the elimination of the governmental control of prices. All of these measures have caused an increase in production costs and a reduction of profits for maize producers.

The case of maize production in Tlaxcala, Mexico, illustrates how climate impacts on food security. The study builds on climate change and climate variability studies that have been carried out in this state since 1997 (Ferrer, 1999; Conde and Eakin, 2003). The state of Tlaxcala is located in the centre of the country, in the Mexican high plateau. It is the smallest state in the country, and 98 per cent of agriculture is developed under rain-fed conditions (INEGI, 1996) There is only one harvest a year (Trautmann 1991), and maize is the most important crop (71 per cent of the total planted area).

During spring, farmers in Tlaxcala wait for the onset of the rainy season by April; should there be a delay in this, they start considering changing varieties of maize or even changing to another crop. This situation could be clearly observed during the strong 1997–1998 El Niño event, when oats (for fodder) were planted. Oats are locally known as the 'hopeless crop' and were planted as a desperate measure just to prevent cattle losses, with the expectation of maize planting being abandoned (Aviles, 2005). When normal climatic conditions returned, farmers reverted to planting maize (Conde and Eakin, 2003), because alternative crops are planted only during extreme climatic events, and not as a rule to adapt to adverse market conditions.

Since maize prices have significantly decreased, the cost of fertilizers and other inputs has increased, and there is a lack of labour force in terms of younger farmers, a drought event can severely affect the capacity of the farming community to cope with its impacts. Furthermore, agricultural policies and supports are more centred towards the production of fruits and vegetables for export, not taking into account the high consumption of water of those products in a context of climate variability and change, associated with past and future droughts in the country.

Other environmental factors raise the risk of increasing losses in maize production. Tlaxcala is the state with the worst soil erosion conditions in the country (SEMARNAT, 1996). Even when farmers are aware of soil conservation techniques (Conde and Eakin, 2003), they cannot practise them, because those require strong collective work, and families are being reduced in number because of migration or changed labour, so they are forced to develop maize monoculture production in extended areas, which reduces soil productivity and increases the soil erosion processes. Furthermore, the reduction of crop diversity (Altieri and Trujillo, 1987) increases climatic risks and reduces the farmers' nutritional opportunities.

Food security

The agricultural policies developed over the last 20 years in Mexico related to food security have shifted from a view of self-sufficiency agricultural production to a policy that seeks to secure access to food resources, following the globalization of economic processes. Government support for the rural population now focuses on programmes that deliver economic help for those needing to acquire basic goods (for example, tortillas or milk) at reduced prices, not on a policy to sustain the traditional maize production (*milpas*). The current government has declared that subsistence farmers have five years to be 'efficient and competitive' in the international markets, or to 'look for another activity' (Bartra, 2003). Besides the impacts of changes in Government policy, the NAFTA provisions have also established that until 2008 the Mexican market will be totally open to corn importations. Maize and tortilla prices have therefore been adjusted to the requirements of international markets, which has resulted in a decrease in national maize prices and an increase in tortilla prices.

Before 1998, tortilla prices were subsidized by the government in a policy that focused on guaranteeing food security for the increasing urban population (Appendini, 2001). The costs of production were mainly transferred to consumers, but the benefits of the increase in prices of tortilla did not reach the maize producers. The massive imports of corn from the US at lower prices than maize produced in the country (Bartra, 2003) reduced the possible profits for Mexican maize producers. Traditional production of tortillas has also been mostly abandoned, and the corn flour production has been controlled since the 1990s by huge companies such as Grupo Maseca (Rosas-Peña, 2005). These companies are free to import forage corn from the US and use it for processing tortillas for Mexico City, for example.

Food insecurity for maize farmers in Mexico, particularly in Tlaxcala, is therefore increasing, due to the described policies and other factors such as the decrease in human resources (migration and farmers' aging) and in environmental resources. The financial support given by the governmental programmes to maize farmers that have suffered the impacts of climatological contingencies, which are delivered late and in reduced amounts (Cortés, 2004), does not solve the decreasing productivity and the lack of a market for their products.

These governmental and macroeconomic policies and trends tend to reduce farmers' ability to manage with adverse climatic events. In this context, new threats, such as transgenic maize or climate change, will be difficult to cope with. However, farmers with rain-fed land continue to plant maize as a means to subsist, making total corn production in the country more or less stable, but increasing planting areas and impacting soil and forest ecosystems.

Several authors have considered that a national food security policy should be linked to environmental sustainability and social equity (Appendini, 2001), particularly related to the social right of rural communities to work (Bartra, 2003) and of consumers to chose the quality of the tortillas they eat.

Analysis and Discussion

These four case studies both exhibit a number of similar trends and demonstrate distinct differences. In the South African case study, it is evident that there is a clear tension between natural environmental stress of precipitation variability and the social system that determines the welfare options and employment options available. If access to money through employment or grants is available, then food can be acquired through exchange, but those depending on household production are directly exposed to climatic variability, as well as market fluctuations. It is important to recognize that those households relying on grants or income might still be impacted through secondary-order sensitivities, where jobs may decline due to climate variability, for example, decreased employment on commercial farms when harvests have failed. Research has shown that the poorer households tend to respond to climate variability in multiple, low-input strategies, whereas the better-off households focus on a few strategies, often with higher risk (Bharwani et al, 2005). Fieldwork has supported the idea that food security interventions need to be sensitive to user characteristics and strategies at the same time as supporting institutional developments that enable vulnerable households to cope with loss of livelihood options through a range of stresses, including climate variability, unemployment or ill health.

Although drought is often regarded as the major cause of food insecurity in semi-arid northern Nigeria, the study found that household factors contributed more to food insecurity than climate factors. These household factors include the size of landholding available to the household for cultivation and the labour available in the household to cultivate the land. The farmers are largely subsistence farmers using crude farming implements with little farm inputs such as fertilizers, irrigation, insecticides, pesticides or improved crop varieties. Where crop production is largely dependent on the size of a household's landholding, a common strategy for increasing production is through land intensification. This usually results in the cultivation of marginal lands that have hitherto been occupied by pastoralists. This encroachment often results in conflicts and destruction of cattle and crops, further reinforcing food insecurity in the region. Belonging to a community organization was another major factor in food security in the region. There is no organized welfare system in Nigeria, and these local community organizations provide safety nets to their members in times of crisis. The study estimated that about 15–20 per cent of cereals and up to 40 per cent of perishable crops produced are lost before they can be consumed. Food storage was thus an important issue in food security. Minimizing this level of waste would make more food available for consumption.

Food insecurity in northern Nigeria is also a 'food access problem'. This could be linked to poor governance, whereby infrastructure such as roads are concentrated in the urban centres with very little being provided in the rural areas. This makes it difficult for farmers to transport their goods from the farms to the markets. Besides the general lack of roads and transportation services, the high cost of fuel adds to the cost of transportation, which makes the final prices of the goods very expensive and beyond the reach of the majority of the rural poor. It could also be linked to poverty and the inability of poor people to access food and other resources. Over the longer term, poverty contributes further to food insecurity as it restrains households' potential for accumulation and growth. In view of this, it is important that government seeks to provide physical infrastructure in the rural areas, as well as provide seasonal input credit and long-term financing of farm investments. In Sudan and Mexico, it was also clear that climate variability alone does not determine vulnerability to climate change. Rather, it is the livelihood characteristics overlain with social and economic environments and climate variability that determine the vulnerability of households to food insecurity and climate change.

In order to assess the similarities across the cases more systematically, the key vulnerabilities in each case study have been compared by assessing the role of determinants in five groups: climate, environment, food economy, household factors, and social and human environment. The determinants were scored on a scale ranging from 0 to 2 (where 0 indicates that the factor does not appear to be a key determinant of vulnerability, 1 suggests it is an important determinant and 2 that it is very important). These scores were derived from the expert judgement of the authors, based on their interpretation of stakeholder perspectives. This method has its limitations, as it does not incorporate stakeholder feedback, but it provides an initial analysis of where similarities and differences between the cases lie. It is important to note that this comparison is based on the four case study sites – Mangondi village in South Africa, Gireigikh Rural Council in Sudan, Chingowa village in Nigeria and Tlaxcala in Mexico – rather than on the countries as a whole.

Table 9.1 *Summary of the importance of determinants*

Ranked as very important by 3 or more case studies	Ranked as very important by 2 case studies	Ranked as a combination of very important and important by all case studies	Ranked as important by all case studies
Trends in precipitation	Recent drought	2-year/seasonal drought	Ability to subsist
Input price	Area cultivated	3–5 year ENSO	Household size
Income diversification	Labour available per hectare	5–10 year drought	Health
Income	Off-farm employment	Land degradation	Poor training and education
Local community institutions	Poor health services		Poor nutrition and human health
Disintegration of social fabric			

Note: Very important = score of 2; and Important = score of 1

A summary of the key determinants is presented in Table 9.1. It is clear from the comparison that there are many common factors that influence household food security. The most important determinants of household vulnerability to food insecurity across all four case studies are trends in precipitation, input price, household income, income diversification, belonging to local community institutions and disintegration of social fabric. The next most important determinants include the occurrence of recent droughts, the size of landholding cultivated, the labour per hectare of farm land, poor health services and participation in off-farm employment. It is clear that there is a mix of physical, social and economic factors that determine vulnerability to food insecurity in all of the case studies.

Given that the common vulnerabilities have been established, an objective way of comparing the strengths of the determinants across the various study sites is needed. The key determinants for five categories (climate, environmental, food economy, household factors, and social and human environment), as mentioned above, were ranked as to their role in determining vulnerability in each case study. The mean score for each group of determinants is plotted on a radar graph for each case study (Figure 9.2). This illustrates that climate factors played a similar role in determining vulnerability to food insecurity in Mangondi village, Gireigikh Rural Council and Chingowa village. Climate did not appear to be a major factor in Tlaxcala. Generally, household factors played a more dominant role among all four countries and appeared to have the largest influence on vulnerability to food insecurity. This is a significant finding that should be explored further.

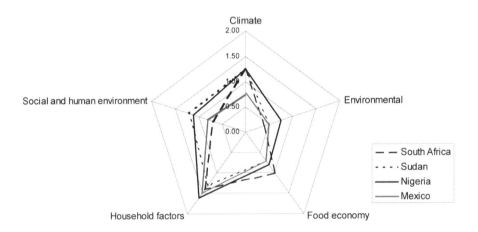

Figure 9.2 *Determinants of vulnerability to food insecurity in study villages*

Another way to compare the relative importance of the factors affecting food security is to place each factor in a conceptual framework. For the purposes of this synthesis, we chose a straightforward set of factors that link the underlying use of resources, exposure to drought and the consequences of food shortage

(Figure 9.3). The focus on drought is justified, as this is the major climatic factor affecting food security in these four case study areas. Of course, drought alone is not a sufficient cause of food insecurity, and the framework attempts to place drought in context.

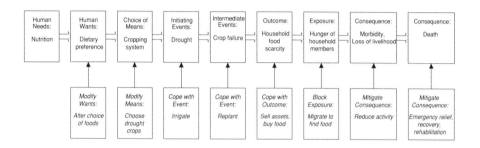

Figure 9.3 *Causal chain of drought risk*

The upstream context begins with the identification of human needs (nutrition) and wants (the choice of diet to fulfil nutritional needs), along with the choice of cropping systems (or food procurement systems, more generally) to fulfil the dietary preferences. The hazard-sensitivity elements include the initiating events (drought, or a combination of drought and other factors) and the first-order impacts (such as crop failure), leading to initial outcomes, including household food scarcity. Differential vulnerability is apparent in the range of exposures to the first-order impacts and sensitivity to the consequences (from increased disease burden to death, plus environmental, social, economic and political consequences). At each stage, a range of actions can intervene to disrupt the causal chain (in other words to prevent further impacts and consequences) or to shift the chain of events to other pathways (for instance, to shift household food scarcity to regional markets, leading to increased food prices and imports to the region).

This framework is used to map the determinants from the case studies against the causal chain as shown in Table 9.2. The most striking similarity, based on the interpretations of the expert teams, is in the initiating events – the importance of trends in decreasing precipitation, generally accompanied by drought. Health status and health services are seen as the major factors influencing the outcomes of climatic stress. The range of factors under the categories of structural vulnerability and impact sensitivity are similar, but often with different degrees of importance. For example, off-farm employment is a major factor for the wealthier two countries, South Africa and Mexico. These two countries show subsidies, pensions and welfare systems as the most important structural factors, but these are not as prominent in Sudan and Nigeria. This could be due to the fact that a healthier economy leads to more job opportunities.

Table 9.2 *Determinants of vulnerability situated in a causal chain of drought risk*

	Structural vulnerability: Needs Wants Means	Initiating events: Climatic Economic Environmental	1st order sensitivity: Impacts Exposure	Consequences: Nutrition Health Livelihood Death
Sudan	**Water harvesting** **Land degradation** Deforestation Land pressure Pests & disease Market access **Storage** Market prices Welfare	⬇**Precipitation** Drought **ENSO** Early warning	**Area cultivated** **Income/** **diversification** **Training/** **education** **Community** **institutions** Off-farm employment Size of holding Household size	**Health/health** **services**
Nigeria	Land degradation Deforestation Land pressure Pests & disease **Storage** Market access **Market prices**	⬇**Precipitation** **Drought** ENSO Floods Early warning	**Area cultivated** **Labour per ha** **Income/** **diversification** Off-farm employment **Community** **institutions** Training/education	Health/health services
South Africa	Land degradation Water harvesting Storage **Welfare** Market access Market prices	⬇**Precipitation** **Drought** ENSO Heat waves Floods Early warning	Area cultivated **Off-farm** **employment** **Income/** **diversification** Community institutions	Health/health services
Mexico	Land degradation Deforestation Pests Market access Market prices **Welfare**	⬇**Precipitation** Drought ENSO Heat waves Floods Early warning	Area cultivated **Labour per ha** **Off-farm** **employment** **Income/** **diversification** Training/education **Community** **institutions**	Health/health services

Key: **Bold** = very important (2); regular font = important (1) from Table 9.1.

Conclusion

Vulnerability to food insecurity is common across the world in semi-arid areas where marginal groups rely on rain-fed agriculture. This chapter has started to compare some of the dynamics associated with these commonalities. This is particularly important because it is well established that food insecurity is not solely about climate, but about a range of social, economic and political factors that are linked to physical factors. At the same time, the shift in climate patterns associated with climate change requires an understanding of how climate variability has an impact on food security in conjunction with other determinants.

The causal chain of drought risk helps to highlight the process of becoming vulnerable to drought. In most of the case studies, the determinants of vulnerability are spread throughout the continuum, indicating that there are multiple ways to modify and change the risks. This highlights the need to understand the problem so that interventions can be appropriate in nature and timing.

If one looks at the four case studies, it can be seen that household factors played a dominant role in determining vulnerability. Although this is not unexpected, it suggests that there needs to be a continued emphasis on the multidimensional integrated approach to assessing vulnerability to climate variability. This needs to be followed through when responding to climate variability, whether through climate adaptation options or through development policies to support drought-affected households. Another determinant that cut across all cases was the health status and health services that households have access to. Health stress is related to climate variability but can also be seen as a basic service and need that should be addressed to reduce vulnerability at multiple stages in the chain of drought risk. Off-farm income is important for case studies located in the two countries that are relatively wealthy, Mexico and South Africa. This highlights the differences that national-level policies might have on local impacts of drought on food security.

In many places, the term 'food security' is still equated with 'food availability'. The result is that government strategies to address food security, such as strategic grain reserve programmes and various agricultural development strategies, end up addressing only availability. These do not achieve the desired goal of improving food security, however, other key determinants that impact directly on that goal have not been integrated by government into their policies. There is the need to develop effective long-term agricultural policies that are situated within a wider development framework. For example:

1   productive commercially-oriented smallholder farming systems that employ cheaper means of enhancing farm productivity could be promoted;
2   irrigation development for drought-mitigation strategies and sustainable food production could be encouraged;
3   barriers to land ownership and secure tenure could be addressed; and
4   the capacity of farmers and rural institutions to continue to provide safety nets in times of food crisis could be better supported.

The implications of this study for climate policy as related to food security are clear. The impacts of climate change on food security cannot be seen solely as food production issues. Food security depends on livelihood security that, in turn, depends on many factors, including social, economic and environmental determinants. The second key policy issue is that understanding the context is of paramount importance. Depending on the local and national situation, certain institutions support access to, availability and utilization of food. It is difficult to generalize about coping strategies in response to stress. Support for adaptation measures therefore needs to be grounded in the local context. What might be effective and contribute to improving food security in South Africa might be ineffective in Sudan and end up increasing the vulnerability of marginal groups. It is therefore critical to verify and screen adaptation options and support.

This chapter has highlighted that there are commonalities and differences in understanding food security in the light of climate extremes such as drought. In cases in which there are commonalities, more could be done to look at how other countries have managed both the response to drought and the efforts to reduce the impact of drought. A potential increase in drought frequency and increased temperatures requires that understanding these processes of risk is a priority in order to respond appropriately with support for the most vulnerable groups.

Notes

1   For further details on the four case studies in this chapter, see Chapters 10, 11, 12, 13 and 14 in this volume.

References

Altieri, M. A. and J. Trujillo (1987) 'The agroecology of corn production in Tlaxcala, México', *Human Ecology*, vol 15, pp189–220

Appendini, K. 2001. *De la Milpa a los Tortibonos: La restructuración de la política alimentaria en México,* 2nd edn, Instituto de Investigaciones de las Naciones Unidas para el Desarrollo Social, El Colegio de México, Mexico

Archer, E. M. (2003) 'Identifying underserved end-user groups in the provision of climate information', *Bulletin of American Meteorological Society*, vol 84, pp1525–1532

Arnell, N. W., M. G. R. Cannell, M. Hulme, R. S. Kovats, J. F. B. Michell, R. J. Nicholls, M. Parry, M. J. Livermore and A. White (2002) 'The consequences of CO_2 stabilisation for the impacts of climate change', *Climatic Change*, vol 53, pp413–446

Aviles, K. (2005) 'Ofensiva neoliberal crea pueblos fantasmas en zonas agrícolas', *La Jornada*, vol 7

BancodeMexico (2004) 'Informe Anual 2004', www.banxico.org.mx

Bartra, A. (2003) *Del Teocintle a los Corn Pops: Sin maíz no hay país*, Conaculta, Museo Nacional de Culturas Populares, Mexico, pp219–250

Bharwani, S., M. Bithell, T. E. Downing, M. New, R. Washington and G. Ziervogel (2005) 'Multi-agent modelling of climate outlooks and food security on a community garden scheme in Limpopo, South Africa', *Philosophical Transactions of the Royal Society: B*, vol 360, pp2183–2194

Bryant, C. R., B. Smit, M. Brklacich, T. Johnston, J. Smithers, Q. Chiotti and B. Singh (2000) 'Adaptation in Canadian agriculture to climatic variability and change', *Climatic Change*, vol 45, pp181–201

Carney, D. (ed) (1998) *Sustainable Rural Livelihoods: What Contributions Can We Make?* Department for International Development (DFID) Natural Resources Advisers' Conference (July 1998), DFID, London

Chambers, R. (1989) 'Vulnerability, coping and policy', *IDS Bulletin*, vol 20, pp1–7

Clover, J. (2003) 'Food security in sub-Saharan Africa', *African Security Review*, vol 12, pp1–11

CONAPO (2004) 'Población nacida en México que reside en Estados Unidos: 1990 a 2004', www.conapo.org.mx

Conde, C. and H. Eakin (2003) 'Adaptation to climatic variability and change in Tlaxcala, Mexico', in R. K. J. Smith and S. Huq (eds) *Climate Change, Adaptive Capacity and Development*, Imperial College Press, London

Cortés, S. (2004) 'Criterio 2: Beneficios del Programa', Evaluación Externa 2003 al Fondo para Atender a la Población Rural Afectada por Contingencias Climatológicas (FAPRACC), Centro de Ciencias de la Atmósfera, UNAM, Mexico

Devereux, S. and J. Edwards (2004) 'Climate change and food security', *IDS Bulletin*, vol 35, no 3, pp22–30

Devereux, S. and S. Maxwell (eds) (2001) *Food Security in Sub-Saharan Africa*, Intermediate Technology Development Group Publishing, London, UK

Dixon, J., A. Gulliver and D. Gibbon (2001) *Farming Systems and Poverty: Improving Farmers' Livelihoods in a Changing World*, Food and Agriculture Organization and World Bank, Washington, DC, US

Döös, B. R. and R. Shaw (1999) 'Can we predict the future food production? A sensitivity analysis', *Global Environmental Change*, vol 9, pp261–283

Dougherty, B., A. Abusuwar and K. A. Razig (2001) *Sudan Community-Based Rangeland Rehabilitation for Carbon Sequestration and Biodiversity*, Terminal Evaluation Report, SUD/93/G31.UNDP GEF

Downing, T. E. (2002) 'Linking sustainable livelihoods and global climate change in vulnerable food systems', *Die Erde*, vol 133, pp363–378

FAO (2000) *Guidelines for National FIVIMS: Background and Principles*, Food and Agriculture Organization of the United Nations, Rome

Ferrer, R. M. (1999) 'Impactos del cambio climático en la agricultura tradicional de Apizaco, Tlaxcala', thesis, Facultad de Ciencias, Universidad Nacional Autónoma de Mexico, Mexico City, Mexico

Florescano, E. and S. Swan (1995) *Breve Historia de la Sequía en México*, Biblioteca Universidad Veracruzana, Veracruz, Mexico

Gregory, P. J., J. S. I. Ingram and M. Brklacich (2005) 'Climate change and food security', *Philosophical Transactions of the Royal Society: B*, vol 360, pp2139–2148

Hoelzmann, P., D. Jolly, S. P. Harrison, F. Laarif, R. Bonnefille and H. J. Pachur (1998) 'Mid-Holocene land-surface conditions in northern Africa and the Arabian peninsula: A data set for the analysis of biogeophysical feedbacks in the climate system', *Global Biogeochemical Cycles*, vol 12, pp35–51, www.ncdc.noaa.gov/paleo/abrupt/references.html#hoelzmann1998

Hoerling, M. P., J. W. Hurrell, J. Eischeid and A. Phillips (2006) 'Detection and attribution of 20th century northern and southern African monsoon change', *Journal of Climate,* vol 19, no 16, pp3989–4008

Hulme, M. (2001) 'Climatic perspectives on Sahelian desiccation: 1973–1998', *Global Environmental Change*, vol 11, pp19–29

INEGI (Instituto Nacional de Estadistica, Geografia e Informatica) (1996) Sonora. Datos por Ejido y Comunidad Agraria. XI Censo General de Poblacion y Vivienda. Aguascalientes, Ags. INEGI, Hermosillo

Lozano, F. and F. Olivera (2005) 'Impacto económico de las remesas en México: un balance necesario', presented at Problemas y Desafíos de la Migración y el Desarrollo en América seminar, Cuernavaca, Mexico, April 7–9, 2005, available at www.migracionydesarrollo.org.mx

McCarthy, J. J., O. F. Canziani, N. A. Leary, D. J. Dokken, K. S. White (eds) (2001) *Climate Change 2001: Impacts, Adaptation, and Vulnerability*, Contribution of Working Group II to the Third Assessment Report of the Intergovernmental Panel on Climate Change, Cambridge University Press, Cambridge, UK

McConnell, W. J. and E. F. Moran (eds) (2000) *Meeting in the Middle: The Challenge of Meso-Level Integration*, LUCC Report Series no 5, International Workshop on the Harmonization of Land Use and Land Cover Classification, Ispra, Italy, 17–20 October, Indiana University Press, Bloomington, IN, US

Moser, C. O. N. (1998) 'Reassessing urban poverty reduction strategies: the asset vulnerability framework 1998', *World Development*, vol 26, pp1–19

Nadal, A. (2000) 'The environmental and social impacts of economic liberalization on corn production in Mexico', study commissioned by Oxfam, GB and WWF International

Osman-Elasha, B. (2006) 'Environmental strategies to increase human resilience to climate change: Lessons for eastern and northern Africa', Final Report, Project AF14, Assessments of Impacts and Adaptations to Climate Change, International START Secretariat, Washington, DC, US, www.aiaccproject.org

Parry, M., C. Rosenzweig, A. Iglesias, G. Fisher and M. Livermore (1999) 'Climate change and world food security: A new assessment', *Global Environmental Change*, vol 9, ppS51–S67

Parry, M. L., C. Rosenzweig, A. Iglesias, M. Livermore and G. Fischer (2004) 'Effects of climate change on global food production under SRES emissions and socio-economic scenarios', *Global Environmental Change*, vol 14, pp53–67

Perry, A. H. and L. J. Symons (1994) 'The wind hazard in the British Isles and its effects on transportation', *Journal of Transport Geography*, vol 2, pp122–130

Reilly, J. (1995) 'Climate change and global agriculture: Recent findings and issues', *American Journal of Agricultural Economics*, vol 77, pp727–733

Rosas-Peña, A. M. (2005) 'Un mercado hecho bolas', *La Jornada en la Economia*, vol 5

Scoones, I. (1998) 'Sustainable rural livelihoods: A framework for analysis', Working Paper no 72, Institute of Development Studies, University of Sussex, Brighton, UK:

SEMARNAT (1996) 'Estadísticas Selectas: Agua: Balance de agua superficial y subterránea', Secretaría de Medio Ambiente y Recursos Naturales, www.semarnap.gob.mx/naturaleza/estadística-am/

Smit, B., E. Harvey and C. Smithers (2000) 'How is climate change relevant to farmers?' in D. Scott, B. Jones, J. Audrey, R. Gibson, P. Key, L. Mortsch and K. Warriner (eds) *Climate Change Communication: Proceedings of an International Conference*, Environment Canada, Kitchener-Waterloo, Canada, ppF3.18–F3.25

Stephen, L. and T. E. Downing (2001) 'Getting the scale right: A comparison of analytical methods for vulnerability assessment and household-level targeting', *Disasters*, vol 25, no 2, pp113–135

Trautmann, W. (1991) 'Los cultivos indígenas de Tlaxcala y la Mesa Central: Tipología y problemas de su datación' in Historia y sociedad en Tlaxcala (ed) *Memorias del 4º y 5º Simposios Internacionales de Investigaciones Socio-Históricas sobre Tlaxcala*, Gobierno del Estado de Tlaxcala, Tlaxcala, Mexico, pp62–65

USAID (United States Agency for International Development) (1992) *Policy Determination 19: Definition of Food Security*, United States Agency for International Development, Washington, DC, US

Vogel, C. and J. Smith (2002) 'The politics of scarcity: conceptualizing the current food security crisis in southern Africa', *South African Journal of Science*, vol 98, pp315–317

Watson, R. T. and the Core Writing Team (eds) (2001) *Climate Change 2001: Synthesis Report*, Contribution of Working Groups I, II and III to the Third Assessment Report of the Intergovernmental Panel on Climate Change, Cambridge University Press, Cambridge, UK and New York, US

Winters, P., R. Murgai, A. de Janvry, E. Sadoulet and G. Frisvold (1999) 'Climate change and agriculture: effects on developing countries', in G. Frisvold and B. Kuhn (eds) *Global Environmental Change and Agriculture*, Edward Elgar Publishers, Cheltenham, UK

Ziervogel, G. (2004) 'Targeting seasonal climate forecasts for integration into household level decisions: The case of smallholder farmers in Lesotho', *The Geographical Journal*, vol 170, pp6–21

Ziervogel, G. and R. Calder (2003) 'Climate variability and rural livelihoods: Assessing the impact of seasonal climate forecasts', *Area*, vol 35, pp403–417

Ziervogel, G., S. Bharwani and T. E. Downing (2006) 'Adapting to climate variability: Pumpkins, people and policy', *Natural Resource Forum*, vol 30, pp294–305

10

Vulnerability in Nigeria: A National-level Assessment

James O. Adejuwon

Introduction

Vulnerability to climate change is the extent to which climate change may damage or harm a system and is a function of a system's exposure, sensitivity and adaptive capacity (McCarthy et al, 2001). Applying this conception of vulnerability, an index of vulnerability of peasant households is constructed and used to rank the 30 states of the Nigerian Federation from least to most vulnerable. The analysis produces a depiction of the spatial distribution of vulnerability that is a synthesis of several investigations of climate variability, climate change and food security in Nigeria, the details of which are reported in Adejuwon 2005a, 2006a and 2006b.

The components of the vulnerability index correspond to the three main aspects of vulnerability: exposure, sensitivity and adaptive capacity. Exposure is the nature and degree to which a system is physically exposed to climatic variations and changes. Sensitivity is the degree to which a system is affected, either adversely or beneficially, directly or indirectly, by climate-related stimuli. Adaptive capacity refers to the ability of a system to adjust to climate change, including variability and extremes, to moderate potential damages, to take advantage of opportunities, and to cope with the consequences. Indicators of each of these three components of vulnerability are selected, secondary state-level data for the indicators are collected from various sources, and the indicators are combined into an aggregate measure of vulnerability and mapped. In addition, analyses have been made of the contemporary pattern of climate variability in Nigeria, projected future climate change and the impacts of climate change on future crop yields in major ecological zones of Nigeria.

Climate Variability and Climate Change

The contemporary regional climate

The ecological zones of Nigeria, depicted in Figure 10.1, are determined large-ly by climatic conditions. The lowest and highest mean monthly minimum and maximum temperatures are presented in Table 10.1 for the major ecological zones. Maximum temperatures during the warmer months generally increase as you travel from south to north, from the forest zone, through the Guinean savannahs and to the savannahs of the Sudan and Sahel zones. But in the coolest month, January, temperatures are higher as you travel south. The obser-vations confirm the well-known fact that diurnal variations in temperature are more pronounced than intra-annual variations and the common conceptual-ization that night is the winter of the tropics.

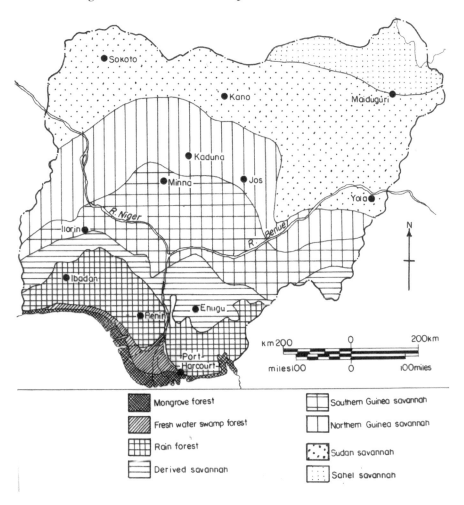

Figure 10.1 *The ecological zones of Nigeria*

Table 10.1 *Mean monthly minimum and maximum temperatures by zone in Nigeria, 1971–2000*

Zone	Mean monthly minimum temperature (°C)		Mean monthly maximum temperature (°C)	
	Lowest (month)	Highest (month)	Lowest (month)	Highest (month)
Forest	21 (Jan)	24 (Apr) 2	8 (Aug)	34 (Mar/Apr)
Guinea savannah	17 (Jan)	24 (Apr)	30 (Aug)	38 (Mar/Apr)
Sudan/ Sahel savannah	12 (Jan)	26 (May)	28 (Dec/Jan)	40 (May)

Within the forest zone, mean annual rainfall varied between 1250 and 3000mm. Although rain can be expected during each month, there is usually a dry period of two to four months with significantly lower rainfall. During the dry period, the air remains humid. In the Guinea savannah zones constituting the Middle Belt of the country, the year is sharply divided into rainy season and dry season. During part of the dry season, a dry air mass, which comes in from the Sahara Desert, overlies the area. Dryness is expressed in terms of both low rainfall and low humidity of the air. There is little difference between the northern, drier boundary and the southern wet boundary in terms of total annual rainfall. However, the dry season is about seven months long in the northernmost areas, whereas it is only five months long in the south. The boundaries between the Northern Guinea Zone and the Sudan correspond to a sharp drop in mean annual rainfall from 1200mm to about 900mm, while the boundary between the Sudan and the Sahel corresponds to a mean annual rainfall of 600mm. In the Sahel, the rainy season is barely three months long, whereas in the Sudan, the rainy season extends over a period of four months.

Inter-annual variability of maximum temperature (Table 10.2) is spectacularly low, averaging less than 5 per cent across the ecological zones and from January to December. The implication of this is that each year is very much like another with respect to daytime temperatures. The stability of high daytime temperatures from month to month and from year to year is a well-known marker of typical tropical climates. This notwithstanding, one can discern temporal and spatial patterns in the variability of mean monthly maximum temperatures. In forest zone locations, variability is uniformly low compared with the other zones. In the Sudan and Sahel zones, variability appears to be higher in the months of December, January and February compared with the other months of the year.

Variability of minimum temperature (Table 10.3) demonstrates an unmistakable contrast between December–February on the one hand and the rest of the year on the other. In almost all of the stations, the highest coefficients were for January, followed by December. This pattern is much more pronounced in the drier northern areas than in the south. Although the average for December is more than 10 per cent, the averages for April, May, June, July, August, September and October are less than 5 per cent.

Table 10.2 *Variability of monthly maximum temperature, 1971–2000*

Ecological Zone	Climate Station	Jan	Feb	Mar	Apr	May	Jun	Jul	Aug	Sep	Oct	Nov	Dec
Sahel	Maiduguri	5	6	3	2	3	10	4	4	4	5	3	5
Sudan	Kano	9	7	4	3	5	2	4	5	3	2	3	9
N. Guinea	Bauchi	10	6	3	2	5	3	10	3	3	2	4	5
N. Guinea	Jos	6	5	1	2	5	3	6	3	2	2	1	2
S. Guinea	Minna	3	3	3	3	5	3	2	3	2	1	3	2
S. Guinea	Ilorin	6	2	2	3	4	2	2	3	2	2	3	2
S. Guinea	Lokoja	4	2	3	4	3	2	1	1	1	2	2	2
Dry Savanna	Enugu	3	3	4	4	2	2	2	2	1	2	2	3
Forest	Ibadan	2	3	3	3	2	2	4	3	3	2	3	2
Forest	Benin	1	2	5	3	2	3	3	2	7	2	2	2
Forest	Lagos	3	2	2	2	1	2	2	2	2	1	1	2
Forest	Calabar	2	2	4	3	1	2	4	3	2	1	1	2
Forest	Port Harc	3	2	4	1	1	3	11	3	1	1	2	2

Note: Numbers in the table are the coefficients of variation of monthly maximum temperature, or the standard deviation of monthly maximum temperature as a percentage of the mean.

The generally low variability of temperature depicted in Tables 10.2 and 10.3 explains why these parameters are usually relegated to a minor role in the literature on climate variability compared to the emphasis placed on rainfall. Although the coefficient of variation of monthly temperature normally falls between 1 and 5 per cent, that of rainfall can be as high as 600 per cent and hardly ever falls below 20 per cent. Table 10.4 presents the monthly and total annual coefficient of variation of rainfall. The low coefficients of variability of

Table 10.3 *Variability of monthly minimum temperature, 1971–2000*

Ecological Zone	Climate Station	Jan	Feb	Mar	Apr	May	Jun	Jul	Aug	Sep	Oct	Nov	Dec
Sahel	Maiduguri	13	9	9	4	4	4	3	4	4	6	9	12
Sudan	Kano	13	7	10	4	3	3	4	3	3	5	5	8
N. Guinea	Bauchi	12	8	9	3	12	2	3	12	2	3	6	8
N. Guinea	Jos	13	18	7	5	3	3	2	3	4	6	8	12
S. Guinea	Minna	4	3	7	2	4	2	1	2	2	2	2	5
S. Guinea	Ilorin	10	6	2	3	4	3	2	2	2	2	5	11
S. Guinea	Lokoja	18	17	12	6	4	4	2	1	1	1	5	16
Dry Savanna	Enugu	8	6	2	3	2	2	2	2	2	3	5	8
Forest	Ibadan	8	3	2	2	2	2	2	3	1	2	3	3
Forest	Benin	10	4	3	3	3	8	6	2	1	2	4	3
Forest	Lagos	6	4	4	4	4	4	4	4	2	3	5	4
Forest	Calabar	5	3	4	3	4	2	3	4	3	3	2	4
Forest	Port Harc	10	3	3	2	2	2	2	1	1	1	2	4

Note: Numbers in the table are the coefficients of variation of monthly minimum temperature, or the standard deviation of monthly minimum temperature as a percentage of the mean.

the annual totals compared with the variability of monthly totals are noteworthy: while the coefficients for annual totals vary from 9 to 26 per cent, those of monthly totals vary from 0 to 600 per cent. There is no significant spatial pattern in the variability of annual total rainfall. However, one can discern a tendency for variability of annual totals to increase as the total rainfall decreases. The station with the least variable annual total, Jos, is distinguished by being the only high-altitude location among the list selected for this analysis.

Table 10.4 *Variability of monthly rainfall, 1971–2000*

Ecological Zone	Climate Station	Jan	Feb	Mar	Apr	May	Jun	Jul	Aug	Sep	Oct	Nov	Dec	Year
Sahel	Maiduguri	0	0	493	183	74	59	41	39	59	174	0	500	22
Sudan	Sokoto	0	500	292	148	76	65	37	32	44	145	600	0	21
Sudan	Kano	0	415	477	176	72	51	39	46	63	160	0	0	26
N. Guinea	Bauchi	0	500	240	102	50	45	29	23	51	72	50	0	18
N. Guinea	Yola	0	0	228	78	76	41	31	28	40	76	271	0	16
N. Guinea	Kaduna	0	321	211	82	43	31	29	30	33	83	462	0	14
N. Guinea	Jos	379	326	128	68	34	18	23	24	18	80	291	0	9
S. Guinea	Minna	582	372	138	102	49	33	27	29	34	61	244	0	26
S. Guinea	Ilorin	308	162	75	52	40	31	50	66	35	67	187	384	24
S. Guinea	Lokoja	296	204	89	62	37	37	48	57	31	43	225	489	16
Dry Savanna	Enugu	188	143	75	46	32	35	38	41	32	45	137	226	18
Forest	Ibadan	223	136	71	41	44	38	39	105	49	32	109	165	25
Forest	Benin	170	175	51	38	28	29	36	53	28	42	82	96	11
Forest	Lagos	143	100	63	53	41	38	73	115	49	63	75	136	20
Forest	Calabar	115	116	52	37	27	33	35	32	35	26	60	152	12
Forest	Port Harc	104	76	62	49	31	31	35	39	23	36	68	102	14

Note: Numbers in the table are the coefficients of variation of monthly rainfall, or the standard deviation of monthly rainfall as a percentage of the mean.

December and January are perennially dry in the Northern Guinea, Sudan and Sahel zones. Therefore the coefficients of variability for these months and for these stations are zero. Apart from these, dry season months throughout the country are characterized by very high coefficients of variability. The dry season months with coefficients greater than 100 per cent in the Sudan and Sahel zones are February, March, April, October and November. In the Northern Guinea zone, the affected months are February, March, April and November. In the areas extending from the coast through the forest zone to Southern Guinea, coefficients greater than 100 per cent are recorded for December, January and February. Within the rainy season, very high coefficients are recorded for the months representing onset and cessation of the rains throughout the country. Such months include June and September in the arid zones and March, April, October and November in the forest zone. In summary, the percentage of periodic change is greatest in months with the smallest average precipitation and decreases as rainfall increases.

Climate change

The most recent assessment of climate change projections concludes that Africa is very likely to warm more than the global average. The median projection of 21 global climate models for annual mean temperature increase is 3.3°C for West Africa from 1980–1999 to 2080–2099, with a range of 2.7 to 3.6°C for 25–75 per cent of the projections, compared to a global mean increase of 2.8°C (Christensen et al, 2007). Rainfall could either decrease or increase. Projected rainfall changes for West Africa range from decreases (9 per cent annually and 18 per cent for the wet months of June–August) to increases (13 per cent annually and 16 per cent for June–August). These projections correspond to the A1B emission scenario of the Intergovernmental Panel on Climate Change (IPCC, 2000), which assumes rapid economic and population growth and a balanced mix of energy technologies and yields emissions in the upper-mid range relative to other scenarios.

Our analysis for Nigeria is based on earlier projections of climate change. Specifically, we used experiments of the Hadley Centre's HadCM2 model for emissions of greenhouse gases that increase at annual rates of 0.5 and 1.0 per cent. The climatic parameters included in the analysis are precipitation, minimum temperature, maximum temperature, cloud cover and vapour pressure. The patterns of change with respect to maximum temperature and precipitation for the higher emission scenario, applied to selected stations in Nigeria, are shown in Figures 10.2 and 10.3. This scenario projects increases in mean temperatures of the order of 5°C or more by 2099, with minimum temperatures increasing more than maximum temperatures. On average, mean vapour pressure may rise by as much as 5–8hPa (hectopascals, equal to 100 pascals) with the potential for a significant increase in atmospheric energy. One would expect from this scenario an increase in the frequency and intensity of stormy weather (IPCC, 2001). A general decrease in mean cloudiness is projected. This could improve the availability of sunlight for primary biological productivity.

There has been an observed trend toward aridity in sub-Saharan West Africa (Adejuwon et al, 1990; Nicholson, 2001; Hulme et al, 2001). The HadCM2 model projects increasing rainfall for the region, suggesting that this trend could be put on hold or reversed as the century progresses. Note, however, that some other models project decreases in rainfall for West Africa and that there is not sufficient agreement across models to conclude whether rainfall will increase or decrease (Christensen et al, 2007). One aspect of the current climate pattern that seems likely to be carried forward into the climate of the future is more pronounced zonation. Rainfall, cloudiness and humidity are projected to decrease with distance from the ocean, whereas temperature and incident solar energy are projected to increase.

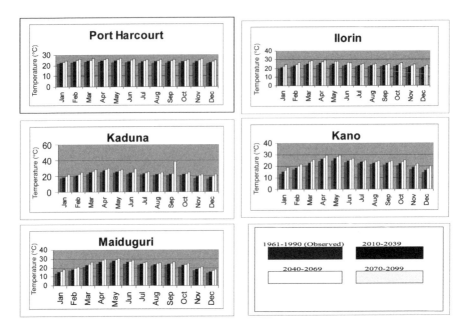

Figure 10.2 *Mean monthly maximum temperature projections, 1961–2099*

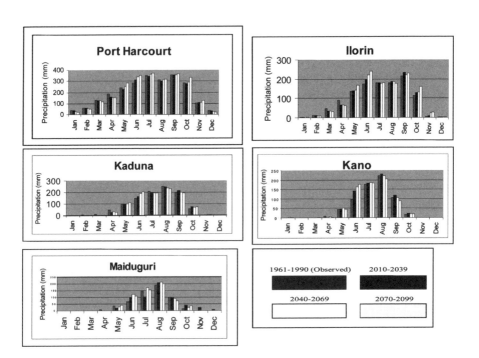

Figure 10.3 *Mean monthly precipitation projections, 1961–2099*

Sensitivity of Crop Yield to Climate Variability and Change

Sensitivity of yields to contemporary climate variability

Adejuwon (2005a) investigated the sensitivity of crop yield to climate variability in a case study of sites in the arid region states of Bornu and Yobe. The study area covers 70,000km^2 and lies between latitudes 10°N and 13°N and between longitudes 10°E and 15°E in the northeastern corner of the country. The climatic data used for the analyses are from the records of the two meteorological stations within the study area, namely Maiduguri (11.53°N, 13.16°E) and Potiskum (11.40°N, 11.03°E). The crop yield and climate data cover the 17-year period from 1983 to 1999. The major food crops included in the analyses are maize, sorghum, rice, millet, cowpeas and groundnut.

Bivariate correlation, multiple correlation and regression analyses were employed to demonstrate the relationship between crop yield and climate variability. The predictive models generated for cowpeas, groundnut, millet and sorghum are statistically significant with $\alpha < 0.05$. Among the more powerful determinants of crop yield were rainfalls in the onset and cessation months of the growing season. Inter-annual changes in the yields of maize and rice are less sensitive to rainfall variability. In general, the predictive models failed to incorporate the separation of crop yield variability from rainfall at higher levels of precipitation. During the long periods with normal and above normal rainfall, crop yield sensitivity to rainfall tended to be weak. However, during the years with unusually low precipitation, crop yield sensitivity became more pronounced. Thus, for purposes of developing the appropriate adaptation strategies, a distinction should be made between drought, with its associated disasters, and the less hazardous but more frequent inter-annual climate or rainfall variability.

Sensitivity of yields to projected climate change

Our analyses of sensitivity of crop yield to projected climate change are based on simulations using the crop model Erosion Productivity Impact Calculator (EPIC) (Williams et al, 1989; Adejuwon, 2005b) and the HadCM2 climate projections. The simulations indicate both benefits and risks. The case of maize is depicted in Figure 10.4 as an example. Port Harcourt (forest zone), Ilorin (S. Guinea), Kaduna (N. Guinea), Kano (Sudan) and Maiduguri (Sahel) represent different zones along the climatic profile from the humid to the semi-arid areas. Jos is presented as an example of a zonal high-altitude ecology. Outputs of the EPIC runs include biomass production, economic yield, water stress, temperature stress, nitrogen stress, phosphorus stress and aeration stress. These are useful in identifying the limiting environmental factors.

The general pattern of projected changes in the yield of maize, as depicted in Figure 10.4, is an initial increase from 1961–1990 to 2010–2039, followed by a decline towards the end of the 21st century. The exception is at Jos, representing a high-altitude ecosystem, where yield increases from less than 3 metric tons per hectare in Jos for the 1961–1990 period to more than 6 metric tons per hectare during 2070–2099. For Kano, representing the Sudan savannah

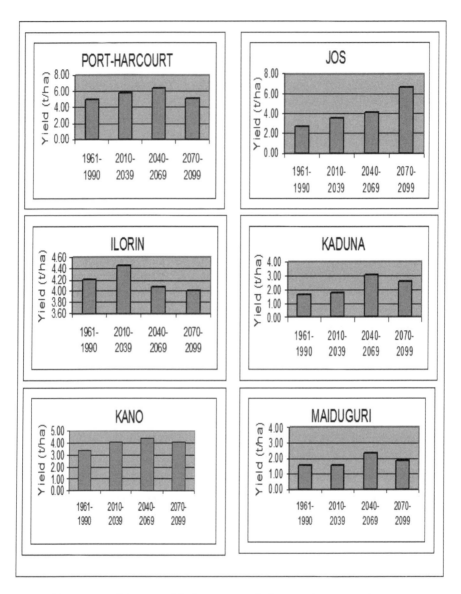

Figure 10.4 *Maize yields for projected climate change, 1961–2099*

ecology, Maiduguri, representing the Sahel ecology, Kaduna, representing northern Guinean ecology and Port Harcourt, representing the forest zone ecology, peak yields are projected for 2040–2069. For Ilorin, representing the southern Guinean ecology, peak yields are projected for 2010–2039. The yield predicted for the end of the 21st century is lower than the yield for 1960–1990. This means that over the 140-year period, a net decrease in the maize yield is projected for Ilorin.

The general increase in yield is explained in part by the effects of increases in the atmospheric concentration of carbon dioxide, the principal greenhouse gas, on plant water use efficiency and photosynthesis. The steady increase in yield at the high-altitude location of Jos corresponds to a steady decline in water stress from 47 days during 1961–1990 to 15 days during 2070–2099. Temperature stress is also projected to decline from 2.6 days to 0.5 days. Because the high-altitude site also experiences the projected general warming trend, it might be concluded that the current temperature levels are suboptimal in the region represented by Jos and that the warmer days ahead will provide environmental conditions for enhanced yield of maize in that region. However, it seems clear that the steady and significant increases in the yield of maize projected for Jos are related to increased rainfall and not increased temperature.

In Maiduguri, which falls in the Sahel ecological zone, the increases in yield from 1961–1990 to 2040–2069 correspond to a decline in the level of water stress from 46 to 28 days. However, the further decline to 25 days during 2070–2099 seems not to be reflected in continued increase in crop yield. It appears that by the time of the 4th time slice, the rising temperature would have taken over as the limiting factor. In other words, the decline in crop yield from 2.75 metric tons per hectare to 2.31 metric tons per hectare could be ascribed to the increase in temperature stress from 8 to 11 days.

It is important to bear in mind that the above analysis is based on a single climate change scenario that projects increases in rainfall for the region, while other scenarios of climate change indicate the potential for rainfall to decrease. Should rainfall fail to increase, or if it should become more variable, rainfall would not offset the temperature stress effects of warming and the potential for yield losses would be greater. One should also note here that across the country and across the four time ranges, the experiments did not show any stress related to nitrogen, phosphorus or aeration. In selecting the soil with which to create the soil file used in the EPIC model simulations, we adopted the more commonly cultivated soil series, which, in most cases, are of moderate productivity. In addition, the simulations assume that 300kg/ha of NPK is applied as part of the operations schedule.

Climate-driven risks and benefits

Risks are the expected losses (losses of life, persons injured, property damaged and economic activity disrupted) because of a particular hazard for a given area and reference period (Downing et al, 2001). From the foregoing analysis, the risks to the livelihood of peasant households are related strongly to the potential for reductions in the yields of their crops. The risks vary from widespread crop failure affecting all crops in the arid zone or some of the crops throughout the country, to regional, local and individual farm-level crop failures affecting the more sensitive crops. Depending on its severity, crop failure could result in food inadequacy and famine, loss of livelihood, and long-distance emigration from the arid zone to the rainforest belt. Usually it is the able-bodied young men that emigrate. A large proportion of those left behind, especially the women and the children, pay with their lives. Moreover, the crop production systems are constrained by poor soils, disease, pest infestation and chronic peasant production diseconomies. These serve as amplifiers of the climate factor as the chief driver of the risks.

The drivers of crop failure are droughts; in other words, inadequate growing season rainfall. Droughts have always been a common, though irregular feature of the arid region of Nigeria. The areas most exposed to the incidence of disastrous droughts are the Sudan and Sahel ecological zones, which cover about 240,900km^2 and 20,700km^2 respectively and thus constitute nearly 27 per cent of the country's land area. These areas are characterized by a mean annual rainfall averaging 600 to 800mm and a short rainy period of 100 to 120 days. From the records, five major drought periods resulting in human deprivation were documented in the Nigerian arid zone during the 20th century. These were the 1913–1914, 1931–1932, 1942–1943, 1972–1973 and 1983–1984 droughts (Mijindadi and Adegbesin, 1991). Recurring drought periods were not limited to the 20th century. Oladipo (1988) traced the occurrence of periodic droughts in Africa from before the birth of Christ up to the 20th century.

The farmers in the arid zones are quite conscious of the weather factors in their lives. According to the farmers interviewed during field work (Adejuwon, 2005a and 2006a), when the seasonal rains come early (in May), crop performance is high. When seasonal rain onset is delayed until July, however, crop yield is low. This is because unless cessation of rain is also delayed, the growing season is shortened and there is insufficient time for crops to mature. Rain coming in June is judged to be favourable and is associated with good yields of crops. Most crop failures are, however, associated with premature cessation of the rainy season. There can also be a low yield of crops when there are prolonged dry spells within the growing season. However, the most significant negative impacts of climate on crop production are delivered by extreme events such as season-long droughts with decadal frequencies of occurrence. Disaster usually comes in the form of a late arrival and/or a premature termination of the growing season. In the broad band of years that could be described as normal, noticeable, rather than significant, responses of crops to changes in climate can be observed. These responses reflect changes in the environmental drivers from one locality to another.

For the rest of the current century, the risks outlined above will most likely remain for the Nigerian peasant household. However, the severity, spatial resolution and temporal resolution could differ as the century progresses. Instead of oscillating or periodic timing, the risks could gather momentum as the century progresses. Instead of cellular occurrence, the risks could affect the entire country with comparable severity. For the scenario of increasing rainfall that was analysed using the EPIC model, risks would most likely be least during the first half of the century, during which crop yields increase in response to higher levels of solar radiation, atmospheric humidity, rainfall and carbon dioxide. As the century progresses, however, the risks will be driven by a new set of climatic factors. The favourable moisture-based drivers projected for the first half of the century will be overshadowed by temperature-based factors in the second half. In the context of ecological factor interaction, the negative impacts of supra-optimum temperatures will tend to mask the positive impacts of increases in solar radiation, moisture and carbon dioxide during the second half of the century.

Indirect Sensitivity of Peasant Households to Climate

By definition, a peasant household depends on agriculture and related activities for whatever livelihood its members are able to eke out of their environment. It is the view in certain quarters that 'one major cause of vulnerability to climate change is dependence of the exposure unit on sectors such as agriculture, forestry and fishery that are sensitive to changes in climate' (Sperling, 2003). The logic of this viewpoint is quite easy to appreciate. Crop production, on which the peasant householder depends for his livelihood, is sensitive to climate variability and climate change. Whatever effects climate has on crop production affect the peasant household. In essence, sensitivity of crop production to climate is thus a good measure of the sensitivity of the peasant household to climate variability and climate change.

The National Agricultural Sample Survey (FOS, 1983–97) indicates that 94 per cent of agricultural holdings are involved in crop farming. A good measure of the extent of dependence on agriculture is the percentage of employed persons in the sector. For the country as a whole, 65 per cent of employed persons worked in the agricultural sector in 1993 (FOS, 1996b). The data for 1993 also indicate that the percentage was above 50 in 20 out of the 30 states in the country. In general, the proportion of employed persons in agriculture tends to be higher in the northern, drier parts of the country than in the wetter south.

The major crops grown by the households include maize, guinea corn and cassava. During the 1993/1994 crop season, maize was the most widely cultivated crop and was grown on 54 per cent of the household land holdings, while guinea corn (sorghum) was cultivated on 48 per cent and cassava on 47 per cent of the holdings (FOS, 1983–1997). Most of the states of the Nigerian Federation recorded high percentages for maize. The exceptions were Jigawa, Sokoto and Yobe, located in the Sudan and Sahel ecological zones, where less than 10 per cent of land is planted in maize. Sorghum cultivation was concentrated in the same Sudan and Sahel zones, where more than 90 per cent of the households cultivated the crop. 60 to 70 per cent of the households in the Guinean (middle belt) zones cultivated guinea corn, whereas in the southern forest zone less than 10 per cent of the households were engaged in cultivating the crop.

The core of high-intensity cultivation of cassava is in the southeastern states of Anambra, Imo, Enugu, Akwa Ibom and Abia and extends westward into Delta, Edo and Oyo states, all lying outside the cocoa belt. The intensity of cultivation of cassava decreases northward. The Sudan and Sahel zones could be considered as lying outside the proper cassava growing areas. What all this implies is that any disaster overtaking maize, sorghum or cassava cultivation as a result of climate variability or climate change would also be a disaster for the Nigerian peasant household. Beans, millet, yams and groundnuts are also regionally important crops, cultivated by between 30 and 40 per cent of the households during the 1993/1994 growing season. Yam cultivation is intensive in the southeast and the middle belt, while beans and millet are important crops in the far north.

Constraints to Adaptive Capacity

A low capacity to adapt to climate change automatically implies vulnerability. Among the factors imposing limitations on adaptive capacity, the most significant is persistent poverty, which signifies absence of the resources necessary for adapting to climate change (Sperling, 2003). In addition, there are disabilities such as poor health that could undermine labour availability for the farming activities both in quality and in quantity. Relatively low levels of educational attainment in parts of the country could also constrain the ability to acquire the technological capacity for combating the negative consequences of climate change. The rate of population increase, which at present stands at 28 per 1000, could also increase the rates of child dependency, increase pressure on social infrastructure and impose limitations on the capacity to cope with the negative impacts of climate change.

Poverty

Widespread poverty has been cited as the main cause of a low capacity to adapt to climate change in Africa (Desanker et al, 2001). Resources, including social, financial, natural, physical and human capital, are required for planning, preparing for, facilitating and implementing adaptation measures. Poor persons, poor communities and poor nations do not have enough of these resources, hence their low adaptive capacity. Existent or pre-impact poverty connotes vulnerability. A summary of the latest results from the National Integrated Survey of Households of 1995 (FOS, 1996b) showed that practices that could have boosted the adaptive capacity of the peasant households were still being constrained by lack of funds at the individual household level. With respect to crop production, the use of pesticides and insecticides was limited to 4 per cent; the use of improved seeds was limited to 11 per cent and the use of chemical fertilizers was limited to 32 per cent of the peasant holdings. Among those who did not use fertilizer, 51 per cent considered the cost too high, 8 per cent found the distance to the source to be too far, 23 per cent did not know where to obtain fertilizer and 12 per cent felt they did not need fertilizers. Of those who were not using pesticides and insecticides, 36 per cent felt the cost was too high, 24 per cent felt no need for them and 22 per cent did not know where to obtain them.

All of these reasons are due to inadequate financial resources and ignorance, which are the hallmarks of the poor. Ninety-four per cent of the holders had no credit for their farm work. Only 1 per cent had credit through formal banking and a cooperative society system. Informal credit systems accounted for only 2.6 per cent. Friends and relatives were the source of credit for 2 per cent of households, while 0.4 per cent obtained credit from money lenders (FOS, 1996b).

There are currently two official poverty lines that are set relative to the standard of living in the country (FOS, 1999). There is a moderate poverty line, which is equivalent to two thirds of the mean per capita expenditure, and a core poverty line, which is equivalent to one third of the mean per capita expenditure. Using the two lines, households are classified into three mutually exclusive groups: core poor, moderately poor and non-poor. There has been a change for the worse in the poverty structure of the country in recent years. The incidence of poverty increased from 27.2 per cent in 1980 to 46.3 per cent in 1985 and 65.6 per cent in 1996. Over the same period, the incidence of core poverty increased from 6.2 per cent in 1980 to 12.1 per cent in 1985 and 29.3 per cent in 1996 (FOS, 1999). Whether poor or non-poor, most of the income is derived from basic cash (i.e. from wages, salaries, rents, interests on investments, etc., as opposed to COP (consumption of own production) income such as gifts in kind, loans of all types etc.). However, basic cash is 10 per cent higher in the income of the non-poor compared with the income of the poor. On the other hand, the consumption from the own production component in the income of the poor is as high as 20 per cent compared with 12 per cent in the income of the non-poor. The core poor and the moderately poor spent 76.2 and 72.9 per cent, respectively, of their total income on food compared with 58 per cent spent for the same item by the non-poor in 1996 (FOS, 1999). There are significant differences between the poor and the non-poor with regard to the proportion spent on non-food items. The respective percentages for the core poor, moderately poor and non-poor were 24, 27, and 41 in 1996 (FOS, 1999).

The incidence of poverty is considerably higher among households engaged in agriculture compared with households employed in the other sectors. In 1996, 77 per cent of farming households were classified as poor compared with 65.6 per cent for the total population. Among the farming households, 48 per cent fell into the core poor category compared with 29.3 per cent for the country as a whole (FOS, 1999). There are also regional disparities in the incidence of poverty. In 1996, householders in the southern forest-based states were less poor compared with those in the middle belt (Guincan) states, while those in the Sudan and the Sahel states were the poorest.

Demography-induced constraints

Nigeria has a youthful population (FOS, 1996c). Going by the estimates for 1995, children under the age of 15 years constituted 44.0 per cent of the population. The youthful age structure creates a built-in momentum for future population growth. Even if it were possible to reduce the growth rate to replacement level, births would outstrip deaths and the population would continue to increase until the very large number of young females had passed through their reproductive years. The percentage of the female population that is in the reproductive age bracket, after declining between 1980 and 1990, increased from 1990 to 1995, giving indications that the growth rate might be accelerating. In 1993, women in the reproductive age brackets constituted 46.0

per cent of the female population (FOS, 1996c). With such high percentages within the reproductive age bracket, coupled with the youthful nature of the population, policies aimed at reducing fertility may not produce the desired results within a short time. In the short run, the population of children would remain high relative to total population even if the fertility rate declined.

The youthfulness of the population is directly responsible for the high rate of child dependency burden in the country. Child dependency burden is calculated as the population of children below the age of 15 divided by the population of working adults aged from 15 to 59. (Going on the data for 1993, the southwest has the least burden, followed by the southeast and the northwest.) The main consequence of this at the household level is that each adult household member must strive to provide for many more persons than can be conveniently accommodated. In countries with such high proportions of children relative to the proportions of the working age population, a high percentage of national income is expended on consumable goods for children. The higher the percentage of income expended on these consumables, the lower the percentage of income left for savings and investments. Thus a high dependency burden has an effect similar to poverty. The capacity to cope with any additional stress in the form of negative consequences of climate change will thus be lower in situations with high dependency burden because the first inclination would be to care for children rather than to prepare for a future under a changed climate.

The rapidly expanding population is exerting increasing pressure on the social and economic infrastructure of the country. Schools, hospitals and houses become inadequate almost as soon as they are completed. Similarly, electricity, water and waste disposal facilities designed for a given population are being made to serve much more than the population on the day they are commissioned. In other words existing facilities are being used to a higher capacity than that for which they were designed. The result is a high rate of infrastructure deterioration. There is the possibility that these inadequacies will tend to command greater attention from policymakers and draw away funds from proactively responding to the consequences of a potential climate change.

Educational status

Education definitely enhances personal, community and national capacity to respond to external stresses placed on human livelihood and well-being. Therefore inadequate or substandard education is a measure of the vulnerability of human exposure units to expected negative impacts of climate change. It is easy to appreciate the fact that education is one of the means for achieving the goals of better health, higher labour productivity and more rapid GDP growth, all of which are required as the need arises to anticipate, manage or adapt to a worsening climatic factor (Basher et al, 2000). The higher levels of education are especially necessary to enable individuals and countries to understand and participate more fully in the technological and administrative processes of the modern global economy. Since achieving independence from colonial rule in 1960, a considerable proportion of the national income has been invested in raising the standard of education. Because of this, enrolment ratios have been trending upwards (FOS, 1996c). The national adult literacy rate averaged 25 per cent in 1970. By 1995, it had climbed to 49 per cent. However, regional disparities are well marked. In 1995, literacy rates among male adults varied from a low of 19 per cent in Jigawa state in the far north, to a high of more than 93 per cent in Lagos state, located in the humid forest zone. In general, the northern parts of the country are chronically handicapped in terms of the necessary literacy level for adapting to climate change.

Health and adaptive capacity

The view has been expressed that climate change's impact on human health will increase vulnerability and reduce opportunities by interfering with education and the ability to work (Sperling, 2003). In the absence of mechanization and other forms of modernization, the main input to crop and animal production in Nigeria is labour. Most of the labour used on peasant farms is supplied by members of the household. In households headed by women, hired labour could be employed for the more strenuous activities such as tilling in preparation for planting. Households engaged in cash crop production use more hired labour than households engaged in food crop production. During the harvest season, households cooperate to ensure that farm output is brought in as soon as possible. There is always limited time available for harvests as delay may expose the harvested crops to pests, diseases and destruction by the weather. Thus sufficient and timely availability of labour is crucial to the level of yield realized.

The effect of the HIV/AIDS epidemic in limiting farm productivity is common knowledge. Hands that could have been employed in production are either lost through death or immobilized by sickness. Statistics on morbidity and mortality due to HIV/AIDS are not yet in the public domain and estimates supplied through the news media are largely unreliable. The rates of losses in farm worker days due to the disease are probably now as high as those reported for more traditional human ailments. However, most of the reported cases of death and sickness are children under the age of 5. Sick children are likely to reduce the normally substantial contributions of their mothers to farm labour.

Spatial Pattern of Vulnerability

An aggregate index of vulnerability is constructed from three groups of attributes: exposure to climate variability and projected climate change, the sensitivity of households to climate, and the inherent capacity of the households to adapt to climate-related risks. Exposure to climate variability is ranked according to the variability of the onset of rainfall. The variability indices of rainfall in March, April/May and June are used as indicators of exposure to climate variability for the forest zone, Guinean zones (north and south) and semi arid zones respectively. The variability index of the onset of the rainy season can be as low as 34 per cent and as high as 65 per cent. The index is lowest at Jos and highest at Maiduguri. Hence Plateau state, where Jos is located, is ranked first, or least exposed, while Bornu state, in which Maiduguri is located, is ranked 30th, or most exposed.

Our simulations of crop yields found that temperature effects have a negative effect on yields in most zones of Nigeria and that temperature becomes the dominate driver of yield changes towards the latter half of the 21st century. Consequently, exposure to climate change is measured by the projected average temperature for the growing season for the 2070–2099 time range. Growing season mean temperature for 2070–2099 is projected to be lowest along the coast and highest at the boundary with the Sahara Desert in the north. Hence, coastal states are ranked highest, or least exposed to climate change stresses, followed by the middle belt states, while the northernmost states are ranked lowest, or most exposed.

As noted previously, high proportions of land holdings devoted to agricultural activities and of dependence of households on agriculture for livelihoods connote a condition of high sensitivity to climate stresses. We measure the sensitivity of households to climate by their dependence on crop production as indicated by the percentage of the households employed in agriculture. Hence Lagos state, where the percentage of households employed in agricultural production is lowest, is ranked first, or least sensitive, while Jigawa state, where the percentage is highest, is ranked 30th, or most sensitive.

The attributes of adaptive capacity include economic, health, education and demographic conditions of the households. The indicators used to measure adaptive capacity are poverty head count for the economic attribute of adaptive capacity, the under-five mortality rate for the health attribute, adult literacy rate for education and the child dependency ratio for the demographic attribute. The state with the lowest percentage classified as poor, the lowest under-five mortality, the highest adult literacy rate and the lowest child dependency burden was ranked first in adaptive capacity. Other states were ranked lower in succession with respect to each attribute.

To construct the index of vulnerability, the ranks for exposure, sensitivity and adaptive capacity for each state were averaged; the results of the ranking are summarized in Figure 10.5. The mean rankings show clearly that the peasant households in the arid zone states of the Sudan and Sahel are potentially the most vulnerable to climate change, followed by those in the middle belt or Guinea savannah, while households in the forest-based states are potentially the least vulnerable.

The spatial pattern of vulnerability depicted in Figure 10.5 can be explained in terms of differences in cultural, historical and environmental attributes. The north is predominantly Moslem while the south is predominantly Christian. Because of this, European influence in the form of development has been consistently stronger in the south than in the north. Thus attributes favouring higher levels of adaptive capacity such as the provision of health and education facilities and availability of non agricultural employment tend to favour the south. Also the south, with its longer rainy season, is characterized by less

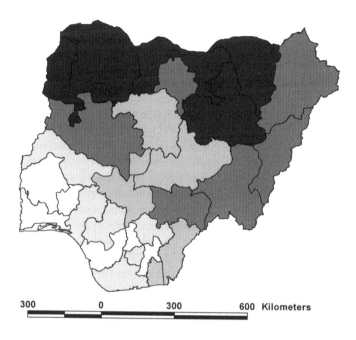

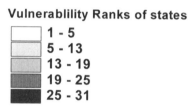

Vulnerablility Ranks of states
- 1 - 5
- 5 - 13
- 13 - 19
- 19 - 25
- 25 - 31

Figure 10.5 *Vulnerability of peasant households to climate change by state*

exposure to water stress, less sensitivity to climate due to greater diversity of agricultural products and a higher degree of resilience against the hazards and risks of a changing climate. This is based not only on a multiplicity of crop products – including cocoa, oil palm, coffee, cassava, yam, plantain and banana – but also on the plant and animal natural resources of the rainforest zone. Contemporary average temperature in the north is higher than the average temperature in the south; thus a general increase in temperature of the same magnitude will attain levels that will breach the upper limits of tolerance for crops earlier in the north than in the south. For this reason, the risks confronting peasant householders in the event of a changed climate are greater in the north than in the south.

Summary and Conclusions

Exposure of crop production to contemporary climate variability, especially to droughts of varying severity, is a major source of existing vulnerability for the Nigerian peasant household. Climate change during the 21st century in Nigeria will be manifested by a statistically significant rise in temperature. Precipitation changes are projected with less confidence and either increases or decreases are possible. For the scenario of increased precipitation and atmospheric humidity analysed in our study, crop yield is projected to increase substantially during the first half of the century. Such increases, if they occur, would tend to relieve contemporary vulnerability. However, during the second half of the century, benefits from increases in precipitation and atmospheric humidity would tend to be overshadowed by the negative consequences of the higher temperatures. The net result of these higher temperatures could be that climate change will pose considerable risks to peasant household livelihood, health, crop production and food security. The risks will most likely be intensified towards the end of the century and will tend to be greater in the north than in the southern parts of the country.

Peasant households of Nigeria are vulnerable to climate change because they are dependent on agricultural livelihoods that are highly sensitive to climate, because exposures to climate stresses are likely to become increasingly adverse for crop production as temperatures rise and because their capacity to adapt is low. The low adaptive capacity derives from poverty, food insecurity, poor health, low educational attainment, inadequate social and economic infrastructure, and explosive population growth. Vulnerability seems to be highest in the northern areas of Nigeria, where current and projected climate are less favourable for crop production and adaptive capacity is lowest. Vulnerability is lower in the coastal and high-altitude regions, where there are indications that the projected climate change may present opportunities for improving the quality of human life.

References

Adejuwon, J. O. (2005a) 'Food crop production in Nigeria: I – Present effects of climate variability', *Climate Research*, vol 30, pp53–60

Adejuwon, J. O. (2005b) 'Assessing the suitability of EPIC Crop Model for use in the study of impacts of climate variability and climate change in West Africa', *Singapore Journal of Tropical Geography*, vol 24, pp44–60

Adejuwon, J. O. (2006a) *Food Security, Climate Variability and Climate Change in Sub-Saharan West Africa*, Final report of AIACC Project Number AF 23, The International START Secretariat, Washington, DC, US

Adejuwon, J. O. (2006b) 'Food crop production in Nigeria: II – Potential effects of climate change', *Climate Research*, vol 32, pp229–245

Adejuwon, J. O., E. E. Balogun and S. A. Adejuwon (1990) 'On the annual and seasonal patterns of rainfall fluctuations in Sub-Sahara West Africa', *International Journal of Climatology*, vol 10, pp839–848

Basher, R., C. Clark, M. Dilley and M. Harrison (2000) *Coping with the Climate: A Way Forward*, International Research Institute for Climate and Society, Palisades, NY, US

Christensen, J. H., B. Hewitson, A. Busuioc, A. Chen, X. Gao, I. Held, R. Jones, R. Koli, W. Kwon, R. Laprise, V. Rueda, L. Mearns, C. Menendez, J. Raisanen, A. Rinke, A. Sarr and P. Whetton (2007) 'Regional Climate Projections', in S. Solomon, D. Qin, M. Manning, Z. Chen, M. C. Marquis, K. Averyt, M. Tignor and H. L. Miller (eds), *Climate Change 2007: The Physical Science Basis*, Contribution of Working Group I to the Fourth Assessment Report of the Intergovernmental Panel on Climate Change, Cambridge University Press, Cambridge, UK and New York, US

Desanker, P., C. Magadza, A. Allali, C. Basalirwa, M. Boko, G. Dieudonne, T. E. Downing, P. O. Dube, A. Githeko, M. Githendu, P. Gonzalez, D. Gwary, B. Jallow, J. Nwafor and R. Scholes (2001) 'Africa', in J. McCarthy, O. Canziani, N. Leary, D. Dokken, and K. White (eds) *Climate Change 2001: Impacts, Adaptation and Vulnerability*, Contribution of Working Group II to the Third Assessment Report of the Intergovernmental Panel on Climate Change, Cambridge University Press, Cambridge, UK and New York, US

Downing, T., R. Butterfield, S. Cohen, S. Huq, R. Moss, A. Rahman, Y. Sokona and L. Stephen (2001) *Vulnerability Indices: Climate Change Impacts and Adaptations*, Policy Series No 3, United Nations Environment Programme, Nairobi, Kenya

FOS (1983–1997) *National Agricultural Sample Survey*, Annual Series, Federal Office of Statistics, Lagos, Nigeria

FOS (1996a) *General Household Survey*, Federal Office of Statistics, Lagos, Nigeria

FOS (1996b) *The Nigerian Household 1995: Summary of latest results from the National Integrated Survey of Households*, Federal Office of Statistics, Lagos, Nigeria

FOS (1996c) *Socio-Economic Profile of Nigeria*, Federal Office of Statistics, Lagos, Nigeria

FOS (1999) *Poverty Profile for Nigeria 1980–1996*, Federal Office of Statistics, Lagos, Nigeria

Hulme, M., R. Doherty, T. Ngara, M. New and D. Lister (2001) 'African climate change: 1900–2100', *Climate Research*, vol 17, pp145–168

IPCC (2000) 'Summary for policymakers', in N. Nakicencovic and R. Swart (eds) *Emission Scenarios*, Special report of the Intergovernmental Panel on Climate Change, Cambridge University Press, Cambridge, UK

IPCC (2001) 'Summary for policymakers', in J. Houghton, Y. Ding, D. Griggs, M. Noguer, P. van der Linden and D. Xiaosu (eds) *Climate Change 2001: The Scientific Basis*, Contribution of Working Group I to the Third Assessment Report of the Intergovernmental Panel on Climate Change, Cambridge University Press, Cambridge, UK and New York, US

McCarthy, J., O. Canziani, N. Leary, D. Dokken and K. White (eds) (2001) *Climate Change 2001: Impacts, Adaptation and Vulnerability*, Contribution of Working Group II to the Third Assessment Report of the Intergovernmental Panel on Climate Change, Cambridge University Press, Cambridge, UK and New York, US

Mijindadi, N. B. and J. O. Adegbesin (1991) 'Drought, desertification and food production in Nigeria', *Savannah*, vol 12, pp25–40

Nicholson, S. E. (2001) 'Climatic and environmental change in Africa during the last two centuries', *Climate Research*, vol 17, pp124–144

Oladipo, E. O. (1988) 'Drought in Africa: A synthesis of current scientific knowledge', *Savannah*, vol 9, pp64–82

Sperling, F. (ed) (2003) *Poverty and Climate Change: Reducing the Vulnerability of the Poor*, World Bank, Washington, DC, US

Williams, J. R., C. A. Jones, J. R. Kiniry and D. A. Spaniel (1989) 'The EPIC growth model', *Transactions of the American Society of Agricultural Engineers*, vol 32, no 2, pp497–511

11

Vulnerability in the Sahelian Zone of Northern Nigeria: A Household-level Assessment

Anthony Nyong, Daniel Dabi, Adebowale Adepetu, Abou Berthe and Vincent Ihemegbulem

Introduction

The arid and semi-arid region of West Africa commonly known as the Sahel is characterized by a strong gradient of decreasing annual rainfall from south to north. Rains fall during a single wet season consisting of short intense storms over a 3- to 5-month period, with about 90 per cent of the rains falling during the months of July, August and September. Total seasonal rainfall ranges from 100 to 650mm in the northern region and from 650mm to over 1000mm in the semi-humid Sudan climate of the south (Ingram et al, 2002). Drought has been a recurrent feature in this region, with early records dating back to the 1680s. Annual rainfall levels decreased in the region over the course of the 20th century, with an increase in inter-annual and spatial variability (Dai et al, 2003; Brooks, 2004) and southward shifts of isohyets by 200km (L'Hôte et al, 2002).

Whether this trend of increasing dryness in the western Sahel will continue or be exacerbated as a result of climate change is very unclear, as there is presently no convergence in predictions of climate change for the region. A comparison of climate change projections for Sub-Saharan West Africa, encompassing the Sahel, finds quite different outcomes (Dietz et al, 2001). Recent studies have suggested that increases in atmospheric carbon dioxide will lead to an enhanced West African Monsoon, wetter conditions in parts of the Sahel and an expansion of vegetation into the Sahara (Claussen et al, 2003; Maynard et al, 2002; Haarsma et al, 2005; Hoerling et al; 2006). Other models, however, project a significant drying (Hulme et al, 2001; Jenkins et al, 2005). Other studies have noted that the models that project a trend to wetter conditions do not take into account land-use changes and degradation, which are capable of inducing drier conditions (Huntingford et al, 2005; Kamga et al, 2005).

One area of agreement between most models, however, is that the response of the African Monsoon to increased carbon dioxide concentrations is likely to be highly non-linear, and the Sahel is likely to continue to experience a high degree of climatic variability on a range of timescales for the foreseeable future (see Wang and Eltahir, 2002; Mitchell et al, 2000). Rainfall will likely remain highly variable, and drought and associated conflicts could still pose a major problem in many areas in the Sahel (FAO, 2005). This could negatively affect the major livelihood systems of the Sahelians and increase their vulnerability, particularly to food insecurity.

In climate change research, two distinct notions of vulnerability have been recognised – biophysical vulnerability and social vulnerability. Biophysical vulnerability is concerned with the ultimate impacts of a hazard event, and is often viewed in terms of the amount of damage experienced by a system as a result of an encounter with a hazard. Social vulnerability, on the other hand, is viewed more as a potential state of human societies that can affect the way they experience natural hazards (Vincent, 2004; Adger, 1999; Adger and Kelly, 1999). Social vulnerability depends on a range of factors including composition of resource endowments of the household, social relations in the community and the institutional capacity of local organizations. The most vulnerable are considered those who are most exposed to shocks, who possess a limited coping capacity and who are least resilient to recovery (Adger and Kelly, 1999). The nature of social vulnerability will depend on the nature of the hazard to which the human system in question is exposed, as certain properties of a system will make it more vulnerable to certain types of hazard than to others.

In this chapter, we focus on the social vulnerability of rural farm households to drought in the Sahel region of West Africa, using a case study of selected villages in northern Nigeria. While the effects of future climate change on the frequency and intensity of drought in the Sahel is uncertain, drought is and very likely will remain the greatest climatic hazard faced by people of the region. Adapting to reduce climate risks in the future will necessarily require improved understanding of present day vulnerability to drought.

Developing meaningful adaptation initiatives at the local level to reduce vulnerability to drought should begin by assessing household vulnerability among local populations. To be able to assess the vulnerability and adaptive capacity of rural households, we adopt a livelihood systems framework. This framework recognizes that a household's vulnerability to drought is affected by its exposure to drought and its first order effects on the biophysical environment and on the livelihood assets at its disposal to ameliorate the impacts of the drought or to adapt to the situation. The main objective of this chapter is to identify the determinants of the vulnerability of farm households to drought in northern Nigeria and the implications for policy. The study uses a participatory process to identify indicators of vulnerability and rank households into various classes of vulnerability.

The remainder of the chapter is organized as follows. The next section describes the study region and the study villages; the physical and socioeconomic characteristics are presented in order to better situate drought impacts in the region. This is followed by a description of the study methodology and then the results of our household vulnerability assessments. The chapter ends with a summary of findings and recommendations.

The Study Area

Semi-arid northern Nigeria is characterized by low and variable rainfall. The Sahel is intermediate between the desert and the sub-humid zones of Africa, with average departures from the annual mean rainfall of 20 to 40 per cent over the period 1901 to 1973 (Janowiak, 1988). The key source of variation – and of drought – is seasonal rainfall. Two distinct seasons are observed, dry and wet. The dry season lasts about seven to eight months, from October to April or May, while the wet season lasts about four to five months, from May or June through September. Since the major droughts of the early 1970s, droughts have become persistent in the region (Lamb, 1982), and in 1983–1984 some stations recorded even lower rainfall than in the early 1970s (Mortimore, 1998).

From the beginning of the 20th century, drought events have been recorded in Northern Nigeria in 1904–1912, 1914–1930, 1942, 1950–1952, 1966–1968, 1969–1974, 1983–1984 and 1987 (Apeldoorn, 1981, Okechukwu, 1997). During the 1968–1974 droughts, the region lost about 300,000 animals (13 per cent of the livestock population in northeastern Nigeria), agricultural yields fell to about 40 per cent of normal yields and the population at risk was about 14 million persons. Between 1983 and 1984, there was localized drought in Borno, Jigawa and Yobe resulting from deficient rainfall. In parts of Borno, the impact was as severe as the drought of 1971–73. During this drought, about 5 million metric tons of grains was lost, accompanied by constraints on biological productivity and forced migrations (Tarhule and Lamb, 2003; Ojo and Oyebande, 1985).

The patterns of drought, as computed using the Bhalme and Mooley Drought Intensity Index (BMDI) for selected stations in the study area between 1930 and 1983 (Bhalme and Mooley, 1980), are presented in Figure 11.1. For the purposes of this chapter, the BMDI nine-class schema was reduced to five: BMDI values >3.00 = extreme wet, >2 = wet, >1 = Normal, –1 to –3 = mild to moderate drought and <–3 = severe drought. Observed data show that the region has experienced a trend towards increased aridity, as can be seen in the figure.

Based on the 1991 census, the region has an estimated population of 47.3 million. Infrastructure to serve this population is extremely weak in terms of the quality and distribution of roads, schools and health facilities. Major indigenous ethnic groups in this region include the Hausa, Fulani, Kanuri, Shuwa, Burbur, Gerewa and Ningawa. Members of other ethnic groups have also migrated into the region from within and beyond Nigeria in recent decades. The different groups have different interests in the resource base, possess different skills with which to use it, and claim rights over different resources and areas.

The region is rich in agricultural production, but the large inter-annual variability of rainfall subjects it to frequent dry spells, which sometimes result

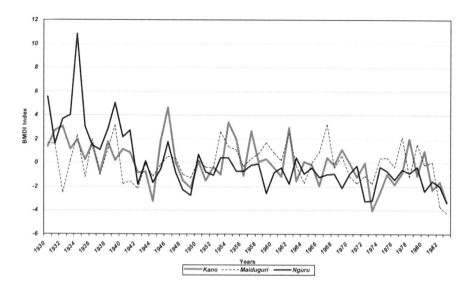

Figure 11.1 *Bhalme and Mooley drought intensity (BMDI) index for selected stations in northern Nigeria, 1930–1983*

in severe and widespread drought that can impose serious socioeconomic constraints. Irrigated agriculture is widely practised and agricultural crops include rice, wheat, soybeans, beans, maize, millet, cotton, sorghum and groundnut. Besides arable farming, pastoralism is the main economic activity in the region. A particularly large stock of cattle is found in this zone, originating mainly from the neighbouring countries of Chad, Niger and Cameroon. These countries are currently experiencing particularly dry periods, and so livestock has been transferred from them to the transitional zone in Nigeria, where fodder is still available around the patches of wetland areas, fadamas (flood plains of rivers) and those river valleys that still contain water.

Two major pastoral corridors exist in the region and 3 million hectares of wetlands dot these corridors, with an average livestock density of 13 animals per hectare, well above the carrying capacity. Herders traditionally move along these corridors on a seasonal basis, following the rains as they move from north to south and back. The land for these corridors was acquired by the federal government, which has created a number of consequent problems. The original owners of the land did not believe they were adequately compensated and have since attempted to repossess their lands. The movements of pastoralists are not monitored, and in many instances pastoralists have allowed their herds to stray from the corridor to graze on farmland, provoking conflicts. This continues because the density of herds using the corridors is greater than the forage available along them, and vegetation is consequently unable to regenerate sufficiently.

Data Collection

Data were collected to examine vulnerability to droughts in 27 communities in northern Nigeria. The data collection started with a reconnaissance survey that took the research team from the east to the west of northern Nigeria, covering all the states that fall within the study area. The states that we visited include Bauchi, Gombe, Borno, Yobe, Kano, Jigawa, Katsina, Sokoto, Zamfara, Kebbi and Adamawa. The essence of the reconnaissance survey was to familiarize ourselves with the study area, identify the major livelihood systems and identify the major drought and other issues faced by households. We attempted to learn from members of the surveyed communities the nature and magnitude of the problem of drought and climate change. A major problem noted in the visit was the high water deficit in the area. Hand dug wells exploiting ground water are common features and it is currently estimated that the rate of abstraction of ground water in this zone is highly unsustainable, with a continuous decline in the water table. It is also common to find once perennial rivers having turned to dry valleys.

We identified four major livelihood structures in the study: fishing, pastoralism, sedentary farming, and other informal livelihood systems such as mat making. We found that livelihood systems are differentiated spatially across the study region. Villages that are farther north are home predominantly to pastoralists, while those in the south are largely home to sedentary farmers. At the interface of these two livelihood systems lies a zone of mixed livelihood systems comprising both pastoralists and arable farming.

Using information from the reconnaissance survey, we selected a number of communities for more comprehensive study using a three-tier sampling strategy. First, we selected all the states that are vulnerable to drought resulting from climate change. We then listed all the local government areas (numbering 250) in all the affected states. From the list, we aggregated these into larger units, numbering 27, and selected 1 community each from the larger units. The factors that we considered in selecting the study villages included the occurrence of past and/or repeated drought disasters, willingness of the women to participate in the survey, the main livelihood system in the village and the size of the village. We grouped the villages into three classes based on their population and physical size – large, medium and small. We ensured that the villages selected represented a mix of these classes.

Data collection in the selected villages was done through the administration of questionnaires, focus group discussions and stakeholder analysis. The questionnaire comprises 17 sections that solicit information about household processes and relations, socioeconomic and drought-related variables, and livelihood systems and strategies. The questionnaire was developed in conjunction with relevant stakeholders identified during the reconnaissance survey and pre-tested in three communities to assess its validity and reliability in collecting pertinent information for the study. After the pre-test, some questions were modified to suit local norms and customs.

910 questionnaires were administered to household heads in 27 communities in Nigeria, of which 828 were completed.[1] We define a household as a social and economic unit consisting of one or more individuals, whether they

are relatives or not, who live together and share both 'the pot and the roof' (in other words dwelling and food). The questionnaire administration was supplemented by focus group discussions. The questionnaires could only reveal past and present vulnerabilities; they do not explain the processes that are at the root of the households' present situation of vulnerability. Focus-group discussions served to achieve this latter goal.

Self-Assessed Perceptions of Risk

Although the focus of the study is to assess drought vulnerability, it is important to situate this within the overall risks faced by communities and groups in the study region. The inhabitants' perception of risk may be based not only on the objective risk they face, but also on their subjective assessment of risk. The vulnerability of households and groups to these risks may differ and also affect the way they respond to them. In this work we asked broader questions about what worries the people face in their lives overall in order to look at how their perceptions of these worries can inform our understanding of their vulnerability. These worries were translated into risks. The risks that respondents identified are presented in Table 11.1. It should be noted that households listed more than one risk or worry and respondents were not restricted in the number of risks they could list. The risk incidence index, Ij, presented in Table 11.1, is a measure of the proportion of respondents that mentioned a particular risk.

Table 11.1 *Self-perceived risks*

Serial no	Perceived Risk	Incidence Index (Ij)	Severity Index (Sj)	Risk Index (Rj)
1	Insufficient food for people	0.55	1.03	0.93
2	Shortage of water for domestic use	0.55	1.14	0.91
3	Shortage of water for animals	0.52	1.24	0.86
4	Shortage of crops for cultivation	0.50	1.25	0.77
5	Insufficient pasture for animals	0.40	1.47	0.60
6	Animal diseases	0.37	1.55	0.47
7	Limited land for cultivation	0.37	1.62	0.44
8	Crop failure	0.34	1.63	0.33
9	Human diseases	0.31	1.74	0.30
10	Conflicts/insecurity	0.28	1.76	0.18
11	Low prices for animals	0.26	1.89	0.15
12	Lack of employment	0.25	1.92	0.14

Note: The incidence index (Ij), is a measure of the proportion of respondents that mentioned a particular risk; the severity index (Sj), measures the severity of each risk on a scale from 1 (most severe) to 2 (least severe); and the risk index (Rj), is the ratio of the Incidence index (Ij) to the severity index (Sj)

Severity and risk indices also were computed using a methodology adopted from Quinn et al (2003). The severity index measures the severity of each risk on a scale from 1 (most severe) to 2 (least severe). It was calculated for each risk identified by each respondent as:

$$Sj = 1 + \frac{(r-1)}{(n-1)}$$

where Sj is the severity index value for a particular risk, r is its rank, based on the order in which it was mentioned by the respondent, and n is the total number of problems identified by that respondent. The mean value of Sj was then calculated for the subset of respondents who identified the particular problem. Finally, for each risk, a risk index was calculated as:

$$Rj = \frac{I_j}{S_j}$$

Since higher values for Ij indicate higher incidence and lower values for Sj indicate more severity, Rj increases with the overall risk associated with each type of problem. The risk index ranges between 0 (no incidence of risk) and 1 (severe risk).

The results in Table 11.1 show that the greatest concern of the respondents was the risk of insufficient food, followed by shortage of water for domestic use. Without the respondents specifically mentioning drought, the table shows that most of the concerns are problems related to drought, an indication that drought is a major problem in the study area. This justifies the focus of the study on drought vulnerability.

Household Drought Vulnerability Assessment

An index of drought vulnerability

Vulnerability is a relative term differing between socioeconomic groups or regions, rather than an absolute measurement of deprivation. The analyst or decision maker must assign the thresholds of vulnerability that warrant specific responses. For our study, we developed a drought vulnerability index (DVI), which is constructed from indicators developed through a combination of top–down and bottom–up approaches. In conjunction with stakeholders, 14 indicators of vulnerability were identified along with their weights (Table 11.2). Indicators that directly impact on vulnerability are given a weight of 1, while those that affect vulnerability indirectly have a weight of 0.5. The original scores for the indices are transformed linearly so that the scores for each indicator range from 0 to 1. Adding up the weighted household scores on the 14 indices resulted in an overall vulnerability score for each household in the sample, with the scores ranging from 0.89 to 10 (see Table 11.2). Indicators that respondents felt directly explain vulnerability include crop yield, dependency ratio, livestock ownership, livelihood diversification and drought preparedness.

Table 11.2 *Indicators and weights for vulnerability assessment in northern Nigeria*

Indicator	Weight	Derived from:	Mean	Min	Max
Acreage under cultivation	0.5	Hectares/consumer units	0.21	0.04	1
Crop yield	1	Total bags of cereals harvested/consumer unit	0.50	0.06	1
Dependency ratio	1	Labour units/consumer units (inverted)	0.63	0.38	1
Livestock ownership	1	Tropical livestock units/ consumer units	0.45		
Gender of household head Dummy: 1 if the household head is male, 0 otherwise	0.5	Value given to sex of household head	0.91	0	1
Livelihood diversification	1	Weighted number of non-agricultural income generating activities/ consumer units	0.29	0	1
Annual cash income	1	In 1000 naira/consumer units	0.43	0.25	1
Drought preparedness Dummy: 1 if the household uses drought resistant crops or received drought-related information, 0 otherwise	1	Value given to use of drought resistant crops and livestock and received drought-related information and advice	0.34	0	1
Educational background of the household head Dummy: 1 if household had completed at least primary education, 0 otherwise	0.5	Value given to highest school level attained by the head of the household	0.28	0	1
Land tenure situation Dummy: 1 if household owns more than 50% of the land it cultivates, 0 otherwise	0.5	Value given to land tenure situation	0.57	0	1
Type of house Dummy: 1 if house is a modern house, 0 otherwise	0.5	Value given to type of house lived in	0.13	0	1
Self-sufficiency in food production	0.5	Logged number of years surplus foodstuffs were sold/number of years foodstuffs were bought in the past 10 years	0.56	0	1
Family and social networks	0.5	Number of organizations the household is involved in	0.33	0	1
Quality of household	0.5	Number of able persons/ number of disabled and/or sick persons in the household (inverted)	0.14	0.02	1

Note: Mean, minimum and maximum values from household surveys are normalized to [0,1] interval, with 1 representing lowest vulnerability.

The next step in constructing the DVI was to identify different thresholds within which households can be grouped into various levels of vulnerability. We could have adopted the Delphi method using 'expert judgement' or a top–down approach based only on the earlier computations of vulnerability. However, we considered neither of these methods satisfactory, as we believe that the respondents should contribute to defining their vulnerability. We therefore adopted a methodology that combined a top–down and bottom–up approach to delineating vulnerability thresholds.

During the questionnaire administration, respondents participated in a vulnerability ranking exercise in which they placed themselves in any of three classes of vulnerability: very vulnerable, vulnerable and least vulnerable. These allowed us to factor in their perceptions and self-reported assessments of vulnerability. We took all those who put themselves in each group, found the average scores for each group based on our earlier computation and used those as the midpoints of the various vulnerability classes and then built class intervals about them. We arrived at the following ranges: those that scored less than 4 were categorized as highly vulnerable, scores between 4 and 7 were categorized as vulnerable and those above 7 as least vulnerable. The distribution of households by vulnerability class for each of the 27 communities is presented in Table 11.3.

A model of household vulnerability to drought

As described in the previous section, households' self-assessments of their level of vulnerability to drought and contributing factors were established through household surveys and participatory exercises. We then performed a multivariate analysis with the aim of identifying how these and other factors influence the probability of a household being classified as less vulnerable, vulnerable or highly vulnerable. Our model of vulnerability to drought, which is based on the sustainable livelihoods framework, postulates that a household's vulnerability is a function of the household's exposure to droughts and the livelihood assets available to the household, which provide capacity to cope with, recover from and adapt to drought and its impacts. Four classes of assets were used in the analysis – natural, financial/economic, human and social.

The statistical analysis was performed using ordinal logistic regression analysis. The ordinal logit model is used when the outcome variable is categorized on an ordinal scale, as in this case where vulnerability is ordered as (1) least vulnerable, (2) vulnerable and (3) highly vulnerable (McCullagh and Nelder, 1989). This model is particularly useful in that it can show movement between vulnerability classes, explaining who moves in and out of vulnerability. Following Green (1993), the reduced form of the ordinal logit model is given as:

$$y^* = \beta'Z + \varepsilon$$

where y* is the given state of vulnerability, Z is the set of explanatory variables,

Table 11.3 *Distribution of households by vulnerability class*

Serial no.	Community	Latitude (°N)	Major occupation	Vulnerability class of household			Total
				Less vulnerable	Vulnerable	Highly vulnerable	
1	Buni Yadi	11.578	farming	8	10	13	31
2	Dan Matamachi	12.612	pastoralism	10	13	7	30
3	Kalalawa	13.210	pastoralism	6	9	15	30
4	Maimallamri	11.425	farming	8	11	12	31
5	Daki Takwas	11.908	farming	7	13	11	31
6	Shanga	11.214	farming	7	7	17	31
7	Maguru	12.466	pastoralism	8	9	15	32
8	Kofin Soli	12.501	pastoralism	7	8	16	31
9	Guruma	12.118	mixed	6	10	16	32
10	Marnona	13.212	pastoralism	9	9	12	30
11	Tabanni	11.098	farming	11	11	8	30
12	Garin Ahmadu	13.090	pastoralism	6	10	14	30
13	Dabai	11.480	farming	7	9	14	30
14	Auki	12.185	mixed	7	13	10	30
15	Madara	11.690	farming	7	10	15	32
16	Zangon Buhari	11.663	farming	8	9	14	31
17	Kwanar Gaki	12.429	mixed	9	8	13	30
18	Chanchanda	12.524	pastoralism	11	10	11	32
19	Sara	11.349	farming	9	10	11	30
20	Jinjimawa	12.290	pastoralism	8	11	12	30
21	Damasak	13.098	pastoralism	7	11	12	30
22	Badrama	11.715	farming	7	8	16	31
23	Zandam	11.300	farming	6	9	15	30
24	Chingowa	12.045	mixed	7	9	15	31
25	Andarai	11.899	farming	5	10	16	31
26	Kajiji	12.537	pastoralism	9	12	9	30
27	Kubani	11.018	farming	8	13	10	31
	Total			208	272	349	828

β' is the vector of coefficients to be determined and ε is a random error with zero mean and unit variance. y* is unobserved; what we do observe is:

$$y = 1, \text{ if } y^* \le \mu_2$$
$$y = 2, \text{ if } \mu_2 < y^* \le \mu_3$$
$$y = 3, \text{ if } \mu_3 \le y^*$$

The μ-values (μ_2, μ_3), referred to as cut-off points, are unknown parameters to be estimated along with β. A positive coefficient indicates an increased chance that a respondent with a higher score on the independent variable will be observed in a higher class of vulnerability. A negative coefficient indicates the chances that a respondent with a higher score on the independent variable will be observed in a lower class of vulnerability.

The explanatory variables are grouped as exposure, natural assets, economic assets, human assets and social assets. Following Ziervogel and Calder (2003), we emphasize livelihood assets rather than capitals, which tend to have economic associations. The explanatory variables used in the model are described in the Appendix to this chapter.

Variables used to characterize household exposure to drought include the number of drought episodes previously experienced by the household, receipt of drought information, use of drought-resistant practices and existence of a household drought contingency plan. Previous exposure to drought could either increase vulnerability by depleting household assets or decrease vulnerability by increasing a household's knowledge about and adoption of drought-resilient practices. However, we hypothesize that the greater the number of droughts experienced by a household, the more vulnerable it is. Receipt of drought-related information, either in the form of seasonal forecasts or information about drought-resilient crop varieties or management practices, and current use of drought-resistant crop varieties or livestock breeds are expected to reduce vulnerability. Some households have drought contingency plans and those that do are expected to be less vulnerable than those that do not.

Most rural livelihoods in the West African Sahel are substantially reliant on the natural resource base. The natural asset variables used in the logit analysis capture the ability of the natural production system to maintain productivity when exposed to drought. The explanatory variables include self-assessed fertility of the soil, size of household landholdings and the proportion of household landholdings under irrigation. We hypothesize that households with soils that they consider fertile, larger landholdings and more than 50 per cent of their land under irrigation are less vulnerable than those that have infertile soils, small landholdings and less than 50 per cent of their lands irrigated.

Another group of variables represents the economic capital base of the household, which is essential for the pursuit of any livelihood strategy (Scoones, 1998). Each household's main occupation is identified as farming, pastoralism, agro-pastoralism or other. Households that engage in agro-pastoralism are expected to be less vulnerable than the other occupations. Financial asset related variables used in the analysis include identification of the main occupations of the household, number of income sources, level of cash income per capita, access to credit, existence of a savings account and percentage of income spent on household upkeep. Variables were also included for non-financial economic assets such as per capita livestock ownership, per capita cereal harvest, number of years in last ten that the household was self-sufficient in food, use of modern farm equipment, distance of the household to the nearest road suitable for motor vehicles and distance of the village to the nearest market. All of the financial and non-financial asset variables are hypothesized to confer lesser vulnerability to drought.

Household composition and structure – gender relations, household cycle, the number of members and the number of potential contributors to the household economy – are crucial to understand households' and household members' vulnerability. Variables related to human assets that are included in the analysis include the age and gender of the household head, the highest level of education attained by any member of the household, the ratio of household labour units to consumer units and household size. Studies elsewhere have shown that age is a major factor that affects poverty (UNDP, 1998). For example, data from Lebanon and Palestine suggest that households headed by young and old workers – in the early stage and the dispersion years of the domestic cycle – are much more vulnerable to poverty than households whose providers are between 40 and 54 years old. There exist divergent views among researchers regarding the vulnerability of female- versus male-headed households, with some suggesting that female-headed households are more vulnerable (Buvinic and Gupta 1994) and others arguing that female-headed households are as economically and socially viable as male-headed ones (Chant, 1997). Households with more education and more workers per dependent are expected to be less vulnerable, while larger households could be associated with either greater or lesser vulnerability.

Social assets also play a vital role in sustaining livelihoods, particularly through benefits coming from networks of community based organizations and relatives. Membership of community organizations provides safety nets at times of crisis and the number of organizations a household belongs to reduces its vulnerability to droughts. Assistance that households receive from community organizations and from family members and relatives outside the community in the form of remittances can also reduce vulnerability.

Results from the Statistical Model of Vulnerability

The results of our empirical estimation of the model are presented in Table 11.4. All the exposure variables are significant either at the 95 or 90 per cent confidence levels and have the expected signs. The most significant exposure variable is the use of drought-resistant crop and livestock varieties. Using drought-resistant varieties reduces the likelihood of being in a higher vulnerability class. While many of the households are using drought-resistant varieties, a significant proportion do not. Some of the reasons given by households who do not use them ranged from not knowing where to buy them to not having the services of extension workers to explain how to use them.

Another exposure variable that is very significant is the number of drought episodes experienced. The higher the number of drought episodes a household has experienced, the higher the likelihood of belonging to a higher vulnerability class. The odds of a household's vulnerability being above any level (j) are estimated to be 1.3 times higher for every additional exposure to drought. About 57 per cent (476) of the households reported experiencing droughts, 11 per cent of these in a previous settlement, 57 per cent in their present location and about 33 per cent in both previous and present locations. These included households who had migrated because of droughts in their previous communities only to experience them again in their destination communities. This category of people are very likely to be highly vulnerable as many lost almost all their assets in their previous communities to warrant migration, which is often seen as a last resort.

Table 11.4 *Ordinal logit results for determinants of drought vulnerability*

Variable	Coefficient	p>|z|	Odds ratio
Exposure			
Drought episodes experienced	0.2596443	0.004	1.3
Drought information received	−0.1936687	0.052	0.8
Use of drought resistant varieties	−0.3356348	0.002	0.7
Drought preparedness	−0.2849131	0.051	0.8
Natural Asset			
Soil fertility	−0.1370299	0.034	0.9
Cultivated land size	−0.0421065	0.121	1.0
Land under irrigation	−0.5540021	0.027	0.6
Economic/Financial asset			
Main occupation of household head			
Farming	0.4037844	0.039	1.5
Pastoralism	0.0295531	0.048	1.0
Agro-pastoralism	−0.3861327	0.024	0.7
Income diversification activities	−0.0318834	0.055	1.0
Total annual income	−0.5844522	0.002	0.6
Tropical livestock units (TLUs) per household	−0.5100647	0.063	0.6
Total crop harvest	−0.5330721	0.046	0.6
Use of modern farm equipment	−0.3383219	0.175	0.7
Access to credit	−0.1439984	0.074	0.9
Existence of savings account	−0.1275478	0.051	0.9
Household expenditure	0.5833401	0.023	1.8
Distance of household from major access road	0.4973665	0.218	1.6
Distance of settlement from market	0.6683497	0.049	2.0
Household type i.e. traditional or modern	−0.0025662	0.258	1.0
Food self sufficiency	−0.492291	0.085	0.6
Human Asset			1.0
Age of household head	0.0161207	0.188	1.0
Sex of household head	0.3218215	0.230	1.4
Highest level of education in household			
Primary	−0.1021783	0.195	0.9
Secondary	−0.2410995	0.047	0.8
Tertiary	−0.4805231	0.203	0.6
Household dependency ratio (labour/consumers)	0.7230225	0.000	2.1
Household size	0.0026388	0.093	1.0
Social Asset			
Membership of community organizations	−0.1921738	0.381	0.8
Assistance from organizations	−0.4529962	0.047	0.6
Assistance from family outside the community	−0.5562897	0.033	0.6
cut1	−0.5684523		
cut2	0.8932861		
Sample size	828		
Log likelihood statistic	−14925.141		
Pseudo R^2	0.401		

Note: For a detailed description of the variables in Table 11.4, please refer to the Appendix at the end of the chapter.

Availability of drought information, including forecasts and information about drought-resilient practices, can be used by households to reduce their exposure to drought impacts. But, as the study shows, about 58 per cent of the population is not aware of the existence of drought and rainfall forecast information. Only 27 per cent regularly receive forecasts, while 15 per cent are aware of but do not receive them. Lack of information, therefore, reduces the coping capacity to drought, hence increasing vulnerability to drought hazards.

The population that receives forecast information gets the information from different sources, including radio, television, agricultural extension officers, village heads and farmers' associations. Those who have access to the forecasts generally consider them satisfactory in terms of reliability and presentation. But often the forecast information is not used. Reasons given for non-use of the forecasts include language constraint, poor user friendliness and lack of timeliness. Greater efforts are needed to make forecasts available to a larger proportion of households, to provide forecasts in local languages and in forms that are more easily understood and used, and to issue forecasts farther in advance of forecasted events.[2]

While one cannot stop the onset of droughts, it is assumed that the extent of one's preparedness affects the impacts of the droughts when they do occur. The statistical analysis confirms that those with contingency plans for drought are less vulnerable.

The three natural asset variables had the expected signs, although only soil fertility and land irrigation were significant at the 95 per cent confidence limit. Most of the farmers practise rain-fed farming and harvests are strongly affected by rainfall variability. But those that do use irrigation on more than 50 per cent of their land are 40 per cent more likely to fall within a lower vulnerability class compared to households that do not irrigate or irrigate less than 50 per cent of their land.

The data collected show that only 13 per cent of the farmlands are irrigated. There are five major sources of water for irrigation in northern Nigeria. These include rain harvesting, ponds and dams, streams and rivers, and wells and boreholes. The few households that have land under irrigation were those that live close to streams and rivers or are engaged in rainwater harvesting. Digging of boreholes and wells is an expensive venture and the technology to pump water from the ground is also expensive for most of these farmers. Efforts to make rainwater harvesting more widely available and the cost of pumping water more affordable could help to reduce vulnerability to drought.

With respect to the economic and financial assets, the variables for main livelihood occupation are all significant. Being a farmer increases by 50 per cent the likelihood of belonging to a higher vulnerability class compared to other occupations. On the other hand, households whose main occupation was agro-pastoralism are 30 per cent more likely to belong to lower classes of vulnerability than those with 'other' occupations. Pastoralism is positively associated with vulnerability, but the odds ratio is statistically insignificant.

Farming is the most common livelihood in the study area, followed by pastoralism. Pastoralism is the main economic activity in 33 per cent of the sampled villages and is the main livelihood for about 37 per cent of the sampled households. The most common domesticated animals in the research area are cattle, poultry, goats and sheep. Cattle are generally kept at the commercial level, while the smaller animals – goats, sheep and poultry – are kept at the subsistence level. When expressed in tropical livestock units (TLUs), cattle are the most important type of animal among households, followed by goats, poultry and sheep. The poultry include chickens, ducks, turkeys and guinea fowl. Virtually every household keeps poultry and some goats and sheep. However, the distribution of livestock in the sample was very unequal in the communities and among the various vulnerable groups, with the less vulnerable households owning more livestock per household than the other groups.

Livelihood diversification has become a well-accepted adaptation strategy in the Sahel. Households are less vulnerable to climatic stress if they have multiple sources of livelihood to fall back on in times of scarcity. The survey obtained information from households regarding all their non-agricultural income-generating activities and assigned weights to them based on the reliability and the income generated by each activity as reported by the respondents. The assumption is that the greater the number of non-agricultural income-generating activities, and the more income generated from them, the less vulnerable a household was.

Income diversification activities identified in this study are separated into four main types: crafts, trade, labouring and hunting/gathering. Labouring on other people's farms is a widespread phenomenon and to many a primary method of supplementing their own farm income. Labouring is the largest income diversification activity in the region, followed by trading. Migration on its own was not considered as an income diversification activity, rather what the migrant does to generate income. Many of the migrants go outside their immediate communities to work on other people's farms or work in non-farm income generating activities. Hunting/gathering is the least practised income diversification activity in the region.

Income and per capita crop harvest were all significant at the 95 per cent confidence level, and households with higher values of these were less likely to belong to higher vulnerability classes. Crops cultivated in the area include maize, millet, sorghum, beans and rice. About 28 per cent of households harvested less than 20 bags of cereals, 38 per cent harvested between 20 and 60 bags, 23 per cent harvested between 60 and 150 bags, while 11 per cent harvested more than 150 bags of cereals.

Households that spent more than 70 per cent of their income in running the household were 1.8 times more likely to belong to a higher class of vulnerability. Also, longer distances from the house to a major road (inaccessibility) increased by 80 per cent the likelihood of belonging to higher classes of vulnerability. The same holds true for market distance, where the odds of belonging to a higher vulnerability class is estimated to be 2.0 times for every additional kilometre increase in distance. It is instructive to note the importance that distance to market plays in farm household vulnerability. Many of the farmers harvest their crops and cannot transport them to the markets because of distance. This inaccessibility to markets makes them receive suboptimal prices for their crops, reducing their income and further exacerbating their vulnerability. Investment in rural infrastructure is needed to improve access to markets, which can improve farmers' livelihoods and lessen their vulnerability to drought.

With regards to human assets, the household dependency ratio is the most significant variable. A household that has more mouths to feed than pairs of hands to cultivate the land is very vulnerable as the cycle of subsistence is reinforced. Regarding education, only secondary education is significant, with those with secondary education more likely to be less vulnerable than those without any education. Household size and age and gender of household head are not statistically significant determinants of vulnerability.

Of the social asset variables, assistance from community organizations and from family are significant at the 95 per cent confidence level. Those who receive assistance are less vulnerable than those who do not. This is where migration plays an important role in reducing vulnerability. The data show that remittances decline the farther relatives are from home. For example, there is more assistance from those within the villages than from those outside the village but within the country, and there is more assistance from those outside the community but within the country than from those outside the country.

Membership of community organizations is not statistically significant. About 60 per cent of the population in the study area do not belong to any group or organization. Those that do are members of organizations such as farmers' associations, trade unions, aid groups and religious associations. The most common type of organization among the rural communities under study is the farmers' association. Those that belong to some organization have varied reasons for being members, such as for economic progress and membership benefits, for assistance from government, to praise and worship God, and to assist one another in the community.

Conclusion

Drought is a persistent problem in the West African Sahel and has contributed to the under-development of the region. Many of the sampled households have experienced and been impacted by multiple droughts. But vulnerability is not a physical entity that can be seen or measured directly. It is a relative term differentiating between socioeconomic groups or regions, rather than an absolute measure of a physical characteristic. In our study villages, there was no agreement on what is meant by vulnerability to drought. Rather, households experience and perceive risks in terms of the consequences of the occurrence of events such as drought. For example, most households are more concerned about the risk of hunger or shortage of water for domestic use, which can be triggered by drought, than they are about the risk of drought itself.

The perceived risks, filtered through various household assets and conditions, form the basis for households' understanding of vulnerability. These fears or vulnerabilities vary among households and are shaped by economic, social and environmental processes. Because of the lack of uniformity in measuring vulnerability, the usual practice in assessing vulnerability is that the analyst or decision maker assigns thresholds of vulnerability that warrant specific responses. We took a different approach, combining top–down and bottom–up methods to construct an index of vulnerability from indicators and weights derived from the literature and through stakeholder analysis.

Using a simple self-assessment procedure in combination with statistical classification, households in the study were classified as highly vulnerable, vulnerable or less vulnerable. About 25 per cent of the households classified themselves as less vulnerable, 33 per cent as vulnerable and about 42 per cent as highly vulnerable. Numerous potential explanatory variables of vulnerability levels were identified with respondents. Some of these variables have direct impacts on vulnerability (for example, size of crop harvest, dependency ratio, livestock ownership, livelihood diversification and drought preparedness), while others act indirectly on household vulnerability. We consider this method of vulnerability assessment to be more robust as it captures both objective and subjective vulnerabilities and incorporates the perceptions of the local people.

A multivariate analysis was conducted to statistically test which factors explain the vulnerability of rural farm households to droughts. This was based on a conceptual framework that postulates that vulnerability is a function of exposure and resilience, where resilience is determined by the availability to the household of natural, economic, human and social assets. Exposure variables found to be significant determinants of household vulnerability include the number of droughts a household was exposed to, the availability of drought information for planning and the use of drought-resistant varieties. Of the household assets, household dependency ratio and income are the most significant, but many others contribute to shaping the household's vulnerability. These include soil fertility, use of irrigation, main source of livelihood, diversification of income, distance from markets, and assistance from community organizations and family.

The needs of rural households in the Sahelian zone of Nigeria are still very basic, and efforts to build resilience to drought in these communities should first address issues of access to food and water, and to help households to build the assets that are needed to sustain their livelihoods. Concerns about food, water and livelihood assets cut across pastoralist groups and sedentary farmers. Issues such as human diseases and conflicts, though often considered important in the literature, did not feature very prominently among the risks perceived by respondents.

Notes

1   The study in Nigeria was conducted as part of a larger project that included research on vulnerability to drought in Mali. Six hundred questionnaires similar to the ones used in the Nigerian analysis were administered in 16 communities in Mali between April 2003 and March 2004. Information about the full project can be found in the AF92 Project 'Final Report to Assessments of Impacts and Adaptation to Climate Change' (forthcoming; www.aiaccproject.org).

2   In Chapter 10 of this volume, James Adejuwon presents a more complete analysis of the provision and use of seasonal weather forecasts and provides further recommendations for their improvement.

References

Adger, W. N. (1999) 'Social vulnerability to climate change and extremes in coastal Vietnam', *World Development*, vol 27, pp249–269

Adger, N. and M. Kelly (1999) 'Social Vulnerability to Climate Change and the Architecture of Entitlements', *Mitigation and Adaptation Strategies for Global Change*, vol 4, pp253–266

Apeldoorn, G. J. van (1981) *Perspectives on Drought and Famine in Nigeria*, George Allen and Urwin, London

Bhalme, H. N. and D. A. Mooley (1980) 'Large-scale drought/floods and monsoon circulation', *Monthly Weather Review*, vol 108, pp1197–1211

Brooks, N. (2004) 'Drought in the African Sahel: long-term perspectives and future prospects', Tyndall Centre Working Paper no 61, Tyndall Centre for Climate Change Research, Norwich, UK

Buvinic, M. and G. R. Gupta (1994) *Poor Woman-Headed Households and Woman-Maintained Families in Developing Countries: Views on a Policy Dilemma*, International Center for Research on Women, Washington, DC, US

Chant, S. (1997) *Women Headed Households: Diversity and Dynamics in the Developing World*, Macmillan, London

Claussen, M., V. Brovkin, A. Ganopolski, C. Kubatzki and V. Petoukhov (2003) 'Climate change in northern Africa: The past is not the future', *Climate Change*, vol 57, pp99–118

Dai, A., P. J. Lamb, K. E. Trenberth, M. Hulme, P. D. Jones and P. Xie (2004) 'The recent Sahel drought is real', submitted to *International Journal of Climate Change*, available online from www.cgd.ucar.edu/cas/adai/publication-dai.html

Dietz, A. J., R. Ruben and A. Verhagen (2001) 'Impacts of climate change on drylands with a focus on West Africa', Report No. 410 200 076, Dutch National Research Programme on Global Air Pollution and Climate Change, ICCD, Wageningen

FAO (2005) 'West African food crisis looming: Millions at risk of food shortages', news release, 20 June, Food and Agriculture Organization of the United Nations, Rome

Greene, W. H. (1993) *Econometric Analysis*, Second Edition, Macmillan, New York

Haarsma, R., F. Selten, N. Weber and M. Kliphuis (2005) 'Sahel rainfall variability and response to greenhouse warming', *Geophysical Research Letters*, vol 32, pL17702

Hoerling, M., J. Hurrell, J. Eischeid and A. Phillips (2006) 'Detection and attribution of 20th century northern and southern African monsoon change', *Journal of Climate*, vol 19, pp3989–4008

Hulme, M., R. Doherty, T. Ngara, M. New, and D. Lister (2001) 'African climate change: 1900–2100', *Climate Research*, vol 17, pp145–168

Huntingford, C., F. Lamber, J. Gash, C. Taylor and A. Challinor (2005) 'Aspects of climate change prediction relevant to crop productivity', *Philosophical Transactions of the Royal Society: B*, vol 360, no 1463, pp1999-2009

Ingram, K. T., M. C. Roncoli and P. H. Kirshen (2002) 'Opportunities and constraints for farmers of West Africa to use seasonal precipitation forecasts with Burkina Faso as a case study', *Agricultural Systems*, vol 74, pp331–349

Janowiak, J. E. (1988) 'An investigation of interannual rainfall variability in Africa', *Journal of Climate*, vol 1, pp241–255

Jenkins, G., A. Gaye and B. Sylla (2005) 'Late 20th century attribution of drying trends in the Sahel from the Regional Climate Model (RegCM3)', *Geophysical Research*

Letters, vol 32, pL22705

Kamga, A., G. Jenkins, A. Gaye, A. Garba, A. Sarr and A. Adedoyin (2005) 'Evaluating the National Center for Atmospheric Research Climate System model over West Africa: Present day and the 21st century A1 scenario', *Journal of Geophysical Research-Atmospheres*, 110(D3), D03106.

Lamb, P. J. (1982) 'Persistence of sub-Saharan drought', *Nature*, vol 299, pp46–47

Lebel, T., F. Delclaux, F. Le Barbe and J. Polcher (2000) 'From GCM scales to hydrological scales: Rainfall variability in West Africa', *Stochastic Environmental Research and Risk Assessment*, vol 14, pp275–295

L'Hôte, Y., G. Mahé, B. Somé and J. P. Triboulet (2002) 'Analysis of a Sahelian annual rainfall index from 1896 to 2000: The drought continues', *Hydrological Sciences Journal*, vol 47, pp563–572

Maynard, K., J. F. Royer and F. Chauvin (2002) 'Impact of greenhouse warming on the West African summer monsoon', *Climate Dynamics*, vol 19, pp499–514

McCullagh, P. and J. Nelder (1989) *Generalized Linear Models*, second edition, Chapman and Hall, London

Mitchell, J. F. B., T. C. Johns, W. Ingram and J. A. Lowe (2000) 'The effect of stabilising the atmospheric carbon dioxide concentrations on global and regional climate change', *Geophysical Research Letters*, vol 27, no 18, pp2977–2980

Mortimore, M. (1998) 'Roots in the African dust: Sustaining the sub-Saharan drylands', Cambridge University Press, Cambridge, UK

Mortimore, M. J. and W. M. Adams (2001) 'Farmer adaptation, change and "crisis" in the Sahel', *Global Environmental Change*, vol 11, pp49–57

Ojo, O. and L. Oyebande (1985) 'Trends in occurrences and severity of droughts in Nigeria', in *Ecological Disasters in Nigeria: Drought and Desertification*, Proceedings of the National Workshop on Ecological Disasters, Kano, pp19–53

Okechukwu, G. C. (1997) 'Survey of drought history in northern Nigeria', sub-project report no 8, Jos–McMaster Drought and Rural Water Use Project, University of Jos, Nigeria and McMaster University, Canada

Quinn, C. H., M. Huby, H. Kiwasila and J. C. Lovett (2003) 'Local perceptions of risk to livelihood in semi-arid Tanzania', *Journal of Environmental Management*, vol 68, pp111–119

Scoones, I. (1998) 'Sustainable rural livelihoods: A framework for analysis', IDS Working Paper 72

Tarhule, A. and P. J. Lamb (2003) 'Climate research and seasonal forecasting for West Africans: Perceptions, dissemination, and use', *Bulletin of the American Meteorological Society*, vol 84, pp1741–1759

UNDP (1998) 'Mapping of living conditions in Lebanon: An analysis of the housing and population database, 1998', United Nations Development Programme/ Ministry of Social Affairs

Vincent, K. (2004) 'Creating an index of social vulnerability to climate change for Africa', Tyndall Centre Working Paper 56, Tyndall Centre for Climate Change Research, Norwich, UK

Wang, G. L. and E. A. B. Eltahir (2002) 'Impact of CO_2 concentration changes on the biosphere-atmosphere system of West Africa', *Global Change Biology*, vol 8, pp1169–1182

Ziervogel, G. and R. Calder (2003) 'Climate variability and rural livelihoods: Assessing the impact of seasonal climate forecasts in Lesotho', *Area*, vol 35, no 4, pp403–417

Appendix

Variables in the ordinal logit model of determinants of drought vulnerability in northern Nigeria

Variable	Variable description	Min	Max	Mean	Std Dev
Exposure					
Droutepi	Number of drought episodes experienced	0	4	2.18	1.19
Droutinfo	Dummy variable: 1 if household has ever received formal drought-related information, 0 otherwise	0	1	0.15	0.34
Droutvar	Dummy variable: 1 if household uses drought-resistant varieties, 0 otherwise	0	1	0.57	0.41
Droutpln	Dummy variable: 1 if household has any drought preparedness plan, 0 otherwise	0	1	0.49	0.36
Natural Assets					
soilfert	Dummy variable for self-assessed fertility of farmlands: 1 if fertile, 0 otherwise	0	1	0.42	0.56
landsize	Total size of land cultivated/number of consumer units in the household (ha)	0.1	3.5	0.84	1.22
irrigland	Dummy variable for proportion of land under irrigation: 1 if more than 50% of the land is under irrigation, 0 otherwise.	0	1	0.34	0.46
Economic/Financial Assets					
mainocc	Categorical variable representing the main occupation of the household head: 1 if farmer, 2 if pastoralist, 3 agro-pastoral, 4 other occupations	1	4	1.98	1.72
incomdiv	Weighted number of income diversification activities in the household/consumer units	0	3.1	1.05	0.95
income	Total annual income to the household from all sources/consumer units (1000 naira)	2.3	10.6	4.7	2.41
TLU	Tropical livestock unit in the household/number of consumer units.	0	11.2	5.3	4.33
crophvst	Crop total bags of cereals harvested/consumer unit	1.2	24.6	11.3	5.44
farmquip	Dummy variable for use of modern farm equipment: 1 if household uses modern farm equipment, 0 otherwise.	0	1	0.32	0.51
credit	Dummy variable: 1 if household has access to credit, 0 otherwise	0	1	0.21	0.65
banksav	Dummy variable: 1if any household member has a savings account, 0 otherwise	0	1	0.27	0.44

Variable	Variable description	Min	Max	Mean	Std Dev
hhexpen	Dummy variable for proportion of household expenditure spent in running the household: 1 if more than 70%, 0 otherwise	0	1	0.64	0.44
roadist	Distance of home to major access road (km)	0.01	3.8	1.02	1.27
Markdist	Distance of settlement to major market (km)	0.5	12.8	6.3	2.41
foodsuff	Food self sufficiency: number of years in the past 10 years that household produced enough food to feed itself	0	10	4.23	5.1
Human Assets					
Age	Age of household head in completed years	15	83	49.26	22.4
Sex	Dummy variable for sex of household head: 1 if male, 0 otherwise	0	1	0.96	0.12
educat	Categorical variable for highest level of education completed by any member of the household: 0 for none, 1 for primary, 2 for secondary and 3 for tertiary	0	3	1.02	1.79
depend	Household dependency ratio (labour units/consumer units)	0.24	0.88	0.61	0.37
hhsize	Number of persons in the household	1	31	12.9	9.3
Social Assets					
comorg	Number of community organizations household belongs to	0	4	1.5	1.3
orgasist	Receives assistance from organizations	0	1	0.45	0.24
famasist	Has family member outside the community that sends money and other forms of assistance	0	1	0.23	0.38

12

Livelihoods and Drought in Sudan

Balgis Osman-Elasha and El-Amin Sanjak

Introduction

Drought is a primary agent of famine in Africa today, where the agricultural production environment is under increased stress from many factors. Studies of past environmental change and the northern African archaeological record indicate just how variable climatic and environmental conditions are in the Sahel-Sahara zone on timescales of centuries to millennia. Such studies also illustrate the sensitivity of rainfall in this region to hemispheric and global-scale changes in climate (Brooks, 2006). In Africa, where around half of cultivable land is arid and semi-arid, about 65 per cent of the croplands and 30 per cent of pastureland have been affected by degradation, with resultant declines in crop yields and food insecurity. High seasonal rainfall variability is endemic to the arid regions of Sudan and the resulting droughts have affected many inhabitants, who live with constant vulnerability and possess weak or poor coping ability to deal with hunger, famine, dislocation and material loss (Osman-Elasha, 2006).

However, such vulnerability is not caused by climate variability or climate change alone. The highly variable climate is an underlying characteristic, a chronic state of the region's fragile livelihood systems. Given the constant exposure to this state of fragility under frequent harsh conditions, most human inhabitants have developed traditional knowledge regarding occurrences and likely consequences of extreme climatic events. However, while they possess the know-how to adapt and modify their livelihood systems to buffer against potential disasters and prepare themselves with whatever means at their disposal for these anticipated threats, more recently, particularly since the 1980s, some human livelihood systems seem to have lost their ability to adapt to or recover from sustained droughts (Teklu et al, 1991). Hence, there is an urgent need to examine the underlying causes and the factors that determine enhanced exposure and declining ability to recover from extreme climate events. Consequently, there is also a need to find answers to questions such as 'How do people manage their livelihoods under current vulnerability?' and

'How could they avoid potential vulnerability in the face of anticipated enhanced future climate variability and change?'

This chapter attempts to address the above questions by exploring the relationship between climate variability and the livelihoods of rural agricultural and pastoral populations in this semi-arid Sahelian region of Africa. While focusing on climate-related vulnerabilities, it also considers the socioeconomic context of the inhabitants by examining the many other stresses they face and how these contribute to increasing their vulnerability.

Climatic events in these parts of Africa, particularly droughts, trigger frequent subsistence crises, sharply increasing crop failures. An example is the drought that occurred in the whole of Sahelian Africa in 1984, resulting in widespread hunger and famine that has been ascribed to a combination of climate variability and socioeconomic factors. According to Braun et al (1998), the genesis of food crises in this region is a result of the interaction between environmental and socioeconomic factors, in both the short and the long terms, and a failure of policy to deal with them. Most survivors of the 1984 drought were left with fewer assets and with an increasingly risky agricultural income base that offers little buffer against future crises (Braun et al, 1991; Teklu et al, 1991). This situation was also a striking example of the collective impact of multiple factors (poor infrastructure, lack of capacity, illiteracy and under-development) undermining the coping abilities and resilience of entire populations, rendering them helpless, limiting their coping abilities, and resulting in extreme suffering and large scale migration away from the region.

Vulnerability to climate variability and change

Vulnerability to climate change is generally understood to be a function of a range of biophysical and socioeconomic factors. According to McCarthy et al (2001), vulnerability may be characterized as a function of three components: adaptive capacity, sensitivity and exposure. Household vulnerability is defined as the capacity to manage shocks. Adaptive capacity describes the ability of a system to adjust to actual or expected climate stresses, or to cope with the consequences. It is considered 'a function of wealth, technology, education, information, skills, infrastructure, access to resources, and stability and management capabilities' (McCarthy et al, 2001, p8). Sensitivity refers to the degree to which a system will respond to a change in climate, while exposure relates to the degree of climate stress on a particular system, represented as a function of either long-term change in climate conditions or changes in climate variability, including the magnitude and frequency of extreme events. In the most general sense, the term 'climate variability' is often used to denote deviations from the mean of climate statistics over a given period of time.

In this analysis, the following scales of variability are recognized:

- *micrometeorological variability*: from fractions of a second to several minutes;
- *mesometeorological variability*: from several minutes to several hours;
- *synoptic variability*: from several hours to two–three weeks; and

- *climate variability*: from three weeks to several decades.

Variability on such a scale characterizes internal climatic oscillations, climate variability or climate fluctuations (Gruza and Rankova, 2004). Variability could also cover isolated extreme events or catastrophic weather conditions, such as floods, droughts or storms.

Severe drought has occurred throughout the recorded history of Sudan. However, the Sudano-Sahelian zone has experienced a general decline in rainfall since the late 1960s (Brooks, 2006). In western Sudan, annual rainfall variability increased from 16 per cent in the 1960s to 21 per cent in the 1970s and 32 per cent in the 1980s. Drought in many cases has been followed by famine. The two greatest famines since 1684, when the historical record begins, are those of 1888–89 and 1984–85, both triggered by consecutive years of poor rain and resulting massive crop failures (Teklu et al, 1991). This study also revealed that drought-associated famine in Sudan tended to occur in the arid and semi-arid zones of the west and northeast, where the resource-base is poor, rainfall generally low and erratic, the income and asset base of the population thin and variable, and the agricultural environment marginal.

In this chapter we focus on the exposure of people to climate variability as documented in the historical records of the meteorological department and as observed by the local communities. Indicators of sensitivity and adaptive capacity are used to represent vulnerability to climate variability, given that local inhabitants have historically been coping with periodic droughts and rainfall variability. Based on this vulnerability profile, in this study we assumed that current exposure to climate variability affects the community's livelihoods such that communities respond to climate changes by trying to employ measures that enhance their adaptive capacity. However, vulnerability is not a passive state, but a dynamic process. Consequently, vulnerable people are caught up in a state of continuous struggle, attempting to lessen their vulnerability and gaining more resilience. Since the future state of the regional climate is uncertain, there is no guarantee that a specific coping mechanism that is appropriate today will still be appropriate in 20 or 30 years. Nevertheless, we assume that the social and individual capacity for community action, flexible management of natural resources, and diversification of livelihoods are valuable strategies for years to come (Osman-Elasha, 2006).

Impacts of Climate Variability

The severe drought of 1984 is considered one of the most devastating in the history of Sudan. Poor rainfall contributed to low and variable food production. For instance, sorghum and millet production in Northern Kordofan declined by 92 and 86 per cent respectively compared with the average of 1974–81 (Osman-Elasha, 2006). The decline in cereal production led to rapid price increases that spread throughout the country. Large losses of cattle and camels among the pastoralists also resulted in great hardships for nomads. At the household level, the large drop in production (crops and rangeland) translated into large reductions in farm employment and income. The drop in income, coupled with rapidly increasing food prices, resulted in a severe and widespread decline in purchasing power and contributed to extreme displacement of the rural population as hundreds of thousands became destitute and moved out of their villages. Farmers and livestock herders sought employment away from their traditional lands and sold their assets in depressed markets to maintain their food entitlements. The dramatic deterioration in purchasing power and in the level and quality of food consumption, combined with a high incidence of disease, translated into an increased incidence of severe child malnutrition (Osman-Elasha, 2006; Teklu et al, 1991). The largest groups of affected households were the poor and those families consisting of the elderly or missing able adult males. By mid-1985 more than 700,000 people in Kordofan and about 800,000 in Darfur were at high nutritional risk. These two regions experienced significant demographic change resulting from high death rates and large-scale emigration (Osman-Elasha, 2006; Teklu et al, 1991).

Climate variability had a similar impact in eastern Sudan, where frequent occurrences of drought and consequent famine in the Red Sea hills were largely the norm during the 20th century. The long-term drought and famine of the 1980s brought devastating effects, shattering the traditional pattern of natural short-term recovery and causing a major depopulation of the herds of the Beja tribe of Sudan, with losses estimated at 80 per cent of their animal wealth. A complex of human and other factors combined to produce a situation wherein the area available for the Beja's livestock rearing was rapidly diminishing, coupled with a complete failure of all their livelihood systems (Osman-Elasha, 2006).

Vulnerability Assessment

Most of the information contained in this chapter was drawn from three case studies conducted plus a number of studies and papers on the subject of impacts and adaptation to climate variability and change in Africa. This project attempted to address the local vulnerability of agro-pastoral people to global environmental changes in the context of sustainable livelihoods. The case studies examined the past experiences and coping capacities of the rural population in the face of drought, in order to assess the likely impacts of future climate change. A system called the 'livelihood asset status tracking system' was used to measure the changing asset base in five livelihood capitals, which could, in turn, serve as a proxy for determining the impacts on households.

Participatory interviews conducted by a team of researchers is the main method used in this assessment. The process involves group discussions, brainstorming and clustering of criteria, field testing and validation. The main objective is to evolve 'word pictures' for livelihood assets tracking. The word picture is a method for constructing verbal descriptions of asset status. Such word pictures can depict 'worst off' and 'better off' households and also intermediate positions. To measure asset status for each of the five capitals available to a household, a locally meaningful scale of stages is considered from the worst known situation to the best, while maintaining a balance between aspects related to production, equity and sustainability. An illustration of the word picture obtained from the case studies is given in Table 12.1. The illustration covers two word pictures of worst off and better off households.

Table 12.1 *Word picture of households' access to/use of livelihood capitals*

Livelihood capital	Worst Picture under drought condition without interventions	Best picture under drought condition with intervention
Natural capital	Degraded land with v. low fertility and low productivity of grains Little water pools insufficient for animals No fodder for livestock Weak and fewer number of animals No access to forest produce	More fertile soil; abundant amount of fodder More moisture retention power; more produce from land; fertile soil that sustains growth of diverse crops, vegetables and fodder; access to forest produce and fuel wood from shelterbelts (some have government permit to grow opium); has many fruit trees
Physical capital	No water pumps or irrigation facilities Poor human health services (few clinics) Poor extension services Poor vet services Poor roads and marketing places Grain stores with small capacity	Irrigation facilities available round the year Availability of extension services Improved health and vet services Large-capacity stores for excess grains Improved marketing Availability of improved inputs and spare parts
Financial capital	Lack of options for income generation Unstable income condition No credit system granted to individuals and no savings	Availability of home grown food throughout the year; more livestock, high returns from livestock Better income levels and stability Introduction of revolving funds and better savings
Human capital	Poor skills (no training or education opportunities) Poor housing type	Improved skills and better access to extension, health, education, training and veterinary services
Social capital	Poor managerial skills Poor organizational set-up Poor participation in the decision making process	Better ability to manage natural resources (pasture, land, water, livestock etc.) Better organizational set-up (local village committees) Improved participation in the decision making process More membership in civil society organizations

The study involved data collection and analysis of 'resilience indicator' data to show how certain sustainable livelihood measures were effectively implemented and supported in order to ensure their lasting impact. In spite of the variation across the five capitals assessed across the three case studies, our study succeeded in reflecting the state of vulnerability of the communities before the employment of interventions as well as in illustrating how some environmental management/sustainable livelihood measures have succeeded in increasing the community's overall resilience.

Coping deficit

Our analysis has shown that, in their attempts to cope with climatic and other related stresses, people may adopt specific measures that further aggravate their vulnerabilities and undermine their productive assets, for example, through overexploiting their over-stressed natural resource base. This is illustrated by the farmers in Kordofan region, who faced decreased land capacity during the 1984 drought. When the per-hectare yields dropped so low that overall production could no longer sustain the households, people tried to compensate for the lost productivity by increasing the agricultural areas and expanding into marginal rangelands. The less productive the land, the more the farmers expanded. This situation eventually led to a situation of high tension and conflict with other tribes and land-users, especially the pastoralists.

At the national level, government policies that encourage expansion of agricultural land through mechanized farming to improve the food security situation and safeguard against food shortages under climate variability, often negatively impact the pastoralists by forcing them onto marginal lands and exacerbating the problems. According to Tekulu et al (1991) and Braun et al (1998), the over-expansion of agriculture and consequent encroachment of pastoralists into historically marginal areas reflect the failure to appreciate the nature of long-term (in other words multi-decadal scale) climatic variability in the region. Well-meant policies have had inadvertent and catastrophic impacts on livelihoods in the arid parts of Sudan, including massive loss of life and livestock, destruction of communities and livelihood systems, and massive societal disruption on a regional scale. This is a typical condition in Sahelian Africa highlighted by Thébaud and Batterby (2001), who mention that the expansion of agriculture during the wet 1950s and 1960s and a shift to agro-pastoralism pushed pastoralists into more marginal areas and led to a breakdown in the networks connecting herders and farmers, contributing to conflict between these groups. Brooks (2006) writes that 'Pushed into more marginal areas, and with their access to pasture regulated and restricted by both colonial and post-colonial government, pastoral communities became more vulnerable to drought'.

Yet this is not always the case, and some local and national strategies have proven viable in producing some positive tangible impacts on the communities' livelihoods (Osman-Elasha, 2006). The results from the three case studies emphasized this and suggest that planners adopt and build on environmental management/sustainable livelihoods, emphasizing the need for the development planning and adaptation to proceed by progressively improving on those proven coping strategies.

The sustainable livelihood approach

Here we define livelihood as the capabilities, assets and activities required for a means of living. Livelihood is sustainable when one can cope with and recover from stresses and shocks and maintain or enhance one's capabilities and assets both now and in the future, without undermining the natural resource base (Carney, 1999). Vulnerability in this context could be taken as the risk that the household's capitals will fail to buffer against impacts of drought. According to Goldman (2000), the sustainable livelihoods approach sees poverty as vulnerability to shocks and seeks to reduce vulnerability by building on the livelihood assets (natural, physical, financial, human and social) of households.

The sustainable livelihood approach provides the 'bottom–up tool' for assessing vulnerability as perceived by the local people themselves. Using this approach we were able to account for climate variability events and the social and economic conditions to model the processes that shape the negative consequences on the livelihoods of the studied communities. In this exercise, we got answers to questions such as 'Who are the most vulnerable groups?', 'To which stresses are they exposed?', 'What sustainable livelihoods/environmental management strategies have they used to improve their coping capacity?' and 'What other factors contributed to improving their coping capacity?' We also gained an insight into their views regarding future adaptation options. Some of the benefits of using a sustainable livelihoods framework are that it 'provides a checklist of important issues and sketches out the way these link to each other, draws attention to core influences and processes, and emphasizes the multiple interactions between the various factors which affect livelihoods' (DFID,2004).

In the context of this analysis, the sustainable livelihood analysis has been used to include considerations of issues related to impacts of policies and institutions on the coping capacity of the rural communities in an attempt to show how macro-, meso- and micro-level policies – ranging from land-tenure and marketing policies to taxes – have played major roles in both security and vulnerability through their effects on different aspects of livelihood capitals. The sustainable livelihoods approach might assist in solving some of the problems inherent to vulnerable regions of Sudan. Our analysis showed that in some cases, vulnerability has been lessened through access to alternative income generating opportunities and productive resources such as land, irrigation, credit, fertilizers and improved seed. Our study also showed that vulnerability to climate variability and change can be reduced through certain carefully selected policies and institutional set ups.

The Case Studies

Our research was conducted in Sudan. Three case studies representing different community settings in eastern, west-central and western parts of Sudan were undertaken. These case studies were selected partly on the basis of advance knowledge that the communities represent successful examples of sustainable livelihood measures for reducing vulnerability to drought.

The first case study focused on a UNDP-funded project, 'Community-Based Rangeland Rehabilitation for Carbon Sequestration and Biodiversity', in a rural area of western Sudan. This UNDP project was introduced into the area after the severe drought period that affected the Sahel zone during the 1980s. The study area lies within Kordofan State in west-central Sudan and is a part of Sahelian Africa that has undergone a general decline in rainfall since the late 1960s. Between 1961 and 1998, episodes of drought have inflicted the region with varying degrees of severity. This period witnessed two widespread droughts, during 1967–1973 and 1980–1984, the latter being the more severe. Available records show that drought episodes were intense and long lasting, resulting in enhanced vulnerability of the local population, particularly during and after the droughts mentioned above (Osman-Elasha, 2006). The droughts resulted in severe impacts in the region, including chronic poverty, socioeconomic marginalization and food insecurity, leading to a rural development crisis which required integrated and cross-sectoral responses (Warren and Khogali, 1991). In response to this, many viable interventions were identified, providing a starting point for addressing adaptation needs through issues of rural development and poverty reduction.

The second case study is an SOS Sahel intervention called the 'Khor Arba'at Rehabilitation Programme'. The study area is located in the Red Sea State in northeastern Sudan, about 50km north of Port Sudan, the state capital. The Red Sea State, one of Sudan's 26 states, falls between latitudes 17°00 and 23°01N and longitudes 33°14 and 38°32E in the extreme northeastern part of Sudan. Administratively, Arba'at is part of the Red Sea locality, one of the four localities comprising the Red Sea State. The area lies in the catchment of the Khor (small stream) Arba'at, after which it is named. The Khor Arba'at drains a catchment of 4750km^2 (Bashir, 1991) and flows in a west–east direction from the Red Sea Hills, where it originates, to the Red Sea. The region is generally characterized by relative isolation and harsh terrain, highly variable rainfall with recurrent spells of drought, small area of cultivable land and low population density. The people who live here are mainly the Beja pastoralist and agro-pastoralist tribal groups, some of whom are transboundary tribes moving between Sudan, Ethiopia and Eritrea. Rainfall is highly variable, but averages recorded between 1900 and 1980 range between 26mm and 64mm per annum. Both rainfall amounts and geographical distribution show a high degree of variability that generally increases from south to north. Available records indicate that over the last four decades, the general trend has been negative, with frequent and successive droughts. The rainwater received in Arba'at is too small to support cultivation, except in exceptional cases. For that reason, since the 1920s agriculture has depended on the Khor Arba'at. Although rainfall in the area has rarely been of significant benefit to agricultural production, it does support the natural growth for livestock to graze on, though even that resource has declined since the 1970s, reaching a minimum in 1984. The volume of runoff (Khor water) varies considerably between a minimum of 168mm³ (90 per cent probability of occurrence) and a maximum of 1662mm³ (10 per cent probability of occurrence), with high evaporation losses (Osman-Elasha, 2006). The hilly nature of the topography and the absence of aquifers due to the basement complex formation of the base rock make surface run-off the only source of fresh water in the Red Sea area. Of the total area of the Arba'at deltaic fan, the arable lands of Arba'at are estimated at 23,215 feddans (9750ha). Of these, about 9285 feddans (3900ha) can readily sustain irrigation agriculture.

The third case study focused on water harvesting techniques as a coping mechanism in the face of climate variability and change in the North Darfur State. North Darfur is situated in western Sudan, on the northern transitional margin of the Intertropical Convergence Zone. Consequently, most of the area is deficient in water even in the wettest months of July to September (80 per cent of the rainfall). During June, the hottest month, temperatures regularly reach over 45°C and in January, the coldest month, temperatures reach 18°C. North Darfur is one of the most drought-affected regions of the Sudan. The drought years of 1983–85 greatly affected the demographic and socioeconomic conditions of the area, leaving large numbers of people homeless and facing the increasing impacts of poverty, famine and social dislocation. This was accompanied by tribal conflicts, particularly between livestock herders and subsistence farmers. During this time, most people lost the majority of their cattle (the animals most vulnerable to droughts), as well as considerable numbers of sheep, goats and camels.

Our study attempted to locate the causes of rural vulnerability and related land degradation under climate fluctuations, taking into consideration other factors such as policies and institutions. In the three case studies, we assessed vulnerability and adaptation across the five livelihood capitals in terms of their productivity, equity and sustainability as well as risk factors. The target groups in the three case studies were the vulnerable households practicing subsistence farming and raising livestock in the most drought-prone areas of Sudan. Table 12.2 below summarizes the main impacts of drought as identified by the local communities in the three case study areas.

Autonomous Response Strategies

Autonomous response strategies are traditional strategies employed by the local communities in response to recurrent climate variability features such as erratic rainfall and severe droughts. Although the details of these response strategies may vary from one region in Sudan to another, broad commonalities appeared in the type and sequence of responses adopted between the three study areas. Great similarities were seen in the two case studies of Kordofan and Darfur, both situated within the same ecological region of western Sudan. The pattern of household response generally involves a succession of stages. Often the pattern starts by the family moving towards more dependence on markets for the acquisition of food in response to crop failure, as well as look-

Table 12.2 *The main impacts of drought identified by the communities across the three case studies*

Stress	Impact	Leading to	Resulting in	Contributing factors
Drought (declining rainfall)	Water scarcity and deteriorating quality	Poor hygiene	Spread of water-borne diseases Poor health	Poor health services High illiteracy rate Poor water harvest and storage
	Loss of soil moisture Erosion of topsoil	Low production Crop failure	Poor nutrition Poor health	Low storage capacity Low inputs Lack of technology Poor extension services
	Reduced vegetation cover, less fodder, reduced carrying capacity and reduced number of animals	Exposure of topsoil Loss of soil fertility Loss of animals Over logging of trees (selling charcoal)	Loss of animal products Protein deficiency Poor health Increasing dust storms (burying of properties)	Lack of skills Poor rural extension services Poor health services Lack of alternative income sources
	Loss of soil moisture Erosion of topsoil	Low production Crop failure	Poor nutrition Poor health	Low storage capacity Low inputs Lack of technology Poor extension services

ing for employment to provide the necessary cash. If conditions get worse and people are unable to pay for their necessities; then they start exchanging their properties and personal possessions for food and water. Some tend to reduce their livestock numbers or change the composition of herds (replacing cattle with smaller animals like sheep and goats). The frequency and size of meals is also reduced. Ultimately, under chronic conditions, they increasingly liquidate their assets and sell their livestock. Those with little or no assets wait either for external assistance to arrive or hope that their livelihoods will improve due to a change in climatic or non-climatic conditions. If nothing happens, then the deteriorating pattern eventually leads to mass migration, including that of whole families. These local measures for coping with climatic shocks do not necessarily represent a standard procedure followed by each and every household in the impacted community, however. Furthermore, the responses may not follow the above-mentioned sequence. Depending on the household's decision, some families may move immediately on the onset of the crisis, while others may stay behind and never move off their lands. During the period when the households follow the response sequence described above, it becomes increasingly difficult for them to decide between the few difficult alternatives. Many sad stories from the famous 1984 drought describe the situation of livestock herders who lost all their animals because they refused to sell them at a depressed price and kept moving around in search of forage and water, mostly in vain.

In the case of Arbaat, aware of their environment's vulnerability to drought and famine outbreaks, the Beja agro-pastoralists have developed over time various mechanisms that worked well for some time, contributing to the preservation of their livelihood system and the post-drought recovery. Unlike the responses identified in the Kordofan and Darfur case studies, household responses in Arbaat are not short-term, immediate responses to climatic events/shocks but a series of gradual changes that have been adopted by the communities exposed to the high variability of the climate system over the long term. The adopted survival patterns therefore involve strategic adjustments of livelihood systems, such as preparing in advance for expected climatic shocks. This early strategic action by the community and local leaders reflects the community's awareness of the fragility of their natural resource base, particularly in view of the frequent droughts and famines that hit the region and the location of the area close to the most populated city in the region, Port Sudan. The ownership of land by the community contributes to the conservation of an important livelihood capital (natural capital). Other community adjustment measures include the adoption of a dispersed pattern of settlements that maintain land carrying capacity and reduce competition and conflict over resources. Another practice is the spatial and temporal migration up and down the Red Sea Hills in pursuit of water, pasture and cultivable lands. This is in addition to the temporary migration for work outside home areas, primarily to Port Sudan. Another significant measure is the strong social sanctioning system that dictates the use of resources, especially pasture and tree conservation, imposed by tribal leaders (the 'native administration') and adhered to by all the community members (Osman-Elasha, 2006). These measures have worked well for a period of time, enabling the Beja to survive their harsh, changing climatic conditions. Unfortunately, this traditional pattern of recovery was shattered with the system failure to re-configure after the long and severe drought of the 1980s (Osman-Elasha, 2006).

Planned Interventions

In the case studies, planned interventions represent specific types of strategies that have been induced by means of external assistance, government agencies or NGOs to assist the local communities to cope with a number of stresses that they face under their harsh environmental conditions, especially the extreme droughts that are the dominant characteristic of arid and semi-arid Africa. Given enhanced climate variability, in the future more robust and sustainable solutions are needed to protect livelihoods and enable the people of the region to better utilize their meagre resources. We sought answers to the following questions:

- What conditions are necessary to cultivate and raise livestock in these dry, arid, and hence drought-prone, areas with the least risk?
- What types of interventions are necessary?
- What kinds of livelihood systems are needed?
- What skills and capacities need to be acquired?
- Who are the targeted stakeholders?

It is generally argued that enhancing the capacity of Africans to handle climate variability is an appropriate means to increase resilience and reduce the vulnerability of the continent to climate variability and change on all time scales (DFID, 2004).

In the three case studies, the assessment of livelihood assets involved analysis of data collected around a set of indicators spanning four areas: productivity, sustainability, equity and risks. It was found that Sahelian Sudan is highly vulnerable to climate variability and change. Many factors were found to contribute to this vulnerability, including the general low level of economic development, the lack of alternative income-generating opportunities and the lack of adaptive technologies. These factors result in heavy dependence on and consequent over-exploitation of natural resources, leading to the tragic conditions such as those faced by the majority of the rural population during the 1980s drought. The identification of these factors guided the efforts of development agencies to reduce the local vulnerability. Major interventions were aimed at increasing ecological sustainability, including water harvesting and conservation, rehabilitation of range lands, creating shelterbelts, employment of a sustainable management system, and the application of strict regulations and sanctions against over-utilization of the meagre resources. The analysis of conditions following the interventions revealed that productivity and ecological management practices have evolved favourably and are, to a great extent, sustainable. Some important interventions aimed at reducing subsistence vulnerability include diversification of income sources, increasing savings and purchasing power, providing better storage facilities, and improving access to markets. Moreover, the formation of locally based organizations (community development committees) has enabled the participation of community members in activities and decision making processes. This has helped in the effective implementation of training and skill development programmes, helped to target local priorities, identify measures acceptable to the community, mobilize community resources and provided a sense of ownership and empowerment that can help sustain efforts.

The failures of the local livelihood system in many parts of the Red Sea State in eastern Sudan have rendered it completely dependent on central government support and foreign aid organizations, and made long-term planning, including that of combating desertification, a low priority. In response to this, the Khor Arba'at Rehabilitation Project (KARP) was launched by the UK-based organization SOS Sahel. Its main objective was to contribute to the development of the Khor Arba'at area through the application of a wide-ranging programme designed to improve community livelihoods and including: the sustainable management of natural resources in order to meet local community needs, provide for food security and enhance grassroots participation in overall development. The main areas of intervention included water management and harvesting, soil reclamation and protection, provision of extension services, community organization, support of education and health services, the empowerment of women and literacy classes. The application of these interventions led to positive impacts on the rural populations through the overall improvement of their livelihood capitals and increased diversity of crop and economic activities through provision of access to resources and livelihood options. This contributed to increased savings and purchasing power for the rural population. We conclude that the control of the Khor waters and the registration and management of land have been the key factors that underpin and shape the resilience pattern in the area. This was substantially helped by the homogeneity and prevailing spirit of cooperation among the community.

In the case of Kordofan, a UNDP-funded project, 'Community-Based Rangeland Rehabilitation (CBRR) for Carbon Sequestration', has been implemented in response to the disastrous conditions that prevailed in the region after the 1984 drought. The project had two main developmental objectives. The first was to sequester carbon through the implementation of a sustainable, local-level natural resources management system that prevents degradation of and rehabilitates or improves rangelands; the second was to reduce the risks of production failure in a drought-prone area by providing alternatives for sustainable production and increasing the number of livelihood alternatives so that out-migration may decrease and population might stabilize. In essence, the project included both mitigation and adaptation outcomes. This was made possible through the implementation of a simple model of community-based natural resource management aimed at preventing the over-exploitation of marginal lands and rehabilitating rangelands for the purpose of biodiversity conservation and carbon sequestration. These activities represented an integrated package of sustainable livelihood measures with tangible impacts in relation to improving the coping capacity of rural communities in the study area. Most important was the development of a new type of social organization, community development committees, that participated in the process of rangeland rehabilitation, land management, livestock improvement, agro-forestry and sand dune fixation to prevent overexploitation and restore the productivity of rangelands. The availability of essential infrastructure, ranging from irrigation, health, veterinary and extension services to marketing facilities, contributed to the overall development. Social security and credit systems are also essential determinants of whether these interventions can be sustained over time.

Given that sheep and goats can survive harsher environmental conditions than cattle, as conditions became drier sheep and goats feature more prominently in the Sahara resource base (di Lernia and Palombini, 2002). However, in the case of Kordofan it was found that goats can contribute to environmental degradation since they graze and browse anything and everything, including young seedlings. This led to the introduction of sheep to replace the goats, which served two purposes: first, they are more readily marketable and could contribute more to income generation, and second, they are less harmful to the environment, being less aggressive grazers and more manageable.

In the case of Darfur, despite the fact that people in this region are able to survive extreme climate conditions and shocks, since the 1984 drought their coping capacity has weakened (Osman-Elasha, 2006). The current situation in Darfur presents a striking example of drought coupled with a number of other factors and stresses creating a devastating cycle of environmental collapse, conflict and displacement. According to Keen (1998), it is often the lack of viable economic alternatives that drives poor people to engage in violence.

One of the important interventions that came in response to the 1980s drought is promoted by the Intermediate Technology Development Group (ITDG). This group started its work in Darfur in 1988 on a livelihood support programme, focusing on increasing poor people's ability to improve their livelihoods through improved food production methods and processing, rural transport and building materials. A key element of ITDG's food security programme has focused on building on the indigenous knowledge regarding water-harvesting techniques with the involvement of local communities. The aim of the water-harvesting component was to harvest as much of the rain that does fall in parched North Darfur as possible and store it for as long as possible in order to provide enough water for irrigation and domestic use. Various methods are used for water harvesting, including the use of earth dams to capture increased amounts of rainy season floodwater from streams. Other response strategies include construction of a central grain store for surplus production to be used in times of scarcity, diversifying income sources (for example, selling fruits and vegetables), establishing a gum garden and taking advantage of other employment opportunities. Training of farmers to manage their resources and diversify production, involvement of women in productive activities and public life, social networks and cooperatives, and the provision of a credit system are additional important factors.

Policy Assessment

We also conducted assessments of policy and institutional aspects by identifying the levels at which policies are developed and implemented, assessing their impacts on the people and identifying the resources that could be influenced by them. We found that it is important in policy analysis to understand contextual factors that shape the policy with respect to the social, political and economic environment. Policy analysis conducted in this context highlighted the possible means by which policies could impact different aspects of people's livelihoods, including their livelihood assets, the vulnerability context within which they operate and their capacity to choose effective livelihood strategies. Since some government policies on land use in arid and semi-arid areas have been considered among the causes of vulnerability (Brook, 2006), it is important to put in place the types of policies that assist in reducing vulnerability, enhance the knowledge base and capabilities, and facilitate adaptation and innovation. Our studies have shown that development/adaptation measures will not be sustainable until they address issues related to land use and resource management, and contribute to the maintenance and development of ecologically sound agricultural practices.

While short-term relief programmes curbed the negative impacts of the drought and famine conditions in the Red Sea State, they rendered the population heavily dependent on central government support and foreign aid organizations and made long-term policies, including that of combating drought, a low priority. This approach is unsustainable as it may undermine traditional coping capacity and contributes to the creation of relief-dependent societies. Instead, it is preferable to support local capacities and help sustain a local food production system. A similar situation was faced by the people in the Bara area of western Sudan. In this case, the appropriate intervention was to avoid the creation of a situation of relief dependency by selling the relief food to the villages participating in the project activities at nominal prices instead of distributing it for free. The revenue generated was used to supplement the revolving funds of the villages. Initially the idea was not favoured by the communities involved, but later on they concluded that it had replenished their financial capital and contributed to their sustainability (Osman-Elasha, 2006). Moreover, the creation of favourable marketing policies and stable infrastructure in the three study areas led to increased inter-state trading opportunities, social networks, and greater freedom and capacity to participate in decision making. The involvement of women in public life enhanced their participation in economic activities and related events, and ultimately reduced household vulnerability.

Conclusions and Lessons Learned

1   Increasing vulnerability of arid and semi-arid lands: Arid and semi-arid lands in Africa are experiencing a state of chronic high climate variability and extremes. Disasters associated with these are expected to become more frequent and more intense in the future (McCarthy et al, 2001). To address this issue, there is a need to deal with many problems faced by the population of the region, including underdevelopment, poverty and other aspects of vulnerability. Use of accumulated knowledge generated by other initiatives such as disaster mitigation, poverty reduction strategies and development programmes, and developing longer-term strategies are both important.

2   Climate change is an additional source of uncertainty and risk: Vulnerability to hunger, famine, dislocation or material loss in arid and semi-arid areas results from the interaction of multiple stresses shaping the socioeconomic system of rural households and impacting their livelihood capitals. Hunger, famine, dislocation and material loss can best be understood and redressed by learning from the past. Analysis of current and historical impacts of climate variability reveals the underlying causes of vul-

nerability and assists in the identification of responses necessary to address
these causes. Sudan has experienced more than 20 years of below average
rainfall, during which there have been many localized droughts as well as
a severe and widespread drought from 1980 to 1984. These events may be
unrelated to the human contribution to global warming. Nevertheless, it is
accepted wisdom that people are changing the Earth's climate and that
changes will be manifested in Sudan. Projections suggest that the climate
of Sudan may become drier in the future. With this may come greater risk
of drought and its impacts.

3   Drought, population pressures and conflict are degrading lands and
undermining resilience: Population and economic pressures have driven
people to intensify cultivation of drylands, extend cultivation into more
marginal areas, overgraze rangelands and over-harvest vegetation.
Recurrent and severe drought overlaid on these activities has degraded
lands, reduced availability of water, depressed production of food, fodder
and livestock, and eroded livelihoods. Competition for resources has been
a source of conflict and has contributed to the tragic violence that engulfs
parts of Sudan.

4   Policies and institutions can contribute to increasing vulnerability or
improving adaptation: Vulnerability is shaped by the ongoing processes of
institutional set-ups, such as different roles played by formal and informal
organizations, macro-, meso- and micro-level policies and conflicting interests, and also by the distribution of and access to livelihood assistance,
including training opportunities, services and social networks. It is not possible to consider the sustainability of the livelihood in a specific area
separately from the broader geographical, social and political-economic
context in which the area is located. Some of the causes of and responsibility for environmental degradation and vulnerability of livelihoods at the
local levels could be attributed to national-level policies and irrational
plans, for example, the expansion of mechanized farming at the expense of
rangelands and forests.

5   Communities are adapting: Sudan's rural communities are adapting to
reduce risks in a harsh, variable and changing environment. The adaptation strategies are not necessarily driven by climate change. Nonetheless,
they do help enhance resilience to climate change. The measures being
adopted include water harvesting and *trus* cultivation, expanding food
storage facilities, managing rangelands to prevent overgrazing, replacing
goat herds with sheep, planting and maintaining shelterbelts, planting of
backyard farms or *jubraka* to supplement family food supply and income,
supplying micro-credit and educating people about the use of credit, and
forming and training of community groups to implement and maintain the
various measures. Adaptation measures will not be sustainable until we
address issues related to the productivity, equity and sustainability of livelihood assets, and contribute to the maintenance and development of
ecologically sound agricultural practices.

6   Adaptation requires local involvement to be effective: In some instances
the adaptation strategies have been initiated within communities and

implemented largely with local resources. In other instances the adaptation strategies derive from externally funded and implemented projects. In both cases, the involvement of local institutions and community leaders has been critical for targeting local priorities, identifying measures that can be accepted by the community, mobilizing community resources and developing ownership that can sustain the effort.

7   Adaptation falls short of what is needed: Existing efforts to cope and adapt are too little to manage present day risks. Drought and other climate disturbances impose an unacceptably high burden on the Sudanese, and this burden is likely to grow with global warming and associated climate change. The adaptive responses that have been applied and shown to be successful in building resilience need to be replicated and expanded, and innovative approaches need to be explored.

8   Use the sustainable livelihoods approach for planning: This approach could enable effective national and international responses to manage reduction of risk and enhance adaptive capacity.

9   Current coping capacities could contribute to future adaptation: The future climate is uncertain. However, by enabling current populations to buffer themselves against today's climatic variations, they will be better able to cope with future contingencies. The social and individual capacity that is being built for community action, flexible management of natural resources and diversification of livelihoods will be valuable for years to come, whatever the climate may be.

References

Bashir, S. (1991) 'Surface Runoff in the Red Sea Province', *RESAP Technical Papers*, no 5, May

Braun, J. von, T. Teklu and P. Webb (1998) *Famine in Africa: Causes, Responses and Prevention*, The Johns Hopkins University Press, Baltimore, MD, US

Brooks, N. (2006) 'Climate change, drought and pastoralism in the Sahel', discussion note for the World Initiative on Sustainable Patoralism, November

Carney, D. (1999) *Approaches to Sustainable Livelihoods for the Rural Poor*, Overseas Development Institute, London, UK

DFID (2004) *African Climate Report*, report commissioned by the UK Government to review African climate science, policy and options for action, Department for International Development, London

Di Lernia, S. and A. Palombini (2002) 'Desertification, sustainability, and archaeology: indications from the past for an African future', *Origini*, vol 24, pp303–334

Goldman, I. (2000) *Micro to Macro: Policies and Institutions for Empowering the Rural Poor*, Department for International Development, London

Gruza, G. and E. Rankova (2004) *Detection of Changes in Climate State, Climate Variability and Climate Extremity*, Institute for Global Climate and Ecology (IGCE), Russia

Keen, D. (1998) 'The economic functions of violence in civil wars', Adelphi Paper, International Institute of Strategic Studies, London

McCarthy, J. J., O. F. Canziani, N. A. Leary, D. J. Dokken and K. S. White (eds) (2001) *Climate Change 2001: Impacts, Adaptation, and Vulnerability*, Contribution of Working Group II to the Third Assessment Report of the Intergovernmental Panel on Climate Change, Cambridge University Press, Cambridge, UK

Osman-Elasha, B. (2006) 'Environmental strategies to increase human resilience to climate change: Lessons for eastern and northern Africa', Final report, Project AF14, Assessments of Impacts and Adaptations to Climate Change, International START Secretariat, Washington, DC, US, www.aiaccproject.org

Teklu, T., J. von Braun and E. Zaki (1988) 'Drought and famine relationships in Sudan: Policy implications', research report no 88, IFPRI, Washington DC, US

Thébaud, B. and S. Batterby (2001) 'Sahel pastoralists: Opportunism, struggle, conflict and negotiation: A case study from eastern Niger', *Global Environmental Change*, vol 11, pp69–78

Warren, A. and M. Khogali (1992) 'Desertification and drought in the Sudano-Sahelian region 1985–1991', United Nations Sudano-Sahelian Office (UNSO), New York, US

13

Social Vulnerability of Farmers in Mexico and Argentina

Hallie Eakin, Mónica Wehbe, Cristian Ávila, Gerardo Sánchez Torres and Luis A. Bojórquez-Tapia

Introduction

Within regions with similar exposure to climate hazards, the sensitivity of particular farm units to climate impacts will vary considerably, as will the capacity of agricultural producers to adapt in relation to a wide variety of socioeconomic, institutional and psychological variables (Easterling, 1996; Brklachich et al, 1997; Eakin, 2002). These variables are not always easily observed or measured at the household level, posing considerable challenges to assessing the vulnerability of specific farm populations.

In response to this challenge, we focus on the analysis of the variety of factors that differentiate farm enterprises and farm households in terms of both their sensitivity to climate events and their capacity to adjust to changing climatic and market circumstances. For this analysis, two case studies are presented in two different Latin American socioeconomic and climatic contexts: the community of Laboulaye, in Córdoba Province, Argentina, and the county (*municipio*) of González, in the state of Tamaulipas, Mexico. Although the cases are quite distinct, their production systems have similar exposure to political and economic uncertainty originating from intensified processes of economic liberalization and market integration in both countries. In very broad terms, the focus of production is also similar: grains and livestock in different combinations for commercial markets. The comparison of the cases, however, also reveals important differences in the distribution of livelihood resources, the relationship between farmers and the public sector, and thus the flexibility of agriculture in the face of both economic and environmental challenges.

Agricultural vulnerability

In this study, the social vulnerability of farm households is considered to be a function of their exposure to climate shocks and extreme events, the sensitivity of the farm to such events in terms of both direct crop impacts and indirect livelihood impacts, and the capacity of households to adapt and adjust to protect themselves from future harm. In the analysis presented below, we explore in depth two of these three attributes of vulnerability: sensitivity and adaptive capacity. Although exposure to climate hazards is in part a product of the social construction of risk through, for example, the historical political and economic factors that have affected the geographic distribution of landholdings, physical infrastructure and populations (see Liverman, 1990), we consider that at the household level these differences in exposure are captured in differential sensitivities to climate impacts.[1]

The sensitivity to climatic hazards in agriculture is often measured in terms of the degree of decline in yields, losses in agricultural profits or farm value, increased costs of production or falls in production quality (Easterling, 1996; Reilly and Schilmmelpfenning, 1999). Thus sensitivity is also a product of the organization of a farm system, the technology and information employed by the system, and its exposure to other socioeconomic and biological factors as mentioned above (Anderson and Dillon, 1992; Chiotti et al, 1997; Smithers and Smit, 1997). If one uses farmers' own assessments of climatic impacts on their production (as we have in this study), then sensitivity becomes a function of risk perception and risk tolerance – variables that are rarely captured in impact studies at sector scales (Risbey et al, 1999; Dessai, et al, 2003).

In general terms, adaptive capacity can be viewed as a function of a system's flexibility, stability and access to key resources, attributes that overlap and interact. Farmers' capacities to respond to stress and uncertainty depend on several factors such as landholding size and soil quality, availability of machinery and equipment, access to credit and insurance, availability of technical assistance and information, social networking, the existence of public support programmes and farmer education and age (Blaikie et al, 1994; Scoones, 1998; Ellis, 2000). Both the degree of diversification within the agricultural production system and the economic diversification of the farm household have also been posited as important factors in determining the sustainability of farm households over time, particularly in peasant farm systems (Ellis, 2000). For example, the importance of non-farm income in a household's income portfolio, or, conversely, the dependence of the household on agricultural income, can be a measure of household sensitivity to climate impacts (Adger, 1999). As described in the following section, the expectation that diversification will enhance adaptive capacity runs counter to current policy trends, which favour specialization.

The political-economic context of vulnerability

The rapid rate of agricultural change that has occurred in Latin America over the last several decades has profoundly altered farmers' relations with markets, their use of technology and their management of resources (de Janvry and Sadoulet, 1993; Loker, 1996; Bebbington, 2000; Berdegué et al, 2001). Neoliberalism, characterized by a suite of policies such as privatization, decentralization, liberalization and deregulation that are designed to open up economies to foreign investment and international trade, has been the driving force behind the sweeping reforms and has become the dominant paradigm of economic development in the region.

In both Mexico and Argentina, agricultural policy reforms have been implemented in concert with substantial changes in macroeconomic policy. Over the course of the 1980s and 1990s, in both countries protectionist policies, price supports and input subsidies for agricultural products were largely withdrawn, farm service agencies privatized and agricultural markets deregulated (Appendini, 2001; Obschatko, 1993; Ghezan et al, 2001). Smaller scale farmers – principally the *ejidatarios* or communal farmers of Mexico and the small family farmers of Argentina – have been particularly sensitive to these changes.

In Argentina, since the beginning of the 1990s, the loss of agricultural income purchasing power has resulted in the concentration of land in larger production units, while those smaller farm units that have remained in production have been forced to restructure and have faced an increasing burden of debt (Wehbe, 1997; Peretti, 1999; Latuada, 2000). The economic crisis of 2002 was followed by an agricultural boom led by growth in soybean production, which helped some farmers get out of debt. The soybean boom, however, is considered to be augmenting soil stress and degradation, particularly under extreme climatic conditions (Cisneros et al, 2004). Beef production and pork and poultry farming have become less profitable in comparison with export crops such as soybeans. Many agricultural analysts in Argentina increasingly fear that these changes are resulting in the exchange of more sustainable agricultural practices for practices that are highly dependent on external inputs (Pengue, 2001; Solbrig and Viglizzo, 1999; Solbrig, 1996).

In Mexico, the *ejidatarios* have been offered title to their land through a federal process initiated in 1992 in the hope that this would encourage the more efficient and entrepreneurial farmers to expand their production, while enabling others to leave agriculture (Ibarra Mendívil, 1996; Cornelius and Myhre, 1998). Today access to and use of technology and farm services (such as credit and insurance) has polarized the sector, dividing those who have 'commercial potential' from those who are considered 'unviable' (Myhre, 1998). While a relatively small number of agribusinesses have enjoyed rapid growth in productivity and exports over the 1990s, rural incomes have generally stagnated or declined in real terms (Kelly, 2001; Hernández Laos and Velásquez Roa, 2003).

Methods

Our analysis employed both quantitative and qualitative data. We undertook an analysis of trends in agricultural and economic policy both at the national scale and the farm level for the two regions of study in order to evaluate some of the non-climatic stress factors that were hypothesized to have affected agricultural sensitivity and capacities in each case. At the farm level, we implemented a household survey using a similar survey instrument in each region to evaluate vulnerability attributes and outcomes. The samples were designed to be representative of the estimated number and diversity of production units in each study site (see Gay, 2006, for more details on the sample design and other methodological details).

In each case study, a selection of the survey variables are grouped according to the particular attributes of adaptive capacity or sensitivity they are intended to represent. In Argentina, adaptive capacity is measured by four attributes: material resources, human resources, management capacity and adaptations. Sensitivity is calculated by the main climatic events affecting each main crop, frequency of adverse events, percentage of area usually affected and type of damage. Crop loss is taken into account as the difference between planted and harvested area within each group and for each of the main crops for the surveyed year. Impacts on livestock production and on infrastructure are also considered. In Mexico, adaptive capacity is measured by five attributes: human resources, material resources, financial resources, information access and use, and economic and agricultural diversity. Sensitivity is defined by variables measuring direct climate impacts on crops and by variables which are hypothesized to indicate greater sensitivity of the farm livelihood to climate shocks.

Using a slightly different method in each of the two case studies, aggregate scores for each attribute are calculated and the attribute scores are combined to create the values of a single multivariate indicator of adaptive capacity and a single multivariate indicator of sensitivity. These two indicators are then combined (qualitatively in the Argentinean case, quantitatively in the Mexican case) to create an overall measure of vulnerability. In the Mexican case study, each household is categorized according to its values for sensitivity and adaptive capacity in one of three vulnerability categories (low, moderate and high). In Argentina, the production units are first grouped into different production systems and then for each system group indices of sensitivity and adaptive capacity are obtained, assigning each group to a particular vulnerability level (low, moderate and high) in relation to both their sensitivity and adaptive capacity. The particular variables that appear to contribute most to the vulnerability of farmers in each case are identified through radar diagrams. The results, described below, illustrate the characteristics of vulnerability in each case and the particular resources that currently differentiate the sensitivity and capacities of farmers.

Case Study 1: Laboulaye, Argentina

Laboulaye City and its surrounding area belong to the Presidente Roque Saenz Peña Department in the southeast of Córdoba Province. It is a region in which agriculture has been a primary activity since the 'Desert Conquest' of the late 19th century, when white settlers were encouraged to expand the agricultural frontier into what was then indigenous territory. Today, agriculture and services for farmers continue to drive the local economy, although the circumstances of production have become increasingly difficult for the area's family farms.

These producers have traditionally pursued a variety of farm strategies based on diverse crops and livestock (Table 13.1).

Table 13.1 *Main production systems of Laboulaye, Córdoba Province, Argentina*

System	Farms		Worked area		Average hectares per farm
	Number	%*	Hectares	%*	
Bovine livestock	641	25.4	284,962	20.4	444.6
Mixed crop/livestock	509	20.2	425,165	30.4	835.3
Small landholdings	222	8.8	21,260	1.5	95.8
Dairy livestock	186	7.4	79,140	5.7	425.5
Cash crop	169	6.7	63,538	4.5	376.0
Dairy – mixed	94	3.7	85,834	6.1	913.1
Bovine and ovine livestock (mixed)	83	3.3	78,126	5.6	941.3
TOTAL	1904	75.4	1,038,025	74.3	545.2

Note: *Farms included in this table are a subset of the 'most representative' of those in the studied area, which is why the percentage columns do not add up to 100.

Source: INTA (2002).

Reflecting the same trends that have been noted at the national scale, these family farmers have been negatively affected by the declining prices for livestock and rising living costs. Official statistics show an expansion of cash-cropping area (by 50 per cent) and a decline in livestock area (by 13 per cent) and in livestock numbers (by 37 per cent) in the region since the late 1980s (INDEC, 2004; INTA, 2002). Although soybean expansion was already apparent before the 2002 crisis, the recent rapid land-use changes have now raised concerns about possible environmental impacts (Moscatelli and Pazos, 2002; Pengue, 2001).

Increasingly these changes in production practices – the lack of crop rotation, mono cropping and the absence of complementary practices to no-tillage systems – are being associated with the increased impacts from flood events (Cisneros et al, 2004). The agro-ecologic zone to which this area belongs to is characterized as a semi-arid to sub-humid region (INTA, 1987). Annual rainfall average (1961–1990) is 842mm, concentrated in spring, summer and autumn, predominating in summer and autumn (67 per cent). As in much of the Pampas, the region is relatively flat, with slight undulations. While the area is exposed to a variety of climatic hazards, in recent decades floods have raised the most concern among farmers. Excessive rainfall can cause the main rivers of the area, Río Cuarto and Río Quinto, and small streams to overflow (Seiler et al, 2002). The floods have incurred a high social cost locally, causing losses in harvests, problems with livestock mobilization, the spread of diseases, and property damage in both rural and urban areas. Flood management thus requires soil and crop management techniques and high investment in infrastructure and sanitation plans (SAGyP/CFA, 1995).

Adaptive capacity and sensitivity of farm systems in Laboulaye

The 47 farm units that were surveyed in Laboulaye are classified according to land use, resulting in 4 groups: cash-cropping farms (6 cases), large-scale mixed cash-crop/livestock units (8 cases, representing those cases with more than 890ha), small-scale mixed cash-crop/livestock ranches (20 cases, representing those cases with less than 890ha) and livestock-specializing farms (13 cases). Measures of sensitivity to climate hazards and adaptive capacity are constructed for each category of farmers.

Variables selected as indicators of adaptive capacity are presented in Table 13.2. Their selection is based on previous knowledge about different production systems in the region and according to hypotheses about what types of resources might enhance the farmers' flexibility to adjust to or cope with climatic variability. Weights for aggregating these variables and variable groupings into a measure of adaptive capacity are decided through a process of consultation with farmers to establish their relative importance for adapting to climate risk.

Table 13.2 *Indicators of the adaptive capacity of farm households in Laboulaye, Argentina, by farm type*

Capacity Attribute	Variable	Cash Crop	Mixed Large	Mixed Small	Livestock
Social/Human Resources	Potential experience (yrs)[a]	32	37	40	47
	Education (yrs)[a]	11.7	12.25	8.9	7.3
Material Resources	Landholding size (ha)[a]	506	2,030	435	426
	(Min/max)	(120/1200)	(900/3600)	(172/800)	(50/1270)
	Machinery index[a]	1.3	2.3	1.3	0.6
	Gross margin (Arg $) (Income)[a]	207,000	807,000	66,000	0
	Good soil quality (% of cases)	66.66	62.50	35.00	30.77
Management Capacity	Rented land (as % of worked area)[b]	89.5	46.4	33.8	40.9
Financial Resources	Other sources of income (% of cases)[c]	17	12	25	54
	Hail insurance (% of cases)	33	70	40	7
Information	No of sources of technical assistance[a]	1	2.25	1.5	1.93
	Consult any type of climate information (% of cases)	83	50	100	84
Diversity	No of crops[a]	1.83	3.0	2.05	0.15
	% of hectares dedicated to cash-crops[a]	98.7	61.7	36.7	0

Notes: a Average data;
b Average data, weighted by landholding size;
c Other sources of income refers only to the same or greater amount of money from activities other than agriculture.

Cash-crop farmers have fewer years of experience than other types of farmers, but more years of education for all groups except the mixed large farm producers. They work farms of moderate size with generally good soil quality and earn an average gross margin greater than do the mixed small and livestock producers. However, a large percentage of the area they cultivate is on rented land and their incomes are not well diversified. Mixed small farm producers and livestock producers have similar human capital, land resources and access to technical assistance but differ in terms of income level and diversity. The mixed large farm producers have the greatest adaptive capacity, with the most years of education, larger farms, higher incomes, greater use of insurance and greater access to technical assistance.

While sensitivity to climate in agriculture is often interpreted as a function of crop physiology, soils and management, farmers' perception of their risk can also contribute to their sensitivity. The farmers are well aware of the implications of recent changes in public policy and land use in the region for their sensitivity to climate. Frustration at the lack of planning and water resource management, poor infrastructure development, and the volatility of the market were also expressed as elements that enhanced their sensitivity to climate impacts.

We develop a sensitivity matrix to differentiate farmers' sensitivity not only by the four farm types of Laboulaye, but also by the type of climate events and the nature of their impacts on crops, livestock and infrastructure. Information to construct the matrix is taken from the survey, and thus is based on farmers' perceptions of the impacts of climate on their enterprises and livelihoods. By summing the sensitivity scores of each type of climate event for those farm groups reporting climate impacts on crops, livestock and infrastructure, each considered separately, weighted aggregate scores are calculated for each group, climate event and impact category. Results for sensitivity to crop impacts from flood, drought and hail are reported in Table 13.3. Similar analyses were performed for impacts on livestock and infrastructure. The analysis reveals that for cash-crop producers, climate is of relatively small concern. Flooding and drought are the most worrisome climate events for the mixed large farm group, while flooding is more important for the mixed small group of farmers. Surprisingly, neither mixed large nor mixed small groups reported impacts on livestock, despite the fact that these groups were both grain and livestock producers, which may be explained by the relatively higher participation of grain production relative to livestock in the total income of these farm units. The scores for impacts on crops are combined with indicator scores for impacts on livestock and infrastructure reported by farmers in all of the groups. The resulting value is the aggregate sensitivity index.

Vulnerability of farm systems in Laboulaye

Aggregate indicators for sensitivity, adaptive capacity and vulnerability are reported in Table 13.4 for the different categories of farmers in Laboulaye. The results suggest that the mixed small and mixed large farmers are the most sensitive of the farm groups to climate hazards. The types of farmers who are most numerous in Laboulaye – the mixed small and livestock farmers – are found to have less adaptive capacity than the mixed large farm systems. According to the survey data, the mixed small and livestock producers tend to have the smallest landholdings and report problems with soil quality. In the case of livestock farmers, their choice of production strategy may be a result of the

Table 13.3 *Sensitivity of farm households in Laboulaye, Argentina,*
to climate impacts on crops by farm type and climate event

	Cash crop	Mixed small	Mixed large	All
Flood	0.8	3.52	2.07	6.39
Drought	0.3	0.58	2.57	3.45
Hail	0.15	0.25	0.28	0.68
All	1.27	4.36	4.92	

Note: Figures in this table are the result of linearly adding weighted values of number, frequency, percentage of area usually affected and type of damage, calculated for the main climatic events affecting each main crop. Weights are determined on the basis of the proportion of agriculture producers concerned with each particular event within their group and by the area dedicated to that particular crop in proportion to the total worked area by each farmer. Crop loss is also taken into account as the difference between planted and harvested area within each group and individually for each of the main crops for the surveyed year.

limitations of the soils they have available to them, which prohibit intensive crop production. Although both these groups report less total income than the other two groups, they tend to be more diversified economically. Cattle constitute a capital asset and source of income that is typically far less sensitive to climate impacts than crop income. The mixed small and livestock farmers also tend to rely more on technical assistance, primarily related to veterinary services, than the other farm groups.

Table 13.4 *Vulnerability of different farm production systems*
within the Laboulaye area

Farmer Group	Vulnerability	Sensitivity	Adaptive Capacity
Mixed Small	*High*	5.21	6.82
Livestock	*Moderate*	1.89	6.27
Cash-Crop	*Moderate*	1.27	6.09
Mixed Large	*Low*	5.67	11.95

Note: Sensitivity indices in this table represent those in Table 13.3 plus impacts on livestock production (such as pasture damages) and on infrastructure (damages to roads, water mills, etc.). Adaptive capacity indices were obtained after weighing indicators through consultation with farmers. The indicators were grouped into four categories: material resources; human resources; management capacity and adaptations. All farmer groups were then assigned to vulnerability classes (High, Medium and Low) according to dispersion criteria (defining three ranges from average values of both indices). This vulnerability ranking is only relative to the considered groups within the studied area.

Cash-crop producers have adaptive capacity that is similar to that of mixed small and livestock farmers, although they report farming at a range of scales (120ha to 1200ha), and the interviewed farm managers have higher average incomes and high education levels. However, unlike the mixed small and livestock farmers, these farmers tend not to own their land or machinery, and do not rely on family labour for production. The highest level of adaptive capacity is associated with the mixed large farm systems, which are able to enjoy relatively high incomes from farming increasing amounts of soybeans on large farms of 900 to 3600ha with high quality soils. These farmers also report high education levels, high crop diversity (although low economic diversity) and high use of machinery and other inputs.

It is the combination of the farm's sensitivity to climate and its capacity to manage its impact that determines its vulnerability, which is assessed qualitatively by comparing the aggregate scores for the sensitivity and adaptive capacity indices (Table 13.4 and Figure 13.1). The four Laboulaye farm groups' sensitivity and adaptive capacity scores are plotted in Figure 13.1. Situations of higher sensitivity (i.e. higher values on the x-axis) and lower adaptive capacity (lower values on the y-axis) correspond to higher vulnerability, as denoted by the arrow in Figure 13.1. For simplicity, vulnerability is assumed to be a linear function of sensitivity and adaptive capacity, implying that points along the diagonals represent equal vulnerability. From the figure it can be inferred that the mixed large group of farmers in the Laboulaye area are less vulnerable than the cash-crop and livestock groups and these three groups are all less vulnerable than the mixed small group. In general, the four groups from Laboulaye are relatively more vulnerable than the majority of other groups of farmers evaluated in the wider south-centre of Córdoba Province, represented by the black dots. This is explained partly because the geomorphology of the Laboulaye area makes it prone to floods in addition to the droughts and hail that occur in the rest of the south-centre of Córdoba.

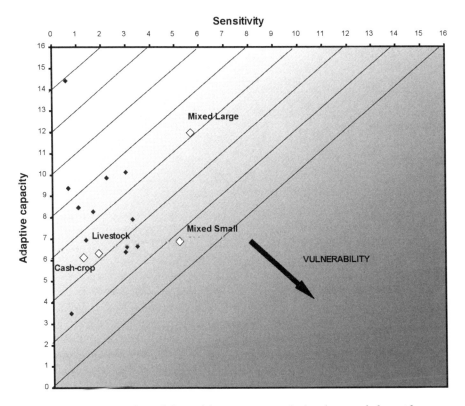

Figure 13.1 *Vulnerability of farm groups in Laboulaye and the wider south-center of Córdoba Province*

Note: Higher sensitivity and lower adaptive capacity represent conditions of higher vulnerability.

The analysis illustrates that while the exposure to climate variability is similar across the Laboulaye area, the sensitivity and adaptive capacity of each group differed according to the nature of their production activities, their soil conditions and use, and their material assets, landholding size and income (Figure 13.2). The livestock and cash-crop groups are attributed with moderate levels of vulnerability, reflecting similar overall scores for sensitivity and adaptive capacities. However, the factors contributing to their vulnerability are quite different. Livestock production is an activity that is less affected by climate, but presently is less profitable and tends to take place in marginal cropping areas more susceptible to floods. Cash-crop farmers (generally soybean farmers) are far more sensitive to the direct impacts of climate events, but tend to rent land for this activity with higher quality soils that are less prone to flooding and offer better probabilities for high-income generation (90 per cent of worked area is devoted to soybeans). While cash-crop farmers are not economically diversified, livestock producers are highly diversified in their sources of income (58 per cent of cases have other income similar or greater than that from agriculture).

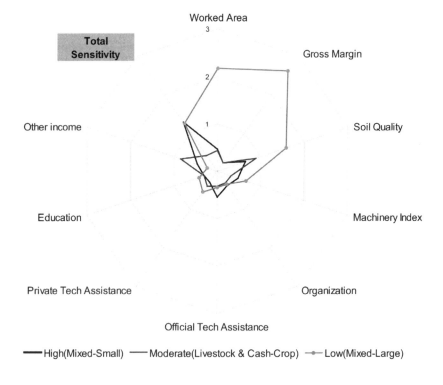

Figure 13.2 *Structure of vulnerability for different farmer groups in Laboulaye, Argentina*

Note: normalized scores for total sensitivity and nine indicators of adaptive capacity show their relative contributions to the level of vulnerability of each group.

The largest differences in vulnerability can be seen between mixed small and mixed large producers in the Laboulaye area (high and low vulnerability respectively). While both of these groups show a high sensitivity to a variety of climate events, the very high adaptive capacity of the mixed large producers outweighs this sensitivity and differentiates the two groups. The landholdings of the mixed large group are, on average, five times those of the mixed small, and, on average, the former group devotes more than 60 per cent of their land area to cash crops compared with the 37 per cent for small landholdings. This translates into 12 times greater income for mixed large producers than that of mixed small farmers (net of direct production and land renting costs). Farmers' participation in organizations is not a distinguishing factor between the groups, a result that was expected given the general perception among all farmers that farmers' organizations are not particularly helpful for the less favoured rural sectors. In summary, we find that the social vulnerability of agricultural producers is highly related to access to physical and material resources that allow producers greater flexibility in a changing economic and institutional environment.

Case Study 2: González, Mexico

The *municipio* of González is located in the southern extension of the northeastern state of Tamaulipas, Mexico. Unlike much of the state of Tamaulipas, which tends to have a relatively arid climate, González is characterized by sub-humid conditions with an average temperature of 24°C and average annual rainfall totals of 850mm. Historical precipitation records illustrate a decadal pattern rather than any defining trends (Conde, 2005). Some analysts have also observed a correlation between winter precipitation, the Pacific North American Oscillation and El Niño Southern Oscillation events in this region (Cavazos 1999). In addition to periods of drought and flooding, the southern part of the state is particularly susceptible to the impact of the hurricanes that occasionally climb the Gulf of Mexico, as occurred in 1955, 1966, 1988, 1995 and 2000. Frost is relatively infrequent, although hailstorms cause occasional crop losses. Other than climate variability, pests have been a consistent problem in the state. Recently, locusts have been causing significant damage to annual grain crops.

In contrast to the northern *municipios* of Tamaulipas, González has few factories or assembly plants and is primarily agricultural, with 28 per cent of land under crops and 24 per cent under pasture. The *municipio*'s 3491km² area is also relatively flat, averaging 56 metres above sea level, which facilitates mechanized agriculture and contributes to the relatively uniform climatic conditions. In 2000, 51 per cent of the population was rural, living in localities of less than 2500 people, and 44 per cent of the economically active population was dedicated to agriculture. It is a relatively poor *municipio*, with 47 per cent of its economically active population earning less than 2 minimum salaries (INEGI, 2000). Although 87 per cent of adults are literate, over one third have not completed primary school.

As in other *municipios* in Mexico, the cultivated area in González is divided between private farmers (*pequeños propietarios*), representing 30 per cent of landholders and farming 70 per cent of agricultural land, and smaller-scale communal farmers (*ejidatarios*), who represent 70 per cent of landholders but farm only approximately 30 per cent of the *municipio*'s land. Several of the *municipio*'s *ejidos* (communal farms) are incorporated into irrigation districts along the Tamesi and Guayalejo rivers, and this provides farmers with the opportunity to plant irrigated vegetables, grains and fruit trees. The remainder of the *municipio* specializes in the crops for which Tamaulipas is best known: sorghum, maize, safflower and soybeans. Sorghum was introduced to the region in the 1950s and 1960s to supply the US' and Mexico's growing livestock industries and to address what was perceived as Tamaulipas' vulnerability to drought (Barkin and DeWalt, 1988). Ironically, given the initial marketing of sorghum as a drought-tolerant crop, sorghum is now being actively discouraged in the more arid northern part of Tamaulipas, in response to the government's observation of a progressive desertification of soils that they believe is associated with sorghum farming under persistent drought conditions in the 1990s (ASERCA, 1997).

Adaptive capacity and sensitivity of farm systems in González

As described in the previous section, the agricultural population of González consists of both communal and private farmers (*ejidatarios* and *pequeños propietarios*). Of the sample of 181 farm households used to analyse vulnerability in González, 34 cases are private farmers and 147 are communal farmers. Data was collected from the households for variables related to their human capital, material and financial resources, information access, and diversification of livelihood, which we consider to be indicators of their adaptive capacity. As Table 13.5 shows, the two groups are distinguished not only in terms of landholding size, but also in terms of education, age and access to key resources such as credit and insurance.

The survey data reveal that the average values for attributes of adaptive capacity are generally higher for private farmers than those of communal farmers. The private farmers are more educated, younger (and thus hypothetically more likely to be receptive to new technologies and ideas), and have far more land with which to experiment with alternative crops. The *pequeños propietarios* reported a higher average number of crops planted, but tend to devote more of their total landholding to crop cultivation than to livestock. Farmers with private tenure are thus, on average, less diverse in terms of land use, while only slightly more diverse in terms of crop choice. A higher per cent of private farmers report having received credit and insurance and are far more likely to have the mechanical equipment necessary for farmland production. These physical and financial resources could give these farmers more flexibility to respond to unexpected challenges in the future – whether from market shocks or climatic events.

The sensitivity of farmer households in González to climate hazards is measured in terms of perceptions and impacts of past climate events and the

Table 13.5 *Selected indicators of adaptive capacity of farm households in González, Mexico*

Capacity Attribute	Variable	Private	Communal
Human capital	Age of farmer (yrs)	46	52
	Education (yrs)	4.6	3.2
	Adults with primary school education	1.5	2.15
Material resources	Landholding size (ha)	332	23
	Animal units	30	10
	Tractor ownership (%)	91	31
	Irrigation (%)	15	37
Financial resources	Credit access (%)	44	15
	Insurance access (%)	21	7
Information	Technical assistance (%)	29	29
	Consult climate information (%)	53	70
Diversity	Number of crops	2.2	1.5
	Land allocated to crops (%)	90	69

Note: Mean values are given for private and communal farmers.

degree of dependency on crop income (Table 13.6). Results from the survey indicate that sensitivity, both indirect (for example, impact on livelihoods) and direct (for example, impact on crop yields), are similar for the *ejidatarios* and the private tenure farmers. For example, despite the apparent drought-tolerant nature of sorghum, all farmers reported equally variable yields for sorghum as for maize and similar spatial extent of impacts on land planted with sorghum and maize. Farmers report that yields decline by an average of 73 per cent for all crops in bad years relative to good years. In the 2002–2003 season, the percentage of planted area adversely affected by climate ranged between 40 and 43 per cent for sorghum and 47 to 48 per cent for maize.

Table 13.6 *Selected indicators of sensitivity of farm households in González, Mexico, to climate hazards*

Sensitivity Attributes	Private	Communal
Average number of past climate events remembered	2.0	1.6
Average number of pests and diseases that frequently affect crops and livestock	2.4	1.7
Average % area affected by hazards, summer 2002	35	45
Average decline in yields of summer crops between good and bad years (%)	72	74
Farmers who think climate is changing (%)	71	92
Farmers reporting loss in income 1998–2003 (%)	32.4	35.4
Dependency of household on crop income (%)	60	37

Note: Mean values are given for private and communal farmers.

The two groups do differ in some respects. Although private farmers tend to recall more damaging climate events in the past than communal farmers, the communal farmers are more inclined to believe that the climate is changing. The *ejidatarios* also report less frequent problems with pests and crop diseases compared to the *pequeños propietarios*. Communal farmers in general also rely more heavily on non-farm income sources, either as the primary income source or in combination with crop income, while crop income was the primary income source for 47 per cent of private farmers (see Figure 13.3).

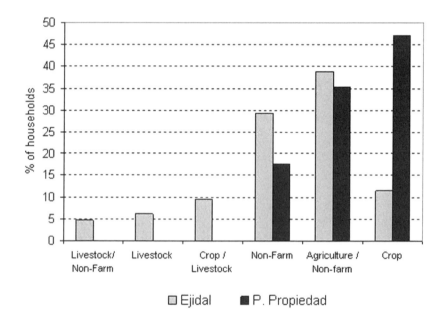

Figure 13.3 *Sources of income for communal and private tenure farmers in González, Mexico*

Note: Data represent percentage of households receiving 66 per cent or more of income from different sources (farm or non-farm).

Vulnerability of farm systems in González

Each of the variables associated with adaptive capacity and sensitivity were transformed into a 0 to 1 scale and weighted using the analytical hierarchy process (Saaty, 1980). This process produced two indicators for each household, with values between 0 and 1, representing 'absence of adaptive capacity' and 'degree of sensitivity'. The average score for 'absence of adaptive capacity' is predictably higher for the *ejidatarios* than for the private farmers (0.70 vs 0.59), reflecting the long history of unequal access to services and resources between the two groups (see Yates, 1981; Sanderson, 1986). However, the opposite is true for sensitivity. Average sensitivity scores are 0.38 for *ejidatarios* and 0.51 for private farmers. The higher sensitivity scores for private farmers can be attributed to higher reported sensitivity to crop pests and diseases, as well as their greater dependence on crop income.

To analyse the overall vulnerability of the households, the values for the sensitivity and adaptive capacity indicators were combined using fuzzy logic (see Bojórquez et al, 2002, for a description of this method). The resulting values are used to assign each household to one of three vulnerability classes: low, moderate and high. In the overall sample, 57 per cent of households are classified as moderately vulnerable, 39 per cent as highly vulnerable and only 4 per cent in the low vulnerability class. In comparison with the *ejidatarios*, a higher percentage of private farmers are, as expected, associated with the low vulnerability category. However, these farmers are also proportionally better represented in the high vulnerability class (Figure 13.4), suggesting that the land tenure classes alone are not good predictors of vulnerability.

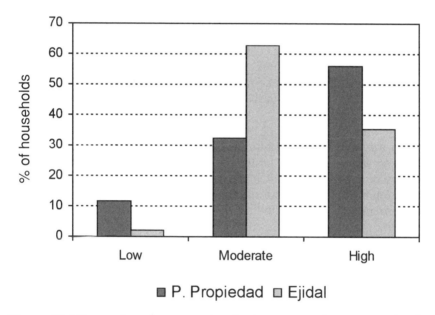

Figure 13.4 *Proportion of communal and private tenure farmers associated with each vulnerability class in González, Mexico*

By plotting the transformed values of the variables that were used to construct the indices for adaptive capacity and sensitivity on radar diagrams, one can see that for both *pequeños propietarios* and *ejidatarios*, access to financial resources (credit and insurance) and technical assistance, together with crop-income dependence and problems with crop pests, are what primarily distinguishes the households in the high and low vulnerability classes (Figure 13.5). It is interesting to note that in both of the tenure groups, income diversity and crop diversity are associated with both low and high vulnerability classes. This may reflect the fact that income diversity – particularly diversification into temporary low-skilled positions – is a coping strategy for income insecure households, and thus could equally be an indicator of poverty and marginalization as an indicator of flexibility in the face of risk, depending on the type of non-farm activity and the other endowments of the household. While crop diversity (in this case, the number of crops planted by the household in 2002/2003) theoretically provides households with alternatives should a climatic hazard affect one particular crop, greater diversity can also mean increasing one's exposure to a broader variety of climatic hazards and thus increasing the probability that a household will experience crop loss. The greater sensitivity of diversified households was also seen with the mixed small and mixed large farm systems of the Laboulaye case study.

Discussion and Conclusions

Despite the differences in the agricultural histories and structure of farming in the two countries of Argentina and Mexico, the case studies reveal important similarities. First, the drivers of vulnerability are similar. In the context of neoliberalism, farmers in both regions are feeling renewed pressure to specialize in one or two commercially viable commodities, and the bias in policy is in favour of larger-scale more entrepreneurial farm units, putting the smallholder farm system at a disadvantage.

In Argentina, the importance of agricultural diversification in climate risk mitigation may also be diminishing in the face of the changing technologies and markets, which encourage farmers to accept greater climate risks whenever these risks are coupled with higher economic returns. However, if crop specialization is pursued without the support of financial mechanisms such as insurance to assist in coping with loss, this strategy can be associated with high vulnerability. Pursuing soy monocultures entails higher production costs and, as a result, some households have been forced by debt and economic hardship to rent out their land or abandon agriculture altogether.

In González, it is apparent that income diversification still remains the primary risk reduction strategy for farmers operating on the economic margins. These farmers – almost exclusively *ejidatarios* – are spreading the impact of their losses through access to a variety of income sources. In contrast, for private farmers pursuing a crop specialization strategy, the determining factor in their vulnerability is their access to financial and material resources that can buffer a large-scale producer against climatic risk.

Our study provides a snapshot of vulnerability in a particular tumultuous period in the histories of both countries. While our selection of indicators reflects the vulnerability of farm units to very dynamic social and climatic processes, we cannot argue that our assessment captures the changing nature of vulnerability in either location. We can, however, consider our assessment in the context of plausible scenarios for each region. One such scenario would be the continuation of current policy trends, with the likely result – particularly in Laboulaye – of further land concentration, the continued expansion of monocropping, and the continued economic marginalization of the small family farm. The particular resources identified in our case studies as important in

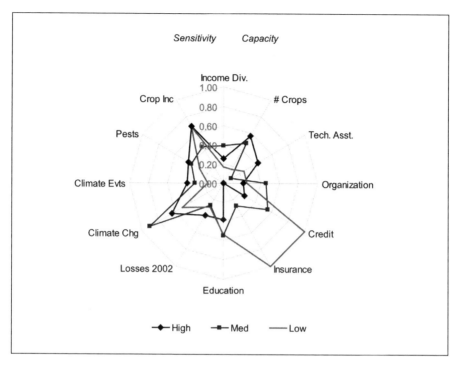

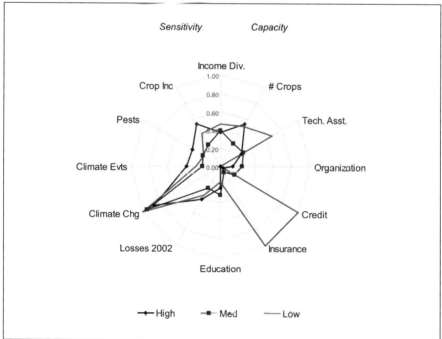

Figure 13.5 *Structure of vulnerability for low, medium and high vulnerability classes among communal farmers (top) and private tenure farmers (bottom) in González, Mexico*

adaptive capacity (credit, insurance, landholding size and farm profit) would continue to play an important role in determining future vulnerability, by facilitating adaptations, reducing sensitivity or improving coping capacities.

Under this scenario, the farmers who would be most likely to exit the agriculture sector are those who have been unable to engage fully and profitably in commercial markets and those who have assumed too much economic risk in the face of both volatile markets and climatic conditions. This scenario has environmental implications at the local and regional levels that could – and likely would – feed back into increased vulnerability at the scale of the farm enterprise. For several decades researchers have cautioned that very capital intensive models of agricultural development may, in some cases, make production systems less resilient by creating an unsustainable dependency on exogenous inputs and increasing the sensitivity of production to ecological and economic disturbances such as salinity, water scarcity and pests (Conway, 1987; Buttel and Gertler, 1982; Marsden, 1997).

In one sense, the González case offers a good example of this process. According to the state's agricultural ministry, the problem of erosion and soil degradation from sorghum mono-cropping are beginning to be evident in northern Tamaulipas, illustrating the environmental consequence of what was imagined in the 1960s to be a perfect adaptation to both water scarcity and market opportunity. A similar future could await Laboulaye, with disturbing implications for the regions' susceptibility to floods and droughts.

Another scenario is possible, although less probable. In Argentina, greater concern over the environmental impacts of expansive agriculture might encourage the development of new regulations to conserve fragile lands and enable more diversified land use once again. A drop in soy prices and increased support for Argentina's livestock industry, perhaps in response to renewed consumer interest in locally-produced organic beef, would help revive the opportunities for small-scale family farms. In Mexico, although the promotion of pasture as an alternative to sorghum may, in the long run, also produce unconsidered environmental consequences (particularly because the promoted pasture is buffle grass, an invasive plant that has become very controversial in the Sonoran Desert, see Tobin, 2004, and Tucson Weekly, 1996), such a policy might provide those farmers practicing mixed grain/livestock farming with the resources they need to adjust to new opportunities. One of the benefits of globalization is that it can also facilitate the growth of new approaches that can improve the resilience of production – such as low-tillage farming, rainwater harvesting for irrigation and improved management of organic manures – by spreading information about these techniques and linking producers to consumers who are increasingly interested in the production process. Tamaulipas is already home to a large number of Mennonite farmers, who have practised low-input, high-yielding agriculture for decades. Public support for the formation of farm associations and producer groups would be a key element in such a scenario.

Regardless of the future scenario, it is clear that vulnerability in both regions will continue to be a product of the incidence and biophysical impact of climate events, the structure and resources of the affected farm units, and the institutional and policy environment in which farmers are operating. The complex and multivariate nature of vulnerability challenges any simple interpretation of current sensitivities and makes evaluating future risk problematic. The methodologies we used in this study we hope provide useful insights into how the evolving strategies of farm households are changing the landscape of vulnerability at the local level. Our analysis identifies not only processes presently occurring which may well have important implications for future risk, but also some areas of possible intervention, both at macro and micro levels, that could enhance farmers' coping capacities to climate risks today and in the future.

In our analysis we have raised important questions about the sustainability of current agricultural development pathways and the implications of these trajectories for future climate risk. The particular variables that make a farm system adaptive are not absolute or invariable but rather products of the ambitions and visions of progress held by the broader society and articulated through policy. Who will be adapting and by what means is thus ultimately a normative question inseparable from the ideology and outcomes of present development processes.

Note

1   Exposures to climate hazards in the two study areas in Argentina and Mexico are examined in Chapter 14 of this volume.

References

Adger, N. (1999) 'Social vulnerability to climate change and extremes in coastal Vietnam', *World Development*, vol 27, no 2, pp249–269

Anderson, J. and J. Dillon (1992) *Risk Analysis in Dryland Farming Systems*, FAO, Rome

ASERCA (1997) 'El sorgo Mexicano: Entre la autosuficiencia y la dependencia externa', *Claridades Agropecuarias*, vol 46, pp3–13

Appendini, K. (2001) *De la Milpa a los Tortibanos: La reestructuracion de la politica alimentaria en Mexico*, Colegio de Mexico City, Mexico City, Mexico

Barkin, D. and B. R. DeWalt (1988) 'Sorghum and the Mexican food crisis', *Latin American Research Review*, vol 23, no 3, pp30–59

Bebbington, A. (2000) 'Re-encountering development: Livelihood transitions and place transformations in the Andes', *Annals of the Association of American Geographers*, vol 90, no 3, pp495–520

Berdegué, J., T. Reardon and G. Escobar (2001) 'Rural non-farm employment and incomes in Chile', *World Development*, vol 29, no 3, pp411–425

Blaikie, P., T. Cannon, I. Davis and B. Wisner (1994) *At Risk: Natural Hazards, People's Vulnerability and Disasters*, Routledge, London

Bojórquez-Tapia, L. A., L. Juárez and G. Cruz-Bello (2002) 'Integrating fuzzy logic, optimization and GIS for ecological impact assessments', *Environmental Management*, vol 30, no 3, pp418–433

Brklachich, M., D. McNabb, C. Bryant and J. Dumanski (1997) 'Adaptability of agriculture systems to global climate change: A Renfrew County, Ontario, Canada pilot study', in B. Ilbery, Q. Chiotti and T. Rickard (eds) *Agricultural Restructuring and Sustainability: A Geographical Perspective*, CAB International, Oxon and New York, pp185–200

Buttel, F. H. and M. E. Gertler (1982) 'Agricultural structure, agricultural policy and environmental quality', *Agriculture and Environment*, vol 7, pp101–119

Cavazos, T. (1999) 'Large-scale circulation anomalies conducive to extreme precipitation events and derivation of daily rainfall in northeastern Mexico and southeastern Texas', *Journal of Climate*, vol 12, pp1506–1522

Chiotti, Q., T. Johnston, B. Smit and B. Ebel (1997) 'Agricultural response to climate change: A preliminary investigation of farm-level adaptation in southern Alberta', in B. Ilbery, Q. Chiotti and T. Richard (eds) *Agricultural Restructuring and Sustainability*, CAB International, Oxon and New York, pp201–218

Cisneros, J. M., J. de Prada, A. Degioanni, A. Cantero Gutiérrez, H. Gil, M. Reynero, F. Shah and B. Bravo Ureta (2004) *Erosión Hídrica y Cambio de Uso de los Suelos en Córdoba. Evaluación Mediante el Modelo Rusle 2*, unpublished manuscript Universidad Nacional de Río Cuarto, (In Spanish)

Conway, G. (1987) 'Properties of agroecosystems', *Agricultural Systems*, vol 24, pp95–117

Cornelius, W. and D. Myhre (eds) (1998) *The Transformation of Rural Mexico: Reforming the Ejido Sector*, Center for US–Mexico Studies, San Diego, CA, US

Conde, C. (2005) 'El Clima de Tamaulipas', powerpoint presentation to stakeholders, Gonzalez, Tamaulipas, 6–7 May

de Janvry, A. and E. Sadoulet (1993) 'Market, state, and civil organizations in Latin America beyond the debt crisis: The context for rural development', *World Development*, vol 21, no 4, pp659–674

Dessai, S., W. N. Adger, M. Hulme, J. Köhler, J. Turnpenny and R. Warren (2003) *Defining and Experiencing Dangerous Climate Change*, Tyndall Center for Climate Change Research, University of East Anglia, Norwich

Eakin, H. (2002) 'Rural households' vulnerability and adaptation to climatic variability and institutional change', unpublished doctoral dissertation, Department of Geography and Regional Development, University of Arizona, Tucson, AZ

Easterling, W. (1996) 'Adapting North American agriculture to climate change in review', *Agricultural and Forest Meteorology*, vol 80, pp1–53

Ellis, F. (2000) *Rural Livelihoods and Diversity in Developing Countries*, Oxford University Press, Oxford

Gay, C. (2006) 'Vulnerability and adaptation to climate change: The case of farmers in Mexico and Argentina', Final Report AIACC Project No. LA29, International START Secretariat, Washington, DC, US, www.aiaccproject.org

Ghezan, G., M. Mateos and J. Elverdin (2001) *Impacto de las Políticas de Ajuste Estructural en el Sector Agropecuario y Agroindustrial: El Caso de Argentina*, Serie Desarrollo Productivo no 90, Red de Desarrollo Agropecuario, ECLAC (UN), Santiago de Chile

Hernández Laos, E. and J. Velásquez Roa (2003) *Globalización, Desigualdad y Pobreza: Lecciones de la Experiencia Mexicana*, Universidad Autónoma Metropolitana, Mexico City, Mexico

Ibarra Mendívil, J. L. (1996) 'Recent changes in the Mexican constitution and their impact on agrarian reform', in L. Randall (ed) *Reforming Mexico's Agrarian Reform*, M. E. Sharpe, Armonk, NY, pp49–60

INDEC (2004) www.indec.mecon.ar/

INEGI (2000) XII Censo General de Población y Vivienda, 2000. INEGI, Aguascalientes

INTA (1987) *Análisis de la Evolución, Situación Actual y Problemática del Sector Agropecuario del Centro Regional Córdoba*, INTA Centro Regional Córdoba

INTA (2002) *Plan de Tecnología Regional (2001–2004) Centro Regional Córdoba*,

Ediciones INTA, Buenos Aires, Argentina

Kelly, T. (2001) 'Neoliberal reforms and rural poverty', *Latin American Perspectives*, vol 28, no 3, pp84–103

Latuada, M. (2000) 'El crecimiento económico y el desarrollo sustentable en los pequeños productores agropecuarios Argentinos de fines de siglo XX', Conferencia Electrónica sobre Políticas Públicas, Institucionalidad y Desarrollo Rural en América Latina, www.rlc.fao.org/foro/institucionalidad

Liverman, D. (1990) 'Drought impacts in Mexico: Climate, agriculture, technology and land tenure in Sonora and Puebla', *Annals of the Association of American Geographers*, vol 80, pp49–72

Loker, W. M. (1996) '"Campesinos" and the crisis of modernization in Latin America', *Journal of Political Ecology*, vol 3, pp69–88

Marsden, T. (1997) 'Reshaping environments: Agriculture and water interactions and the creation of vulnerability', *Transactions of the Institute of British Geographers*, vol 22, no 3, pp321–337

Myhre, D. (1998) 'The Achilles' heel of the reforms: The rural finance system', in W. Cornelius and D. Myhre (eds) *The Transformation of Rural Mexico: Reforming the Ejido Sector*, The Center for US–Mexico Studies, San Diego, CA, US

Moscatelli, G. and M. S. Pazos (2002) 'Soils of Argentina: Nature and use', www.elsitioagricola.com/articulos/moscatelli/soils%20of%20argentina%20-%20nature%20and%20use.asp

Obschatko, E. (1993) *Efectos de la Desregulación Sobre la Competitividad de la Producción Argentina*. Grupo Editor Latinoamericano, Buenos Aires, Argentina

Pengue, W. (2001) 'The impact of soybean expansion in Argentina', www.grain.org/seedling/?id=116

Peretti, M. (1999) 'Competitividad de la empresa agropecuaria Argentina en la década de los '90', *Revista Argentina de Economía Agraria*, vol 11, pp27–42

Reilly, J. M. and D. Schilmmelpfenning (1999) 'Agricultural impact assessment, vulnerability and the scope for adaptation', *Climatic Change*, vol 43, pp745–788

Risbey, J., M. Kandlikar and H. Dowlatabadi (1999) 'Scale, context and decision making in agricultural adaptation to climate variability and change', *Mitigation and Adaptation Strategies for Global Change*, vol 4, pp137–165

SAGyP/CFA (1995) *El Deterioro de las Tierras en la República Argentina*, SAGyP Ed.

Saaty, T. (1980) *The Analytic Hierarchy Process*, McGraw-Hill, New York and London

Sanderson, S. (1986) *The Transformation of Mexican Agriculture: International Structure and the Politics of Rural Change.* Princeton University Press, Princeton, NJ, US

Scoones, I. (1998) 'Sustainable rural livelihoods: A framework for analysis', IDS Working Paper, Institute for Development Studies, Brighton, UK

Seiler, R., M. Hayes and L. Bressan (2002) 'Using the standardized precipitation index for flood risk monitoring', *International Journal of Climatology*, vol 22, pp1365–1376

Smit, B., D. McNabb and J. Smither (1996) 'Agricultural adaptation to climatic variation', *Climatic Change*, vol 33, pp7–29

Smithers, J. and B. Smit (1997) 'Agricultural system response to environmental stress', in B. Ilbery, Q. Chiotti and T. Richard (eds) *Agricultural Restructuring and Sustainability: A Geographical Perspective*, CAB International, Oxon and New York

Solbrig, O. (1996) 'Towards a sustainable Pampa agriculture: Past performance and prospective analysis', Working Paper No.96/97-6, The David Rockefeller Center for Latin American Studies (DRCLAS), Harvard University, Cambridge, MA, US

Solbrig, O. and E. Viglizzo (1999) 'Sustainable farming in the Argentine Pampas: History, society, economy, and ecology', Working Paper No.99/00-1, The David Rockefeller Center for Latin American Studies (DRCLAS), Harvard University, Cambridge, MA, US

Tobin, M. (2004) 'Exotic grass vs. palo verde', *The Arizona Daily Star*, 8 August, Accessed online: http://www.azstarnet.com/dailystar/printDS/33361.php

Tucson Weekly (1996) 'The grass that ate Sonora', cover story, *The Tucson Weekly*, 18–24 April, www.tucsonweekly.com/tw/04-18-96/cover.htm

Wehbe, M. B. (1997) 'Regional consequences of the agro-food system: Rural changes in the south of Córdoba (Argentina)', unpublished thesis, Institute of Social Studies, The Hague, The Netherlands

Yates, P. L. (1981) *Mexico's Agricultural Dilemma*, The University of Arizona Press, Tucson, AZ

14

Climatic Threat Spaces in Mexico and Argentina

Cecilia Conde, Marta Vinocur, Carlos Gay, Roberto Seiler and Francisco Estrada

Introduction

Extreme climatic events associated with climate variability have exposed the vulnerability of human systems to such events (Le Roy, 1991; Jáuregui, 1995; Florescano and Swan, 1995; Stern and Easterling, 1999). In response, human systems have generated various adaptation strategies and measures according to their differing socioeconomic capacities to cope. Economic globalization processes have, on the one hand, extended, in principle, the access to knowledge and technology that can support a wide range of coping capabilities. On the other hand, in the developing countries, they have also influenced an accelerated loss of resources for many social groups and contributed to a deterioration of the social organizations that have applied and supported these capabilities. These kinds of globalization impacts are especially true for the climate sensitive agricultural sector and as O'Brian and Leichencko (2000) have stated, climate change and economic globalization are two 'external' processes that affect agricultural systems in the developing world.

Mexico and Argentina are two examples of developing countries that are currently under the pressure of economic globalization. Current social conditions here are such that a relatively small change in normal climatic conditions might trigger important impacts on agricultural activities and generate varying responses based on their specific circumstances.

In order to better understand the vulnerability of these two countries to present and future climate risks we analysed coffee and maize cultivation in two regions in Mexico and Argentina respectively (Gay et al, 2002): the central region of Veracruz, Mexico, and Roque Sáenz Peña Department in Córdoba Province, Argentina. Farmers in both countries aim to export most of their agricultural production and are, therefore, highly susceptible to both climatic and market variations. We have used the term 'climatic threat spaces' to describe cases in which climatic variables have played a major role in agricultural losses. In cases where no climatic explanation is found for agricultural losses, other non-climatic stressors that could be responsible are examined. The detection of other stressors – different from climate – that affect agricultural production is particularly important since events such as changes in agricultural policies or prices have in the past, affected crop production even when climate conditions have been favourable.

The concept of threat spaces developed in this analysis is therefore intended to aid in the description of climatic variability in the regions under study. The concept could help in attributing losses in agricultural production during a particular year to specific climate anomalies and, in the absence of any climate-related explanation for the losses, would point to the need to examine other stressors in the socioeconomic and sociopolitical spheres in the region during the period. The establishment of threat spaces for current climate variability could additionally help to determine future vulnerability to climate change using outputs from climate scenario projections. At the same time, the assessment of current adaptation strategies to these climate threats can serve to inform future options for coping with climate impacts.

Methods

Climatic threat spaces (Conde, 2003) used in this analysis were constructed by means of seasonal or monthly scatterplots of precipitation and temperature, similar to those constructed for climate change scenarios (see, for example, Hulme and Brown, 1998; Parry, 2002). For current climate anomalies, we used the interquartile range of the two variables to determine the threat space for crop cultivation. This can also be done using the one standard deviation criterion, which is currently used (Gay et al, 2004b) by the Mexican Ministry of Agriculture to determine economic support for farmers affected by extreme climatic events (*contingencias climatológicas*). However, this approach has certain limitations and therefore the interquartile range method is proposed, because it is more robust. According to Wilks (1995, p22) the interquartile range is 'generally not sensitive to particular assumptions about the overall nature of the data'. Also, the interquartile range 'is a resistant method that is not unduly influenced by a small number of outliers' (Wilks, 1995, p22) because the 50 per cent of the distribution (25 per cent in each tail, independent of the shape of the distribution) in which extreme values occur is excluded in this process. To get a more precise description about the tails of the data, a crossed schematic plot can be used to classify extreme values with respect to their degree of unusualness.

Climatic data included in the plots cover a period of more than 30 years, with the years 1961–1990 as the reference period. Years of extreme conditions in temperature and/or precipitation are selected as potential circumstances under which crop production might have been affected. Particularly, El Niño or La Niña years are specified in the plot to visualize the possible effects of strong El Niño Southern Oscillation (ENSO) episodes, which have been documented in previous studies (Podesta et al, 2000; Magaña, 1999; Seiler and Vinocur, 2004) in these regions. For the purposes of this study, El Niño and La Niña years in the threat spaces are considered when the bimonthly values of the multivariate ENSO index (see Wolter) are above (or below) 1 (or -1). Particular attention is given to the strongest ENSO events since 1950.

The quartile range for climatic variables is considered as a first order approximation of the limits of the coping range for agricultural activities. The hypothesis is that normal climatic conditions (with respect to 1961–1990) should be within the optimal or near-optimal conditions for crop production in the regions under study and that small variations around that average are tolerable for the system. Most of the crop models used to analyse the crops' sensitivity to climate are based on this hypothesis (for example, Baier, 1977; Jones and Kiniry, 1986).

Optimal conditions for a specific crop can be described within the threat space to help determine whether the region provides optimal or near-optimal conditions, or whether the climatic circumstances represent an important threat for that particular crop production. Thus the coping range's boundaries, which were initially defined in terms of the interquartile range, could then be redefined in terms of the climatic requirements for the specific crop.

In our research, we studied the impacts of climate on two specific crop production systems: coffee production in Mexico and maize production in Argentina. We analysed a series of crop production years and those showing relevant decreases or increases were searched within the threat space for a potentially responsible climatic factor. Such climatic anomalies are, however, only one of the possible stressors that affect production. Other stressors that can impact production in a given critical year include changes in markets and pricing, changes in agricultural policies, and environmental factors such as soils and pests. Documentation of such non-climatic factors that cannot be addressed within the threat spaces helps to determine the relative weight of climatological factors on agricultural production and therefore aids in assessing farmers' vulnerability. Importantly, such factors can help to explain important crop losses in years when climatic conditions were favourable. In this analysis, we relied on the historical records of prices and agricultural policies; rural studies (Eakin, 2002); in-depth interviews and focus group discussions with producers (Gay et al, 2002; Maurutto et al, 2004; Maurutto, unpublished); and newspaper articles (Martínez, 2002; La Red, 2004, Diario La Communa, 1979a, b and c) and other secondary sources of information as tools to account for the influence of non-climatic stressors.

In summary, threat spaces seen under the scope of the specific crop requirements can be used as a tool to assess the current vulnerability of agricultural production to extreme climatic extreme events (drought, floods, frosts, heat waves) in a particular region.

Once the role of climatic factors in current vulnerability of crop production is established, future vulnerability under a changed climate can be determined using climate change scenarios. We obtained future climate scenarios for 2020 and 2050 from three general circulation models (GCMs), EH4TR98, GFDLTR90 and HAD3TR00, using the Model for the Assessment of Greenhouse Gas-Induced Climate Change and a Scenario Generator (Magicc/Scengen Model; version 4.1) (Wigley, 2003; Hulme et al, 2000), and considering the two emission scenarios A2 and B2 (Nakicenovic et al, 2000; IPCC, 2001). Simple interpolation methods have been applied to obtain the possible changes in mean temperature and precipitation values for specific locations (Sánchez et al, 2004; Palma, 2004). The changes in these variables are then introduced into the threat spaces constructed to assess current vulnerability, to visualize possible future climatic threat conditions and to assess future vulnerability to climate change. When the anomalies for both variables are outside the limits of the coping range defined above, the climate threat is considered to increase considerably under the particular climate scenario.

Finally, besides the analysis of anomalies in the means of temperature and precipitation, the distribution or variability of the mean is also important. This can be determined by a simple approach that tracks changes in the variability of the mean, assuming no change in the other parameters of the distribution of the data. The distribution then gets transposed to the new mean without any alteration in its shape. Changes in the frequency of extreme events can be used to describe the possible increase in climatic threat. Another approach to include variability in climate change threat spaces is to draw schematic plots constructed with observed data around the future mean value, providing a plot of future minimum, lower quartile, median, upper quartile and maximum values. Thus the probability of having climatic events outside the coping range of a given crop (or activity) can be estimated. Although these methods are based on the assumption that current and future variability are the same, they can provide a rough scenario of future variability that can guide stakeholders and decision makers.

Case Studies

Case Study 1: Coffee production in Veracruz, Mexico

Veracruz is one of Mexico's largest states (Figure 14.1), located in the Gulf of Mexico between Tamaulipas and Tabasco. Agriculture is an important economic activity here, generating 7.9 per cent of the state's gross domestic product (GDP) and providing jobs for 31.7 per cent of the state's labour force (Gay et al, 2004a). Veracruz is the second largest coffee producer in the country, with 153,000 hectares devoted to coffee production and coffee production involving 67,000 producers in 2000. Ninety-five per cent of this coffee was exported, with a production value of 151.1 million dollars (Gay et al, 2004a).

Coffee plantations in Veracruz State are a relatively recent development, with coffee production becoming an important agricultural activity in the 1940s and 1950s, particularly because of the good prices after World War II (Bartra, 1999). Until the 1980s, favourable governmental policies led to an increase in production of nearly 75 per cent on that of the 1940s and a doubling of the number of coffee producers in the country, most of them with plantations of less than 10ha. However, since the late 1980s and early 1990s

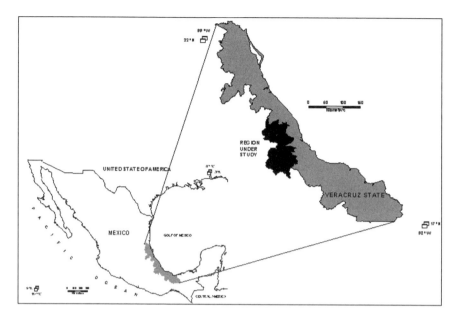

Figure 14.1 *The state of Veracruz and the region under study*

Note: Locations described here are situated between about 1000m and 1500m above sea level.

there has been a 'megacrisis' (Bartra, 1999) in the coffee sector, brought on by a saturation of production in the coffee market and decreasing international prices for coffee. The current trend of importing Vietnamese coffee into Mexico has also affected the producers' competitiveness within the national coffee markets. At the same time, government support for coffee producers to cope with adverse market or environmental conditions has declined (Castellanos el al, 2003, Eakin et al, 2005; Eakin et al, 2006). These conditions have contributed to the exacerbation of poverty in the state, with about half the number of municipalities classified under very high and high poverty levels in 2000 (Consejo Estatal de Población, undated).

Besides the economic and policy-oriented concerns (Bartra, 1999), historical records of crop losses as well as results from a recent study (Gay et al, 2004b) show that changes in temperature and precipitation have severely affected coffee production in Mexico. However, awareness regarding such current climatic threats is very low, and this lack of knowledge, in combination with declining government support, serves to increase the vulnerability of coffee production and reduces the response capacity of the producers to adverse climatic events.

For the purpose of our analysis we selected a region in the central part of the state of Veracruz (Figure 14.1), between latitudes 18°30' and 20°15'N and longitudes 95°30' and 97°30'W. It occupies an area of about 183,600 km² (Palma, 2004), with high altitudes providing almost optimal conditions for coffee production. It currently contributes almost 90 per cent of the total coffee production in Veracruz (Araujo and Martínez, 2002). The region was analysed as a single unit, given that precipitation and temperature regimes (depending on altitude) are similar in the majority of the meteorological stations or *munici-pios* (Palma, 2004).

The optimum average annual temperature range for coffee production is from 17 to 24°C, and the optimal annual precipitation is between 1500 and 2500mm (Nolasco, 1985). These climatic conditions are observed in Teocelo, in central Veracruz, which has a mean annual temperature of 19.5°C and an annual precipitation of 2046.9mm (Nolasco, 1985) (Figure 14.2).

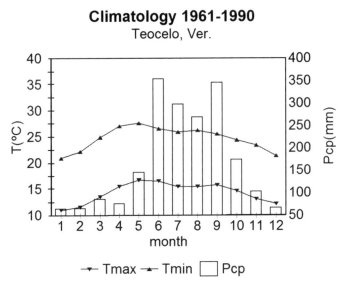

Figure 14.2 *Normal climatic conditions for Teocelo*

Note: Tmax = Maximum temperature; Tmin = minimum temperature; Pcp = precipitation

Specific seasonal requirements for coffee include dry weather just before flowering: a small decrease in precipitation or 'relative drought' during one or two months in spring (March, April, May: MAM) is considered optimal (Nolasco, 1985; Castillo et al, 1997). Excess rain during this period could damage the flowering process. Figure 14.2 shows this condition for the month of April in Teocelo. This decrease in precipitation must, however, not be confused with an actual drought, since a drought can severely impact production, as has been noted during strong El Niño events (Martínez, 2002, La Red, 2004), particularly during May 1970, May 1983 and May 1998. In Figure 14.3, spring anomalies for minimum temperature and precipitation are shown for Atzalan, Veracruz (19°80'N, 97°22'W, 1842m above sea level), also located in the same region, but with a more reliable and complete data series (Bravo et al, 2006).

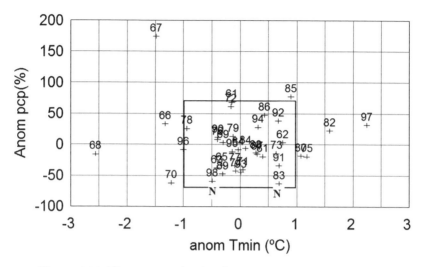

Figure 14.3 *Threat space for Atzalan, Veracruz, in spring (MAM)*

Note: Anomalies for minimum temperature (Tmin°C) and for precipitation (%) and the year they occurred are indicated by the dots. Years are represented by their last two digits (97 equals 1997). The rectangle represents the quartile range (1961–1990) for this season. N represents strong El Niño years. Years with greater anomalies lie outside the rectangle.

In winter and spring, minimum temperature is another critical factor that can affect coffee production. In summer, critical variables include maximum temperature and precipitation since heat waves, drought or floods can affect the development and maturity of the coffee cherry. In autumn, the coffee fruits mature and therefore damaging factors such as climatic extreme events and pests are important.

Factors such as high relative humidity, high temperatures and drought can increase the danger of crop pests (Castillo et al, 1997). Harvesting occurs during the end of autumn, winter and the beginning of spring. Adverse climatic conditions, particularly colder and wetter winters during strong El Niño events, can affect labour activities by preventing access to plantations located far into the forests or at higher altitudes.

The effects of climatic events on coffee agrosystems in Mexico are unfortunately difficult to detect, since these systems are typically classified as rustic, immersed in a complex forest ecosystem that makes coffee plants quite resilient to climatic variations (Nolasco, 1985). For this reason, the anomalies reported for the extreme climatic events that have severely affected coffee production in the past will be taken as the thresholds to which the system is more vulnerable to determine current and future climatic threats (see Figure 14.2).

Given the vulnerability of coffee plantations to spring drought (Castellanos, 2003), this factor was used in the determination of a coping range for the crop. The average reduction in accumulated (total) spring precipitation during the El Niño years of 1970, 1983 and 1998 was around 60 per cent in the region under study, severely affecting several plantations in the study area. Losses of 25 per cent and 17 per cent in coffee production occurred in Veracruz in 1970 and 1998 respectively (Figure 14.4).Given this damaging impact of a 60 per cent reduction in average rainfall, the lower boundary of total precipitation should be established at -50 per cent of the conditions (approximately 300 mm). At the higher boundary, precipitation should not exceed +50 per cent, as this could diminish the relative drought necessary for coffee. Excess rain can also affect the plant and soil conditions by favouring the spread of pests.

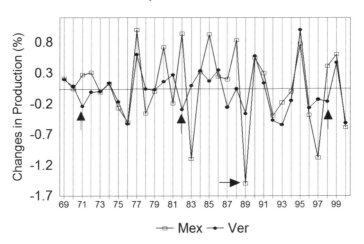

Figure 14.4 *Coffee production anomalies for Mexico and for the state of Veracruz*

Note: Arrows show critical years in coffee production, either for both the country and the state (1989) or for only the state (1971, 1982 and 1998)

The temperature anomaly for spring of 1970 was a 'mixed' signal, since during April the temperature rose to more than 40°C, but during May, after the intense heat-wave, one of the worst frosts to affect the region occurred. This combination of high temperatures and very low precipitation during April, followed by the very intense frost with a continued drought during May, caused great damage to the coffee crop (see data for 1970 in Figures 14.3 and 14.4) that was to be exported (El Universal, in La Red database, 2004). This frost event occurred on several days, but the seasonal averages used in developing the threat spaces might obscure such climatic events (for example, frost or heavy rains). This highlights a shortcoming of the threat spaces, which cannot substitute for the analysis of daily data to study the behaviour of extreme climatic events. Information on such events must therefore be obtained from other sources.

Considering the requirements for coffee with respect to precipitation and minimum temperature, the threat space for spring should include those cases in which minimum temperature could be below 10°C, which is damaging to the coffee plant (Castillo et al, 1997). Thus minimum temperature anomalies of ≤–1°C during spring would lie in the threat space for coffee in Veracruz (Figure 14.5). No limitation is depicted for an increase in minimum temperature, because even +3°C is within the range of optimal requirements.

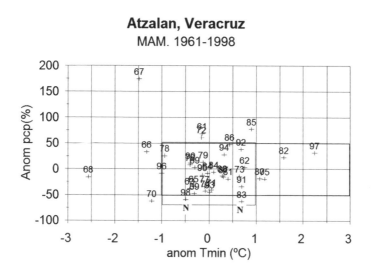

Figure 14.5 *Climatic threat space for coffee during spring (MAM), considering the minimum temperature and precipitation requirements of the coffee plant*

Note: The square box represents the initial coping range proposed. Climatic anomalies outside the rectangle are considered to be risky for coffee. **N** represents strong El Niño years.

A threat space that considers the anomalies for maximum temperature and precipitation indicates possible combinations of climatic threats that could occur when anomalies for maximum temperature are greater than +1.5°C, combined with a 20 per cent reduction in precipitation, a situation that occurred in 1975 (when almost half the coffee production was lost in the central region of Veracruz (see Figure 14.4). The greater losses in other years were caused by other stressors, in other words, different from climatic extreme events, such as changes in the political or economic conditions (Figure 14.4).

It must be noted that adverse climatic conditions during spring could increase the sensitivity of the coffee plants and their environment such that in the subsequent seasons changes in climatic conditions even inside the coping range could cause crop damages. This issue is not discussed here, but it is certainly an important element in the ecological study of this agrosystem.

In summer (June, July, August: JJA), total precipitation is quite high in the central region of Veracruz. Nevertheless, exceeding the optimal limit for coffee can cause important damages through flooding or severe storms (Figure 14.6). Such floods were recorded in 1970, 1973, 1996, 1997 and 1981 (La Red, 2004; Martínez, 2002). Generally, for a good coffee crop, rainfall should be neither more that 30 per cent above nor more that 40 per cent below normal.

Strong ENSO years might be associated with important drought periods, for example, the episodes of 1982, 1989 and 1997. They may also be associated with an increase in maximum temperature, such as the episodes of 1982 and 1991 (see Figure 14.6). Significant losses in production can be attributed to these events, such as the 30 per cent loss in production in 1982 and the 36 per cent loss recorded in 1989.

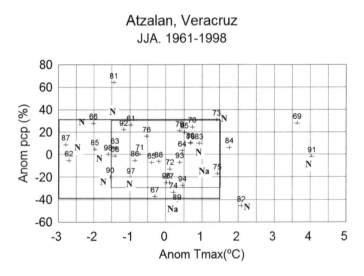

Atzalan, Veracruz
JJA. 1961-1998

Figure 14.6 *Threat space for Atzalan, Veracruz, in summer (JJA)*

Note: Anomalies for maximum temperature (Tmax°C) and for precipitation (%).

The rectangle represents the limits of the proposed coping range. The square box represents the quartile range calculated for the 1961–1990 period. **N**: El Niño year. **Na**: La Niña year.

The scale is adjusted to the minimum and maximum values in the series; for visual purposes, it is not the same as in Figures 14.3 and 14.5

Another interesting observation about the climatic threat space for Veracruz is that there were years when climatic conditions inside the box characterized normal conditions and yet resulted in important losses in coffee production in

Veracruz and indeed throughout Mexico (for example, 1992 and 1993, see Figure 14.4). In such cases, precise studies must be developed to analyse in greater detail monthly and daily data distributions, identifying possible extreme events that were lost in the seasonal averages. If no important climatic signal is detected, then it is highly probable that other stressors impacted the coffee production system, which must be investigated.

An important example is the ENSO year 1989, which not only had a strong climatic influence but also coincided with the economic 'megacrisis' that additionally affected coffee production. In this year the central region of Veracruz was affected by a severe frost, and during this period the governmental institute (Instituto Mexicano del Café – INMECAFE) that regulated coffee prices and the coffee market was also abolished. The effects of the unfavourable climatic conditions combined with the very low coffee prices due to market restructuring resulted in a significant reduction in coffee production (Figure 14.4). Even before 1989, coffee prices were already on the decline and coffee producers had begun to substitute coffee plantations with sugar plantations, clearing the shade trees on the plantation in this process and causing severe ecological damage (Martínez, 2002). The tendency to switch from coffee to sugar cane has persisted and has intensified in Veracruz, despite an overall increase in total coffee production in the region. The abandonment of the agro-ecosystem caused by low coffee prices and the occurrences of extreme climatic events described above could also be responsible for the spread of pests (such as *broca, Hypothenemus hampei*), which is an important environmental stressor in plantations in the lower altitudes.

According to farmer surveys, climatic events such as drought, heat-waves, strong winds and frosts were the most worrisome climatic events and have been responsible for most of their losses (Gay et al, 2004a; Eakin and Martinez, 2003; Castellanos et al, 2003). However, coffee farmers did not find climate as relevant a variable to their activity as the economic factors. Although such survey responses must be interpreted with care, since respondents could be biased by recent climatic events, it is important to note that a low perception of climatic threats might serve to increase the vulnerability of producers to extreme climatic events in the future.

This analysis of the central region of Veracruz in Mexico thus highlights the importance of threat spaces in assessing the significance of climatic factors in coffee cultivation. Coffee production was found to be highly correlated with climate variables, with spring precipitation and summer and winter temperatures being the most relevant climatic variables (Gay et al, 2004a). These findings are also supported by data from newspaper sources and other literature. A separate regression analysis and fieldwork were also undertaken, which arrived at the same conclusions noted above.

Case Study 2: Maize production in Roque Sáenz Peña County, Argentina

Argentina is an agro-exporter country with most of the agricultural production based on the pampas, one of the world's major agricultural regions. Córdoba province, in the centre of the country, has 83 per cent of its area dedicated to different agricultural activities developed under variable edaphic (soil related) and climatic conditions. The province is ranked fifth in size among all the Argentine provinces and its agricultural outputs represent 25 per cent of the state gross geographical product[1] (INTA, 2002). It contributes approximately 14 per cent of national agricultural GDP, with 14 per cent of the national live-stock, 17 per cent of the cereal and 25 per cent of the oilseed production. The province is the second largest maize producer in the country, accounting for about 32 per cent of the total national production (SAGPyA, 2004).

For our case study, we selected the city of Laboulaye (34°08'S, 63°14'W), situated in Presidente Roque Saénz Peña County in the southern half of Córdoba Province (Figure 14.7). This is a flood-prone area and is typical of the poorly drained plains in the south of Córdoba Province, characterized by semi-arid/subhumid temperate conditions (INTA, 1987). Annual mean precipitation here is 845mm (1961–1990) with most of the precipitation con-centrated during the warm period (October to March). Seasonal distribution shows that 28.5 per cent of the rain occurs in the autumn, 38.4 per cent in the summer, 26.4 per cent in spring and only 6.7 per cent in winter. Mean annual temperature is 16.3°C, with the month of July being the coldest (8.8°C) and January the warmest (23.7°C). Mean annual precipitation and maximum and minimum temperatures are shown in Figure 14.8.

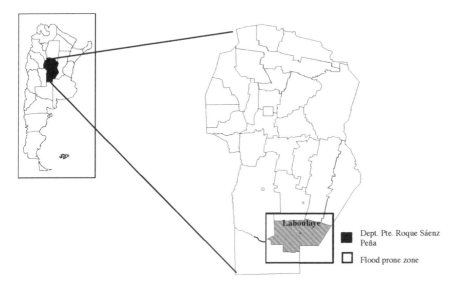

Figure 14.7 *Study region: Location of the city and flood-prone area*

Climate and climatic variability are major factors driving the dynamics of agri-cultural production in the area. Inter-annual and inter-seasonal climatic fluctuations result in a high variability in crop production, thus negatively affecting the local and regional economy. Floods and droughts of varying fre-

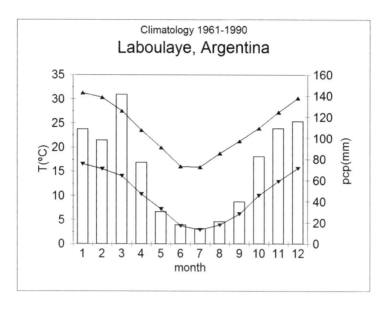

Figure 14.8 *Normal climatic conditions for Laboulaye, Argentina, in terms of maximum temperatures (Tmax), minimum temperatures (Tmin) and precipitation (Pcp)*

quencies, intensities and extents alternate in occurrence. Floods are caused mainly by excess rainfall in the flood-prone basin and by the overflowing of rivers and streams. Additional factors (some of them human-induced) such as soil saturation, volume of runoff, physical characteristics of the area, control structures and management characteristics also play a significant role in their occurrence (Seiler et al, 2002).

Besides the climatic and soil characteristics, ethnographic research (including surveys, in-depth interviews and focus groups meetings) involving key regional and local actors such as farmers, government officials and cooperative managers also informs us of the perception of climate threats and the importance of climate in agricultural decision making. Farmers here were found to have a 'naturalized' perception of climate, since it is a part of their daily life and relates to their living reality as well as to their historical past (Maurutto et al, 2003). Droughts, floods and hailstorms were identified as the most important events affecting farming activities, with flood being the most damaging threat (Rivarola et al, 2002; Vinocur et al, 2004).

In particular for the maize crop, air temperatures between 10°C and 34°C are necessary during the growing period, with different thresholds depending on the stage of the crop in the growth cycle (Andrade et al, 1996, Andrade and Sadras, 2002). High temperatures during plant germination to flowering could shorten the development period, as the thermal time required by the crop for flowering is completed earlier. This will result in a shorter time for the interception of solar radiation, leading to a yield reduction (Andrade, 1992). Water requirements for maize are around 450–550mm during the crop cycle. Water shortage is very critical during the period from 15 days before flowering to 21 days after flowering. During this period, the number of grains per square meter, the principal component of maize yield, is determined (Uhart et al, 1996). The magnitude of yield losses depends on the time of occurrence and the intensity and the duration of any water stress. Because the probability of water stress is higher in January, the time of planting becomes important to ensure that flowering occurs before 15 December of the previous year.

Precipitation and maximum temperature anomalies for summer (December, January and February: DJF) for the city of Laboulaye are shown in Figure 14.9. The summer season is critical for maize since the principal components of the crop's yield are determined during this season. The importance of temperature and precipitation values during this period has been explained above. The box in Figure 14.9 represents values of the interquartile range for maximum temperature and rainfall in Laboulaye for the 1961–1990 period. The anomalies of rainfall and maximum temperature can be related to maize yield deviations from the linear trend (Figure 14.10) to identify events that may cause yield reduction or surplus.

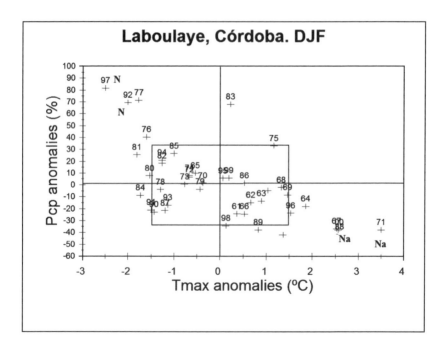

Figure 14.9 *Climatic threat space for Laboulaye, Córdoba,
for summer season (DJF)*

Note: Quartile ranges for the anomalies of the climatic variables are shown as a box. Years are represented by the last two digits (97 equals 1997). N and Na represent an El Niño and a La Niña year respectively.

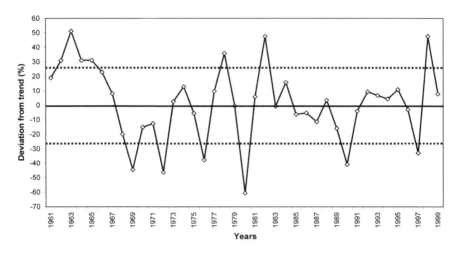

Figure 14.10 *Maize yield deviations from linear trend of the series 1961–1999 for the Department of Roque Sáenz Peña (Córdoba, Argentina)*

Note: 1961 = 1960–1961 cropping season. The dotted lines above and below zero represent plus and minus one standard deviation.

Yields above the trend of the crop yield series 1961–1990 (linear regression, R^2 = 0.68, $P < 0.00001$) were observed for different crop seasons (for example, 1961–1967, 1973–1974 and 1992–1995). If a coping range of one standard deviation from the trend is established (SD = ±26.2 per cent), maize yields exceeded this threshold in the 1962, 1963, 1964, 1978, 1982 and 1998 crop seasons. Despite the above average yields, three of these seasons (1998, 1982 and 1978) were also identified in the risk space (see 97, 81 and 77 in Figure 14.9) due to high rainfall anomalies during the summer, indicating that exceeding this threshold does not imply yield losses. Crop yield during the crop seasons of 1969, 1972, 1976, 1980, 1990 and 1997 was below the one standard deviation threshold (Figure 14.10). Some of these seasons can be identified in the risk space due to low rainfall and high maximum temperatures (for example, 71 and 89 in Figure 14.9). Although a discussion about the effects of La Niña/El Niño events is outside the scope of this chapter, it is interesting to point out that some of the years characterized by high/low rainfall anomalies during summer and high/low yields coincide with El Niño/La Niña events (for example, 1971–1972, 1988–1989 and 1997–1998). In this region, precipitation tends to be low from October to December in cold events (La Niña) and high from November to January during warm events (El Niño) (see Magrin et al, 1998), periods coinciding with the critical period of the maize crop when the grain number is determined.

Extreme events in the area, such as floods and droughts, which can be obscured by the seasonal average used to construct threat spaces were documented from newspaper and other literature records (*Diario* (newspaper) *La*

Comuna, Laboulaye; Holguín de Roza, 1986). Severe droughts were recorded in February 1967 and June 1988 and during 1989 (La Niña events) causing decreases in maize yield (Figure 14.10). Flood events were documented in 1979 (from January to August), in 1986–1987 (from May 1986 to June 1987) and in 1998–1999 (from March 1998 to May 1999) (Holguín de Roza, 1986). The 1986–1987 flood event (also an El Niño event) resulted in significant yield reductions in the affected local area. The impact of this flood event, however, shows up only as a small reduction in maize yield in Figure 14.10 since maize yields in this case have been determined for the entire study area, including areas not affected by floods. Heat-waves or unusual frost events were not documented for the area during the period of analysis.

Based on anomalous values for summer precipitation and maximum temperatures, we identified events that exceed normal values, depicting a risk space for maize for Laboulaye. When rainfall anomalies are below 30 per cent and maximum temperature anomalies are above 1.5°C, important yield decreases are found (for example, in the 1971–1972, 1967–1968 and 1988–1989 crop seasons; see Figures 14.9 and 14.10). In contrast, when the summer precipitation anomaly is above the quartile threshold and the maximum temperature is below that threshold – in other words, events are located in the upper left portion of Figure 14.9 – maize yields are not affected, indicating that scenarios tending toward these conditions, at least for the summer, will be harmless for maize. Finally, there are very few examples of years with conditions representing those in the upper right corner of Figure 14.9 (summer precipitation and temperatures above the quartile threshold), so we were unable to assess their effects on maize yield and production.

Climate Change Scenarios for Mexico

As stated in the introduction, climate change scenarios were constructed for 2020 and 2050 using the MAGICC/SCENGEN model version 4.1 (Wigley, 2003; Hulme et al, 2000). The outputs of the EH4TR98, GFDLTR90 and HAD3TR00 models were used under A2 and B2 emission scenarios (Nakicenovic et al, 2000). Simple interpolation methods (Sánchez et al, 2004) and a downscaling technique (Palma, 2004) were applied to obtain the possible changes for specific locations. The results obtained were also compared with those from the IPCC Data Distribution Center (http://ipcc-ddc.cru.uea.ac.uk/) and the Canadian Institute for Climate Studies (www.cics.uvic.ca/scenarios/data/ select.cgi).

The EH4TR98 model (German Climate Research Centre/Hamburg Model) model and the HAD3TR00 model from the Hadley Centre provided the best approximations to the observed climate for Mexico (Morales and Magaña, 2003; Conde, 2003). The GFDL (US Geophysical Fluid Dynamics Laboratory) model was also used to generate climate change scenarios, since it has been used in previous research (Gay, 2000) in Mexico.

Using the month of July to illustrate climate changes for summer, Figures 14.11a and 14.11b show the possible changes in temperature and precipitation for the central region of Veracruz. Considering all the GCM outputs, the projected temperature changes range from an increase of 0.9°C in 2020 to an increase of 2.7°C in 2050. The projected changes in precipitation range from a decrease of 29 per cent to an increase of 42 per cent, depending on the year and the model used.

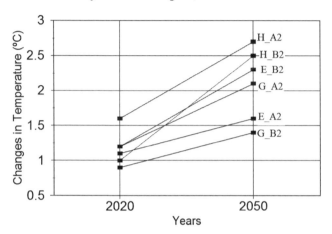

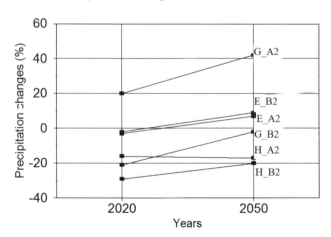

Figure 14.11 *Projected changes in* a) *temperature and* b) *precipitation for the central region of Veracruz (2020 and 2050)*

Note: Projections made using 3 GCM (G: GFDL; H: Hadley; E: ECHAM) outputs and two SRES scenarios (A2 and B2).

In order to determine the combinations of temperature and precipitation that could represent a climatic threat in the future, changes in temperature and precipitation for each scenario could be introduced in the threat spaces described in the previous sections. When the anomalies for both variables are outside the limits of the coping range (Figure 14.12), the climate scenario is considered to significantly increase the climate threat in the future, and therefore special attention must be paid to it in terms of assessing its potential future impacts on agricultural activities in the regions.

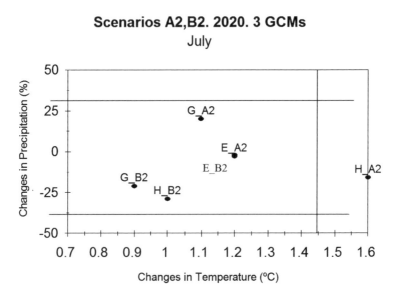

Figure 14.12 *Climatic threat space (outside the rectangle) for coffee production in the central region of Veracruz, considering climate change scenarios*

Note: The projected changes are based on the models ECHAM4 (E_A2 and E_B2), GFDL (G_A2 and G_B2) and Hadley (H_A2 and H_B2).

Figure 14.12 shows the limits of the threat space for coffee production for July (similar to that for summer discussed previously) that is related to precipitation and to maximum temperature. In this case, the proposed coping range is such that precipitation must not exceed an increase of 30 per cent or a decrease of 40 per cent, and maximum temperature must not exceed an increase of 1.5°C. Using the results of future climate scenarios for 2020 described in this section, it is observed that the projected changes from ECHAM4 (A2 and B2) and GFDL (B2) models are within the coping range for coffee. On the other hand, the projected changes for the Hadley model, in the emission scenario A2 (H_A2, Figure 14.12) lie within the threat space, implying possible important decreases in production, considering the historical impacts and the current climatic threat spaces.

However, if climate variability is considered, then even the scenarios that are within the coping range could represent a climatic threat. As an example, if the ECHAM4 (E_A2 and E_B2) scenarios are considered, which are within the coping range (Figure 14.12), it can be observed in Figure 14.13 that instead of 2 years (5 per cent) with temperatures equal to or greater than 30°C, there could be 4 years (11 per cent) with maximum temperatures equal to or exceeding 30°C. This means that while anomalies in the mean temperature for the period continue to fall within the coping range, there is a possibility of an increase in the occurrence of extreme temperature events, which could have negative impacts on the coffee crop. Thus, areas that are not threatened now could be threatened in the future due to the impacts of climate variability, and these scenarios should be further explored and accounted for in future vulnerability studies.

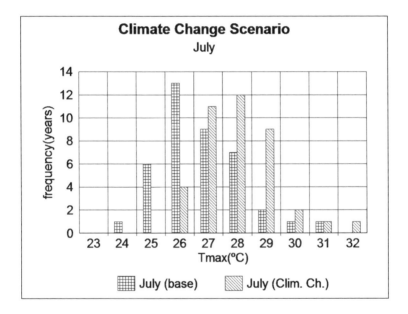

Figure 14.13 *Frequency maximum temperatures (Teocelo, Veracruz, 1961–1998)*

Note: Frequency maximum temperatures considering the observed data (July-base) and with the increase in temperature as proposed by the ECHAM4 (A2) model (July, Clim. Ch.) for 2020.

According to the models' projections for the future climatic mean values, a relocation of the observed minimum, lower quartile, median, upper quartile and maximum values can be performed, providing a scenario of possible changes in climate variability. Each marker in Figure 14.14 represents different means and variability in temperature (horizontal lines) and precipitation (vertical lines). Current mean and variability are represented by the markers TO and PO, and all of the other markers are future scenarios for the emission scenario A2. The box represents the coping range for July (see Figure 14.12) and it is used to illustrate how, once a variability scenario is provided, relatively small and moderate changes in mean can imply important changes in the probability of adverse conditions for a specific crop. These changes in probability could be interpreted as changes in the viability of a certain crop (or activity) given climate change conditions. It also reveals the possible increase in future vulnerability of the coffee producers to climatic hazards.

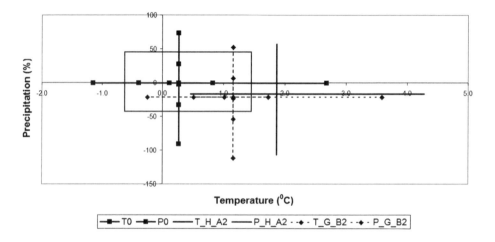

Figure 14.14 *Current mean and variability conditions and climate change scenarios for 2020*

Note: The crosses show a mean value and variability for current and for each future scenario of temperature and precipitation. T0 and P0 are current temperature and precipitation conditions and the black box represents the coping range (Figure 14.12). The scenarios were constructed using mean temperature (T) and precipitation (Pcp) for HadCM3 (A2 scenario) and GFDL (B2 scenario), which project the highest and lowest changes in temperature respectively (see Figure 14.11a).

Using regression equations constructed in previous work (Gay et al, 2004a), which relate climate and economic variables with coffee production, we observed that the most important decreases are expected to occur when the projected changes in spring, summer and winter precipitation are considered. The regression parameters derived are presented in Equation 1.

$$P_{coffee} = -35965262 + 2296270(T_{summ}) - 46298.67(T_{summ})^2 + 658.01618(P_{spr})$$
$$+ 813976.3(T_{win}) - 20318.27(T_{win})^2 - 3549.71(MINWAGE)$$

where:

P_{coffee} = projected changes in coffee production,

T_{summ} = mean summer temperature,

T_{win} = mean winter temperature,

P_{spr} = mean spring precipitation, and

MINWAGE = the real minimum wage.

Considering that optimal temperatures for coffee in the summer and winter are 24.8°C and 20.0°C respectively, and that the mean precipitation for spring is ~81mm, the expected production of coffee in the central region of Veracruz is 549,158.4 tons. Changes in these variables based on scenario results for April, July and January indicate a decrease of 9 per cent to 13 per cent in coffee production by 2020.

Climate Change Scenarios for Argentina

The same models and methodology used above were applied to develop climate change scenarios for Argentina. The results show minor increases in temperature, compared to the Mexican case study. The likely changes in temperature and precipitation for 2020 and 2050 for Laboulaye in January are shown in Figures 14.15a and 14.15*b*. The projected changes in precipitation range from decreases of 0.7 per cent to 4 per cent, while the projected changes in temperature range from increases of 0.2°C to 1.5°C, depending on the model used. These projections are consistent with the findings of other authors (Ruosteenoja et al, 2003) for southern South America (2010–2039), which have ranged from -3 per cent to +5 per cent changes in precipitation during summer (December, January, February: DJF) and an increase of about 1°C in temperature for the same season.

   In this case, even though the increase in temperature is minimal (+0.33°C as projected by the ECHAM4 scenario for 2020 for January), changes in extreme events should be considered. If the distribution of values of maximum temperature prevails under climate change conditions, the frequency of extreme values for that variable might increase. The situation in Laboulaye is depicted in Figure 14.16, with two events with maximum temperature above 34.0°C (4.3 per cent) in the baseline years and a projected increase to 4 (10.3 per cent) events with maximum temperature crossing 34.0°C in 2020.

   With reference to the threat space constructed for the region (see Figure 14.9), it can be stated that the climate change scenarios that might represent future threats are the ones that project increases in temperature and decreases in precipitation, similar to the climatic conditions during strong La Niña years. However, all the models project a decrease in precipitation for January in 2020 and 2050 (Figure 14.15b), indicating risky conditions for maize. When the summer season (DJF) is considered (data not shown), all the climate change scenarios projected increases in both temperature and rainfall, although the

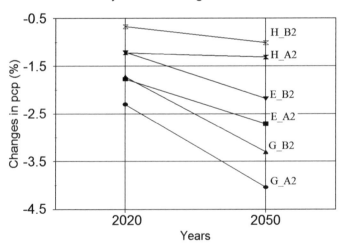

Figure 14.15 *Projected changes in* a) *temperature and* b) *precipitation for January in the southern region of Cordoba, Argentina (2020 and 2050)*

Note: Projected changes using 3 GCM (G: GFDL; H: Hadley; E: ECHAM) outputs and two SRES scenarios (A2 and B2)

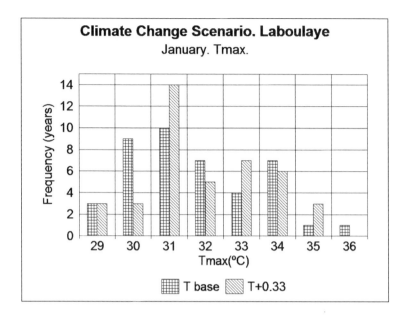

Figure 14.16 *Observed (1960–2002) and projected DJF maximum temperature (2020) based on ECHAM4 under the A2 emissions scenarios for Laboulaye, Argentina*

increases varied between the different scenarios. This latter situation, similar to the conditions in 1975, could lead to decreases in maize yields, but as there are few previous events that could illustrate the farmers' responses to these conditions, it is difficult to determine the ultimate effects of these climatic changes on crop yield. Sensitivity analyses using crop models, which also include changes in variability besides changes in the mean values of rainfall and temperature, will help to better assess the conditions that could affect crop yield (Vinocur et al, 2000).

Conclusions

Analysis of regional climatic variability can help in defining the current climatic threat via the construction of climatic threat spaces, which can serve as a useful tool for defining 'threat' for stakeholders and decision makers and for communicating risk. The dispersion diagrams for temperature and precipitation used in this study help to define the coping range and also illustrate the climatic threat for specific agricultural crops. The magnitude of the hazard and of the crop losses incurred due to unfavourable changes in climatic variables can be used to characterize the existing vulnerability of agricultural producers. The outputs of regional climate change scenarios can then be introduced into these climatic threat spaces to determine any future threats or opportunities that can once again serve to inform key stakeholders in the region.

It is important to note that even though the changes in the mean values of climatic variables projected by the outputs of several GCMs may appear to be within the coping range for a particular crop, the pattern of extreme events in the future must also be considered. Even though climate change variability under future conditions is similar to the current observed variability, there could be an increase in the future frequency of extreme climatic events that would contribute to increased future vulnerability of the system under study. Climate threat spaces are limited tools in this regard: they are unable to analyse the frequency of extreme events since they are constructed using seasonal means, which can hide the effects of daily extreme values. However, other data sources such as newspaper articles, interviews and surveys, along with specific daily climatic studies, can help to overcome this limitation.

Climate threat spaces can thus serve as a valuable tool to provide an initial assessment of potential risks to crop production or other climate-dependent activities under a changing climate. In combination with other analytical tools such as frequency analysis and sensitivity analysis, a more detailed understanding of present and future climate-related risks can be determined.

Notes

1   The gross geographic product (GGP) of a particular area amounts to the total income or payment received by the production factors (land, labour, capital and entrepreneurship) for their participation in the production within that area. It is a regional GDP.

References

Andrade, F. A. (1992) *Radiación y Temperatura Determinan los Rendimientos Máximos de Maíz* [*Radiation and temperature determine maximum yields of maize*], Boletín Técnico no 106, Estación Experimental Agropecuaria Balcarce, Instituto Nacional de Tecnologia Agropecuaria, Buenos Aires, Argentina

Andrade, F. A., A. Cirilo, S. Uhart and M. Otegui (1996) *Ecofisiología del Cultivo de Maíz* [*Ecophysiology of maize*], Dekalb Press, Buenos Aires, Argentina

Andrade, F. and V. Sadras (eds) (2002) *Bases Para el Manejo del Maíz, el Girasol y la Soja* [*Basis for the management of maize, sunflower and soybean*], Estación Experimental Agropecuaria, Instituto Nacional de Tecnologia Agropecuaria Balcarce – Facultad de Ciencias Agrarias, Universidad Nacional de Mar del Plata Buenos Aires, Argentina

Araujo, R. and J. Martínez (2001) AIACC workshop presentation, Vulnerabilidad Social de la Producción de Café en el Estado de Veracruz, Mexico

Araujo, R. and J. Martínez (2002) 'Vulnerabilidad Social de la Producción de Café en el Estado de Veracruz' ['Social Vulnerability of Coffee Production in the State of Veracruz'], AIACC workshop presentation, Centro de Ciencias de la Atmósfera, UNAM, Mexico, D.F. May 17– 21

Baier, W. (1977) *Crop-Weather Models and their Use in Yields Assessment*, WMO no 458, technical note no 151, World Meteorological Organization, Geneva

Bartra, A. (1999) 'El aroma de la historia social del café' [The smell of the coffee social history'], *La Jornada Delcampo*, 28 July, pp1–4

Bravo, J. L., C. Gay, C. Conde, F. Estrada (2006) 'Probabilistic description of rains and ENSO phenomenon in a coffee farm area in Veracruz, Mexico', *Atmosfera*, vol 19, no 2, pp49–74

Castellanos, E., C. Conde, H. Eakin and C. Tucker (2003) *Adapting to Market Shocks and Climate Variability in Mesoamerica: The Coffee Crisis in Mexico, Guatemala and Honduras*, Final Report IAI SGP 1-015

Castillo, G., A. Contreras, A. Zamarripa, I. Méndez. M- Vázquez, F. Holguín and A. Fernández (1997) *Tecnología para la Producción del Café en México* [*Technology of Coffee Production in Mexico*], Instituto Nacional de Investigaciones Forestales, Agrícolas y Pecuarias, Folleto Técnico no 8. Div. Agrícola Veracruz, Mexico

CONAPO (1995) Índices de Marginación por Entidad Federativa: Resultados Principales [Marginality Indices for Federal Entities: Principal Results]. Consejo Nacional de Población. CONAPO – Secretaria de Gobernación. México

Conde, C. (2003) 'Cambio y variabilidad climáticos: Dos estudios de caso en México' ['Climate variability and change. Two case studies in Mexico'], postgraduate thesis, Universidad Nacional Autónoma de México, Distrito Federal, Mexico

Diario La Comuna (1979a) *Inundaciones: No hay Solución a Nivel Oficial. Delicada Situación por el Avance de las Aguas* [*Floods: There is No Solution at Official Level. Delicate Situation Due to the Advance of the Water*] 17/05/1979 – Año LIV, N° 2628. Laboulaye, Córdoba

Diario La Comuna (1979b) *Inundaciones: Gestiones de la Sociedad Rural.* [*Floods: Management of the Rural Society*] 07/06/1979 – Año LIV, N° 2630

Diario La Comuna (1979c) *Inundaciones: Las Aguas Llegaron a la Ciudad.* [*Floods: Water Reached the City*] 19/07/1979 – Año LIV, N° 2686

Eakin, H. (2002) 'Rural households' vulnerability and adaptation to climate variability and institutional change: Three cases from central Mexico', PhD dissertation, Department of Geography and Regional Development, The University of Arizona

Eakin, H. and J. Martínez (2003) Presentation to coffee farmers and experts in Coatepc, Veracruz, 6–8 December, unpublished

Eakin, H., C. M. Tucker, E. Castellanos (2005) Market shocks and climate variability: The coffee crisis in Mexico, Guatemala, and Honduras', *Mountain Research and Development*, vol 25, no 4, pp304–309

Florescano, E. and S. Swan (1995) *Breve Historia de la Sequía en México* [*Brief History of Drought in Mexico*], Biblioteca Universidad Veracruzana, Xalapa, Veracruz, Mexico

Gay, C. (2000) *México: Una Visión hacia el siglo XXI: El Cambio Climático en México* [*Mexico: Climate Change in Mexico: A Vision Towards XXI Century*], Instituto Nacional de Ecología (INE), US Country Studies Program (USCSP), SEMAR-NAP, Universidad Nacional Autónoma de México

Gay, C., C. Conde, H. Eakin, M. Vinocur, R. Seiler and M. Wehbe (2002) 'Integrated assessment of social vulnerability and adaptation to climate variability and change among farmers in Mexico and Argentina', Final report, Project LA29, Assessments of Impacts and Adaptations to Climate Change, International START Secretariat, Washington, DC, US, www.aiaccproject.org

Gay, C., F. Estrada, C. Conde and H. Eakin (2004a) 'Impactos potenciales del cambio climático en la agricultura: Escenarios de producción de café para el 2050 en Veracruz (México)' ['Potential impacts of climate change in agriculture: Scenarios of coffee production for 2050 in Veracruz (Mexico)'], in J. C. García, C. Diego, P. Fernández, C. Garmendía and D. Rasilla (eds) *El Clima, Entre el Mar y la Montaña*, Asociación Española de Climatología, Santander, Spain, pp651–660

Gay. C, C. Conde, N. Monterroso, H. Eakin, F. Echanove, B. Larqué, A. Cos, H. Celis, S. Cortés, R. Ávila, J. Gómez, H. García, A. Monterroso-Rivas, M. P. Medina, G.

Rosales and R. Araujo (2004b) 'Evaluación externa 2003 del Fondo para Atender a la Población Afectada por Contingencias Climatológicas (FAPRACC)' ['External evaluation of the Fund to Support Rural Population Affected by Climatological Contingencies'], Project supported by the Mexican Minister of Agriculture

Holguín de Roza, M. C. (1986) *Laboulaye, Cien Años de Vida [Laboulaye, One Hundred Years of Life]*, Dirección General de Publicaciones, Universidad Nacional de Córdoba, Córdoba, Argentina

Hulme, M., T. M. L. Wigley, E. M. Brown, S. C. B. Raper, A. Centella, S. Smith and A. C. Chipanshi (2000) *Using Climate Scenario Generator for Vulnerability and Adaptation Assessment: MAGICC and SCENGEN*, Version 2.4 Workbook, Climate Research Unit, Norwich, UK

Hulme, M. and O. Brown (1998) 'Portraying climate scenario uncertainties in relation to tolerable regional climate change', *Climate Research*, vol 10, pp1–14

INTA (Instituto Nacional de Tecnologia Agropecuaria) (1987) *Análisis de la Evolución, Situación Actual y Problemática del Sector Agropecuario del Centro Regional Córdoba [Analysis of the Evolution of the Current Situation and Problems in the Agricultural Sector of the Central Region of Cordoba]*, Ediciones INTA, Centro Regional Córdoba, Buenos Aires, Argentina

INTA (2002) *Plan de Tecnología Regional (2001–2004) [Regional Technological Plan (2001–2004)]*, Ediciones INTA, Centro Regional Córdoba, Buenos Aires, Argentina

IPCC (2001) 'Summary for policymakers', in B. Metz, O. Davidson, R. Swart and J. Pan (eds) *Climate Change 2001: Mitigation*, Contribution of WGIII to the Third Assessment Report of the Intergovernmental Panel on Climate Change, Cambridge University Press, Cambridge, UK and New York, US

Jáuregui, E. (1995) 'Rainfall fluctuations and tropical storm activity in Mexico', *Erkunde: Archiv Für Wiseenschagtliche Geographie*, vol 49, pp39–48

Jones, C. A. and J. R. Kiniry (1986) *CERES–Maize: A Simulation Model of Maize Growth and Development*, Texas A&M Press, College Station, TX

La Red (2004) Social Studies Network for Disaster Prevention in Latin America website, www.desinventar.org/desinventar.html

Le Roy, E. (1991) *Historia del Clima Desde el Año Mil [History of Climate since the Year One Thousand]*, Fondo de Cultura Económica, Mexico City, Mexico

Magaña, V. (ed) (1999) *Los Impactos de El Niño en México [Impacts of El Niño in México]*, Centro de Ciencias de la Atmósfera, Universidad Nacional Autónoma de México, Mexico, with Dirección General de Protección Civil, Secretaría de Gobernación, Mexico, http://ccaunam.atmosfcu.unam.mx/cambio/nino.htm

Magrin, G., M. Grondona, M. Travasso, D. Boillón, Rodríguez and C. R Messina. (1998) *Impacto del Fenómeno ENSO Sobre la Producción de Cultivos en la Región Pampeana Argentina [Impacts of ENSO Phenomenon on the Crop Production in the Argentinean 'Pampas' Region]*. Instituto Nacional de Tecnología Agropecuaria, Instituto de Clima y Agua, Cautelar, Argentina.

Martínez, J. (2002) 'Work Report: Newspaper analysis 1980–2002', unpublished report, El Diario de Xalapa, Veracruz

Maurutto, M. C., M. Vinocur, C. Quiroga and R. Seiler (2003) 'Assessment of social vulnerability and change among farmers in central Argentina: Importance of the subjective dimension', Open Meeting of the Global Environmental Change Research Community, Montreal, Canada, 16–18 October, http://sedac.ciesin.columbia.edu/openmtg/absSrch results.jsp

Maurutto, M. C. (2004) 'Assessment of social vulnerability and adaptation to climate variability and change among farmers in central Argentina: importance of the subjective dimension', Informe final Beca de Investigación, unpublished, Universidad Nacional de Río Cuarto, Argentina

Morales R., V. Magaña, C. Millán and J. L. Pérez. (2003) *Efectos del Calentamiento*

Global en la Disponibilidad de los Recursos Hidráulicos de México [*Effects of Global Warming on the Availability of Hydrological Resources in Mexico*], Proyecto HC-0112, Instituto Mexicano de Tecnología del Agua (IMTA), Centro de Ciencias de la Atmósfera, Universidad Nacional Autónoma de México (CCA–UNAM)

Nakicenovic, N., J. Alcamo, G. Davis, B. de Vries, J. Fenhann, S. Gaffin, K. Gregory, A. Grübler, T. Y. Jung, T. Kram, E. L. La Rovere, L. Michaelis, S. Mori, T. Morita, W. Pepper, H. Pitcher, L. Price, K. Riahi, A. Roehrl, H. H. Rogner, A. Sankovski, M. Schlesinger, P. Shukla, S. Smith, R. Swart, S. van Rooijen, N. Victor and Z. Dadi (2000) *Special Report on Emissions Scenarios*, Special Report of Working Group III of the Intergovernmental Panel on Climate Change, Cambridge University Press, Cambridge, UK

Nolasco, M. (1985) *Café y Sociedad en México* [*Coffee and Society in Mexico*], Centro de Ecodesarrollo, Mexico City, Mexico

O'Brian, K. L. and R. M. Leichenko (2000) 'Double exposure: Assessing the impacts of climate change within the context of economic globalization', *Global Environmental Change*, vol 10, pp221–232

Palma, B. (2004) 'Generación de escenarios de cambio climático para la Zona Centro del Estado de Veracruz, México' ['Generation of climate change scenarios for the central region of Veracruz State, Mexico'], postgraduate thesis, Universidad Nacional Autónoma de México, Mexico City, Mexico

Parry, M. (2002) 'Scenarios for climate impacts and adaptation assessment', *Global Environmental Change*, vol 12, pp149–153

Podesta, G., D. Letson, J. Jones, C. Messina, F. Royce, A. Ferreyra, J. O'Brien, D. Legler and J. Hansen (2000) 'Experiences in application of ENSO-related climate information in the agricultural sector of Argentina', in *Proceedings from the International Forum on Climate Prediction, Agriculture and Development*, IRI-CW/00/1, International Research Institute for Climate Prediction (IRI) Publications, Palisades, NY

Rivarola, A. del V., M. G. Vinocur and R. A. Seiler (2002) 'Uso y demanda de información agrometeorológica en el sector agropecuario del centro de Argentina' ['Use and demand of agrometeorological information in the agricultural sector of the centre of Argentina'], *Revista Argentina de Agrometeorología*, vol 2, pp143–149

Ruosteenoja, K., T. Carter, Jylhä, K. and H. Tuomenvitra (2003) *Future Climate in World Regions: An Intercomparison of Model-Based Projections for New IPCC Emission Scenarios*, Finnish Environmental Institute, Helsinki, Finland

SAGPyA (Secretaría de Agricultura, Ganadería, Pesca y Alimentos de la República Argentina) (2004) 'Estimaciones agrícolas para maíz', www.sagpya.mecon.gov.ar/

Sánchez, O., C. Conde and R. Araujo (2004) 'Climate change scenarios for México and Argentina', AIACC internal report, supported also by CONACYT, SEMARNAT project SEMARNAT-2002-CO1-0615

Seiler, R. A., M. Hayes and L. Bressán (2002) 'Using the standardized precipitation index for flood risk monitoring', *International Journal of Climatology*, vol 22, pp1365–1376

Seiler, R. and M. G. Vinocur (2004) 'ENSO events, rainfall variability and the potential of SOI for the seasonal precipitation predictions in the south of Cordoba-Argentina', in *Proceedings of the 14th Conference on Applied Climatology*, CD. JP1.10., http://ams.confex.com/ams/pdfpapers/71002.pdf

Stern, P. C. and W. E. Easterling (eds) (1999) *Making Climate Forecasts Matter*, National Academy Press, Washington, DC, US

Uhart, S., F. Andrade and M. Frugone (1996) *Producción Potencial de Maíz. Impacto de la Sequía Sobre el Crecimiento y Rendimiento* [*Potential Production of Maize: Impacts of Drought on Maize Development and Yield*], Material Didáctico no 12, Estación Experimental Agropecuaria, Instituto Nacional de Tecnologia Agropecuaria, Buenos Aires, Argentina

Vinocur, M. G., R. A. Seiler and L. O. Mearns (2000) 'Predicting maize yield responses to climate variability in Córdoba, Argentina (Abstract)', in *Proceedings of the International Scientific Meeting on Detection and Modelling of Recent Climate Change and its Effects on a Regional Scale, Tarragona, Spain, May 29–31, 2000*

Vinocur, M., A. Rivarola and R. Seiler (2004) 'Use of climate information in agriculture decision making: Experience from farmers in central Argentina', in *Proceedings of the Second International Conference on Climate Impacts Assessment (SICCIA)*, Grainau, Germany, 28 June–2 July, www.cses.washington.edu/cig/outreach/workshopfiles/SICCIA/program.shtml

Wigley, T. (2003) *MAGICC/SCENGEN 4.1*, technical manual and user manual, Boulder, CO, US

Wilks, D. (1995) *Statistical Methods in Atmospheric Sciences: An Introduction*, International Geophysics Series, vol 59, Academic Press, San Diego, CA, US, pp21–27

Wolter, K. (no date) 'Multivariate ENSO Index', Earth System Research Laboratory, National Oceanic and Atmospheric Administration, US, www.cdc.noaa.gov/ENSO/enso.mei_index.html

15

Climate Variability and Extremes in the Pantabangan–Carranglan Watershed of the Philippines: An Assessment of Vulnerability

Juan M. Pulhin, Rose Jane J. Peras, Rex Victor O. Cruz, Rodel D. Lasco, Florencia B. Pulhin and Maricel A. Tapia

Introduction

In the Philippines, watershed areas are among those likely to be adversely affected by climate change. Watersheds are critical to sustainable economic development and environmental protection. More than 70 per cent of the country's total land area lies within watersheds, including much of the remaining natural forests, which provide a host of environmental services. An estimated 1.5 million hectares or more of agricultural lands presently derive irrigation water from these watersheds. Moreover, around 20 to 24 million people – close to a third of the country's total population – inhabit the uplands of the many watersheds, the majority depending on their resources for survival.

Previous studies relevant to climate change in watershed areas have focused on the biophysical aspects (see, for instance, Jose et al, 1996). Completely lacking are studies that delve into the human dimension of climate change in these areas. In particular, there is little information on the impacts of climate change on local communities inhabiting watersheds. Even more limited is knowledge about the vulnerability of these communities to climate variability and extremes, and their capacity and mechanisms for coping with and responding to climate stresses.

This chapter tries to fill this gap. It synthesizes the results of pioneering research on the vulnerability of local communities to climate variability and extremes within the Pantabangan–Carranglan watershed located in northern Philippines. The focus is on the local scale, that is to say on households and communities living within the watershed. Specifically, the study sought to answer questions about exposures of communities in the watershed to stresses from climate variability and extremes in recent decades; the nature and degree of vulnerability to negative impacts from these exposures; the distribution of vulnerability demographically and geographically within the watershed; the social and economic factors that determine vulnerability; and the implications for coping with and responding to human-driven climate change. In the following sections, we outline the key concepts and analytical framework that guided our assessment of the present vulnerability of watershed households and communities to climate variability and extremes, describe the study area and research methodology, present key findings, and conclude by pointing out key research and policy measures that could help advance the body of knowledge and improve policy responses to managing risks associated with climate variability and extremes.

Analytical Framework

Vulnerability has many different definitions and is subject to various interpretations and usage. A number of authors have reviewed the various definitions and approaches to vulnerability in relation to climate change (see, for instance, Cutter, 1996; Adger, 1999; UNEP, 2001; Brooks, 2003; Leary and Beresford, 2007). Despite this, confusion appears to continue, and the term seems to defy consensus usage (Few, 2003).

In our assessment of vulnerability in the Pantabangan–Carranglan watershed, we define vulnerability as the likelihood of households and communities suffering harm and their ability to respond to stresses resulting from climate variability and extremes. This conceptualization is consistent with Moss (1999), who views vulnerability as a function of at least two major variables: sensitivity of the system to climate-related events and its coping capacity.

Climate variability refers to the variations in the mean state and other statistics of the climate (such as standard deviations and the frequency of extremes) on all temporal and spatial scales beyond that of individual weather events (IPCC, 2001). It may be due to natural internal processes within the climate system (internal variability) or to variation in natural or anthropogenic external forcing (external variability). This definition of climate variability encompasses human-driven climate change. A climate extreme is an event that is rare within its statistical reference distribution at a particular place. For the purposes of our study and in consideration of the climatic type in the study area, the occurrence of the following forms of climate variability and extremes are assessed: El Niño, La Niña, early onset or delay of the rainy season, prolonged rains and the occurrence of typhoons.

At the operational level, the nature and degree of people's vulnerability to the above-mentioned climate-related events are examined at two levels: the community and the household. At the community level, the degree of vulnerability of various socioeconomic groups is assessed by looking at the extent of impacts (positive or negative) of climate variability and extremes on four major areas of concern to local communities, namely food availability, water supply, livelihoods and health. In addition, the communities' adaptation strategies are identified and their effectiveness determined as a measure of their degree of vulnerability.[1]

To better understand the nature of the household's vulnerability to climate variability and extremes, an index of vulnerability is constructed from selected indicators that are related to the above-mentioned four major areas of concern. This approach is based on the framework of Moss (1999) using multiple indicators of vulnerability to climate variability and climate change, from which a vulnerability index was developed on the basis of the system's sensitivity and coping capacity. In the present study, a number of factors are hypothesized to influence vulnerability: demographic factors (age, gender, ethnic affiliation, educational attainment, household size and migration); socioeconomic factors (income, household assets, expenditures, land ownership, farm size, farm practices, number of organizations, and access to transportation, credit and information); geographic factors (distance to market); and a number of coping mechanisms.

The Pantabangan–Carranglan Watershed

Physical characteristics

The Pantabangan–Carranglan watershed lies between 15°44' and 16°88'N and 120°36' and 122°00'E, roughly 176km north of Manila on the island of Luzon (Figure 15.1). Located within the watershed are the municipalities of Pantabangan and Carranglan in the province of Nueva Ecija, the municipalities of Alfonso Castañeda and Dupax del Sur in the province of Nueva Vizcaya, and the municipality of Maria Aurora in the province of Aurora. The watershed has a total area of 97,318ha, of which 4023ha comprise the water reservoir (Saplaco et al, 2001). It is considered to be a critical watershed under the government's classification as it supports a multipurpose dam for irrigation and hydroelectric generation.

The Pantabangan reservoir provides water for domestic and industrial uses and serves to tame the flood waters, which for years damaged farm crops in Central Luzon. At present, it supplies the irrigation requirements of 24 municipalities in the provinces of Nueva Ecija, Bulacan and Pampanga. The reservoir serves an area of 102,532ha, which is divided into 4 districts. A total of 369 irrigators' associations, consisting of 62,039 farmers, depend on the watershed and reservoir for their farm irrigation needs. The dam also generates 100,000 kilowatts of hydroelectric power, which supplies electricity to the adjacent region of Central Luzon (NPC, 1997).

The Pantabangan–Carranglan watershed area largely falls under the Philippine Climatic Type I, with a pronounced dry season from December to April and a wet season the rest of the year. A small portion of the watershed, especially at the boundary of the province of Aurora, falls under Climatic Type II, characterized by no dry season and very pronounced maximum rainfall from November to January. Annual rainfall, based on measurements from 1960

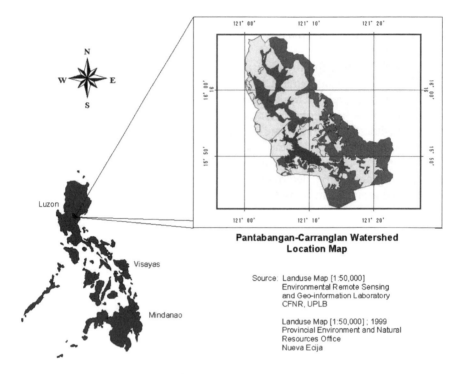

Figure 15.1 *Location of the Pantabangan–Carranglan watershed
on Luzon Island in the Philippines*

to 1999 in four gauging stations within and adjacent to the watershed area,
ranges from 1800 to 2300mm (Saplaco et al, 2001). Minimum and maximum
monthly temperatures are recorded as 23°C and 34°C respectively, while the
average annual relative humidity is 83 per cent (NPC, 1995 and 1997).

The topography of the Pantabangan–Carranglan watershed is characterized by complex land configuration and mountainous, rugged terrain. It ranges
from nearly level, through undulating and sloping, to steep hilly landscapes. Its
soils originated mostly from weathered products of meta-volcanic activities
and diorite. Surface soil textures are silty clay loam and clay loam to clay. There
are four types of soils in the watershed, known locally as Annam, Bunga,
Guimbaloan and Mahipon (Saplaco et al, 2001).

The major land-use types found in the watershed are forestlands, open
grasslands and reforestation sites (Figure 15.2). Vegetation in the watershed is
predominantly second growth. Since the logging boom of the 1960s, primary
forest in the watershed has greatly declined, though remnants of dipterocarp
forest can still be found (Saplaco et al, 2001). Nevertheless, there has been a
significant increase in the area of reforested sites, although these sites are now
under intense pressure from increasing population. Residential and *barangay*
(the smallest unit of local government) sites, as well as cultivated areas, are
included in the alienable and disposable areas.

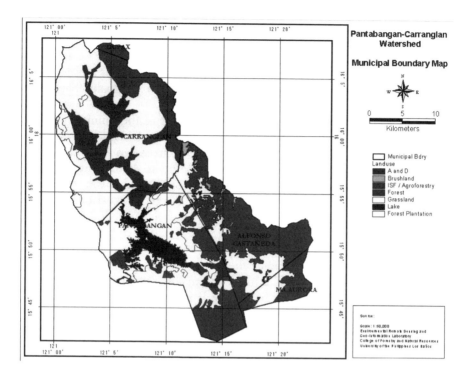

Figure 15.2 *Land uses in the Pantabangan–Carranglan watershed, 1999*

Administrative, demographic and socioeconomic characteristics

Spearheading the management of the Pantabangan–Carranglan watershed are three national government agencies, the Department of Environment and Natural Resources (DENR), the National Irrigation Administration (NIA) and the National Power Corporation (NPC). Each institution has specific areas within the watershed under its jurisdiction. This institutional arrangement comes from the need to sustainably manage the watershed so that there will be sufficient water in the reservoir for irrigation and hydroelectric power generation (Cruz, 2003). Supporting these institutions in the performance of their functions are the local government units, or *barangays*, which through the process of devolution instituted under the 1991 Local Government Code were given the mandate to conserve, manage and protect natural resources. There are a total of 36 *barangays* found in the Pantabangan–Carranglan watershed – 17 in Carranglan, 14 in Pantabangan, 3 in Alfonso Castañeda and 2 in Maria Aurora. As of 2000, about 61,000 people resided in the watershed, which comprises around 12,400 households (National Statistics Office, 2000). Three ethnic groups inhabited the watershed long before the Spanish occupation: the Aetas, Irol-les and the Italengs. They were later joined by several groups of migrants, among them the Pangasinensis, Ibaloi, Ifugao, Waray, Bicolano, Pampango, Kalinga, Kankanai, Ibanag, Cebuano and Ilongot.

However, the construction of the Pantabangan Dam in 1971 has led to relocation of the residents of the town and caused waves of out-migration through the 1970s and 1980s. Today, residents in the Pantabangan–Carranglan watershed are predominantly Tagalog and Ilocano. Other groups present in the area are Pangasinensis, Pampango, Waray, Bicol, Ifugao and Ibaloi (Saplaco et al, 2001).

The largest portion of the watershed is located in the municipalities of Pantabangan and Carranglan in the province of Nueva Ecija. More than half of the productive population of Pantabangan and Carranglan are in the labour force. However, unemployment is a problem due to limited employment opportunities in these areas (Municipality of Pantabangan, undated; Municipality of Carranglan, undated), hence many residents depend on the goods and services provided by the watershed for their livelihood.

The major source of livelihood in these municipalities comes from agricultural activities. In Pantabangan, about 5400ha (12 per cent of the total land area) is devoted to agriculture, while the corresponding figure for Carranglan is about 19,700ha (28 per cent). Among the major crops produced are rice, corn, onions and vegetables. Although the Pantabangan reservoir is located within the area, it only stores irrigation water for the Central Luzon area. Farmlands in the watershed are unirrigated and dependent on rain because of the topography, and slash-and-burn farming (*kaingin*) is commonly practised.

Fishing is the second largest industry in these areas, much of it located in Pantabangan. This is because the area houses the dam reservoir, which is one of the biggest fishing reservoirs in Asia. The municipality of Carranglan, on the other hand, depends on large fishponds for their fish production. Other sources of income of the residents are cottage and business activities, which include wood and rattan craft, animal grazing and small stores (Municipality of Pantabangan, undated; Municipality of Carranglan, undated). Charcoal-making is also common.

History of development intervention in the area

The human-made lake that forms part of the Pantabangan Dam reservoir submerged the old Pantabangan town and seven outlying *barangays* (Saplaco et al, 2001). Residents of the old town were resettled in the upper portion of Pantabangan. This resettlement process, which was a joint responsibility of the NIA and the Department of Agrarian Reform (DAR), started in May 1973 and was completed in August 1974 (Toquero, 2003). Because of the displacement of people caused by the construction of the dam, the area has continually received support from various agencies and institutions in the form of projects or programmes. Raising the economic conditions of the relocated settlers was a prime concern of the government, and the DAR was the leading agency that took care of this mission.

One of the most prominent projects implemented in the watershed was the RP-Japan reforestation project, which was launched in partnership with the DENR. The project commenced in 1976 and ended in 1992. It aimed to reforest the open and denuded areas of the watershed and provide technical support through the establishment of the Afforestation Technical Cooperation Center and the Training Center for Forest Conservation. The project has not only rehabilitated the denuded parts of the watershed but also created jobs for the local residents. Moreover, more than 600 Filipino forestry personnel were trained through this project and are now actively working in environment departments (Yoshida, 2000).

Aside from the joint project with the Japanese government, the DENR launched several reforestation programmes, particularly in the municipality of Pantabangan. These are the Regular Reforestation Program, covering a total area of 823ha, and the Integrated Social Forestry Program, which reforested about 856ha. The department also engaged in the Contract Reforestation Program with the NIA from 1989 to 1990. In this programme, the DENR contracted the NIA to reforest a total of 900ha in the Pantabangan–Carranglan watershed (Municipality of Pantabangan, undated).

The NPC and the NIA also have their share of projects implemented in the watershed area. Aside from training and extension services, the NPC conducts yearly reforestation and extension projects in the three sectors under its jurisdiction. The reforestation projects cover an average of 30–40ha a year. The biggest project implemented by the NIA in the Pantabangan–Carranglan watershed has been the Watershed Management and Erosion Control Project, which lasted from 1980 to 1988. This project was funded by the World Bank and aimed to control soil erosion and minimize sedimentation and siltation in the reservoir. It had the following components: reforestation; a feasibility study of an integrated development, waste management and smallholder agroforestry pilot project; and an integrated forest protection pilot programme. Aside from opening employment opportunities for 3800 residents in Pantabangan in 1982, the project also provided revenue and profit sharing to the communities in the watershed in the form of facilities such as domestic water supply, school building and road improvements

The Casecnan Multipurpose and Irrigation Project, which began operations in 2001, was designed to collect some of the water from the Casecnan and Taan rivers in Nueva Vizcaya and transport it to the Pantabangan reservoir. It was designed to irrigate 35,000 new hectares of agricultural lands and stabilize the water supply of the current areas serviced by the Pantabangan–Carranglan watershed. Moreover, it will generate approximately 150MW of hydroelectric capacity for the important Luzon grid (Calenergy Company, 2004).

As already mentioned, the above projects have significantly helped the residents in the watershed through the provision of jobs, livelihood programmes and various forms of assistance. But despite the three-decade-long development effort of the government, amounting to PHP1.5 billion or US$30million, there is still widespread poverty in the resettlement, as shown by a high percentage of families with income below the poverty threshold of PHP7377. The residents also perceived the services provided by the government organizations to be unsatisfactory. This implies the failure of the government in providing an economically viable resettlement area for the residents.

A point of contention which could have contributed to this failure is the lack of participation of the residents in the planning and monitoring of the development projects or programmes. Consequently, some residents were unfamiliar with the livelihood activities that were introduced by the projects. Moreover, these development projects and programmes, which were temporary, may have resulted in the dependency of some people on these forms of assistance. With the recent completion of these development projects and programmes, the local people resort to charcoal-making and open *kaingin* or slash-and-burn farming practices, livelihoods that are practised by more than 50 per cent of the residents in the watershed (Toquero, personal communication, 2005). These practices are negatively impacting the watershed and areas reforested by the various projects.

Research Methodology

Household survey

A household survey was conducted to collect information about the vulnerability of households to climate variability and extremes and the socioeconomic factors influencing their vulnerability. The survey included question about 1) the socioeconomic profile of the respondent; 2) the household's use of and benefits from the Pantabangan–Carranglan watershed; 3) climate variability and extremes experienced in the last few decades and their impacts; 4) food availability, water supply, livelihood and heath; and 5) adaptation strategies. The survey was administered in the four municipalities of the three different provinces encompassing the watershed. These are Pantabangan and Carranglan in Nueva Ecija, Alfonso–Castañeda in Nueva Vizcaya, and Maria Aurora in Aurora. Twenty-six of the 36 *barangays* within the watershed area were represented. The other 10 *barangays* were excluded because only small portions of their respective areas are within the watershed boundary and very few of their inhabitants live within the watershed. A total of 375 respondents were randomly selected using the *barangay* records. This sampling technique employed was adopted from Chua (1999), which allows a 0.05 permissible error and 95 per cent confidence interval level.

Focus group discussions also were conducted in 21 *barangays* to complement the household survey. Of the 26 *barangays* included in the household survey, invited representatives from four *barangays* did not show up for the scheduled discussions. A minimum age of 40, equal distribution of males and females, and representation of different socioeconomic groups were considered in the selection of participants.

The focus group discussions employed a combination of participatory techniques such as time-line analysis, stakeholder analysis, participatory vulnerability assessment and community mapping of vulnerable areas (see Pulhin, 2002, for discussions of these techniques). Time-line analysis was used to determine the local communities' exposures to climate variability and extremes from the 1960s to the present. A combination of stakeholder analysis, participatory vulnerability assessment and community mapping techniques were used to identify which socioeconomic groups in the communities are more vulnerable, their location in the watershed, and the extent and nature of their vulnerability. A scenario-building activity was conducted to explore the potential impacts of more extreme climate conditions that might be experienced in the future as a consequence of human-driven climate change and the vulnerability of the different socioeconomic groups to the impacts of climate change. The focus group discussions were also used to incorporate the communities' perspectives in determining the weights of the different indicators for construction of a vulnerability index.

Direct field observations were also conducted to validate information gathered through the household survey and focus group discussions. Vulnerable areas identified by the participants during the community mapping were verified on the ground and documented through photographs. In addition, GPS readings of vulnerable areas were taken for purposes of mapping these areas.

Index of vulnerability

A multi-level index of the vulnerability of households to climate variability and extremes was constructed from information gathered in the household surveys. The index consists of four major component sub-indices: food, water, livelihoods and health. These indices are further divided into subcategories. Drawing on the framework of Moss (1999), the subcategories comprised relevant variables that involved certain characteristics of the component indicators in relation to climate variability and extremes (representing the household's sensitivity in relation to these components) and the presence or absence of adaptation strategies (representing the household's coping capacity). The sub-indices and their component indicator variables are shown in Table 15.1.

The vulnerability index is constructed as a weighted aggregation of the four major sub-indices, which, in turn, are weighted aggregations of their component indicators. The weights are selected such that the maximum possible weighted vulnerability score is 100. Two different schemes are used to determine the weights for the sub-indices and indicators. One scheme applies the researchers' judgements while the second scheme uses results of focus group discussions to develop weights that represent the perspectives of local stakeholders.

The vulnerability index computation based on the researchers' judgements assigns equal weights of 25 to all of the 4 sub-indices (food, water, livelihood and health). The subcategories under each major index were also given equal weights (see Table 15.1). For instance, the food index, assigned a total possible weighted score of 25, has two sub-components – availability of seeds and crop yield – each with a total possible weighted score of 12.5. The sub-component for availability of seeds is further divided into three separate indicators: seasonality of seed availability, sensitivity of seed availability to climate variations and availability of strategies to adapt to constraints on seed availability. Each of these indicators is assigned a total possible weighted score of 4.17 (a third of the 12.5 weight for seed availability). Thus, if seeds are available to a household only seasonally, a score of 4.17 is given, whereas year-round availability would result in a score of zero for the indicator for seasonality of seed availability.

Table 15.1 *Multi-level indicator of vulnerability of households to climate variability and extremes (CV and E) using varying weights*

Sub-Indices and Indicators	Weights Provided by Researchers	Weighted Scores		
		Weights Provided by Local Communities		
		Pantabangan	Carranglan	P&C Combined
A. Food	25	25	40	32.5
a.1. Seed availability	12.5	20	15	17.5
a.1.1. Availability of planting materials	4.17	8	7	7.5
i. Available any time of the year	0	3	2	2.5
ii. Seasonal or hard to find	4.17	5	5	5
a.1.2. Is it affected by CV and E?	4.17	9	5	7
i. Yes	4.17	9	4	6.5
ii. No	0	0	1	0.5
a.1.3. Adaptation strategies	4.17	3	3	3
i. With adaptation	0	2	1	1.5
ii. Without adaptation	4.17	1	2	1.5
a.2. Crop yield	12.5	5	25	15
a.2.1. Per cent (%) lost in rice production	4.17	1.5	10	5.75
a.2.2. Is it affected by CV and E?	4.17	2	10	6
i. Yes	4.17	2	7	4.5
ii. No	0	0	3	1.5
a.2.3. Adaptation strategies	4.17	1.5	5	3.25
i. With adaptation	0	0.5	2	1.25
ii. Without adaptation	4.17	1	3	2
B. Water	25	40	40	40
b.1. Domestic water	12.5	33	15	24
b.1.1. Sources of domestic water	2.5	11	7	9
i. Natural sources	2.5	8	6	7
ii. Through agencies 1	.25	3	1	2
b.2.1. Distance of house to sources of water	2.5	5	2	3.5
i. 0–250m	0.62	0.4	0.2	0.3
ii. 251–500m	1.25	1	0.3	0.65
iii. 501–1000m	1.88	1.5	0.5	1
iv. >1000m	2.5	2.1	1	1.55
b.1.3. Observation for the supply of domestic water	2.5	7	2	4.5
i. Declining supply	2.5	3	1	2
ii. Increasing supply	0	2	0.5	1.25
iii. No change	1.25	1	0.5	0.75
b.1.4. Is domestic water supply affected by CV and E?	2.5	5	2	3.5
i. Yes	2.5	3	1.5	2.25
ii. No	0	2	0.5	1.25
b.1.5. Adaptation strategies	2.5	5	2	3.5
i. With adaptation	0	1	0.5	1.25
ii. Without adaptation	2.5	4	1.5	2.75

Table 15.1 (*continued*)

Sub-Indices and Indicators	Weights Provided by Researchers	Weighted Scores		
		Weights Provided by Local Communities		
		Pantabangan	Carranglan	P&C Combined
b.2. Irrigation water	12.5	7	25	16
b.2.1. Regularity/problem with supply?	4.17	3	10	6.5
i. Problem with supply	0	1	3	2
ii. No problem with supply	4.17	2	7	4.5
b.2.2. Effects of scarcity	4.17	2	10	6
i. Decrease in production/ income	2.78	1	7	4
ii. No (zero) production/ income	4.17	0.5	1	0.75
iii. Delayed harvest	1.39	0.5	2	1.25
b.2.3. Adaptation strategies	4.17	2	5	3.5
i. With adaptation	0	0.56	2	1.28
ii. Without adaptation	4.17	1.44	3	2.22
C. Livelihood	25	15	10	12.5
c.1. Seek sources of income in cases of CV and E?	8.33	6	2	4
i. Yes	0	4	0.5	2.25
ii. No	8.33	2	1.5	1.75
c.2. Is income from other sources sufficient?	8.33	6	6	6
i. Sufficient	0	2	2	2
ii. Not sufficient	8.33	4	4	4
c.3. Adaptation strategies	8.33	3	2	2.5
i. With adaptation	0	2	0.5	1.25
ii. Without adaptation	8.33	1	1.5	1.25
D. Health	25	20	10	15
d.1. Experienced health problems during CV and E?	6.25	6	2	4
i. Yes, experience health problems	6.25	4	1.5	2.75
ii. No	0	2	0.5	1.25
d.2. Kinds of health problems experienced during CV and E	6.25	7	4	5.5
i. Diarrhoea, amoebiasis, dehydration, dysentery	4.17	3	2	2.5
ii. Dengue, typhoid, malaria	6.25	2	1	1.5
iii. Others: hepatitis, bronchitis, sore eyes, etc.	2.09	2	1	1.5
d.3. Access to medical services	6.25	3	2	2.5
i. Sufficient	0	1	0.5	0.75
ii. Not sufficient	6.25	2	1.5	1.75
d.4. Adaptation strategies	6.25	4	2	3
i. With adaptation	0	1.8	0.5	1.15
ii. Without adaptation	6.25	2.2	1.5	1.85

Similarly, the indicator for sensitivity of seed availability to climate is scored 4.17 if availability to the household is sensitive and zero if it is not, and the lack of adaptation strategies for the household would result in a score of 4.17 for the adaptation indicator, while existence of adaptation strategies would give a score of zero. Similar logic is followed in giving weights to the other subcategories under the other three component indicators of vulnerability, water, livelihood and health.

As an alternative to the researchers' equal weighting of indicators, we used the local communities' perspectives to determine the weights. In two separate focus group discussions conducted with two different clusters of *barangays* in the municipalities of Pantabangan and Carranglan, participants were asked to provide their own weights for the indicators. The objective was to determine whether there would be significant variation in the weights provided by the two groups and to determine the likely implications of this in the use of multi-level indicators of vulnerability. Consensus was sought from the participants during the focus group discussions on the specific weights that they should assign for each component indicator at various levels.

The computed vulnerability indices, which are the weighted summations of the food, water, livelihood and health sub-indices are correlated with factors hypothesized to influence vulnerability using Spearman correlation. These include a combination of demographic, socioeconomic and geographic factors, as well as the number of coping mechanisms practised by each household. Regression analysis is used to determine the combined effects of the hypothesized determinants of household vulnerability.

Mapping of vulnerable areas

Vulnerable areas within the watershed are mapped using two different approaches. One uses spatially referenced data for biophysical variables considered to be associated with the vulnerability of different land-use categories to map vulnerability. The other uses a participatory mapping approach in which stakeholders identify vulnerable areas. In the first approach, areas of grassland/ brushland, cultivated land and forests are classified as having low, moderate and high vulnerability using five parameters: slope, elevation, distance from the nearest road, distance from the nearest river and distance from the nearest community centre. A single vulnerability map is developed by overlaying all of the individual maps produced for each of the five parameters.

The vulnerability of grassland and brushland in the watershed is assessed in terms of their susceptibility to human-induced fire, which is common in the watershed and which has been observed to increase during a prolonged dry season. Proximity to human activities is a key determinant of vulnerability to fire. The closer an area is to a road, river or community, the greater is the chance that the area may suffer from human-induced fire. On the other hand, vulnerability to fire is low when the slope gradient and elevation of an area are low, as it is easier to control fire in favourable terrain.

In agricultural areas, vulnerability is assessed in terms of their susceptibility to soil erosion from large rain events, a commonly observed problem associated with climate variability and extremes in the watershed, and in terms of their accessibility to farmers. Higher elevation and more steeply sloped farmlands are more vulnerable to erosion than are lands at lower elevations or with less slope, while farms that are far from a road, river, or community centre are more difficult to manage and therefore more vulnerable.

For forests, the vulnerability level is assessed in terms of ease of management and protection, associated with terrain conditions. Areas with favourable gradient and elevation are rated with low vulnerability since management and protection are less challenging here than in areas with adverse terrain. Forests that are more accessible (closer to roads, rivers and community centres) are rated as more vulnerable than forests that are difficult to access due to the greater chances of their being encroached on or cleared and converted to cultivated areas.

The alternate approach had local communities identify vulnerable places during the focus group discussions using a participatory vulnerability mapping technique. Unlike the GIS-generated vulnerability map, which categorized the physical vulnerability of the watershed into low, moderate and high levels, the places identified by the communities as vulnerable do not have these categories. Instead, the participants of focus group discussions were just asked to identify locations of vulnerable areas on the *barangay* map, which they themselves had drawn, and to explain the reasons why they think these areas are vulnerable. GPS readings were made of the vulnerable places and plotted on the vulnerability map of the watershed developed using GIS. The idea is to examine the congruences and divergences between vulnerable areas identified using biophysical parameters and the areas that stakeholders judge to be vulnerable.

Results and Discussion

Past climate variability and extremes in the Pantabangan–Carranglan watershed

Considering the watershed's geographic location, it can be said that all the communities living there are significantly exposed to natural hazards such as climate variability, climate extremes and other natural calamities like earthquakes. Data available from the Philippine Atmospheric, Geophysical and Astronomical Services Administration (PAGASA) indicate that from 1980 to 1995 a total of 58 strong typhoons – an average of about 4 typhoons per year – inflicted major damage in the area. In addition, three major drought episodes occurred during the same period, with an average interval of only about four years between episodes. These drought episodes occurred in 1983, 1987 and 1991, the three years with the lowest total annual rainfall and water inflow in the period 1980–2001.

Participants in our focus group discussions were asked to recall past climate variations and extremes; the major events they identified are listed in Table 15.2. The respondents recalled two particularly strong typhoons that occurred in the 1970s, the local names of which, *Kading* and *Didang*, left an indelible mark in the minds of the respondents because of the great destruction that they brought to the communities within the watershed. Respondents also noted several symptoms of El Niño episodes in 1979–1980, 1982–1983 and 1997–1999, which correspond with El Niño events as recorded by PAGASA. Prolonged rains were also observed by the respondents in 1984, which marked the occurrence of a weak La Niña event.

Table 15.2 *Major climate events identified by participants in key informant interviews and focus group discussions*

Year	Climate Variability and Extremes
1974	Typhoon Didang
1978	Destructive typhoon Kading
1979–1980	Drought/El Niño
1982–1983	El Niño
1984	Prolonged rains
1989	Delay in the onset of rainy season
1997–1999	El Niño
2000	Delay in the onset of rainy season
2001	Early onset of rainy season
2002	Delay in the onset of rainy season
2003	Early onset of rainy season

Greater variability in the onset of the rainy season has been observed since 2000, making the onset of rains less predictable. Forest fires have been more frequent in the area since the 1980s. Between 1980 and 1988, the DENR recorded an average of 43 forest fires annually in the Pantabangan–Carranglan watershed, damaging a total area of 25,783ha over the 9 years. Although the high frequency of forest fires coincided with the almost cyclic occurrences of climate variability and extremes, such as El Niño and delays in the onset of the rainy season, greater fire frequency cannot be attributed to climate factors with high confidence. This is because most forest fires, according to respondents, are set off intentionally by people practising *kaingin* (slash-and-burn farming) and charcoal-making, practices that have also increased since the 1980s.

Although the exact value of damages inflicted by past climate-related events in the watershed is not available, anecdotal evidence gathered during the survey and focus group discussions affirm that significant losses have been incurred. These losses include human lives, property and infrastructure, and sources of livelihood, especially farmlands and fishing areas. Pronounced decreases in crop yields have been observed in years with climate patterns that are unfavourable for the region's agriculture. For instance, records from the NIA indicate that rice yield fell by more than two cavans (1 cavan = 50kg) per hectare below average in both the wet and dry season cropping periods of 1990 as a result of drought and typhoons. Individual yield changes, however, can vary substantially from the average, and locals reported that crop loss from droughts and floods can be as much as 100 per cent for individual farms. Indeed, some community members are so vulnerable that even before they can fully recover from the adverse impacts of previous events, another calamity will strike again and force them back to their original desperate state.

Mapping vulnerable areas

Our assessment of the spatial distribution of biophysical vulnerability of different land-use types using the five parameters discussed earlier (slope, elevation, distance from the nearest road, distance from the nearest river and distance from the nearest community centre) results in more than 65 per cent of the entire watershed being classified as moderately vulnerable and more than 25 per cent as highly vulnerable (Figure 15.3). Most of the forest and brushland areas are classified as highly vulnerable, with forests comprising most of the highly vulnerable land area, mainly due to their location in steep and highly elevated areas. Some grassland areas are also classified as highly vulnerable, but most grasslands are classified as moderately vulnerable, as are most of the forest plantations. The alienable and disposable lands, which consist of residential and cultivated areas, are mostly classified as moderately vulnerable, with some patches of low and high vulnerability.

Also shown in Figure 15.3 are the places identified as vulnerable by the local communities themselves during focus group discussions. The participants tended to emphasize risks to people and their livelihoods over biophysical parameters in their identifications of vulnerable places. Places identified as vulnerable include low-lying flood-prone settlement areas, agricultural areas prone to floods and drought impacts, intermittent streams/rivers, farmlands at the tail end of irrigation canals, highly erodible areas on steep slopes along riverbanks, unstable areas with steep slopes that support infrastructure, and grasslands, forests and forest plantations near roads and settlements that are susceptible to fire.

In total, 86 places were identified as vulnerable by participants in the participatory mapping exercises. These tend to cluster in areas of human settlement and cultivated farmlands, reflecting the concern with potential impacts on people and their livelihoods. Most of these (74 per cent) lie in areas classified as moderately vulnerable based on biophysical parameters, while 15 per cent and 11 per cent are in areas classified as having high and low vulnerability respectively. None are located in the forest areas along the northeastern border or in the southeastern corner of the watershed, which are classified as highly vulnerable in biophysical terms but which are relatively distant from the main population centres.

While the vulnerable places identified by the local communities do not distinguish between areas of moderate and high vulnerability, they are more specific in their location. They also reflect the concerns of local communities with respect to risks associated with climate variability and extremes such as flood damages, soil erosion, water shortage and forest fires. On the other hand, the vulnerability map based on biophysical parameters and land-use categories

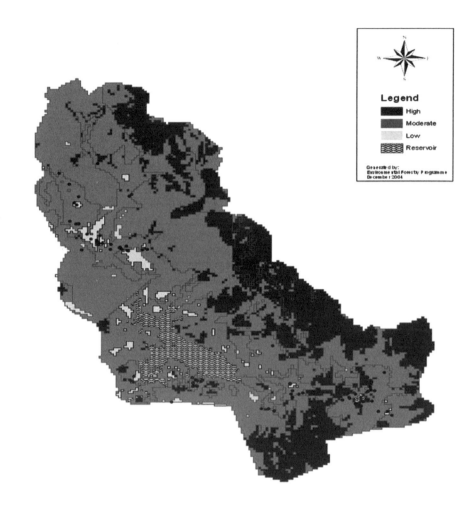

Figure 15.3 *The location of vulnerable areas in the Pantabangan–Carranglan watershed as identified by analysis of biophysical data and by participatory mapping with community members*

can have advantages for macro-level planning to reduce vulnerability in the entire watershed. An approach that combines the two methods of identifying vulnerable areas could thus produce a more comprehensive assessment of vulnerable areas to be used to better address vulnerability in the watershed.

Groups vulnerable to climate variability and extremes

Vulnerability indices were calculated for 108 households using data collected from the household survey and the 2 different schemes for weighting the component indicators. Mean, minimum and maximum values of the indices for the entire sample and for farmers and non-farmers are presented in Table 15.3.

Farmers, in general, are more vulnerable to climate variability and extremes compared to non-farmers. This finding is true regardless of the source of the weights used in the index, in other words whether determined by the researchers or the local communities themselves. However, the index developed using the researchers' weights produced both the highest (67) and lowest (4) index values (the index developed with weights provided by the local communities had 59 as the maximum and 12 as the minimum).

Table 15.3 *Vulnerability index values for farmers, non-farmers and the full sample, based on weights provided by researchers and local communities*

Source of Index Weights	No of Respondents	Vulnerability Index (Possible Value from 0 to 100)		
		Mean	Minimum	Maximum
Researchers				
Farmers	70	38	7	67
Non-farmers	38	25	4	43
Combined	108	33	4	67
Local Communities				
Farmers	70	43	19	59
Non-farmers	38	26	12	55
Combined	108	37	12	59

The values of the index are sensitive to the perceptions or experiences of whoever is giving the weights. For example, under the seed availability sub-index, households with an adaptation strategy get a weighted score of 2, but those with no strategy are scored 1. This suggests that those with an adaptation strategy are more vulnerable, which appears counter-intuitive. However, when asked in the focus group discussions if this was a mistake, participants maintained that the weights are logical. They noted that some adaptation strategies used in response to the lack of seeds, for example, shifting to other crops or buying hybrid varieties of seeds, can result in higher risk because of the high cost and the possibility that financial debt would be incurred. If the higher cost seeds fail to produce an adequate crop, for example, due to flooding or dryness, the indebted farmers are exposed to even greater financial losses and even the risk of losing their farms. Sometimes, in the experience of the farmers, doing nothing but waiting until seeds become available (no adaptation) can be a better option.

Farmers are not a homogeneous group and are not all equally vulnerable. During the focus group discussions, the local community members identified at least three categories of farmers, as well as other socioeconomic groupings in the Pantabangan–Carranglan watershed, that have varying degrees of vulnerability to climate variability and extremes. These are small, average and rich farmers, fishermen, employees and small-business entrepreneurs (see Table 15.4). The focus group discussions identified small farmers as the most vulnerable group. These farmers are characterized as having very low educational attainment, not owning land, having meagre income, and lacking capital and access to other productive resources. Often they live in places considered to be vulnerable and have adaptation strategies for managing risks caused by variable and extreme climate that are ineffective.

Table 15.4 *Groups vulnerable to climate variability and extremes*

Description	Socioeconomic Groups			
	Small Farmers	**Average Farmers and Fishermen**	**Employees/Small Entrepreneurs**	**Rich Farmers and Overseas Workers**
General socioeconomic characteristics	Landless; low educational attainment; no capital; very low income; almost no access to other productive resources.	Elementary and some secondary education; some access to productive resources such as land, capital and technology	College or high-school graduates; some access to productive resources such as land, capital and technology	College or high-school graduates; more access and control over productive resources
Nature of impacts of climate variability and extremes	Decline in crop production, food, livelihood, health condition; more debt incurred	Decline in crop/fish harvest and income, food availability, livelihood sources; health condition may or may not be affected	Increase in prices of commodities; reduced sales	Decline in production and income
Degree of negative impacts	High	Moderate	Moderate	Low
Examples of adaptation strategies	High-interest loans or borrowing from relatives; plant vegetables along rivers; plant other crops; work in nearby towns; engage in other jobs	Plant vegetables along rivers, plant other crops; engage in other sources of livelihood	Government loans; engage in backyard projects; store food supply and other farm inputs for sale	Store food and farm inputs
Effectiveness of adaptation strategies	Some effective, others not	Effective	Effective	Effective
Location of settlement/ properties relevant to vulnerable areas	Some are located in vulnerable areas	Some are located in vulnerable areas	Some are located in vulnerable areas	Generally located in secure areas
Degree of vulnerability	High	Moderate	Moderate	Low

The groups considered to be moderately vulnerable include fishermen, average farmers, owners of small enterprises, *sawali* makers (*sawali* is a walling material made from bamboo), and employees of various agencies and businesses. These groups generally are better educated than the small farmers and have greater access to productive resources such as land, capital and technology, although they don't always have control over them. Incomes are modest but usually sufficient to provide for basic necessities, though some have incomes below the annual per capita poverty threshold (13,843 pesos per year in the Central Luzon region). Some live in vulnerable places such as low-lying flood-prone areas and those with limited water sources. Compared to the most vulnerable group, they are relatively less sensitive to climate-related losses because of their greater access to resources and have more effective options for adaptation.

The least vulnerable groups are the rich farmers and households with family members working overseas. Affluent farmers in general are the best educated among the three groups of farmers. They usually own large tracts of farmland, possess investment capital, own farm machinery and tools, and have control over other factors of production. They live in areas that are less susceptible to flooding and have effective adaptation strategies. Overseas workers are also among the better educated, have access to financial resources and have linkages with other institutions outside the community. Their families are considered among the least vulnerable group because the financial support they provide is stable and not affected by variable and extreme climate events in the local area. Similar to the well-off farmers, their families also live in safe places and have effective options for adaptation.

Vulnerability to future climate change

Projected annual mean temperature increases over Southeast Asia from 1980–1999 to 2080–2099, from climate model simulations reviewed in the recent report of the Intergovernmental Panel on Climate Change (IPCC), have a median of 2.5°C and a 25th–75th percentile range of 2.2 to 3.0°C (Christensen et al, 2007). Most of the models project increases in the average annual precipitation for Southeast Asia, with a median of 7 per cent and a 25th–75th percentile range of 3 to 8 per cent. Seasonal changes vary strongly, with areas away from the Intertropical Convergence Zone showing a tendency for precipitation decreases. However, results from different models are as yet too varied to generalize about the effects of global warming on precipitation in the region (Boer and Faqih, 2004). With respect to extremes, Southeast Asia is likely to share the global tendency for daily extreme precipitation to become more intense, particularly in areas where mean precipitation increases, and tropical cyclones in the Pacific are likely to see an increase in the intensity of rain and wind (Christensen et al, 2007).

Changes in the climate are likely to have far reaching consequences for the Pantabangan–Carranglan watershed. Participants in the focus group discussions were engaged in a scenario building exercise to explore vulnerabilities to a future with higher temperatures, greater variability of rainfall and more intense precipitation events. Through this exercise, potential outcomes are identified that are of concern to the participants and to which they consider themselves to be vulnerable. The outcomes identified as concerns are not predictions or projections of future impacts, but they do provide information about where potential vulnerabilities lie and indications of priorities for directing efforts to prevent or adapt to adverse impacts.

Declines in crop production, greater risk of poverty, hunger and malnutrition, greater indebtedness, loss of access to farms due to unpaid debts, and shortages of water for farm and domestic use were identified as concerns by small farmers. Strategies that small farmers say they could apply to reduce risks of climate impacts include labour on other people's farms and non-farm labour both locally and distant from their homes, adoption of drought tolerant crops, and *sawali* production. Access to high-interest loans may no longer be an option since they may not have sufficient collateral to guarantee them. Temporary relocation in times of extreme weather events such as typhoons can be used to reduce risks, but permanent relocation to safer areas is not an option.

Average farmers, fishermen, employees and small entrepreneurs are concerned about and would be moderately vulnerable to potential climate impacts on the productivity of farmland, fisheries and other livelihood resources, incomes, prices of commodities, and water scarcity. Future climate impacts are not seen as major threats to the livelihoods, food security or health of these groups as a few adjustments in their expenditures, investments and other activities would enable them to cope with potential negative impacts. Available adaptation options include use of short-cycle crops, food storage, changes in household expenditure patterns, investment in other businesses to diversify risks and employment in other areas. Should the need arise, they also have the capacity to transfer to less vulnerable places.

Rich farmers generally have low vulnerability to future climate impacts. Adverse impacts are expected to be readily managed and would not pose important threats to their health or food security. Participants in the scenario building exercise think that rich farmers could even benefit from the situation by gaining farmlands and other possessions from poor farmers who default on their debts.

Factors that influence vulnerability

While communities and households in the Pantabangan–Carranglan watershed are generally vulnerable to climate variability and extremes by virtue of their geographic location, their degree of vulnerability varies based on a combination of factors. These factors include the demographic and socioeconomic characteristics of the households, as well as the broader sociopolitical and institutional contexts of the communities.

Spearman correlation analysis was conducted to identify household characteristics that are correlated with the two vulnerability indices; results are presented in Table 15.5. For the vulnerability index constructed using the researchers' weights, we found three factors that have significant correlation with vulnerability: farm income, monthly food expenditures and farm distance to market. Farm income and distance to market are positively correlated with vulnerability, while monthly food expenditures are negatively correlated. In the case of farm income, those with high farm income tend to be more dependent on a source of income that is highly sensitive to climate. Farmers who are more distant from markets can be cut off from markets and other services during the rainy season and floods, which can amplify their vulnerability. Monthly food expenditures are postulated to be negatively correlated with vulnerability because larger expenditures suggest greater financial capacity to acquire food and other necessities.

Table 15.5 *Results of Spearman correlation analysis of vulnerability indices*

Postulated Factors	Weights by Researchers		Weights by Communities	
	Vulnerability Coefficients	Level of Significance	Vulnerability Coefficients	Level of Significance
1. Demographic				
age	−0.079		−0.12	
gender				
ethnic affiliation				
educational attainment	−0.06		−0.04	
household size	0.014		0.001	
2. Socioeconomic				
total income	0.03		0.03	
household assets	−0.18		−0.08	
number of organizations joined	0.18		0.22*	0.05
farm size	−0.12		0.32*	0.01
farm income	0.26*	0.01	0.44	
number of transportation vehicles	−0.07		−0.017	
monthly food expenditures	−0.30*	0.01	−0.30*	0.01
number of loans applied for	0.07		0.13	
number of information sources	0.01		0.11	
3. Geographic				
farm distance to market	0.24	0.05	0.21	
4. Overall coping mechanisms				
number of coping mechanisms	−0.09		0.03	

*Indicates correlation coefficient estimates that are significant at 0.05 or 0.01 confidence levels.

The correlation analysis for the vulnerability index constructed using weights from the local communities also identified monthly food expenditure as significant and negatively correlated with vulnerability. Two other factors were also found to have a significant correlation with vulnerability: the number of organizations joined and farm size. A positive relationship is found between the number of organizations joined by farmers and their vulnerability. This positive correlation might result from more vulnerable households having greater motivation to join organizations, or it might be that the number of organizations joined fails to capture the nature and quality of organizations that can help households to cope with climate hazards. A positive correlation is also found between farm size and vulnerability, which runs counter to our finding that rich farmers, who have the largest farms, are the least vulnerable households in the watershed. Perhaps this can be explained by the fact that most farmers in the watershed usually devote their farms to a single commodity, rice, which could enhance their vulnerability.

To further evaluate the influences of the different household characteristics on the households' vulnerability, we conducted stepwise multiple regression analyses for both vulnerability indices. In the regressions for the vulnerability index based on weights provided by researchers, 5 of the 17 postulated predictor variables are found to be statistically significant determinants of household vulnerability (Table 15.6). The significant predictors are sex of household head, ethnic affiliation, number of organizations joined, land ownership and distance of farm to market. Households headed by women are found to be more vulnerable compared with male-headed households. The vulnerability of female-headed households may be attributed to overwhelming family burdens, lack of adult male labour, limited livelihood opportunities and higher poverty rates. Ethnic affiliation serves as a proxy to identify households that are migrants to the region. Ethnic groups that are migrants are found to be more vulnerable, which may reflect their difficulty in gaining access to land for cultivation since the watershed area is mostly classified as government land and therefore legally protected from further encroachment and cultivation by new settlers. Migrants are also unfamiliar with the area and may be unable to develop appropriate adaptation strategies or draw on social networks to cushion the adverse impacts of variable and extreme climate conditions. The number of organizations joined by the farmers is estimated to increase vulnerability, consistent with results of the correlation analysis. Land ownership is a significant factor, with households that don't own land found to be more vulnerable than households that do. The distance of farms to market is positively and significantly related to vulnerability, affirming the relationship found in the correlation analysis.

For the vulnerability index based on weights provided by the communities, we found four variables to be significantly related to households' vulnerability. Two of the significant variables (ethnic affiliation and distance to market) that were significant predictors of vulnerability as measured using weights from the researchers are also found to be significant predictors of household vulnerability using the weights provided by the communities. Larger households are found to be more vulnerable compared with smaller households, probably because the former have more mouths to feed compared with the latter. Monthly food consumption is also found to be negatively and significantly related to vulnerability, consistent with the correlation analysis results. On the basis of the computed coefficient of determination, 46 and 44 per cent of the total variation in vulnerability using the weights provided by the researchers and the local communities respectively is explained by the above-mentioned significant variables (Table 15.6). This means that roughly 55 per cent of the vulnerability variance of the 2 indices is still unaccounted for at an aggregate level. There is therefore a need to look for other factors that may help explain household vulnerability apart from those identified in the regression model.

In addition to the above-mentioned factors, the broader sociopolitical context in which communities interact influences their level of vulnerability. As mentioned earlier, the chain of development projects implemented in the area

Table 15.6 *Results of stepwise regression analysis*

Predictors	Weights by Researchers		Weights by Communities	
	Regression Coefficients	Level of Significance	Regression Coefficients	Level of Significance
1. Demographic				
age				
gender	−9.66	0.01		
ethnic affiliation	−10.11	0.01	−0.29	0.01
educational attainment				
household size			0.28	0.05
2. Socioeconomic				
total income				
household assets				
number of organizations joined	9.74	0.01		
farm size				
farm income				
number of transportation vehicles				
monthly food consumption			−0.39	0.01
number of loans applied for				
number of information sources				
land ownership	−8.3	0.05		
3. Geographic				
farm distance to market	0.0006	0.01	0.40	0.01
4. Overall coping mechanisms				
number of coping mechanisms				
Intercept	46.25		43.73	
Coefficient of determination	0.46		0.43	

Note: Variables without corresponding coefficient values do not meet the 0.05 level of significance.

from 1971 to the present has in some ways created a sense of dependency on the part of the local communities on external assistance. This is because these projects, especially the resettlement scheme, were oriented to providing hand-outs with very little attempt towards building local capacities. Consequently, a culture of self-reliance was not fully developed, contributing to the vulnerability of some members of the local community, especially with the termination of these projects.

   Instead of perpetuating external dependency through such projects, it would be possible to create more positive impacts by implementing national policies and crafting a more responsive institutional support system to improve livelihoods and the capacities of households to cope with and manage risks. For instance, forest policy could be reformed to provide communities with greater participation in and control of forest projects in their localities so that they might reap a greater portion of the benefits. At present, the national forest policy prohibits timber harvesting in all watershed areas that support big infrastructure projects (like the Pantabangan–Carranglan watershed, which supports the Pantabangan dam), even if the communities themselves are involved in plantation establishment. This has discouraged their active participation in reforestation and forest protection activities and has led in many cases to deliberate burning of established plantations. In the absence of direct benefits from established plantations and because of limited sources of livelihood opportunities in the area, community members are compelled to engage in illegal cutting and charcoal-making to augment their meagre income. This has contributed to the degradation of some parts of the watershed and increases in biophysical vulnerability.

The presence of the different institutions in the area, such as the NIA, NPC and DENR, could be a catalyst for increasing opportunities and resources for building local capacity. However, the main focus of these institutions is on protecting their investments. The interests of the local communities are only a secondary priority. Previous institutional efforts have not given attention to the provision of more sustainable sources of livelihood. Moreover, institutional support to anticipate and adequately plan for the occurrence of variable and extreme climate conditions has yet to be developed. Similarly, there are as yet no initiatives directed at enhancing current adaptation strategies and building capacity at the local level.

Finally, the prevailing inequity that characterizes the Philippine social structure is evident in the Pantabangan–Carranglan watershed and contributes to the vulnerability of the poor community members. The communities' own typology of small, average and rich farmers is a concrete reflection of the inequitable social structure that prevails in the area. The well-off members of the community have better access to and control over productive resources and have the option to live in safer places, putting them in a less vulnerable situation. They are also better able to capture most of the benefits from the different development projects due to stronger associations and linkages with the institutions that implement them.

Conclusions

Given the same climate stressors, vulnerability varies among different socioeconomic groups depending on their access to production resources and other assets, options to live in or have their assets in less vulnerable areas, and the effectiveness of coping mechanisms or adaptation strategies. In addition, components of broader societal, policy and institutional contexts can exacerbate the adverse impacts of climate change, compounding the vulnerability of certain groups.

Looking at the multiple stressors that contribute to people's vulnerability – which include a combination of climate and non-climatic factors both at the micro and macro levels – is a useful way of understanding this complex concept. There is a need for bottom–up assessment and planning to address vulnerability and enhance adaptive livelihoods at the local level. Participatory action and research that engages the different stakeholders, particularly the local communities, should be pursued to minimize the vulnerability of the poor and enhance adaptive capacity at the local level.

To reduce vulnerability, policies and development programmes should aim to empower the local communities to broaden their range of choices of appropriate adaptation strategies, rather than making them dependent on external support. This should not, however, preclude questioning the large-scale structural causes of vulnerability such as poverty, inequity, and institutional and economic barriers to development.

Note

1   Adaptation strategies for the Pantabangan–Carranglan watershed are explored in Lasco et al (2008).

References

Adger, W. N. (1999) 'Social vulnerability to climate change and extremes in coastal Vietnam', *World Development*, vol 27, pp249–269

Boer, R., and A. Faqih (2004) 'Current and future rainfall variability in Indonesia', Technical Report, AIACC Project no AS21, International START Secretariat, Washington, DC, US

Brooks, N. (2003) *Vulnerability, Risk and Adaptation: A Conceptual Framework*, working paper no 38, Tyndall Centre for Climate Change Research, University of East Anglia, Norwich, UK

Calenergy Company (2004) 'Worldwide projects: Caseccnan (Philippines)', www.calenergy.com/html/projects5b.asp

Christensen, J. H., B. Hewitson, A. Busuioc, A. Chen, X. Gao, I. Held, R. Jones, R. Koli, W. Kwon, R. Laprise, V. Rueda, L. Mearns, C. Menendez, J. Raisanen, A. Rinke, A. Sarr and P. Whetton (2007) 'Regional climate projections', in S. Solomon, D. Qin, M. Manning, Z. Chen, M. C. Marquis, K. Averyt, M. Tignor and H. L. Miller (eds) *Climate Change 2007: The Physical Science Basis*, Contribution of Working Group I to the Fourth Assessment Report of the Intergovernmental Panel on Climate Change, Cambridge University Press, Cambridge, UK and New York, US

Chua, L. A. (1999) *Understanding the Research Process*, Department of Agricultural Education and Rural Studies, College of Agriculture, UP Los Baños, College, Laguna

Cruz, R. V. O. (2003) 'Watershed level SDI for global change', in *Sustainable Development Indicators for Global Change: A Multi-Scale Approach*, Completion Report, Environmental Forestry Programme, College of Forestry and Natural Resources, University of the Philippines, Los Baños, Philippines

Cutter, S. L. (1996) 'Vulnerability to environmental hazards', *Progress in Human Geography*, vol 20, pp 529–539

Few, N. (2003) 'Flooding, vulnerability and coping strategies: Local responses to global threat', *Progress in Development Studies*, vol 3, pp43–58

IPCC (Intergovernmental Panel on Climate Change) (2001) *Climate Change 2001: Impacts, Adaptation and Vulnerability*, edited by J. McCarthy, O. Canziani, N. Leary, D. Dokken and K. White, Contribution of the Working Group II to the Third Assessment Report of the Intergovernmental Panel on Climate Change, Cambridge University Press, Cambridge, UK

Jose, A. M., L. M. Sosa and N. A. Cruz (1996) 'Vulnerability assessment of Angat Watershed Reservoir to climate change', *Water, Air, Soil Pollution*, vol 92, pp191–201

Lasco, R., R. Cruz, J. Pulhin and F. Pulhin (2008) 'Spillovers and tradeoffs of adaptation: Examples from a Philippine watershed', in N. Leary, J. Adejuwon, V. Barros, I. Burton, J. Kulkarni and R. Lasco (eds) *Climate Change and Adaptation*, Earthscan, London, UK

Leary, N. and S. Beresford (2007) 'Vulnerability of people, places and systems to environmental change', in G. Knight and J. Jaeger (eds) *Integrated Regional Assessment*, Cambridge University Press, Cambridge, UK

Moss, R. (1999) *Vulnerability to Climate Variability and Change: Framework for Synthesis and Modeling: Project Description*, Battelle Pacific Northwest National Laboratory, Richland, WA, US

Municipality of Carranglan (undated) *Development Master Plan of the Municipality of Carranglan, 2003–2007*, Nueva Ecija

Municipality of Pantabangan (undated) *Master Plan of the Municipality of Pantabangan, 1998–2000*, Nueva Ecija

NPC (National Power Corporation) (1995) *Pantabangan Watershed Rehabilitation Project*, Watershed Management Department, Quezon City, The Philippines

NPC (1997) *Pantabangan–Carranglan Watershed Management Plan*, Watershed Management Department, Quezon City, The Philippines

National Statistics Office (2000) *Census 2000: Philippines Population*, CD-ROM, Barangay

Pulhin, J. M. (2002) 'Climate change and watershed communities: Methodology for assessing social impacts, vulnerability and adaptation', paper discussed during the AIACC–AS 21 Regional Capability-Building Training Workshop on Climate Change Impacts, Adaptation and Vulnerability, College of Forestry and Natural Resources, 25 November to 8 December, University of the Philippines, Los Baños, College, Laguna, Philippines

Saplaco, S. R., N. C. Bantayan and R. V. O. Cruz (2001) *GIS-based ATLAS of Selected Watersheds in the Philippines*, Department of Science and Technology, Philippine Council for Agriculture, Forestry and Natural Resources Research and Development (DOST-PCARRD) and Environmental Remote Sensing and Geo-Information (UPLB-CFNR-ERSG)University of the Philippines Los Baños, College of Forestry and Natural Resources

Toquero, F. D. (2003) 'Impact of involuntary resettlement: The case of Pantabangan resettlement in the province of Nueva Ecija', PhD thesis, Central Luzon State University, Science City of Muñoz, Nueva Ecija

UNEP (United Nations Environment Programme) (2001) *Vulnerability Indices: Climate Change Impacts and Adaptations*, edited by T. E. Downing, R. Butterfield, S. Cohen, S. Huq, R. Moss, A. Rhaman, Y. Sokona and L. Stephen, Policy Series, United Nations Environment Programme, Nairobi, Kenya

Yoshida, S. (2000) 'Pantabangan forestry development assistance project', www.jica.go.jp/english/news/2000/16.html

16

Climate Risks and Rice Farming in the Lower Mekong River Basin

Suppakorn Chinvanno, Somkhith Boulidam,
Thavone Inthavong, Soulideth Souvannalath,
Boontium Lersupavithnapa, Vichien Kerdsuk
and Nguyen Thi Hien Thuan

Introduction

Agriculture is one of the most important activities in the lower Mekong river basin. It is a source of livelihood for a large portion of the population and a significant contributor to national incomes. For example, in Lao PDR, agriculture employs 76.3 per cent of the country's 5.7 million people (UNESCAP, undated) and agricultural products contributed 44.8 per cent of Lao PDR's gross domestic product (GDP) of US$2.9 billion in 2005 (World Bank, 2007). In Thailand, agriculture contributed a much smaller 9.9 per cent of total GDP (US$176.6 billion) (World Bank, 2007), yet the sector employs 44.9 per cent of Thailand's 63.1 million people (UNESCAP, undated).

Rice is the most important agricultural product of the region in terms of the proportion of land area used, the quantity and value of output, and contribution to diet. In Thailand, rice is cultivated on 88 per cent of land used for cereal production and represents 43 per cent of the per capita daily caloric intake (FAO, 2004a). Rice is even more predominant in Lao PDR, where 94 per cent of cereal lands is planted in rice and 64 per cent of daily caloric intake is provided by it (FAO, 2004b). Most rice and other cereals are grown under rain-fed conditions as the irrigated land area is limited, accounting for 19 and 30 per cent of total harvested area in Lao PDR and Thailand respectively (Barker and Molle, 2004).

Because of the high dependence on rain-fed rice cultivation, and the sensitivity of rain-fed rice yields to rainfall amounts and other climate conditions, the region is strongly affected by variations or changes in climate that adversely affect rice cultivation. Farmers of rain-fed rice are among the most vulnerable groups in the lower Mekong basin as their livelihood depends heavily on their annual production of rice, which is directly exposed to climate risk. In addition, most of these farmers are poor and have limited resources and other capacity with which to cope with the impacts of climate variability and change. The risk profile and vulnerability of rice farmers of the Mekong basin vary from place to place due to differences in the changes in climate to which they will be exposed, the sensitivity of the production systems to climate change, the socioeconomic condition and lifestyle of each community, and the condition of the surrounding natural environment (IPCC, 2001a).

As part of a larger study of climate change in the lower Mekong basin, we investigated the existing climate risks faced by rice farmers in selected villages in Lao PDR and Thailand and how their risks may change with climate change (see Snidvongs, 2006). This chapter presents the results of our investigations. Our approach, which follows the Adaptation Policy Framework of the United Nations Development Programme (Lim et al, 2004), is outlined in Figure 16.1. The analysis includes development of climate change scenarios for the region, estimation of climate change impacts on rice yields, and assessment of the vulnerability of farm households to climate variations and change as a function of their sensitivity to climate risk, exposure and coping capacity. Strategies for adapting to climate change were also examined and are evaluated in Chinvanno et al (2008).

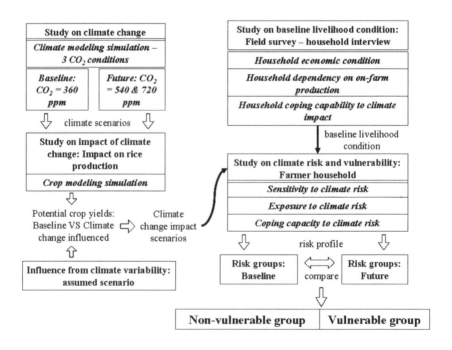

Figure 16.1 *Framework for climate risk and vulnerability assessment*

The Study Sites

Our study encompassed three countries of the lower Mekong basin: Lao PDR, Thailand and Vietnam. In this chapter, we focus on study sites in Savannakhet Province in Lao PDR and Ubon Ratchathani Province in Thailand. These two countries of Southeast Asia represent opposite ends of the scale of socioeconomic development, resulting in very different conditions that lead to differences in their farmers' vulnerability to climate hazards and climate change. Thailand is far more economically developed than Lao PDR, as reflected by the per capita gross national income levels in 2005 of US$2720 in Thailand and US$430 in Lao PDR (The World Bank, 2007), and has a higher population and population density. The different level of development and socioeconomic conditions are reflected in different livelihoods (commercial farming vs subsistence), structure of household expenses, resources for coping and adapting to stresses, institutional support, and agricultural practices. But despite the differences, farmers of rain-fed rice in the two countries share the same cultural roots and are among the poorest members of their respective societies; in both countries their well-being is highly dependent on climatic conditions.

We selected four villages for study in Lao PDR: Seboungnuantay, Lahakhoke, Khouthee and Dongkhamphou. The villages, all located within the Songkhone district of Savannakhet Province, have a total land area of 1851ha and a population of 2490 living in 434 households. Savannakhet Province is in the central to southern part of Lao PDR, has a land area of 21,774km² and consists of 15 districts. The topography of the province is lowland with a slight slope from east to west towards the Mekong river. Savannakhet Province has the largest area of rice fields in the country, nearly 140,000ha or 19 per cent of all rice fields in Lao PDR (Committee for Planning and Cooperation, 2003). It is also the most populated province of the country, with a total population of 811,400, or approximately 15 per cent of the population of Lao PDR.

Songkhone district, where the study villages are located, is in the southwest of Savannakhet Province. It is the largest district of the province, with a total area of 1406km². The district consists of 142 villages with 13,919 households and a total population of 86,855. Most of the inhabitants are subsistence farmers who grow rice mainly for their own consumption and sell only a small amount of their farm output in markets. Rice farming is rain-fed and a single crop is grown each year. Households supplement their food supply and livelihoods by harvesting natural products from surrounding natural ecosystems, which are relatively intact.

Eighteen villages were selected for study in Thailand, all located in Ubon Ratchathani Province in the lower northeastern region of Thailand. The province covers an area of 16,112km². Most of the land area consists of highlands, averaging 68 metres above sea level, with mixed sandy soils of low fertility. The Mekong river and mountains form the border between the province and Lao PDR to the east and high mountains form the border between the province and the Democratic Republic of Cambodia to the south. Major rivers include the Chi river, which merges with the Mun river and flows through Ubon Ratchathani Province from west to east before joining the Mekong in Khong Chiam district. In 2005, Ubon Ratchathani maintained a total population of 1,774,808 in 432,923 households, which are mostly in the agricultural sector (Department of Provincial Administration, undated).

The study area is part of the Ubon Ratchathani Land Reform Area (ULRA), which covers 55,000ha on the east bank of the Dome Yai river. This area has three slope classes: level to gently sloping, sloping to undulating, and undulating to rolling. Soils are generally sandy and of low fertility. Korat series is the major soil type in this area; these soils are fairly well drained and strongly acidic.

Most of the area is cultivated for paddy rice, with some areas cultivated for upland crops. There are small patches of degraded forests. Water is plentiful in the wet season, but severe shortage occurs in the dry season. Average rainfall is about 1600mm, 90 per cent of which falls in the period May to October. Average monthly temperature ranges from a minimum of 17.0°C in December and January to a maximum of 35.9°C in March and April. There is very limited irrigation and cropping is mainly a wet season activity (Ubon Ratchathani Province Administration, undated). Farmers are mostly commercial farmers who grow a single rice crop each year on farms of moderate size and using mechanized farming methods. The study area is divided into five zones, which are characterized in Table 16.1.

Table 16.1 *Villages by zone in Thailand*

Zone	Characteristics of zone	Villages studied
#1	Deep sandy soils. Cropping patterns are rice plus plantation and forest. The forest trees are eucalyptus and cashew nut.	1. Ban Mak Mai 2. Ban Mek Yai 3. Ban Khok Pattana
#2	This area lies along the Lam Dom Yai river. Soil has high fertility. It is a wet area. The dominant cropping system is rice and upland crops such as vegetables, cassava or kenaf.	1. Ban Fung Pa 2. Ban Muang 3. Ban Bung Kham 4. Ban Bua Thaim
#3	The area is partly upland rice. The cropping system is an encroached forest area.	1. Ban Nong Sanom 2. Ban Udom Chart 3. Ban Pa Rai 4. Ban Non Sawang
#4	This area has an intensive rice system. Mostly commercial farming practice. There is low tree density.	1. Ban Bua Ngam 2. Ban Nong Waeng 3. Ban Rat Samakee 4. Ban Non Yai
#5	This area is similar to zone # 3 but has more lowland characteristics. Rice cultivation encroaches into forest areas.	1. Ban Pa Pok 2. Ban Sok Seang 3. Ban Non Deang

Projected Climate Change in the Lower Mekong Basin

Our analyses of potential impacts of climate change on rice production are based on climate change scenarios constructed for our study areas from projections of the conformal cubic atmospheric model (CCAM), a high- resolution regional climate model. The CCAM is a second-generation regional climate model developed for the Australasian region by the Commonwealth Science and Industrial Research Organization (McGregor and Dix, 2001). Evaluations of the model in several international model inter-comparison exercises have shown it to be among the best climate models for reproducing key features of the climate of the Southeast Asian region (Wang et al, 2004).

The baseline climate for the analysis is developed using a steady state simulation of the CCAM with an atmospheric concentration of carbon dioxide (CO_2) of 360ppm, which corresponds to the CO_2 concentration during the 1980s. Scenarios of future climate are developed using steady state simulations for CO_2 concentrations of 540ppm and 720ppm, which correspond to 1.5 times and double the baseline level. These concentrations would be reached by roughly the 2040s and 2070s, respectively, for the IPCC's A1FI scenario of greenhouse emissions, the highest of the IPCC emission scenarios (IPCC, 2001b).

Figures 16.2 and 16.3 display baseline temperatures and precipitation for the region and the changes projected by the CCAM for CO_2 concentrations of 540ppm and 720ppm. The CCAM simulations have a spatial resolution of 0.1 degree, or approximately 10km². No results are shown for Cambodia due to insufficient observational data. For the 540ppm scenario, the CCAM projects that the region would get slightly cooler. For the 720ppm scenario, warming of less than 1°C is projected over most of Thailand and Lao PDR. Annual precipitation is projected to increase throughout the region for both climate change scenarios, with greater precipitation projected for the 720ppm CO_2 concentration scenario than for the 540ppm scenario. The increases are greatest in the eastern and southern part of Lao PDR.

Climate change in the study areas

To create climate scenarios for our study sites, the outputs of the CCAM model must be adjusted to match local climate conditions. The adjustment focused on precipitation and used observed data from weather stations throughout the region. The statistical procedure used to adjust the model output is based on cumulative rainfall using a non-linear log–log function to exponentially increase the daily variability. An arbitrary rainfall threshold of 3mm/day was applied to reduce the number of rainy days.

In Savannakhet Province in Lao PDR, the rainy season is extended slightly for the 540ppm CO_2 scenario as the onset of the rainy season is projected to shift approximately 10 days earlier. Total annual rainfall increases roughly 10 per cent from the baseline average of 1624mm to 1780mm. In comparison, the rainy season length would settle back to the same condition as the baseline when the CO_2 concentration rises to 720ppm. However, total rainfall increas-

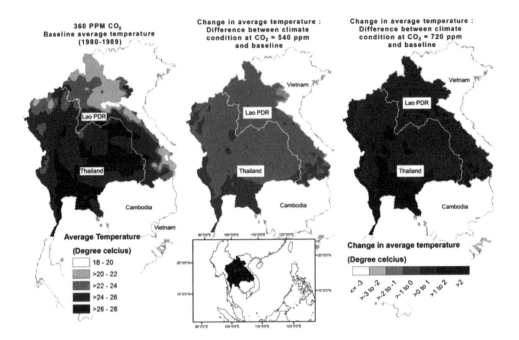

Figure 16.2 *Average temperature in the lower Mekong river basin:*
Baseline and projected changes

es by a larger amount, about 20 per cent above the projection for 540ppm, to
2120mm. Projected temperatures for Savannakhet only change within the
range of +/-1 degree C as more cloud cover locally dampens the global warming trend.

In Ubon Ratchathani Province of Thailand, the onset of the rainy season is
projected to start much earlier, by about 20 days, for both the 540 and 720ppm
CO_2 scenarios. The simulated 10-year average annual rainfall is 1688mm during the baseline period and it rises to 1734mm and 1901mm for the 540 and
720ppm scenarios, respectively. However, despite the increased rainfall, the
mid-season dry spell becomes more prominent for the 540ppm simulation. The
temperature in the area would change within a narrow range of +/-1°C, which
is also projected for the study site in Lao PDR, again because more cloud cover
in the region dampens the warming trend.

Comparison to other projections of climate change for Southeast Asia

To put the CCAM-derived scenarios in context, it is useful to compare them to
the range of climate projections from other models. The projections of future
temperature increases in Southeast Asia that are assessed in the IPCC's most
recent report range from 1.5 to 3.7°C average annual warming over the 100-

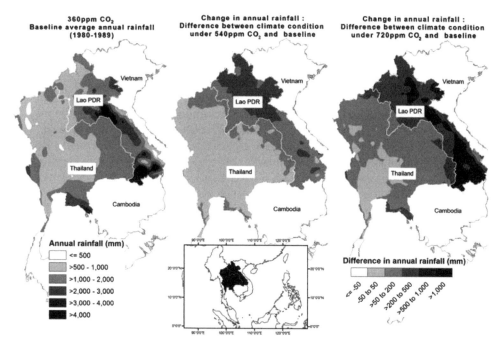

Figure 16.3 *Average rainfall in the lower Mekong river basin: Baseline and projected changes*

year period from 1980–1999 to 2080–2099 (Christensen et al, 2007). Seasonal warming is roughly the same for each season as the projected change in average annual temperature. The median projected warming for the region is 2.5°C, similar to the global average, while the 25th and 75th percentile projections span a range of 2.2 to 3.0°C. Somewhat greater warming is projected over Indochina and the larger land masses of the archipelago. Note that none of the projections assessed in the new IPCC report indicate cooling for the region and that the CCAM projection of temperature changes for 720ppm is below the range projected by other models. So, our analyses are based on scenarios that are significantly cooler than other models have projected.

The projected increase in precipitation from the CCAM is consistent with other model projections for the region. Most of the models reviewed by the IPCC project increases in precipitation averaged over all Southeast Asia, with a median increase of about 7 per cent in all seasons (Christensen et al, 2007). But there is potential for substantial local variations in precipitation changes, as demonstrated by McGregor and Dix (2001). For example, precipitation decreases are often projected in areas away from the Intertropical Convergence Zone (ITCZ) (Christensen et al, 2007). In areas where mean precipitation is projected to increase there is also the potential for more intense daily extreme precipitation.

Impact of Climate Change on Rice Yields

The Decision Support System for Agrotechnology Transfers (DSSAT) version 4.0 crop modelling software (Hoogenboom et al, 1998) and the climate scenarios generated from the CCAM climate model are used to simulate the impacts of climate change on rain-fed rice yields at the study sites. The crop modelling software uses daily climate data, including maximum and minimum temperature, precipitation and solar radiation, coupled with the crop management scheme and soil property of the study sites, to calculate the rice yields. By using daily climate data for the simulation process, our study is able to capture the impact of climate change on rain-fed rice productivity not only with respect to changes in average climate parameters such as rainfall and temperature, but also with respect to changes in temporal aspects of climate such as shifts in the onset of rains, changes in the length of the rainy season or changes in the pattern of the mid-season dry spell. The DSSAT simulations also incorporate the direct effects of higher CO_2 concentrations, which can increase yields by increasing photosynthesis and plant water-use efficiency.

The crop management scheme used in the simulations assumes homogeneous practice in each site. The crop management scheme is comprised of choice of rice cultivar, planting date, initial condition of the field before planting, planting method and density, water management, and application of organic and inorganic fertilizers. Results of the simulations are shown in Table 16.2. Simulation results for the baseline case differ somewhat from actual yields as recorded from field interviews. Differences in yields are due, in part, to differences between modelled and actual farm management practices and differences between the dataset used for the simulations and actual field conditions, particularly for soil properties. However, the simulations provide useful indicators of the future trend and potential impacts of climate change on rice productivity in the study areas.

Table 16.2 *Simulated rice yields under different climate scenarios*

Climate Scenario	Rice Yields (kg/ha)			Change from Baseline	
	360ppm CO_2 (Baseline)	Average Climate for 540ppm CO_2	Average Climate for 720ppm CO_2	540ppm CO_2	720ppm CO_2
Lao PDR					
Savannakhet Province					
Songkhone District	2535	2303	2470	−9.1%	−2.6%
Thailand					
Ubon Ratchathani Province					
Zone 1	1154	1235	1331	7.0%	15.3%
Zone 2	1920	2002	2072	4.3%	7.9%
Zone 3	2364	2408	2439	1.9%	3.2%
Zone 4	2542	2575	2592	1.3%	2.0%
Zone 5	3024	3051	3069	0.9%	1.5%

According to the climate change scenarios simulated by the CCAM, climate change has a slight negative impact on rain-fed rice production in Savannakhet Province in Lao PDR. The simulated rice yield is reduced by nearly 10 per cent under climate conditions corresponding to a CO_2 concentration of 540ppm, but for the 720ppm CO_2 scenario, yields rise back to almost the same level as the baseline scenario. The simulated rice yields at the study sites in Ubon Ratchathani Province in Thailand show positive impacts from climate change. The increase in rice yield varies from zone to zone and is greater for the 720ppm CO_2 scenario than for the 540ppm scenario. The increases range from roughly 1 to 7 per cent for the CO_2 concentration of 540ppm and 1.5 to 15 per cent for the 720ppm climate.

The mild impact of climate change on rice yields in the Lao PDR sites and the positive impacts at the Thai sites are due primarily to three factors: the beneficial effects of carbon dioxide and increased rainfall for rice cultivation and the relatively modest temperature changes of the climate scenarios used in the analysis. Scenarios with greater warming would likely result in less beneficial outcomes or even negative outcomes. It is also worth noting that the simulations do not take account of the potential effects of more intense rainfall, flooding and changes in the timing of rainfall, which are discussed in the following section.

Farmers' Concerns and Extreme Events

Interviews with farmers in the study areas revealed that farmers are already threatened by climate variability. Farmers are highly concerned about extreme climate events that can cause substantial losses of farm output and threaten their livelihoods. Extreme events identified by farmers as threats to rice cultivation in the study areas include prolonged mid-season dry spells, floods and late-ending rainy seasons. Farmers of rain-fed rice sow their rice at the start of the rainy season, typically in May, or transplant seedlings into their fields in mid-June to mid-July, and harvest their crop in October or November after the end of the rainy season. A mid-season dry spell after sowing or transplanting rice is common to the region. The dry spell can damage young rice plants or impose additional costs on farmers for water procurement to sustain the rice plants while waiting for the rains to resume. If plants are lost but the resumption of rains does not come too late, the farmer can replant to salvage his harvest, but again incurring additional expenses. In the worst case, the mid-season dry spell is prolonged and rains resume too late for replanted rice to mature before the rainy season ends. When very prolonged dry spells occur, farmers are at risk of losing a substantial portion of their crop and income.

Floods are also a significant threat to rice cultivation in the lower Mekong basin. Floods commonly occur near the end of the rainy season, around the months of October and November, when water flow is at its highest in the Mekong river and its tributaries. This period of frequent flooding coincides with the middle to end of the crop season. Late season floods have caused severe damage to rice production, and recovery is difficult as it is too late in the rainy season to replant. Another source of risk is a late end to the rainy season. Rains during and after harvest can damage the harvest or result in higher costs for drying the rice.

Our simulations of the impacts of climate change on rice productivity do not take into account potential changes in the timing, duration or severity of events such as dry spells, heavy rains and floods. But the greatest climate risks to farmers are currently from extreme events and it is changes in extremes that are of greatest concern to farmers. Thus, a complete assessment of climate change risks and vulnerability needs to consider potential changes in the distribution frequencies of extreme events. However, this requires climate scenario simulations for longer time periods than the 10-year time slices constructed for our study.

In order to gauge the sensitivity of farmers to the occurrence of extreme climate events, we examine the impacts of a hypothetical extreme event on farm household risk profiles. Group discussions with farmers and community leaders in the study sites indicate that an event causing a loss of approximately one third of rice production or higher would be a severe situation that would significantly affect a farmer's livelihood. Therefore, a loss of 30 per cent of rice production is used as a proxy for an extreme climate event in our analysis.

Baseline Climate Risk

The level of climate risk faced by farm households is a function of three broad determinants: the sensitivity of the household to stresses in climate variations and changes, the exposure of the household to climate stresses, and the capacity of the household to cope with climate impacts. A variety of indicators are used to measure these three determinants of risk (see Table 16.3).

Indicators of household economic condition are used to measure the sensitivity of the farmer household to climate stresses. Households with current consumption that is sustainable within the limits of household income, land ownership and farm size, allowing self-sufficient food production, have low sensitivity to climate stresses. The degree of dependency on farm production and rice production are used to measure the exposure of the farmer household, with low levels of dependency indicating low exposure. Coping capacity is measured by the diversity and amount of resources available to the farmer household for responding to and recovering from climate impacts. Within this conceptual framework, farmer households are at high risk if they have an unstable or unsustainable household economic condition, are highly reliant on rice production for their livelihood, and have few resources for coping with climate impacts.

Data on the indicators was collected through field interviews of 560 farmer households in Thailand and 160 farmer households in Lao PDR. The field assessment activity in Thailand was conducted by researchers from the Faculty of Agriculture of Ubon Ratchathani University during May–July 2004. The assessment in Lao PDR was conducted by researchers from the National University of Laos during September 2004.

Table 16.3 *Indicators used in evaluating farmers' risk from climate impact*

Criteria	Indicator	Measurement	Scoring	Min score	Max score
Household Economic Condition	Sustainability of household consumption	Total household production (or income)/total household consumption (or expenditure)	>1 = 0; 1–0.7 = 1; <0.7 = 2	0	2
	Stability of household production	Farmland: own or rent	Own = 0, Rent = 1	0	1
	Self-sufficiency of household food production	Farmland/capita 0.8ha/capita for Lao PDR and 0.65 for Thailand are thresholds to produce annual food consumption for one family member	≥0.8 = 0; <0.8 = 1 (Thailand ≥0.65 = 0; <0.65 = 1)	0	1
Sub-total				0	4
Household Dependency on On-Farm Production	Availability of income from non-climate sensitive sources	Total household consumption/income from livestock + Fixed off-farm income	>1 = 0; 1–0.7 = 1; <0.7 = 2	0	2
	Dependency on rice production to sustain basic needs	Total rice production/total food expenditure (or Total household fixed expenditure)	>1 = 0; 1–0.7=1; <0.7 = 2	0	2
Sub-total				0	4
Coping Capacity	Ability to use non-farming income to maintain livelihood	Total household consumption + Total cost of production/total household saving + Total off-farm income + Income from livestock + Extra income	≤1 = 0; 1–1.3 = 1; >1.3 = 2	0	2
	Ability to use non-farming income to maintain household basic needs	Total food expenditure (or Total fixed expenditure)/total household saving + Total off-farm income + Income from livestock + Extra income	≤1 = 0; –1.3 = 1; 1>1.3 = 2	0	2
Sub-total				0	4
			Total	0	12

The collected indicator data were combined into an index of climate risk using the scoring system outlined in Table 16.3. Farm households are grouped into three risk categories according to their scores as follows:

- Low risk: households with risk scores in the range 0–4;
- Moderate risk: households with risk scores in the range 5–8; and
- High risk: households with risk scores in the range 9–12.

The proportions of farm households classified as having low, moderate and high risk in the current climate for each of the study sites are shown in Figure 16.4. Farm communities in Savannakhet Province in Lao PDR are found to be highly resilient to climate stresses relative to the farm communities of Ubon Ratchathani Province in Thailand. More than 80 per cent of the households in the Laotian villages are classified as low risk and less than 5 per cent are classified as high risk. In comparison, farmers at the study sites in Thailand are at greater risk from climate impacts. Only about a third of the surveyed population are classified as low risk, while approximately 15–25 per cent are in the high risk category. The moderate risk group is the largest group of the population, in some study sites accounting for as many as half of the total surveyed population.

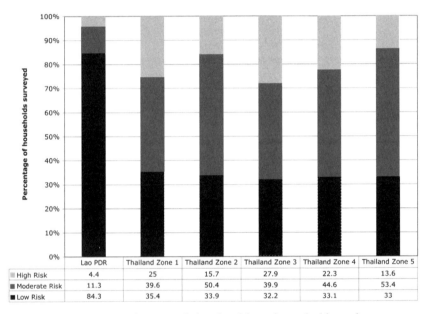

	Lao PDR	Thailand Zone 1	Thailand Zone 2	Thailand Zone 3	Thailand Zone 4	Thailand Zone 5
High Risk	4.4	25	15.7	27.9	22.3	13.6
Moderate Risk	11.3	39.6	50.4	39.9	44.6	53.4
Low Risk	84.3	35.4	33.9	32.2	33.1	33

Figure 16.4 *Climate risk levels of farm households under current climate conditions*

The contributions of exposure, sensitivity and coping capacity to household risk scores are displayed in the risk profiles in Figure 16.5. The low risk groups in every location have risk profiles that differ substantially from the moderate and high risk groups. Their risk scores are low in every criterion. In most cases the biggest difference between the low risk and higher risk groups is that the higher risk groups have much less coping capacity. Greater exposure to climate stresses is also a significant contributor to the greater risks faced by households classified as moderate and high risk. The total risk scores of the low risk groups in Lao PDR and Thailand range roughly from 1 to 2 points, while the total risk scores of the moderate and high risk groups average close to 7 and 10 points respectively.

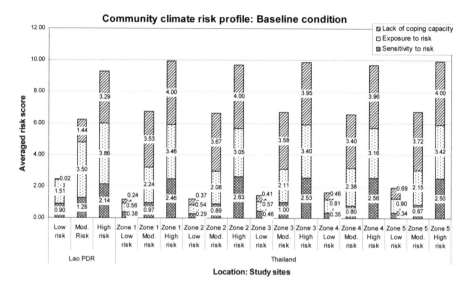

Figure 16.5 *Climate risk profiles under current climate conditions*

The large proportion of rain-fed rice farmers in Lao PDR that are at low risk from climate stresses have high coping capacity relative to other farmers in the study. This is partly because their household production is diversified over various activities, including both on-farm and off-farm sources. Consequently they can accumulate and draw on a wide range of resources with which to cope with climate and other stresses. Rice production for these farmers does not dominate household production and accounts for less than a third of total household output. Another advantage of farmers living in rural areas of Lao PDR is that, due to the low population, natural systems are still able to provide a significant alternate food source and forest products that can be converted or exchanged for other products required for daily use or sold for cash. In addition to relying on natural ecosystems as a coping mechanism, farmers in Lao PDR also have savings in the form of stored rice and cash-convertible livestock to help them cope with impacts from climate stresses, even though cash saving is almost non-existent. In addition, the debt level of farmers in Lao PDR is virtually zero, partly due to the limited availability of loans or other institutional lending mechanisms, but also to social norms that are against indebtedness (Boulidam, 2005).

The majority of surveyed farmers in Thailand are categorized as moderate or high risk. The most important factor contributing to their risk level is very limited coping capacity due to their having few savings and high debts. In addition, the surveyed farmers in Thailand have little diversification in their production and income sources and are highly dependent on income from rice production. Their dependency on rice production creates conditions of high exposure and sensitivity to climate impacts.

Vulnerability to Climate Change

Our analysis thus far has addressed current or baseline climate risks to farmers. Climate change will change the stresses to which farm households are exposed and result in a variety of impacts. Potential impacts include changes in yields of rice and other crops, the availability of water, costs of planting, replanting and water procurement, and the frequency and severity of crop losses to floods and dry spells. Here we examine the potential impacts of climate change on rice production and how these impacts would affect the risk scores and risk profiles of farm households.

Changes in rice yields for four scenarios are presented in Table 16.4. These include scenarios of average climate conditions corresponding to the steady-state CCAM projections for CO_2 concentrations of 540 and 720ppm. The changes in rice yields are those derived from the DSSAT simulations, which indicate potential yield reductions in Savannakhet Province and yield increases in Ubon Ratchathani Province for the average projected climates. Climate change may also bring changes in extremes, such as late season flooding. To investigate how future climate extremes might affect farm households, we construct two scenarios of rice yields that assume that extremes reduce yield by 30 per cent relative to the simulated yields for average climate conditions.

Table 16.4 *Scenarios of changes in rice yields in response to changes in average climate and extreme climate*

	540ppm CO₂		720ppm CO₂	
	Average climate	Extreme climate	Average climate	Extreme climate
Lao PDR:				
Savannakhet Province				
Songkhone district	−9.1%	−39.1%	−2.6%	−32.6%
Thailand:				
Ubon Ratchathani Province				
Zone 1	7.0%	−23.0%	15.3%	−14.7%
Zone 2	4.3%	−25.7%	7.9%	−22.1%
Zone 3	1.9%	−28.1%	3.2%	−26.8%
Zone 4	1.3%	−28.7%	2.0%	−28.1%
Zone 5	0.9%	−29.1%	1.5%	−28.5%

We use these yield changes to recalculate our measures of household economic condition, dependency on rice and coping capacity. New risk scores and risk profiles are then constructed for the climate change scenarios and compared to baseline risks to determine the proportion of households that are vulnerable to climate change. We define households to be vulnerable if the change in climate increases their risk score. Figure 16.6 shows the percentage of households whose risk scores increase or decrease for each scenario.

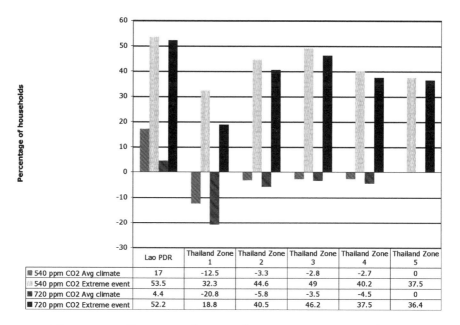

	Lao PDR	Thailand Zone 1	Thailand Zone 2	Thailand Zone 3	Thailand Zone 4	Thailand Zone 5
540 ppm CO2 Avg climate	17	-12.5	-3.3	-2.8	-2.7	0
540 ppm CO2 Extreme event	53.5	32.3	44.6	49	40.2	37.5
720 ppm CO2 Avg climate	4.4	-20.8	-5.8	-3.5	-4.5	0
720 ppm CO2 Extreme event	52.2	18.8	40.5	46.2	37.5	36.4

Figure 16.6 *Changes in climate risk scores in response to climate change and extremes*

In Lao PDR, there are no substantial changes in the proportion of households classified as low, moderate and high risk for any of the climate change scenarios compared to the baseline case. More than 80 per cent of households are still classified as low risk for each scenario. While the majority of households would still be in the low risk category, however, some households would experience an increase in their risk score. Under average climate conditions, 17.0 and 4.4 per cent of households would face increased risk for the 540ppm and 720ppm CO_2 scenarios, respectively, and are therefore defined as vulnerable. For the scenarios of extreme climate, more than 50 per cent would experience an increase in risk and are thus vulnerable.

In Thailand, there is also no substantial change in the risk groups for the scenarios of changes in average climate, with the moderate risk group still the largest. Because rice yields are projected to increase at the Thai sites for the CCAM-projected changes in average climate, risk scores decrease by 3 to 6 per cent for households in zones 2, 3 and 4 and by 12 to 20 per cent in zone 1. The decrease in climate risk is more pronounced for the 720ppm CO_2 case than for the 540ppm case.

In the extreme climate scenarios, there are noticeable changes in the moderate and high risk group, with some households moving from the moderate to the high risk group. In zone 3, the number of households classified as high risk increases for the extreme climate scenarios and accounts for more than one-third of households. Approximately 18 to 50 per cent of households have higher risk scores for the climate extreme scenarios compared to the baseline case.

Conclusion

Our analysis shows that the relation between the level of development and climate risk is not a simple one and that development level is not a major determinant of risk profiles. Vulnerability to climate impacts is a place-based condition that depends on the socioeconomic, environmental and physical conditions of each location that shape the exposure, sensitivity and coping capacity of households. The profile of climate risk differs from community to community. Households with low climate risk tend to have high coping capacity and low exposure and sensitivity. Comparing the communities in Lao PDR and Thailand, coping capacity emerges as the most important factor contributing to the low risk of the majority of households in the Laotian communities. Households in the Thai communities have lower coping capacity than their counterparts in Lao PDR. They also tend to have higher exposures and sensitivity to climate stresses due to high dependence on rice production for their livelihoods. Consequently, the majority of Thai farm households face moderate to high climate risks.

Changes in average climate conditions are found to have relatively small effects on the degree of climate risk faced by rice farmers in the lower Mekong. For the specific climate change scenarios analysed, average yields would increase in Ubon Ratchathani Province in Thailand, resulting in reductions in climate risks. Vulnerability to changes in climate extremes is potentially greater, as suggested by the increases in climate risk scores for our hypothetical scenario of extreme climate.

Our study is an attempt to develop a quantitative assessment of vulnerability that captures the influences of local context. However, it should be viewed only as a pilot study on the subject in the Southeast Asia region, and there are many gaps in the approach that need to be improved. First of all, we did not cover other non-climate stresses, particularly changes in socioeconomic conditions, which are impacting and changing farmers' livelihoods. Future socioeconomic conditions such as the cost of living, market structure and condition, and national and regional development policy could differ greatly from the current situation, especially in the timescales relevant to the study of climate change. These non-climate factors are important drivers that are likely to have a significant influence on the future vulnerability and risk of any social group. Appropriate scenarios of socioeconomic change should therefore be developed and used in future risk analyses.

Impact on rice production was used as the single proxy of climate stress in the analysis of risk and vulnerability. While changes in rice production are critically important for farmers in the lower Mekong, climate change will have other impacts that also need to be considered. Our categorization of households into risk groups is based on our own judgements; future research should attempt to establish empirical thresholds of farmers' tolerance to climate stresses for delineating low, moderate and high risk households. In addition, the cumulative impact on the household of multi-year or consecutive occurrences of extreme climate event should also be taken into consideration.

The issue of accumulated risk and vulnerability condition may be a serious one, especially in the case of farmers in Thailand, whose coping capacity is low. Most of the Thai farmers have limited resources to buffer climate impacts on their on-farm output and sustain themselves until the next cropping season. In addition, most of the households have debt, which, in many cases, is higher than their annual income. The impact from multi-year climate stresses, especially consecutive years of extreme climate events, may drive them into a very difficult economic state. Such cumulative effects can drain away a household's resources for coping and recovery, and surpass thresholds for the sustainability of their livelihood. For example, they may not be able to repay their debts and end up losing their farmland, which is their most important resource, and be forced to change their way of life or social status from that of an independent farmer to that of a hired farm labourer or leave farming permanently to work in another economic sector. Future study might include annual household cash flow analysis over periods of time under different scenarios in order to understand the effects of multi-year climate stresses on household financial conditions.

Only two projections of climate change were used in this analysis, both from the same climate model and both representing cooler climates for Southeast Asia than are projected by most other models. Future analyses should examine a broader range of future climate projections. Our assessment focused on impacts in a single year for the average climate projected for the future and for artificially constructed extreme climates. But in order to understand climate change vulnerability and adaptation of farmers in the lower Mekong region, it may be necessary to consider the impacts of climate variability over a number of years. Analyses are needed of potential changes in the frequency and magnitude of extreme climate events and their cumulative impacts over multiple-year time horizons.

References

Barker, R. and F. Molle (2004) *Evolution of Irrigation in South and Southeast Asia*, Comprehensive Assessment Secretariat, Colombo, Sri Lanka

Boulidam, S. (2005) 'Vulnerability and adaptation of rainfed rice farmer to impact of climate variability in Lahakhok, Sebangnuane Tai, Dong Khamphou and Koudhi Villages of Songkhone District, Savannakhet Province, Lao PDR', Mahidol University, Nakhon Pathom, Thailand

Chinvanno, S., S. Souvannalath, B. Lersupavithnapa, V. Kerdsuk and N. Thuan (2008) 'Strategies for managing climate risks in the Lower Mekong River Basin: A place-based approach', in N. Leary, J. Adejuwon, V. Barros, I. Burton, J. Kulkarni and R. Lasco (eds), *Climate Change and Adaptation*, Earthscan, London, UK

Committee for Planning and Cooperation (2003) *Statistical Yearbook 2002*, National Statistical Center, Vientiane, Lao PDR

Christensen, J. H., B. Hewitson, A. Busuioc, A. Chen, X. Gao, I. Held, R. Jones, R. Koli, W. Kwon, R. Laprise, V. Rueda, L. Mearns, C. Menendez, J. Raisanen, A. Rinke, A. Sarr and P. Whetton (2007) 'Regional Climate Projections', in S. Solomon, D. Qin, M. Manning, Z. Chen, M. C. Marquis, K. Averyt, M. Tignor and H. L. Miller (eds) *Climate Change 2007: The Physical Science Basis*, Contribution of Working Group I to the Fourth Assessment Report of the Intergovernmental Panel on Climate Change, Cambridge University Press, Cambridge, UK and New York, US

Department of Provincial Administration (undated) website fo Department of Provincial Administration, Ministry of Internal Affairs, Thailand: www.dopa.go.th/xstat/p4834_01.html (in Thai)

FAO (2004a) 'FAO statistical yearbook country profile: Thailand', available at www.fao.org/countryprofiles

FAO (2004b) 'FAO statistical yearbook country profile: Lao PDR', available at www.fao.org/countryprofiles

Hoogenboom, G., P. W. Wilkens and G. Y. Tsuji (eds) (1999) DSSAT version 3 v4, University of Hawaii, Honolulu, HI

IPCC (2001a) 'Summary for policymakers', in J. McCarthy, O. Canziani, N. Leary, D. Dokken and K. White (eds) *Climate Change 2001: Impacts, Adaptation and Vulnerability*, Contribution of Working Group II to the Third Assessment Report of the Intergovernmental Panel on Climate Change, Cambridge University Press, Cambridge, UK and New York, US

IPCC (2001b) 'Summary for policymakers', in J. Houghton, Y. Ding, D. Griggs, M. Noguer, P. van der Linden, X. Dai, K. Maskell and C. Johnson (eds) *Climate Change 2001: The Scientific Basis*, Contribution of Working Group I to the Third Assessment Report of the Intergovernmental Panel on Climate Change (IPCC), Cambridge University Press, Cambridge, UK and New York, US

Lim, B., E. Spanger-Siegfried, I. Burton, E. Malone and S. Huq (eds) (2005) *Adaptation Policy Frameworks for Climate Change: Developing Strategies, Policies and Measures*, Cambridge University Press, Cambridge, UK

McGregor, J. L. and M. R. Dix (2001) 'The CSIRO conformal-cubic atmospheric GCM', in P. F. Hodnett (ed) *IUTAM Symposium on Advances in Mathematical Modelling of Atmosphere and Ocean Dynamics*, Kluwer, Dordrecht

Shukla, P. R., S. K. Sharma, N. H. Ravindranath, A. Garg and S. Battacharya (2003) *Climate Change and India: Vulnerability Assessment and Adaptation*, University Press, India

Snidvongs, A. (2006) *Vulnerability to Climate Change Related Water Resource Changes and Extreme Hydrological Events in Southeast Asia*, Final Report of AIACC Project no AS07, International START Secretariat, Washington, DC, US, www.aiaccproject.org

Ubon Ratchathani Province Administration (undated) Ubon Ratchathani Province Administration website: www.ubonratchathani.go.th/

UNESCAP (undated) 'Annual core indicators', United Nations Economic and Social Commission for Asia and the Pacific (UNESCAP), available at http://unescap.org/stat/data/main/datatable.aspx

Wang, Y., L. R. Leung, J. L. McGregor, D. Lee, W. Wang, Y. Ding and F. Kimura (2004) 'Regional climate modeling: Progress, challenges, prospects', *Journal of Meteorological Society of Japan*, volume 82, pp1599–1628

World Bank (2007) 'Country data profiles', available at www.worldbank.org/

17

Vulnerability of Sri Lankan
Tea Plantations to Climate Change

*Janaka Ratnasiri, Aruliah Anandacoomaraswamy,
Madawala Wijeratne, Senaka Basnayake, Asoka Jayakody
and Lalith Amarathunga*

Introduction

Sri Lanka is an island state located to the southeast of the Indian sub-continent. It is the third largest tea producer in the world, after India and China, and ranks first as an exporter. Tea plantations in Sri Lanka currently cover a land area of approximately 210,000ha, which is about 3.1 per cent of the total land area or 12 per cent of the cultivable land of the country, and stretch from the lowlands below 50m in elevation to the highlands above 2000m in elevation.

Tea was initially introduced to Sri Lanka in 1867 by British companies who established large plantations by clearing virgin forest in the central hill country. By the turn of the century, more than 120,000ha had been brought under tea cultivation, which doubled to 240,000ha by 1965. In the 1960s, the Government of Sri Lanka nationalized all foreign-owned plantations, and in the early 1990s, the management of plantations was handed back to the private sector. These changes in ownership and management over the years have also significantly impacted the productivity of the industry.

Despite these changing circumstances within the industry, export of tea remains one of the key foreign exchange sources of the country. It is the second highest net foreign exchange earning industry on the island, second only to the clothing industry. During 2000–2004, the total foreign exchange earning of the country was in the range 420–584 billion rupees (US$5.25–5.58 billion), of which the tea industry alone contributed 53–75 billion rupees (US$664–716 million) or about 13 per cent (CBSL, 2005). Tea plantations also provide livelihoods for over 1 million people in Sri Lanka.

The tea crop is very sensitive to climatic and other environmental factors (Devanathan, 1975; Wijeratne and Fordham, 1996) and has specific requirements of rainfall, humidity and soil conditions. Any sustained changes in any of these conditions could adversely affect the yield and thus cause a significant drop in national revenue. This would also affect the livelihoods of the many involved in various aspects of tea growing, processing and other allied operations. Therefore an understanding of the vulnerability of this economically important crop to environmental stressors would serve as an important tool for stakeholders and decision makers in Sri Lanka.

One of the biggest concerns for crop production presently is the environmental threat of future climate change whose specific impacts on individual crops are still not exactly clear. Climate change could have important implications for the tea producing sector in Sri Lanka, depending on the nature of the impacts and the sector's capacity to adapt. An assessment of the vulnerability of tea production in Sri Lanka to the impacts of a changing climate was therefore undertaken in order to generate a knowledge base that can inform current understanding of the strengths and weaknesses of this sector with respect to its ability to cope. A crop simulation model was developed to study the specific impacts of climate change on tea production in the different tea growing regions of Sri Lanka, and a vulnerability matrix was developed for the assessment of regional and national vulnerability. The findings of this study are discussed in the sections that follow.

Current Climate and Future Climate Scenarios for Sri Lanka

Current climate

Sri Lanka has a hot and humid tropical climate except in the central uplands. Based on data on daily temperature observations made at 19 meteorological stations for the 30-year period 1961–1990, the mean annual temperature in the lowlands is 27.5°C, while that in the highlands is 18.0°C. A significant feature of Sri Lanka's mean monthly temperature is its small seasonal variation, which rarely exceeds 3°C at any location, while the diurnal temperature range may vary between 5 and 10°C depending on the location and the season (DCS, 2003).

According to past studies on long-term temperature variations carried out using linear regression analyses, the mean surface temperature in Sri Lanka increased during the 30-year period 1961–1990 at a rate of 0.016°C per year (Chandrapala, 1996). The annual mean maximum surface temperatures have shown increasing trends for almost all stations examined, with the maximum rate of increase 0.021°C per year at Puttalam, a station midway along the west coast. The night-time annual mean minimum surface temperatures have also shown increasing trends, with a maximum rate of increase reported as 0.02°C per year at Nuwara-Eliya, the highest central hill station.

When 30-year (1961–1990) averaged values of temperature were interpolated and mapped into island-wide patterns, incorporating variation in elevation (using a software package, ANUSPLINE, developed by the Australian National University (Hutchinson, 1989)), the baseline annual mean temperature distribution was obtained as shown in Figure 17.1.

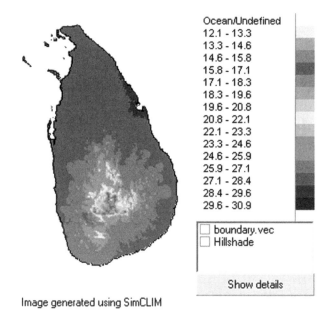

Ocean/Undefined
12.1 - 13.3
13.3 - 14.6
14.6 - 15.8
15.8 - 17.1
17.1 - 18.3
18.3 - 19.6
19.6 - 20.8
20.8 - 22.1
22.1 - 23.3
23.3 - 24.6
24.6 - 25.9
25.9 - 27.1
27.1 - 28.4
28.4 - 29.6
29.6 - 30.9

☐ boundary.vec
☐ Hillshade

Show details

Image generated using SimCLIM

Figure 17.1 *Baseline temperature distribution*

The average annual rainfall in Sri Lanka is 1861mm (1961–1990 data), pre-dominantly from the two monsoonal wind patterns: the southwest monsoon (SWM) period from May to September, experienced mostly in the southwestern part of the country; and the northeast monsoon (NEM) period from December to February, experienced mostly in the northeastern and eastern parts of the country. There is a wide variation in rainfall across the country, with mean annual rainfall received in certain parts of the western slopes of the hill country exceeding 5000mm, while that in the northeastern coastal area is less than 100mm. Based on the rainfall patterns, Sri Lanka has traditionally been divided into 3 climatic zones: the wet zone, covering roughly the south-west quadrant, receives an annual rainfall more than 2500mm, mostly from the SWM; the dry zone, covering the other three quadrants, receives less than 1750mm, mostly from the NEM; and the intermediate zone receives rainfall in the range 1750–2500mm. Figure 17.2 shows the baseline annual rainfall distri-bution determined for the 30 year period 1961–1990 derived using the ANUSPLINE software.

When rainfall variations are analysed, it is found that the average annual rainfall over Sri Lanka for the 30-year period 1961–1990, 1861mm, was about 7 per cent less than that during 1931–1960. Further, the rates of decrease are observed to be higher in the wet regions than in the intermediate regions. The NEM rainfall over Sri Lanka decreased between the periods 1931–1960 and 1961–1990, also with increasing variability, while the SWM rainfall did not show any significant change between the two periods.

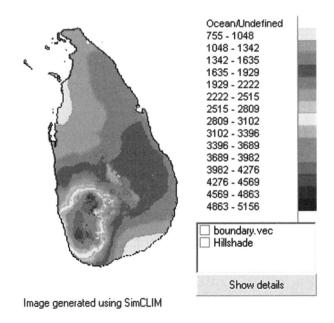

Ocean/Undefined
755 - 1048
1048 - 1342
1342 - 1635
1635 - 1929
1929 - 2222
2222 - 2515
2515 - 2809
2809 - 3102
3102 - 3396
3396 - 3689
3689 - 3982
3982 - 4276
4276 - 4569
4569 - 4863
4863 - 5156

☐ boundary.vec
☐ Hillshade

Show details

Image generated using SimCLIM

Figure 17.2 *Baseline rainfall distribution (mean of 1961–1990)*

Future climate scenarios

Future climate scenarios for Sri Lanka were determined on the basis of region-
al climate projections developed using several global circulation models
(GCMs) (Cubasch et al, 2001) and with reference to the emission scenarios
developed by the Intergovernmental Panel on Climate Change (IPCC) in its
Special Report on Emission Scenarios (SRES) (Nakicenovic and Swart, 2000).
Software developed by the International Global Change Institute (IGCI) at the
University of Waikato, New Zealand, was used to downscale the GCM results
to locations within the country using an interpolation technique (Warrick et al,
1996).

The GCM results considered for our analysis were the outputs of HadCM3
(UK), CSIRO (Australia) and CGCM (Canada) (McAvaney, 2001). The
HadCM3 gives the worst scenario for temperature rise, while CGCM gives the
worst scenario for rainfall. These GCMs results were found to be closely comparable to the observed baseline data for the 1961–90 period, especially with
regard to temperature. The SRES emissions scenarios used were those representing the highest emissions (A1FI), median emissions (A2) and the lowest
emissions (B1).

For the mid-2100 year, the highest projected mean temperature rise, of
about 2.7°C, was obtained with the HadCM3/A1FI scenario, while the lowest,

about 1.0°C, was obtained with the CGCM/B1 scenario. Projections made with all other scenarios show increases of intermediate magnitude, as shown in Table 17.1.

Table 17.1 *Projected change in mean temperature under different emission scenarios at mid-2100*

Emission Scenario	Range in Temperature rise (°C) at mid-2100 within Sri Lanka			
	HadCM3	CSIRO	CGCM	Mean
A1FI	2.5–3.0	2.2–2.4	2.0–2.2	2.38
A2	2.1–2.5	1.9–2.0	1.7–1.8	2.00
B1	1.1–1.4	1.0–1.1	0.9–1.0	1.08

The range of values indicated for a given scenario is the variation within the country as interpolated by IGCI software. These projections are slightly lower than those in the IPCC Data Distribution Centre maps for the zone covering Sri Lanka (see IPPC-DDC, undated). The future projected temperature distributions applicable under any emission scenario are obtained by adding the corresponding changes to the baseline data. The distribution of the increased temperature corresponding to the HadCM3/A1FI scenario for mid-2100 is shown in Figure 17.3.

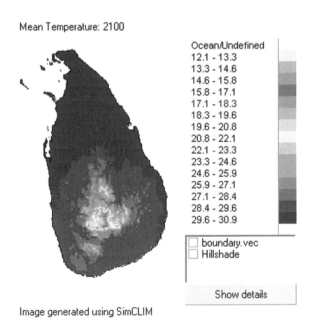

Figure 17.3 *Increased mean temperature during mid-2100 corresponding to HadCM3/A1FI scenario*

Rainfall change projections show both increases and decreases with different GCMs relative to baseline values. Both the HadCM3 and CSIRO models project increasing rainfall while the CGCM projects decreasing rainfall. The HadCM3 projects an increase in the range 0–476mm above the baseline rainfall for the A1FI scenario for June–August 2100. The CGCM projects a decrease in rainfall in the range 190–6mm for the A1FI scenario for the same period. The projected changes in rainfall for the three GCMs and the three emission scenarios are given in Table 17.2. The future rainfall in absolute terms for a given scenario is obtained by adding the corresponding changes to the baseline values. The rainfall scenario projected by the HadCM3/A2 emission scenario for June–August 2100 is shown in Figure 17.4.

Table 17.2 *Projected change in rainfall under different emission scenarios for June, July and August 2100*

| Emission Scenario | Range in Temperature rise (°C) at mid-2100 within Sri Lanka | | |
	HadCM3	CSIRO	CGCM
A1FI	0 to 476	2 to 157	−190 to −6
A2	0 to 403	2 to 133	−161 to −5
B1	0 to 215	1 to 71	−86 to 3

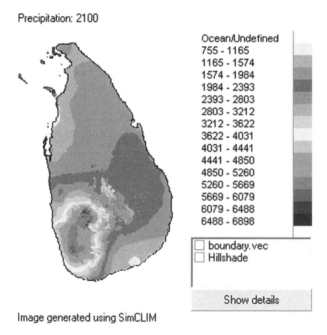

Figure 17.4 *Increased precipitation during mid-2100 corresponding to HadCM3/A1FI scenario*

Climate and Tea Production

Sri Lanka is divided into 24 agro-ecological regions (AERs), based on rainfall, annual rainfall distribution, elevation, soils and landforms (Panabokke, 1997), as shown in Table 17.3. The elevation component is, in turn, divided into three ranges – low-country (LC) (<300m), mid-country (MC) (300–900m) and up-country (UC) (>900m). Of the 24 agro-ecological regions, only 11 are suitable for tea cultivation (Watson, 1986). Their distribution within the country is shown in Figure 17.5. Of the three climate zones in Sri Lanka (the wet zone, dry zone and intermediate zone described in the previous section), the wet zone and a substantial portion of the intermediate zone are suitable for tea cultivation. No tea is grown in the dry zone or low-country intermediate zone.

Table 17.3 *Agro-ecological regions where tea is grown and their characteristics*

Elevation Range (amsl)	Description	Mean Temp (°C) (1961–1990)	Climate Zone	
			Wet Zone	Intermediate Zone
0–300m	Low-country	27.3	Wet zone low-country (WL)	No tea grown
300–900m	Mid-country	24.6	Wet zone mid-country (WM)	Intermediate zone mid-country (IM)
>900m	Up-country	18.1	Wet zone up-country (WU)	Intermediate zone up-country (IU)

Figure 17.5 *Agro-ecological regions where tea is cultivated*

Note: See Table 17.3 for explanation of codes.

The tea industry uses its own classification of elevation ranges, different from those used in the classification of agro-ecological regions. The industry classifications for tea produced are low-grown (<600m), mid-grown (600–1200m) and high-grown (>1200m). Generally, the traditional tea plantations owned by large companies with resident labour produce mid- and high-grown tea. Low-grown tea is mostly produced by smallholders who have recently taken up tea cultivation. Mid-grown tea is produced by both estates and smallholders. Here we use the term 'region' to express division of elevations according to agro-ecological regions and the term 'category' to express division of elevations as per industry classification.

Since the early 1990s, the extent of high- and mid-grown tea estates has declined while the extent of low-grown estates has increased. This can be attributed to the government's decision in 1992 to hand over the management of government-owned plantation estates to the private sector while at the same time increasing financial assistance to smallholders for investing in new plantations. The tea-land survey of 1994 conducted by the Tea Small Holdings Development Authority shows that there were 206,652 smallholdings (below 20ha), covering a total area of 82,918ha. The average size of the smallholdings is thus 0.40ha. A survey carried out by the Census and Statistics Department in 2002 has shown that the area under estate plantations decreased from 168,627ha in 1982 to 118,754ha in 2002 – a decrease of 49,673ha or 29 per cent (DCS, 2004). This decrease is partly due to fragmentation of larger estates into smaller units and partly due to abandonment of unproductive plantations. Concurrently there has also been a significant increase in low-grown tea production since the early 1990s, while the production of the high-grown and mid-grown categories has remained the same.

Annual production and yield

In order to evaluate yield on a regional basis and determine the effect of the most influential climatic factors (rainfall and temperature), yield data and meteorological data were collected for selected tea estates. Only estates with time series monthly yield and weather data for a period of more than 20 years and tea plants of an age below 20 years were selected. The average climatic factors and yield data for the selected stations are shown in Table 17.4. For production data,[1] the period 1996–2005 was selected; production in each of the three elevation categories is shown in Table 17.5. The mean productions of 161.06kt, 53.78kt and 80.40kt for the low-, mid- and high-grown categories respectively were used as the baseline data for determining future projections under various climate change scenarios.

Effect of temperature on yield

The correlation between temperature and productivity in each agro-ecological region was less evident than that between rainfall and productivity. Hence all data were pooled and the relationship between temperature and productivity was established. Dry months were excluded in this analysis in order to elimi-

Table 17.4 *Climate and yield data at four sites representing four agro-ecological regions*

Location	Maximum (°C)	Minimum (°C)	Rainfall (mm)	Yield kg/ha/yr
Ratnapura (WL)	32.0	22.9	3617	2489
Kandy (WM)	29.0	20.2	1863	2217
NuwalaEliya(WU)	20.5	11.5	1907	2454
Badulla (IU)	28.7	18.5	1777	2651

Table 17.5 *Annual (baseline) production of made tea during 1996–2005*

Year	High-grown	Mid-grown	Low-grown	Total
	\multicolumn{4}{c}{Annual Production (tonnes)}			
1996	72,447	48,211	138,312	258,970
1997	83,999	57,255	136,174	277,428
1998	77,638	52,542	150,494	280,674
1999	81,471	53,660	149,060	284,191
2000	83,867	56,492	166,430	306,789
2001	83,982	56,578	166,571	307,131
2002	75,342	53,943	169,334	298,619
2003	87,632	54,363	168,149	310,144
2004	82,137	54,371	184,270	320,778
2005	75,525	50,391	181,826	307,742
Mean	80,404	53,781	161,062	295,247
Percentage	27.2	18.2	54.6	100.0

Source: SLTB (2005).

nate the effect of moisture stress on productivity. Analysis of pooled data for all regions shows an increasing trend in productivity with rising temperature up to about 22°C, above which productivity dropped with increasing temperature as shown in Figure 17.6.

Similar results have been observed in controlled experiments carried out under laboratory conditions (Wijeratne and Fordhum, 1996). It can therefore be expected that in the low-country, where the ambient temperature is above 22°C a drop in productivity is likely, while in the up-country, where the temperature is below this value, an increase is likely with rising temperatures. The equation below, which explains this relationship, was established taking temperature and yield during wet weather when there is no moisture stress. Thus the rainfall effect was removed to get the temperature response.

$$Y = -508+63.7\ T - 1.46T^2,$$

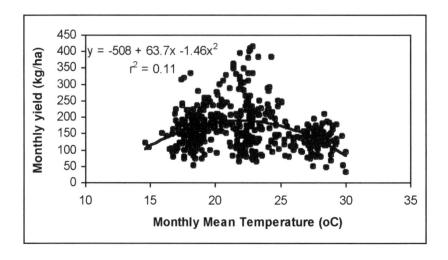

Figure 17.6 *Variation of monthly yield with ambient temperature with optimum value at 22°C*

Source: STLB (2005).

where, Y = yield in kg of made tea/ha/month and T = temperature in °C. ('Made tea' refers to processed tea available in the market as loose tea; it is also referred to as 'black tea'. To produce 1 kilogram of made tea, around 4 kilograms of green leaves are generally needed. Statistics usually give made tea values rather than green leaves'.)

Effect of rainfall on yield

The rainfall effect was determined by considering only the relatively dry months. The effect of rainfall on the productivity of tea lands was studied by scatter diagrams and regression analyses with a one-month lag period, thus comparing yield with the rainfall of the previous month. The optimum rainfall for each region was first established using curvilinear relationships. The rate of reduction in yield expressed in kg/ha per millimetre loss of rainfall below optimum was next estimated by linear regression analysis. Analysis of productivity with rainfall showed that a 1 millimetre change in rainfall could change productivity by 0.3–0.8kg of made tea per ha during a dry month. The highest positive response to rainfall was seen in the mid-country intermediate zone, where soil fertility and the amount of solar radiation were high compared to other regions. The lowest response, again positive, was seen in the low-country wet zone with less fertile soil. The optimum rainfall and the gradient values of the variation of yield with rainfall for each of five climate zones are given in Table 17.6. The variation observed in one zone – intermediate up-country – is shown in Figure 17.7.

Table 17.6 *Effect of rainfall on productivity of tea lands*

Agro-ecological zone	Optimum rainfall (mm)	Productivity change (kg (made tea)/mm rain)
Up-country wet zone	223±38	0.55±0.07
Up-country intermediate zone	303±34	0.39±0.03
Mid-country wet zone	417±49	0.36±0.06
Mid-country intermediate zone	227±10	0.81±0.11
Low-country wet zone	350±20	0.29±0.03

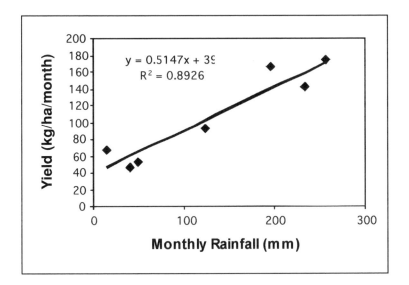

Figure 17.7 *Variation of yield with rainfall up to optimum rainfall for the intermediate up-country region*

Effect of drought on yield

In 1992 a severe drought was experienced in many parts of the country and data from this year were used to assess the effect of drought on tea production. Data collected from different tea growing regions for this year show that the yield loss due to drought in 1992 was in the range of 14–28 per cent compared to the previous year. The total loss was estimated to be worth about US$70 million. The drought was particularly severe in the intermediate up-country region and relatively mild in the intermediate mid country region in comparison to other regions (Figure 17.8). Generally, drought effects are more pronounced in the low- and mid-country tea growing regions due to the poor soil conditions resulting from the absence of proper conservation measures and the adoption of ecologically unsound practices in tea lands. The degree of drought impact thus varies between different tea growing regions.

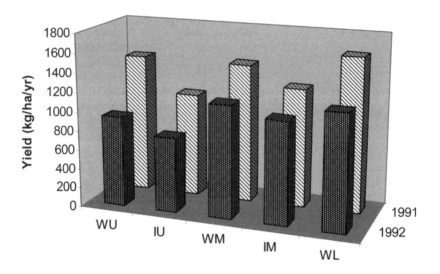

Figure 17.8 *Variation of annual yield in different agro-ecological regions in the drought year (1992) and the previous year*

Yield response to CO_2 elevation

The growth rate of mature tea bushes planted in a CO_2-enriched enclosure with CO_2 concentration maintained at 550±50ppm was compared with that of bushes planted in a control enclosure maintained at ambient CO_2 level. This control enclosure had four sides closed and the top open. These trials were conducted at both up-country and low-country locations. It was observed that the tea yield increased with the enhancement of CO_2 levels at both elevations, by 33 per cent at the low elevation and 37 per cent at the high elevation. The increase in yield with raised CO_2 was attributed to increases in shoot density, growth rate, shoot weight, net photosynthesis rate and enhanced water-use efficiency, factors that are also dependent on the ambient temperature (Wijeratne, 2001).

Climate Change and Tea Production

A simple empirical simulation model incorporating the effects of temperature, rainfall, radiation, CO_2 and soil organic carbon was developed to quantitatively describe climate impacts on tea yield. The model was based on similar work carried out at the Indian Agricultural Research Institute (Kalra and Aggarwal, 1996). The total biomass production was considered to be a function of leaf area index (LAI) and radiation use efficiency (RUE) of canopy, as well as of radiation level (Monteith, 1977). Solar radiation was determined based on maximum and minimum temperatures using an empirical relationship (Kalra, personal communication, 2004). Nutrient levels were not considered limiting as the growers practise recommended fertilizer applications which ensure that nutrients will be supplied adequately. Since there is no data on how soil organic carbon or plant population are affected by climate change, a crop model incorporating only rainfall, temperature and CO_2 was used to predict tea yield under varying climatic conditions for a given set of soil conditions and cultivars.

In developing the model, it was assumed that there are 12,000 tea bushes per hectare and that a mature tea bush at its maximum productivity has about 2kg of above ground biomass. Therefore, the initial biomass (above ground) was taken as 24000kg/ha. The radiation use efficiency value for tea was taken to be 0.3gMJ^{-1} of total radiation (Carr and Stephens, 1992) and the leaf area index for a healthy tea bush at its maximum productivity was taken to be 5. Of the total carbohydrates produced, it is assumed that 60 per cent is lost through respiration, about 20 per cent is lost through harvesting and only the remaining 20 per cent accumulates as biomass in the bush (Barbora and Barua, 1988; Tanton, 1992; Magambo et al, 1988). The basic flow chart of the model is shown in Figure 17.9. The crop model was linked to the IGCI software, enabling the determination of changes in crop yield for different elevations corresponding to future climate scenarios.

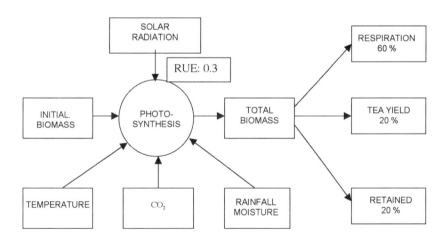

Figure 17.9 *Basic flow chart of the crop simulation model*

The model runs on monthly data, generating accumulated yield per month (kg/ha/month), which can be summed up to obtain total annual yield in kg/ha/yr. The crop model was validated under varying field conditions in the different agro-ecological regions. It was found that the model can account for 70–96 per cent of yield variations, pointing to the fact that further improvements are possible by including other ecological (for example, soil) and plant (variety) factors influencing tea yield.

The variation of tea yield under conditions of increased temperature and higher CO_2 levels at one location in the wet zone mid-country region, as estimated by the crop model, is shown in Figure 17.10. At this location, a temperature rise beyond the optimum temperature of 22°C was found to reduce the tea yield, while a CO_2 rise enhanced it. Under the combined effect yield increased, but by less than that due to the CO_2 effect alone due to the negative impact of temperature rise.

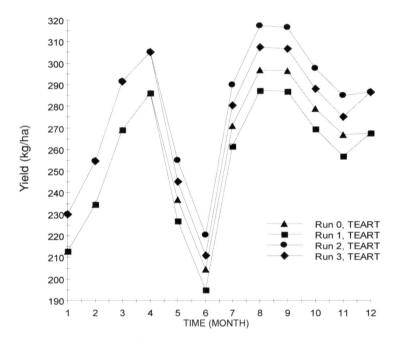

Figure 17.10 *Variation of tea yield in wet zone mid-country estimated by the tea crop model with change of climatic conditions*

Note: Run 0: present climate; Run 1: temperature rise by 1°C only; Run 2: 400ppm CO_2 only; Run 3: temperature rise by 1°C and 400ppm CO_2. 1–12 denote months from January to December.

The projected yield changes for the three GCMs and emission scenarios considered are shown in Table 17.7. According to this analysis, yields are likely to fall in the low-country, where the present ambient temperature is higher than the critical value of 22°C. In the mid- and up-country regions, the yield is also expected to reduce by 2100 since by then the temperature in these regions is also projected to exceed this critical value (Figure 17.11). The reductions expected by 2100 are in the ranges of 19–35 per cent, 9–17 per cent and 0.9–6 per cent, for the low-, mid- and up-country regions respectively, with the high emission scenario HadCM3/A1FI projecting the high end of the ranges and

Table 17.7 *Projected yield changes under different climate change scenarios*

Model/Emission Scenario	Projected Yield Change (%)								
	Low-Country			Mid-Country			Up-Country		
	2025	2050	2100	2025	2050	2100	2025	2050	2100
HadCM3+A1FI	−0.32	−5.66	−34.67	−0.63	−1.94	−16.78	1.92	3.75	−6.13
HadCM3+A2	0.04	−3.66	−29.33	−0.68	−1.44	−15.02	1.69	3.51	−4.18
HadCM3+B1	−0.24	−2.81	−19.37	−0.77	−1.26	−11.05	1.89	3.25	−2.35
CGCM+A1FI	−2.09	−7.03	−31.14	0.32	0.45	−13.17	0.23	3.02	−3.17
CGCM+A2	−1.73	−5.14	−30.57	0.27	0.50	−11.41	−0.07	2.25	−2.29
CGCM+B1	−2.05	−4.38	−18.80	0.32	0.50	−8.84	−0.07	1.82	−0.83
CSIRO +A1FI	1.85	−3.54	−33.95	0.90	1.31	−15.47	2.39	4.97	−6.13
CSIRO +A2	2.25	−1.49	−30.57	0.81	1.35	−13.04	2.09	4.38	−4.18
CSIRO +B1	1.97	−0.68	−20.41	0.90	1.26	−9.70	2.35	3.98	−0.93

the low emission scenario CGCM/B1 producing the low end. In all three regions, yield changes are observed to be relatively small up to 2050 and could be either positive or negative depending on the time frame and scenario adopted. By 2050, the highest increase of 5 per cent is predicted for the up-country using the CSIRO/A1FI scenario while the highest reduction of 7 per cent is predicted for the low-country under the CGCM/A1FI scenario.

The majority of tea plantations appear to be adversely affected by rising temperatures. This is mainly because the present mean temperatures in tea growing regions in the wet zone low-country, wet zone mid-country, intermediate zone mid-country and intermediate zone up-country are above the optimum temperature for high productivity (22°C). Hence beneficial effects of temperature rise can be expected only in the wet-zone up-country region. Given that more than 50 per cent of national production comes from the wet zone low-country and wet zone mid-country regions and this tea also fetches a higher price on the world market, the implications for revenue could be significant.

Impact on national production and revenue

The projected yield obtained from the crop model as biomass accumulated per ha per year for each elevation region can be used to determine total production by multiplying this quantity by the corresponding area of plantation for a particular region. However, given that accurate records of productive plantation areas are not available, future projections were instead made using production values. Plantation areas are not expected to change significantly due to a government freeze on the further expansion of tea cultivation, largely because of declining market prices, and also due to a control on encroachment of forested land by smallholder tea cultivators. The production values in the low-, mid- and high-country regions for 2025, 2050 and 2100 were obtained using the baseline production values computed from 1996–2005 data (Table 17.5) and the percentage regional yield changes corresponding to different

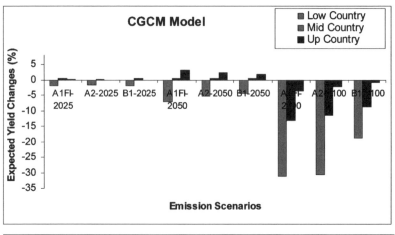

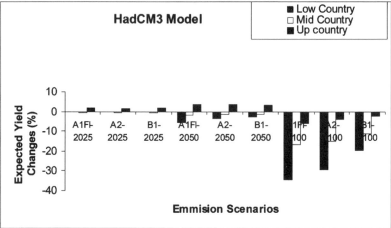

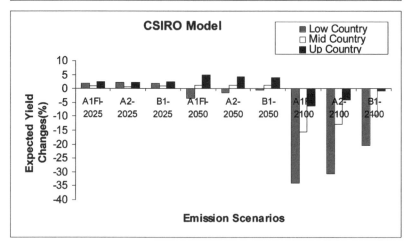

Figure 17.11 *Percentage yield change expected with respect to baseline values for 2025, 2050 and 2100 and emission scenarios A1FI, A2 and B1 under the three GCMs in low-, mid- and up-country regions*

emission scenarios and climate models (Table 17.7). It is assumed that the yield changes based on elevation regions would also apply to the elevation categories for which production data are available. The new regional production values corresponding to a given time and climate scenario were then summed up to obtain the national production values under similar conditions, with their deviations from the baseline values expressed as percentages (Table 17.8).

Table 17.8 *National projected production changes under different models and climate change scenarios*

GCM/Emission Scenario	National production of made tea (kt per annum)					
	2025		2050		2100	
Baseline	295.24	% change	295.24	% change	295.24	% change
HadCM3+A1FI	295.93	0.23	288.10	−2.42	225.45	−23.64
HadCM3+A2	296.30	0.36	291.39	−1.30	236.56	−19.87
HadCM3+B1	295.96	0.24	292.65	−0.88	256.21	−13.22
CGCM+A1FI	292.23	−1.02	286.59	−2.93	235.45	−20.25
CGCM+A2	292.54	−0.91	289.04	−2.10	238.03	−19.38
CGCM+B1	292.05	−1.08	289.92	−1.80	259.54	−12.09
CSIRO +A1FI	300.63	1.82	294.24	−0.34	227.31	−23.01
CSIRO +A2	300.98	1.94	297.09	0.63	235.63	−20.19
CSIRO +B1	300.79	1.88	298.02	0.94	256.40	−13.15

A very significant finding is that for both 2025 and 2050, the expected changes in national production are relatively small for all scenarios and models, at less than ±3 per cent, while the changes expected for 2100 would be in the range −12 per cent to −23 per cent, depending on the scenario and the model. A 3 per cent variation is of the same order of magnitude as that due natural climatic variability, land fragmentation, loss of fertility and various socioeconomic factors. When the expected temperature rise is small and rainfall increases (under HadCM3 and CSIRO models), the overall production change is positive, while with the CGCM model, in which rainfall shows a decrease, there is a negative trend. The positive effects of increasing CO_2 concentration and the increasing rainfall more than compensate for the negative effects of increasing temperature. For 2100, however, when the temperature rise exceeds the critical temperature of 22°C for all three regions, the overall effect overrides the positive effects of the CO_2 increase and rainfall increase and causes a significant reduction in production under all scenarios and models.

Assuming that all other factors remain unchanged, the impacts of climate change on tea production could bring about a reduction in national revenue by approximately 2–4 per cent by 2100. This amount represents the direct loss of revenue from exports, but there could be additional economic losses due to loss of employment for estate workers and the loss of auxiliary industries and services that are associated with various aspects of tea production and processing prior to export.

Vulnerability Assessment

Vulnerability in this case is considered to be the difference between the degree of impact and the degree of adaptive capacity; it will thus vary between different elevation regions (where the impacts differ) and for different owners (whose adaptive capacities differ). Based on the results obtained for changes in yield for the different regions using different models and scenarios (Table 17.7), it can be determined that yield reductions of 20–35 per cent, 9–17 per cent and 1–6 per cent are likely for the low-, mid- and up-country regions respectively by 2100, the ranges indicating the variability due to different models and scenarios. The mean impacts would then be –28 per cent, –13 per cent and –3.5 per cent for low-, mid- and up-country respectively, and the relative impacts would thus be 8, 4 and 1.

In order to assess the coping capacity of planters, which depends on the ownership of land, information on tea land ownership was extracted from the 2002 survey by the Census and Statistics Department (DCS, 2004). Landholdings of over 20 acres (8 hectares) fall into the category of estates. Most owners of land have holdings of under about 2 acres and cultivate tea in their home gardens, with very little capital and depending mostly on government subsidies. They also usually lack resources to implement adaptation measures in response to adverse climate conditions and hence their adaptive capacity is considered to be zero. The smallholders with over 2 acre landholdings have relatively higher incomes and a better capacity to adapt in comparison to those with less than 2 acres, and hence they are assigned a capacity index of 1. Among the estate holdings, there are wide disparities in size and ownership. There are the relatively recent estate holdings of less than 100 acres, developed using capital raised from banks and depending on government subsidies for their running expenses. These are located mostly in the low-country and are assigned an index of 2. Then there are the estates, several hundred acres in extent, which are the successors to the British-owned companies and have adequate financial resources. These exist in the mid- and up-country and are assigned the highest adaptive capacity index of 3.

Using the above information on yield impacts and adaptive capacity indices, a vulnerability matrix was constructed to determine vulnerability of the various classes of landholders. In order to place the impact index in the same range as the adaptive capacity index, the relative impacts derived earlier are normalized to be in the range 0.5–4, with the index 4 assigned to low-country, 2 to mid-country and 0.5 to up-country. The vulnerability index, computed as the difference between the impact index and the adaptive capacity index, shows that the vulnerability of low-country holdings, both smallholdings and estates, is high, with the index lying between –3 and –4. The vulnerability of mid-country smallholdings for both categories (less than and greater than 2 acres), on the other hand, is low, and mid-country estates show no vulnerability at all. In the up-country scenario, the estates and larger smallholdings show a positive response, which indicates a higher than necessary adaptive capacity, while the smallholdings below 2 acres show low vulnerability (Table 17.9).

Table 17.9 *Matrix of indices of impact, adaptive capacity and vulnerability vs. ownership*

Elevation Region	Ownership	Impact Index	Adaptive Capacity Index	Vulnerability Index	Vulnerability Rank
Low-country	EH	−4	2	−2	Low (L)
	SH<2A	−4	0	−4	High (H)
	SH>2A	−4	1	−3	High (H)
Mid-country	EH	−2	3	1	Nil
	SH<2A	−2	0	−2	Low (L)
	SH>2A	−2	1	−1	Low (L)
Up-country	EH	−0.5	3	2.5	Positive
	SH<2A	−0.5	0	−0.5	Low (L)
	SH>2A	−0.5	1	0.5	Positive

Note: EH: estate holding; SH: smallholding; 2A: 2 acres

The vulnerability of individual holdings would, in turn, impact the national economy depending on their individual contribution to national production. Since production is generally dependent on the size of the landholding, this was used as the contributory factor. Using the landholding sizes for each of the ownership categories described above (Table 17.9), the size index for each category was obtained by dividing the landholding sizes by 20,000 and rounding off to the first decimal (Table 17.10). The vulnerability of the entire area under each ownership category is then obtained by multiplying the individual vulnerability by the size index and this gives the regional vulnerability. The mean for the three regions is then taken as the national vulnerability (Table 17.10).

Table 17.10 *Vulnerability of tea plantations at regional/national level*

Elevation Region	Ownership	Size (Acres)	Size Index	Individual Holding Vulnerability	Regional/ National Vulnerability	Vulnerability Rank
Low-country	EH	30,147	1.5	−2	−3	High
	SH<2A	65,668	3.3	−4	−13	Ex-High
	SH>2A	40,085	2.0	−3	−6	V-High
Mid-country	EH	85,905	4.3	1	4	Positive
	SH<2A	39,230	2.0	−2	−4	High
	SH>2A	23,947	1.2	−1	−1	Low
Up-country	EH	135,191	6.7	2.5	16	Positive
	SH<2A	17,440	0.9	−0.5	−0.5	Low
	SH>2A	10,646	0.5	0.5	0.3	Positive
National		448,259			−0.8	Low

The contribution to the regional vulnerability is extremely high from low-country smallholders with landholdings below 2 acres, while that from larger smallholders (above 2 acres) is very high. The contributions from low-country estates and mid-country smallholders with landholdings of below 2 acres are also both high. The mid-country larger smallholders (above 2 acres) as well as the up-country smallholders with landholdings below 2 acres show low vulnerability. The up-country larger smallholders show a marginal adaptation capacity to counteract the adverse impacts from climate change. Not surprisingly, the mid-country and up-country estates have more than the required capacity to mitigate any adverse impacts. The country's tea sector as a whole shows low vulnerability to climate change because of the high positive contribution from the large up-country estates.

Discussion and Conclusion

In terms of future climate change in Sri Lanka, the projected outputs of three GCMs for three emissions scenarios for the period up to 2100 indicate an increase in temperature with mean increases in the range 1.0–2.4°C for all cases considered. Rainfall, on the other hand, shows different trends under different GCMs. The HadCM3 and CSIRO models project increases in rainfall while the CGCM model projects decreases. The extent of change varies with the emission scenario, with A1FI producing the highest changes and B1 producing the lowest changes. Temperature and precipitation are critical factors in tea production and our vulnerability analysis suggests a varying range of vulnerability depending on the size and location of the tea estate. Tea production in the low-country displays the highest vulnerability and could suffer a decline in productivity of up to 35 per cent by 2100 according to the HadCM3/A1FI emission scenario or somewhat lower declines of up to 19 per cent according to other scenarios. In contrast, the corresponding decreases for up-country are in the range 6–1 per cent. When impact indices for the different regions are compared it can be observed that for shorter time frames, up-country plantations in fact show increases in yields because the ambient temperature there is still less than the critical temperature of 22°C, unlike in the low-country, where it has already been exceeded.

Similarly, when adaptive capacity and vulnerability indices are considered, it is the smallholders with landholdings below 2 acres in the low-country that would display the highest vulnerability, in contrast to the estate owners in the up-country, who display greater than the required adaptive capacity to deal with any adverse impacts of climate change. Climate change impacts would thus have important socioeconomic implications, especially in the low-country, by affecting the livelihoods of smallholders, who have few or no capital assets. In turn, the viability of industries and businesses associated with various aspects of tea production and processing could also be impacted. This could also have socioeconomic implications, especially for the low income groups associated directly or indirectly with this sector.

In terms of climate change impacts on the national economy, a reduction in foreign exchange revenue by about 2–4 per cent by 2100 is likely due to the direct loss of revenue from tea exports. However, the actual loss of revenue would probably be higher due to the losses incurred by allied industries and businesses that support the tea production sector. It would therefore be in the national interest for the government to intervene by providing financial assistance to planters with low adaptive capacity in highly vulnerable areas so that they are able to implement the necessary adaptation measures. Several options, such as irrigation, fertilization, application of potassium sulphate and management of shade, have been suggested. The evaluation of potential adaptation options in order to determine the most appropriate strategies for the management of the tea production sector in Sri Lanka under a changed climate is therefore an important subject for future studies.

Note

1   Land production data are more accurate than land extent data. This is because the tea produced across the country is traded through the weekly auctions and statistics of quantities traded are maintained both by elevation category and product type (bulk tea, tea packets, teabags, green tea and instant tea) by the Sri Lanka Tea Board (SLTB, 2005).

References

Barbora A. C. and D. N. Barua (1988) 'Respiratory losses and partitioning of assimilates in tea bushes (*Camellia sinensis* L.) under plucking', *Two and a Bud*, vol 35, pp75–82

Carr, M. K. V. and W. Stephens (1992) 'Climate, weather and the yield of tea', in K. C. Wilson and M. N. Clifford (eds) *Tea: Cultivation to Consumption*, Chapman and Hall, London, pp87–135

CBSL (2005) *Annual Report 2004*, Central Bank of Sri Lanka, Colombo, Sri Lanka

Chandrapala, L. (1996) 'Long Term Trends of Rainfall and Temperature in Sri Lanka', in Y. P. Abrol, S. Gadgil and G. B. Pant (eds) *Climate Variability and Agriculture*, Narosa Publishing House, New Delhi, India

Cubasch, U., G. A. Meehl, G. J. Boer, R. J. Stouffer, M. Dix, A. Noda, C. A. Senior, S. Raper and K. S. Yap (2001) 'Projections of future climate change', in J. T. Houghton, Y. Ding, D. J. Grggs, M. Noguer, P. J. van der Linden, X. Dai, K. Maskell and C. A. Johnson (eds) *Climate Change 2001: The Scientific Basis*, Contribution of Working Group I to the Third Assessment Report of the Intergovernmental Panel on Climate Change, Cambridge University Press, Cambridge, UK and New York, US

DCS (2003) *Statistical Abstract: 2003*, Department of Census and Statistics, Colombo, Sri Lanka

DCS (2004) *Sri Lanka: Census of Agriculture – 2002*, Department of Census and Statistics, Colombo, Sri Lanka

Devanathan, M. A. V. (1975) 'The quantification of the climatic constraints on plant growth', *Tea Quarterly*, vol 45, pp43–72

Hutchinson, M. F. (1989) 'A new method for gridding elevation and stream line data with automatic removal of pits', *Journal of Hydrology*, vol 106, pp211–232

IPCC–DDC (undated) website for the Data Distribution Centre of the Intergovernmental Panel on Climate Change, www.ipcc-data.org/sres/gcm_data.html

Kalra, N. and P. K. Aggarwal (1996) 'Evaluating the growth response for wheat under varying inputs and changing climate options using Wheat Growth Simulator

WTGROWS', in Y. P. Abrol, S. Gadgil and G. B. Pant (eds) *Climate Variability and Agriculture*, Narosha Publishing House, New Delhi, India, pp320–338

McAvaney, B. J., C. Covey, S. Joussaume, V. Kattsov, A. Kitoh, W. Ogama, A. J. Pitman, A. J. Weaver and R. A. Wood (2001) 'Model evaluation', in J. T. Houghton, Y. Ding, D. J. Grggs, M. Noguer, P. J. van der Linden, X. Dai, K. Maskell and C. A. Johnson (eds) *Climate Change 2001: The Scientific Basis*, Contribution of Working Group I to the Third Assessment Report of the Intergovernmental Panel on Climate Change, Cambridge University Press, Cambridge, UK and New York, US

Magambo, M. J. S., J. G. Omolo and C. O. Othieno (1988) 'The effect of plant density on yield, harvest index and dry matter production', *Bulletin of United Planters Association of South India*, no 40, pp7–14

Monteith, J. L. (1977) 'Climate and efficiency of crop production in Britain', *Philosophical Transactions of the Royal Society of London, Series B*, vol 281, pp277–294

Nakicenovic, N. and R. Swart (eds) (2000) *Special Report on Emissions Scenarios*, Special Report of Working Group III of the Intergovernmental Panel on Climate Change, Cambridge University Press, Cambridge, UK and New York, US

Panabokke, C. R. (1997) 'Agro ecological regions', in T. Somasekaram, M. P. Perera, M. B. G. de Silva and H. Godellawatta (eds) *Arjuna's Atlas of Sri Lanka*, Arjuna Consulting Co. Ltd., Dehiwala, Sri Lanka, pp79–80

STLB (2005) *Statistical Bulletin 2005*, Sri Lanka Tea Board, Colombo, Sri Lanka

Tanton, T. W. (1992) 'Tea crop physiology', in K. C. Wilsion and M. N. Clifford (eds) *Tea: Cultivation to Consumption*, Chapman and Hall, London, pp173–199

Warrick R. A., G. J. Kenny, G. C. Sims, N. J. Ericksen, Q. K. Ahmad and M. Q. Mirza (1996) 'Integrated model system for national assessment of climate change applications in New Zealand and Bangladesh', *Journal of Water, Air and Soil Pollution*, vol 92, no 1–2, pp221–227

Watson, M. (1986) 'Soil and climatic requirements', in P. Sivapalan, S. Kulasegaram and A. Kathiravetpillai (eds) *Handbook on Tea*, Tea Research Institute, Talawakelle, Sri Lanka, pp3–5

Wijeratne, M. A. (2001) *Shoot Growth and Harvesting of Tea*, The Tea Research Institute of Sri Lanka, Talawakelle, Sri Lanka

Wijeratne, M. A. and R. Fordham (1996) 'Effect of environmental factors on growth and yield of tea (*Camellia sinensis (L) Kuntze*) in the low-country wet zone of Sri Lanka', *Sri Lanka Journal of Tea Science*, vol 64, pp21–34

Part V:

Human Health

18

Vulnerability to Climate-Induced Highland Malaria in East Africa

Shem O. Wandiga, Maggie Opondo, Daniel Olago, Andrew Githeko, Faith Githui, Michael Marshall, Tim Downs, Alfred Opere, Pius Z. Yanda, Richard Kangalawe, Robert Kabumbuli, Edward Kirumira, James Kathuri, Eugene Apindi, Lydia Olaka, Laban Ogallo, Paul Mugambi, Rehema Sigalla, Robinah Nanyunja, Timothy Baguma and Pius Achola

Introduction

Malaria is a mosquito-borne (*Anopheles gambiae* species) viral illness, which causes the greatest morbidity and mortality in tropical and subtropical countries, with an especially high prevalence in Africa. Approximately 90 per cent of the 1 million global annual deaths due to malaria occur in Africa and nearly three-quarters of these are children under the age of five (WHO, 1996; McMichael et al, 1996;). It is also associated with several complications such as severe anaemia (especially in children and pregnant women) and cerebral malaria. Low birth weight caused by malaria is responsible for about 6 per cent of the infant mortality.

In Kenya, Uganda and Tanzania malaria is endemic in most regions, accounting for a third or more of the outpatient morbidity in the population. In Kenya, malaria accounts for 40,000 infant deaths annually. In Uganda, there were 5.7 million and 7.1 million cases of malaria in 2002 and 2003 respectively, resulting in 6,735 and 8,500 deaths. In Tanzania, malaria causes between 70,000 and 125,000 deaths annually, accounting for 19 per cent of the health expenditure (De Savigny et al, 2004). Thus malaria is also an economic burden, and deprives Africa of US$12 billion every year in lost gross domestic product (GDP) (Greenwood, 2004).

Because of climatic and ecological diversity, there is regional variation in the epidemiology of malaria transmission in Africa: from negligible to high risk in high-altitude areas, low but stable transmission along the Indian Ocean, and intense, high transmission around the Lake Victoria basin. A recently observed phenomenon of an increased frequency of malaria in the highlands of Africa has become a matter of serious concern, given that its prevalence here is typically low. Fifteen per cent of the African population live in the highlands and are therefore at high risk from the impacts of epidemic malaria, particularly in the eastern and southern African regions (Worrall et al, 2004). The concern is relatively small for the lowland areas, where the disease is endemic and the population has developed immunity to it.

In East Africa, highland malaria has been recorded since the 1920s and 1950s, when it was first reported (Garnham, 1945; Fontaine et al, 1960; Roberts, 1964; Githeko and Clive, 2005), but the early epidemics were not as severe or as frequent as they have been within the last two decades, with virtually no recorded epidemics between 1960s to the early 1980s. The recent resurgence of malaria epidemics in this region in the last couple of decades has been closely associated with climate variability and change by several scientists (Matola et al, 1987; Lepers et al, 1988; Fowler et al, 1993; Khaemba et al, 1994; Loevinsohn, 1994; Some, 1994; Lindsay and Martens, 1998; Malakooti, et al, 1998; Mouchet et al, 1998; Githeko and Ndegwa 2001; Zhou et al, 2004).[1] In fact such zones of unstable malaria, are generally observed to be more sensitive to climate variability and environmental changes (Mouchet et al, 1998). There is concern therefore that future climate change could result in minimum temperature and precipitation thresholds for malaria transmission being surpassed in various parts of the region (Githeko et al, 2000), thus favoring further disease outbreaks. Short-term climate extremes, such as El Niño that similarly affect temperature and precipitation have also been implicated in increased malaria transmission (Kilian et al, 1999; Lindblade et al, 1999).

The sensitivity of malaria transmission to climate variability and change is influenced by several factors pertaining to the development and propagation of the vector and the virus, the vector's preference for human blood feeding, and suitability and availability of disease habitat. In the East African highlands, increases in human population density have led to deforestation and swamp reclamation (Mouchet et al, 1998, Afrane et al, 2005; Minakawa et al, 2005) leading to the creation of puddles and providing ideal breeding sites for mosquitoes. The removal of vegetation, especially Papyrus, in swampy areas, also results in relatively higher temperatures, further aiding disease transmission (Walsh et al, 1993; Minakawa et al, 2005; Munga et al, 2006; Mouchet et al, 1998; Lindblade et al, 2000).[2] Other non-climatic factors implicated in disease transmission include environmental and socio-economic change, deterioration of healthcare and food production systems, and the modification of microbial/vector adaptation (Epstein, 1992, 1995; Morse, 1995; McMichael et al, 1996).

Given this outlook for a potentially increased incidence of highland malaria in the Lake Victoria region of East Africa, we undertook a study to better examine the relationship between climatic factors and disease outbreaks in three high altitude communities in Kenya, Uganda and Tanzania. Available climate, health and hydrological data from 1960 to 2001 were utilized for this purpose. An integrated vulnerability assessment mechanism for malaria in the affected communities was developed and the manner in which sources of vulnerability are differentiated within the population of this region was analysed. The coping and adaptive capacities of those affected were also identified in this process. The key questions addressed by this research include:

1   Which target groups are the most vulnerable, i.e. how are sources of vulnerability differentiated within the population of the Lake Victoria region?
2   What excess risk (the added risk above the normal malaria incidence in a community/household) could be attributable to climate variability?

A more comprehensive description about this study and the important findings that emerged is outlined in the sections that follow.

Study Sites

One characteristic of highland malaria epidemics is that affected communities have yet to develop resistance/immunity to the disease, due to the fact that it has not been historically endemic to this area, which was formerly a high-altitude, colder region. As a result we selected communities that were located at altitudes higher than 1100 meters above sea level, where the existence of malaria vectors is limited by the cool temperatures. Households from various elevations above the 1100m level were included because previous studies (for example, Githeko et al, 2006) have shown that prevalence of highland malaria is affected by elevation. Other factors considered include proximity to a hospital and a meteorological station with reliable data. Kabale (Uganda), Kericho (Kenya) and Muleba (Tanzania) were selected as study sites (Figure 18.1) since these sites not only have a recorded history of malaria epidemics in the last two decades but also have been experiencing climate variability and change since the turn of the 20th century.

Climate data (temperature and rainfall) were obtained from the nearest meteorological station for Kabale, Kericho and Bukoba (for Muleba, Tanzania) for the period 1961 to 2001 (for Kericho the temperature data were from 1978 to 2001). Streamflow data were obtained from National Water Ministries or Meteorological Agencies for rivers passing or close to the study sites. Only data for the Sondu-Miriu and Yurith rivers from the Kericho site (Kenya), covering the period 1961–1991, could be used because data from the Ugandan site were found to be of poor quality and the Tanzanian site lacked sufficient streamflow data (Table 18.1).

An integrated approach using both quantitative and qualitative techniques was employed in assessing the vulnerability and adaptability of highland communities to malaria epidemics. A household survey using 150 semi-structured interviews[3] was conducted in each study site at Kabale, Kericho and Muleba to establish the health, demographic and socioeconomic characteristics of the affected communities. The key variables collected include location, sociodemographic data, incomes, household food security, wealth indicators, health issues, knowledge of disease and coping mechanisms.

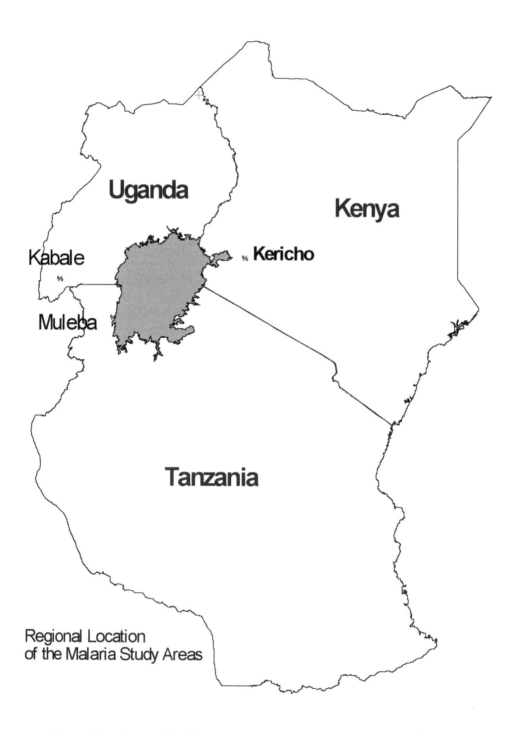

Figure 18.1 *Geographical information system maps of the three study sites in Uganda, Kenya and Tanzania*

Table 18.1 *Geographical positions of streamflow gauging stations, Kericho area*

ID	Longitude	Latitude	Altitude	Name
IJG01	35°00′30″E	0°23′35″S	1500m	Sondu
1JD03	35°04′45″E	0°28′35″S	>1500m	Yurith

Hospital records of the number of monthly malaria cases (both in- and out-patients) were collected for Kabale, Kericho and Muleba over a 30-year period (1971–2001), though only 6 years of data (1996–2001) could be analysed due to the poor quality of data from other years. A trial check on some of the earlier data indicated little variability of malaria cases with seasons. An alarming 750 per cent increase in malaria cases in Kericho was observed over a 13-year period from 1986 to 1998 (Shanks et al, 2000). Similarly, in Kabale, malaria cases increased from 17 to 24 cases per 1000 individuals per month during 1992–1996 and 1997–1998 (Kilian et al, 1999; Lindblade et al, 1999), yet this is not reflected in the health data collected, highlighting the poor quality of records, largely resulting from the fact that highland malaria epidemics were not recognized as a national health concern by the East African governments until recently. Health data were collected from Kabale Regional Referral Hospital, Litein Mission Hospital (Kericho) and Rubya District hospital (Muleba).

Additionally, qualitative data derived from focus group discussions and participatory stakeholder meetings with community, health and local administrative officials were also used. A total of 12 focus group discussions (4 in each study site) were conducted in communities where households had been previously interviewed; issues discussed include indicators of wealth, knowledge of disease, attitude towards the disease, disease prevention and management practices and impact of disease, coping mechanisms, and interventions. Two participatory stakeholder meetings were conducted in Kabale, Kericho and Muleba, where stakeholders were invited to actively articulate their knowledge, values and preferences regarding vulnerability and adaptation to malaria epidemics.

Climate and Hydrology of the Study Sites

Temperature

Analysis of the temperature data sets indicates increases in maximum (T_{max}) and minimum (T_{min}) temperatures at both lowland and highland sites during various periods (Table 18.2). The temperature change (increases in both T_{max} and T_{min}) has generally been greater in the highlands than in the lowlands and of note is the marked increase in T_{max} (3.6°C) in Kericho (a highland site). An increasing trend in T_{max} and T_{min} was also noted for the lowland sites of Kisumu and Kampala, but there was a declining trend in Mwanza. The trend of temperatures increasing from the lowlands to the highlands is probably a factor that has enabled the malaria transmitting mosquitoes to find new habitats in the highlands; hence the creeping altitudinal ascent of unstable malaria epidemics.

Table 18.2 *The long-term context of temperature changes in the Lake Victoria basin, showing results for highland sites based on linear regression*

Station	Period of analysis	Temperature change (°C)	
Kericho	1978–2001	Max	3.6
		Min	0.5
Kabale	1960–2003	Max	1.1
		Min	1.6
Bukoba	1960–2002	Max	0.7
		Min	1.1

The ranked T_{max} and T_{min} values in Table 18.3 indicate that the high T_{max} years within the Lake Victoria region as a whole are associated with El Niño occurrences and concomitant high streamflow and flooding in the lake basin area.

Table 18.3 *Ranked T_{max} and T_{min} with high T_{max} and low T_{min} for the period 1978 to 1999, compared with occurrence of El Niño and La Niña years*

Site	High T_{max} years	Low T_{max} years	High T_{min} years	Low T_{min} years	El Niño years	La Niña years
Kericho	**1981, 1991, 1994–1995, 1997,** *1999*	**1978,** 1985	**1987,** *1989*	1981, **1991**	**1977–1978, 1982–1983, 1986–1987** **1991–1992,**	 *1988–1989.*
Kabale	**1982–1983, 1995, 1997**		**1983, 1997**	1978, 1985, 1993	**1992–1993, 1994–1995,**	 *1995–1996.*
Bukoba	**1983, 1987, 1997,** *1999*	1985	*1996,* **1997–1998**	**1987,** 1993	**1997-1998**	 *1998–1999.* *1999–2000*

Note: Bold – El Niño years; bold/italic – La Niña years; normal font – non-El Niño/La Niña years.

Precipitation

Rainfall analyses for the period 1961–2002 show that Kericho (annual rainfall range from 897 to 2420mm) and Bukoba (884–2736mm) received relatively high amounts of rainfall with relatively high coefficients of variation, while Kabale (755–1282mm) received the least. Generally, annual time series analysis for the period 1961–2001/2 shows a decreasing trend in rainfall at all the stations except Kabale. In all the stations, March to May (MAM) received more rainfall than September to December (SOND). On a seasonal basis only Bukoba showed a statistically significant downward trend for the JF, MAM and JJA seasons.

Table 18.4 *Ranked mean monthly cumulative precipitation with wet years (≥1 standard deviation from long-term mean) and dry years (≤1 standard deviation from long-term mean) for the period 1978 to 1999, compared with occurrence of El Niño and La Niña years*

Site	Wet years	Dry years	El Niño years	La Niña years
Kericho	**1982,**	**1978,**	**1977–1978,**	
	1988–1989,	1980,	**1982–1983,**	
	1992,	1984,	**1986–1987,**	
	1994,	**1986,**		*1988–1996,*
	1996,	*1993,*	**1991–1992,**	
		1999,	**1992–1993,**	
Kabale	**1978,**	1979,	**1994–1995,**	
	1998,	**1982,**		*1995–1996,*
	1996,	*1993,*	**1997–1998**	
	1998,	*1999,*		*1998–1999,*
				1999–2000
Bukoba	1985,	1980,		
	1986,	1981,		
	1994	**1982–1983**		

Note: Bold – El Niño years; bold/italic – La Niña years; normal font – non-El Niño/La Niña years.

The ranked mean monthly cumulative precipitation data (1978–1999) show that in Kericho, wet years occur either during El Niño or La Niña years (Table 18.4), with the exception being the El Niño period 1997–98, which was not significantly wetter. In Kabale, wet years also appear to be associated with La Niña and El Niño, more consistently with La Niña. In Bukoba, wet years are associated with El Niño, though not as strongly, with one high rainfall episode during a non-El Niño/La Niña year (1985). Dry years in Kericho occur during both El Niño and non-El Niño/La Niña years. In Kabale, dry years occur during El Niño, with single occurrences of dry years during a La Niña and non-El Niño/La Niña year. In Bukoba, dry years are associated with non-El Niño/La Niña years, but it is of significance that during the strong El Niño of 1982–83, Bukoba was dry but experienced a 'normal' rainfall season in SOND. The observed heterogeneity in the rainfall patterns around Lake Victoria may partly be accounted for, to varying degrees, by a combination of factors such as differences in topography and aspect, changes in land use, the influence of Lake Victoria and land–ocean interaction (see Ogallo et al, 1989; Ropelewski and Halpert, 1987).

Hydrology

No significant trends in the annual flows for the Sondu-Miriu and Yurith rivers were noted during the period of analysis (1961–1990), although moving averages showed some fluctuations in river flows. An association of high flows with El Niño years (1968, 1970, 1978–1979, 1982, 1988 and 1990) was observed.

The mean and median flows for the Sondu-Miriu and Yurith rivers show that highest flow occurs in the MAM 'long rains' season, with a subdued peak in August and a high flow in the SOND 'short rains" season with a peak in November. The peak river flow lags behind two of the three observed rainfall peaks (April and August) by one month, but is coincident with the rainfall peak in November.

Flood frequency analysis on the Sondu-Miriu river indicates that the return period for maximum flow is between two and five years. This suggests that besides the influence of El Niño (occurring approximately every two to seven years) in generating abnormally high flows in either or both MAM and SOND, other simultaneous mesoscale climate and weather systems can also account for the flooding events. The results of streamflow analyses demonstrate that precipitation and resulting flow in rivers within the area are a tightly coupled system, which means that the streamflow is directly dependent on the precipitation.

Possible links between climate, hydrology and malaria outbreaks

The climate and hydrological data provide some important insights into the links between vulnerability to malaria outbreaks and climate variability and change. Positive trends in maximum temperature are significantly linked to the El Niño Southern Oscillation (ENSO) (Table 18.3), which, in turn, has been associated with serious malaria epidemics in the lake basin. These results indicate that the malaria exposure risk of the highland lake communities is dramatically increased during ENSO periods when anomalously high temperatures and widespread flooding favour the proliferation of the mosquito vector. Secondly, anomalously wet years are not always necessarily accompanied by anomalously high temperatures (see Tables 18.3 and 18.4), which indicates that other mesoscale climate or weather patterns, such as the Indian Ocean dipole reversal (Conway, 2002), that can generate heavy precipitation events equalling or even exceeding ENSO effects do not necessarily increase the risk of epidemic malaria in the highlands. This notwithstanding, the increasing trend in mean temperatures across the study sites in the lake basin region over the past three decades or so suggests that perhaps a critical threshold in this relationship could be breached in the near future if the warming trends continue, and that this could potentially lead to increased non-ENSO-related malaria epidemics in the highlands. From the flood frequency analysis, it can be deduced that the frequency of occurrence of conditions conducive to highland malaria epidemics could double in the future, assuming that the global warming trends do not significantly disrupt the current prevailing weather patterns in the region.

Climate-Related Trends in Malaria Outbreaks

In East Africa, malaria causes 30–40 per cent of all hospital admissions. Available hospital-based morbidity records were reanalysed to indicate percentage departure of mean monthly in-patient admissions from long-term means (six years) obtained from in-patient records from 1996 to 2001 (Figure 18.2). The data were also assessed for seasonal departures from the long-term mean and for long-term trends from 1996 to 2001. A monthly increase of 50 per cent in malaria admissions above the long-term mean from the respective study sites was taken as a threshold for malaria epidemic outbreaks. The first upsurge in malaria cases in Muleba was observed in May to July 1997, and that in Litein from June to July 1997. In Kabale, the number of cases during this period remained below normal (Figure 18.2).

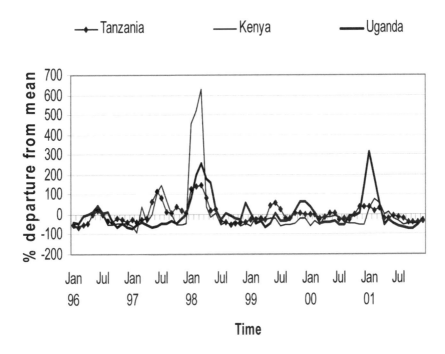

Figure 18.2 *Trends in malaria hospital admissions in Kenya, Tanzania and Uganda*

Comparing trends in malaria cases for children under five and older individuals indicated that children under five were much more susceptible to malaria attacks (Figure 18.3). Children under 5 were 1.5 times more likely to be admitted than older individuals, which points to the fact that younger children have lower immunity.

The most significant change in seasonal outbreaks was observed from January to March 1998 in Tanzania and Kenya, but the trends extended to May of the same year in Kabale, Uganda, which implies that the epidemic lasted for six months. In Tanzania, the epidemic caused a peak increase in cases of 146

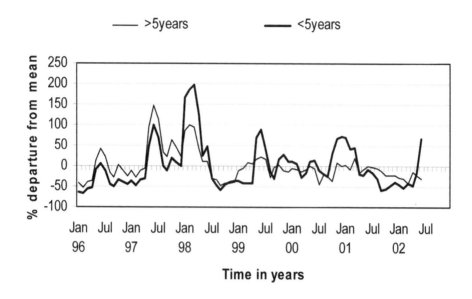

Figure 18.3 *Trends in malaria in children <5 years in Muleba, Tanzania*

per cent, while in Kenya and Uganda the increases were 630 per cent and 256 per cent respectively. The peak month for admissions in all countries was March. It should be noted that in Kenya, government hospital workers were on strike during this period, so most of the cases were treated in Mission hospitals, which probably accounts for the large increase, since the Kenyan hospital used in this study is a Mission hospital. It is more likely that the increases in malaria cases in Tanzania and Uganda give the true picture.

Uganda had further malaria outbreaks in November–December 1999 (with epidemic increase of 63 per cent) and again in December 2000–February 2001, when the outbreak peaked at 312 per cent in January. A small outbreak was observed in Kenya (with an increase of 78 per cent) in February 2001. Data from Uganda indicate that outbreaks are more common after the short rainy season (September–November).

The most significant anomalies in temperature and rainfall were observed during the El Niño period of 1997–1998, after which there were severe malaria outbreaks. In all cases, seasonal malaria outbreaks were associated with anomalies in temperature. This observation is consistent with the well-established biology of malaria transmission. For example, anomalies were observed at Kericho in the mean monthly maximum of 2.2–4.5°C in January–March 1997 and of 1.8–3.0°C in February–April 1998.

The overall data did not show significant annual trends in malaria cases over the period 1996–2001. The data from Litein, Kenya, and Muleba, Tanzania, showed a declining trend in malaria cases, while data from Kabale showed a slightly increasing trend. Data from the three study sites were compared by regression analysis to determine the degree of association among sites. Data from Tanzania and Kenya had the best association of ($R^2 = 0.59$), while R^2 for Kenya and Uganda was 0.3 and R^2 for Uganda and Tanzania was 0.29. These results indicate that there is likely a common effect modulating the outbreaks and this is most likely a climate phenomenon.

Non-Climate Factors that Influence Vulnerability to Malaria Outbreaks

Self-medication

Chloroquine was initially the drug of choice for the treatment of malaria in East Africa, but this was later replaced by sulfadoxine and pyremithamine (SP) combinations due to the development of drug resistance by about 70 per cent of the parasites by 1990. SP was in turn replaced by the more expensive artemisinin-based drugs, once again due to resistance. A fourth drug, quinine, which is still very effective, is only used in cases of hospitalization. Interviews with residents in Kericho, Kenya, revealed that many people (49 per cent) still relied on chloroquine for home treatment, despite 85 per cent of the malaria parasites being resistant to the drug. The next most popular drug, used by 39 per cent of the people, was Fansidar (an SP), to which about 50 per cent of the parasites are resistant. Other drugs used were quinine and antibiotics, which are prescription drugs. Thus people treating themselves in Kericho are at a high risk of developing severe and complicated malaria due to drug failure or under-dosage. This can contribute to high morbidity and mortality, particularly in populations with low immunity.

Knowledge of disease

Knowledge of malaria among the communities and local health officials was found to be couched in myths. For example, the Public Health Act still requires clearing of bushes around houses to prevent yellow fever even though recent studies have demonstrated that such bush clearing instead creates a favourable microclimate for the mosquitoes that spread malaria (Walsh et al, 1993). A second misconception is regarding the role of climate in triggering the outbreak of malaria epidemics. For example, there was a malaria epidemic episode in 2002, which was a relatively hot year, followed by the absence of any outbreaks in 2003, when the temperature was 2°C cooler. However, the Clinical Officer at Litein in Kericho attributed the low incidences of malaria in 2003 to the effectiveness of a government introduced campaign promoting the use of insecticide treated nets to protect against mosquito bites. In reality, this campaign has not been as successful as claimed due to a lack of supply of insecticide treated nets and also their unaffordability. Although the use of bed nets (treated or not) may have contributed to preventing malaria to some extent in 2003, the lack of association of the low disease incidence with a lower temperature points to vulnerability arising from inadequate knowledge about the disease.

Generally, a significant proportion of the respondents (83.2, 94.5, and 52.7 per cent in Kabale, Kericho and Muleba respectively) could establish a link between the health of household members and weather conditions. The awareness of symptoms of malaria is also high. However, knowledge regarding the causes and prevention of malaria is once again largely based on myths. One such myth from Kenya associates consuming food cooked with an edible oil called Chipsy with immediate malaria outbreaks. This brand of edible oil was introduced in 1990, a year that coincided with the El Niño rains and malaria epidemics. In Muleba, Tanzania, people believe that eating maize meal instead of bananas causes malaria. But maize meal is generally consumed only during periods of food shortages that usually result from above and/or below average rains (for example, El Niño rains and/or La Niña droughts), periods when malaria is also more rampant. Similarly, in Uganda, malarial complications such as convulsions (neuropsychiatric events) are attributed to supernatural forces, and hence considered to be best treated with traditional medicine (Nuwaha, 2002). This often leads to delays in medical care, thereby increasing malaria morbidity, severity and mortality. Monthly household income, gender and levels of education also had a significant correlation with the level of awareness on prevention of malaria.

Socioeconomic characteristics

The surveys do reveal that the interplay of poverty and other variables intensifies the vulnerability of a population to malaria. This is because of a lack of economic resources for investing in healthcare that can reduce susceptibility to the disease and help offset the costs of adaptation. Socioeconomic characteristics of the population suggest certain poverty indices that reflect the vulnerability of these communities to malaria epidemics. Most of the households in the survey area live below the poverty line (less than one dollar a day), relying predominantly on either farming or self-employment (Table 18.5). Only a privileged few are formally employed with a source of steady income, accounting for 19, 15 and 2 per cent of the populations of Kabale, Kericho and Muleba respectively. Indeed, when disaggregated by income group, formal employment is the most common source of income for the households found in the higher income brackets (US$91–100 and US$101+). In addition to poor incomes, these communities also experience household food security issues, with a significant proportion of the households in the study areas indicating days of household food shortages and the poorer households more likely to experience food shortages. For example, 50 per cent of households with a monthly income of less than US$30 experience days of food shortage (Table 18.5). Kabale and Muleba have a significantly higher proportion (54.5 and 46.7 per cent) of households experiencing food shortages than Kericho (20.5 per cent).

Table 18.5 *Selected indicators of vulnerability to malaria epidemics*

	Monthly household income (US$)[a] (%)	Proportion of households (%)	Predominant source of income	Average household size	Days of food shortage (%)	Households without bed-nets (%)	Household malaria mortality (1998–2002) (%)	Most common mode of transport (%)
HIGH	≤30	47.8	Farming (54.5%)	8.0	50	76.2	30.0	Bicycle (46.7)
	31–40	12.2	Farming (73.5%)	7.4	47.2	69.0	16.7	Bicycle (32.4)
	41–50	7.1	Self-employment (50%)	5.7	40	20.0	5.9	Bicycle (70.0)
	51–60	6.4	Farming (94%)	7.6	38.9	13.0	0	Bicycle (37.5)
	61–70	7.1	Farming (60%)	6.0	35	10.0	0	Bicycle (52.9)
	71–80	2.4	Farming (57.1%)	6.4	34.4	10.0	0	Bicycle (57.1)
	81–90	3.2	Self-employment (66.7%)	5.3	23.5	3.0	0	Bicycle (100)
	91–100	2.0	Formal employment (60%)	7.6	14.3	1.0	1	Bicycle (80)
LOW	101+[b]	11.8	Formal employment (54.5%)	7.0	0	1.0	1	Motor vehicle (56.3)
	Total	100.00 (n = 450)						

Notes: [a]The average monthly income is US$50.2; the most common income (mode) is US$25.6.
   [b]The highest monthly income in this class is US$580.3.

Lack of adequate healthcare systems coupled with persistent poverty greatly compromise the capacity of individuals and communities to cope with the consequences of malaria epidemics. Most households surveyed in Kericho indicated that they relied on local dispensaries rather than the provincial or district hospitals that are better equipped and have professional staff and in-patient facilities (Table 18.6). Only Kabale reported more use of the district hospital (59.2 per cent) and private clinics (28.7 per cent). Reliance on local dispensaries and private clinics for treatment often results in misdiagnosis due to lack of qualified staff or self-medication by the respondents. Quick treatment was one of the main reasons for the preference for private clinics over public health facilities, which are often overcrowded with long patient queues and have generally unfriendly staff. Accessibility to health facilities is also an issue since the predominant mode of transport is the bicycle for all income groups apart from the highest income group (Table 18.5), primarily due to the high cost of motorized transport. This is also reflected in the low frequency of visits to health facilities (Table 18.7). Consequently, the malaria mortality rate appears to be more prevalent among the low-income households: 30 per cent of households living below the poverty line had lost a household member in the past five years (Table 18.5). Poverty indices indicate that vulnerability increases as monthly household incomes decrease and days of food shortage and household mortality increase, while the proportion of bed-nets in use decreases (Table 18.5).

Table 18.6 *Type of health facility visited*

Health facility	Kericho	Kabale	Muleba
Provincial hospital		0.6%	0.7%
District hospital	1.0%	2.5%	11.7%
Health centre	5.5%	59.2%	15.3%
Local dispensary	91.5%	20.3%	50.3%
Mobile dispensary			5.3%
Herbalist			10.0%
Private hospital	1.0%	6.4%	6.7%
Private clinic	1.0%	11.0%	
Total	**100%**	**100%**	**100%**

Table 18.7 *Visits to hospitals in the last three months by household members*

No of Visits	Kericho	Kabale	Muleba
0	44.4%	31.4%	28%
1	24.5%	37.1%	41.3%
2	15.9%	21.4%	16%
3	9.9%	7.5%	9.3%
4	2.0%	1.3%	2%
5	1.3%	0.6%	2%
6	1.3%		0.7%
9	0.7%		
10+			0.7%
Total	**100%**	**100%**	**100%**

Existing coping and adaptation mechanisms

The use of insecticide treated nets (ITNs) is one of the preventive measures advocated by the Malaria Global Control Strategy, as well as the national malaria control programmes in East Africa.[4] However, the survey revealed that the use of ITNs is not very widespread, particularly among the households with monthly incomes of less than US$30 and US$31–40, of which 76.2 per cent and 69 per cent respectively do not have bed nets (Table 18.5). In Kabale, the proportion of household members sleeping under a bed net was observed to increase with increase in average income. The weak economic base of these highland communities, who rely largely on farming and self-employment for income generation, is a critical issue that leaves them vulnerable to external shocks and to seasonal and climatic variability and change.[5]

The World Health Organization's (WHO, 2002) 'Roll Back Malaria' programme has been adopted by most countries in Africa. The Kenyan, Ugandan and Tanzanian governments actively promote this programme, whose objectives are to increase the use of ITNs, early diagnosis and treatment of malaria, and the use of effective antimalarial drugs. The programme has attracted several local and international civil society organizations, such as Population Services International (PSI), which is supported by the British and US governments and aims to increase the use, ownership, availability and accessibility of ITNs in the malaria-endemic areas of Kenya, Uganda and Tanzania. However, the cost of the subsidized ITNs (about US$1.50) is still beyond the reach of households living below the poverty line (Table 18.5).

Even households that do own bed-nets are unable to provide them for all members. A household may have as many as 16 members with an average size of 3.7 persons. The number of bed-nets, on the other hand, may range from 1 to 6. Our analysis showed that for those who own bed-nets, only 37 per cent could afford to have more than three quarters of household members sleeping under them. Furthermore, a majority of those using bed-nets tend not to treat them with insecticides (about 75 percent of bed net users). Among those who do treat the nets, many do so only once or twice a year, which is considered insufficient for them to remain effective. These factors together tend to reduce the overall effectiveness of the 'Roll Back Malaria' programme in combating malaria.

From the survey results we found that there are very few coping mechanisms available for the households. In the likely event of a malaria epidemic, the majority (75.5 per cent) sell their food crops to cover the cost of treatment. Other ways of coping include borrowing or relying on remittances from relatives. In Kabale, focus group discussions revealed that a number of people have resorted to selling land in order to cope with malaria. Out of the 30 participants in the group, 13 reported having sold land at some stage in the last 8 years in order to cope with malaria in the family. Such coping mechanisms deplete the resources of those affected and may lead to increased food shortage, debt and poverty.

The common adaptation to highland malaria in Muleba, Kericho and Kabale is largely the use of traditional curative measures that rely on local herbs as insect repellents or antimalarial treatments, primarily because of their affordability to the large populations of poor people in these areas. Surveys carried out by the National Institute for Medical Research (NIMR) in Tanzania noted that traditional healers that give out these treatments do possess knowledge and skills useful for malaria disease management. Further, NIMR laboratory analyses of traditional herbs have also established their safety and efficacy, although this often varied depending on the herb (Mwisongo and Borg, 2002).

Predicting Malaria Epidemics Using Climate Data

The observed increase in maximum or both minimum and maximum temperatures and the relatively higher temperature variability in the highlands, as compared to the lowlands, have possibly increased mosquito productivity in vector habitats, thus leading to increased malaria transmission rates. This would partly explain why episodic malaria outbreaks have been increasing at higher altitudes in recent years. Githeko and Ndegwa (2001) have reported evidence to support this view, including improved larval survival at warmer temperatures and increased mosquito biting frequency in deforested areas of the western Kenyan highlands (in comparison to forested areas) due to a rise in temperature of 2°C (Githeko et al, 2006).

The period March–May (MAM) receives more rainfall than the September–November (SON) or September–December (SOND) season throughout the three study sites. During MAM, when the highest rainfall occurs, rivers overflow their banks and flood their basins, while in much wider areas the soils get saturated, encouraging retention of standing water. There is a one-month lag between the peak rainfall and the peak river flow, as the rivers are largely recharged by land runoff and groundwater flow from their drainage basins. The malaria epidemics tend to occur from July to September, with a minimum lag of two-months after the peak rainfall in April; this is related to the one-month lag between peak rainfall and peak streamflow, and a further one-month lag necessary for the development of the malaria vector. During El Niño years, when the short rains (SOND) are anomalously heavy and temperature is high, a similar potential for malaria exists in January–February (JF) as the characteristic conditions of the MAM season are replicated.

Figure 18.4 indicates that malaria outbreaks are sensitive to maximum temperature, with a lag of one to four months after the maximum peak to the onset of the malaria episode (Githeko and Ndegwa, 2001), which agrees with the hydrological data. Other factors, such as the shape of the valleys, which determine vector habitat availability and stability, can also account for large variations in transmission intensities and malaria prevalence at the same altitude (Githeko and Ndegwa, 2001). Thus, although the general principle of the model developed by Githeko and Ndegwa (2001) is valid, there is a need to fine-tune it to specific ecological zones. Furthermore, changes in malaria treatment policies can affect the outcome of the model, as the use of effective antimalarial drugs in primary healthcare can dramatically reduce the number of cases in hospitals.

Analysis of trends in temperature data indicated that in Kabale, Uganda, there was an increase of 1.17°C in mean annual minimum temperature between 1960 and 2001. In Kericho, Kenya, the mean annual maximum temperature increased by 3.5°C. In Bukoba, Tanzania, the mean annual maximum and minimum temperatures were found to have increased by 0.21 and 0.49°C respectively between 1960 and 2001.

While climate data are collected at regular intervals, the same is not true for malaria data, which is of relatively poor quality. The long-term climate data demonstrated a trend towards warming in the highlands, which suggests improved transmission conditions. Although the five-year malaria data available (1996–2001) cannot be used to detect long-term trends in transmission, it nevertheless demonstrated an association between malaria cases and climate variability.

Additionally, every 1°C increase in temperature is equivalent to a reduction of 154 metres in altitude. Therefore transmission conditions at 1500 metres above sea level would be equivalent to conditions at approximately 1200 meters above sea level for a temperature increase of 2°C, thus making malaria at 1200 metres above sea level stable and hyperendemic due to the favourable temperature conditions. Such a situation could be reality for Bukoba located at 1100m above sea-level, even below the 1200m level.

The risk of malaria epidemics is associated with positively anomalous temperatures in the months preceding and during the rainy season. Temperature controls the rate of larval and parasite development, with higher temperatures shortening the development time of the larvae as well as parasites in the mosquitoes. The logistic model for the effects of temperature and rainfall developed by Githeko and Ndegwa (2001) indicates that the rate of growth of a mosquito population is dependent on the initial population size before the rainy season. Rainfall increases the availability of mosquito breeding habitats, thus contributing to the size of the mosquito population, which directly influences the intensity of malaria transmission. Recent studies (Zhou et al, 2004) indicate that the availability and stability of mosquito breeding habitats and the initial vector population size before the rainy season are also a function of drainage efficiency and epidemic propagation and intensity.

Githeko and Ndegwa (2001) also showed that malaria epidemics in Kakamega district in western Kenya could be predicted using simple temperature and rainfall data. The model was able to identify climatic conditions that enabled a rapid growth of mosquito populations leading to epidemics one or two months later. One of the problems with the model is its inability to account for the incidence of temperature and precipitation anomalies around January and February, which are associated with the Indian Ocean dipole reversal episodes that cause non-El Niño rains in East Africa (Nicholson, 1996; Conway, 2002). In the case of the 1997–1998 El Niño period, rainfall continued from November 1997 into January and February 1998 creating perfect breeding habitats for malaria vectors.

We used the data from the three sites to determine whether the model of Githeko and Ndegwa was applicable to other sites in East Africa. Our preliminary results show that, with slight modification, the model was able to identify major epidemics in Kericho, Kabale and Muleba (Figure 18.4). In all cases the epidemics were associated with anomalies in the mean monthly maximum temperature one or two months before the epidemic. The other necessary condition was a significant increase in rainfall one month before the peak of the epidemic. The model is currently being further refined to take into consideration the drainage characteristics of individual sites as this affects the rainfall thresholds used in the model. The ability to forecast an epidemic about two months beforehand is critical for decision making and the logistics of putting preventative and curative measures in place in a timely fashion.

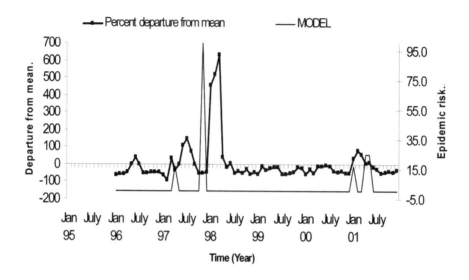

Figure 18.4 *Modelled climate and malaria data for Litein, Kenya*

Conclusion

Changes in climate have been noted at the three study sites in Kenya, Tanzania and Uganda, and these changes are consistent with what has been observed and documented by previous research in other parts of the highlands of East Africa. The maximum and minimum temperatures have changed, with significant increases generally recorded at all sites. The temperature change has been more pronounced at the higher altitudes than in the lowlands. The observed temperature increase has enabled malaria vector mosquitoes to find new habitats in the highlands. Similarly, the rainfall pattern has changed. Generally, time series analyses for the 1961–2001 period show decreasing trends in rainfall for all of the stations except Kabale. Hydrological data show that for the Kericho site, the peak riverflow lags behind two of the three observed rainfall peaks (April and August) by one month, but is coincidental with the rainfall peak in November.

Malaria epidemics often occur in the months of July to September; since peak rainfall occurs in April and there is a minimum two-month lag between the peak rainfall and the epidemics. If, for a given year, the maximum and minimum temperatures are consistently conducive for development and growth of the malaria vector, then the two-month lag between peak rainfall and the onset of the epidemics can largely be accounted for by the one-month lag in peak streamflow.

During the 1997–1998 El Niño episode, malaria admission data from the study sites indicated that the epidemic months corresponded with the onset of abnormally high rainfall during the short rains season and abnormally high maximum temperatures during the months preceding the rainy season. This was confirmed with the observation of anomalies in the mean monthly maximum of 2.2–4.5°C between January and March 1997 and 1.8–3.0°C between February and April 1998. Other cases of malaria epidemics follow the trends described above, with the highest incidents in March–May and July–September associated with the long and short rainy seasons respectively.

Poverty seems to play a very important role in determining the vulnerability of the communities to climate change and variations in the social system. Poor communities lack effective strategies for coping with climate-induced shocks such as disease and weather extremes. Household incomes in our study sites were generally very low and derived largely from insecure and uncertain sources, which exposes them to external shocks. The impacts of climate variability and change tend also to affect crop production and therefore the socioeconomic stability of the region. Shortages of food can lead to malnutrition, especially in poor households, and further increase vulnerability to diseases such as malaria. The inability to afford preventive and curative measures such as protective bed-nets and effective medical treatment can lead to high malaria mortality rates among this group.

The absence of adequate early warning mechanisms for potential epidemic outbreaks and the lack of a good information system that can communicate predictable effects of climate change are some of the institutional shortcomings that further increase vulnerability to malaria outbreaks. The East African governments also have no comprehensive programmes or fiscal facilities to deal with climate variability and extremes. The few malaria programmes that exist are run by civil society or state governments with assistance from major external resources such as aid agencies, international institutions and donor country programmes. Therefore, the local capacity to develop adaptive strategies to cope with climate variations and extremes is still very poor at all levels and remains a major challenge.

Future adaptation programmes should therefore take into account the diversity of factors that influence a society's capacity to cope with these changes. Such programmes should have as major inputs demographic trends and socioeconomic factors, since these have an effect on land use, which may, in turn, accelerate or compound the effects of climate change. Positive trends in demographic, economic and social development would contribute towards better living conditions and therefore increase the ability to cope with the potential consequences of climate change. Diseases such as HIV/AIDS, malaria, diarrhoeal diseases and respiratory diseases are significant factors that affect not only people's health but also their productivity and responsiveness to external threats. The trends in dealing with these diseases must therefore be factored into the analysis of climate change-related vulnerability. The implementation of policies and measures to enable the development of adequate early warning systems and sound communication systems with respect to climate variability and change would contribute towards the better management of disease epidemics. Institutional programmes that are geared towards anticipatory adaptation measures would be best able to address the climate-related vulnerabilities of the population.

Notes

1 Hay et al (2002) have disputed the association of malaria outbreaks with climate variability and change and reported finding no significant changes in temperature or vapour pressure at any of the highland sites that had reported high malaria incidences. However, these results have been challenged by Patz et al (2002) (and later others), who report a warming trend and claim that the use of a downscaled gridded climate data set by Hay et al (2002) ignores climate dependencies on local elevation, which compromises the accuracy of the results.
2 The natural swamps in the valley bottoms contain papyrus, which, due to its cooling properties and its mosquito-inhibiting natural oil secretions, is believed to hamper mosquito development (Lindblade et al, 2000; Reiter, 2001).
3 This sample represents 4, 5 and 7 per cent of the total number of households in the lowest level of administrative unit in Kabale, Kericho and Muleba.
4 Malaria programmes and strategies in East Africa are guided by the overall health policy, whose goal is to provide universal primary healthcare. Such strategies seek to reduce malaria through the promotion of primary healthcare, increasing access to healthcare services and encouraging private sector participation in the delivery and financing of healthcare services. Coexisting with national health policies are international programmes like the Global Malaria Control Strategy, which advocates four technical measures:

- sustainable preventive measures such as the use of ITNs;
- early diagnosis and treatment;
- early detection and prevention of epidemics; and
- strengthening local research capacities.

5 Subsistence farmers in Kabale, for instance, are worried that they can no longer accurately predict the onset of rains and that the rains have reduced in amount. This is affecting their agricultural productivity, income and nutritional status, and hence increasing their vulnerability to climate-related diseases.

References

Afrane, Y. A., B. W. Lawson, A. K. Githeko, G. Yan (2005) 'Effects of microclimatic changes caused by land use and land cover on duration of gonotrophic cycles of *Anopheles gambiae* (Diptera: Culicidae) in Western Kenya Highlands', *Journal of Medical Entomology*, vol 42, pp974–980

Conway, D. (2002) 'Extreme rainfall events and lake level changes in East Africa: Recent events and historical precedents', in E. O. Odada and D. Olago (eds) *The East African Great Lakes: Limnology, Palaeolimnology and Biodiverity*, Kluwer Academic Publishers, Dordrecht, Germany, pp64–92

De Savigny, D., E. Mewageni, C. Mayombana, H. Masanja, A. Minhaji, D. Momburi, Y. Mkilindi, C. Mbuya, H. Kasale, H. Reid, and H. Mshinda (2004) 'Care-seeking patterns in fatal malaria: Evidence from Tanzania', *Malaria Journal*, vol 3, no 27, available at www.pubmedcentral.nih.gov/articlerender.fcgi?artid=514497

Fontaine, R. E., A. E. Najjar, J. S. Prince (1961) 'The 1958 malaria epidemic in

Ethiopia', *American Journal of Tropical Medicine and Hygiene*, vol 10, pp795–803
Fowler, V. G. Jr., M. Lemnge, S. G. Irare, E. Malecela, J. Mhina, S. Mtui, M. Mashaka, and R. Mtoi (1993) 'Efficacy of chloroquine on *Plasmodium falciparum* transmitted at Amani, eastern Usambara Mountains, Northeast Tanzania: An area where malaria has recently become endemic', *Journal of Tropical Medicine and Hygiene*, vol 6, pp337–345
Garnham, P. C. C. (1945) 'Malaria epidemics at exceptionally high altitudes in Kenya', *British Medical Journal*, vol 11, pp45–47
Githeko, A. K. and S. Clive (2005) 'The history of malaria control in Africa: Lessons learned and future perspectives', in K. L. Ebi, J. Smith and I. Burton (eds) *Integration of Public Health with Adaptation to Climate Change: Lessons Learned and New Directions*, Francis and Taylor, London
Githeko, A. K., J. M. Ayisi, P. K. Odada, F. K. Atieli, B.A. Ndenga, I. J. Githure and G. Yan (2006) 'Topography and malaria transmission heterogeneity in the western Kenya highlands: Prospects for vector control', *American Journal of Tropical Medicine and Hygiene* (in press)
Githeko, A. K. and W. Ndegwa (2001) 'Predicting malaria epidemics in the Kenyan Highlands using climate data: A tool for decision makers', *Global Change and Human Health*, vol 2, pp54–63
Githeko, A. K., S. W. Lindsay, U. E. Confaloniero and J. A. Patz (2000) 'Climate change and vector-borne disease: a regional analysis', *Bulletin of World Health Organization*, vol 78, pp1136–1147
Greenwood, B. (2004) 'Between hope and a hard place', *Nature*, vol 430, pp926–927
Hay, S. I., M. Simba, M. Busolo, A. M. Noor, H. L. Guyatt, S. A. Ochola and R. W. Snow (2002) 'Defining and detecting malaria epidemics in the highlands of western Kenya', *Emerging Infectious Diseases*, vol 8, pp555–562
Khaemba, B. M., A. Mutani and M. K. Bett (1994) 'Studies of anopheline mosquitoes transmitting malaria in a newly developed highland urban area: A case study of Moi University and its environs', *East African Medical Journal*, vol 3, pp159–164
Kilian, A. H. D., P. Langi, A. Talisuna and G. Kabagambe (1999) 'Rainfall pattern, El Niño and malaria in Uganda', *Transactions of the Royal Society of Tropical Medicine and Hygiene*, vol 93, pp22–23
Lepers, J. P, P. Deloron, D. Fontenille and P. Coulanges (1988) 'Reappearance of falciparum malaria in central highland plateaux of Madagascar', *Lancet*, 12 March, p586
Lindblade, K. A., E. D. Walker, A. W. Onapa, J. Katunge and M. Wilson (1999) 'Highland malaria in Uganda: Prospective analysis of an epidemic associated with El Niño', *Transactions of the Royal Society of Tropical Medicine and Hygiene*, vol 93, pp480–487
Lindblade, K. A., E. D. Walker, A. W. Onapa, J. Katunge and M. L. Wilson (2000) 'Land use change alters malaria transmission parameters by modifying temperatures in a highland area of Uganda', *Tropical Medicine International Health*, vol 5, pp263–274
Lindsay, S. W. and W. J. M. Martens (1998) 'Malaria in the African highlands: Past, present, and future', *Bulletin of World Health Organization*, vol 76, pp33–45
Loevinsohn, M. E. (1994) 'Climate warming and increased malaria in Rwanda', *Lancet*, vol 343, pp714–748
Malakooti, M. A., K. Biomndo and G. D Shanks (1998) 'Reemergence of epidemic malaria in the highlands of western Kenya', *Emerging Infectious Diseases*, vol 4, pp671–676
Matola, Y. G., G. B. White and S. A. Magayuka (1987) 'The changed pattern of malaria endemicity and transmission at Amani in the eastern Usambara mountains, northeastern Tanzania', *Journal of Tropical Medicine and Hygiene*, vol 3, pp127–134
McMichael, A. J., A. Hames, R. Scooff and S. Covats (eds) (1996) *Climate Change and*

Human Health: An Assessment Prepared by a Task Group on Behalf of the World Health Organization, World Meteorological Organization and the United Nations Environment Programme, Geneva, Switzerland

Minakawa, N., S. Munga, F. Atieli, E. Mushinzimana, G. Zhou, A. K. Githeko and G. Yan (2005) 'Spatial distribution of anopheline larval habitats in Western Kenyan highlands: Effects of land cover types and topography', *American Journal of Tropical Medicine and Hygiene*, vol 73, pp157–165

Morse, S. S. (1995) 'Factors in the emergence of infectious diseases', *Emerging Infectious Diseases*, vol 1, pp7–15

Mouchet, J., S. Manuin, S. Sircoulon, S. Laventure, O. Faye, A. W. Onapa, P. Carnavale, J. Julvez and D. Fontenille (1998) 'Evolution of malaria for the past 40 years: Impact of climate and human factors', *Journal of American Mosquito Control Association*, vol 14, pp121–130

Munga, S., N. Minakawa, G. Zhou, E. Mushinzimana, O. O. Barrack, A. K. Githeko and G. Yan (2006) 'Association between land cover and habitat productivity of malaria vectors in Western Kenyan highlands', *American Journal of Tropical Medicine and Hygiene*, vol 74, pp69–75

Mwisongo, A. and J. Borg (eds) (2002) *Proceedings of the Kagera Health Sector Reform Laboratory 2nd Annual Conference*, Ministry of Health, United Republic of Tanzania

Nicholson, S. E. (1996) 'A review of climate dynamics and climate variability in Eastern Africa', in T. C. Johnson and E. O. Odada (eds) *The Limnology, Climatology and Palaeoclimatology of East African Lakes*, Gordon and Breach, Australia, pp25–56

Nuwaha, F. (2002) 'People's perceptions of malaria in Mbarara, Uganda', *Tropical Medicine International Health*, vol 7, pp462–470

Ogallo, L. J. (1989) 'The spatial and temporal patterns of the East African rainfall derived from principal components analysis', *International Journal of Climatology*, vol 9, pp145–167

Patz, J. A., K. Strzepek, S. Lele, M. Hedden, S. Greene, B. Noden, S. I. Hay, L. Kalkstein and J. C. Beier (1998) 'Predicting key malaria transmission factors, biting, and entomological inoculation rates, using modeled soil moisture in Kenya', *Tropical Medicine International Health*, vol 3, pp818–827

Patz, J. A, M. Hulme, C. Rosenzweig, T. D. Mitchell, R. A. Goldberg, A. K. Githeko, S. Lele, A. J. McMichael and D. Le Sueur (2002) 'Regional warming and malaria resurgence', *Nature*, vol 420, pp627–228

Reiter, P. (2001) 'Climate change and mosquito-borne diseases', *Environmental Health Perspectives*, vol 109, supplement 1, pp141–161

Roberts, J. M. D. (1964) 'Control of epidemic malaria in the highlands of Western Kenya, Part I: Before the campaign', *Journal of Tropical Medicine and Hygiene*, vol 61, pp161–168

Ropelewski, C. F. and M. S. Halpert (1987) 'Global and regional-scale precipitation patterns associated with the El Niño/Southern Oscillation', *Monthly Weather Review*, vol 115, pp1606–1626

Shanks, G. D., K. Biomondo, S. I. Hay and R. W. Snow (2000) 'Changing patterns of clinical malaria since 1965 among a tea estate population located in the Kenyan highlands', *Transactions of the Royal Society of Tropical Medicine and Hygiene*, vol 94, pp253–255

Some, E. S. (1994) 'Effects and control of highland malaria epidemic in Uasin Gishu District, Kenya', *East African Medical Journal*, vol 7, pp2–8

Walsh, J. F., D. H. Molyneux and M. H. Birley (1993) 'Deforestation: Effects on vector-borne disease', *Parasitology*, vol 106, pp55–75

WHO (2002) 'Roll back malaria', World Health Organization, Geneva, Switzerland, www.rbm.who.int

WHO (1996) *World Health Report: Fighting Diseases, Fostering Development*, World

Health Organization, Geneva, Switzerland

Worrall, E., A. Rietveld, C. Delacollette (2004) 'The burden of malaria epidemics and cost-effectiveness of interventions in epidemic situations in Africa', *American Journal of Tropical Medicine and Hygiene*, vol 71, supplement 2, pp136–140

Zhou, G., N. Minakawa, A. K. Githeko and G. Yan (2004) 'Association between climate variability and malaria epidemics in the East African highlands', *Proceedings of National Academy of Sciences*, vol 101, pp2375–2380

19

Vulnerability to Dengue Fever in Jamaica

Charmaine Heslop-Thomas, Wilma Bailey,
Dharmaratne Amarakoon, Anthony Chen, Samuel Rawlins,
David Chadee, Rainaldo Crosbourne, Albert Owino,
Karen Polson, Cassandra Rhoden, Roxanne Stennett
and Michael Taylor

Introduction

Dengue fever is one of the most severe insect-borne viral infections; it is potentially fatal and is currently endemic in more than 100 countries in Africa, the Americas, the Eastern Mediterranean, Southeast Asia and the Western Pacific, with Southeast Asia and the Western Pacific being the most seriously affected (WHO, 1997). It is a flu-like illness but may develop into the more serious dengue haemorrhagic fever/dengue shock syndrome, which can result in death. In the Caribbean, virological evidence of dengue fever was first obtained in the 1950s, although the disease is believed to have existed there for the past 200 years (Ehrenkranz et al, 1971). The outbreak of dengue haemorrhagic fever in Cuba in 1981, which affected almost half the population, is considered to be one of the most important events in the history of dengue in the Americas (CAREC, 1997). Since this event there have been confirmed or suspected cases of dengue haemorrhagic fever almost every year in the American region. The last large epidemic in Jamaica occurred about ten years ago.

Transmission of the disease from a sick to a healthy person occurs via the bite of the *Aedes* mosquito, of which the tropical and subtropical species, *Aedes aegypti*, is common in the Caribbean. This mosquito species has a large variety of breeding places and especially thrives in urban environments with poor sanitation. It can be found breeding in water storage containers and receptacles within the home; in water collected in blocked drains, improperly discarded tyres, bottles and coconut shells (World Resources Institute, 1998);

and in rain water accumulated in tree holes and herbaceous plants. The eggs can resist desiccation for up to one year and hatch when sites are flooded with water. This results in the sudden emergence of mosquitoes at the end of long, dry spells. Vector abundance and the frequency of vector–human contact have been identified as the most significant factors that influence dengue outbreaks in the Caribbean region.

The dengue virus itself exists as four distinct serotypes, which further adds to the risk of acquiring infection. Infection with one serotype leads to protection against homologous re-infection but provides only brief protection against heterologous infection (WHO, 1997). Currently all four serotypes of the dengue virus are in circulation in Jamaica. The risk of acquiring dengue haemorrhagic fever/dengue shock syndrome increases with sequential dengue virus infections (Valdes et al, 2000).

The potential impact of climate change on the incidence of dengue in the Caribbean has emerged as an important cause for concern because the development, dynamics, abundance and geographical distribution of vectors as well as viruses tend to be affected by elements of climate (Martens et al, 1997). Temperature is an especially important factor, influencing mosquito development as well as viral multiplication and development within the mosquito (Wilson, 2001). It is expected that an increase in temperature will shorten the incubation period of the dengue virus within the mosquito and result in potentially higher transmission rates (Watts et al, 1987). It has already been demonstrated that increasing temperatures are altering the geographic range of *A. aegypti*, which is now appearing at higher elevations than before (Suarez and Nelson, 1981; Koopman et al, 1991). Previously limited to locations below 1000m above sea level, dengue appeared for the first time at 2000m sites in Colombia in 1980 (Suarez and Nelson, 1981) and at 1700m in Mexico in 1986 (Koopman et al, 1991).

The situation is somewhat more complex for countries like Jamaica, where the disease is currently endemic and where conditions are already favourable for the vector and virus. The high level of poverty here, especially in rural areas and inner city regions, results in poor environmental sanitation and further encourages the existence and spread of the disease. Higher temperatures resulting from climate change are expected to cause *Aedes aegypti* to become infective faster, reproduce more rapidly and bite more frequently – factors that could increase transmission rates in dengue endemic areas (Focks et al, 1995) and also increase the risk of dengue haemorrhagic fever (Patz et al, 1998; WHO, 2002). Preliminary studies have also shown a link between El Niño Southern Oscillation phenomena and the incidence of dengue in some Pacific island nations (Hales et al, 1999).

Given the important influence of climate on the status of dengue in the Pacific island nations, our objective here is to assess the existing vulnerability of the population of Jamaica to dengue outbreaks and to identify the specific factors that put communities at risk. This is examined at two levels: at the government/ministry level by means of stakeholder interviews with key individuals and at the community level by means of a local case study using survey questionnaires. The results of this assessment can then serve to inform further evaluation of the ability of the country to respond to a possible future increase in the transmission of dengue fever due to climate change as well as to stressful events in general. It will also help to lay the ground for the identification of potential adaptation options in successive studies.

Background

A significant warming trend has been noted for the Caribbean region over the past two decades, and a similar, though less significant, increasing trend has been observed for rainfall over the past four decades (Peterson et al, 2002). Dengue data obtained from the Caribbean Epidemiological Centre (CAREC) in Trinidad and Tobago for the corresponding period also shows a higher incidence of the disease in the 1990s than in the 1980s.

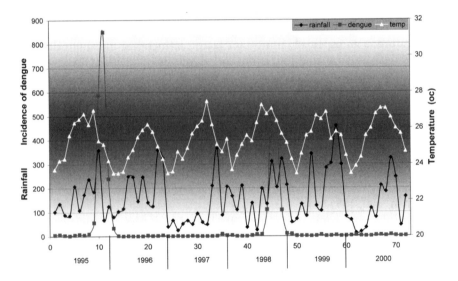

Figure 19.1 *Time series graph of reported cases of dengue with rainfall and temperature for Jamaica*

Source: Stennett (2004).

On a seasonal basis, dengue epidemics have been observed to peak in the latter part of the year, after a few warm months when maximum temperatures have been attained and usually when the rain is receding. There is thus a distinct lag between the attainment of maximums in temperature and rainfall and epidemic outbreaks (Figure 19.1), with a greater lag correlation observed for temperature than for rainfall. The stronger association of the disease with temperature can be explained by the fact that temperature not only results in shorter viral cycles within the mosquito (Koopman et al, 1991; Focks et al, 1995; and Hales et al, 1996) but also results in increased biting frequency of mosquitoes (McDonald, 1957), leading to greater vector–human contact. The association with rainfall, though weaker, is nonetheless important since either an increase in or lack of rainfall results in the increased availability of breeding grounds in the form of accumulated rainwater or stored water respectively, resulting in increased vector abundance.

The majority of dengue outbreaks have also been found to occur in the El Niño and El Niño+1 years (Table 19.1 and Figure 19.2), which is possibly due to the existence of warmer temperatures and drier than normal conditions during the latter part of El Niño years and warmer and wetter than normal conditions during the first half of El Niño+1 years (Chen and Taylor, 2002; Taylor et al, 2002). These temperature and rainfall conditions are once again conducive to vector abundance and viral propagation.

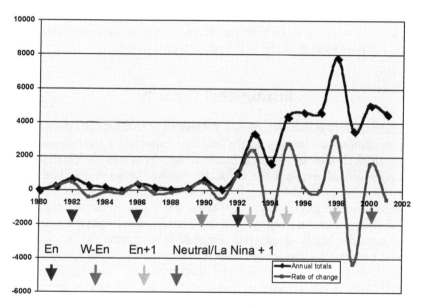

Figure 19.2 *Variation of annual reported cases and rate of change*

Note: Key: En – El Niño; W-En – Weak El Niño; En+1 – El Niño+1; Ln+1 – La Niña+1.

Table 19.1 *Distribution of epidemic peaks among ENSO phases, 1980–2001*

Region	Total	El Niño and El Niño+1	La Niña	Neutral
Caribbean	8	7	–	1
Trinidad and Tobago	8	6	–	2
Barbados	6	5	–	1
Jamaica	5	4	–	1

Source: CSGM (2004).

Mean temperature projections for stations in Jamaica and Trinidad for 2020, 2050 and 2080, using statistical downscaling methods and based on the A2 and B2 scenarios from the Intergovernmental Panel on Climate Change's Special Report on Emissions Scenarios (SRES), indicate a possibility of increased warming in the next century, with an increase of nearly 2°C by 2080 (CSGM, 2004). The trend in rainfall is not as pronounced (CSGM, 2004). Some climate models also indicate an increase in the frequency of El Niño Southern Oscillation events due to the projected changes in climatic parameters (Timmermann et al, 1999). Given the association between dengue incidences and temperature, these future climate conditions may serve to enhance dengue transmission rates in the Caribbean and increase the possibility of epidemic outbreaks. The present overall public immunity to the disease in this region is also likely to be low since the last large outbreak occurred almost a decade ago, though there have been smaller outbreaks. There are also other individual and contextual circumstances that could modify vulnerability to dengue and make communities more or less susceptible. The various issues that affect vulnerability to dengue in the Caribbean region, especially in the context of climate change, are presented in detail in the sections that follow.

Institutional Capacity

An important factor that determines vulnerability to a future increased incidence of dengue in Jamaica is the existing capacity of institutions in the country to deal with such health impacts. An effort was therefore made to assess institutional preparedness to handle climate change-related health challenges, the manner in which key individuals and decision makers interpreted their roles, and current efforts at sensitizing the public to climate change and its implications. For this purpose, at a more generic level, interviews were conducted with the heads of agencies responsible for preparing Jamaica's First National Communication to the United Nations Framework Convention on Climate Change, namely the National Environmental Planning Agency, the National Meteorological Division, and the Office of Disaster Preparedness and Emergency Management. At a more specific level, six officials in key positions in the Ministry of Health were interviewed: the principal budget holder, two medical officers in the surveillance department, the environmental health officer, the chief public health officer and a health educator. These officers not only served as key informants but also as stakeholders who could become involved in the study right from the initial stages and could use the results for the benefit of their constituents. Additionally, scientists in the Climate Change Group of the University of the West Indies were also interviewed.

Generic institutional capacity

The Office of Disaster Preparedness and Emergency Management has a mandate to manage all aspects of disaster management and risk reduction. It does so by an inclusive approach, working in partnership with other agencies, which allows it to pursue programmes that would otherwise be impossible to implement and also to influence national risk reduction. Sea-level rise and the inundation of coastal areas resulting in population displacement were stated as key areas of concern during interviews. However, climate change risk information was not included in the agency's public education campaign, even though such communication was considered important. The topic was thought to be too complicated for the general population, which usually did not worry about issues that did not affect them immediately. The organization heads at this office also exhibited little awareness about the possible health effects of climate change, since health was not regarded as a part of their mandate. Resource constraints were also stated as a factor.

The National Environment and Planning Agency's mission is to promote sustainable development by ensuring protection of the environment (NEPA, undated). The issue of climate change was addressed indirectly in their public education programmes, though the specific term was not used since it was once again considered complicated. The attitude of this agency was found to mirror that of the Office of Disaster Preparedness and Emergency Management: instead of looking for ways to communicate climate change concerns to the public, they presumed a lack of intelligence and avoided the issue altogether. They, too, did not find the need for the inclusion of the health threats in their mandate.

In contrast, the National Meteorological Service was the only agency that specifically included in its mission climate change research and communication of climate change-related risk information to stakeholders and the general public to enable adaptation by affected sectors. Unlike officials at the previous agencies, the expert interviewed here demonstrated a full appreciation of the health implications of climate change and considered public access to this kind of information to be important. There is some information on health impacts in the literature produced by the Meteorological Service, but implementation of public education programmes was only considered feasible if more resources were available, and even then addressing sea-level rise would always take precedence over other impacts.

What was curious about the above agencies was the narrow interpretation of their mandates and the unwillingness to acknowledge health as a part of their purview. Since its establishment in 1980, the Office of Disaster Preparedness and Emergency Management has routinely been called on to deal with three types of hazards – hurricanes, landslides and floods caused by intense rainfall – and such extreme events have been noted to have increased in frequency and intensity in the recent past. Displacement of population resulting from hurricanes and floods has often been accompanied by outbreaks of communicable diseases in shelters managed by this office (Bailey, 1989), and this is one of the most critical areas in shelter management. Yet there was no acknowledgment of an interest in diseases resulting from hazards. The recent increase in the frequency and intensity of hurricanes and floods was also not viewed as a possible consequence of climate change and was not considered as a more immediate threat than the effects of sea-level rise.

Concerning the National Environment and Planning Agency, it is interesting to note that its interpretation of its mission objective of sustainable development for environmental protection does not seem to include any aspect of population health, despite the direct linkage between environmental health and population health. The interviewee from the National Environment and Planning Agency completely denied any interest in health within the agency or any plans to incorporate health impacts into the education programme of the organization. The preoccupation with sea-level rise was observed to be at the forefront at all three organizations, and health issues were considered the responsibility of the Ministry of Health. Though the Meteorological Service was the only agency of the three that demonstrated a good awareness of climate-related health issues it was nonetheless reluctant to see itself in partnership with the Ministry of Health.

Specific institutional capacity

Interviews with key officials at the Ministry of Health showed that there was overall a good awareness about the potential for increased temperature and precipitation in the Caribbean due to climate change. All but one official interviewed agreed that such climatic impacts could lead to an increase in dengue transmission. However, despite the relatively high level of awareness, there are no long-term strategies in place or under consideration to address the possible negative impacts of climate change. Dengue fever is classified as a Class 2 disease and given significantly less priority than Class 1 diseases,[1] especially HIV/AIDS. The problem of inadequate financial resources, largely due to cuts in budgetary allocations, and the resulting need to establish priorities, was repeatedly cited as a major issue during interviews. There is a growing feeling, however, that the competition between HIV/AIDS and diseases such as dengue is not so much due to financial issues but rather stems from a lack of attention. For example, the Global Fund for HIV/AIDS brings large sums of money into the country and this has the unfortunate effect of diverting attention and manpower away from other health issues.[2] The present approach to dengue prevention and control in the Caribbean therefore tends to be mostly reactive.

There is also no vaccine against dengue or dengue haemorrhagic fever, and the only effective method of prevention is the elimination of vectors and their breeding places. The World Health Organization (WHO) has very clearly outlined priorities for the control of dengue, including epidemiological surveillance (WHO, 2002)[3], but Jamaican health authorities often find these requirements difficult to meet, largely due to staff shortages of as much as 50 per cent at various levels in the ministry and to shortages of entomologists and public health inspectors. This situation is not expected to improve in the near future since many of these positions come with heavy workloads and unattractive salaries and are not considered respectable. There is also no routine vector surveillance and control programme in place, due to the expense involved and the lack of any budgetary allocation to such an exercise, according to one official from the Ministry of Health in the parish of St James. As a result, there are only knee-jerk responses to reports of heavy infestation in specific communities or special venues, such as important official meetings or events.

Identification of dengue cases was also cited as an issue, as there is only one under-equipped virology laboratory on the island and blood samples from sick persons must be sent to Trinidad and Tobago for disease identification.

The position of the Ministry of Health is that environmental sanitation must be the responsibility of community members since their actions to a large extent determine the existence of mosquito breeding sites. It felt that government intervention could result in a shift of responsibility from the community to the state and generate a false sense of security among the public, who would then do nothing to control breeding sites, as has been the experience in Asia and the Americas (Gubler, 2002). Jamaican communities, on the other hand, considered dengue prevention and control to be entirely a government responsibility.

On the positive side, the country does have a well-organized system of primary healthcare under a recently decentralized health services programme, which divides the island into four autonomous health regions (Figure 19.3) under four regional authorities. The system is based on a nested system of health centres, offering different levels of care. There is a health centre within five miles of every community on the island (Figure 19.4), which ensures greater sensitivity to local needs. This system could potentially be mobilized during emergency situations and could help facilitate greater responsiveness in the event of epidemic outbreaks, despite the financial constraints plaguing the Jamaican health system. There are only a few areas on the island that may experience difficulty in accessing health services due to geographic and socio-organizational factors.

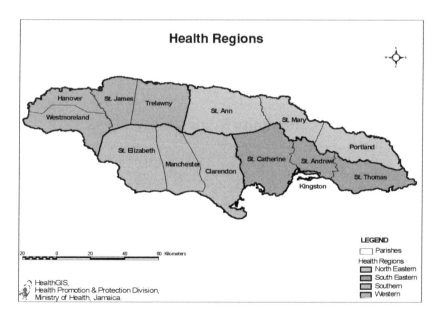

Figure 19.3 *Health regions in Jamaica*

Source: Ministry of Health, Jamaica (2006)

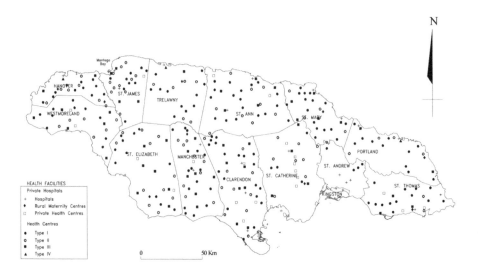

Figure 19.4 *Health centres in Jamaica*

Source: Ministry of Health, Jamaica (2006)

The Ministry of Health also has a long tradition of involvement in policy-oriented research and there have been occasions when research/policy collaborations have been initiated by the ministry to investigate the effects of its policies on vulnerable groups (Gordon-Strachan et al, 2005). This kind of interest and involvement on the part of the ministry could potentially be further developed to facilitate continued research on dengue in Jamaica and serve to inform policymakers to enable appropriate decision making.

Community Vulnerability

To determine vulnerability to dengue fever at the community level and thus provide a more comprehensive assessment, a local case study was undertaken in a section of the parish of St James in the northwest of Jamaica. According to the dengue records for this parish, there had been a concentration of cases within the city of Montego Bay and sporadic cases within the vicinity of a permanent stream and its associated seasonal streams and gully banks (Figure 19.5). Three communities along this hydrological feature were selected: Granville/Pitfour, a suburb of the parish capital Montego Bay; Retirement, immediately beyond the boundaries of the urban area; and rural John's Hall. A 10 per cent sample of heads of households in these communities (Table 19.2) was then surveyed using a questionnaire to determine socioeconomic conditions of householders, support systems available, their knowledge of the disease, and cultural practices that might have important implications for the spread of dengue fever.

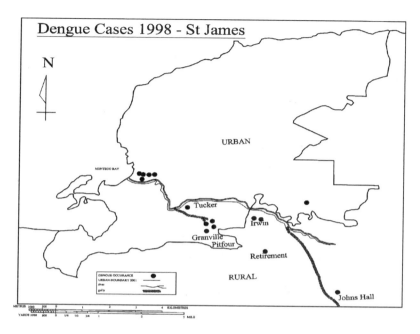

Figure 19.5 *Distribution of dengue cases in St James, Jamaica, 1998*

Table 19.2 *Sample size*

Community	Number of households	Sample
Granville/Pitfour	1507	151
Retirement	485	49
John's Hall	572	57
Total	2564	257

Of the three communities surveyed, Granville/Pitfour is a low-income community of about 6300 people on the outskirts of the tourist centre of Montego Bay and comprises a mix of formal and informal structures. Most of the informal structures are one-roomed dwellings with a room density of 4.2 persons per room, among the highest of the three communities under study. Heads of households were either self-employed or worked in the service sector in Montego Bay. A few miles to the southeast is Retirement, a lower middle-income community of about 1780 people with few obvious informal dwellings. Heads of households here are employed in the service sector in Montego Bay and in public service. Further southeast is John's Hall, a poor community of rural squatters. It consists of small, crudely built houses, most lacking basic amenities and scattered over rugged terrain. Roughly 60 per cent of the households here are headed by women, who typically have very little education or training and are employed in domestic service and petty trading activities with incomes at the minimum wage or below. Male heads share similar characteristics and are employed as gardeners and labourers on construction sites. Unemployment in this community stands at 33 per cent.

Even for Jamaica as a whole, a little over 66 per cent of single parent households living in poverty in 2002 were in fact headed by females (PIOJ/STATIN, 2002). This is significant in light of the fact that gender is recognized globally as an extremely important factor in explaining poverty. In our survey, responses to questions such as the frequency with which households were forced to borrow money or take food on credit, had to rely on relatives or friends, and survived on restricted food intake were combined to form an index of coping, and the general picture obtained was one in which large numbers were 'struggling to make ends meet'. Such conditions serve to greatly limit the coping capacity of the population to added health stresses.

About 50 per cent of household heads in the survey also suffered from chronic illnesses, mainly hypertension and diabetes. It has been noted that households with disabled or ill members display greater vulnerability since this reduces the number of members available for productive labour and puts a strain on household resources (Kouri et al, 1989; Nyong et al, 2003). The strongest association was found with chronic illnesses, which are often incapacitating and require strict adherence to therapeutic and dietary regimes. Rapid access to health facilities can minimize vulnerability, and geographically Granville/Pitfour is the best positioned in terms of access to comprehensive public-sector services in Montego Bay, with John's Hall the least.

With respect to access to services, households in which there is no piped water are more at risk than those with a piped supply. In the three communities investigated, 23 per cent had no water piped into their homes or yards, and even when there was piped supply, it was often irregular, necessitating storage of some sort. This is especially true for the squatter communities in urban areas, which are, by law, not permitted piped water supply. The degree of risk varies with the mode of storage. Focks and Chadee (1997), working in Trinidad and Tobago, found that the outdoor drum was one of the most productive *Aedes* breeding containers and was most commonly found in homes with no access to piped supply. Four types of containers – outdoor drums, tubs, buckets and small containers – accounted for more than 90 per cent of all *Aedes aegypti* pupae discovered. Focks and Chadee concluded that the provision of an adequate water supply system and targeted source reduction had the potential to reduce pupal production in the country by more than 80 per cent. In our survey in St James, 54 per cent of the respondents stored water in drums, which were usually left uncovered to facilitate the entry of rain water and for easy access to the stored water.

The overall awareness about dengue in the three communities surveyed was generally low. Many respondents were unfamiliar with the vector and had little knowledge about the habits of mosquitoes, which contributed to their inability to adequately protect themselves against the disease. The *Aedes* species typically bites in the early mornings and at dusk, so bed-nets that protect against mosquitoes at night are ineffective in controlling dengue fever. The best forms of protection have been found to be screens or mesh on windows and doors (Ko et al, 1992) to keep mosquitoes out of homes. Studies in Taiwan have shown that screens can eliminate as much as 63 per cent of dengue infection, and in Puerto Rico, the absence of screens showed a strong correlation with the occurrence of dengue fever (Dantes et al, 1988; Ko et al, 1992; Morens et al, 1978). Installation of screens or mesh is, however, expensive and low-income households usually depend on repellents and mosquito destroyers, which often simply force mosquitoes into cupboards and other hiding places from which they later emerge. Screens were only used on some houses in the formal settlements in Granville/Pitfour and Retirement. Eight per cent of the sample used repellents, but the majority used no form of protection at all.

Responsibility for vector control remained an issue, and it was observed that members of communities often do not appreciate the importance of their role in disease management. About 78 per cent of community members considered dengue control to be entirely a government responsibility. Community cooperation was also found to be low in insecticide spraying activities undertaken by the government in response to complaints of high mosquito infestation levels. This activity requires that all doors and windows be kept open during the spraying, but only about 44 per cent of individuals said they abided by this directive.

Ranking of communities

Table 19.3 gives a ranking of the three communities using specific indicators of vulnerability. For each indicator, a score of 1 represents the lowest and a score of 3 the highest level of vulnerability.

In tandem with poverty, vulnerability was found to increase outwards from the urban area. The score was the lowest for Granville/Pitfour and highest for John's Hall, the rural squatter community. The difference between Granville/Pitfour and Retirement was small and this was attributed to the mix of formal and informal settlements in the Granville community, which resulted in depressed scores. In order to more accurately differentiate between the groups a vulnerability index was prepared based on survey responses and using indicators of vulnerability. Scores of 0 and 1 were assigned for the absence and presence of vulnerability respectively. A test of normality (mean ±3 standard deviations) was applied to the results and the data were observed to be normally distributed with a mean of 5.7 and standard deviation of 1.96. On this basis, five groups displaying varying degrees of vulnerability were created as shown in Table 19.4. The most vulnerable group (Group 5) comprised 24 respondents or 9 per cent of the sample, while the least vulnerable group (Group 1) accounted for 14 respondents or about 5 per cent of the sample.

Most of those in the most vulnerable group, Group 5, lived in the community of John's Hall, while 64 per cent of those classified as least vulnerable (Group 1) lived in Granville/Pitfour (Table 19.5). The overwhelming majority of the most vulnerable had no knowledge about the disease, its symptoms or mode of transmission. Together with the high level of poverty this means that they are not in a position to effectively protect themselves from the vectors of the disease. Most households headed by women were found to be at risk.

Table 19.3 *Composite of ranking for communities in St James*

Vulnerability indicators	John's Hall (%)	Score	Retirement (%)	Score	Granville/ Pitfour (%)	Score
No knowledge of dengue fever	52.6	2	53.1	3	42	1
No knowledge of disease symptoms	72	3	69	2	59	1
No protection	95	3	92	2	89	1
Income minimum wage or less	68	3	33	1	61	2
Inability to cope	63	3	51	2	50	1
No pipe at home	46	3	12	2	11	1
Water storage in drums	65	3	53	2	44	1
Chronic illness	53	2	37	1	54	3
Distance from health facility	70	3	49	2	13	1
Female household head	60	3	47	1	55	2
Believe dengue control is public health responsibility	56	3	47	1	51	2
Total Score		31		19		16

Note: **1** = least vulnerable; **2** = vulnerable; **3** = highly vulnerable.

Finally, Table 19.6 shows the characteristics of Groups 4 and 2 (high and low vulnerability groups), both of which interestingly contain a majority of respondents from Granville/Pitfour. This exercise therefore brings out the effect of the mix of formal and informal settlements in Granville/Pitfour, which results in its dual nature in terms of vulnerability and highlights the situation of squatter settlements within this community and elsewhere on the island.

Discussion and Conclusion

Vulnerability to dengue fever in Jamaica thus emerges as a multifaceted issue that stems from weaknesses at the social, economic and political levels. A potentially increased incidence of dengue in the future resulting from the projected continuation of the warming trend observed in Jamaica over the past

Table 19.4 *Identification of vulnerable groups*

Group	Vulnerability	Total	Measure
5	Most vulnerable	24	Mean +1.5SD >8.64
4		67	Mean + 0.5SD to Mean + 1.5SD 6.68–8.64
3	Average	51	Mean ±0.5SD 5.72–6.68
2		101	Mean -0.5SD to Mean -1.5SD 2.76–5.72
1	Least Vulnerable	14	< Mean -1.5SD <2.76 Normality Mean ±3SD Mean = 5.7 SD = 1.96 Mean ±3SD = 0.18–11.58

couple of decades raises serious concerns about the impacts of such outbreaks and the capacity of the island to cope. These findings are especially significant given that a substantial number of people in the Caribbean are poor and often live in situations conducive to the proliferation of the vector and the virus.

Lack of decent living conditions and lack of access to infrastructure and services are at the forefront of issues that stem from poverty and greatly affect coping capacity in the face of climate-related stresses. In Jamaica, about 15 per cent of the population lived below the poverty line in 2002 (PIOJ/STATIN, 2002), earning the minimum wage or below. The majority of these people

Table 19.5 *Characteristics of the most and least vulnerable groups*

Characteristics	Group 5 (%)	Group 1 (%)
1. No knowledge of vector	92	7
2. No knowledge of dengue symptoms	96	14
3. No Protection	92	57
4. Minimum wage or less	92	21
5. Inability to cope	83	0
6. Female head	83	21
7. Storage in drums	79	21
8. No piped water	50	0
9. Distance from health facility	79	7
10. Chronic disease	79	21
11. No personal acceptance of responsibility for dengue control	83	7
Community with highest proportion	**Johns Hall – 67%**	**Granville/Pitfour – 64%**

Table 19.6 *Characteristics of Groups 4 and 2*

Characteristics	Group 4 (%)	Group 2 (%)
1. No knowledge of vector	75	21
2. No knowledge of dengue symptoms	83	48
3. No protection	100	89
4. Minimum wage or less	69	38
5. Inability to cope	75	37
6. Female head	69	44
7. Storage in drums	54	44
8. No piped water	31	10
9. Distance from health facility	48	16
10. Chronic disease	70	36
11. No personal acceptance of responsibility for dengue control	63	39
Community with highest proportion	**Granville/Pitfour – 48%**	**Granville/Pitfour – 69%**

resided in informal settlements Although the precise number of persons who live in such settlements in Jamaica is not known, it has been estimated that about 60 per cent of the population of the city of Montego Bay (about 55,000 to 60,000 people) live in informal settlements (Ministry of Environment and Housing, 1997). A significant number of these poor households were also headed by women, which serves to highlight gender-associated vulnerability to climate-related health stresses.

In terms of infrastructure and services, access to piped water supply came across as a critical factor, with a lack of piped water increasing susceptibility to dengue fever by necessitating water storage, which, in turn, created additional breeding grounds for mosquitoes. Furthermore, there was a complete lack of awareness about the disease and its vector among the population surveyed. More than a half of those interviewed in the communities could not say what causes the disease, and the overwhelming majority had no knowledge of its symptoms (Table 19.3).

The impact of the socioeconomic situation is compounded by the complete absence of any programme to address even the current threat of dengue fever at the policy and planning level. This is partly due to the classification of dengue as a Class 2 disease in comparison to the more serious Class 1 diseases like HIV/AIDS which warrant much global attention. Moreover, sea-level rise garners most of the attention in terms of climate change-related concerns, and many representatives from ministries responsible for articulating the country's position on climate change are in fact unaware of the health implications thereof. As a result, the current capacity to deal with large outbreaks is quite low. Responses to outbreaks are typically reactive in nature and largely limited to spraying insecticide in mosquito-infested areas. There are also no public education programmes in place to increase awareness about the prevention and control of dengue. Distribution of responsibility for dengue control is itself a big question at the moment.

This situation in Jamaica thus raises serious concerns about its capacity to cope with the future health impacts of climate change. While there is merit to the Ministry of Health's position that communities must take some responsibility for vector control, at the same time communities cannot be expected to take action unless they are made aware about the disease. Public education that can adequately inform and empower communities therefore comes across as a strong necessity to address the knowledge gap revealed in the study and encourage collective action. Supporting initiatives to arrange provision of low-cost water storage options such as covered drums and for granting security of tenure to those who, because of their status, are denied access to running water, would also be important.

Additionally, the narrow focus on sea-level rise must be revised to include a broader range of climate change impacts that can be equally devastating for affected communities. Health-related threats must be included among environmental hazards and addressed by institutions responsible for dealing with hazards, such as the Office of Disaster Prevention and Emergency Management. Similarly, the National Environment and Planning Agency and the National Meteorological Service must also specifically target climate-related health threats in their public education programmes. A concerted effort by the various ministries dealing with climate related issues would lend support to the Ministry of Health, which, by itself, is in no position to meet the challenge of increased disease transmission on the island. Strong government initiatives can help draw attention to the issue and enable the generation of additional resources for its management and control. Resources must also be targeted at the existing healthcare system in Jamaica, which is a definite strength and must be adequately equipped for mobilization in the case of epidemic outbreaks.

Due recognition to the issue from national authorities would also be conducive to encouraging community participation in the implementation of measures to prevent and control dengue. A partnership approach that includes the government, communities and the private sector has the best potential to enable the development of appropriate policies and measures to reduce the vulnerability of Jamaica to the growing threat of increased dengue epidemics due to a changing climate in the Caribbean.

Notes

1   Class 1 diseases are those which must be reported immediately to the Ministry of Health and include HIV/AIDS, malaria and diseases preventable by immunization. Class 2 diseases are reportable weekly in line listing.
2   This problem arising out of specific disease-focused funding programmes is currently being researched by the Alliance for Health Policy and Systems Research, an initiative of the Global Forum of Health Research and the WHO (2005).
3   Priorities for the control of dengue outlined by the WHO include epidemiological surveillance, in other words both entomological surveillance and monitoring of human behaviours that contribute to larval habitats (WHO, 2002). Health authorities are also expected to improve emergency preparedness and response and strengthen national control programmes; promote behavioural change by developing guidelines for the prevention and control of vectors; and support dengue

research programmes that can also help build national and international partnerships (WHO, 2002).

References

Alliance for Health Policy Systems Research/WHO (2005) *Effects of Global Health Initiatives on Health Systems Development*, Alliance for Health Policy Systems Research and World Health Organization, Geneva, Switzerland

Bailey, W. (1989) 'Disease outbreak in ODPEM shelters: Hurricane Gilbert 1988', *Disaster Report*, no 5, Pan American Health Organization

CAREC (1997) *Epinote: An Update of Dengue Fever in the Caribbean*, Caribbean Epidemiological Centre, Trinidad, West Indies

Chen, A. A. and M. A. Taylor (2002) 'Investigating the link between early season Caribbean rainfall and the El Niño+1 year', *International Journal of Climatology*, vol 22, pp87–106

CGSM (Climate Studies Group Mona) (2004) 'The threat of dengue fever in the Caribbean', Project of the Climate Studies Group Mona, University of the West Indies, Jamaica

Dantes, H., J. S. Koopman, C. Laddy, M. Zarate, M. Magin, I. Longini, E. Guttierez, V. Rodriquez, L. Garcia, and E. Mirelles (1988) 'Dengue epidemics on the Pacific coast of Mexico', *International Journal of Epidemiology*, vol 17, pp178–186

Ehrenkranz, N., A. Ventura and R. Cuadrado (1971) 'Pandemic dengue in Caribbean countries and the Southern United States: Past, present and potential problems', *New England Journal of Medicine*, vol 285, pp1460–1469

Focks, D., E. Daniels, D. Haile and J. Keesling (1995) 'A simulation model of the epidemiology of urban dengue fever: Literature analysis, model development, preliminary validation, and samples of simulation results', *American Journal of Tropical Medicine and Hygiene*, vol 53, pp489–506

Focks, D. and D. Chadee (1997) 'Pupal survey: An epidemiologically significant surveillance method for *Aedes Aegypti*: An example using data from Trinidad', *American Journal of Tropical Medicine and Hygiene*, vol 56, no 2, pp159–167

Gordon-Strachan, G., W. Bailey, S. Lalta, E. Ward, A. Henry-Lee and E. LeFranc (2005) 'Linking researchers and policy makers: Some challenges and approaches', Ministry of Health/ University of the West Indies, Mona, Jamaica

Gubler, D. (2002) 'Epidemic dengue/dengue hemorrhagic fever as a public health, social and economic problem in the 21st century', *Trends in Microbiology*, vol 10, no 2, February

Hales, S., P. Weinstein, Y. Souares and A. Woodward (1996) 'Dengue fever epidemics in the South Pacific Region: Driven by El Niño Southern Oscillation', *Lancet*, vol 348, pp1664–1665

Hales, S., P. Weinstein, Y. Souares and A. Woodward (1999) 'El Niño and the dynamics of vector-borne disease transmission', *Environmental Health Perspectives*, vol 107, pp99–110

Ko, Y., M. Chen and S. Yeh (1992) 'The predisposing and protective factors against dengue virus transmission by mosquito vector', *American Journal of Epidemiology*, vol 136, pp214–220

Koopman, J. S., D. Prevots, M. Mann and H. Dantes (1991) 'Determinants and predictors of dengue infection in Mexico', *American Journal of Epidemiology*, vol 133, pp1168–1178

Kouri, G. P., M. G. Bravo, M. Guzman and C. Triana (1989) 'Dengue hemorrhagic fever/dengue shock syndrome: Lessons from the Cuban epidemic, 1981', *Bulletin of the World Health Organization*, vol 67, pp375–380

Martens, W., T. Jetten and D. Focks (1997) 'Sensitivity of malaria, schistosomiasis and dengue to global warming', *Climate Change*, vol 53, pp145–156

McDonald, G. (1957) *The Epidemiology and Control of Malaria*, Oxford University Press, London, UK

Ministry of Environment and Housing (1997) 'Low-income settlement policy design and development project', draft final implementation plan, report IDB ATN/SF 5104-JA, Ministry of Environment and Housing, Kingston, Jamaica

Ministry of Health, Jamaica (2006) *Ministry of Health Annual Report: 2005*, Ministry of Health, Kingston, Jamaica

Morens, D., J. Rigan-Perez and R. Lopez-Correa (1978) 'Dengue in Puerto Rico, 1977: Public health response to characterize and control an epidemic of multiple serotypes', *American Journal of Tropical Medicine and Hygiene*, vol 35, pp197–211

NEPA (undated) 'About NEPA', National Environment and Planning Agency website, www.nepa.gov.jm/about/aboutnepa.htm#mission

Nyong, A. (2003) 'Vulnerability of rural households to drought in Northern Nigeria', *AIACC Notes*, vol 2, no 2, p7

Patz, J. A., W. J. M. Martens, D. A. Focks and T. H. Jetten (1998) 'Dengue fever epidemic potential as projected by general circulation models of global climate change', *Environmental Health Perspectives*, vol 106, pp147–153

Peterson, T. C., M. A. Taylor, R. Demeritte, D. L. Duncombe, S. Burton, F. Thompson, A. Porter, M. Mercedes, E. Villegas, R. S. Fils, A. K. Tank, A. Martis, R. Warner, A. Joyette, W. Mills, L. Alexander and B. Gleason (2002) 'Recent changes in climate extremes in the Caribbean region', *Journal of Geophysical Research*, vol 107, p4601, doi: 1029/2002JD002251

PIOJ/STATIN (2002) *Economic and Social Surveys of Jamaica*, Planning Institute of Jamaica/Statistical Institute of Jamaica, Kingston, Jamaica

Stennett, R. (2004) 'Retrospective study: Climate and dengue fever in the Caribbean', unpublished document, Climate Studies Group, Mona, Jamaica

Suarez, M. F. and M. J. Nelson (1981) 'Registro de altitude del Aedes Aegypti en Colombia', *Biomedica*, vol 1, p225

Taylor, M. A., D. B. Enfield, and A. A. Chen (2002) 'The influence of the tropical Atlantic vs. the tropical Pacific on Caribbean rainfall', *Journal of Geophysical Research*, vol 107, p3127, doi: 10, 1029/2001JC001097

Timmerman, A., J. Oberhuber, A. Bacher, M. Esch, M. Latif, and E. Roeckner (1999) 'Increased El Niño frequency in a climate model forced by future greenhouse warming', *Nature*, vol 398, April 22

Valdes, K., M. Alvarez, M. Pupo, S. Vázquez, R. Rodríguez and M. G. Guzmán (2000) 'Human Dengue Antibodies against Structural and Nonstructural Proteins', *Clinical and Diagnostic Laboratory Immunology*, publication of the American Society of Microbiology, vol 7, no 5, September, pp856–857

Watts, D. M., D. S. Burke, B. A. Harrison, R. E. Whitmire and A. Nisalak (1987) 'Effect of temperature on the vector efficiency of *Aedes aegypti* for Dengue-2 virus', *American Journal of Tropical Medicine and Hygiene*, vol 36, pp143–152

WHO (1997) 'World Health Report: Communicable disease surveillance and response', in *Dengue Haemorrhagic Fever: Diagnosis, Treatment, Prevention, and Control*, 2nd edition, World Health Organization, Geneva, Switzerland

WHO (2002) 'Fifty-fifth World Health Assembly Provisional Agenda', Item 13.14, March 4, Annecy, France

Wilson, M. L. (2001) 'Ecology and infectious disease in ecosystem change and public health', in J. L. Aron and J. Patz (eds) *Ecosystem Change and Public Health*, Johns Hopkins University Press, Baltimore, MD

WRI (1998) *World Resources 1998–1999: A Guide to the Global Environment: Environmental Change and Human Health*, World Resources Institute, Oxford University Press, New York

Index